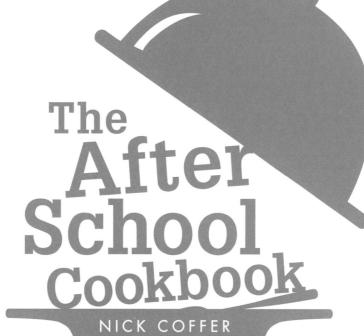

The After School Cookbook

NICK COFFER

HODDER &
STOUGHTON

First published in Great Britain in 2014 by
Hodder & Stoughton
An Hachette UK company

1

Copyright © Nick Coffer 2014

A CIP catalogue record for this title is available from the
British Library

Trade Paperback ISBN 978 1 444 79525 7
Ebook ISBN 978 1 444 78327 8

Designed by Bobby Birchall, Bobby&Co
Typeset in Glypha LT Std

Printed and bound in China by C&C Offset Printing Co. Ltd.

Hodder & Stoughton policy is to use papers that are natural,
renewable and recyclable products and made from wood grown
in sustainable forests. The logging and manufacturing processes
are expected to conform to the environmental regulations of the
country of origin.

Hodder & Stoughton Ltd
338 Euston Road
London NW1 3BH

www.hodder.co.uk

Contents

Introduction

With a six-year-old son at school and a three-year-old daughter growing up too quickly, the need for after-school food inspiration is acute in our house. And, if what I hear from fellow parents is anything to go by, our house is certainly not unique.

That's why I actually need this book! And I am confident that you do too.

Schoolchildren of any age need nutritious and tasty food, fast. They need energy food. They need food to keep them going before they go to football or Brownies or music practice. They need lunch boxes with fun things in them to make a change from jam sandwiches. They need parents who can cope with a group of school friends coming home for unplanned and chaotic play dates.

And as for us parents, we need time. But we don't have any of that. So we need food that will save us time. Food that is hassle-free. Food that fits into an ever-tighter family budget. Food our children will actually eat and which we can just as happily enjoy ourselves, either with our children or later in the evening when they are in bed asleep.*

7

* In our house, being in bed and actually being asleep are not necessarily concurrent activities.

Our children would love us to consistently produce marvellous treats in an eye blink. But with our own busy schedules to contend with, we need to find meals to keep everyone happy that we can cook around all of our timetables. And, most importantly, we need to juggle all of this to get food on the table at the *right* time because their tired heads can't cope with waiting.

There have been times when I have felt that reconciling all of the above was actually impossible. Especially when you throw children's unpredictable food tastes into the mix: when a curry can be a hero on a Tuesday and a pantomime villain on a Wednesday.

And all that is why I have written this book.

In the **Speed of Night** chapter you will find dishes that can be on the table literally minutes after you walk through the door. There are meals you can stretch over two days in two different forms in **Here Today, Still Here Tomorrow. Inspired Lunchboxes** goes well beyond soggy sandwiches (and all of the recipes here will act as great lunches or light meals in their own right too) and there are loads of fantastically frugal ideas in **Saving your Bacon**. I have also picked out some of the most popular supermarket ready-meals and turned them into **Ready-Made Meals, Made by You**. Crispy pancakes, chicken Kievs and a cheat's lasagne are among many home-made treats to beat the ping-and-ding of microwave meals with limited effort. There's also a brilliant chapter of food which can be prepared in advance with minimum fuss so it can be **Ready When You Get Home** and, not forgetting the fun, there is a raft of wonderful **Genius Treats** to round off any meal in style.

2+2=7 turns mealtimes into the main event when you have a full house. This chapter is packed with low-effort meals for unexpected play dates. Sociable, fun and guaranteed to impress your discerning young guests, all of these recipes have been stress-tested during the most stressful of after-school shenanigans.

And, by popular demand in my house, I have addressed the ever-pressing issue of The Gap. The Gap is when your child comes out of school, hungry and in need of instant refuelling but it's too early for supper and they quite possibly have somewhere to shoot off to before they will be able to eat a full meal. Maybe they are heading to an activity or you are planning to do some shopping with them in tow. The chapter entitled **Mind the Gap** deals with that need perfectly.

As with everything I cook, the food in this book is not simplified 'kids' food'. This is food for adults to love too. And if you plonk a coriander leaf on top or serve it in a posh bowl, nearly all of the food here wouldn't look out of place at a dinner party among friends either.

All the signature elements of my first book are still here. This is a book chock-full of great family recipes, for everyone to cook together and eat together. Equally, all of the recipes can be served early for the children and eaten later by their parents when the house is a little calmer.

And, as before, techniques are always simple, recipes are forgiving and foolproof and ALL the ingredients are widely available. In fact, I'd even go as far as to say that all but a very small handful of the ingredients are available from the smaller local versions of the big supermarkets. This is important for me as lack of time (and planning) often means I stop off on the way home from work to grab some simple ingredients to throw together for an emergency supper.

So, while the nature of my recipes has not changed in the three years since I published my first book, much else has. Archie is at school, I'm no longer a stay-at-home dad, as I've started a new career, Matilda has joined the family, and my wife is a busy psychotherapist.

Which takes me back to what I said at beginning: **I need this book!**

Cooking with children

As I have always said, once you accept the inevitable mess, cooking with your children is one of the most fun things you can do together. That's why what I really do miss are the almost daily cooking mash-ups I used to enjoy with Archie when he was little and not yet at school and I was a stay-at-home dad. As I have documented so many times before, this was always precious quality time for both of us, and a wonderful learning experience to boot. It's no exaggeration to say that his hours in the kitchen have led to him being a proper little cook.

It's not that we don't cook together any more. We just do it less, which in some ways makes it all the more fun and precious when we do. If Archie isn't too tired after his school day, he loves creating havoc with me in the kitchen. In truth though, weekends are now the preferred time for cooking together. The funniest part is that his sister is following exactly the same path as he did. Everyone knows how children try to emulate their elder siblings and the time spent in our kitchen is a prime example of that. It's rather lovely really, as Archie adopts a gentle helping-hand approach with his firebrand little sister, showing the kind of patience I always tried to show him when he was a toddler. It has also been interesting to see that it wasn't just a one-off with Archie; when children help in the kitchen there is more chance of them eating what they have prepared.

I've not made suggestions for what steps your children can help with, as it really depends on how confident they are in the kitchen and what they've done before. I'd suggest very young children stick to mixing and stirring, and then progress to simple chopping with a normal dining knife when they're a bit older. It goes without saying that only older children should be in charge of hot saucepans and the oven, and always with your eyes on them at all times!

New ingredients, new equipment

As my family kitchen has evolved, so has my cooking and the equipment I use for it. A slow cooker is a wonderfully affordable addition to any busy family home. And, at the other end of the speed scale, my pressure cooker enables me to make dishes in barely 20 or 30 minutes that would take 2 or 3 hours if cooked conventionally. The rather cumbersome (and slightly unsafe) pressure cookers I remember my mum using 30 years ago are now long gone and forty quid will see you buying a good model which will last an age. Both these cookers are investments you won't regret making, not least because they both love turning cheap cuts of meat into meltingly flavoursome meals. For that alone, they pay for themselves in time. I have got back into fondues recently too, and as such have included three fondue recipes in the 2+2=7 chapter (although two of them can be made without an actual fondue kit). Ours was just a cheap version and, again, it has more than paid for itself in the number of times it has been used.

There is nothing in this book that cannot be made from ingredients that are easily to hand. You may want to make sure your spice cupboard is well stocked, and some good wine vinegars and cider vinegars will come in handy, as will a block of creamed coconut. And with beans so good for you – and so cheap too – they are used a lot in this book, so a few spare tins on the shelves will stand you in good stead. The same goes for lentils. Basically, as long as you have a good range of staples in your kitchen, you'll be able to make fantastic meals every night of the week.

As you will find as you cook the recipes in this book, nothing will fall apart if you are missing an ingredient or two. Feel free to leave out what you don't have – and to add in what you do. This book is all about flexible recipes, which will forgive on even the most stressful of evenings.

Vegetarian recipes and special dietary requirements

I'm conscious of the growing interest in meat-free cooking, and so over half of the recipes in this book are vegetarian or can be easily adapted to be meat-free.

VEGETARIAN

I've also considered the growing need for gluten-free and dairy-free diets and so there are lots of recipes here that are suitable for anyone following these diets. There are also some specifically gluten-free desserts in the Genius Treats chapter.

Preparation, cooking times and portions

All the recipes in this book have been tested by me and by a wonderfully generous group of mums and dads who offered to try out the recipes to make sure they are popular with adults and children alike when served at the dinner table.

I want everyone to enjoy these recipes, no matter how experienced you are in the kitchen, so I have rated them: 'very very easy', 'very easy' or 'easy'. Every recipe is wholly manageable even for a moderately confident cook.

VERY VERY EASY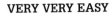

VERY EASY

EASY

The time each recipe takes is ranked as 'really really quick', 'really quick' or 'quick'. With the focus on simplicity, no recipe in the book merits long preparation.

REALLY REALLY QUICK

REALLY QUICK

QUICK

You'll also notice that some recipes are labelled 'slow'. These are perfect for when you want to put a meal on to cook and forget about it while you get on with something else.

SLOW

You can share your thoughts about the recipes in this book on twitter: @nickcoffer, facebook/MyDaddyCooks, and my blog: MyDaddyCooks.com.
Happy cooking!

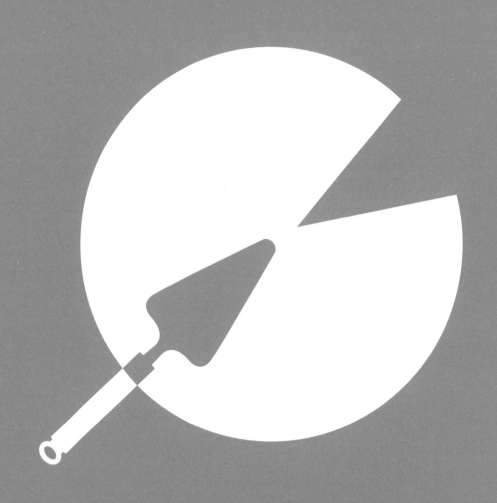

Mind the Gap

When you pick up your children from school, you may still be a couple of hours away from suppertime. And during that gap they may be going off to football practice, Guides or Scouts, they may have a music lesson, or you may be (bravely) about to drag them around the shops. This is where this chapter comes into its own. These recipes are not quite meals (although some come close) but they are mostly much more than snacks. Guaranteed to fill the gap, refuel and tide your children over until supper.

Italian eggy bread croque-monsieur

You are going to have to cut me a bit of slack here! I just couldn't think of the right title so, I figured, if in doubt, just tell it like it is. So this is indeed an Italianesque sandwich, which really is halfway between a croque-monsieur and eggy bread (as we always call it in our house). Most importantly, this is a filling and frankly delicious after-school snack. If you are not serving it immediately, wrap it in some aluminium foil and it will keep while you take it on the school run.

Makes 2 sandwiches

1 tablespoon tomato purée

A small handful of fresh basil, chopped

1 small garlic clove, crushed

4 slices of bread

1 ball of mozzarella cheese, sliced

4 thin slices of ham

Salt and freshly ground black pepper

1 large egg, beaten

4 tablespoons milk

Olive oil

Butter

1. Mix together the purée with basil and garlic. Spread it over 2 of the slices of bread.
2. Layer over the mozzarella and the ham, leaving a border of around 2cm (to prevent the cheese dripping out when frying). Season with salt and pepper.
3. Top each sandwich with another slice of bread and squash together firmly.
4. Mix the eggs and milk in a shallow bowl, dip the sandwiches into the mixture and coat well.
5. Heat a dash of olive oil and a large knob of butter in a wide frying pan on a medium heat. Fry the sandwiches on each side until golden brown.
6. Serve immediately or wrap in foil for later.

Cheddar, Parma ham and courgette scones

Break time, lunchtime or, in this case, at the school gates, these light and flavoursome scones are almost a meal in their own right. If Archie wolfs down three of these, he is happily full for the rest of the evening. And why not? Meat, veg and dairy, all in a very simple and light traditional scone. As with the fritters on page 155, making scones is a great way of using up whatever cold meats and vegetables you may have in your fridge that are reaching the point of no return.

Preheat your oven to 220°C/425°F/Gas Mark 7.

1. Mix the flour and paprika with a little salt and pepper in a bowl. Add the butter and rub it in using the tips of your fingers until it looks like a crumble mix.
2. Give the grated courgette a good squeeze to remove any excess water, and then stir it into the crumb mix with the cheese and ham.
3. Mix the eggs and buttermilk together in a bowl. Make a well in the flour mix and pour in the wet mixture. Stir it lightly with your hands to combine and form a dough.
4. Turn out the dough onto a floured surface and knead it lightly until smooth (you won't get a perfectly smooth dough, thanks to the added courgette, cheese and ham).
5. Roll out the dough to a thickness of around 3cm and cut into rounds, preferably using a scone cutter but you can really use any roundish cutter shape you have (I like to use the rim of a tall tumbler).
6. Place the scones on a non-stick baking tray. Brush with the beaten egg and sprinkle with cheese.
7. Bake in the oven for 20 to 25 minutes until the scones have risen and are golden brown.
8. These scones can be eaten warm or they can keep for a maximum of a day in an airtight container (they will dry out a little overnight though).

Makes about 12 scones

450g self-raising flour, plus extra for dusting

½ teaspoon paprika

Salt and freshly ground black pepper

175g butter, broken into small lumps

1 smallish courgette, grated

100g grated extra-mature Cheddar cheese

50g Parma ham, chopped (or regular ham)

2 eggs

6 tablespoons buttermilk

For the topping

1 egg, beaten

Freshly grated Parmesan or Cheddar cheese, for sprinkling

Tuna and tomato empanadillas

Life is definitely too short to make your own puff pastry so a store-bought block is at the heart of these empanadillas. Capers are funny things, really. Individually, they have such a strong flavour and yet they work so well with tuna and tomatoes. The capers and olives will likely be more than salty enough so there is no need to season the filling with salt. If you prefer, instead of baking the empanadillas, you can fry them for a couple of minutes either side in oil on a medium heat, which will save you a little time.

Makes 8–10

2 tablespoons olive oil

1 small onion, finely chopped

3 ripe tomatoes, finely chopped

185g tin tuna (preferably in oil or spring water), drained

1 tablespoon green olives, finely chopped

1 tablespoon capers, rinsed and chopped

Freshly ground black pepper

1 hard-boiled egg, chopped

Flour, for dusting

500g packet of puff pastry

1 egg, beaten

Preheat the oven to 200°C/400°F/Gas Mark 6.

1. Heat the olive oil in a frying pan over a medium heat and cook the onion for 4 to 5 minutes until soft. Add the tomatoes and cook until reduced and only very slightly wet.

2. Remove the pan from the heat and stir in the tuna, olives and capers. Season with pepper and then very gently stir in the hard-boiled egg. You want the filling to be quite dry so that it doesn't make the pastry wet.

3. On a floured worktop, roll out the puff pastry to a thickness of 3–5mm and cut out as many 15cm rounds as you can (I use a small plate or saucer as a template). You should get 8 to 10.

4. Spoon a heaped tablespoon of the mixture onto each round, a little off centre. Now, wet the edge of the pastry with some of the beaten egg, fold one side over and seal gently. Crimp with a fork and brush with more beaten egg. Place the empanadillas on a non-stick baking tray.

5. Bake in the oven for 20 to 25 minutes until nicely puffed up and golden brown. Serve warm or cold.

Vegetarian scotch eggs

It goes without saying that you can turn these into classic sausage Scotch eggs by using the meat from a couple of sausages to replace the vegetable and chickpea mix, but this vegetarian version is just as, well, meaty and full of good stuff. These Scotch eggs work well as stopgap snacks because eggs themselves are filling, without being unnecessarily heavy. And, if your children are crafty types (I mean crafty as in they like doing crafts, not as in sneaky, naughty and cheeky!), they will enjoy assembling these Scotch eggs.

1. Cook the eggs in simmering water for 5 minutes exactly, then cool them down immediately in ice-cold water (or, better still, a bowl of ice). This will stop them cooking and leave the yolks a little runny.

2. Now make the filling. Heat some olive oil in a pan on a medium heat and fry the onion, carrot, beetroot and garlic for about 5 minutes until soft. Add the spices and lemon zest and stir well.

3. Crush the chickpeas using a fork or masher (you don't want them to be completely smooth) and mix them in with the other filling ingredients. Remove the pan from the heat.

4. To assemble, peel the eggs, dry them with kitchen paper and dust them in flour.

5. Divide the filling into 4 equal pieces. Dust your hands with flour and flatten each piece into a large oval about one and a half times the size of the egg (it will be roughly 3–4mm thick). Mould each piece around an egg so that the filling completely covers the egg.

6. Dip each egg in the beaten egg and then coat in breadcrumbs, making sure they're evenly and fully covered.

7. Heat a deep-fat fryer to 180°C (or a saucepan, one-third full with oil – test the temperature of the oil by dropping in a small cube of bread. If it browns and crisps up in 15 seconds, it is hot enough). Fry the eggs until golden brown – around 3 minutes. You can also shallow fry them in 5mm oil – just keep turning them so they brown evenly all over.

Makes 4

4 large eggs, plus 1 egg, beaten

Olive oil

1 onion, finely chopped

1 carrot, grated

1 small beetroot, finely grated

2 garlic cloves, crushed

1 teaspoon cumin

A pinch of ground cinnamon

Zest of 1 lemon

400g tin chickpeas, rinsed and drained

2–3 tablespoons plain flour

Fine breadcrumbs (panko breadcrumbs are excellent for this)

Vegetable oil, for deep-frying

Chicken and butternut squash pasties

Makes 6

Olive oil

Butter

1 onion, finely chopped

1 clove garlic, crushed

1–2cm cube of fresh ginger, grated

150g butternut squash, cut into small cubes

2 chicken breasts, skin removed, cut into cubes

1 teaspoon curry powder

Salt and freshly ground black pepper

A squeeze of lime juice

2 tablespoons crème fraîche

Flour, for dusting

1 x quantity of shortcrust pastry (see recipe for chard and Gruyère tart on page 42)

1 egg, beaten

To think that my conversion to butternut squash is relatively recent! Up until about five years ago, I just couldn't even consider eating it. It was one of those totally irrational food dislikes, possibly going back to soggy carrots at school when I was six. Squash is now a regular feature in our house, be it in soups, casseroles or, as is the case here, as a filling for a pie or pasty. The sweetness of the squash is a great match for the ginger and squeeze of lime juice, and the crème fraîche ensures the chicken breast stays moist. And of course, their grabbability (I think I may have made up that word) makes these the perfect mind-the-gap snack.

Preheat your oven to 190°C/375°F/Gas Mark 5.

1. Heat a good drizzle of olive oil and a small knob of butter in a frying pan on a medium heat. Throw in the onion and cook for 4 to 5 minutes until it is softened, then add the garlic, ginger, butternut squash and chicken. Keep stirring until the chicken is just cooked on the outside.
2. Sprinkle over the curry powder, season with some salt and pepper and add a splash of water. Leave this to cook for about 5 minutes – you need it to be quite dry so that it doesn't make the pastry wet.
3. Squeeze in some lime juice and stir in the crème fraîche.
4. On a floured worktop, roll out the pastry to a thickness of 4–5mm. Cut out six rounds, each about 15cm in diameter (a small plate or saucer makes a good template.)

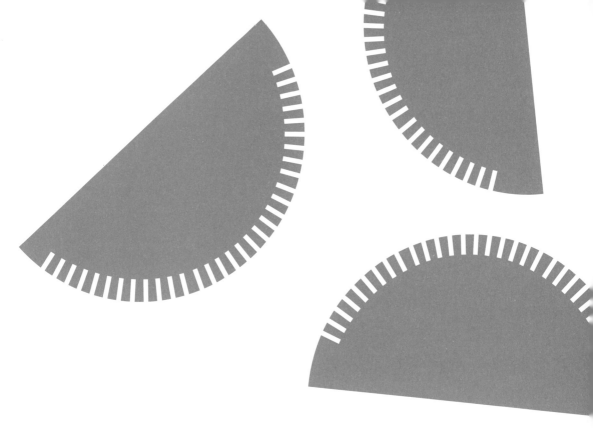

5. Divide the chicken mixture into 6 and place a portion in the middle of each round (keeping away from the edges or else the mixture will splodge out when you seal the pasties).

6. Wet the edge of the pastry with some of the beaten egg and fold one side over, pressing it together firmly. Either press around the edge with a fork or crimp with your fingers to seal.

7. Brush with more of the beaten egg, place on a baking tray and bake for 25 to 30 minutes until golden brown.

8. You can serve these fresh out of the oven or chilled.

Quick nachos with melted cheese and tomato salsa

Serves 2 children

For the salsa

4 tomatoes, deseeded and chopped

½ red onion, finely chopped

Juice of 1 lime

A pinch of sugar

½ teaspoon cumin

Salt and freshly ground black pepper

A small handful of coriander (leaves and stems), chopped

A pinch of cayenne pepper or chilli powder, to taste (optional)

A drizzle of olive oil

For the nachos

200g tortilla chips

100g grated Cheddar cheese

A small handful of chopped jalapeños (optional)

You can make a more elaborate version of this with your own guacamole, but we are talking quick, after-school gap fillers here and time is of the essence. Ideally, you would cook these in the kind of foil trays you get with takeaways and take them to school with you in the car. You can also create your own trays by using a double layer of aluminium foil. At the risk of contradicting the quick USP of this recipe, you can also make your own tortilla chips very easily using tortilla wraps cut into triangles and baked in the oven (see below). It will add an extra 10 minutes to your cooking time but, if you prefer to serve baked rather than fried crisps, this is a good option.

Preheat your oven to 220°C/425°F/Gas Mark 7.

1. Make the salsa by simply mixing together all the ingredients.
2. Divide the tortilla chips between a couple of foil trays and sprinkle with the cheese (and the jalapeños, if using). Cook in the oven for about 5 minutes until the cheese has melted.
3. Take the trays out of the oven, spoon over the salsa and either serve immediately or wrap well in foil to keep warm.
4. To make your own tortilla chips, cut 4 corn tortillas each into 6 triangles. Brush them lightly with oil, sprinkle with salt and arrange them on a couple of baking trays, making sure they aren't touching. Bake in the oven at 180°C for 8 to 10 minutes until crisp and golden.

Chewy flapjacks with seeds, coconut and dried fruit

Give your children a power boost with these flapjacks, which are brimful of good things. The beauty of flapjacks is that they are almost impossible to get wrong as they basically involve two steps: mix then bake. These flapjacks will last a good while in an airtight container and can easily be made totally vegan by replacing the butter with coconut oil and the honey with maple syrup.

Preheat your oven to 190°C/375°F/Gas Mark 5.

1. Put the butter, sugar and honey in a saucepan on a low heat. Melt them together, then simply stir in all the remaining ingredients.
2. Tip the mixture into a greased 20 x 30cm baking tray (or you can line the tray with greaseproof paper instead) and smooth it out with a knife.
3. Bake for 15 to 20 minutes until the top is nice and golden brown.
4. Allow to cool slightly before cutting into squares, then leave in the tin to cool completely. Once cool, store the flapjacks in an airtight container.

Makes 24 pieces

You will need a 30 x 20cm deep baking tray

250g butter or coconut oil, plus extra for greasing

125g soft light brown sugar

6 generous tablespoons honey or maple syrup

400g porridge oats

100g desiccated coconut

50g chopped dates

50g currants, raisins or sultanas

50g mixed seeds

Traditional Spanish omelette

The perfect quick French omelette is cooked in a searing pan and is ready on the table in a matter of minutes. Spanish omelette, however, is at totally the opposite end of the scale in terms of preparation and technique. Whereas the French one is a screechy sports car of an omelette, this Spanish omelette is a gentle meander down a breezy seafront on a warm late-summer's day. With a stop-off for beer. In less poetic terms, the Spanish omelette needs time and a little love. Still incredibly simple, it will not want to be rushed. The reward will be a truly traditional omelette, with the lovely rich, deep, sweet onion flavour that typifies the dish. The other reward I get for the TLC I put into this omelette is seeing my children almost inhale the end result. Needless to say, although this works as a mind-the-gap snack, it is just as much at home in a lunch box or as an evening meal, served with a green salad.

Makes 8 portions

250ml olive oil

1 large white onion, thinly sliced

550g waxy potatoes (e.g. Maris Piper or Desiree), peeled and cut into 3–4mm thick slices

6 large eggs, beaten in a large bowl

Salt and freshly ground black pepper

1. Heat the olive oil in a large frying pan with a lid on a medium heat. You don't want the oil to be smoking hot. Add the onions and potatoes, partially cover the pan and cook for 25 to 30 minutes. They need to cook nice and slowly, on a low simmer. There's no need to stir or mix them at this stage, but they will need an occasional nudge in the pan with a wooden spoon so they don't burn or stick to the bottom.

2. When the onions are translucent and the potatoes are soft, drain them in a colander set over a heatproof bowl and save the cooking oil.

3. Season the egg generously with salt and pepper, then mix the potatoes and onions into the bowl too. It is very important to do it this way round, rather than pouring the egg on to the cooked vegetables, so that they get a nice even coating.

4. Put the pan back on the same medium heat and pour in a really good glug of the cooking oil. Carefully add the egg mixture and give the pan a gentle shake to even out the surface. Leave it until the omelette is about 80 per cent cooked – again, no mixing or stirring. It will be coming away from the edge of the pan and still be a little liquid in the middle.

5. Place a large plate (bigger than the pan) on top of the pan (with the base of the plate facing up) and hold it tightly while flipping the pan over. The omelette will drop on to the plate. Slide it back into the pan, complete with any juices, and cook for a further 5 minutes until fully cooked through – although it should have a slight springiness when you press down on the middle.

6. Turn the omelette out on to a plate and serve warm or chilled.

Toasted gap-fillers

This is not quite as obvious as it may sound. I wanted to include some quick toasted snacks without simply saying Marmite on toast (although I do believe that Marmite on toast with Cheddar cheese is one of the greatest things ever). So, beyond the obvious, I wanted to create two lovely toppings for toast, which are very portable (meaning that they don't easily fall off), perfect for the car journey between school and Brownies or football practice. I am making these two toasted treats as open sandwiches (going the whole hog on lovely thick-cut doorstep single slices) but you can also turn them into toasted sandwiches, by lightly toasting the bread, then frying the sandwich in a pan or, of course, by simply putting it in a sandwich maker. Oh, and one more thing: you can combine these sweet and savoury suggestions: banana, peanut butter and bacon is said to have been Elvis's favourite sandwich! (Probably best to leave out the avocado from that combo though!)

The sweet
Banana and peanut butter

I enjoy omitting the sugar here and adding a spread of jam instead. Cherry or plum work particularly well.

For 2 slices of toast

Peanut butter

1 large banana, sliced very thinly

A squeeze of lime juice

A pinch of ground cinnamon

A sprinkling of brown sugar

1. Spread each slice thickly with the peanut butter.
2. Put the banana in a bowl and mix with the lime juice, cinnamon and brown sugar.
3. Mash very lightly, so it is still very chunky (you really don't want a mush). Pile on top of the nut butter and press down.

Mashed avocado with bacon and tomatoes

1. Put the chopped bacon or lardons in a frying pan with a little drizzle of oil and fry it until it browns and crisps up.
2. Add the lime juice to the mashed avocado and season with salt and pepper.
3. Stir the bacon, tomato and red onion into the avocado, adding the cayenne pepper or hot sauce if you'd like some heat.
4. Pile it all on to hot buttered toast and push down firmly.

For 2 slices of toast

2 rashers of bacon, chopped (or a handful of lardons)

Olive oil

1 tablespoon lime juice

1 avocado, mashed

Salt and freshly ground black pepper

1 tomato, deseeded and finely chopped

¼ red onion, finely chopped

A pinch of cayenne pepper or a dash of hot sauce (optional)

Lemony nut, seed and chickpea mix

This tangy, home-baked nut-and-seed mix is so moreish that I think I should market it myself! Not sure what I would call the brand though. Actually, how about 'Nutty Kids'?! This full-of-goodness snack will act as a wholesome energy boost when it is most needed. I have used citric acid, as it is fairly easily available in supermarkets, chemists and high street health food shops, but don't drive yourself mad trying to find it: lemon juice works fine, as does the North African spice, sumac.

Makes 4 servings

400g tin chickpeas, rinsed and drained

Olive oil

Salt and freshly ground black pepper

1 teaspoon of curry powder or garam masala or ½ teaspoon ground cumin and ½ teaspoon ground coriander

A pinch of ground cinnamon

½ teaspoon citric acid or 1 teaspoon lemon juice

50g nuts of any sort (almonds are perfect)

50g mixed seeds (pumpkin, sunflower and sesame all work well)

50g raisins

Preheat the oven to 200°C/400°F/Gas Mark 6.

1. Put the chickpeas on a clean tea towel, fold it over and rub gently. Some of the chickpea skins will now be stuck to the tea towel, but it's not essential to remove them all.
2. Put the chickpeas in a shallow baking dish, add a good glug of olive oil, season with salt and pepper and add the spices, including the citric acid (or lemon juice or sumac). Mix well to coat the chickpeas.
3. Cook in the oven for 20 to 30 minutes, shaking the dish every so often, until the chickpeas have dried out a little and are turning dark brown. When you think they are close to being done, stir in the nuts, seeds and raisins for a final 5 minutes.
4. Remove from the oven and leave to cool. This nut and seed mix will keep for up to a week in an airtight container.

Fruit and nut chocolate balls

This is really a three-word recipe: melt, mix, roll. Simple, failsafe, full of good stuff and, as with so many of the recipes in this book, extremely versatile. Oh, and they are pretty too! You can slip these into a school bag for a break-time snack and energy boost or just as easily pop them on a breakfast plate for a nutritious early morning treat. Just a little tip with ingredients like desiccated coconut: hunt them out in the specialist food aisles of your supermarket and you will find them at half the price of the major UK brands.

1. Melt the peanut butter and honey or maple syrup in a saucepan on a gentle heat. Remove the saucepan from the heat and stir in all the other ingredients.
2. Form into small balls in the palm of your hand, then roll the balls in the desiccated coconut and chill in the fridge.
3. These can be kept in an airtight container in the fridge for a good few days.

Makes as many as you want!

200g peanut butter

100ml honey or maple syrup

75g finely chopped nuts (almonds or cashews are especially good here)

75g dried fruit, finely chopped (I like to use a mixture of dates, apricots, raisins and blueberries)

75g mixed seeds (a combination of sunflower, pumpkin and sesame works well)

2 tablespoons cocoa powder

50g desiccated coconut, plus around 100g for rolling

Ready When You Get Home

If this book could play music, right now it would be
playing some very laid-back lounge-style music while you
nonchalantly pick a recipe, prepare it and cook it, in the full
knowledge that it will be sitting there ready for when you
get back from the school run. You certainly don't need a slow
cooker to make these recipes but, if you have one, it will come
into its own in this chapter. I think some of the recipes will
surprise you. The pork chilli con carne is a big favourite in my
house – and a lighter, cheaper alternative to beef. And my love
of all things French (from living there for most of my twenties)
means I couldn't resist sharing my wonderful garbure recipe
with you (see page 40). Your children will love
this thick, soupy casserole.

Beef stew with herbed dumplings

**Serves 2 adults and
2 children**

2 tablespoons plain flour

1 teaspoon freshly ground
black pepper

½ teaspoon cayenne pepper
or mustard powder

Salt

Olive oil (or beef dripping)

750g beef stewing steak

1kg root vegetables (try a
mixture of carrots, swede,
celeriac and even beetroot),
cut into 3cm chunks

2 sticks of celery, thickly
sliced

1 onion, thickly sliced

2 garlic cloves, chopped

1 teaspoon crushed fennel
seeds or star anise

1 strip of orange zest
(optional)

A bouquet garni made from
sprigs of thyme and flat-leaf
parsley and a bay leaf tied
together (or a store-bought
one)

100ml red wine or cider

1 tablespoon wholegrain
mustard

400ml beef stock or water

If you want to make this stew extra-economical, seek
out ox cheeks to use instead of stewing steak – they
are very similar in flavour, but with a moister texture
(you can probably only find them at your butcher's
though). Don't for a moment think this is a spicy
stew; lightly spiced is the best way to describe it.
A traditional stew with a little warming edge. My
notoriously spice-averse children don't view this
as spicy, which is a pretty good barometer for me.
The dumplings are the perfect accompaniment for
mopping up the juices left on your plate.

If you want to make this in a slow cooker, simply
brown everything as described below and cook in
a slow cooker for 4 hours on high or 8 hours on low.
Add the dumplings for the last 45 minutes.

Preheat the oven to 160°C/325°F/Gas Mark 3.

1. In a shallow bowl, mix the flour with the black pepper
   and cayenne pepper and some salt. Toss the steak in the
   flour mixture to coat it on all sides.
2. Heat a glug of olive oil (or some beef dripping for total
   authenticity) in a large casserole over a medium to high
   heat and fry the beef in batches until brown all over.
3. Remove the beef and transfer it to a plate. Add the
   vegetables (including the celery and onion) and garlic to
   the casserole and cook, stirring occasionally until they
   are lightly browned.
4. Stir in the fennel seeds and orange zest, if using, and add
   the bouquet garni, then pour over the wine or cider and
   allow it to bubble for a minute or so. Give everything a
   good stir, scraping off anything stuck to the bottom of the
   casserole for extra taste.

5. Add the mustard and stock and return the beef to the casserole. Put the lid on and cook in the oven for around 2 hours.

6. To make the dumplings, mix together all the ingredients and season with salt and pepper. Add water, 1 tablespoon at a time, mixing until you have a fairly sticky dough. Break this into 8 pieces and form rough dumpling shapes.

6. After the 2 hours of cooking time is up, drop the dumplings on top of the beef casserole and return it to the oven, uncovered, for a further 15 to 20 minutes until they are golden brown.

7. Serve immediately.

For the dumplings

200g self-raising flour

100g suet (vegetarian or beef)

1 teaspoon mixed dried herbs

1 teaspoon mustard powder

Salt and freshly ground black pepper

Pork chilli con carne

Serves 2 adults and 2 children

Vegetable oil

500g pork, cut into 1cm cubes

1 onion, finely chopped

3 garlic cloves, finely chopped

2 teaspoons ground cumin

2 teaspoons ground oregano

A small bunch of coriander

400g tin chopped tomatoes

1 tablespoon chipotle paste, or less to taste (any variant of chilli sauce or cayenne pepper can be used, but you won't get the lovely smoky warmth of the chipotle chillies)

400g tin beans (pinto, black or kidney beans all work here), rinsed and drained

200ml stock or water

Sour cream and grated Cheddar cheese, to serve

Using diced pork instead of minced beef makes this chilli slightly lighter and also cuts down on eating too much red meat, which is something we have been trying to do in our house. The pork also seems to perfectly complement the gentle spicing of the dish. I am a convert to chipotle paste, which is readily available in all large supermarkets and adds a smoky warmth to the chilli. Ideally you should add the paste during cooking so that the flavours can really develop in the sauce, but I tend to put just a drop in and then add some more to my own plate at the table, so as not to inflict my love of hot spice on the rest of the family! This is, of course, best served with rice but Archie simply loves flour tortillas and insists on rolling his chilli into a wrap.

1. Pour a really good glug of vegetable oil into a large casserole on a medium to high heat.
2. Throw in your diced pork and cook until it has browned nicely on all sides. Then add your chopped onion. Keep stirring the pork and the onion for about 5 minutes until the onion softens.
3. Add the garlic, cumin and oregano. Finely chop the coriander stems, reserving the leaves for the end of the cooking. Add the chopped stems to the casserole, along with the tomatoes, chipotle paste and beans. Pour in the stock or water.
4. Cover the casserole, reduce the heat and simmer gently for 45 minutes. Remove the lid and simmer for a further 15 minutes to reduce and thicken the sauce.
5. Coarsely chop the coriander leaves and chuck them in right at the end.
6. Serve with rice and top with sour cream and Cheddar.

For a vegetarian version

Replace the pork with 90g dried red lentils or 400g tinned red lentils, rinsed and drained. Throw the dried lentils in once the tomato sauce is made and cook the chilli following the rest of the recipe instructions. If you're using tinned lentils, add them for the final 15 minutes of cooking time, while it's reducing and thickening. Keep an eye on the sauce in case it needs a little extra water while cooking.

Chicken and mushroom cannelloni

Serves 2 adults and 2 children

You will need a 20 x 30cm baking dish

25g dried mushrooms, soaked in warm water for 15 minutes

Olive oil

Butter

100g mushrooms (preferably chestnut mushrooms), sliced

1 garlic clove, finely chopped

1 teaspoon thyme, chopped

2 chicken breasts, skin removed, cut into small pieces

Salt and freshly ground black pepper

200g ricotta cheese

50g grated hard cheese (such as Cheddar or Parmesan), plus extra to sprinkle on top

A squeeze of lemon juice

6 tubes of cannelloni (approx. 250g)

In recent years, the cost of dried mushrooms has dropped significantly and they have become a great store-cupboard staple. I always try to have a packet in my own cupboard, because with them there I know I can make a simple pasta dish in a matter of minutes (just soak them in water for a few minutes, then fry them in a little olive oil with a couple of cloves of garlic and a handful of chopped fresh flat-leaf parsley). They add a lovely hearty flavour to this cannelloni bake but, if you prefer not to use them, extra chestnut mushrooms (which have more flavour than white mushrooms) will do the trick well enough.

Preheat your oven to 190°C/375°F/Gas Mark 5.

1. Drain the dried mushrooms, reserving the liquid but making sure there is no grit left in it (grit is never going to taste nice in any dish!). Finely chop the mushrooms.
2. Heat a drizzle of olive oil and a knob of butter in a frying pan over a medium heat. Add the dried and fresh mushrooms, along with the garlic and thyme and cook for a couple of minutes, stirring.
3. Throw in the chicken and continue to stir for a few minutes until it is cooked through.
4. Season with salt and pepper and pour in the mushroom-soaking liquid. Simmer for a couple of minutes and then remove from the heat.
5. Stir in the ricotta and hard cheese. Taste, and season with a little more salt and pepper if you think it needs it. Add a squeeze of lemon juice. The filling is now ready. Set aside while you make the sauce.

6. Fry the onion and garlic in a glug of olive oil over a medium heat for 4 to 5 minutes until soft. Add the tomatoes, a pinch of sugar and 200ml water. Season with salt and pepper, then simmer until the sauce is slightly reduced. Be aware that you need the sauce to be quite wet in order to cook the cannelloni.
7. Carefully spoon the mushroom and chicken mixture into the cannelloni tubes.
8. Spread a little tomato sauce across the bottom your baking dish. Arrange the stuffed cannelloni tubes on top and pour over the rest of the sauce. The sauce should cover the surface of the cannelloni, but they won't be completely submerged. Sprinkle over some extra cheese.
9. Bake for around 30 minutes until everything is cooked through and nicely browned on top.

For the sauce

1 onion, finely chopped
2 garlic cloves, crushed
Olive oil
400g tin chopped tomatoes
A pinch of sugar
Salt and freshly ground black pepper

Ready When You Get Home

Prawn, sausage and bacon 'bog'

This recipe is not dissimilar to a jambalaya and has it roots in the southern states of the USA. Think of it as a rice dish with a slightly soupy feel – hence the term 'bog'. The prawns can be viewed as an optional extra, but I love the added flavour they bring and they also mean the dish offers up a full 'surf and turf' experience! This is proper hearty, honest cooking and, bearing in mind my love of sausages and bacon, not far from my ideal supper. As an added bonus, throwing in the green beans at the end turns this into a true one-pot meal.

Serves 2 adults and 2 children

Olive oil

100g smoked streaky bacon or smoked gammon, cut into small cubes

6 pork sausages, sliced into rounds

1 onion, finely chopped

½ teaspoon dried oregano

250g long-grain rice, rinsed well

750ml chicken stock or water

2 ripe tomatoes, finely chopped

Juice of ½ lemon

1 teaspoon Worcester sauce

½ teaspoon cayenne pepper or paprika, to taste

100g green beans, sliced into 2cm lengths

250g shelled king prawns

Chopped flat-leaf parsley, to serve

1. Heat a small drizzle of olive oil in a large casserole or saucepan over a medium heat. Fry the bacon until the fat starts running off and the bacon has crisped up, then transfer the bacon to a plate. Add the sausages to the pan, fry them until they are browned all over, then remove them from the pan and add them to the plate with the bacon.
2. Add the onion and oregano to the pan and fry them in the flavoured oil for 4 to 5 minutes, until the onion is soft.
3. Pour in the rice, give it a good stir and then add the chicken stock, tomatoes, lemon juice, Worcester sauce and cayenne pepper or paprika. Stir to combine everything, then season with a little salt and pepper and simmer for 20 minutes.
4. Return the bacon and sausages to the pan along with the green beans and cook for 10 minutes. Finally, the prawns go in and you want to carry on simmering until they are cooked through (they will be completely opaque and pink). The texture should be soupy, not dry. If it looks as though it might be drying out, add a little more stock or water and if it, conversely, looks just a little too wet, continue to cook it for a minute or two to get the right consistency.
5. Just before serving, taste for seasoning and add more lemon juice, Worcester sauce or cayenne pepper if necessary.
6. Serve with lots of chopped parsley sprinkled over the top.

Slow cooker Boston baked beans with bacon, pork and sausages

This recipe will definitely result in leftovers but I think it tastes even better the next day, and it freezes beautifully (defrost before reheating or cook from frozen in the microwave). With recipes like this – where making extra doesn't actually require any extra effort – it makes sense to err on the side of making a very large batch. Using a slow cooker will give you a richer, sweeter finished dish, but you can easily cook these lovely beans in a normal oven.

1. If your slow cooker has a browning function, heat a glug of olive oil in its base; otherwise, heat some oil in a frying pan on a high heat. Quickly fry the bacon, pork belly and sausages until lightly browned on all sides.
2. Put all the ingredients into your slow cooker and pour in enough water to cover by 2cm. Season with salt and pepper – you won't need much salt, as the bacon and sausages will already be quite salty. Cook for 8 hours on low or 4 hours on medium. Most of the liquid will have reduced down and the sauce should be thick and sweet. Taste and add more treacle if you think it needs it. If it looks just a little too liquid, cook for a bit longer.
3. If you are not using a slow cooker, brown the meat in some olive oil in a casserole over a medium heat. Pour in the red wine and boil it off before chucking in everything else. Cover and cook in an oven preheated to 140°C/275°F/Gas Mark 1 for about 3 hours, uncovering the casserole dish for the final 30 minutes. Add a little extra water if needed.

Serves 2 adults and 2 children

Olive oil

100g smoked bacon, cut into 2cm chunks

250g pork belly, cut into 2cm chunks

8 pork sausages

3 x 400g tins haricot beans, rinsed and drained

1 onion, studded with 2 cloves

2 bay leaves

100ml red wine

400g tin chopped tomatoes

1 tablespoon Dijon mustard

1 tablespoon black treacle

1 tablespoon brown sugar

Salt and freshly ground black pepper

Garbure

Serves 2 adults and 2 children

2 duck legs (skin on)

6 Toulouse sausages (or other strongly flavoured sausages)

½ white cabbage, sliced into wedges

2 carrots, sliced

1 small swede, cut into chunks

2 small turnips, cut into wedges

2 potatoes, cut into chunks

2 leeks, sliced into rounds

1 onion, halved and sliced

4 garlic cloves, chopped

A bouquet garni made from sprigs of thyme and flat-leaf parsley and a bay leaf tied together (or a store-bought one)

A pinch of ground cloves (optional)

1 teaspoon dried oregano

500ml chicken stock or water

2 x 400g tins cannellini beans (you can also use haricot beans), rinsed and drained

Salt and freshly ground black pepper

Chopped flat-leaf parsley, to serve

I really wanted to put a duck dish in this book. Duck legs are excellent value in most supermarkets and butchers. Also, both my children love eating duck (a habit that started, no doubt, in our local Chinese restaurant). This is a simple take on a French cassoulet-style dish. In simple terms, it's meat, beans and root veg in a flavoursome broth, and it goes a very long way. This lot will serve four people with plenty to spare.

1. Heat a large casserole on a high heat. Put the duck legs (without oil) in the hot pan and fry them until they are very well browned and have released a lot of fat. Remove the duck legs and transfer them to a plate. Quickly brown the sausages in the hot fat, and then remove them too.
2. Fry all the vegetables in the duck fat until they start to take on a little colour. You might have to do this in more than one batch, depending on the size of your pan. Add the garlic, bouquet garni, cloves, if using, and oregano. Return the duck legs and sausages to the pan and pour over the stock or water with an extra 250ml water.
3. Finally, add the beans, season well with salt and pepper, and simmer on the lowest heat for around an hour, until the vegetables are cooked through and the meat is falling away from the duck legs. Check regularly to make sure it doesn't dry out – add a splash more water if you think it needs it. You want the texture to be thick, but not dry, like a heavy soup.
4. To serve, remove the duck legs from the casserole. Leave them to cool for a few minutes then pull the meat away from the bones before stirring the chunks back through the garbure. You can also cut up the sausages.
5. This is a meal in one so all that needs to be done is to serve the garbure in bowls, sprinkled with lots of chopped parsley.

Spanish-style chicken with chickpeas and potatoes

Is there a better value ingredient than chorizo? A good-quality chorizo sausage immediately adds three things to any dish: flavour, texture and, of course, colour. That's a lot to get from one ingredient. Tomatoes and chicken are two of its favourite bedfellows, and they combine here to make a wonderful evening meal. If you prefer, you can cut back a little on the chicken by adding more chickpeas.

Serves 2 adults and 2 children

2 cooking chorizo sausages (regular sausage length) cut into rounds *

8 chicken thighs or drumsticks, skin and bone removed, cut in half **

4 garlic cloves, crushed

Zest of ½ lemon

1 teaspoon sweet paprika

Cayenne pepper or hot paprika, to taste

A pinch of saffron, soaked in water (optional)

1 bay leaf

500ml chicken stock or water

400g tin chickpeas, rinsed and drained

250g small new potatoes, left whole

Salt and freshly ground black pepper

2 tomatoes, chopped (or a good glug of passata)

1 tablespoon sherry (optional)

A squeeze of lemon juice

A handful of chopped flat-leaf parsley

1. Put the chorizo in a large casserole on a medium heat and fry it until its lovely red oil is released. Add the chicken pieces, coating them in the oil, and fry until they are nicely browned (or should that be reddened?!).
2. Add the garlic and lemon zest, and sprinkle over the paprika and cayenne pepper, if using. Stir to coat, then chuck in the saffron along with the bay leaf, the chicken stock (or water), the chickpeas and the potatoes. Season with some salt and pepper.
3. Simmer for half an hour or so until the potatoes are cooked. Add the tomatoes and continue to simmer for another 30 minutes, topping up with a little water if it starts to dry out.
4. Just before serving, stir through the optional sherry and a good squeeze of lemon juice and sprinkle over the chopped parsley.

* if you can't find the semi-cured cooking chorizo, use the fully cured, hard, chorizo instead

** to remove the skin from the drumsticks, use a piece of kitchen paper for extra grip. Start at the meaty end of the drumstick and keep pulling, then give it a good tug

Gruyère and chard (or Tenderstem broccoli) tart

Makes 8 slices

You will need a 25cm round tart tin

200g Swiss chard or broccoli, roughly chopped

A squeeze of lemon juice

125g grated Gruyère or other flavoursome hard cheese (Emmental works well, as does Cheddar)

3 eggs, beaten

200ml single cream

Salt and freshly ground black pepper

Freshly grated nutmeg, to taste

For the shortcrust pastry

300g roll of shortcrust pastry
OR
200g plain flour, plus extra for dusting

Salt

50g chilled butter, broken into small lumps

50g chilled lard, broken into small lumps

Chard, the allotment growers' favourite, works especially well in a tart like this. It is readily available in most supermarkets but, if for any reason you are struggling to find it, Tenderstem broccoli makes a great alternative. In fact, you have carte blanche when choosing which greens to use here. Serve with simple boiled potatoes and some lovely sliced ripe tomatoes and vinaigrette. Any leftovers will sneak perfectly into a lunch box the day after. The addition of lard to the pastry adds to the flakiness, while the butter gives it flavour. If you don't have lard, you can simply replace it with an equal quantity of butter. Of course it goes without saying that you can just as easily buy your pastry from the supermarket.

Preheat oven to 200°C/400°F/Gas Mark 6.

1. To make the pastry, either put the flour, a pinch of salt and the fats in a food processor and pulse until you get fine breadcrumbs, or rub it together by hand in a bowl. Add 1–2 tablespoons of water until the pastry comes together into a ball. You don't want it too crumbly, as it will be harder to roll. Chill the pastry for 15 to 30 minutes in the fridge, loosely wrapped in some cling film.

2. On a floured worktop, roll out the pastry to about the thickness of a pound coin (roughly 5mm). Use it to line your tart tin, pressing the pastry down into the base and pushing it gently up the sides. Don't trim the pastry at this stage – leave it to flop over the edges of the tin. Prick the pastry all over with a fork and then line it with greaseproof paper. Add baking beans or rice and bake the pastry 'blind' in the oven for 15 minutes. This will give it a nice crisp base and stop it shrinking when you cook it with the filling. Remove the beans and paper and cook

it for another 5 minutes or so to lightly brown the base. Remove from the oven and turn down the temperature to 180°C/350°F/Gas Mark 4.

3. To make the filling, bring a large pan of salted water to the boil and blanch the Swiss chard or broccoli for 3 to 4 minutes. Drain it well, removing as much liquid as possible. Squeeze over a little lemon juice and toss together.

4. Mix the chard or broccoli with the cheese and sprinkle it over the cooked pastry case. Stir together the eggs and single cream, season with a little salt and pepper and grate in a little nutmeg. Pour the mixture into the pastry case over the greens. Give the side of the tart tin a little tap to even out the surface.

5. Bake for around 30 minutes until the tart is golden brown on top and just set – a slight wobble in the middle is good, not least because the tart will carry on cooking inside as it cools down.

6. Using a sharp knife at a 30-degree angle to the rim of the tart tin, gently cut away the extra pastry hanging over the edge. This will give you a lovely clean and straight finish. You can serve this tart warm or chilled.

Jewelled lamb pilau

Serves 2 adults and 2 children

750g diced lamb (shoulder is ideal)

2 garlic cloves, roughly chopped

2.5cm cube of fresh ginger, sliced

½ stick of cinnamon

1 teaspoon green cardamom pods

1 teaspoon coriander seeds

1 bay leaf

1 teaspoon black peppercorns

Salt

Vegetable oil

1 onion, sliced

2 tablespoons plain yoghurt

For the rice

250g basmati rice, rinsed well

½ teaspoon turmeric

50g golden raisins or sultanas

25g dried goji berries, barberries or cranberries

Seeds from 1 small pomegranate (or 100g prepared pomegranate seeds)

A handful of coriander leaves (optional)

I always say that my recipes are very forgiving with regards to the ingredients I suggest using and that they won't fall down if you are missing one or two. That said, pork ribs are never going to work without, well, pork ribs, and in this recipe, the pomegranate is surprisingly central, as it add a huge amount of flavour. The fact that both my children could quite happily live on pomegranate alone is, of course, a bonus. It is very easy (and much cheaper) to deseed a pomegranate yourself. Just cut it in half and, over a large bowl of water, whack the skin with a wooden spoon. All the seeds will come out and sink to the bottom of the water. Any pith will just float to the top. Be careful though: pomegranate juice is the most stainy thing I have ever come across. There's no point in even trying to get it out of your white T-shirt if you splash yourself with it. If you prefer, chicken will work in place of the lamb here and, if you don't want to use the individual dried spices, a tablespoon or two of your favourite curry powder will be a good substitute.

1. Put the lamb in a large casserole along with the garlic, ginger, spices and peppercorns. Season with salt and cover with water. Bring to the boil and use a spoon to skim off any scum that has formed on the surface. Cover with the lid, turn down the heat and simmer for about 30 minutes, until the lamb is tender.

2. Reserving the cooking liquid, strain the lamb through a sieve, getting rid of as many of the spices as possible. Keep the lamb to one side in a bowl.

3. Heat some vegetable oil in the same casserole over a medium heat and cook the onion until it is golden brown. Mix the lamb with the yoghurt, then add it to the casserole and stir until it is a lovely brown colour.

4. Add the rice, along with the turmeric. You need 650ml liquid in total, so use the reserved cooking liquid and make up the rest with water. Pour in the liquid, give it a good stir, and keep cooking until the rice has absorbed most of the water. This will take about 20 minutes. When you are ready to serve, stir in the raisins and berries and sprinkle with the pomegranate seeds and coriander leaves.

Chicken pot pie with mushroom and tarragon

Serves 2 adults and 2 children

You will need a deep 20 x 30cm baking dish or pie dish

Olive oil

A very large knob of butter

2 leeks, sliced into rounds

1 carrot, cut into small cubes

250g white or chestnut mushrooms, halved

600–650g skinless chicken breasts or combination of breasts and thighs, cut into small chunks

A large sprig of tarragon

1 bay leaf

Salt and freshly ground black pepper

50g plain flour, plus extra for dusting

50ml white wine

250ml chicken stock or water

150ml milk

50ml single cream

100g frozen peas

Flour, for dusting

500g block puff pastry

1 egg, beaten

If you've never made one before, I know a pie can seem a bit daunting. But they really aren't at all tricky. This recipe is basically a simple chicken casserole, topped with puff pastry. Easy! If you need to make your food dairy-free, you can replace the milk and cream with more stock or water; because of the flour in the sauce, you will still get a relatively 'creamy' consistency.

Preheat your oven to 190°C/375°F/Gas Mark 5.

1. Heat the oil and butter in a large saucepan and cook the leeks, carrots and mushrooms for a few minutes until the carrots start softening around the edges.
2. Add the chicken along with the tarragon sprig and bay leaf. Season with salt and pepper and keep stirring until the chicken is lightly browned.
3. Sprinkle over the flour and give everything a good stir, then pour in the wine and continue to mix well.
4. Gradually add the stock or water, followed by the milk and finally the cream. Keep stirring until you have a thickened sauce, slightly lighter than Béchamel consistency – like a thin custard.
5. Add the peas and then pour everything into a pie dish.
6. Flour your work surface and roll out the block of pastry to the size of your pie dish. You want it to be around 5mm thick.

7. Dampen the rim of your pie dish with water and place the pastry over the pie (trying to avoid it actually touching the filling). Trim away any excess around the edge and then press down around the rim, crimping if you wish. Brush with the beaten egg and bake for 40 to 45 minutes, until the pastry is golden brown and puffed up.
8. Serve immediately. In my house, this goes on the table with mash.

Malaysian spiced beef (beef rendang)

**Serves 2 adults and
2 children**

For the curry paste

8 dried red Kashmiri
chillies, deseeded and
soaked for 15 minutes in
warm water

1 teaspoon cumin seeds

1 teaspoon coriander seeds

3cm cube of fresh ginger,
chopped

5 garlic cloves, chopped

1 small onion or 2 shallots,
finely chopped

1 lemongrass stalk, tough
outer leaves removed,
chopped

1 teaspoon turmeric

A while back on the radio food programme I present,
we had a lovely guest called Endang and she made
an equally lovely beef curry called a rendang. As you
can imagine, I had much fun talking about Endang's
rendang, the most poetic dish we have ever had on the
show. This is not her recipe but the ethos is the same:
simple, gentle spices marry with coconut to create a
mild and creamy coconut sauce. Please don't be put off
by the ingredients list; it's the depth of flavour that will
make the curry a favourite in your house. That said, as
with all my recipes, the dish will not fall down if it is
missing a few components. If you have a slow cooker,
this recipe is particularly well suited to using one.
Because of the slightly longer ingredients list, I am using
1kg of beef to make full use of any extra effort in getting
the spices together – this dish will freeze beautifully.
The Kashmiri chillies in the paste are very mild. If you
can't find them, you can substitute them with any others
you know to be mild or with half a teaspoon of ground
red chilli and 1 teaspoon sweet paprika.

1. Put all the paste ingredients in a small blender with
    around 50ml water. Blitz until you have a smooth paste,
    adding a splash more water if necessary. Alternatively,
    you can use a pestle and mortar.
2. Toast the coconut in a large, dry casserole on a medium
    to high heat until it is a light golden brown colour.
    Remove it from the pan and set to one side in a bowl.
3. Heat the oil in the same casserole and fry the beef,
    stirring constantly, until it is lightly browned all over.
    Depending on the size of your casserole, you may need to
    do this in a couple of batches – don't overcrowd the pan.

For the curry

50g desiccated coconut

Vegetable oil

1kg stewing steak

1 small stick of cinnamon

1 lemongrass stalk, bruised

1 star anise

400ml coconut milk

1 tablespoon palm sugar or soft light brown sugar

2 tablespoons tamarind paste (Bart does a good one in a jar)

6 Kaffir lime leaves, finely sliced (replace these with a little extra lemongrass if you can't get them in your supermarket)

Cooked rice, to serve

Coriander leaves, to garnish

4. Add the curry paste, the cinnamon stick, lemongrass, star anise, coconut milk, sugar, tamarind paste and lime leaves with about 150ml water. Bring to the boil, then turn the heat down to very low and simmer, uncovered, for about 2 hours, stirring every so often. Keep an eye on it in case it needs a little extra water. The sauce should have reduced and thickened and the meat be meltingly tender.

5. Serve with rice and garnish with coriander leaves.

Ready When You Get Home

Saving Your Bacon

All the recipes in this book are frugal in one way or another and so there are many recipes I could have easily slipped into this chapter. I never use expensive ingredients and I try to keep waste to a minimum, and this is reflected in everything I make. Still, the recipes in this chapter go that step further. I have steered clear of using much meat and fish, as the prices of both of these are forever on the rise but, as you will see when you cook these dishes, frugal cooking does not in any way mean boring, flavourless meals.

Bacon, leek, onion and potato boulangère

Pommes boulangère is a superb way of cooking potatoes. Think potato gratin but without any milk or cream. By layering the potatoes with flavoursome leeks, onions and bacon, this simple dish turns into a frugal classic. The leeks and onions are naturally sweet and you don't need to be worried by the presence of the mustard powder – its effect is warming and sweetening and this is in no way a spicy dish. Perfect for a chilly autumnal evening, hunks of crusty bread with some real butter are all this needs to become a true family favourite.

Serves 2 adults and 2 children

1 large knob of butter

3 white onions, halved and thinly sliced

400g unsmoked lean bacon, chopped (as much fat removed as possible)

1 large leek, washed and cut into 1cm slices

5 large potatoes, peeled and cut into 3mm slices

Mustard powder, to taste

1 bay leaf

1L chicken or vegetable stock (because of the flavour from the bacon and vegetables, you can simply use water if you don't have stock)

Crusty bread, to serve

Preheat your oven to 180°C/350°F/Gas Mark 4.

1. Put a large ovenproof casserole on a medium heat and melt the butter – be careful not to burn it.
2. Put a layer of onions in the bottom of the dish, followed by some bacon, leek and a layer of potatoes.
3. Sprinkle a little mustard powder over the potatoes and then repeat the exact same layering process, seasoning with mustard powder each time. Be sure to pop the bay leaf in too, about halfway up.
4. Make sure your top layer is made up of potato and, when all the ingredients are used up, pour in your stock or water, so that it is just covering the potatoes – you may not need it all.
5. Put the casserole dish in the oven and cook for 1 to 1½ hours. It is ready when all the potatoes are soft through (a skewer is a good way of checking the potatoes in the middle).
6. Ladle it out and serve with the crusty bread.

Braised sausages with a butterbean mash

Our summer holiday in 2013 resulted in a new nickname for my daughter, Matilda. Her insistence on asking for mashed potatoes every single time we went out for supper meant she was henceforth known as, you've guessed it, Mash. This 'bangers and mash' recipe has two nice twists to it. First, the braising liquid makes a perfect onion gravy, rather than making it separately. And, secondly, to make a change from mashed potato (don't worry, Matilda loves this too), I am serving the sausages with a butterbean mash. It is slightly lighter than mashed potatoes and is also a particularly useful addition to your cooking repertoire if you have low GI dietary requirements. I have made this recipe with vegetarian sausages too, and it worked beautifully.

Serves 2 adults and 2 children

For the sausages
1 tablespoon olive
8 large sausages
2 onions, halved and sliced into crescents
½ teaspoon fresh or dried thyme
2 teaspoons plain flour
100ml red wine or water
250ml beef or chicken stock
Salt and freshly ground black pepper

For the butterbean mash
2 tablespoons olive oil
1 garlic clove, crushed
2 x 400g tins butterbeans, rinsed and drained
Salt and freshly ground black pepper
50ml full-fat milk or single cream

1. In a large, deep frying pan or casserole, heat the olive oil on a medium heat and brown the sausages all over. Then take them out and leave them to one side.
2. Add the onions and thyme and cook for about 5 minutes until the onions are soft.
3. Stir in the flour, turn up the heat a little, add the red wine (or water) and then the stock.
4. Return the sausages to the pan, season well with salt and pepper, turn down the heat and simmer until the sausages are cooked through. This will probably take 15 to 20 minutes.
5. While the sausages are simmering, make the butterbean mash. Heat the olive oil in a saucepan on a low heat, chuck in the garlic and then, after 10 seconds or so, add the butterbeans and season with salt and pepper.
6. Stir in the milk or cream (and the mustard if you are using it) then crush up the beans using the back of a metal spoon. You don't want a totally smooth texture. Serve it alongside the sausages and gravy.

Minced beef minchi

This is great grub to fill up a family frugally. Originating from Macau, in China, minchi is a dish of simple flavours and pleasures. A gentle beef ragù, served with potatoes and rice. Traditionally, the potatoes are deep-fried separately, but I prefer to boil mine and add them in at the end. If the thought of having rice and potatoes in the same dish leaves you thinking 'carb overload', don't worry as, somehow, this dish remains light. That said, if you go the full hog and add the traditional fried egg on top, you will definitely be veering into heavy territory!

Serves 2 adults and 2 children

1 large potato, cut into small cubes

Vegetable oil

I onion, finely chopped

3 garlic cloves, crushed

1 teaspoon ground cumin

450g minced beef (or you can use half-and-half of pork and beef)

1 bay leaf

4–5 tablespoon dark soy sauce

A pinch of sugar

Worcester sauce, to taste

Cayenne pepper, to taste (optional)

Cooked rice, to serve

4 fried eggs, to serve (optional)

1. Boil the potato pieces in salted water for 10 minutes until just cooked but not falling apart. It is important they keep their shape. As soon as they are cooked, drain them and cool them down with lots of cold water then set aside. (Alternatively, you can deep-fry them or bake them, drizzled in olive oil, in an oven at 200°C/400°F/Gas Mark 6 for 30 minutes.)

2. Drizzle some oil into a wok or deep frying pan on a medium heat, and fry the onion for 3 to 4 minutes, until just soft.

3. Stir in the garlic and cumin and cook for a further minute.

4. Turn up the heat to high and add the meat, sealing it nicely all over and breaking it up as it cooks.

5. Chuck in the bay leaf and several glugs of soy sauce. Then in goes a pinch of sugar, several generous drops of Worcester sauce, the cayenne pepper, if using, and a splash of water. Cover and leave to simmer for 5 minutes.

6. Serve the beef ragù on some rice, with the potatoes scattered over the top and, for full Macanese authenticity, a fried egg too. Steamed broccoli goes especially well with this.

Smoked haddock, pea and potato gratin

My early memories of smoked haddock are not good. We used to be served a very pungent kedgeree at my infant school which, single-handedly, put me off smoked haddock for many years. Which was a shame because using smoked haddock is a great way of adding oily fish goodness and flavour to any dish. The beauty of this delicious recipe is that the potatoes take the most of tummy-filling strain, meaning you only need a relatively small amount of fish to feed the whole family.

Preheat the oven to 200°C/400°F/Gas Mark 6.

1. Boil the potatoes in salted water for 10 minutes until they are just cooked but not falling apart. Drain them and then run them under lots of cold water. When they are cool enough to handle, peel them and then cut them into 3–4mm slices.
2. Meanwhile, put the haddock in a saucepan, cover with the milk and add the bay leaf and peppercorns. Bring to the boil, then lower the heat and simmer for 1 minute. Take the pan off heat, leave it for 4 to 5 minutes and then strain the milk into a jug or bowl. Discard the bay leaf and peppercorns and flake the fish (removing any skin and bones).
3. Butter your baking dish. Arrange half the potatoes in the bottom of the dish and season with salt and pepper. Cover with the flaked haddock and peas, and season again. Finally, top with the remaining potatoes.
4. Mix the reserved milk with the crème fraîche and pour it over the potatoes. Sprinkle over the cheese (and breadcrumbs, if using) and dot the surface with butter.
5. Bake the gratin in the oven for 15 to 20 minutes, until it is well browned on top. Serve immediately.

Serves 2 adults and 2 children

You will need a 20 x 30cm baking dish

750g waxy potatoes (e.g. Maris Piper or Desiree), left whole and unpeeled

250g smoked haddock fillet

150–200ml milk (enough to cover the fish)

1 bay leaf

1 teaspoon black peppercorns

Butter

Salt and freshly ground black pepper

100g frozen peas

100ml crème fraîche

100g grated Cheddar cheese

50g breadcrumbs (optional)

Saving Your Bacon

55

Sweetcorn and smoked haddock chowder

Smoked haddock lends itself really well to this lovely thick chowder as it adds both texture and flavour to the finished dish – and the same can be said for the sweetcorn too. I would recommend buying un-dyed smoked haddock if you can as I find its flavour to be more gentle than the yellow dyed equivalent. This is perfect winter-warming comfort food and I often make a double or triple batch. It freezes particularly well and acts as an emergency supper after a defrosting blast in the microwave.

Serves 2 adults and 2 children

400g smoked haddock fillet

600ml milk

A large knob of butter

1 small onion, finely chopped

1 garlic clove, crushed

2 leeks, sliced into rings

2 large potatoes, cut into small cubes

340g tin sweetcorn, drained (or frozen equivalent)

50ml single cream (optional)

2 tablespoons finely chopped flat-leaf parsley, to garnish (optional)

1. Put the smoked haddock in a saucepan and cover it with the milk. Add 150ml water, bring to the boil and then remove the pan from heat. Leave everything to cool.
2. Meanwhile, heat the butter in a large saucepan on a medium heat. Cook the onion for 4 to 5 minutes, until it softens. Chuck in the garlic, leeks and potatoes and give it all a good stir.
3. Strain the milk from cooking the fish into a jug, then flake the fish (removing any skin and bones).
4. Pour the milk over the potatoes in a saucepan and simmer until the potatoes are cooked. Mix in the sweetcorn and flaked haddock and gently heat through.
5. Stir in the cream and garnish the chowder with the chopped parsley. Serve immediately with crusty bread.

Root vegetable gratin with ham and cheese

Grab whatever combination of root vegetables you can get your hands on and chuck them into this lovely gratin. All you need to bear in mind is to have the same weight in potatoes. You want the vegetables to be sliced as thinly as possible – a mandolin works well for this, or you can use the slicer part of a grater. Or just use a sharp knife and think 'as thin as possible' when cutting. This gratin can be prepared well in advance then baked later in the day when you are ready to serve it. The dish won't suffer from having the ham left out, making it fully vegetarian too.

Preheat your oven to 180°C/350°F/Gas Mark 4.

1. Peel all the vegetables and slice them as thinly as you can.
2. Rub the garlic all over your baking dish and follow it with a generous coating of butter.
3. Arrange the vegetables in layers in the gratin dish, seasoning each layer with salt and pepper and sprinkling with the ham and crushed fennel seeds as you go.
4. Mix together the milk, cream and egg and pour it over the vegetables.
5. Top with the cheese and breadcrumbs and bake in the oven for 50 minutes to 1 hour, until the vegetables are all cooked through. A skewer is a good way of checking the potatoes in the middle.

Serves 2 adults and 2 children

You will need a 20 x 30cm baking dish

500g root vegetables (a mixture of one or more of carrot, swede, celeriac, parsnip, turnip, sweet potato and squash or pumpkin)

500g potatoes

1 garlic clove, cut in half

Butter

Salt and freshly ground black pepper

100g ham, cut into cubes or small pieces

2 teaspoons fennel seeds, crushed

200ml milk

300ml single cream

1 egg, beaten

100g grated cheese (Cheddar works well, as always, but you can vary it with any hard, grate-able cheese)

50g breadcrumbs (optional)

Vegetable tagine with couscous

Serves 2 adults and 2 children

2 tablespoons vegetable or olive oil

1 onion, chopped

2 garlic cloves, crushed

1 tablespoon ground cumin

1 tablespoon ground coriander

½ teaspoon ground ginger

1 teaspoon ground cinnamon

3 large carrots, cut into 1.5cm chunks

1 large courgette, cut into 1.5cm chunks

1 small butternut squash, cut into 1.5cm chunks

1 red pepper, deseeded and cut into small cubes

400g tin chickpeas, rinsed and drained

400g tin chopped tomatoes

50g dates, pitted and chopped up

A drizzle of honey

Salt and freshly ground black pepper

During the autumn and winter months, I make a version of this tagine, in one form or another, almost every week. This was always a bit of a risk with Matilda when she was very little, as couscous, covered in tomato, has a wonderful habit of ending up absolutely bloody everywhere when being eaten by a small child armed with a spoon. Still, it is one of our go-to recipes so we always trade off the fear of the mess with the knowledge that the children will love their dinner and get loads of great minerals to boot. In our house, Archie loves the added chickpeas, but Matilda meticulously picks them out one by one and refuses to eat them! We often have leftovers from the quantities given here.

1. Heat the oil in a large saucepan on a medium heat and throw in the onion. Cook, stirring, for 3 to 4 minutes, until just softened.
2. Add the garlic and all the spices, and cook for a further minute, stirring all the time.
3. Chuck in all the vegetables and chickpeas and coat them in the onions and spices.
4. Pour in the chopped tomatoes, add the dates, a squirt of honey and enough water to just cover the contents of the saucepan. Season with salt and pepper and simmer for 25 to 30 minutes until all the vegetables are nice and soft and the tagine is not watery. If you feel the sauce is getting a little dry, simply add some extra water; conversely, if it seems a little liquid at the end, keep simmering for a few more minutes.

5. About 10 minutes before the end of the tagine cooking time, make the couscous. Heat a saucepan and put the dry couscous in it, stirring so it heats up (this seals it and helps make it nice and flaky). Drizzle over some olive oil and add the butter. Season with salt and pepper and give it a stir. Remove the pan from the heat and allow it to cool for a minute. Pour over the water, standing back a little in case it bubbles up. Cover and leave the couscous to steam for 5 to 6 minutes. Fluff up with a fork just before serving and mix through the herbs, if using.

For the couscous

250g couscous (pour it into a cup and then measure out exactly the same volume in water)

Olive oil

25g butter, broken into small lumps

Salt and freshly ground black pepper

Mixture of chopped mint and flat-leaf parsley (optional)

Mushroom and spring greens barley 'risotto'

Beware the mistrust you may meet when serving barley! I have served this dish so many times to guests and I can palpably feel their concern at a risotto that is not made with rice. The lovely thing is that this concern quickly dissipates once they realise how lovely and creamy the barley is, with its almost nutty flavour and pasta-like texture. The other bonus, that they are probably not spotting, is that barley is ridiculously cheap. Barley also has that indescribable quality of just feeling comforting and warming to eat – perfect for a chilly after-school evening. Although this is very much a frugal dish, you can add a bag of dried mushrooms for extra flavour, although this will obviously make the dish a little more expensive.

Serves 2 adults and 2 children

Olive oil

Butter

250g mushrooms, sliced or quartered (chestnut mushrooms give the best flavour)

1 onion, finely diced

25g dried mushrooms, soaked in a little water (optional)

3 garlic cloves, crushed

1 teaspoon fresh thyme leaves

1 teaspoon fennel seeds, crushed

250g pearl barley

Salt and freshly ground black pepper

1.25L vegetable or chicken stock

250g spring greens (such as Savoy cabbage), shredded

50g freshly grated Parmesan cheese, plus extra to serve

A handful of chopped flat-leaf parsley, to serve

1. Heat a glug of olive oil and a knob of butter in a deep pan or saucepan and fry the fresh mushrooms over a high heat for a couple of minutes until they are nicely browned. Don't pack the pan, but try to keep them in roughly one layer, otherwise the mushrooms will start to 'steam'. You may need to do this in a couple of batches. Remove the mushrooms from the pan and set aside.
2. Add a bit more butter and oil to the pan and soften the onion for 3 to 4 minutes. Meanwhile, if you are using dried mushrooms as well, drain them now, saving the soaking liquid but making sure there isn't any grit at the bottom. Chop them roughly.
3. Add the garlic, thyme and fennel seeds to the onion, stir for a couple of minutes and then pour in the pearl barley. Mix well and season with salt and pepper. Stir in the chopped dried mushrooms, if using.

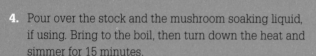

4. Pour over the stock and the mushroom soaking liquid, if using. Bring to the boil, then turn down the heat and simmer for 15 minutes.

5. Mix in the cooked fresh mushrooms and the spring greens and simmer for 5 minutes. The barley will now have a risotto-like texture. If it is still a little liquid, let it cook for a few extra minutes.

6. Finally, stir in a large slice of butter and the Parmesan. Serve with extra grated cheese and the chopped parsley.

Cheese and sweetcorn pudding

Delicious family food doesn't get much simpler than this recipe. This lovely savoury pudding puffs up and feeds your family with ingredients that are most likely already in your kitchen and which will have cost you next to nothing. It is lovely served with sliced ham, or you can add some diced ham or fried bacon to the mix just before putting it in the oven. Any leftovers can be kept in the fridge for a couple of days and reheated.

Serves 2 adults and 2 children

You will need a deep 20 x 30cm baking dish or pie dish

Butter

500g sweetcorn, either tinned or frozen

250g grated mature Cheddar cheese

2 large eggs

A pinch of cayenne pepper

2 tablespoons plain flour or fine cornmeal

Salt and freshly ground black pepper

Preheat your oven to 160°C/325°F/Gas Mark 3.

1. Butter your baking dish and then melt 25g butter in a small saucepan or in a dish in the microwave.
2. Purée about two-thirds of the sweetcorn in a food processor or blender, then add two-thirds of the cheese, both eggs, the cayenne pepper, melted butter and flour and blitz again. Season with salt and pepper.
3. Stir in the remaining sweetcorn and cheese, and then pour the mixture into the buttered ovenproof dish.
4. Bake for 40 to 45 minutes until the pudding is a deep golden brown on top. Serve with some lightly steamed greens, such as broccoli.

Rice and peas (risi e bisi)

How can something so simple be so very tasty? This classic Venetian money-saving dish does exactly what Italian food always does so well: it uses a few tasty ingredients, prepares them without fuss and creates a totally delicious dish. This is not a risotto, although the cooking technique is not far from the traditional risotto method. It is more of a warming, soupy dish and should be able to be eaten with a spoon. Lovely.

1. On a medium heat, melt 50g of the butter in a large saucepan with a little drizzle of olive oil.
2. Throw in your chopped onion and continue to cook for 4 to 5 minutes until it softens nicely and starts to colour a little.
3. Next add the peas, mixing them well with the onions.
4. Pour in the stock, simmer for a couple of minutes and then add the rice. Give it a good stir and then leave it to simmer until the rice is just cooked and it is still very soupy. This will take 15 to 20 minutes. Make sure you check it regularly. If it looks as though it is getting a little dry, add some hot water. Remember, you don't want it to thicken like a risotto.
5. When the rice is cooked, beat in the remaining butter and the Parmesan, season with salt and pepper then stir in the parsley if you are using it.
6. Serve with extra grated Parmesan and some crusty bread.

Serves 2 adults and 2 children

75g butter

Olive oil

1 onion, finely chopped

250g frozen peas (or fresh if you have good ones)

750ml good-quality chicken or vegetable stock

200g risotto rice

2 good handfuls of freshly grated Parmesan cheese, plus extra to serve

Salt and freshly ground black pepper

1 tablespoon finely chopped flat-leaf parsley (optional)

Honey glazed chicken wings

**Serves 2 adults and
2 children**

12–16 chicken wings,
pointed tips removed
(you can cut the wings
in half if you want to)

Salt and freshly ground
black pepper

For the marinade

1 small onion, finely
chopped

2 garlic cloves, crushed

2.5cm cube of fresh
ginger, grated

1 tablespoon vegetable oil

50ml dark soy sauce

For the glaze

1 tablespoon honey

1 teaspoon Dijon or
wholegrain mustard

1 tablespoon ketchup or
tomato purée

1 teaspoon white wine
vinegar

1 tablespoon dark soy sauce

Salt and freshly ground
black pepper

If you have a friendly local butcher, he will sell you a
bag of chicken wings for next to nothing. If not, you
should be able to find the wings for this recipe in your
local supermarket for just a few pounds. These sticky-
fingered wings have a double layer of flavour: first with
a simple ginger and garlic marinade and then thanks
to the sticky glaze they are baked in. If you are really
pushed for time, add the ginger and garlic to the glaze
and make the wings without marinating them first.

1. First blitz the marinade ingredients in a food processor
    or blender until they are nice and smooth. If you don't
    have a food processor or blender, try to ensure that the
    ingredients are finely chopped and grated and perhaps
    give them a whack in a pestle and mortar.
2. Put the chicken wings in bowl then pour over your
    marinade ingredients. Leave the wings for as long as
    possible – overnight is best but an hour will be sufficient.
3. Now preheat your oven to 200°C/400°F/Gas Mark 6. Drain
    the marinade from the chicken.
4. Mix together the glaze ingredients and pour them over
    the wings. This is a messy job best done with your hands.
5. Season the wings with salt and pepper, then arrange
    them in one layer in a baking dish.
6. Cook the wings for around 30 minutes, turning them
    every so often, until they are well browned and cooked
    through. Serve hot or cold.

Mussels with bacon and garlic broth

I am not going to lie to you, this was one of a handful recipes that I filed in a category loosely entitled 'controversial'. These mussels are totally tasty and lightning quick to make. I guess you are either going to have children who love mussels or who hate them; I have one of each in my house. If the children don't like them, I'd still recommend cooking this dish as an adult treat. It is worth noting that a bag of fresh mussels (when they are in season) is an inexpensive addition to your shopping trolley.

Remember the golden rule when dealing with mussels: before cooking, discard any that are open and after they have cooked, discard any that haven't opened.

1. Heat a glug of olive oil and a big knob of butter in a large pan on a medium heat. Fry the bacon and leek until the bacon is starting to crisp and brown.
2. Stir in the garlic and cook for a further minute or two – be careful not to burn it.
3. Pour in the cider, bring to the boil and season lightly with salt and pepper.
4. Add all the mussels, cover the pan and cook for 3 to 4 minutes, shaking regularly, until they have all opened. Discard any that are still closed.
5. Pour in the cream and gently turn over the mussels to coat and combine everything.
6. Sprinkle over lots of parsley and serve with hunks of buttered bread – or go Belgian and serve with lots of chips. Or both!

Serves 2 adults and 2 children

Olive oil

Butter

100g chopped bacon or lardons

1 leek, sliced into rounds

4 garlic cloves, crushed

100ml cider

Salt and freshly ground black pepper

1kg mussels, cleaned

100ml cream

Fresh flat-leaf parsley, to serve

Egg and potato curry with flatbreads

Serves 2 adults and 2 children

For the flatbreads *

250g strong white bread flour, plus extra to dust

2 teaspoons dried instant yeast

1 teaspoon salt

1 teaspoon sugar

1 tablespoon plain yoghurt

4 tablespoons olive oil

For the curry

1 tablespoon vegetable oil

1 teaspoon cumin seeds

1 onion, finely chopped

2cm cube of fresh ginger, grated

2 garlic cloves, crushed

1 tablespoon of your favourite curry powder

400g tin chopped tomatoes

4 tablespoons plain yoghurt

Salt and freshly ground black pepper

200g new potatoes, boiled and cut into chunks if large

4 hard-boiled eggs

100g frozen peas

A handful of fresh coriander leaves, to serve

I often make this the day after we've eaten new potatoes with our supper. A kilo of new potatoes (the standard supermarket packet weight) is difficult to use up in one go and so this dish provides the perfect opportunity to make sure none is wasted. The curry sauce is a great one to have in your cooking locker, as it works with almost any meat or vegetables you care to add to it. And the flatbreads are fun to make, easy to get right and the ingredients cost pennies.

1. To make the flatbreads, mix the flour with the yeast, salt and sugar in a large bowl. Add the yoghurt, olive oil and 100ml water. Form into a dough with your hands, then knead lightly for around 5 minutes until smooth. Cover the bowl with cling film and leave the dough to rise in a warm place for about an hour until doubled in size. After about 45 minutes, make a start on the curry.

2. Heat the oil in a large saucepan over a high heat. Add the cumin seeds and when they start to splutter, add the chopped onion and cook for 4 to 5 minutes until soft. Add the ginger, garlic and curry powder and cook for 2 minutes.

3. Stir in the tomatoes and yoghurt and season with salt and pepper. Leave to simmer for 15 minutes.

4. When the dough has finished rising, lightly flour your worktop. Divide the dough into equal-sized balls. You can make 4 large, 8 medium or 12 small flatbreads with this quantity. Roll out the balls to a thickness of roughly 3mm.

* you can also buy some or use plain pittas

5. Heat a frying pan with no oil in it over a medium heat and cook the flatbreads one at a time in the pan. The flatbreads will need no more than thirty seconds on each side and are ready when they start to puff up a little. Keep the cooked flatbreads on a plate and cover them in foil to keep them warm.

6. While you are cooking the flatbreads, chuck the potatoes, eggs and peas into the curry, lower the heat a little and simmer for a couple of minutes until everything is warmed through.

7. Stir through the chopped coriander leaves and serve immediately with the flatbreads.

Spinach and sweet potato dhal

Serves 2 adults and 2 children

1 tablespoon vegetable oil

1 teaspoon cumin seeds

1 onion, finely chopped

A small bunch of coriander, stems and leaves separated, stems chopped

2 garlic cloves, finely chopped

2.5cm cube of fresh ginger, grated

1 teaspoon turmeric

1 tablespoon curry powder (see below)

1 large sweet potato (or 1 small butternut squash), cut into small cubes

250g dried red lentils

200g tin chopped tomatoes or chopped fresh tomatoes

Salt

2 tablespoons grated block coconut cream

8 cubes of frozen spinach (or 100g fresh spinach)

A squeeze of lime juice

Chilli powder or cayenne pepper, to taste

Lentils rock. They are so cheap (especially if you hunt them out in the specialist food aisle) and they are remarkably filling. In many ways, they are the ultimate frugal ingredient and can be used to bulk up most casseroles and stews. This dhal has a lovely creaminess, enhanced by the use of creamed coconut. Creamed coconut is a great ingredient to have in your cupboard because it keeps very well if stored in a dry airtight container. It also makes a good substitute for coconut milk if a recipe calls for less than a full tin (however, don't confuse it with the thick liquid coconut cream). I have given you a recipe for your own curry powder in case you fancy making one. Alternatively, just use 1½ or 2 tablespoons of your favourite curry powder. If your family is spinach averse, replace it with peas or beans.

1. If you are making your own curry powder, toast the spices in a dry frying pan for a minute or two – be careful not to burn them. Remove them from the pan and leave them to cool, then grind them in a spice grinder or using a pestle and mortar.
2. Heat the vegetable oil in a saucepan on a medium heat. Add the cumin seeds and when they splutter, stir in the onion and cook for 4 to 5 minutes until soft.
3. Mix the chopped coriander stems into the onion, along with the garlic, ginger, turmeric and curry powder.
4. Add the sweet potato (or squash) and the lentils, stirring until everything is well coated in the spices. Pour in the tomatoes, followed by 750ml water. Season with a little salt, bring to the boil and then simmer until the lentils are soft. This will take around 20 minutes.

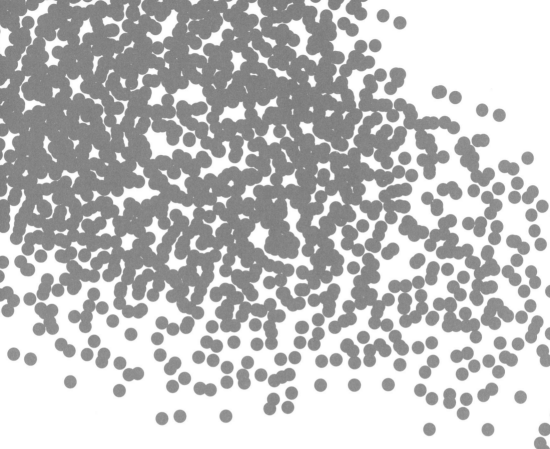

5. Stir in the grated creamed coconut and the spinach and simmer for 2 minutes.
6. Taste, and season with a little extra salt if you think it needs it. Squeeze in a little lime juice.
7. Sprinkle the coriander leaves over the dhal and serve with flatbreads (see page 66) or basmati rice. If you want some extra heat, stir through the chilli powder or cayenne pepper at the table.

For the curry powder

½ stick of cinnamon

1 bay leaf

2 cloves

4 green cardamom pods

1 teaspoon coriander seeds

1 teaspoon cumin seeds

1 teaspoon fenugreek seeds

1 teaspoon black peppercorns

Simple chicken soup and my mum's *kneidlach*

Serves 2 adults and 2 children

For the chicken soup

Olive oil

1 large onion, chopped

3 carrots, chopped

3 sticks of celery, chopped

1 tbsp plain flour

1.5L chicken stock

A couple of good handfuls of leftover cooked chicken, shredded (around 300g)

100g vermicelli pasta, crushed into short strands

A handful of chopped flat-leaf parsley, to serve

For the kneidlach

25g margarine or butter

1 medium white onion, finely chopped

1 large egg

100ml water

125g medium matzo meal (I like Rakusen's)

Jewish food is traditionally thrifty, especially the kind of food my great-grandparents would have made when they were newly arrived immigrants in the East End of London. Suppertime was all about feeding many mouths as wholesomely and as cheaply as possible, using leftovers and simple ingredients. Chopped liver is a prime example, as is perhaps the best-known Jewish dish of all: chicken soup. Throughout my whole life, my Grandma, my Nanny and my mum have plied me with chicken soup, certain in the knowledge that it is not called Jewish penicillin for no reason. The centrepiece of chicken soup is *kneidlach*, the hearty and filling soup dumplings. It took several stages of delicate negotiation to get my mum to give me her *kneidlach* recipe (I may or may not have mentioned it was going in the book!) but they are a frugal favourite in our family and fit perfectly into this chapter so I had to have them. My mum always makes the full-length chicken soup, cooked slowly using chicken bones but I have opted for a cheat's version here using readymade chicken stock. If you make too many kneidlach, you can freeze them after cooking them. They are brilliant in bowls of tinned tomato soup. Matzo meal is very widely available in supermarkets and doubles up as excellent breadcrumbs too, so it's well worth having a bag of it in your store cupboard.

1. Heat a glug of olive oil in a large saucepan on a medium heat. Add the onion, carrot and celery and fry for 5 to 6 minutes until they start to soften.
2. Chuck in the flour and stir it into the vegetables.
3. Pour in the chicken stock and bring to the boil. Turn down the heat and leave the soup to simmer for 20 minutes.

4. Meanwhile, make the *kneidlach*. Melt the margarine or butter in a pan on medium heat and gently fry the onion for 5 minutes until soft. Transfer the onion and the fat in the pan to a bowl and stir in the egg and water.

5. Add the matzo meal and mix together well. You are looking for a firm but not too dry consistency. You can always add a little extra matzo meal if necessary but be careful it doesn't become too hard. (This mixture can be kept in the fridge, covered in cling film, for up to a day.)

6. Bring a saucepan of water to the boil. Roll pieces of the *kneidlach* dough, each about the size of a walnut, between your hands.

7. Carefully drop the *kneidlach* into the boiling water and cook for 10 minutes.

8. Once the soup has been simmering for 20 minutes and the vegetables have softened, add the shredded chicken and the vermicelli. Cook for a further 3 to 4 minutes before finally adding the *kneidlach*.

9. Mix in the chopped parsley and serve the soup immediately with some crusty bread.

Speed of Night

When time is of the essence (I don't know about you, but it very rarely isn't of the essence in my house), these dishes will ensure that food is on the table quickly and without fuss. As well as the obvious pastas and stir-fries, I have included two pressure cooker meals. They can also be made conventionally, but who isn't tempted by a risotto that takes only 5 minutes to cook?

Salmon, courgette and tomato linguine

All hail the wonderful tomato purée! OK, that is probably a little over the top but I do think tomato purée is terribly underrated, especially when it comes to pasta sauces. Maybe it's just that we have been a little bit spoilt by passatas, chopped tomatoes and sauces in jars. The thing is, tomato purée creates a lovely, dry, almost sticky red sauce when stirred into pasta and that's why I often use it at home for the quickest pasta sauce imaginable. It is also very cheap indeed, so it really would be a shame not to have it among your staples. Here, I am jazzing it up a little with courgette, red onion and a couple of fillets of salmon, which are cooked in the pasta water, meaning this pasta dish is on the table in 15 minutes.

Serves 2 adults and 2 children

350g linguine

2 x 170g salmon fillets, skin removed

Olive oil

1 red onion, cut in half and finely sliced

1 courgette, cut into 1cm cubes

3 garlic cloves, chopped

200g tomato purée

Salt and freshly ground black pepper

A good handful of freshly grated Parmesan cheese, to serve

1. Cook the pasta in a large saucepan of salted boiling water according to the packet instructions. With 7 minutes of the cooking time left, drop in the salmon fillets.
2. Meanwhile, pour a glug of olive oil into a large frying pan on a medium heat and gently fry the onion and courgette for 5 to 6 minutes, until soft. Add the garlic, stirring for a further minute.
3. Squirt in all the tomato purée, season with salt and pepper and keep the 'sauce' moving around the pan, stirring it occasionally. You will find that the vegetables stick together in a bit of a tomato purée ball. Don't worry: they will be stirred out once the pasta is added.
4. Drain the pasta and rinse under cold water. Flake the salmon and then mix the pasta and salmon into the vegetables in the pan. Keep mixing until the pasta is heated through and fully covered in tomato.
5. Serve immediately with the freshly grated Parmesan.

Greek-style lamb chops with butterbeans

Lamb chops are not the cheapest cuts of meat but when we do have them as a treat, they are always wolfed down, full carnivore style. It may seem as though two lemons is a lot but the recipe does need them, both for flavour and also to tenderise the meat slightly. You can use any kind of bean here (such as cannellini or flageolet), but I use butterbeans, as they are the closest to the kind of giant Greek beans you may well have enjoyed on your Mediterranean holidays.

Serves 2 adults and 2 children

12–16 small lamb chops or cutlets

Juice and zest of 2 lemons

4 garlic cloves, roughly chopped

A good pinch each of dried thyme and oregano

Olive oil

Salt and freshly ground black pepper

For the butterbeans

Olive oil

1 onion, finely chopped

1 bulb of fennel, finely chopped

1 garlic clove, crushed

4 tomatoes, chopped

A pinch of sugar

A pinch of ground cinnamon

2 tablespoons chopped flat-leaf parsley

400g tin butterbeans, rinsed and drained

1. Put the lamb chops in a large bowl or a bag (make sure it doesn't have any holes in it!). Throw in the juice and zest of the lemons, the garlic, herbs and a generous glug of olive oil. Season with salt and pepper, massage the marinade into the meat and leave it to rest for 10 to 15 minutes.
2. For the butterbeans, heat some olive oil in a saucepan, add the onion and fennel and cook for 4 to 5 minutes until they start to soften. Throw in the garlic and cook for a further minute, then follow with the tomatoes, sugar, cinnamon, parsley and butterbeans. Simmer on a low heat while you cook the lamb, but keep an eye on it and add a splash of water if it looks like it's starting to dry out.
3. Drain the lamb chops, brushing off most of the garlic.
4. Cook the chops under a hot grill, on a hot griddle pan or on the barbecue. Depending on the thickness of your meat, you want to cook them for around 4 minutes on each side for medium. Leave them to rest for a minute or two before serving.
5. Crush the beans very lightly with the back of a spoon (you are NOT looking for a mash here) and serve them with the cooked lamb chops.

Smooth cheese and garlic pasta with sun-dried tomatoes (no-cook sauce)

Serves 2 adults and 2 children

1 whole head of garlic, fully intact

Salt and freshly ground black pepper

400g pasta (you can use anything you like, including spaghetti)

Olive oil

200g cream cheese

Zest of 1 lime (yes, that's lime. Trust me on this one)

Around 10 sun-dried tomatoes, in oil, drained and chopped (see below)

A bunch of basil, torn

Freshly grated Parmesan cheese, to serve

I know I say so myself, but this is clever. Cooked garlic has a far more mellow flavour than raw garlic so, for this simple store-cupboard sauce, I cook a whole head of garlic in the boiling pasta water. A head may seem like an awful lot, but boiling it results in a creaminess and a wonderful mild taste that marries beautifully with the cheese. And there's another clever trick here: if you want to avoid the cost of the sun-dried tomatoes, make them yourself, thanks to the brilliant method outlined underneath the recipe. This was given to me by James Harkin, who runs a lovely restaurant called The Alpine, in Bushey. Using the heat of an oven – which you are already using for something else – costs nothing in terms of gas or electricity. It's a brilliant way of saving money, without compromising on flavour.

1. Peel away some of the outer skin of the garlic bulb but go gently – you want it to remain fully intact. Bring a large pan of water to the boil and salt it generously. Throw in the garlic head.
2. Assuming your pasta requires the classic 11 or 12 minutes of cooking time, wait for 5 or 6 minutes before adding it to the boiling water and garlic.
3. With 3 or 4 minutes of the pasta's cooking time remaining, remove the garlic and let it cool down. After a couple of minutes, squish the flesh out of its skin into a bowl. Drizzle with olive oil and add the cream cheese and lime zest. Beat it all together before mixing in the sun-dried tomatoes. Season with salt and pepper.

4. Drain the pasta, reserving a good ladleful of the cooking water, and mix it (while it is still hot) into the sauce. If it seems a bit thick, stir in some of the reserved cooking water a little at a time.
5. Scatter over the torn basil and serve with lots of grated Parmesan.

To make your own sun-dried tomatoes

1. Heat your oven to its highest temperature (for example, after making a roast). Take medium-sized tomatoes and cut them in half. Arrange them on a baking tray. Sprinkle them with salt and drizzle with olive oil. Put them in the hot oven, then immediately turn the oven off. Leave the tomatoes in the oven overnight. They will dry out beautifully. Store them in an airtight container in olive oil, along with some peeled cloves of garlic. They should keep for several weeks.

Wok-braised aubergines with tofu and black bean sauce

Serves 2 adults and 2 children

2 tablespoons vegetable oil

2 garlic cloves, finely chopped

2cm cube of fresh ginger, finely chopped

2 spring onions, finely sliced

2 medium aubergines, cut into 2–3cm cubes

1 small red or green pepper, deseeded and sliced lengthways

1 carrot, cut into thin batons

1 courgette, cut into thin batons

¼ white cabbage, shredded

100g firm tofu, cut into cubes

3 tablespoons black bean sauce

½ teaspoon sugar

1 teaspoon rice wine vinegar or cider vinegar

A pinch of Chinese five spice

100ml stock or water

A good glug of soy sauce

Salt and freshly ground black pepper

225g fine egg noodles

Coriander leaves, to serve

I am not ashamed to admit that on a busy day a pack of pre-cut vegetables does the trick very nicely in this recipe. Sometimes life is just too hectic to be chopping up veg. The aubergine is braised, meaning it keeps its shape and holds lots of flavour. It also requires less supervision to braise vegetables than fry them. This dish is absolutely packed with vitamins and the addition of tofu gives this simple stir-fry a lovely texture.

1. Heat the oil in a wok on your highest heat. Add the garlic, ginger and spring onions and cook for 30 seconds – be careful not to burn the garlic.
2. Add all the vegetables and stir-fry for 3 minutes before throwing in the remaining ingredients (apart from the noodles and coriander leaves).
3. Turn the heat down a little and cook, uncovered, until the vegetables are just tender. This will take around 10 minutes. Keep an eye on the wok and add a splash of water if it looks like it's drying out. Conversely, if you find that the sauce needs reducing further, turn the heat up again for a minute or two.
4. Meanwhile, cook the noodles according to the packet instructions. Drain and serve with the stir-fry and coriander leaves sprinkled over the top.

Wonderful shakshouka

This shakshouka may have to be one of those recipes where I ask you just to trust me. This is always very popular with everyone who eats it, and with good cause. Why do eggs work so well with peppers and tomatoes? I am not sure but, my word, they do! Think of this dish as ratatouille meets a fry-up and you are part of the way to getting a sense of what it is. It is a staple in North Africa, as well as in Israel. And Mexico can lay claim to a similar dish with its huevos rancheros. The lamb is entirely optional, as many shakshouka recipes are vegetarian. If you want a runny egg yolk, use the yoghurt during cooking as described, as it will act as protection for the yolk. If you prefer your yolk to be set, simply add the yoghurt at the end.

1. Heat the olive oil in your large frying pan. Cook the onions and peppers for 5 minutes until they soften, then add the garlic, spices and lamb (if you are using it) and cook for a further minute or so, until the lamb has browned a little all over.
2. Stir in the tomato purée and cook for 2 minutes before adding the tomatoes. Season with salt and pepper, then bring to the boil and simmer for 3 to 4 minutes until the sauce thickens a little.
3. Make 4 wells in the sauce and break an egg into each hole. Spoon yoghurt over each egg yolk, then put the lid on the pan and cook until the whites are set and cooked through – this will take around 5 minutes.
4. Serve with the fresh herbs sprinkled over the top, and lots of crusty fresh bread.

Serves 2 adults and 2 children

You will need a large frying pan with a lid

2 tablespoons olive oil

1 red onion, cut into thin wedges

2 red peppers, deseeded and sliced lengthways

2 garlic cloves, finely chopped

1 teaspoon ground cumin

½ teaspoon paprika

150g lamb mince (optional)

1 tablespoon tomato purée

200g tin chopped tomatoes or chopped fresh tomatoes

Salt and freshly ground black pepper

4 large eggs

4 tablespoons thick Greek yoghurt

Fresh herbs (mint, flat-leaf parsley and coriander all work well), to garnish

Sweet pork and green bean stir-fry

Serves 2 adults and 2 children

225g fine egg noodles

Vegetable oil

500g pork mince

1 onion, finely chopped

2 garlic cloves, crushed

3cm cube of fresh ginger, grated or chopped

1 lemongrass stalk, hard outer layers removed, finely chopped

2 heaped tablespoons soft dark brown sugar

Dark soy sauce

Thai fish sauce

200g green beans, cut in half lengthways (fine ones work best)

A bunch of coriander, chopped

It is no understatement to say that this is in the top five most popular dishes in our house, and has been for some time now. It just has that indefinable x-factor for my children and yet is very simple in its execution. We all have our turn-to dishes that we are able to cook on autopilot and this is one of mine. It is sweet and richly coloured and makes use of very underrated (in my opinion) pork mince. I may be splitting hairs here but I prefer the drier texture of pork mince compared with beef. I also find it has more flavour and it is, of course, a bit kinder on cholesterol levels too. The addition of green beans makes this very much a whole meal in one wok.

1. Cook the noodles according to the packet instructions.
2. Meanwhile, heat a really good drizzle of vegetable oil in a wok or deep frying pan on your highest heat. Add the pork and fry for 3 minutes, breaking it up with your spoon as you go.
3. Throw in the onion, garlic, ginger and lemongrass and continue to stir and cook for 5 to 6 minutes until the onion is soft and the pork is lightly browned all over.
4. Stir in the sugar followed by several good glugs of soy sauce and a few drops of the fish sauce. Continue to stir until everything is a lovely dark brown colour, then add the green beans. Pour in a small glass of water, cover the wok and cook for a further 4 minutes. The sauce should be dry but if it seems at all liquid at this stage, simmer for an extra minute or so with the lid off.
5. Stir in the coriander. Chop the noodles with some scissors to create shorter strands and mix them into the sauce, making sure all the noodles are well covered. Serve immediately.

Matzo brei

Matzos are unleavened bread crackers traditionally eaten during the Jewish festival of Passover but widely available all year round in supermarkets. A box will set you back about a pound. Matzo brei is an ultra-quick dish, made by soaking broken pieces of matzo in egg and then frying them in a hot pan. Think of it as a Jewish take on eggy French toast. This is a true taste of my childhood that I have passed on to Archie and Matilda, both of whom regularly request it from their Nana. Trust me on this one: although you may be struggling to visualise it, your children will love it. Feel free to add things to the brei to jazz it up. Ironically, some crispy bacon would be marvelous!

Serves 2 adults and 2 children

300g packet of matzos
2 eggs, beaten
Salt and freshly ground black pepper
Olive or vegetable oil

1. Boil the kettle. Break the matzos into a bowl – each piece should be about 2.5cm square. Cover them with boiling water and leave to soak and soften for a minute.
2. Drain the matzo pieces in a colander, then return them to the bowl and pour over the beaten egg. Mix well so all the pieces are nicely coated, then season with salt and pepper.
3. Pour a good glug of oil into a large frying pan on a medium to high heat and add the soaked matzo pieces.
4. Cook for 4 to 5 minutes, stirring all the time. You want the matzo pieces to be fairly dry in the middle and a little crisp on the edges. Serve immediately.

Chicken, butternut squash and sage risotto

Serves 2 adults and 2 children

Olive oil

Butter

1 leek, finely chopped

4 chicken thighs, skin and bone removed, chopped

1 small butternut squash (approx. 500–600g), cut into small cubes

1 teaspoon dried sage

1 teaspoon lemon zest

300g risotto rice

100ml white wine

750ml chicken stock

Salt and freshly ground black pepper

25g freshly grated Parmesan cheese, plus extra to serve

Basil leaves, to serve

I have memories of my mum using pressure cookers 35 years ago. Back in the day they were a little, shall we say, unreliable and, if truth be told, not always completely safe. Nowadays, they are brilliant contraptions and you can get a very good one fairly inexpensively. Amazingly, they can make a risotto like this one in less than 10 minutes. My friend Catherine Phipps' book, *The Pressure Cooker Cookbook*, is a superb bible for pressure cooking. In truth, it is what inspired me to buy my own and I have not looked back since. If you don't have a pressure cooker, you can bake this risotto in the oven.

1. Heat a good drizzle of olive oil and a large knob of butter in your pressure cooker. Add the leek and cook on a medium heat until soft, then turn up the heat slightly and brown the chicken.
2. Add the butternut squash, sage, lemon zest and risotto rice, stirring to coat in the oil and butter.
3. Turn up the heat to high, pour in the wine and allow it to bubble until evaporated. Pour over the stock, season with salt and pepper then close the lid and bring to high pressure. Cook for 5 minutes then release the pressure quickly.
4. Beat in the Parmesan and 25g butter, put the lid back on and leave the risotto to steam for a couple of minutes or so off the heat to finish cooking.
5. Sprinkle over torn basil leaves and serve with more grated Parmesan.

Note

If you are making this in the oven, use an ovenproof casserole and follow all the steps until the method says to bring the cooker to high pressure. At this stage, simply cover the dish and cook it for 20 to 25 minutes in an oven preheated to 180°C/350°F/Gas Mark 4, until all the water is absorbed and the rice is cooked and creamy. Finish off with butter and cheese and serve as above.

One-pot caponata pasta

This pressure cooker recipe demonstrates quite how quick a pressure cooker meal can be. The pasta cooks with the sauce and, once the lid is closed and the pressure is set to high, it only takes 5 minutes. This is very much a vegetarian pasta dish but there is no reason why you can't add some meat. Bacon, sausage, chorizo, leftover chicken and meatballs are all going to work well here.

Serves 2 adults and 2 children

Olive oil

1 onion, finely chopped

1 carrot, cut into small cubes

1 stick of celery, sliced

1 small aubergine, cut into small cubes

1 courgette, cut into small cubes

2 garlic cloves, chopped

Zest of 1 lemon

1 tablespoon capers

A small handful of olives, sliced

½ teaspoon chilli flakes (optional)

A handful of chopped flat-leaf parsley

300g pasta (such as farfalle, penne or conchiglie)

400g tin chopped tomatoes

2 tablespoons cream cheese

Freshly grated Parmesan cheese and chopped flat-leaf parsley, to serve

1. Heat a good glug of olive oil in the pressure cooker. Add all the vegetables and cook them for 2 minutes on a medium to high heat until they start to brown a little. Throw in the garlic, lemon zest, capers, olives, chilli flakes and parsley and give it all a good stir.
2. Spread an even layer of the pasta over the vegetables and stir lightly. Spoon the tomatoes on top of the pasta without mixing them in. Use the empty tomato tin to add enough water to almost cover the pasta.
3. Close the pressure cooker lid, bring it to high pressure, then turn down the heat and leave it to cook at high pressure for 5 minutes, then release the pressure quickly.
4. Add the cream cheese to thicken the sauce and stir thoroughly. Leave the pasta to sit for a couple of minutes, then serve with freshly grated Parmesan and chopped parsley.

Salt and pepper squid with lemon mayonnaise

My children never cease to surprise me, not least in their willingness to try new foods. We've always encouraged them to be adventurous at mealtimes and, as such, they now have some unusual favourites! Squid is one of those random things that my children really love: easy flavour and simple texture – as long as I never give them the tentacles! This recipe is a simple version of classic fried calamari – lovely with the lemony dipping mayonnaise. You can make your own mayonnaise but you can also simply add the lemon zest and juice, mustard and cayenne pepper to a good-quality shop-bought mayonnaise. I view this more as a snacky supper rather than a full meal for four.

Serves 2 children, with some extra

50g plain flour

Salt and freshly ground black pepper

350g squid rings (you can buy the squid whole or ready-prepared)

Vegetable oil

Lemon wedges, to serve

For the mayonnaise

1 egg yolk

Zest of 1 lemon, plus juice of half

½ teaspoon salt

1 teaspoon Dijon mustard

A pinch of cayenne pepper

300ml vegetable or sunflower oil

1. For the mayonnaise, mix together the egg yolk, lemon zest and juice, salt, mustard and cayenne pepper in a bowl. Start dribbling in the oil very slowly, whisking all the time until it thickens and emulsifies. Once it emulsifies, you can start to add the oil a little more quickly. Continue until all the oil is incorporated. If you prefer not to do this by hand, follow the same instructions but use a food processor.

2. To make the squid, season the flour with salt and pepper in a bowl. Add the squid, mixing thoroughly so that it is well coated in the flour.

3. You are going to deep-fry the squid so heat the vegetable oil in either a large, wide saucepan or in a deep-fat fryer to around 190°C. If you are using a saucepan, be careful not to fill it more than one-third of the way up. To test the oil is hot enough, use a thermometer or drop in a cube of bread – it should fizz and turn golden brown within about 10 to 15 seconds.

4. Shake off any excess flour from the squid and carefully fry in two batches for 1 minute only. The squid should crisp up and turn a light golden brown almost immediately. Drain on kitchen paper.

5. Serve with lemon wedges and the mayonnaise.

Gnocchi with a spinach and creamy tomato sauce

Clever little things, gnocchi. We often eat fried gnocchi in our house. Just fry them in butter in a pan for 3 to 4 minutes on each side and then serve them mixed with pesto, roasted vegetables and Parmesan. For this recipe, I am using the classic cooking method and boiling them. Serve with this simple and quick creamy tomato sauce (with spinach added in for extra goodness) and they will rapidly become one of your store-cupboard essentials. You can jazz up this sauce in all the usual ways: chorizo works nicely and I'd never say no to chucking cooked bacon into a pasta either.

1. Cook the gnocchi according to the packet instructions. Drain it as soon as it is ready, so it doesn't become mushy.
2. While the gnocchi is cooking, drizzle the olive oil into a pan and fry the onion for 3 minutes. Throw in the garlic and stir for a further 30 seconds.
3. Pour in the passata, let the sauce bubble up and then stir in the cream.
4. Mix in the spinach, season with salt and pepper and stir in the cooked gnocchi.
5. Serve with lots of freshly grated Parmesan.

Serves 2 adults and 2 children

500g pack of fresh gnocchi

Olive oil

1 red onion, finely chopped

1 garlic clove, chopped

500ml tomato passata

100–150ml double cream

3 blocks of frozen spinach, defrosted and squeezed (or 250g fresh leaves)

Salt and freshly ground black pepper

Freshly grated Parmesan cheese, to serve

Middle Eastern spiced salmon with orange and mint couscous

Serves 2 adults and 2 children

4 x 150g salmon fillets, skin removed

Olive oil

For the sauce

50ml pomegranate molasses

1 tablespoon honey

1 teaspoon ground cumin

1 teaspoon ground coriander

½ teaspoon ground cinnamon

½ teaspoon harissa paste (a rose-scented one is good here) or some chilli powder, to taste

Salt and freshly ground black pepper

Zest and juice of 1 orange

There are lots of fresh, sweet and typically Middle Eastern flavours on show here. Pomegranate molasses is an excellent addition to any kitchen cupboard and it keeps very well. It has a slightly bitter-sweet flavour and a wonderful aroma. You'll be able to find it in most supermarkets, although you may have to go to the world food aisle. If you have not used pomegranate molasses before, it's the kind of ingredient you will find yourself chucking into all manner of things once you have it close to hand.

1. Mix together the sauce ingredients, apart from the orange juice, with a splash of water until the honey has dissolved. Coat the salmon thoroughly in the sauce and drain any excess back into the bowl (this is not a marinade, so there's no need to leave the salmon in the sauce for any extra time).
2. Rub a large frying pan with olive oil (you want a relatively dry pan, so don't pour the oil in).
3. Heat the pan over a medium heat and cook the salmon fillets on one side for around 5 minutes, then turn them over and cook for a further 4 to 5 minutes, basting with the sauce at intervals.
4. Meanwhile, make the couscous. Heat a saucepan and put the dry couscous in it, stirring so it heats up (this seals it and helps make it nice and flaky). Drizzle over the olive oil and add the butter. Season with salt and pepper and give it a stir. Remove the pan from the heat and allow it to cool for a minute. Pour over the water, standing back a little in case it bubbles up. Cover and leave the couscous to steam for 5 to 6 minutes.

5. By this point, the salmon will be ready – it should give a little when pressed, but should still be slightly pink in the middle. Don't over-cook it, as it will continue to cook when you take it out of the pan. Remove the salmon and set aside. Add any remaining sauce to the pan and pour in the orange juice. Simmer until it has reduced to a very thin syrup.
6. Add the orange zest and juice to the couscous and fluff it up with a fork.
7. Sprinkle over the pistachios, mint and pomegranate seeds and serve alongside the salmon.

For the mint and orange couscous

200g dried couscous (pour it into a cup and then measure out exactly the same volume in water)

1 tablespoon olive oil

25g butter, broken into small lumps

Salt and freshly ground black pepper

Juice of 1 orange and zest of half

2 tablespoons roughly chopped pistachios or pistachio nibs

1 small bunch of mint, torn

Seeds from 1 small pomegranate (or 80g prepared pomegranate seeds)

Grilled chicken breasts with romesco sauce

This delicious Catalan sauce will instantly become one of your kitchen staples once you have made it. Not only does it go superbly with chicken, it will also go with pretty well anything else, not least of all fish. Roasting the tomatoes for a short period of time enhances and intensifies their flavours and it's then a simple case of blitzing all the sauce ingredients together.

Serves 2 adults and 2 children

4 chicken breasts, skin removed

Salt and freshly ground black pepper

Olive oil

For the sauce

200g small tomatoes, halved

6 garlic cloves, unpeeled

Salt and freshly ground black pepper

Olive oil

1 slice of stale thick white bread, cut into cubes

15g hazelnuts

1 teaspoon sweet paprika

A pinch of cayenne pepper or chilli flakes

1 tablespoon red wine vinegar or sherry vinegar

Preheat your oven to 190°C/375°F/Gas Mark 5.

1. First, make a start on the sauce. Put the tomatoes in a shallow roasting dish with the garlic, season with salt and pepper and drizzle with olive oil. Roast in the oven for 10 minutes.
2. Meanwhile, lay each chicken breast between two sheets of cling film or greaseproof paper and flatten them slightly by whacking with a rolling pin.
3. Add the bread and the hazelnuts to the baking dish, drizzle over a little more oil and cook for a further 10 minutes (keeping an eye on it to make sure the bread doesn't burn). When you put the bread and nuts in, you can start cooking the chicken breasts.
4. Season the chicken with salt and pepper, brush with olive oil and cook in a pan on a medium heat for 5 minutes on each side. Leave to one side to rest. If you think the chicken breasts are not fully cooked through, just bung them in the oven for a minute or two when you take out the romesco ingredients.
5. Remove the garlic cloves from their skins and blitz them in a blender or food processor, along with the tomatoes, croûtons, nuts, paprika, cayenne pepper or chilli flakes, the vinegar and an extra glug of olive oil. You want a nice thick paste. If it is too dry, add a little more oil.
6. Serve the chicken with the sauce on top and chips or mash.

Speedy Moroccan tomato and chickpea soup

This is very much the 'Ronseal' of soups. It really does exactly what it says on the tin. It also demonstrates that making soup needn't be a long, laborious task. This turbo-charged version of a classic chickpea soup can be on the table in about 20 minutes. Frugal, simple and extremely quick, plus you can easily add some greens in too – just wilt in some spinach or chard right at the end.

Serves 2 adults and 2 children

Olive oil

1 onion, finely chopped

1 carrot, cut into small cubes

1 stick of celery, sliced

1 small aubergine, cut into small cubes

1 courgette, cut into small cubes

2 garlic cloves, chopped

Zest of 1 lemon

1 tablespoon capers

A small handful of olives, sliced

½ teaspoon chilli flakes (optional)

A handful of chopped flat-leaf parsley

300g pasta (such as farfalle, penne or conchiglie)

400g tin chopped tomatoes

2 tablespoons cream cheese

Freshly grated Parmesan cheese and chopped flat-leaf parsley, to serve

1. Heat a glug of olive oil in a saucepan on a medium heat and fry the onion for 4 to 5 minutes until it is soft.
2. Add the garlic, spices and mint, stirring well to coat the onion thoroughly.
3. Then simply pour in the tomatoes, stock and chickpeas. Season with salt and pepper then bring to the boil and simmer for 10 minutes.
4. Drizzle in half of the lemon juice. Taste it, and if it is tangy enough, stop there. If not, you can add the rest.
5. Serve this soup with lots of parsley or mint on top and spoonfuls of yoghurt swirled through. I like to add some chilli sauce (or harissa) to my bowl, just to give it an extra kick.

Lightly spiced beef noodles with cashew nuts

Serves 2 adults and 2 children

400g steak (sirloin or rump), thinly sliced

225g egg noodles

Sesame oil

Vegetable oil

1 small red onion, thinly sliced

1 red pepper, deseeded and sliced lengthways into thin strips

A small head of broccoli, broken into small florets

130g baby corn

Soy sauce

50g whole roasted cashew nuts

It can be tricky to stir-fry beef, as the quick cooking time means that the cut has to be a very tender one. And if you need a tender cut of beef, it is always going to be more expensive than stewing cuts. However, in this recipe, your marinade will work hard for you, so most types of beef escalope or steak will do the job. Sirloin would be best for flavour, but it's fair to say this would be lost on my children! When you're slicing your beef, make sure you cut across the grain of the meat instead of along it. This will instantly give you more tender meat.

1. Put the steak in a bowl with all the marinade ingredients and a tablespoon of water. Mix to coat and then leave it to marinate for at least 15 minutes. The beef can be left quite happily overnight in the fridge too.
2. Cook the noodles according to the instructions on the packet, then drain them and stir through a little sesame oil.
3. Heat a good glug of vegetable oil in a wok until the work is literally smoking. Fry the beef, stirring constantly and quickly, until it is seared all over. Remove the beef from the wok and keep it to one side in a bowl, complete with its cooking juices.

4. Add a little extra oil to the wok, if necessary, then throw in the onion, pepper, broccoli and baby corn. Cook on a high heat for 2 minutes, then pour over a little water and let it sizzle. Cover the wok, reduce the heat and simmer for 5 minutes.
5. Return the beef to the wok, including any juices. Drizzle in a good glug of soy sauce, then stir through the noodles and the nuts. You can also add a little sesame oil right at the end if you have some to hand. Serve immediately.

For the marinade

2 garlic cloves, finely chopped

1 teaspoon finely chopped fresh ginger

1 teaspoon ground cumin

A generous pinch of curry powder (mild or medium, depending on your preference)

1 tablespoon dark soy sauce, plus extra to serve

2 teaspoons rice wine vinegar or cider vinegar

1 tablespoon sweet chilli sauce

A pinch of sugar

Speed of Night

Here Today, ~~Gone~~, still Here Tomorrow

There is nothing revolutionary about this style of cooking organisation. My mum was a master at cooking something and then making it stretch out over more than one meal. Our freezer was full of basic meat and tomato sauce, which she would turn into anything from a Bolognese to a chilli con carne. This was the inspiration for my cheats' lasagne and my take on a classic shepherd's pie, using a cobbler topping instead of mashed potatoes. In this chapter, I've taken the idea a step further, throwing in a few of my absolute favourite things to eat: pulled pork, Mexican bean tacos and a very simple Vietnamese noodle salad. I find there's no extra effort involved in making more of something, so this chapter uses the tasty leftovers of one meal to make a different dish the following day or later in the week.

Ham hock with white beans and lemony gremolata

Serves 2 adults and 2 children

1 x 1kg ham hock, preferably smoked (or 800g smoked gammon joint)

1 onion, peeled and halved

2 cloves

1 bay leaf

1 teaspoon peppercorns

For the beans

Olive oil

1 onion, chopped

2 garlic cloves

2 x 400g tins cannellini beans, rinsed and drained

Salt and freshly ground black pepper

For the gremolata

Zest of 1 lemon

1 garlic clove

2 tablespoons chopped flat-leaf parsley

It's odd to think that I only really came to ham hock in the last few years. I don't know why I had not previously been tempted by the wonders of meltingly tender braised meat, from a really good value joint. Pre-cut joints of gammon work very well in this recipe, but if you can get a proper hock of ham (on the bone) it will give you even more flavour and be especially moist. It may seem a bit of a faff to discard the first lot of water, but it will ensure the meat is not too salty. For an extra-sweet flavour, cover the meat with cola instead of water when you slowly braise it. The leftovers can be used to make the ham and pea pasta bake on page 95.

1. Put the ham hock or gammon in a large saucepan and cover it with water. Bring to the boil, allow it to boil for 1 minute then remove from the heat and discard the water.
2. Rinse the ham, return it to the pan and cover again with water (or cola). Add the onion, cloves, bay leaf and peppercorns then bring to the boil. Turn down the heat and simmer for around 2 hours, until the ham is cooked and flaky.
3. Strain the ham, reserving the liquid (**important:** you will need the cooking liquid for the pasta bake the following day, see page 95). Use a knife to pull the ham apart into chunky slices, discarding the skin and bone (if there is one).
4. Heat a glug of olive oil in the saucepan over a medium heat and cook the onion for 4 to 5 minutes before adding the garlic for an extra minute. Mix in the beans and then fill the tin with the reserved ham cooking liquid and add that too. The liquor may still be quite salty, so make sure you taste it at this stage before seasoning with salt and pepper if needed.
5. Add most of the ham hock to the beans (reserving a few handfuls for the pasta bake) and warm through.
6. Chop the lemon zest, garlic and parsley together finely to make the gremolata.
7. Serve the ham and beans and sprinkle over the gremolata.

Ham and pea pasta bake

Next Day

What better way to use up the leftover ham from the ham hock and white beans with gremolata (see page 94) than in a pasta bake? By saving the cooking liquid from the ham and beans the day before, this pasta bake is rich in flavour but by no means heavy. You can, of course, make this dish as a standalone; just replace the cooked ham with store-bought ham and the ham stock with a chicken stock – make sure to season the bake with salt and pepper, as the stock will not have the saltiness of the ham hock stock.

Preheat oven to 180°C/350°F/Gas Mark 4.

1. Cook the pasta according to the packet instructions, then drain it and cool it down with cold water.
2. Meanwhile, heat the butter and olive oil in a saucepan over a medium heat. Add the onion and cook it for a few minutes, until soft, then add the garlic for a further minute.
3. Stir in the flour and cook for 2 minutes, stirring all the time, until it is nutty brown.
4. Pour in the wine, stir quickly to emulsify, then gradually add the ham hock stock until you have a thin sauce – you may not need to use it all. Mix in the crème fraîche, then the mustard and tarragon.
5. Combine the sauce, pasta, peas and ham in your baking dish, sprinkle liberally with cheese and bake for 10 to 15 minutes, until nicely brown on top. Serve immediately with extra freshly grated Parmesan.

Serves 2 adults and 2 children

You will need a 20 x 30cm baking dish

350g penne, rigatoni or other pasta shapes

A big knob of butter

1 tablespoon olive oil

1 onion, finely chopped

2 garlic cloves, crushed

50g plain flour

100ml white wine

500ml reserved ham hock stock

100ml half-fat crème fraîche

2 teaspoons Dijon mustard

1 teaspoon chopped tarragon

200g frozen peas

100g reserved ham hock, cut into small cubes

100g grated cheese (Parmesan or Cheddar), plus extra to serve

One-pot chicken with vegetables

Serves 2 adults and 2 children

Olive oil

Butter

100g smoked bacon, cut into small cubes

2 large carrots, cut into large chunks

200g small new potatoes left whole or halved if large

2 turnips, cut into wedges

1 x 1.5kg chicken

A sprig of tarragon

4 garlic cloves, unpeeled

Salt and freshly ground black pepper

250ml white wine

250ml chicken stock (If you prefer, you can replace part or all of the wine and stock with water)

2 leeks, cut into 2cm slices

50ml single cream (optional)

A squeeze of lemon juice (if using cream)

Everyone loves a traditional roast chicken, but I thought I'd try something a bit different here. Pot-roasting (without an oven in sight) is a great way of cooking a whole chicken, resulting in meat that is always moist and tender. What's more, the veg is cooked with the chicken, so this really is the kind of supper you can put on the heat and say goodbye to, in the knowledge that your whole meal is cooking together nicely. The leftover chicken can then go on to make my delicious Vietnamese salad on page 97.

1. Heat a generous glug of olive oil and a big knob of butter in a casserole or saucepan large enough to hold all the vegetables and the chicken. Fry the bacon until it's just starting to colour, then remove it from the pan and set aside.
2. Add all the vegetables, apart from the leeks, to the pan and cook them until browned. Then remove them and set aside.
3. Finally, brown the chicken on all sides, adding a little more oil and butter if necessary.
4. Leave the chicken breast-side up in the pan, and throw in the bacon, vegetables (not the leeks, yet!), tarragon and garlic. Season with a little salt and pepper, then pour in the wine. Allow the wine to bubble up, before pouring in the stock. The liquid needs to almost cover the chicken, without fully covering the breasts, so top it up with water if you need to. Bring everything to the boil, cover with a lid, lower the heat a little and simmer for about an hour.
5. For the last 10 minutes, add the leeks to the broth.
6. To serve, transfer the chicken and vegetables (except for the garlic cloves) to a large bowl and cover the bowl with foil. Remove the cloves of garlic and when they are cool enough to handle, squeeze the garlic from their skins into the cooking liquid. Boil for 5 minutes to reduce, then stir in the cream and lemon juice, if using.
7. Serve the chicken and vegetables with the gravy.

Vietnamese chicken salad

This minty-sweet fresh salad has become a real favourite in our house – it makes a lovely light supper, but it also sits very nicely in a lunch box. If the title sounds a little exotic, just think of this as a home-made version of the sweet noodle dishes you can buy in the supermarket for lunch. When I serve this for supper, I also make some spring rolls and dip them in the nuoc cham. This is a great way of using up any leftovers from the one-pot chicken on page 96.

Serves 2 adults and 2 children

300g rice noodles

Shredded leftover chicken from the pot roast (approx. 200g)

1 iceberg lettuce, finely shredded

½ cucumber, grated

1 large carrot, grated

A large handful of chopped coriander

A large handful of chopped mint, plus extra to serve

A large handful of plain roasted peanuts, crushed

For the nuoc cham

1 garlic clove, crushed

1 fresh chilli, very finely chopped (choose the chilli according to your heat tolerance. You can also leave it out completely, if you prefer, or add it to individual portions when serving)

Juice of 1 lime

2 tablespoons fish sauce

1 teaspoon sugar

1. Cook the noodles according to the packet instructions then drain and cool them completely under cold water.
2. Make the nuoc cham by simply mixing all the ingredients together until the sugar dissolves. Taste the sauce and add a tablespoon of water at a time, until you get a flavour you are happy with – don't make it too runny though.
3. In a large bowl, mix together all the salad ingredients (apart from the nuts) and stir in the sauce.
4. Serve in individual bowls, topped with lots of chopped mint and the chopped peanuts.

Mexican black beans with baked eggs and tortillas

I am a huge fan of beans, of all colours and sizes. They are a brilliant, cost-effective way of feeding a family, not to mention that they are full of fine minerals. As a resolute meat-lover, they also never leave me missing the meat. No one knows how to use beans better than the Mexicans and these black beans work superbly both here and in the tacos with black beans, squash and sweetcorn on page 99. Simply save half the beans from this recipe for your tacos later in the week (they will keep well in the fridge for 2 to 3 days). If you think beans can taste bland, I am convinced that these two recipes will change your opinion! If for any reason you are put off by this way of doing the eggs, you can poach or fry them separately.

Serves 2 adults and 2 children

Olive oil

2 red onions, finely diced

2 red peppers, deseeded and chopped into 1cm pieces

4 garlic cloves, finely chopped

1 tablespoon ground cumin

1 teaspoon ground coriander

A bunch of coriander, stems finely chopped and leaves left whole

Chipotle paste or sauce, to taste (according to how hot you want it)

400g tin chopped tomatoes

2 x 400g tins black beans, rinsed and drained (or any other type you like, e.g. pinto or red kidney)

A pinch of sugar

Salt and freshly ground black pepper

Juice of 1 lime

1 tablespoon sherry (optional)

4 eggs

4–6 warm tortillas, to serve

1. Heat a good glug of olive oil in a large pan, throw in the onions, red peppers and garlic and cook for 2 to 3 minutes – no more. You don't want the vegetables to be soft; this dish needs bite.
2. Add the cumin, ground coriander, the coriander stems and the chipotle paste, stirring to combine everything well.
3. Pour in the tomatoes, 200ml water and the black beans. Finish off with a pinch of sugar, some salt and pepper, the lime juice and the sherry, if you're using it. Simmer for about 10 minutes, until you have a fairly thick sauce.
4. Spoon half the beans into a large frying pan (the reserved beans are for making the tacos on page 99). Make 4 wells in the beans and break an egg into each one. Cook on a medium heat, until the white is set and the yolk is still runny. (Leave it for a little longer if you prefer your yolks set.)
5. Either place the pan in the middle of the table or spoon the beans into separate bowls. Sprinkle with the coriander leaves and serve with warm tortillas for scooping.

Tacos with black beans, squash and sweetcorn

A friend once said to me that cooking butternut squash is a labour of love and I know exactly what she means! Since becoming a dad, I don't have time to spend hours preparing complicated ingredients. So, underneath this recipe I have given you my step-by-step instructions for peeling and cutting butternut squash without any of the faff. I have deliberately not made these tacos spicy but you can easily add some sliced fresh chillies if you want a bit more heat. You will need half the bean quantity from the Mexican black beans on page 98.

1. Put the olive oil in a saucepan on a medium heat, throw in the butternut squash and 100ml water. Cook the squash, partially covered with the lid, until it is nice and soft but not breaking up.
2. Mix in the beans and sweetcorn and continue to heat through for a minute or so.
3. The salsa is quick to make: just combine the red onion, tomato, avocado, lime juice, cumin and coriander leaves in a bowl.
4. To serve, pile a portion of beans in a taco shell, and top with salsa, crème fraîche and cheese.

Note

To peel a butternut squash, put it in the microwave on high for 30 seconds. This softens the skin. Cut a thin slice off the base to make it flat and cut the squash in half at the point where it becomes round. Stand up the straight part of the squash and peel it using a sharp knife, cutting from the top downwards. Do the same with the round base of the squash. To deseed the round base, cut it in half vertically, then cut those two chunks in half. This leaves four nicely shaped chunks with very easy access to the seeds; use a knife to cut away the flesh where the seeds sit.

Serves 2 adults and 2 children

1 tablespoon olive oil

1 small butternut squash (approx. 500g–600g), cut into 1–2cm cubes

½ x quantity of the black beans on page 98

340g tin sweetcorn, drained

1 pack of taco shells

100ml crème fraîche or sour cream

100g grated Cheddar cheese

For the salsa

1 small red onion, finely diced

1 tomato, deseeded and finely chopped

1 avocado, cut into small cubes

Juice of 1 lime

½ teaspoon cumin

A handful of chopped coriander leaves

Here Today, Gone, Still Here Tomorrow

One-pot pork with cabbage, apples and potatoes

**Serves 2 adults and
2 children**

A small knob of butter

A small drizzle of olive oil

1 onion, finely chopped

1kg–1.5kg pork shoulder,
cut into large chunks

2 garlic cloves, finely
chopped

1 teaspoon juniper berries,
crushed

1 tablespoon wholegrain
or Dijon mustard

1 teaspoon dried oregano

350ml cider or apple juice

350ml water or chicken
stock

Salt and freshly ground
black pepper

350g baby new potatoes
(or cut them to a similar
size)

1 small cabbage, cut
into wedges

2 eating apples, peeled,
cored, cut into eighths

Single cream and crème
fraîche, to serve (optional)

Relatively cheap, I find that the flavour of pork marries well with so many spices and aromatics, maybe more so than any other meat. And it can easily hold its own alongside strong flavours. That's why I have added juniper berries to this stew, and also because their sweet aromatic flavour goes so well with the apples. By cooking an extra-large amount of meat, you can enjoy the leftover pork in delicious pulled-pork sandwiches the day after (see page 101). If you own a pressure cooker, the casserole cooking time can be reduced to 30 minutes. If you own a slow cooker, you are looking at 4 to 8 hours, but this is a recipe that works particularly when cooked without rushing.

1. Heat the butter and olive oil in a large casserole on a medium heat. Throw in the onion and cook it for 4 to 5 minutes until soft.
2. Whack up the heat to full and brown the pork all over.
3. Stir in the garlic, juniper berries, mustard and oregano.
4. Pour in your cider or apple juice and the water or stock and season with salt and pepper. Bring the casserole to the boil, then turn down the heat and simmer, covered, for an hour and a half. Keep an eye on it and if the casserole looks like it is drying out at any point, add a little water.
5. Throw in the potatoes and cabbage and cook for a further 20 minutes. Finally, in go the apples; they only need 10 minutes.
6. Serve immediately, with a swirl of cream, if you like. Keep any leftover meat and cooking liquid for the pulled pork on page 101.

Pulled pork in barbecue sauce with coleslaw

After you have made your big vat of pork casserole (see page 100), I guarantee you will have some meaty leftovers. This 'pulled pork' is a totally delicious way of using it up. Pulled pork is traditionally smoked in a smoker or on a barbecue, so it would be ideal if you could get some of that smokiness into the barbecue sauce here. Smoked sweet paprika is the easiest way to achieve this. You could also add a pinch of smoked salt (now widely available in the big supermarkets) or, for full authenticity, a few drops of liquid smoke but, in all honesty, that is a fairly tricky ingredient to get your hands on. Any leftover sauce will keep for about a week in the fridge in an airtight container.

1. First make the barbecue sauce. Heat the oil in a saucepan, add the crushed garlic and fry over a low heat for 1 minute. Stir in the tomato purée and then add all the rest of the ingredients. Simmer for 15 minutes, until the sauce has thickened and reduced – it should coat the back of the spoon. Taste and adjust the seasoning with a little salt and pepper if needed.
2. While the sauce is simmering, make the coleslaw by putting all the vegetables in a large bowl. Mix together the dressing ingredients and coat the vegetables, adding a drop of water if it needs loosening up.
3. Shred the pork using a couple of forks. Put it in a saucepan with the leftover cooking liquid and cook over a high heat until the liquid has evaporated and the pork is starting to crisp up around the edges.
4. Add a couple of tablespoons of the barbecue sauce, stir to coat the pork and continue to crisp the meat a little. You want some of the meat to be quite soft, while the rest is a bit brown and little crunchy.
5. To serve, pile the meat into soft bread baps and top with extra barbecue sauce and the coleslaw.

Serves 2 adults and 2 children

2 or 3 handfuls of leftover pork, along with the cooking liquid
4 soft baps

For the barbecue sauce
Olive oil
2 garlic cloves, crushed
1 tablespoon tomato purée
200g tin chopped tomatoes
1 tablespoon tomato ketchup
1 tablespoon maple syrup
1 tablespoon Dijon mustard
1 tablespoon cider vinegar
1 tablespoon dark brown sugar
½ teaspoon smoked sweet paprika
Salt and freshly ground black pepper

For the coleslaw
1 small white cabbage, cored and finely shredded
2 carrots, grated
½ small onion, finely chopped
50g mayonnaise
50g crème fraîche
½ teaspoon sugar
1 teaspoon cider vinegar
A squeeze of lemon juice
Salt and freshly ground black pepper

Cottage pie with cheese cobbler topping

Serves 2 adults and 2 children

You will need a 20 x 30cm baking dish

For the cottage pie filling
Olive oil
1 onion, finely chopped
1 carrot, finely chopped
1 stick of celery, finely chopped
500g beef mince or leftover cooked roast beef, finely chopped
A few sprigs of thyme, rosemary or flat-leaf parsley
150–200ml red wine
A good squirt of tomato ketchup
2 teaspoons brown sauce (I like good old HP sauce)
Salt and freshly ground black pepper

How do you give a fresh spin on something as traditional as a cottage pie? I am not reinventing any wheels here, but I absolutely love the cobbler topping on this pie! It is not as heavy as dumplings – think of it more like a scone dough. I think that a ragù or Bolognese-style sauce tastes great in a roll so, with this bready topping, you get the best of both worlds. What's more, it makes it much easier to eat the leftovers for lunch the next day – and you don't even need to heat them through again (although you can if you want to). To economise on the meat, you can replace some of it with cooked brown lentils – they will make the sauce lovely and creamy as well. And if you prefer a shepherd's pie, follow the same recipe but just replace the beef with lamb. Make a double batch of this ragù and you can use the rest of it in my cheat's beef lasagne on page 104.

1. Heat a glug of olive oil in a large casserole on a medium heat and cook the vegetables for a few minutes, until softened.
2. Turn up the heat, add the meat and fry it, breaking it up with your spoon, until browned all over. (For extra flavour – although a slightly longer cooking time – cook the meat first in a hot pan with a little oil, without breaking it up, until it has browned on its base. Remove it from the pan and cook the vegetables, and then return the beef to the pan to carry on cooking.)
3. Add the herbs, pour over the wine and allow it to bubble up and reduce a little. Squirt in the tomato ketchup and stir in the brown sauce. Season with salt and pepper.
4. Add a splash of water and simmer for around 20 minutes until the sauce has thickened – you don't want it too loose. If it looks as though it's drying out, add a little more water. Preheat your oven to 200°C/400°F/Gas Mark 6.

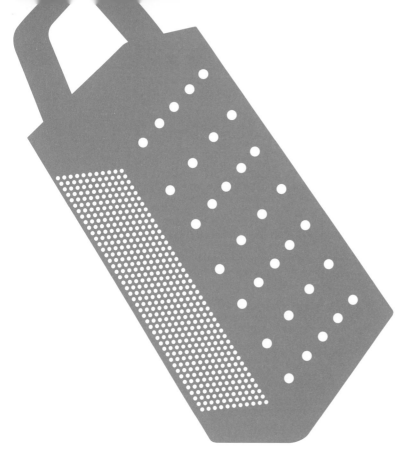

5. While the ragù is simmering, you can make the cobbler topping. Rub together the flour, butter and herbs (if using) and a pinch of salt in a large bowl. Add the cheese and the egg and drizzle in enough milk to make a soft, non-sticky dough. Use your hands to combine the ingredients. Either form the dough into flattish balls, or roll it out to a thickness of about 5mm and cut into rounds of a similar size to small scones.

6. To assemble the dish, spoon the meat mixture into your baking dish and top with the cobbler rounds. Brush the cobbler with the beaten egg and sprinkle with the extra cheese.

7. Bake in the oven for 30 to 35 minutes, until the topping is cooked through and nicely browned.

8. Serve immediately with green vegetables.

For the cobbler topping

200g self-raising flour

50g butter

A pinch of dried oregano or sage (optional)

75g grated Cheddar or other hard cheese

1 large egg

A pinch of salt

Milk, to combine

To finish

1 egg, beaten

Extra grated cheese

Cheat's beef lasagne

**Serves 2 adults and
2 children**

You will need a 20 x 30cm
baking dish

Olive oil

3 garlic cloves, finely
chopped

1 x quantity of beef ragù
from the cottage pie on
page 102

400g tin chopped tomatoes

1 packet of dried lasagne
sheets

250g pot of mascarpone
cheese

3 x 125g balls of mozzarella
cheese, roughly torn

A large handful of basil

Freshly grated Parmesan
or Cheddar cheese, for the
topping, plus extra

By making a big batch of the ragù for the cottage
pie on page 102, this lasagne can be put together
in double-quick time, especially as you don't need
to make a Béchamel sauce. Instead, the creaminess
comes from a pot of mascarpone and some mozzarella
cheese – and I actually prefer the taste and
consistency of this compared to the traditional method.
A final quick tip with lasagne (learned from bitter
experience some time ago): never overlap the lasagne
sheets. Even though it may look harmless, the double-
layered edges simply won't cook!

Preheat the oven to 190°C/375°F/Gas Mark 5.

1. Heat a glug of olive oil in a large saucepan on a low to
   medium heat. Soften the garlic in the pan for a minute,
   then pour in the ragù and the tinned tomatoes. Simmer
   for about 10 minutes, until the tomatoes are cooked and
   the sauce has slightly reduced.
2. To assemble, spoon one-third of the ragù into your
   baking dish and smooth it out to form an even layer.
   Top with a layer of lasagne and one-third of the
   mascarpone and mozzarella cheeses. Scatter over the
   basil leaves and then follow with half of the remaining
   ragù. Top with another layer of lasagne sheets and
   then cover with half of the remaining cheeses. Spoon
   over the rest of the ragù and finish with a final layer of
   lasagne and the rest of the cheeses.
3. Bake in the oven for 35 to 40 minutes until brown and
   bubbling. Serve immediately.

For a lamb alternative

Instead of using the pre-made ragù, fry a chopped onion
for 4 to 5 minutes, then add 2 crushed garlic cloves
followed by 500g lamb mince. Cook the lamb mince until
browned all over, then stir in 1 teaspoon of crushed fennel
seeds and 1 teaspoon chopped rosemary. Add a 400g tin
of chopped tomatoes, a lamb stock cube and a little extra
water, if necessary. Simmer to make a lovely thick tomato
sauce and then assemble the lasagne, as above.

Inspired Lunch Boxes

We all know that eating a proper meal at lunchtime is the key to ensuring children get enough good stuff into them to last the final part of the school day and to fuel their brains until home time. I can also say that lunch box inspiration is one of the most frequently asked questions I get from parents who get in touch with me. Not that there is anything wrong with a cheese sandwich every so often, but these lunch box ideas take the packed lunch to some refreshingly different places. Needless to say, all of these dishes work well as lunches at home in their own right, too.

Tandoori chicken drumsticks with mint raita

Makes 10–12 pieces

1 pack of chicken drumsticks (about 1kg)

Salt and freshly ground black pepper

Juice of 1 lemon, plus lemon wedges to serve

300ml plain yoghurt

2 teaspoons paprika

2 teaspoons ground coriander

2 teaspoons ground cumin

½ teaspoon chilli powder or cayenne pepper

6 garlic cloves, crushed

A small cube of fresh ginger, grated

For the raita

100ml plain yoghurt

1 tablespoon dried mint (or chopped fresh mint)

A pinch of sugar

Salt and freshly ground black pepper

One of my friends, Emma, told me that this recipe went down a storm at her daughter's netball camp. Apparently, it was even better than Emma's friend's mum's jerk chicken, which, up to that point, was the favourite among the girls! High praise indeed for these deliciously simple lunchtime treats. You can buy a readymade tandoori paste but when it's this easy to make one, why would you? These drumsticks will turn a golden yellow when grilled. If you want them to be red, like restaurant tandoori chicken, you will need to add some red food colouring, which is not included in the recipe. If you are really stuck for time and cannot marinate the drumsticks, simply chuck them in a bowl with the lemon juice, yoghurt and spices for 10 minutes before grilling. You will lose some of the depth of flavour but they will still be much tastier than if you grilled them plain.

1. You will need to remove the skin from the chicken drumsticks. This is easily done. The key is to use a piece of kitchen paper for extra grip when pulling off the skin, starting at the meaty end of the drumstick. Keep pulling and give it a good tug to get it off the bottom of the drumstick.
2. Slash the drumsticks all over with a sharp knife, put them in a bowl, season with salt and pepper and cover in the lemon juice. Leave in the fridge for 30 to 60 minutes.
3. Mix the yoghurt with all the spices, the garlic and the ginger. Pour this over the chicken and mix to coat. Leave it in the fridge to marinate, preferably overnight but for at least a few hours.

4. When you are ready to cook the chicken, preheat your grill to high and line your grill pan with foil. Lift the chicken out of the marinade and discard any marinade still in the bowl – the chicken should be lightly coated in the yoghurt but not dripping in it. Grill the chicken pieces for 20 minutes, turning regularly, until the chicken is cooked through and blackened in places. You can test the chicken is cooked by cutting into the fleshy part with a sharp knife; there shouldn't be any pink meat. You can also bake the chicken in an oven preheated to 200°C/400°F/Gas Mark 6 for 30 minutes.

5. Make the raita by simply mixing together the ingredients. Serve the chicken with the raita and lemon wedges to squeeze over the top.

Tuna, carrot and courgette salad

**Makes enough for
4 lunch boxes**

Olive oil

2 carrots, cut into
5mm cubes

2 courgettes, cut into
5mm cubes

160–180g tin tuna, drained

A large handful of finely
chopped flat-leaf parsley

1 orange, cut into segments
(see below)

A few crumbled nuts
(I like walnuts but any
nuts work well)

Fresh mint, to serve

For the dressing

2 tablespoons plain yoghurt

1 garlic clove, crushed

A pinch of curry powder

A pinch of sugar or ½
teaspoon honey

Juice of ½ lemon

1 teaspoon walnut,
hazelnut or olive oil

Salt and freshly ground
black pepper

This is a lovely little salad for a lunch box. It is full of good stuff and rich in gentle flavours – and it's ideal for a summer barbecue too. If you want it to go further, serve it with some lettuce leaves or noodles tossed in a little oil.

1. Heat a good drizzle of olive oil in a pan on a medium heat. Fry the carrots for 3 minutes then add the courgettes. Continue cooking until they have softened slightly but still have a good firm bite, then transfer them to a bowl.
2. Flake over the tuna and stir in the chopped parsley and orange segments.
3. Mix together the dressing ingredients, adding the nut oil if you have any, or a little olive oil if you don't. If the dressing seems very thick, you can thin it slightly with a little water.
4. Pour the dressing over the salad and toss well together.
5. Serve with a few crumbled nuts on top and some chopped fresh mint.

**To remove the orange segments from
the pithy membrane**

1. Cut a small chunk off the top and bottom of the orange. Stand it on a chopping board and peel it by gently slicing downwards using a sharp knife or a knife with a serrated edge. Then cut the orange segments away from the pith. This is easily done by sliding the knife into one of the segments, just inside the pith membrane. From the bottom of the segment, you can then almost peel the orange away from the pith on the other side of the segment using your knife. Repeat for the whole orange.

Smoked mackerel and potato salad

My daughter, Matilda, loves smoked mackerel and one of our fallback lunches is smoked mackerel pâté. She is also very fond of potatoes, so I created this salad so she can enjoy the best of both worlds. Think of it as a potato salad with some extra depth of flavour. Mackerel is also one of the healthiest options around, making this a great choice for your children. From a taste standpoint, some cooked beetroot would also go very well in this salad, as long as you don't mind it creating a rather fetching pink dressing.

1. Cook the potatoes in a saucepan of boiling salted water until tender, then drain and cool them slightly under cold running water.
2. Flake the mackerel into small pieces. Cut the potatoes into chunks, and mix them with the mackerel and the spring onions in a bowl.
3. Simply mix together all the dressing ingredients and spoon over the salad. Toss gently and serve. This will keep well in the fridge for a couple of days.

Makes enough for 4 lunch boxes

300g small new potatoes

2 fillets of cold smoked mackerel

4 spring onions, finely sliced

For the dressing

3 tablespoons crème fraîche

1 teaspoon Dijon mustard

1 teaspoon white wine vinegar

A pinch of sugar

Chopped herbs (flat-leaf parsley or dill are great choices)

Feta, cucumber and watermelon salad

**Makes enough for
4 lunch boxes**

½ cucumber, peeled and
cut into 1cm chunks

1 tablespoon white
wine vinegar

1 teaspoon sugar

200g feta, cubed

A thick and chunky slice
of watermelon, deseeded
and cut into chunks (you
are looking for a slice
roughly the size of a quarter
of a small watermelon)

A small handful of
chopped mint

Olive oil

Freshly ground black
pepper

Juice of ½ lime

I love the mix of flavours in this salad: the saltiness of
the feta (one of my favourite fridge standby ingredients),
the sweetness of the watermelon and the slight tartness
of the dressing. As with all the salads in this chapter,
you needn't limit this to lunch boxes; you can easily
serve it as a starter or an accompaniment to a summer
supper. And try it with the slush on page 180 to use
up more of the watermelon!

1. Chuck the cucumber in a bowl, pour over the vinegar
   and the sugar and toss it all together, making sure the
   sugar dissolves.
2. Add the feta, cucumber and watermelon and mix well.
3. Stir in the mint, then pour over a little drizzle of olive oil.
4. Season with black pepper (no need for salt, as the feta is
   salty enough) and finish with a squeeze of lime juice.

Pittas stuffed with home-made falafel

One day, supermarkets will sell falafel just like the falafel you get in Middle Eastern restaurants: nice and crispy on the outside and deliciously moist and soft inside. In the meantime, I find making falafel at home a lot of fun. This is the traditional method, using raw, soaked chickpeas. The result is classic falafel, which has a lovely texture and a subtle and delicate balance of flavours. You can use tinned chickpeas if you prefer but the resulting falafel will be slightly softer.

Makes 4 large pittas

For the falafel

250g chickpeas, soaked overnight with a pinch of bicarbonate of soda (or 400g tinned chickpeas, rinsed and drained)

1 tablespoon ground cumin

1 teaspoon ground coriander

¼ teaspoon ground cinnamon

2 garlic cloves, chopped

3 tablespoons chopped herbs (preferably a mixture of mint, coriander and flat-leaf parsley)

1 tablespoon plain flour

½ teaspoon baking powder

Salt and freshly ground black pepper

Vegetable oil, for frying

1. Drain the soaked chickpeas and rinse them thoroughly under cold running water.
2. Put all the falafel ingredients in a food processor and blitz until finely chopped but not completely smooth. Chill in the fridge for at least half an hour.
3. Shape about a tablespoon of the chickpea mixture into small, slightly flattened patties.
4. Pour the vegetable oil into a wide, shallow frying pan to a depth of around 5mm. Heat the oil and fry the falafel patties on a medium to high heat until golden on each side – try to turn them only once. Drain on kitchen paper.
5. To make the sauce, mix all the ingredients together and season, to taste, with salt and pepper.
6. To assemble, lightly toast the pitta breads and split into pockets. Fill the pittas with salad of your choice, then add the falafel and drizzle over the sauce. I like to add some chilli sauce to my own pitta.

Note

You can just as easily serve this with the minty raita from the tandoori drumstick recipe on page 108.

For the sauce

100ml tahini

Juice of 1 lemon

2 garlic cloves, crushed

A pinch of cayenne pepper

Salt and freshly ground
black pepper

To serve

1 pitta per person

Chopped lettuce, tomato
and cucumber

Lemon wedges

Freshly chopped coriander,
flat-leaf parsley or mint

Chilli sauce

Dips with a twist

I obviously couldn't do a lunch box section without a few dips.
But you wouldn't have let me get away with traditional hummus
or a simple tzatziki. So I have taken these two classics and given
them a bit of a makeover. In the case of the tzatziki, a reddish-pink
makeover, and for the hummus, I have gone green. I particularly
like using beetroot, because I feel it is a slightly misunderstood
and underappreciated vegetable. Said to reduce fatigue and
rich in loads of good-stuff minerals and vitamins, it's the kind of
vegetable I want my growing children to eat more of. Serve these
dips with sticks of carrot, courgette or cucumber, raw florets of
cauliflower, blanched asparagus or green beans and sliced pitta
bread. They are also very good on the side with meatballs (see
page 144), falafel (see page 114) or some simply grilled fish.

These make enough for 2–4 lunch boxes

Beetroot tzatziki

¼ large cucumber, peeled
and finely grated

2 raw beetroots, peeled
and finely grated

150ml Greek yoghurt

1 teaspoon Dijon mustard

A squeeze of orange juice

A handful of freshly
chopped herbs (dill,
tarragon and flat-leaf
parsley all work well here)

Salt and freshly ground
black pepper

1. Remove as much water as you can from the grated
   cucumber. You can do this by putting it in a tea
   towel and wringing it out or by simply giving it a
   good squeeze in the palm of your hand over the sink.
2. Put all the ingredients in a bowl and mix thoroughly.
   Taste and adjust the seasoning with salt and pepper
   and serve chilled.

Pea and feta hummus

Be careful about adding any extra salt
to this one, as the feta is generally salty
enough – taste first.

1. Cook the peas for a couple of minutes in boiling
   water.
2. Drain the peas and put them in a food processor
   along with the rest of the ingredients, including
   a good glug of olive oil for starters. Blitz until
   smooth, drizzling in some extra oil if needed to
   get the right consistency.
3. Serve with a little extra feta crumbled on top.

250g frozen peas

60g feta, crumbled, plus a
little more to garnish

2 tablespoons chopped
fresh mint (or 3 teaspoons
dried mint)

A good squeeze of
lemon juice

Freshly ground black pepper

Olive oil

Inspired Lunch Boxes

Sichuan chicken with mangetout and spring onions

**Makes enough for
4 lunch boxes**

100g mangetout, topped
and tailed and sliced
diagonally

2 good handfuls of leftover
cooked chicken

3 spring onions, sliced
diagonally

Freshly ground black pepper

1 teaspoon sesame seeds

For the dressing

2 tablespoons soy sauce

1 teaspoon rice wine
vinegar or cider vinegar

1 teaspoon sugar

1 teaspoon finely chopped
fresh ginger

1 garlic clove, finely
chopped

½ teaspoon ground Sichuan
peppercorns

1 tablespoon water or
chicken stock

1 teaspoon sesame oil

Freshly ground black pepper

This is a lovely nibbly salad, and a neat way of using up leftover cooked chicken, although you can very easily make it from scratch. Cook a couple of chicken breasts in a bowl (with a little water) in the microwave for around 10 minutes on medium power, or poach them in gently simmering water for 10 minutes, before taking the pan off the heat and leaving the breasts to continue cooking in the water for 15 to 20 minutes. It is definitely worth seeking out Sichuan peppercorns in the big spice collections in larger supermarkets. It's hard to describe their flavour compared with black peppercorns, but they are less hot and, well, a little more tingly!

1. Boil some water in a saucepan, add a pinch of salt and then blanch the mangetout for a couple of minutes. Drain them and then refresh them in cold water.
2. Put the chicken in a serving bowl with the mangetout and spring onions.
3. Mix together all the ingredients for the dressing and pour it over the salad. Mix to combine, then season with black pepper and sprinkle with the sesame seeds.

Lentils with smoked sausage, courgettes and tomatoes

If there's one thing my children love more than sausages, it is a processed Frankfurter-style sausage! I'm more than OK with this and a good old-fashioned hotdog in a roll is a frequent weekend treat at home. However, this delicious cold salad brings the humble Frankfurter slightly more upmarket, as it is served with wholesome lentils and a sweet dressing. You can, of course, cook your own lentils but, for speed and ease, I can't deny that pre-cooked lentils happily find their way into my shopping basket. I am lucky enough to have a wonderful Polish deli near my work and their kielbasa sausages work really well here, too. There's also no reason not to use chorizo, but make sure you fry it separately and drain it fully, as the oil which comes out of it will set once all the ingredients cool down.

1. If you haven't bought pre-cooked lentils, cook them according the packet instructions. Drain well, tip them into a bowl and leave them to cool a little.
2. Meanwhile, drizzle some olive oil into a frying pan on a medium heat and cook the onion for 2 to 3 minutes, until just softened.
3. Push the onion to one side of the pan and chuck in the sausage and courgette pieces, frying them until they both start browning around the edges and the sausages are hot through.
4. Mix the onion, sausages and courgette with the lentils.
5. Make the dressing by combining the mustard, honey and balsamic vinegar with a glug of olive oil and a splash of water. Season with salt and pepper.
6. Pour the dressing over the lentils, and mix in the tomatoes and torn basil. You can serve this salad while it is still warm, but it is best left to chill completely in the fridge.

Makes enough for 4 lunch boxes

250g cooked lentils (Puy, green or brown) or 100g dried lentils

Olive oil

1 small red onion, sliced lengthways and cut into thin wedges

4 smoked sausages, cut into chunks

1 small courgette, cut into 1cm cubes

4 tomatoes, diced

A handful of torn basil

For the dressing

1 teaspoon mustard (I like Dijon)

1 teaspoon honey

1 teaspoon balsamic vinegar

Olive oil

Salt and freshly ground black pepper

Sweet potato, pea and feta frittata

This frittata could have fitted into almost any of the chapters in this book. Having a good basic frittata in your repertoire will stand you in great stead. I have chucked sweet potato, mint and feta into this recipe but you can use pretty well whatever you want. Most cheeses are great (Cheddar, Parmesan and ricotta, in particular) and any mixture of root vegetables and green vegetables will be lovely. As such, frittatas are a great way of using up any leftover vegetables you may have lurking in the bottom of your fridge.

Makes 8 portions

1 small sweet potato, peeled and cut into cubes

4 eggs

1 teaspoon dried mint (or 1 tablespoon chopped fresh mint)

A pinch of cayenne pepper

Salt and freshly ground black pepper

Olive oil

Butter

100g frozen peas (no need to defrost them)

100g feta, cut into chunks

1. Cook the sweet potato in boiling salted water for 5 minutes, then drain it.
2. Beat the eggs in a bowl and mix in the mint and cayenne pepper. Season with salt and pepper.
3. Heat a really good drizzle of olive oil and a big knob of butter in an omelette pan or frying pan on a medium heat.
4. Evenly arrange the sweet potato and peas over the base of the frying pan, then immediately pour in the eggs. Dot with the cubes of feta. Heat the grill to its highest setting.
5. Cook the frittata until it starts to set and brown around the edges (this will take around 8 minutes), then put the pan under the hot grill for 2 to 3 minutes, until the frittata is slightly puffed and browning. If your frying pan does not have an ovenproof handle, make sure you don't put it directly under the grill.
6. Slide the frittata on to a plate. You can serve it hot, cool or chilled from the fridge.

Prawn, bean sprout and peanut noodle salad

Don't be put off by what may seem like a slightly longer ingredients list than elsewhere in the book. The dressing is very much a store cupboard 'throw-together', and it is also very forgiving. A bit extra, a bit less, a missing ingredient: it will still be delicious.

1. Cook the noodles according to the packet instructions and refresh in iced water. Drain, toss in the oil, then put the noodles in a bowl with the bean sprouts, carrot, cucumber and red pepper.
2. Toss the prawns in the lime juice, season with salt and pepper and add to the noodles and vegetables.
3. Mix together all the dressing ingredients (if you need to, you can loosen it with a little water, a bit more soy sauce or lime juice or some more coconut milk, if you have some to hand.)
4. Pour over the noodle salad and mix gently (hands work best), until everything is well coated. Garnish with coriander leaves, crushed peanuts and lime wedges.

Makes enough for 4 lunch boxes

2 fine egg noodles nests

1 teaspoon sesame or vegetable oil

A handful of bean sprouts

1 carrot, finely cut into strips or grated

¼ large cucumber, cut into small cubes

½ red pepper, deseeded and cut into thin strips

250g cooked prawns

Juice of ½ a lime

Salt and freshly ground black pepper

Coriander leaves

A small handful of peanuts, crushed

Lime wedges, to serve

For the dressing

3 tablespoons peanut butter

1 teaspoon brown sugar or honey

1 teaspoon soy sauce

1 teaspoon fish sauce

Juice of ½ a lime

1 garlic clove, crushed

1cm cube of fresh ginger, finely grated

Chilli sauce or powder, to taste

A little grating of creamed coconut (or you can use 2 tablespoons of coconut milk if you have a tin already open)

Inspired Lunch Boxes

Soy and honey glazed salmon with soba noodles

Makes enough for 4 lunch boxes

4 x 150g salmon fillets, skin removed

Olive oil

250g soba noodles

150g Tenderstem broccoli

2 teaspoons sesame oil

3 spring onions, sliced into rounds

1 teaspoon sesame seeds

For the marinade/dressing

4 tablespoons soy sauce

2 tablespoons honey

½ teaspoon ground ginger

1 garlic clove, crushed

1 tablespoon mirin or rice wine or a little dash of sweet sherry (if you can't find any of these, don't worry)

1 teaspoon rice wine vinegar or cider vinegar

Soba noodles (made from buckwheat) are particularly good eaten cold. That's why they are such a perfect fit for this chapter. If you can't find soba noodles (although most big supermarkets do stock them), any other noodles will work well here. Not only is this a lovely addition to a lunch box, it is also exactly the kind of thing I take on a picnic. Oh, and it goes without saying that this dish can just as happily be eaten warm out of the pan.

1. Mix the marinade ingredients together, stirring to make sure the honey is completely incorporated.
2. Place the salmon in a shallow dish and pour the marinade over the top, then leave it in the fridge for as long as you can – at least half an hour, but overnight would be ideal.
3. When you're ready to cook the salmon, heat a little oil in a large frying pan on a medium to high heat. Drain the salmon fillets, reserving the marinade, and fry them for 2 to 3 minutes on each side, until just cooked. It's good to leave the salmon slightly pink in the middle so that it doesn't dry out, plus the salmon will carry on cooking a little when you take it out of the pan.
4. Meanwhile, cook the soba noodles according to the packet instructions and steam or blanch the broccoli for 2 to 3 minutes. Drain and refresh the noodles in ice-cold water, then toss them in the sesame oil.
5. Cut up the cooked broccoli into bite-sized pieces and toss with the noodles and spring onions, then place the salmon on top. If you prefer, you can also flake the salmon into the noodles.
6. Put the frying pan back on the heat and pour in the saved marinade, swirling it around for a few moments to deglaze the pan.
7. Finally, pour the warm marinade over the salmon and noodles, and sprinkle over the sesame seeds.

Rice pilaf with chicken, apple and pine nuts

Perfectly cooked basmati rice in a very gently spiced pilaf, with a little extra sweetness and crunch thanks to the diced apple and grated carrot. You can serve this warm, but I like it as a cold crispy salad. If you have some leftover chicken, chuck it into the rice at the very end of the cooking process, rather than using fresh chicken breasts and cooking them in the stock (but make sure your leftover chicken is properly reheated). Using leftover chicken will also help stop the pilaf becoming too wet.

**Makes enough for
4 lunch boxes**

Vegetable oil

1 onion, finely chopped

2 garlic cloves, finely chopped

2.5cm cube of fresh ginger, grated

1 teaspoon turmeric

1 teaspoon curry powder

½ stick of cinnamon

2 bay leaves

250g basmati rice, rinsed well

650ml chicken stock or water

Salt and freshly ground black pepper

2 chicken breasts, skin removed and cut into cubes (see intro)

1 apple, peeled and cut into small cubes

Juice of ½ lime

1 large carrot, grated

25g pine nuts, lightly toasted in a dry frying pan

The raita from page 108, to serve

1. Heat a drizzle of vegetable oil in a large saucepan. Add the onion and cook for 4 to 5 minutes, until soft. Add the garlic, ginger and spices and fry for a further minute.
2. Stir in the rice and coat it well in the spices and oil.
3. Pour in the stock and season with salt and pepper. Bring everything to the boil, then turn down the heat to a low simmer and cover the saucepan. Cook for 10 minutes, then carefully mix in the chicken pieces. Try not to stir the rice or it will become creamy, like a risotto.
4. Cover again and cook for 10 minutes, until all the water has evaporated. Keep an eye on it so it doesn't burn or stick to the bottom and make sure the heat isn't too high.
5. Take the pan off the heat and, with the lid still on, leave it to steam for a further 5 to 10 minutes until the rice is soft and fluffy.
6. Just before serving, toss the apple pieces in lime juice and stir them into the rice with the carrot and pine nuts. Serve with the raita.

Ready-Made Meals Made by You

I am not saying we never eat ready-made meals at home.
Far from it. But what with the ever-rising cost of our weekly
shop, there are times when I wonder whether I can really
justify having certain things in our shopping basket. That is
why I enjoy trying to replicate – and better – the kind of pre-
packaged food you find in the supermarket. None of these
dishes will beat a two-minute ping-and-ding microwave
operation, but they will give you all the pleasure of home-
cooked food compared with mass-produced plastic packs.
I decided to have a little fun with this chapter and have gone
a bit retro, featuring crispy pancakes, chicken Kievs and sweet
and sour pork. Old ones, but great ones nonetheless!

Bean burger with tomato relish

A burger made from solely vegetarian ingredients is never going to be a true replacement for a traditional burger. But, with the price of meat forever on the increase, this makes for a frugal and surprisingly, well, 'meaty' alternative. The tomato relish gets made over and again in my house, served with all manner of dishes. Simple and delicious, it's worth the small effort to make your own rather than buy one in a jar.

Serves 2 adults and 2 children

400g tin beans (any beans, around 260–280g drained weight), rinsed and drained

2 eggs, beaten

1 tablespoon finely chopped flat-leaf parsley

1 teaspoon finely chopped thyme

25g freshly grated Parmesan cheese

1 teaspoon Dijon mustard

Salt and freshly ground black pepper

A squeeze of lemon juice

50g fresh breadcrumbs

Olive oil, for drizzling

Preheat your oven to 190°C/375°F/Gas Mark 5.

1. Mash the beans in a bowl using a fork or a masher. You don't want a smooth paste here, so it's best not to use your food processor.
2. Mix in all the remaining ingredients (apart from the oil), making sure everything is well incorporated and leave it to rest for 5 minutes.
3. Divide the mixture into quarters and form each piece into a burger shape.
4. Place the burgers on a non-stick baking tray (or a baking tray lined with greaseproof paper or foil), drizzle them with olive oil and bake for 15 to 20 minutes, turning halfway through. They will be golden when they are ready.
5. While they are cooking, make the tomato relish. Heat a drizzle of oil in a saucepan on a gentle medium heat and cook the onion and garlic for 4 to 5 minutes to soften them.

6. Chuck in the tomatoes, sugar and vinegar and simmer until the tomatoes are just beginning to break down and have started to reduce. You want it to have a slightly jammy consistency. Stir through the chilli sauce, to taste.

7. Serve the burgers in buns with the relish, grated cheese if you fancy it, and any of your favourite burger toppings.

For the tomato relish

Olive oil

1 small red onion, finely diced

1 garlic clove, crushed (optional)

4 medium tomatoes, deseeded and finely chopped (no need to peel)

½ teaspoon brown sugar

1 teaspoon red wine vinegar

Chilli sauce (such as Tabasco), to taste

To serve

Burger buns

Freshly grated cheese (optional)

Your favourite burger topping, such as lettuce and gherkins

Ready-Made Meals, Made by You

Portobello mushroom burger with escalivada and goat's cheese

Portobello mushrooms (or large field mushrooms) are meaty in texture, very filling and fairly cheap to boot. They make a great alternative to the classic burger and are fantastic with all the usual burger toppings – simply grill or bake the mushrooms and then add your favourite extras. I love the Spanish flavours in the escalivada here (a Catalan dish almost like a ratatouille) which elevates these humble mushrooms to a vegetarian spectacular that will satisfy the hungriest of tummies.

Serves 2 adults and 2 children

1 small aubergine, cut into 1–2cm cubes

1 small red pepper, deseeded and thinly sliced

4 tomatoes, quartered

4 garlic cloves, unpeeled

Olive oil

1 teaspoon red wine vinegar

Salt and freshly ground black pepper

4 large portobello or field mushrooms

4 slices of goat's cheese, cut from a log

Rolls or buns, to serve

Preheat your oven to 180°C/350°F/Gas Mark 4.

1. Put the aubergine, red pepper, tomatoes and garlic in a roasting dish and cover them with a really good glug of olive oil. Roast the vegetables for 30 to 40 minutes (stirring halfway through), until they are soft and starting to turn a little bit golden.

2. Remove the dish from the oven (but keep the oven at the same temperature), squeeze the flesh from the garlic cloves and discard the skins. Mix everything together, stir in the vinegar and season with salt and pepper. Set aside to cool a little.

3. Meanwhile, place the mushrooms in a baking dish. Baste them with a little olive oil, season with salt and pepper and cook them in the oven for 10 minutes.

4. Spoon the escalivada equally between the mushrooms (but don't overfill them) and place the goat's cheese slices on top. Drizzle a little olive oil over the cheese, return them to the oven and cook for 10 minutes, until the cheese has melted and the escalivada is warmed through.

5. Serve the stuffed mushrooms in rolls.

Retro sweet and sour pork

I particularly love the fact that this dish carries all the sweet, tangy punch of a true sweet and sour, without any additives or food colouring. But you won't notice the difference between this version and the classic dish we all enjoy at our local Chinese restaurant. To be fully authentic, I have used a batter for the pork, but if you prefer, you can just dust the pork with cornflour after a quick marinade in the soy sauce and Chinese five spice and then simply fry the meat in a little less oil. You can also use chicken breasts or thighs instead of the pork.

1. First make the sauce. Measure out the pineapple juice and top it up with either water or additional juice until you have 150ml liquid. Mix this together with the rest of the sauce ingredients. If you want the end result to be slightly thickened, as in the traditional takeaway dish, mix the cornflour with a little water and stir it into the mixed ingredients. If you leave out the cornflour, the sauce will be looser. Set the sauce aside.
2. In a small bowl toss the pork in the soy sauce and Chinese five spice.
3. Make the batter by simply mixing together the egg and cornflour in a shallow dish. Drain the pork and coat it in the batter.
4. Pour vegetable oil into a wok to a depth of about 5mm. Heat over a high heat and when almost smoking, carefully drop in the battered pork. Cook the pork, turning it a few times in the oil, until golden. Remove and drain on kitchen paper.
5. Drain off most of the oil from the wok and then put it back on the heat. Fry the vegetables until they are just cooked through, then add the water chestnuts, pineapple and sauce. Bring it to the boil, stirring all the time so it thickens evenly (if you are using the cornflour).
6. Return the pork to the wok and heat through for a couple of minutes. Serve with white rice.

Serves 2 adults and 2 children

300g lean pork, cubed
1 tablespoon soy sauce
1 teaspoon Chinese five spice
Vegetable oil
1 red pepper, deseeded and cut into chunks
1 carrot, thinly sliced on the diagonal
4 spring onions, cut into 1cm rounds
225g tin water chestnuts, drained
225g tin pineapple cubes in own juice (reserve the juice)
Sesame oil (optional)
Cooked plain white rice, to serve

For the pork batter

1 egg, beaten
2 tablespoons cornflour, plus extra for dusting

For the sauce

Reserved pineapple juice
1 tablespoon soy sauce
1 tablespoon rice wine vinegar or cider vinegar
1 tablespoon brown sugar
2 tablespoons tomato purée
1 tablespoon cornflour (optional)

Pad Thai

Serves 2 adults and 2 children

225g flat rice noodles

Vegetable oil

10–12 large raw shelled prawns

50g firm tofu, cut into cubes

2 shallots or 1 small onion, chopped

1 carrot, cut into thin batons or grated

A large handful of mangetout, topped and tailed and cut into thirds, diagonally

2 garlic cloves, chopped

1 egg, beaten

For the sauce

1 tablespoon palm sugar (or light brown sugar)

1 tablespoon granulated or caster sugar

1 tablespoon tamarind paste or purée (Bart does a good one in a jar)

2 tablespoons fish sauce

½ teaspoon shrimp paste (optional)

Salt and freshly ground black pepper

Pad Thai is one of those dishes that has a slightly mystical aura surrounding it. It is actually much easier to make than you think, with its signature taste coming from a few key ingredients. Tamarind paste or purée is now readily available in supermarkets, and it is a great addition to your store cupboard, not least for chucking into curries to add extra depth. It's worth pointing out here that the topping really does finish off this dish. The extra crunch from the peanuts really enhances the deliciousness and creates an authentic Pad Thai experience. If you prefer, you can use chicken instead of prawns and interchange whatever vegetables you have to hand.

1. Heat all the sauce ingredients together in a small saucepan, stirring gently, until the sugar has dissolved. Taste and season with salt and pepper if you feel they are needed. Set the sauce aside.

2. Cook the noodles according to the packet instructions. Drain and refresh them in cold water so that they stop cooking.

3. Heat a little vegetable oil in a wok or large frying pan over a high heat. Fry the prawns briskly, stirring all the time, then remove them as soon as they are pink. Add a little more oil and fry the tofu, keeping it moving, and then set that aside too.

4. Stir-fry the vegetables and when they are just cooked through, add the garlic and fry for a moment more.

5. Push all the vegetables to one side of the pan, pour in the beaten egg and stir until it starts to look a little scrambled. Now mix the egg with the vegetables.

6. Chuck the prawns and tofu back into the wok, along with the noodles. Stir gently but thoroughly to warm the noodles and combine all the ingredients.

7. Pour the sauce over the top and toss together. Serve immediately, sprinkled with the spring onions, coriander and peanuts, and with some lime wedges for squeezing over.

To serve

2 spring onions, shredded

A handful of coriander leaves

2 tablespoons roasted peanuts, lightly crushed

Lime wedges

Crispy pancakes

Serves 2 adults and 2 children

For the pancakes
125g plain flour
Salt
2 eggs
300ml milk
A drizzle of vegetable oil
Butter

For the cheese sauce filling
30g butter
30g plain flour
300ml milk
1 teaspoon Dijon mustard
100g grated cheese (pick one with a nice strong flavour like Cheddar or Gruyère)

Optional extras
Chopped ham
Cooked chicken
Mushrooms fried in butter and garlic
Frozen peas
Sweetcorn

I am diving right into the world of Findus here with these crispy pancakes. Do you remember the adverts back in the 1980s? I think the slogan was 'every day has got a different taste'. I also remember a rather clumsy dad trying very hard to amuse an extremely cute little baby. The beauty of these pancakes is that they really do mean that every day can have a different taste, as the fillings can vary enormously, especially if you have leftovers such as ham and cooked chicken. My children enjoy grabbing things and adding them to their own pancakes before they are cooked, so it's a great way to get them involved. If you can't face making the actual pancakes, you have two options: supermarkets sell good-value packets of readymade pancakes (look out for the smaller pancakes) or you can also use small flour tortillas. These have the advantage of being slightly harder to tear than pancakes.

1. If you are making the pancakes, sift the flour into a bowl, then throw in the salt, eggs and milk. Mix with a whisk until nice and smooth. Stir in a drizzle of vegetable oil.
2. Heat a smallish pancake pan or frying pan on a nice high heat. Melt a small knob butter in the pan, swizzle it around then add a small ladleful of batter, swirling it round the base of the pan. You are not looking for big pancakes here – 10cm in diameter is perfect.
3. When the batter has set (this will be quick – just a few seconds), flip over the pancake and cook it for a further 30 seconds. Remove the cooked pancake and repeat with the rest of the batter. It is fine to stack the pancakes on top of each other while you cook the rest; they will not stick together.

4. To make the cheese sauce, melt the butter in a saucepan on a medium heat then stir in the flour. It is important to mix well and keep stirring for a minute or so. Drop in a splash of milk and stir to combine it into the flour and butter. Gradually add the rest of the milk, stirring or whisking the whole time. You will end up with a fairly thick sauce (like custard). Remove the sauce from the heat and whisk in the mustard and cheese. Keep stirring until it is all melted.

5. To assemble the pancakes, place about 2 tablespoons of sauce in the middle of each pancake, just to one side, and add in any of your optional extra fillings.

6. Make a 'glue' by mixing 1 tablespoon of plain flour with an equal amount of water. Add more water if it is too thick. Brush the edge of each pancake with the flour and water mixture, then fold the pancake over and press it gently so you have a sealed half moon.

7. Put the flour in a shallow dish, the egg in another dish and the breadcrumbs in a third. Carefully dip the pancakes first in the flour (shaking off any excess), then in the egg and, finally, in the breadcrumbs. Make sure they are evenly coated all over.

8. Heat a good glug of vegetable oil in a large frying pan over a medium to high heat. When the oil is hot, fry a pancake for a minute on each side, until it is well browned. Drain on kitchen paper and serve immediately. Repeat for the remaining pancakes, making sure to add more oil each time.

To finish
3–4 tbsp plain flour
1 egg, beaten
A large handful of breadcrumbs
Vegetable oil

Chicken Kievs

Serves 2 adults and 2 children

150g butter, at room temperature

5 garlic cloves, crushed

Salt and freshly ground black pepper

Juice of 1 lemon

A handful of flat-leaf parsley, finely chopped

4 skinless chicken breasts, with small fillet attached

50g plain flour, seasoned with salt and pepper

2 eggs, beaten

100g breadcrumbs

Vegetable oil

Lemon wedges, to serve

There is something wonderfully old-fashioned about chicken Kievs. Maybe it's simply the fact that the whole point of them is to have a load of lovely, flavoursome melted butter dripping out when you cut into them! Still, my Gran always said that a little bit of everything is fine, so I am more than happy to serve these at home once in a while. If the preparation seems quite involved to you, the great thing about these Kievs is that they freeze beautifully before the breadcrumb stage so you can make an extra-large batch and save the ones you don't need for a rainy day. The technique of butterflying the chicken breasts is honestly not as difficult as it sounds and is the perfect way to ensure the chicken is nice and flat for cooking.

1. Mix the butter with the garlic, 1 teaspoon of salt, half a teaspoon of pepper, the lemon juice and parsley. If you have the time, chill it until it is firm again.
2. Now you need to butterfly and flatten the chicken breasts. Remove the small fillet from the back of the chicken breast and place the main chicken breast smooth side down. Cut from the top to the bottom along the centre of the breast, about halfway through the flesh – be careful not to cut all the way through. Now make gentle cuts along the same length, working out towards each edge of the breast until you can open it up and lay it out flat. Don't go too close to the edge or you will cut off the top of the breast.
3. Place each breast between cling film or greaseproof paper and bash it with a rolling pin to flatten slightly and tenderize the meat. Season the breasts with salt and pepper.

4. Drop a quarter of the garlic and butter mixture into the centre of each breast, then place the reserved small fillet on top. Fold the chicken breast back together, overlapping the edges slightly and sealing with a little bit of the egg and flour. If you have time, wrap each chicken breast tightly in cling film and chill for a couple of hours in the fridge. You can also freeze them very successfully at this stage if you want to make a larger batch.

5. When you are ready to cook the Kievs, preheat your oven to 200°C/400°F/Gas Mark 6. Tip the flour into a shallow dish, the beaten eggs into another dish and the breadcrumbs into a third. Roll the chicken breasts first in the flour (shaking off the excess), then dip them in the egg and finally coat them in breadcrumbs. Make sure they are evenly coated all over.

6. Lightly oil a frying pan and place on a medium heat. Fry the Kievs for a couple of minutes on each side, until they are golden brown.

7. Transfer the Kievs to a baking tray and cook in the oven for a further 15 minutes. Serve with the lemon wedges, steamed green beans and mashed potatoes to soak up all the lovely garlicky butter.

Traditional chicken and chorizo paella

Serves 2 adults and 2 children

200g chorizo sausage, cut into small cubes

4–6 chicken thighs (approx. 500g), skin and bone removed, cut into cubes

1 onion, finely chopped

4 garlic cloves, finely chopped

1 teaspoon smoked paprika

100g green beans, trimmed and cut in half

100g broad beans

A pinch of saffron, soaked in a little warm water (or a pinch of turmeric)

1L chicken stock or water

300g paella rice

Salt and freshly ground black pepper

Lemon wedges, to serve

This paella is cooked in the traditional way, on the stovetop, as opposed to being baked in the oven. It is also very meaty, rather than being all about the seafood. The beauty of cooking paella on the hob is that it needs virtually no attention at all. Just get all the ingredients in the pan and leave it be. In fact, I would actively encourage you to leave the base of the paella to crisp up a little (not actually burn, but not far off it!). The Spanish call this caramelized crust the socarrat and it is, in some ways, the best part of the dish – for me, anyway. I don't have the luxury of a proper wide, flat-bottomed paella pan (or the space to cook with it) so your normal frying pan will do the trick here.

1. Heat your frying pan over a medium heat and add the chorizo. Cook it until it is crispy (but do not burn it) and its delicious red oil has been released.
2. Add the chicken and the onion and stir to coat in all the lovely chorizo oil. Cook for 3 to 4 minutes until the chicken has browned. Mix in the garlic and paprika and stir for a few seconds.
3. Add the green beans and broad beans to the pan and give them a good stir. Pour over the saffron (and its soaking water) and the stock. Bring to the boil and simmer for a couple of minutes to help the beans along, then pour in the rice.
4. If the rice isn't completely submerged, add enough water to just cover it. Season with salt and pepper and leave the paella to cook for about 12 minutes, checking occasionally to make sure the top hasn't dried out – add a little more water if needed. You want the rice to be nicely puffed and cooked through.
5. Remove the pan from the heat, cover it with the lid or a clean tea towel and allow the rice to finish cooking in the steam for about 10 minutes.
6. Serve immediately with lemon wedges.

Lamb and potato hotpot

Lamb hotpot is like an old friend: you know exactly what to expect, it's reliable, comforting and never lets you down. I have bulked up my version by adding swede and carrots and this recipe is also slightly quicker to cook than traditional hotpot. The key is to use neck fillet, also called the scruff. It is a good-value cut, widely available and, as it is not from a part of the lamb that does the hard work, it is tender and does not require an extended cooking time. However, there is no reason why you can't use shoulder here, or any other cut of lamb for that matter. Shoulder require an extra 30 minutes of cooking time.

Preheat your oven to 200°C/400°F/Gas Mark 6.

1. Chuck your meat into a bowl. Add the flour, mustard powder, salt and pepper and give it a good stir to make sure the meat is evenly coated.
2. Heat a nice glug of olive oil and a knob of butter in an ovenproof casserole and sear the meat to seal it on all sides. Depending on the size of your casserole, you may need to do this in two quick batches so as not to cram it too full.
3. Remove the meat and set aside while you fry the onion for 4 to 5 minutes until soft.
4. Layer the casserole with half the meat, then half the onion, followed by half of the root vegetables. Repeat these layers and tuck in the sprig of thyme.
5. Finish with slices of potato arranged neatly on top.
6. Carefully pour over the stock, cover the casserole with a lid and cook in the oven for 20 minutes, before turning down the heat to 140°C/275°F/Gas Mark 1. Cook for a further 1 hour and 15 minutes.
7. Remove from the oven and dot the potatoes with small pieces of butter. Turn the oven back up to 200°C/400°F/Gas Mark 6 and cook the hotpot, uncovered, for a further 5 minutes, allowing the potatoes to turn a lovely golden colour. Serve immediately.

Serves 2 adults and 2 children

500g neck fillet, sliced into rounds

1 tablespoon plain flour

1 teaspoon mustard powder

Salt and freshly ground black pepper

Olive oil

Butter

1 large onion, halved and sliced

2 carrots, cut into large chunks

½ small swede, cut into chunks

1 sprig of thyme

600g potatoes, peeled and fairly thinly sliced (aim for about 3–4mm)

500ml lamb or chicken stock or water

Southern fried chicken with corn on the cob and greens

Serves 2 adults and 2 children

8–10 thighs or drumsticks, or a mixture (approx. 1kg)

284ml pot buttermilk

Salt and freshly ground black pepper

1 teaspoon onion powder

150g plain flour

½ teaspoon paprika (sweet or hot, it's up to you)

½ teaspoon mustard powder

½ teaspoon dried oregano or sage

Vegetable oil

I am making these finger-licking chicken pieces the traditional way, by frying them. If you prefer, you can cook them in the oven. Heat a baking tray with a little oil in an oven preheated to 180˚C/350˚F/Gas Mark 4. Carefully roll the chicken pieces in the hot oil and then bake them for around 30 minutes. Although it may feel like a bit of a faff to marinate the chicken, it really helps tenderise and flavour the meat. That said, I have also made this chicken without marinating it and it was still lovely.

1. Using a sharp knife, cut some slashes into the chicken pieces. Put them in a bowl and cover them with the buttermilk. Season with 1 teaspoon of salt and pepper, and mix in the onion powder. Give it a good rub to work it into the meat, then leave in the fridge to soak for at least a few hours – and ideally overnight. When you are ready to fry the chicken, let it come back to room temperature first.

2. In a bowl, mix the flour with paprika, mustard powder and dried herbs and season with salt and pepper. Wipe the buttermilk from the chicken and coat each piece in the seasoned flour. Shake to remove any excess.

3. Heat a deep-fat fryer to 160ºC. If you are using a saucepan, make sure the oil is no more than about one-third of the way up the pan. Test the oil with a small piece of bread – it should immediately bubble furiously and turn brown within about 20 seconds. (You can shallow fry the chicken if you prefer, turning it 3 or 4 times while cooking.)

4. Fry the chicken for 10 to 15 minutes until it is deep golden brown and fully cooked through.

5. While the chicken is cooking, bring a large pan of salted water to the boil and cook the corn cobs for 3 minutes. Drain away the water and allow a good knob of butter to melt over the cob pieces, before seasoning with salt and pepper.

6. Shred the greens, then heat 1 tablespoon of olive oil and a large knob of butter in a wide frying pan. Fry the greens for 2 minutes, before adding the garlic. Cook for another couple of minutes then add a splash of water, cover with a lid and cook the greens until they are soft and just starting to collapse down – about 2 to 3 minutes. Season with salt and pepper and a squeeze of lemon juice just before serving with the chicken and the corn cobs.

For the corn

4 corn on the cob,
each cut into 3 wedges

Butter

Salt and freshly ground
black pepper

For the greens

500g spring greens or green
cabbage (don't use spinach,
as it breaks down too
much. If you are using kale,
separate the leaves from the
stems)

Olive oil

Butter

1 garlic clove

Salt and freshly ground
black pepper

A squeeze of lemon juice

Salmon fishcakes with dill and mustard mayonnaise

Serves 2 adults and 2 children

400g floury potatoes (e.g. Maris Piper or King Edward), peeled, cut into chunks

Salt and freshly ground black pepper

400g tin salmon

Zest 1 lemon

4–5 tbsp plain flour

1 large egg, beaten

50g breadcrumbs (panko breadcrumbs are my favourite)

Vegetable oil

For the mayonnaise

1 egg yolk

1 teaspoon Dijon mustard

A dash of Tabasco

Salt and freshly ground black pepper

300ml vegetable oil

1 teaspoon lemon juice

A small bunch of dill, chopped

I have deliberately kept these yummy fishcakes very simple, as there is plenty of extra flavour in the mayonnaise. If you can't be bothered to make your own mayonnaise, feel free to use a small jar of store-bought mayonnaise and just add the lemon juice, mustard and lots of dill to that. I have cheated a little by using tinned salmon. It is, of course, cheaper than fresh salmon and, in all honesty, does the job just fine. If you want to use fresh salmon, you'll need a couple of skinless fillets and the easiest way to cook them (ensuring less washing up) is to pop them in the simmering water with the potatoes for the last 5 minutes of cooking time.

1. Put the potatoes in a saucepan, cover them with water and bring to the boil. Leave them to simmer for 10 to 15 minutes until they are soft. Drain them in a colander and then leave them in the colander for a couple of minutes to dry out. Mash them and season.
2. Mix the salmon and the lemon zest into the potatoes.
3. Shape the fishcake mixture into 4 large or 8 small cakes. Dust each one with flour, shaking off the excess. Dip them into the egg and finally coat in the breadcrumbs.
4. Heat a really good glug of oil in a large frying pan and fry the fishcakes for 3 to 4 minutes on each side until they are a deep golden brown and hot in the middle. (You can also bake the fishcakes for 10 minutes in an oven preheated to 180°C/350°F/Gas Mark 4.)
5. If you are making home-made mayonnaise, mix together the egg yolk, mustard, a dash of Tabasco and a little salt, then dribble in a tiny amount of oil, beating well until it starts to emulsify. Once it starts to emulsify, you can drip in the oil a bit faster, until it has all been added. Right at the end, stir in the lemon juice and chopped dill and season with salt and pepper, if necessary.

Spicy sausage pasta bake

This is a huge hit in my house and beyond. As one of my friends said: 'What's not to like about pasta and sausages?!' I couldn't have put it better myself. When I have a little more time, I squeeze the meat from the sausages and roll it into balls, before frying them like meatballs. I really would recommend using good-quality meaty sausages, as they will hold their shape better during cooking. If you can get hold of some spicy Italian sausages from your butcher, deli or supermarket, this dish will be even lovelier. There is not very much cream here so, if you don't have a leftover dollop to use up, you can omit it. That said, it does add something to the bake, giving it a little, well, creamy texture.

Serves 2 adults and 2 children

You will need a 20 x 30cm baking dish

6–8 large sausages

Olive oil

350g pasta shapes (penne or conchiglie work well here)

100g grated hard cheese (I like to use Parmesan, pecorino or Cheddar)

For the sauce

200ml red wine

A sprig of rosemary

1 x quantity of tomato sauce (from spaghetti and meatballs recipe on page 144)

A pinch of ground cinnamon

1 teaspoon chilli flakes or powder (to taste)

Salt and freshly ground black pepper

50ml double cream

Preheat your oven to 180°C/350°F/Gas Mark 4.

1. Place the sausages in the oven dish you will use for the pasta bake, drizzle them with olive oil and cook them in the oven for 15 to 20 minutes.
2. Meanwhile, cook the pasta in a large pan of salted water according to the packet instructions, then drain in a colander.
3. While the sausages and pasta are cooking, make the sauce. Pour the wine into a saucepan and add the rosemary. Bring to the boil and boil fiercely to reduce by at least half.
4. Add the tomato sauce, cinnamon and chilli, along with 100ml water. Season with salt and pepper, then simmer until the sauce tastes lovely and rich but isn't too thick. Mix in the double cream, if you're using it.
5. When the sauce, pasta and sausages are ready, remove the sausages from the oven, drain away any fat and cut them into rounds.
6. Return the sausages to the oven dish and mix with the sauce and pasta. Sprinkle over the cheese and bake for 20 to 25 minutes. Serve hot from the oven.

Quick chicken curry with pilau rice

Serves 2 adults and 2 children

For the spice blend

1 teaspoon coriander seeds

1 teaspoon cumin seeds

1cm piece of cinnamon stick

2 spokes of star anise

1 cardamom pod

1 bay leaf

1 teaspoon fennel seeds

1 teaspoon black peppercorns

½ teaspoon Nigella seeds

A few gratings of fresh nutmeg

1 teaspoon turmeric

½ teaspoon cayenne pepper or chilli powder, to taste

You may have looked at the ingredients for the spice blend mix and thought, 'Which part of this quick chicken curry is actually quick?!'. Well, if you prefer, you can use your favourite curry powder but I thought it would be a shame not to include a recipe because you can easily make a large quantity of it and store it in a jar. As long as you keep it in a cool dark place (the technical term for this is a cupboard!) it will last a few months. For extra speed, serve the curry with flatbreads, but the pilau rice is rather lovely and goes perfectly.

1. If you are making your own spice mix, put all the whole spices in a dry frying pan and toast them on a medium heat until they give off a lovely aroma – be very careful not to burn them. Remove the spices from the frying pan and tip them on to a plate to cool them down (if you leave them in the frying pan they'll continue to cook). When cool, grind them in a spice grinder or with a pestle and mortar and mix with the rest of the spices.

2. Now make a start on the pilau rice. Heat 2 tablespoons of vegetable oil in a lidded saucepan. Add the spices, cook them for a minute then chuck in the onion.

3. Fry the onion for 2 minutes then mix in the turmeric, rice and sultanas or raisins if you are using them. Stir to combine then add the stock or water and season with salt and pepper.

4. Bring to the boil, then turn down the heat and let it simmer gently. Cover with the lid and leave to cook for 10 to 15 minutes until all the water is absorbed.

5. While the rice is still bubbling away, make the curry. Heat 2 tablespoons of vegetable oil in a large saucepan. Add the onion and cook over a low to medium heat until broken down, soft and a light golden brown. Add the garlic and ginger and cook, stirring for a minute.

6. In go the spices, followed by the tomato purée. Stir to cook the tomato purée for a couple of minutes, then add the tomatoes and a pinch of sugar. Season with salt and pepper and splash in a little water, then cover with the lid and simmer for 5 minutes.
7. The rice should have absorbed all of the water by now, so take the pan off the heat. Remove the lid and place a folded tea towel over the top of the pan and allow the rice to steam for a further 5 minutes or so before serving. (Please make sure you have turned off the gas before leaving the rice to steam. From personal experience, that towel catches fire mighty quickly – and in the ensuing panic, you will ruin the rice too! Trust me.)
8. While the rice is steaming, throw the chicken into the curry, mix well and leave it to simmer for 5 minutes or so, until the chicken is fully cooked through.
9. Stir the yoghurt through the curry and serve with the coriander, chillies (to taste), wedges of lemon and a lovely mound of rice.

For the pilau rice

Vegetable oil

½ teaspoon cumin seeds

½ teaspoon coriander seeds, crushed

1 cardamom pod, seeds only

3cm piece of cinnamon stick

1 bay leaf

1 small onion, finely chopped

½ teaspoon turmeric

250ml basmati rice

50g raisins or sultanas (optional)

650ml chicken stock or water

Salt and freshly ground black pepper

For the curry

Vegetable oil

1 onion, finely sliced

2 garlic cloves, finely chopped

3cm cube of fresh ginger, grated

1 tablespoon spice blend or curry powder (see below)

1 tablespoon tomato purée

100g fresh or tinned chopped tomatoes

A pinch of sugar

Salt and freshly ground black pepper

8 chicken thighs, skin and bone removed, cut into bite-sized pieces

4 tablespoons plain yoghurt

To serve

A handful of coriander leaves

Sliced green chillies (for the adults)

Lemon wedges

Spaghetti with meatballs

Serves 2 adults and 2 children

350g spaghetti
Torn basil and freshly grated Parmesan cheese, to serve

For the sauce
Olive oil
1 onion, finely sliced
2 garlic cloves, crushed
1 teaspoon dried oregano
1 bay leaf
400g tin chopped tomatoes
A pinch of sugar (optional)
Salt and freshly ground black pepper

For the meatballs
250g minced beef
250g minced pork
100g finely chopped smoked bacon
100g fresh breadcrumbs
100ml milk
1 egg
4 tablespoons finely chopped herbs (a mixture of oregano, thyme and flat-leaf parsley)
Salt and freshly ground black pepper

One of the challenges when creating a cookbook is getting the balance right between great new ideas and old favourites. Everyone has had spaghetti and meatballs, but hopefully my ultra-simple recipe will inspire you to revisit this classic dish. In this recipe I bake the meatballs in the oven. I find it is just a little less faffy to cook them in one go like this rather than in a few batches in a frying pan, not least because you could find yourself with three or even four pans on the go, and that leads to two things: mess and lots of washing up.

I recommend making a double-sized batch of the tomato sauce and using the other half for the spicy sausage pasta bake on page 141.

1. First make the tomato sauce. Heat a good glug of olive oil in a saucepan over a medium heat and add the onion. Cook for 4 to 5 minutes, until soft, then add the garlic and cook for another couple of minutes. Chuck in the herbs, tomatoes, sugar (if using) and season well with salt and pepper. Add 100ml water and leave to simmer for 20 minutes.
2. Meanwhile, make the meatballs. Preheat the oven to 200°C/400°F/Gas Mark 6.
3. In a large bowl mix together all the meatball ingredients. Make sure you season it well with plenty of salt and pepper. A trick to check the seasoning is to fry a tiny piece of the mixture and see how it tastes.
4. Shape the mixture into small balls, about 2.5cm in diameter. Place them on a non-stick baking sheet (or a baking sheet lined with greaseproof paper) and cook for around 10 minutes, until the meatballs are hot all the way through and a little browned. When you put the meatballs in the oven, start cooking the pasta in a large pan of salted boiling water according to the packet instructions.

5. Just before serving, add the cooked meatballs to the simmering tomato sauce for a few minutes.
6. Serve the pasta with the sauce and meatballs spooned over the top, sprinkled with basil and freshly grated Parmesan.

Macaroni cauliflower cheese

Serves 2 adults and 2 children

You will need a 20 x 30cm baking dish

300g macaroni (or other pasta, if you prefer)

4 or 5 small cauliflower florets

1 small courgette, cut into cubes

30g butter, plus extra for greasing

30g plain flour

500ml milk

1 teaspoon Dijon mustard

A dash of Tabasco (optional)

75g grated extra-mature Cheddar cheese

½ teaspoon finely chopped thyme

Salt and freshly ground black pepper

2 tomatoes, deseeded and chopped

100g ham, cut into small cubes (optional)

For the topping

25g fresh breadcrumbs

1 tablespoon freshly grated Parmesan cheese

1 tablespoon grated mature Cheddar cheese

1 tablespoon finely chopped basil leaves

I ummed and aaahed about including a mac 'n' cheese recipe, but it fits this chapter so well and it is a staple in our house: two good reasons to include it! I have given it a little twist though by adding some vegetables, which cook in the pasta water, so there's no need for extra pans. You can pretty well use any vegetables you want here, but I have used a combination of cauliflower, courgette and tomatoes, turning it into a kind of macaroni cauliflower cheese! I also like to chuck some ham into this dish but you can, of course, leave it out if you want it to be vegetarian. Oh, and just to be controversial, you can use any other pasta shape too, although don't go calling this a macaroni cheese if you do!

1. Cook the macaroni in a large pan of salted boiling water according to the packet instructions. With 5 minutes left of its cooking time, add the vegetables and let them cook with the pasta. Drain and set aside.

2. Meanwhile, melt the butter in a saucepan on a medium heat. Add the flour and stir together for a couple of minutes, until well combined and the flour is cooked. You are looking for a nice golden brown colour. Gradually add the milk, whisking all the time, until you have a fairly thin white sauce.

3. Remove the sauce from the heat, mix in the mustard, Tabasco, cheese and thyme and stir well until the cheese is melted. Have a taste and season with salt and pepper if you think it needs it. Preheat your grill to its highest setting.

4. Grease a baking dish with butter and tip in the cooked pasta, vegetables, the chopped tomatoes and ham (if you're using it). Pour the sauce over the top and mix everything together.

5. Combine the topping ingredients and sprinkle them over the pasta. Place under the hot grill for about 10 minutes until golden brown. Serve immediately.

Chicken and olive pasta bake

I think I may be addicted to pasta. I would happily eat it several times a week. It has an instant ability to satisfy and soothe, while at the same time, being unbelievably quick and easy to prepare. That said, I am often happy to stretch the cooking time a little to make a pasta bake. The squelch of a big spoon scooping into a delicious bake has something so comforting about it. I'll admit that, on their own, capers are quite feisty but they add so much flavour and depth to all manner of dishes that I use them all the time without complaint from my discerning six- and three-year-old customers.

Serves 2 adults and 2 children

You will need a 20 x 30cm baking dish

350g penne or any other shape pasta

Olive oil

200g chicken thighs or breasts, skin removed and cut into small cubes

1 onion, finely chopped

2 garlic cloves, finely chopped

100ml white wine

2 tablespoons roughly chopped black olives

1 tablespoon capers, rinsed, drained and chopped

Zest of 1 lemon

1 teaspoon fennel seeds, crushed

200g soft cream cheese

Salt and freshly ground black pepper

2 tablespoons finely chopped flat-leaf parsley

50g freshly grated Parmesan cheese

100g grated Cheddar cheese

1. Cook the pasta in a large pan of salted boiling water according to the packet instructions.
2. Make sure it is al dente – you don't want it too soft yet, as it will cook a little more in the oven. Drain, reserving a mug of the cooking water.
3. About 10 minutes before the end of the pasta cooking time, heat some olive oil in a frying pan on a medium heat and add the chicken. Keep it moving around the pan until it is cooked on all sides.
4. Throw in the onion and cook for 3 to 4 minutes until softened, then stir in the garlic.
5. Turn up the heat and pour in the wine. Let it bubble up and then continue to cook for a couple of minutes to reduce. Preheat your oven to 180°C/350°F/Gas Mark 4.
6. Lower the heat and chuck in the olives, capers, lemon zest and fennel seeds.
7. Pour in the reserved pasta cooking water and spoon in the cream cheese. Stir well until the cheese is melted into the sauce. If it's a touch too thick, add a splash of water.
8. Season the sauce with salt and pepper, stir through the parsley and then mix in the pasta.
9. Plonk everything in a baking dish, cover with both the grated cheeses and bake for 20 to 25 minutes until golden on top and bubbling away nicely.

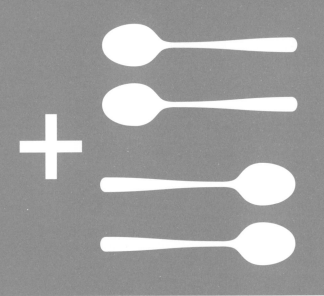

2+2=7

I think this chapter typifies the change in our mealtimes since Archie started school: what to do when, often at the last minute, you find yourself with an extended group of children to feed. Well, you turn to this chapter! Not only will they love eating all these dishes, they will also love how interactive they are. This is where food becomes part of the play date, a centrepiece of the afternoon or evening instead of an afterthought.

Bread and baked beans tartlets

Serves 4 children

You will need an 8-hole muffin tin

Butter

8 medium slices of bread, crusts removed

400g tin baked beans

2 large handfuls of grated Cheddar cheese

I cannot deny that this recipe is, of course, glorified beans on toast, but these tartlets are great fun to make together with children. They look impressive on the plate and can be as posh (or not) as you like. Try them with some fried bacon or sliced leftover sausages added to the beans. Tinned spaghetti works well here too, as does leftover pasta in a tomato sauce. And you can replace the Cheddar with mozzarella or Parmesan. Not only are these tartlets great to wheel out on play dates, but they are so versatile that they have become one of our fallback lunches – and are often eaten at breakfast time at the weekend too. Most importantly, these tartlets are a guaranteed mealtime success in my house, whenever they are served.

Preheat the oven to 180°C/350°F/Gas Mark 4.

1. Grease the muffin tin with butter and spread butter onto each slice of bread.
2. Push a slice of buttered bread gently into each muffin cup (buttered side on the tin), pressing it into the base and against the side. If you tear the bread, simply use a little bit from the corner of the slice to patch up the hole. Repeat with the rest of the bread.
3. Spoon the beans into the bread cups and top with grated cheese.
4. Bake in the oven for 20 to 25 minutes, until the bread is golden and crispy, the cheese has fully melted and the filling is piping hot. Serve immediately.

2+2=7

New York pancakes with bacon and syrup

These are the thicker, fluffier kind of pancakes. If they were big enough, you could have a very comfortable night's sleep on them. Unlike conventional French pancakes, they are dry fried, rather than in oil or butter. This also means that you avoid the perennial problem of the first pancake of the batch not working out properly. The original recipe for the batter comes from a lovely deli in Hitchin in Hertfordshire called Halsey's Deli which is now run by the colourful Damian, who was a Saville Row tailor in a previous life. For a play date, I serve these with crispy rashers of bacon, drizzled with syrup.

Makes approximately 18 pancakes

270 g plain flour

2 tsp baking powder

1 tsp salt

4 tbsp caster sugar

260 ml milk

2 large eggs

4 tbsp melted butter

10 rashers of bacon (smoked or unsmoked)

Golden Syrup or Maple Syrup (2 tbsp)

Vegetable or sunflower

1. First make your batter. Mix together the flour, baking powder, salt and caster sugar. Create a well in the middle and pour in the milk, egg and melted butter. Whisk, all the ingredients together, until you have a thick, gluey batter with no lumps.
2. Fry the bacon rashers in a large frying pan on a medium heat in a little drizzle of oil. When they are crispy, pour in the syrup to coat the bacon. Set the bacon to one side.
3. Heat a clean non-stick pan on a medium heat but don't put any oil into the pan. Dollop a tablespoon of the pancake batter into the pan, spreading it out a little with the back of your spoon. You want a round pancake of 3 inches in diameter.
4. Cook the pancakes up to 3 at a time for a couple of minutes until bubbles form on top, then flip them over and cook for a further minute until brown. Set these pancakes aside then repeat until all the batter is used up. This batter will give you around 18 pancakes. You can make the pancakes in advance and just warm them up for 20 seconds in the microwave or briefly in a frying pan on a low-medium heat.
5. Serve the bacon and pancakes in the middle of the table for the kids to tick into and share, not forgetting some extra syrup for drizzling.

2+2=7

DIY strawberry ice cream sundaes

Serves 4 children

You will need 4 tall glasses
Vanilla and/or strawberry
ice cream

A selection of fillings
Chocolate brownies or any
other kind of cake, broken
into pieces (leftovers work
perfectly)

Cookies or biscuits (the
peanut butter cookies on
page 171 are great in this)

A couple of meringue nests,
crumbled into pieces

Fresh fruit – strawberries,
bananas or pitted cherries
are especially good

For the caramel sauce
100g caster sugar
150g double cream
½ teaspoon vanilla extract

For the strawberry sauce
200g ripe strawberries
Sugar, to taste
A squeeze of lemon juice

My word, are DIY sundaes popular in my house?! Not only are they (of course!) delicious, but they are fun to put together too, especially if you have extra children in the house. I also love the way I can use up the broken ends of the biscuit packets I have lurking in the cupboard – there really are no rules here as to what goes in your sundae. Think of this more as a concept than a single recipe. The caramel sauce is dead easy to make, as is the strawberry sauce and both can be made well in advance (keep them stored in the fridge and reheat gently before using).

To make the caramel sauce

1. Put the sugar in a saucepan in an even layer. Heat it very slowly until it starts to melt around the edges. Now start swirling it gently, until all the sugar has melted and it has started to smoke and darken in colour.
2. Remove the pan from the heat and add half the cream, stirring quickly to make sure it is completely incorporated. Add the remaining cream and the vanilla extract and continue to stir. If you find you have clumps of hardened caramel, put the saucepan back over a very low heat and melt them back into the sauce.

2+2=7

To make the strawberry sauce

1. Hull the strawberries and blitz them in a blender. Add a tablespoon of sugar and give it a taste; add a little more sugar if you think it needs it. Add a squeeze of lemon and blitz again. If you want the sauce to be completely smooth, pass it through a sieve to remove the seeds.

To assemble the sundaes

1. Put everything on the table and let everyone add whatever they like to their sundae dishes. Word of advice: if you are using the squirty cream, keep a close eye on it. Cream 'gun' fights can break out ever so quickly . . . !

Toppings

Marshmallows, chopped nuts, crumbled Flakes, sprinkles

Whipped cream (or squirty cream)

Roast beef French dip

This recipe is a huge crowd pleaser. It successfully turns a fairly traditional joint of beef into a fun and interactive experience, thanks to the dipping gravy. I think it's an ideal dish to feed a group of hungry mouths on a play date, but it is just as effective as a family meal or as a twist on a classic Sunday roast. You can choose how well done you like your beef, but I like to cook mine medium-rare for this, in true French style. It has more flavour and the beef is lovely and tender. Cook it before you head off on the school run and then leave it to rest while you are out. Perfect.

Serves up to 8 children

1 small roasting joint of beef (approx. 750g–1kg)

Salt and freshly ground black pepper

2 teaspoons dried herbs (a mixture of oregano, rosemary and thyme works well)

Olive oil or beef dripping

2 onions, cut in half and finely sliced

1 tablespoon plain flour

100ml red wine

200ml beef stock

A good length of baguette for each person

Preheat the oven to 180°C/350°F/Gas Mark 4.

1. Season the meat with salt and pepper and sprinkle over the herbs. Heat the olive oil or dripping in a roasting dish on a medium to high heat on your hob.

2. Brown the meat well on all sides, then lay the onion slices in the base of the roasting dish and place the beef on top. Add a splash of water and roast the beef to your liking (a good guide is 20 minutes per 500g for rare, 25 minutes for medium-rare or 30 minutes for well done).

3. When cooked, remove the beef from the roasting dish. Cover it with foil and leave it to rest for half an hour.

4. To make the dipping gravy, put the roasting dish back on the hob on a medium heat, sprinkle in the flour and stir together thoroughly. Pour in the red wine and allow it to bubble for a few seconds while you use your spoon to scrape up any bits sticking to the bottom of the dish.

5. In goes the beef stock and simmer gently for 3 to 4 minutes until the gravy is slightly thickened and the onions are well cooked.

6. Remove the onions with a slotted spoon and keep to one side in a bowl. Pour any juices from the rested beef into the roasting dish then pour the whole lot into a wide jug.

7. Slice the beef thinly and serve it with the baguettes, onions and gravy at the table. Allow everyone to assemble a baguette and take it in turns to dip it in the gravy.

Vegetable fritters

These vegetable fritters are incredibly versatile and unbelievably delicious. You can use whatever vegetables you have to hand, plus your choice of cheese, which make them great fun to prepare with children as they can get involved in choosing the ingredients. Feta or Cheddar work very well but there's no need to limit yourself to just these two. The fritters are good served with slices of ham or chicken and go very nicely with some sweet chilli dipping sauce.

1. Whisk the egg whites until they reach the stiff peak stage (technically speaking, they should stay in the bowl if you hold it upside down over your head. You know you want to try this!).
2. Put the flour in a different bowl, pour in the milk and stir to combine. Don't worry: it will be very stiff to start with. Add the egg yolks and the spices and stir again.
3. Gently fold in the egg whites using a metal spoon.
4. Stir in your choice of vegetables and cheese. If you want, you can divide the batter and add different vegetables to each portion to create a variety of fritters.
5. Heat a really good glug of oil in a large frying pan on a medium heat. Drop tablespoonfuls of the fritter mixture into the oil and fry for 2 to 3 minutes on each side until golden brown and cooked in the middle.
6. Serve immediately, as these fritters are best eaten warm.

Serves 4 children

2 eggs, whites and yolks separated

100g plain flour

75ml milk

A pinch of paprika

A pinch of cayenne pepper

Salt and freshly ground black pepper

Your choice of fillings (you can use a combination, but don't use too much or the batter won't hold the filling together)

200g sweetcorn

200g frozen peas

1 courgette, grated

1 carrot, grated

Crumbled feta cheese

Grated hard cheese (Cheddar is great here)

Chopped fresh herbs (a mixture of mint, flat-leaf parsley and basil)

Vegetable oil or olive oil

2+2=7

Chocolate fondue

Serves 4–6 children

200g good-quality chocolate
1 teaspoon vanilla extract
200ml double cream

For dipping

Cubes of cake or brioche
Amaretti biscuits
Marshmallows
Chunks of fruit, such as
strawberries, cherries,
peaches, apricots, plums
or banana
Popping candy

I feel guilty that my sister and I endlessly took the mickey out of my mum for the burgundy-coloured fondue kit she bought and used once. I feel especially guilty because I love eating fondue with the children, especially when we have extra guests in the house. As with the sundaes on page 152, the possibilities here are endless. You can use any kind of chocolate that takes your fancy, although it's worth buying a good-quality chocolate, as it will have a better consistency when melted. Experiment with infusing the cream with different flavours, such as chilli, ginger, cinnamon, orange zest or fennel – simply warm the cream, remove it from the heat, add your chosen flavour and then let it cool down. Or, for an adult twist, mix in some instant espresso powder with a tiny bit of water, or even a teaspoon of rum! For extra fun, dip your fruits in popping candy after coating them in the chocolate. If you don't have a fondue set, both this and the butterscotch version on page 157 can be made without one (see the instructions within the method).

You'll also need wooden or metal skewers (or you can simply use forks)

1. If you have a fondue kit, simply break up the chocolate, put it in the fondue bowl with the vanilla extract and cream and melt it over a gentle heat.
2. If you don't have a fondue pot, put the ingredients in a heatproof bowl set over a saucepan of barely simmering water (don't let the bowl touch the water) and melt the ingredients together.
3. Give the sauce a good stir and serve while it is still warm, either in the fondue pot or in individual dishes or coffee cups, with the dipping ingredients in bowls on the table.

2+2=7

Butterscotch fondue

Butterscotch was made for dipping. Creamy and fudgey, fruit just loves being coated in it! It's the simplicity of this recipe that I really enjoy. Not only will the sauce be just as delicious poured over ice cream or served in a pancake, any leftovers can be kept in the fridge in an airtight container for a good few days. As with the chocolate fondue on page 156, you can make this even if you don't have a fondue kit (see the instructions within the method).

Serves 4–6 children

150g butter
150g dark brown sugar
200g double cream
1 teaspoon vanilla extract
A squeeze of lemon juice

For dipping

Chunks of fruit, such strawberries, cherries, peaches, apricots, plums or banana

You'll also need wooden or metal skewers (or you can simply use forks)

1. Simply cook all the ingredients in your fondue pot or in a saucepan on a low heat, stirring as you go. The sauce is ready when everything is fully melted together and your butterscotch is a lovely rich nutty fudge colour.
2. Leave the butterscotch to cool a little before serving it in the fondue pot or in individual bowls or coffee cups. Pile the fruit in the middle of the table and let everyone get dipping.

2+2=7

Cheese fondue

Serves 4–6 children

1 garlic clove, sliced in half

200ml white wine

1 teaspoon lemon juice

275g grated Emmental cheese

275g grated Gruyère cheese

50g freshly grated Parmesan or Cheddar cheese

2 tablespoons brandy (optional)

1 tablespoon cornflour

Salt and freshly ground black pepper

A pinch of cayenne pepper

For dipping

French bread (preferably a little stale), cut into cubes

Small new potatoes, boiled or roasted

Cherry tomatoes

Chunks of Frankfurter sausages

Button mushrooms

Cooked cauliflower and broccoli florets

If you weren't given a fondue set when you got married (I'm sure it must appear in the top 20 most popular wedding gifts!), there are some very cheap models around, and I promise you, you will get loads of use out of it. They are perfect for hassle-free social occasions and, as such, they are ideal for this chapter. Gruyère, Emmental and Comté are the traditional cheeses used for a fondue but don't be afraid to experiment – you can even create an English-style fondue by using a combination of cheeses such as Red Leicester and mature Cheddar. For a completely English version, use cider or ale instead of the wine. If you want to make this entirely alcohol free, you can replace it with chicken stock but I think a little alcohol adds a lot of flavour and it also cuts through some of the richness of the cheese.

1. Rub the garlic all over the inside of the fondue bowl.
2. Pour in the white wine and lemon juice and heat over a low heat. Gradually add all the grated cheeses, stirring in a figure of eight, until completely melted.
3. If you're using the brandy, blend it with the cornflour; otherwise, mix the cornflour with a couple of tablespoons of water. Stir this into the fondue and cook for a further 2 to 3 minutes.
4. Season with salt, pepper and the cayenne pepper.
5. Put the fondue on the table, keeping a flame underneath. Give everyone a fondue fork and let them select their choice of food to dip.
6. Oh, and don't forget that one of the best bits is the toasted cheesy crust which forms on the bottom, called la réligieuse (which means 'nun'!). Pull it out and eat it when you're done!

2+2=7

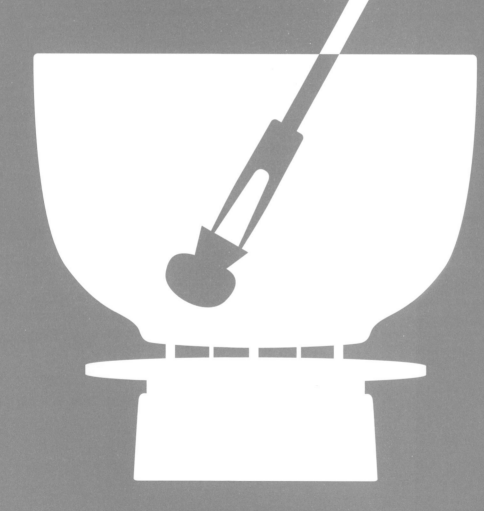

Easy flatbread pizzas

These flatbread pizzas are based on delicious, cheese-free Turkish Lahmacun. This makes them a particularly good option if you are following a diet without dairy. There is no cooking involved in the topping; it is just a case of mixing the ingredients in a bowl and spreading it over the bases! If you want to make these flatbread pizzas ultra quickly, use any of the flatbreads on sale in the supermarket. That said, if you do have a little extra time, the flatbread recipe is lovely to make yourself, or with your children. That would explain why these pizzas often get eaten in my house on a Sunday evening when, at a loose end towards the end of the day, getting Archie and Matilda involved in a bit of dough making is both fun and a great way of killing some tired time.

Serves 4–6 children

For the flatbreads

250g strong white bread flour, plus extra for dusting

2 teaspoons dried instant yeast

1 teaspoon salt

1 teaspoon sugar

1 tablespoon plain yoghurt

4 tablespoons olive oil, plus extra for greasing

Traditional Turkish topping

1 onion, finely chopped

1 garlic clove, finely chopped

250g lamb mince

A good handful of chopped flat-leaf parsley

A pinch of ground cinnamon

A pinch of allspice

1 tomato, finely chopped

1 tablespoon tahini

2 tablespoons lemon juice or a pinch of sumac

2 tablespoons pine nuts

1. In a bowl, mix the flour with the yeast, salt and sugar.
2. Add the yoghurt, olive oil and 100ml water and use your hands to bring everything together to form a dough.
3. On a floured worktop, knead the dough lightly for about 5 minutes until it is nice and smooth (you can also use a dough hook in a food processor if you have one).
4. Lightly oil the bowl, put the dough back in, cover it in cling film and leave it to rise in a warm place for about an hour until it has doubled in size. This will take a little longer if it is a particularly cold day.
5. To make the topping, mix together all the ingredients (except the pine nuts). You can do this well in advance and refrigerate.
6. When you are ready to assemble the pizzas, preheat your oven as high as it will go. Heat a couple of upturned baking trays in the oven to cook the pizzas on.

2+2=7

7. Divide the dough into balls. You can make 4 large, 8 medium or 12 small pizzas from this amount. Give your worktop a good dusting of flour and roll out the flatbreads until they are nice and thin – but be careful not to tear them.

8. Spread some of the topping mixture over each flatbread and sprinkle with the pine nuts.

9. Dust the hot baking trays with flour, place the loaded flatbreads on top and cook them for 8 to 10 minutes – the breads will be cooked and a little crisp around the edge. Serve immediately. I like to put a medium flatbread on each baking tray, cook and serve them, and then cook the next batch while the first lot is being eaten at the table!

2+2=7

Tortilla wraps with home-made refried beans

Serves 4–6 children

I recommend using flour tortillas for this (allowing a couple per person) but tacos work too

For the meat filling
Olive oil

500g chicken meat (breast, leg or thigh), sliced

1 garlic clove

A pinch of ground cinnamon

A pinch of ground cloves

1 teaspoon cumin

½ teaspoon allspice

Salt and freshly ground black pepper

Chilli powder or chipotle paste, to taste (optional)

1 tablespoon tomato purée

This is a great social meal for children to enjoy on a play date or for a family to tuck into at the end of a trying day. I love the variety of textures and flavours and my children particularly enjoy having (almost!) complete control over what they are eating. Be prepared for things to get messy, but they will greatly enjoy filling their wraps and rolling them themselves. Refried beans are readily available in supermarkets but I really like making them myself, with the added benefit that I can control exactly how spicy (or not) I want them to be. Don't limit yourself to a meat filling; you can use mushrooms or firm-fleshed fish instead, cooked in the same way as the chicken. You can also use any kind of mince. I've included rice as one of the optional ingredients as this is a staple in a burrito, but don't try to pack in too much.

1. Heat a glug of olive oil in a frying pan. Add the chicken and cook over a high heat until it starts to brown.
2. Add the garlic, all the spices and seasonings and the tomato purée and stir to coat the chicken. Splash in a little water and simmer for a few minutes until the chicken is cooked through. Add more water if it looks like it's drying out.
3. To make the refried beans, use a masher or fork to mash the beans with a little water. You don't want them to be completely broken down; some texture is good and it's fine to leave a few whole.
4. Heat the butter or lard (or drizzle of oil) in a large frying pan. Cook the onion and garlic on a low heat until softened, add the coriander stems and chilli, and then stir in beans. Cook for a few minutes on a very low heat, stirring regularly so they don't stick to the pan. Add a touch more water if necessary. Season with salt and pepper and remove the pan from the heat.

5. Quickly make the tomato salsa by mixing together all the ingredients. Drizzle with olive oil.
6. Now you are ready to plonk everything on the table and let everyone assemble their wraps! Warm the tortillas in a dry frying pan or in the microwave and then enjoy the free-for-all as everyone chooses their combination of fillings. To create the perfect wrap, place the fillings in a line, about 5cm in from the edge of the tortilla. Fold over the top and bottom edges, then roll the tortilla over itself to create a tight wrap.

For the refried beans

400g tin beans, rinsed and drained (pinto beans or kidney beans work best here)

A large knob butter or lard (or vegetable oil)

1 onion, finely chopped

2 garlic cloves, finely chopped

1 tablespoon coriander stems

½ teaspoon chilli powder or chipotle paste, to taste

Salt and freshly ground black pepper

For the tomato salsa

6 medium tomatoes, deseeded and finely chopped

½ red onion, finely chopped

Juice of 1 lime

A pinch of brown sugar

A pinch of cumin

Salt and freshly ground black pepper

Olive oil

Your choice of fillings

Cooked white rice (for the full burrito experience)

Avocado, sliced and squeezed with lime juice

Sliced mango, squeezed with lime juice

Jalapeño peppers

Grated Cheddar cheese

Sour cream or crème fraîche

Fresh coriander leaves

Crisp lettuce (iceberg is good)

White cabbage, shredded

Grated carrot

Baked eggs

You will need a ramekin for each egg

Butter

I recommend 2 large eggs per person

Salt and freshly ground black pepper

1 tablespoon double cream for each egg

1 tablespoon grated cheese for each egg (Cheddar or Gruyère work well)

Any combination of the following

Cubed ham

Chopped fried bacon

Fried chorizo or any other kind of sausage

Spinach, wilted in butter with a grating of nutmeg

Chopped fresh tomatoes

Sliced roasted red peppers

Tinned tuna or sardines, drained and mixed with a little mayonnaise

Mushrooms fried in butter with herbs and garlic

To serve

Toast soldiers

Blanched asparagus spears or sprouting broccoli florets

Raw courgette and carrot sticks

Oven-baked potato wedges

This simple play date idea works brilliantly when you have a crowd because the ramekins are so much fun to assemble. I would recommend offering a really good choice of fillings and just letting the children do their worst with them! I have found that by putting a dollop of double cream on top of each yolk, it will stay runny while it is baking. If you want a hard yolk, just leave off the cream. This is very much a pick-and-mix recipe, the only constant being the eggs themselves. Everything else is down to your personal taste.

Preheat your oven to 180°C/350°F/Gas Mark 4.

1. Liberally butter each ramekin all around the inside and put a layer of your favourite combination of fillings in the bottom.
2. Carefully, break an egg on top and season it with some salt and pepper. Dollop a tablespoon of cream on top of the yolks if you want them soft set. Sprinkle over the cheese.
3. Place the ramekins on a baking tray and cook in the oven for exactly 12 minutes.
4. Take the ramekins out of the oven and leave them to cool down until they are safe to handle. Serve them at the table with all the dippy bits.

2+2=7

Absolutely instant chocolate mousse

A while back, I had the idea of using yoghurt in a chocolate mousse, thinking it would make a lighter mousse compared with the traditional method that uses egg yolks. I actually discovered that the addition of the yoghurt makes the mousse set almost instantly! No need for it to chill in the fridge, it is ready to eat as soon as you've finished mixing. As such, it's ideal for impromptu play dates – or any last minute-event for that matter. The only downside with this recipe is that as the pay-off for the mousse setting so quickly, the egg yolks are wasted, but you could always keep them fresh in the fridge and use them to enrich an omelette.

Serves 4 children

200g good-quality
dark chocolate

4 egg whites

4 tablespoons caster sugar

140g Greek yoghurt
(0% if possible – I like Total)

Mini marshmallows, to serve

1. Melt the chocolate in a heatproof bowl set over a saucepan of gently simmering water (make sure the bowl doesn't actually touch the water) or in the microwave for 2 minutes, stirring well halfway through. Allow the melted chocolate to cool a little.
2. Whisk the egg whites until they form stiff peaks, then carefully whisk in the sugar, a little at a time.
3. Mix the yoghurt into the cooled chocolate. You will see it starting to thicken already.
4. Using a metal spoon, fold about one-quarter of the whisked egg whites into the chocolate, just to loosen it up a little. Fold in the eggs by moving the spoon in a figure of eight, while at the same time slowly turning the bowl.
5. Gently fold in the rest of the eggs, taking care not to beat the air out of them.
6. Spoon the mousse into bowls, mugs or ramekins and serve immediately with the mini marshmallows scattered on top.

2+2=7

Genius Treats

This is a chapter to put a smile on the faces of adults and children alike, and I had so much fun creating the recipes. I think that cakes, sweets and treats are an important part of my children's diet. Let's face it: there are some mealtimes when a good bit of home-made cake is all that will end up being eaten. I am not the world's most precise baker, which is reflected in this collection of foolproof desserts.

Blocko's blooming brilliant chocolate marshmallow fudge cake

Yes, you read that correctly! Chocolate. Marshmallow. Fudge. Need I say more?! Paul Bloxham is an extremely fine chef. Quality pub grub is his speciality, but he is also a dad to three young children so he knows all about the importance of giving them great food, cooked simply. This is his recipe and he has kindly given me permission to use it. It is quite simply a stunner. A show-stopper for your children and their friends to enjoy. It's best to make this for a group of people, as it does not last well once it has cooled; it loses moisture and you will miss out on all its lovely chocolate-y gooeyness.

Preheat your oven to 180°C/350°F/Gas Mark 4.

1. Line the cake tin with greaseproof paper.
2. Melt your butter gently in a small saucepan or in the microwave and leave it to cool for a few minutes.
3. Sift the flour, half of the cocoa powder, the baking powder and the salt into a large bowl.
4. In a separate bowl, whisk together the eggs, caster sugar, melted butter, milk and vanilla extract.
5. Add the wet mixture to the dry mixture and stir the batter until just combined.
6. Mix in the walnuts and marshmallows and tip the batter into the prepared tin. Smooth the surface to create an even layer.

Makes 10 slices

You will need a 20cm square cake tin

200g unsalted butter

225g plain flour

175g unsweetened cocoa powder

¾ teaspoon baking powder

¾ teaspoon salt

2 large eggs

200g caster sugar

150ml milk

1 teaspoon vanilla extract

125g chopped walnuts

150g marshmallows

For the topping

100g dark chocolate

200g Demerara sugar

225ml boiling water

Crème fraîche or ice cream, to serve

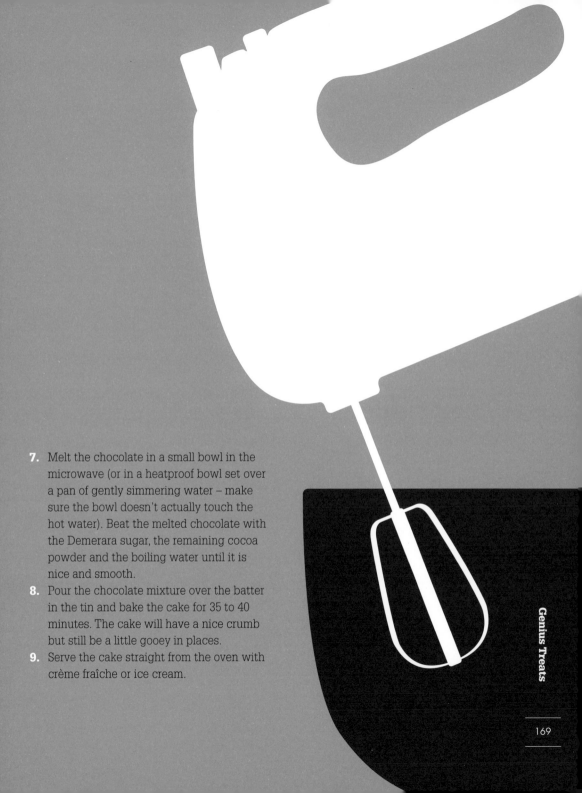

7. Melt the chocolate in a small bowl in the microwave (or in a heatproof bowl set over a pan of gently simmering water – make sure the bowl doesn't actually touch the hot water). Beat the melted chocolate with the Demerara sugar, the remaining cocoa powder and the boiling water until it is nice and smooth.

8. Pour the chocolate mixture over the batter in the tin and bake the cake for 35 to 40 minutes. The cake will have a nice crumb but still be a little gooey in places.

9. Serve the cake straight from the oven with crème fraîche or ice cream.

Genius Treats

Apple and cinnamon tray bake

Makes 16 pieces

You will need a deep
20 x 30cm baking tray

300g plain flour

2 teaspoons baking powder

1 teaspoon ground
cinnamon

1 teaspoon mixed spice

150g butter

250g light soft brown sugar

4 eggs

250ml buttermilk

2 eating apples, peeled,
cored and chopped

2 tablespoons Demerara
sugar

For the crumble topping

50g butter, broken into
lumps

80g plain flour

30g Demerara sugar

1 teaspoon ground
cinnamon

Tray bakes are lifesavers for clumsy bakers like
me. They require less attention than cakes and are
generally more forgiving. This tray bake uses a classic
combination of flavours and the simple addition of a
crumble topping gives it a lovely extra crunch. If you
want to make the method even more simple and quick,
just blitz all of the main tray bake ingredients (except
the apples) in your food processor.

Preheat the oven to 180°C/350°F/Gas Mark 4.

1. Line the baking tray with greaseproof paper.
2. Sift together the flour, baking powder and spices into a
   bowl.
3. In a separate, larger bowl, cream together the butter and
   light brown sugar until fluffy.
4. Add the eggs one at a time to the butter and sugar,
   alternating with heaped tablespoons of the flour mixture
   and the buttermilk, until everything is incorporated.
5. Toss the apple pieces in the Demerara sugar and scatter
   them over the batter. Scrape everything into the prepared
   tin.
6. To make the simple crumble topping, rub the butter into
   the flour until it forms crumbs, then stir in the Demerara
   sugar and cinnamon. Sprinkle over the batter and apples.
7. Bake for 45 to 55 minutes, until the cake is firm and
   starting to shrink away from the sides of the tin.
8. This cake can be served warm or cold.

Peanut butter cookies

These are proper soft and chewy American-style cookies. Despite their name, these cookies don't taste overly 'peanutty', so they probably won't offend anyone who doesn't normally enjoy peanut butter. The actual cookie recipe is a great base for adding other ingredients. I like to mix in a really good handful of chocolate chips for extra flavour and texture.

Makes about 16

110g butter at room temperature, broken into small lumps

100g soft light brown sugar

100g caster sugar

125g crunchy peanut butter

1 teaspoon vanilla extract

1 egg

200g plain flour, plus extra to dust

½ teaspoon baking powder

¼ teaspoon bicarbonate of soda

50g crushed peanuts

Preheat the oven to 180°C/350°F/Gas Mark 4.

1. Line 2 large baking trays with greaseproof paper.
2. Using an electric hand whisk on a low speed or a wooden spoon beat the butter in a large bowl until soft. Add the sugars and then beat together, until very light and fluffy.
3. Continue beating, adding in the peanut butter, vanilla extract and egg until nicely combined.
4. In a separate bowl, sift together the flour with the baking powder and bicarbonate of soda. Add this to the mix, along with the peanuts.
5. On a lightly floured worktop, use a rolling pin to shape small handfuls of the dough into round cookies, about 5cm in diameter and 2cm high.
6. Place the cookies on the prepared baking trays, leaving about 10cm between each one, as they will spread out as they cook. Press down each cookie with the back of a fork.
7. Bake for about 10 minutes until the cookies are set around the edges but still a little soft in the middle. Remove them from the oven and leave them on their baking trays for 5 minutes, where they will continue to cook. Finally, transfer them to a wire cooling rack.

Fizzy lemon and popping candy cake

Makes 8 slices

You will need 2 x 20cm round sandwich tins

225g butter, at room temperature

225g caster sugar

Zest and juice of 2 lemons

4 eggs

225g self-raising flour

A good handful of popping candy (now available in the baking section of supermarkets)

For the filling
150–200g lemon curd, at room temperature

For the icing
300g cream cheese

Zest and juice of 1 lemon

50g icing sugar

2–3 tsp sherbet (from a Dip Dab or Sherbet Fountain)

This is a really fun cake! To this day, the look of bewilderment combined with joy on Archie's face when he first tasted popping candy remains one of my most enduring memories from when he was a toddler. Everyone loves a lemon drizzle cake, and this one is turbo-charged with a big smile! The sherbet does make this a rather sweet cake, but it adds a lovely fizz to the icing, and your children will love it.

Preheat the oven to 180°C/350°F/Gas Mark 4.

1. Line the sandwich tins with greaseproof paper.
2. Cream together the butter and sugar with the lemon zest in a large bowl, until light and fluffy.
3. Add the eggs, one at a time, with alternate spoonfuls of flour. Then fold in the remaining flour. (Alternatively, blitz together the butter, sugar, zest, flour and eggs in a food processor until smooth.)
4. Add the lemon juice, a little at a time, until you have a good dropping consistency (you don't want it to be runny, so you may not need it all).
5. Scrape the mixture into the prepared tins. Bake for 20 to 25 minutes, until golden brown and just starting to come away from the edges of the tins. Leave to cool in the tins for a few minutes then turn out onto wire cooling racks.
6. While the cakes are cooling, make the icing. First, beat the cream cheese until very soft and then add the lemon zest and juice, the icing sugar and sherbet. Continue to beat until it is light and airy.
7. To assemble, spread one of the cakes with a fairly thin layer of the icing, then swirl through the lemon curd. Sprinkle over a couple of good pinches of the popping candy.

8. Place the other cake on top and spread with the rest of the icing. You can also cover the side of the cake, if you like; you'll just need to spread the icing a little more thinly.

9. Decorate the surface with the rest of the popping candy just before serving. You can either sprinkle it all over the cake or, for a pretty effect, cut out a small star from the middle of a piece of paper and use the paper as a stencil to create little stars packed with popping candy.

Classic jammy dodgers

Give me a jammy dodger and I'm thrown straight back to my childhood, hanging out with my grandparents. The beauty of making your own is that you can vary the shape of your biscuits and also use whatever flavoured jam you fancy. In an ideal world, you will use a small cutter, around 1.5cm in diameter, to remove the hole in the top biscuit but, if you don't have one, you can use the point of a sharp knife to cut out a small opening yourself. Being a hit across the generations, these biscuits are also lovely to give as gifts.

Makes 8–10

250g butter, at room temperature

100g caster sugar

Zest of 1 lemon (optional)

350g plain flour, plus extra for dusting

1 egg yolk

1 teaspoon vanilla extract

150g jam of your choice (it should be smooth and not too runny)

Icing sugar, to dust (optional)

1. Using an electric hand whisk or a wooden spoon cream together the butter, sugar and optional lemon zest in a large bowl. Sift in the flour, then add the egg yolk and using your hands bring the dough together to form a ball. Alternatively, you can just whizz all the above ingredients together in a food processor. Wrap the dough in cling film and chill it in the fridge for 30 minutes.

2. Preheat your oven to 140°C/275°F/Gas Mark 1 and line a couple of baking trays with greaseproof paper.

3. Generously flour your work surface, divide the dough in half and knead the balls just a little to make the dough more pliable. Dust your rolling pin with flour, too, and then roll out both pieces of dough to a thickness of about 3mm.

4. Cut out as many biscuits as you can, using a cutter of any shape that is roughly 6cm wide. Cut a small hole (1.5cm) in the middle of half of your biscuits.

5. Arrange the biscuits on the lined baking trays (leaving a good gap between them, as they will spread a little as they cook) and bake for 20 to 30 minutes, until they start turning golden brown round the edges.

6. Remove from the oven and leave to cool on a wire rack.

7. When they have cooled, spread a good layer of jam on to the biscuits without a hole, then top each one with a biscuit with a hole. You want the jam to spread to the edges inside the biscuit. Top up the hole with extra jam then dust with icing sugar, if you like.

8. Your jammy dodgers should keep for at least a week in an airtight container.

Strawberry and apple leather strips

These are a marvellous way of impressing your children and making them believe that you are a genius confectioner. Willy Wonka would have been proud of these. They are like the chewy fruity strips you can buy for babies who are weaning, or the kind of Catherine Wheel sweets you find in pick-and-mix boxes. And yet, they are made from only fresh fruit, honey and lemon, with not a nasty ingredient in sight. I would even be as bold as to say that a strip of this leather could possibly constitute one of your five a day. Healthy and guilt-free snacking. You can use any combination of fruit here, as long as you stick to proportions of 150g of honey to every kilo of fruit.

Depends on the size!

500g strawberries, hulled
500g cooking apples, peeled, cored, chopped
Juice of 1 lemon
150g honey

Preheat your oven to its lowest setting (we're talking 50°C/120°F/ Gas Mark 1/8 here).

1. Put the fruit in a saucepan with a splash of water and the lemon juice. Heat it gently, until the fruit is very soft.
2. Stir in the honey, then push the mixture through a sieve to remove all the bits.
3. Line a couple of baking trays with greaseproof paper. Divide the fruit pulp between the trays, using a spatula to spread it out as evenly as you can. You want a thickness of about 5mm.
4. Put the baking trays in the oven and leave them until the leather has dried out. You still want the leather to be very slightly tacky, as you are going to roll it. This will take between 10 to 12 hours, so is best done overnight.
5. Peel the leather away from the greaseproof paper, cut it into long 2cm-wide slices and then roll the slices into wheels (my children love doing this part).
6. And here's the best part of this recipe: these fruity leathers will keep for several months. Just store them in layers (separated by greaseproof paper) in an airtight container.

Plum and almond crumble

Serves 6

You will need a deep,
20 x 20cm baking dish

750g plums, halved and
stones removed

3–4 tablespoons caster
sugar, depending on the
sweetness of the plums

For the crumble topping

150g chilled butter, broken
into small lumps

250g spelt flour

100g soft light brown sugar

50g flaked almonds

Hand on heart, I have yet to meet a child who
doesn't like a good crumble. There's just something
unbelievably delicious about a melting buttery topping
and slightly sweetened fruit. As a bonus, this is a bit
healthier than the traditional version, as it uses spelt
flour, which is readily available in supermarkets. It gives
the crumble a slightly rougher texture and a bit of a
nutty taste, which I really like, but if you prefer, you can
just use regular plain flour. To make this gluten free, just
swap the flour for gluten-free flour.

Preheat your oven to 190ºC/375˚F/Gas Mark 5.

1. Butter your baking dish, arrange the plums in the bottom
    (cut-side up) and then sprinkle with the sugar.
2. Bake in the oven for 15 minutes. Cooking them in the
    oven first, rather than in a saucepan, will stop the plums
    collapsing and will ensure that they will be perfectly
    cooked through when the crumble is baked.
3. Rub the butter into the spelt flour using your fingers until
    you have a lovely crumbly mixture. Stir in the brown
    sugar and the almonds.
4. Tip the crumble mix on top of the cooked plums,
    spreading it out nice and evenly, but without pressing
    down too much.
5. Bake the crumble for 25 minutes until the crumble
    topping is golden brown.
6. You can serve this crumble warm (with some cream or
    ice cream) or leave it to cool down completely and eat
    it cold.

Egg-free malted chocolate ice cream

Ice cream recipes often ask for egg yolks but this comforting, malty, chocolate ice cream is completely egg–free. This has two benefits. First, it means it is suitable for anyone who is allergic to eggs. Secondly, it means that you can use it as a milkshake instead by simply half-freezing the mixture! I've used milk chocolate here but there's no reason why you can't use dark chocolate or even white chocolate, if you prefer. Whichever you choose, it really is worth buying a good-quality chocolate, as you will notice the different in the final product. Although having an ice cream maker will speed up the whole process, it's not difficult to make this ice cream without one.

Serves 6–8

500ml double cream

50g cocoa powder

200g caster sugar

1 tablespoon malt extract (optional)

150g good-quality milk chocolate

200ml milk

4 tablespoons Horlicks malted drink powder

A packet of crushed and crumbled Maltesers, to serve

Preheat the oven to 180°C/350°F/Gas Mark 4.

1. Put the cream, cocoa powder, sugar and malt extract (if using) in a saucepan. Whisk them together thoroughly and then heat gently on a low heat until the sugar and malt extract have dissolved. Turn up the heat, bring to the boil and then immediately remove the pan from heat.
2. Break up the chocolate and add it to the cream, stirring it gently to melt it through the mixture.
3. Whisk the Horlicks powder into the milk and then add this to the rest of the ingredients and combine well.
4. If you have an ice cream maker, simply cool the creamy chocolate a little, then churn it in the ice cream maker and keep it in your freezer. If you don't have an ice cream maker, pour the mix into a large, shallow container (with a lid) and put it in the freezer. Whisk very thoroughly every 30 minutes until it is completely frozen. This ensures plenty of air gets in giving you a lovely smooth ice cream.
5. Serve with the crumbled Maltesers sprinkled on top.

Genius Treats

Summer fruit jellies

Making jelly at home is absolutely child's play! As with so many recipes in this book, you'll get all the goodness of a traditional treat, without any of the E numbers or additives you would rather avoid. You can use any juice that takes your fancy or, for an extra bit of fun, why not create two different coloured jellies and allow one to set on top of the other in the glasses? As with your choice of juice, play around with what fresh fruit you use too. It's hard to think of any fruits that I wouldn't recommend, although I don't think the texture of banana would work as well in this jelly.

Serves 4

You'll need 4 medium-sized glasses

5 leaves of gelatine

500ml fruit juice of your choice (I think smooth works slightly better)

Juice of ½ a lime

About 2 tablespoons honey

A couple of good handfuls of freshly chopped fruit

1. Break up the gelatine leaves and put them in a small bowl. Pour just a little of your fruit juice over the top and then leave the leaves to soften for a few minutes.
2. Put the rest of the juice in a saucepan with the lime juice and honey and heat through on a low heat until the honey dissolves.
3. Keeping the juice on a gentle heat, add the gelatine and the soaking liquid and stir until everything is combined. Be careful not to boil the liquid.
4. Divide the fresh fruit between the serving glasses and fill each glass about one-third of the way up with the jelly liquid.
5. Put the glasses in the fridge and wait for the jelly to start to set. (Setting it in layers like this is the best way of ensuring that all the fruit doesn't float to the top of your glasses.) If you are tight for time, you can speed up this part of the process by putting the glasses in the freezer.
6. Once the jelly is firming up, divide the rest of the jelly liquid between the four glasses and put them back in the fridge to fully set. This can take 4 to 6 hours.

White chocolate and blueberry blondies

Gooey, cakey and extremely moreish, these blondies are made in a different way from a lot of blondie recipes, as the white chocolate is not melted down as part of the batter but is instead mixed through before baking. This means that they keep their strong butterscotch flavour. Having been known to eat these just before bed, I can confirm that they are perfect at all times of the day.

Preheat the oven to 180°C/350°F/Gas Mark 4.

1. Line your baking tray with greaseproof paper or oiled foil.
2. Melt the butter gently in a small saucepan over a low heat, or in a dish in the microwave. Allow it to cool a little, then mix it with the sugar in a large bowl until nicely combined. Add the eggs and vanilla extract.
3. In a separate bowl, mix the flour and baking powder together and fold this into the wet ingredients.
4. Stir in the chocolate chips and then scrape the batter into the prepared tin.
5. Sprinkle over the blueberries and bake in the oven for 25 to 30 minutes until firm and the top has started to crack. The blondies need to cool completely before being cut up and served.

Makes 16 pieces

You will need a deep
20 x 30cm baking tray

175g butter

300g soft light brown sugar

2 large eggs

1 teaspoon vanilla extract

225g plain flour

1 teaspoon baking powder

100g white chocolate chips (or put a 100g block of white chocolate in a sandwich bag and crush it into small chips using a rolling pin)

150g blueberries

Genius Treats

Watermelon slush

Serves 4

Approx. 900g cubed, deseeded watermelon (this is about one-quarter of a large melon or half of a small one)

150–200g strawberries, hulled

Juice of 1 lime

1 tablespoon honey

A cheekily simple and extremely refreshing summer slush drink. And if you want to be extra cheeky, adults can add a shot of tequila and turn it into a frozen Margarita! Make sure you keep an eye on who has which glass though! For extra speed, buy a seedless watermelon, otherwise you'll need to spend a few minutes cutting around the seeds and then deseeding the rest. Double up the quantities and keep an extra batch in the freezer, then simply allow the slush to defrost a little just before serving. (If you have any leftover watermelon, try making the salad on page 112.)

Mint is a lovely addition to these flavours, but it can make the slush have a rather bitty texture. If you want to use some, melt the honey with 50ml water, add lots of fresh or dried mint and leave it to infuse for 15 minutes. Strain the leaves and add the minty syrup to the watermelon when blitzing.

1. Freeze the watermelon pieces in a covered container for at least 2 hours.
2. Blitz the frozen watermelon with the remaining ingredients in a food processor or blender.
3. If you want the slush to be slightly diluted, add some extra ice while you blitz it.
4. Serve immediately.

Genius Treats

Lime and mango cheesecake pots

These little cheesecake pots are ideal to make in advance because they freeze really well. Leave them at room temperature while you eat your main course and they will be the perfect consistency just in time for dessert! This recipe makes 10 to 12 cupcake-sized pots. You can buy glass ramekins very cheaply, or you can just as easily use a muffin tin lined with paper cupcake cases. If the pots have been frozen, your kids will have loads of fun ripping away the wrapper and eating them with their fingers. There are a couple of important things to note here: first, please use proper cream. If you use one of the cream alternatives, the mixture is likely to split when you add the lime. Secondly, don't over-beat the cream, as that could also cause it to split when you mix everything together.

Makes 10–12 small pots

You will need 10 to 12 ramekins or muffin cases

75g butter

150g biscuits (digestives or ginger nuts are ideal)

300g cream cheese (I like Philadelphia)

75g caster sugar

100ml double cream

Zest and juice of 2 limes

1 mango, peeled and cut into small cubes

Long curls of lime zest, to decorate (optional)

1. Melt the butter in the microwave (it only needs a minute or so) or in a saucepan on a low heat.
2. Put the biscuits in a sandwich bag and bash them with a rolling pin to turn them into crumbs.
3. Mix the biscuits into the butter and divide the mixture between the ramekins or muffin cases. Press down well to get a nice firm base.
4. Beat together the cream cheese, sugar and double cream. Add the zest and juice of the limes and beat again, then gently fold through the mango pieces. Spoon this on top of the biscuit bases.
5. You could do worse than serve these pots immediately, although the cream mixture will not have firmed up. Ideally, leave them to chill in the fridge for a couple of hours or bung them in the freezer for 20 to 30 minutes to firm up.
6. If you are feeling creative, decorate with fine curls of lime zest before serving.

Luxury gluten-free chocolate brownies

Makes 16 pieces

You will need a deep
20 x 30cm baking tray

100g unsalted butter

200g good-quality dark
chocolate (minimum
70 per cent cocoa solids,
and make sure it is
gluten free)

4 large eggs

250g caster sugar
(preferably golden
caster sugar)

100g ground almonds

100g chopped walnuts
(optional)

Slightly crunchy on the outside but still soft and
deliciously gooey in the middle . . . it's not difficult to
achieve pure brownie perfection; you just have to make
sure you don't overcook them. The best brownie I have
eaten recently was made by a chef who is local to me,
called Hendrik Dutson Seinfeld. As is so often the case
with great chefs, he was more than happy to share
his recipe and I have since adapted it to produce this
wonderful flourless, gluten-free version.

Preheat your oven to 180°C/350°F/Gas Mark 4.

1. Line your baking tray with greaseproof paper or oiled foil.
2. Gently melt the butter and chocolate together, either
   in a dish in the microwave, or in a heatproof bowl set
   over a pan of gently simmering water (don't let the bowl
   actually touch the hot water). Allow it to cool a little
   once melted.
3. Meanwhile, in a large bowl, whisk together the eggs and
   sugar for a minute or two. You are looking for the sugar to
   be fully incorporated into the eggs and for the mixture to
   take in a little air, but don't over-whisk.
4. Pour the melted chocolate and butter into the eggs and
   sugar and stir well.
5. Add the ground almonds, together with the walnuts if
   you are using them. Fold them through the batter until
   you have a smooth and even mixture.
6. Scrape the mixture into your prepared tin and bake in
   the oven. Check on it after 20 minutes and if the top has
   already risen and is starting to crack a little, you can
   remove it from the oven. If the surface still looks a little
   raw in the middle, cook for a further 5 minutes and then
   check again.

7. Leave it to cool in the tin (the inside will carry on cooking a little) then cut into brownie-sized chunks.
8. The brownies will taste even better the following day and can be kept for 2 or 3 days in an airtight container. However, the likelihood is they will be gone by morning.

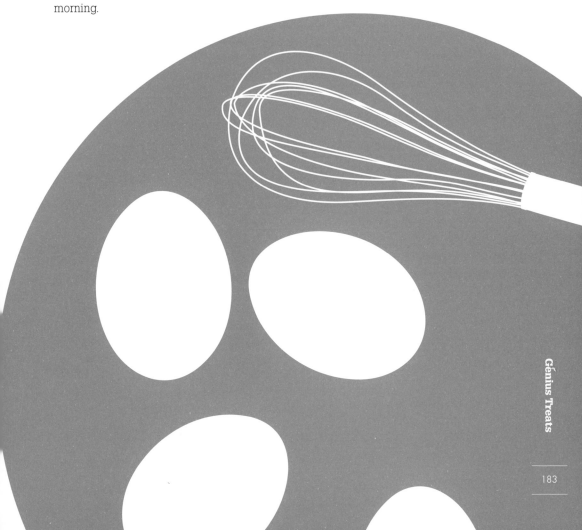

Home-made honeycomb chocolates

Vegetable or sunflower oil

8 tablespoons caster sugar

4 tablespoons golden syrup

1 level teaspoon bicarbonate of soda

200g good-quality dark chocolate

You will need a deep 20 x 20cm baking tray and a good deep saucepan

Archie and I spent a great Saturday morning hanging out together in the kitchen developing these wonderful Crunchie, sorry, crunchy sweet treats. We have since made a slightly odd discovery and so I feel I should give you a small warning about climactic conditions! It would appear that if you make honeycomb on a very hot or very damp and humid day, your chances of success are significantly reduced. I am unsure of the science behind this but it leads me to conclude that autumn and winter are the best seasons for making honeycomb.

1. Line your baking tray with greaseproof paper and then lightly oil the paper with vegetable or sunflower oil (honeycomb is very sticky stuff and it won't leave your paper alone if it can get away with it).
2. Put your deep saucepan on a medium heat. Pour in the sugar and golden syrup and heat, stirring gently, making sure all the sugar dissolves. As soon as the sugar has dissolved, stop stirring. Immediately!
3. Turn down the heat to low and let the syrup bubble and simmer very gently for 5 minutes. You definitely do not want a fierce bubble here, and do not stir it. Let it slowly turn into a caramel. You are going to have to trust your nose and eyes – don't let it smell of burning and make sure it isn't turning too dark. Once or twice, you can ever so slightly fold the mixture with your spatula, to make sure it stays an even colour (but don't overdo it or you will affect the temperature of the syrup – and don't scrape around the edges).

4. When the caramel has reached a nutty brown colour (not too dark; not too light), take the pan off the heat and dust in the level teaspoon of bicarbonate of soda. Fold it in immediately using a whisk but, again, don't overwork it.

5. Now leave it to bubble and rise up inside the saucepan like a volcano (your children will love watching this but remember we are dealing with scalding hot syrup, so this really is for an adult to do).

6. Once it has stopped rising, pour it into the prepared dish. Don't scoop out any of the honeycomb mix that doesn't naturally fall out of the pan. Anything you scoop will have the air knocked out of it and will turn to toffee. At this stage, rush the pan to the sink and fill it with very hot water. If you don't, you will be getting the hammer and chisel out later to get the honeycomb off the inside of your pan!

7. Leave the honeycomb to set. This will take 20 to 30 minutes. When it is set, break it up into bite-sized pieces.

8. Melt the chocolate in the microwave or in a small heatproof bowl set over a pan of gently simmering water (don't let the bowl actually touch the hot water).

9. Using your fingers or a skewer, dip the honeycomb pieces into the melted chocolate and then place them on greaseproof paper to set. The chocolate ensures the honeycomb stays fresh, so make sure you fully cover each piece.

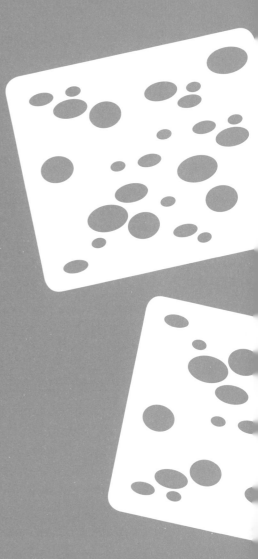

Genius Treats

Yoghurt and lemon curd crème brûlée

Serves 4

You will need 4 x 150–200ml ramekins (7–8cm wide)

300ml Greek yoghurt

100ml half-fat crème fraîche

1 tablespoon honey

4 tablespoons lemon curd (or any flavour you fancy)

4 tablespoons blueberries

4 tablespoons granulated sugar (not caster)

These crème brûlées don't actually involve any cooking, apart from the heat required to give them a crunchy topping. Putting them together is simply a case of mixing the ingredients – the thick Greek yoghurt gives them all the texture they need and the tangy flavour comes from the lemon curd. Don't worry if you don't have a blowtorch in your kitchen, if you grill them under a high heat you will get a more than acceptable finish.

If you are using your grill, preheat it to its very highest setting.

1. Whisk together the yoghurt, crème fraîche and honey until you have a smooth mixture and all the honey is well incorporated.
2. Put a tablespoon of curd in the bottom of each ramekin and top with a tablespoon of blueberries.
3. Divide the yoghurt mixture between the ramekins and sprinkle over the sugar. You want a good, even layer of sugar, covering all the creamy mixture.
4. Either brown the sugar with a blowtorch or place the ramekins on a baking tray and cook them under the very hot grill until the sugar has melted, turned a rich brown and is bubbling away. Under no circumstances touch the melted sugar while it is hot, as it will seriously burn you.
5. Allow the sugar to cool and then chill the brûlées in the fridge before serving. They will have a lovely crisp topping.

Index

Index

Acknowledgements

A huge thank you to everyone who continues to follow my blog and follow me elsewhere, such as on my radio show. Thank you also to everyone who bought the first book – I hope you enjoy this one too. None of this would happen without your brilliant support.

Thank you to my superb team at Hodder & Stoughton – Sarah Hammond, Nicky Ross, Emma Knight and everyone else involved in the various stages on this book – for all their patience and creativity. And more patience.

Catherine Phipps' help, advice and friendship during the recipe development process was invaluable.

Thank you to my two brilliant agents for all their hard work and support – Clare Hulton for my books and Richard Howells at Somethin' Else for all his work on the other aspects of my career.

To all my friends and colleagues at BBC Three Counties Radio, thank you for everything you do which makes being on the radio such a constant pleasure for me.

I am totally indebted to everyone who gave up their time to test my recipes. Their help was priceless: Jenny Boler, Eimear Carvill, Karen Chaplin, Jo Cloke, Lisa Conley, Clare Cuckow, Alison and Graham Dear, Stew Denholm, Nicky Desmond, Miff Dunn, Lyse Edwards, Christine Evans, Rosie Fean, Emma Ferns, Lisa Glanville, Simon Glazier, Karen Goodwin, Michelle Groom, Nicola Guy, Penelope Hankey, Rachel Hartell, Denise Hayes, Judith Hayton, Maddy Hill, Aisling Holmes, Sarah and Jack Holmes, Laura Hoskison, Andy Hurry, Sylvia James, Katie Jansen, Sal Jefford, Kate Jones, Janice Kirkwood, Emily Lamboy, Rachel Locke, David Millar, Clare Morgan, Jennie Moore, Kate Notarianni, Wendy Orr, Cassie Pearse, Anthony Pike, Fiona Preece, Martina Rafter, Clair Rankin, Heidi Roberts, Helen Robinson, Claire Slim, Rachel Suddrick, Anna Story, Louise Teal, Ian Thake, Meg Thomas, Liz Tumner, Lisa Wakefield, Lisa Willes, Sian Williams, Elizabeth Wright, Kate York, Snow Yule.

To my friends and family, thank you for all your love, support, encouragement and patience over the last few years, without which I would be very lost. Thank you Jo for keeping me sane and for being there come what may, and to my parents, sister and in-laws for all their guidance and help and their ability to just drop anything to help us when we need them.

And finally, Archie and his willing sous-chef Matilda. You both have the priceless ability to keep me on my toes, to brighten my days, to keep me grounded and to just make me smile and laugh. I am so proud watching you both grow into your very individual personalities and love you both more than you can know.

UNDER FIRE
A CENTURY OF
WAR MOVIES

UNIVERSITY OF CHICHESTER

UNDER FIRE

A CENTURY OF WAR MOVIES

EDITED BY

JAY SLATER

Ian Allan

PUBLISHING

Dedication

1977 – For Dad who took me to the Wimbledon Odeon. Instead of *Pete's Dragon* as promised, ended up watching *A Bridge Too Far*.

2009 – For Jay Brown and his Schmeisser in a world where there was no VE Day.

First published 2009

ISBN 978 0 7110 3385 6

Published by Ian Allan Publishing

an imprint of Ian Allan Publishing Ltd, Hersham, Surrey KT12 4RG.
Printed by Ian Allan Printing Ltd, Hersham, Surrey KT12 4RG.

Code: 0908/E

Visit the Ian Allan Publishing web site at www.ianallanpublishing.co.uk

CONTENTS:

BIOGRAPHIES:

The Editor:

Jay Slater was born in Wimbledon, London, and was raised on a televised diet of fading Universal horror movies before being exposed to the video revolution in the early 1980s. Jay has written for *Fangoria*, *Rue Morgue* and *The Dark Side* as well as *Hotdog*, *Death Ray*, *Bizarre*, *DVD Review*, *SFX*, *Neo*, *Film Threat*, *PC Format*, *GamesTM*, *Retro Gamer* and *Xbox 360*. In 2002, Jay edited *Eaten Alive: The Italian Cannibal and Zombie Movie* that has become a cult book, and in 2005 edited a range of fiction titles including *The Texas Chainsaw Massacre*, *Blade: Trinity*, *The Butterfly Effect* and *Final Destination 3*.

The Authors:

Ellen Cheshire studied Film and English at London Metropolitan University gaining a BA (Hons). She has subsequently taught Film at FE and Adult Education level, regularly giving talks and lectures on a wide variety of film topics. She has written books on Jane Campion, Ang Lee, Audrey Hepburn and The Coen Brothers for Pocket Essentials. She contributed to *Science Fiction World's Top 100 Fantasy Films*, as well as to numerous film and literature magazines and websites.

James Clarke is the writer of *The Pocket Essentials: Steven Spielberg* and *The Virgin Film Guide: Coppola* amongst other titles. His writing has been published by the British Film Institute, the *Guardian* and *Empire* movie magazine and he has contributed to The Rough Guide to Film and The Wallflower Press critical guides to directors. James is Lecturer and Course Co-Ordinator in the Film and Video Foundation Degree programme at Hereford College of Arts.

Tom Dawson is a freelance film critic and interviewer, specialising in British and European cinema. He has contributed to various newspapers, magazines and websites. These include *Metro*, *The Information*, *Total Film*, *Hot Tickets*, *What's On in London*, *The List*, *BBC Online*, *Channel Four.com* and *Scotland on Sunday*. He still can't decide whether Robert Bresson or Jean-Pierre Melville is his favourite French filmmaker.

After attending high school in England, **Robert Davenport** joined the navy, completed flight training and made two overseas deployments as a plane commander with Patrol Squadron Forty-Four. Upon graduation, he held a succession of creative and business affairs positions at various entertainment companies, including Twentieth Century-Fox, CBS, Viacom and New World Pictures. He is also an author and volunteered as a captain in the US Army where he saw service in the first Gulf war and Kosovo and Afghanistan. He then transferred to the United States Air Force, where he awaits his next tour of duty. Robert has a Master of Fine Arts in Screenwriting from UCLA, and holds the distinction of being the only person to have twice won the prestigious UCLA Screenwriting Showcase. He has received a total of 48 screenwriting awards and is listed in 'Who's Who in America'.

Paul M. Edwards is the Senior Fellow at the Center for the Study of the Korean War at Graceland University. He served with the 31st Field Artillery, 7th Division, in Korea.

He received his doctorate from St. Andrews University, Scotland, taught history and philosophy, and served as a university administrator for several years. He is the author of more than a dozen books on the Korean War, including *A Guide to Films on the Korean War* (Greenwood, 1997).

Daniel Etherington was deputy editor on Channel 4's film website for five years and has also contributed to *Sight & Sound*, *BBC Online*, *Total Film* and BAFTA publications. He loves war movies, but isn't convinced the real thing is always such a good idea.

James Evans is a Senior Lecturer in the School of Historical and Critical Studies at the University of Brighton and Associate Lecturer at both University of the Arts, London and the Film Studies Department at the University of Sussex. He graduated in Fine Art from the Nova Scotia College of Art and Design and then received an MA in Film Studies at the University of Sussex. He also works as a freelance journalist and contributes to, among others, *Cinema Scope* and *Electric Sheep Magazine*. He is currently researching and writing a book on representations of the artist in cinema. He is Canadian born and resides in the UK.

Sean Hogan was born in Slough but thankfully never had to live in the place. The rot quickly set in thereafter with childhood exposure to late night horror double bills; an adolescent diet of video nasties, thrash metal and pulp novels did the rest. Despite later attempts to go straight, he became a genre filmmaker and bears varying degrees of responsibility for the films *Lie Still* (2005), *Summer's Blood* (2009) and the forthcoming *Little Deaths*. His mother still wonders where he got it from.

James Kidd studied English literature at Liverpool University and University College London. Based in London, he has written for the *Observer*, the *Independent on Sunday*, *Time Out*, the *South China Morning Post*, *The Jerusalem Post*, the *Daily Telegraph*, and *Square Meal* magazine.

Mike Mayo is the author of *VideoHound's War Movies*, *Horror Show* and *Video Premieres*. He edited three editions of the *VideoHound's DVD Guide*, and for several years was the host of the nationally syndicated radio show Max and Mike On the Movies (maxandmike.com). He contributed a short history of the movies to *The Encyclopedia of Recreation and Leisure in America* and served as book page editor of *The Roanoke Times*. His most recent book is *American Murder: Criminals, Crime and the Media*. He plays a less than perfect but enthusiastic game of racquetball. He also reviews films for *The Washington Post*.

Karen McCreedy was brought up in Staffordshire and worked in the civil service in London for over twenty years, before moving to the coast for a gentler pace and more 'writing time'. For twelve years, she wrote for and edited a quarterly newsletter for the James Mason Appreciation Society and has written articles about British films, actors and studios for *Classic Television*, *Yours* and *Best of British* magazines. She has also been shortlisted a half-dozen times in *Writing* magazine short story competitions, and hopes to improve on this with a win in 2009.

James Mottram is a journalist who has written on film for numerous publications, including *The Times*, *The Independent*, *Total Film* and *Scotland on Sunday*. He is also the author of four books: *Public Enemies: The Gangster Movie A-Z*, *The Coen Brothers: The Life of the Mind*, *The Making of Memento* and *The Sundance Kids: How The Mavericks Took Back*

Hollywood. In addition, he has contributed to several other works, including *Ten Bad Dates with De Niro*. He lives in London.

Kim Newman is a novelist, critic and broadcaster. His fiction includes *Anno Dracula*, *Life's Lottery* and *The Man from the Diogenes Club*. His non-fiction includes *Nightmare Movies*, *Horror: 100 Best Books* and BFI Classics studies of *Cat People* and *Doctor Who*. He is a contributing editor to *Sight & Sound* and *Empire*. He wrote and directed a short film *Missing Girl* (available online at www.johnnyalucard.com/missinggirl.html), has written radio and TV documentaries (Radio 4's *Dicing With Dragons*, *Time Shift: A Study in Sherlock*) and plays for radio (BBC Online's *Mildew Manor*, Radio 4's *Cry-Babies*). His website is at johnnyalucard.com.

Julian Petley is Professor of Screen Media and Journalism in the School of Arts at Brunel University. His first published book was *Capital and Culture: The German Cinema 1933-1945* (BFI, 1979) and he has published widely on various aspects of German cinema ever since. His most recent books are *Censoring the Word* (Seagull Books/Index on Censorship 2007), *Censoring the Moving Image* (Seagull Books/Index on Censorship 2008), which was co-written with the *Observer*'s film critic Philip French, and *Censorship: A Beginner's Guide* (Oneworld Publications 2009). He is principal editor of the *Journal of British Cinema and Television* and a member of the editorial board of the *British Journalism Review*.

Eddie Robson is a scriptwriter and journalist. He is the author of the books *Film Noir* (2005) and *Coen Brothers* (2003), essays in *The Routledge Companion to Gothic* (2007) and *Postscript: Coen Brothers* (2008), and pieces for the *Guardian*, *Film Review*, *What DVD*, *SFX* and *Shortlist*. He has also written comedy for the BBC radio shows *Broken Arts*, *Play and Record*, *Look Away Now* and *Tilt*, and episodes of *Doctor Who* for BBC Radio 7.

Jamie Russell is the author of *Vietnam War Movies* and *Book of the Dead: The Complete History of Zombie Cinema*. He ardently believes it's better to make love not war, but sadly doesn't seem to be able to get anyone in power to agree with him...

Esther MacCallum-Stewart is a postgraduate research fellow at SMARTlab, the University of East London. Her work specialises in group behaviour in online communities, in particular the ways that people respond to the narratives within game worlds. She has written widely on the developing representations of warfare in games, as well as the ways that people understand virtual worlds. She is currently editing a collection of essays about *The Lord of the Rings Online*, as well as writing her own book on how players form tribal communities within game worlds.

FOREWORD

by Mark Goldblatt

The study of mankind is generally demarcated by the wars that have been fought throughout recorded time. There are pre-war periods, the war campaigns that follow, eventual armistice and finally post-war reconstruction. During this period of calm the balance of power may shift with new political lines drawn, resulting in fresh tensions and ultimately new wars. 'And so it goes…' in the immortal words of Kurt Vonnegut, a writer who is no stranger to exploring this dialectic of mass destruction the human race seems drawn to like the proverbial moth to the flame.

On the face of it, there are always 'good' reasons for war: manifest destiny, political differences, supposed religious or racial 'superiority' ('God is on our side'), economics and even blatant war profiteering. What is perhaps harder for us to comprehend is that our race might just be hardwired for war; that war could be a part of our genetic coding. This might seem simplistic and there is no easy way to prove it, but human history does seem to indicate that the drive towards ritual race slaughter may lie within our own DNA.

This is a pretty dire thesis and certainly not verifiable, but it is one interpretation amongst many as to why war is such a constant in human history. Since war takes place on a vast canvas, cinema, during its relatively short life, has been particularly suited to providing the necessary spectacle and topography within which vast land armies, seas of battleships and squads of flying machines provide an overview, and within which also more personal and precise stories of combat and human conflict may be told.

In this book, Jay Slater has assembled his own vast army of fine writers whose task it is to explore various theses of 'why we fight' and the consequences of doing so within the many sub-genres of war cinema. These sub-genres may reflect pro-war propaganda, anti-war deconstructionism or any shades of grey (or even noir) between them.

Mark Goldblatt and James Cameron with theitr Oscar for *Terminator 2: Judgment Day* 1991

© Mark Goldblatt

They may comment on the individual human condition or the mass national consciousness of the warring parties being portrayed. They can explore past wars, speculative future wars or real-life present conflicts. In other words, the myriad sub-genres of the war film may in fact serve as commentary or metaphor for many aspects of the human condition, as the various essays in this volume will demonstrate.

For example, Esther MacCallum-Stewart in her essay 'Battleground: Storming the Beaches' discusses speculative war films that metaphorically replace naturalistic elements of the genre with science fiction or fantasy elements. Thomas Dawson's essay, '1950s British War Movies and the Myth of World War 2', on the other hand focuses on the classical World War 2 films produced in England, which were representational, often with jingoistic middle class perspectives. Kim Newman zeroes in on the Powell/Pressberger war oeuvre which produced so many wonderful pictures such as *The 49th Parallel*, *One of Our Aircraft is Missing* and the masterpieces *The Life and Death of Colonel Blimp*, *A Matter of Life and Death* and *A Canterbury Tale*, among others. Their work

Mark Goldblatt
with Vincent
Price on
Dead Heat
1998

© Mark
Goldblatt

was certainly patriotic, but infused with a three dimensional complexity that places them in an exalted class of their own, which Karen McCreedy also alludes to in her essay on propaganda films. James Mottram explores the Vietnam War film, kicked off by *Platoon* in 1986 (though actually preceded on a much less inspired level by *A Yank in Vietnam* and *The Green Berets*; interestingly, both directed by their stars. Paul Edwards explores the Korean War film in 'Missing in Action: Where was John Wayne?', postulating an interesting premise as to why John Wayne never starred in a film about that war. [1] James Clarke discusses war films written about children and, in 'Not So Silent Night: The World War 2 Hollywood War Film', James Evans writes about the Christmas-time war movie. Robert Davenport's essay distinguishes between the epic 'A' budget war movie and the lean, claustrophobic 'B' war film. (I think that the late great Manny Farber would have had a lot to say on this subject.)

James Clarke discusses animation and how it can allow us to experience the horrors of war from a distanced perspective. Mike Mayo explores Nazi-tinged exploitation films such as the Ilsa series and *Salon Kitty*, which mix sadomasochism and softcore sex with lots of violence. Eddie Robson journeys into the dark heart of film noir as a post-war phenomenon, often following the exploits of a protagonist (possibly an ex-serviceman) who re-enters a 'dark' society. [2] Jamie Russell discusses the influence of the real life 'grunt video' on contemporary war cinema, analysing such works as *Redacted*, *Stop Loss* and *Battle for Haditha* in 'Lights, Camera, Incoming!: How YouTube Rewrote the War Movie'.

At this point I should mention that the reason for my being asked to pen this foreword stems from my three decades of work as a film editor. I've worked on scores of projects, but a number of them can definitely be described as war films: *Rambo: First Blood Part II*, which James Mottram explores in his Vietnam essay; *Pearl Harbor*, which is essentially a romantic triangle that plays out within the vast carnage of the Japanese sneak attack on Oahu and its aftermath; and *Starship Troopers*, director Paul Verhoeven's subversive take on Robert Heinlein's novel, which is nicely analysed in Jamie Russell's second essay for this volume, 'Goose-Stepping in Space: Fascism, World War 2 and Giant Bugs in *Starship Troopers*'. The one huge constant in these films is that they are all fairly large scale spectacles. They each provide a very large canvas within which we view the daily events of warfare.

In *Rambo: First Blood Part II*, we follow the further adventures of former special forces op John Rambo, years after the Vietnam War has concluded. Incarcerated for going ballistic when pushed too far in his previous screen outing, *First Blood*, Rambo is freed from prison in order to journey back to Vietnam on a government-backed mission to investigate reports that prisoners of war are being held in camps hidden deep in the jungle. Of course, we later learn that the mission is a set up and that Rambo is a pawn supposed to substantiate the non-existence of any POWs. When he does locate them at a hidden prison camp, he is abandoned by the bureaucrats and left for dead, eradicating any evidence that there ever was a mission. He is expendable, just like the

POWs. Rambo, however, is not easily disposed of and he survives captivity and torture to become a one-man army who reboots the war and this time (at least symbolically) wins it.

Rambo: First Blood Part II is very well staged, beautifully shot by the legendary Jack Cardiff. My personal interpretation is that the film plays out as an almost mythic battle film with Rambo as the 'über warrior' vanquishing all foes. I once told the director, George Cosmatos, that with Sylvester Stallone's finely chiselled body, the film seemed to me to be the ultimate Maciste film. Maciste was the muscular hero of most of the Italian 'peplum' films (sometimes called Hercules or Samson in the American dubbed versions, and played by Steve Reeves, Gordon Scott, Reg Park and others) that were extremely popular in the '60s, but date all the way back to 1915. Maciste often befriended and protected the poor farmers and villagers from despotic rulers. He was super strong with rippling muscles and a man of few words.

You might remember that James Cameron wrote the first draft of the screenplay: Rambo is mythic in this film, the way that *The Terminator* is mythic. And the sense of time and place is really irrelevant. Strip away allusions to the Vietnam War and this movie could take place in the future or World War 2 and essentially be the same.

Pearl Harbor is similar to *Rambo: First Blood Part II* in that, despite its tragic historical story, it is ultimately a cathartic patriotic action spectacle. However, it is much more a recreation of actual events. The centrepiece of the film is the Japanese sneak attack on Pearl Harbor, and in preparing these scenes director Michael Bay studied numerous historical news photographs and records in order to accurately recreate them in his film (i.e. the panoramic views of battleship row), albeit through the prism of a late 90s cinematic sensibility. [3] As in *Rambo: First Blood Part II*, there is an internal logic within the depiction of mayhem and devastation, as well as a controlled disorientation that results from putting the viewer within the centre of incomprehensible carnage. This, combined with the very real and terrible human consequences of the attack, creates tremendous pathos that inevitably dwarfs the fictional romantic story meant to provide a structure to the historical events.

Dolph Lundgren and Mark Goldblatt on the set of *The Punisher* 1989

© Mark Goldblatt

Paul Verhoeven's *Starship Troopers* deals with a different sort of horror. The ostensible plot concerns a near-future civilization at war with a seemingly unfathomable enemy: giant arachnids from a distant planet. In fact, it is the armies of Earth who set off the first altercations by attempting to colonise planets already claimed by the bugs. *Starship Troopers*, while speculative science fiction, is also clearly metaphorical, utilising (and sometimes varying) many mainstays of the classic World War 2 film such as the multiracial platoon (which in this case becomes sexually mixed as well), the 'objectification of the enemy' ('the only good bug is a dead bug'), and yes, again, the romantic triangle. But something here is different: the human society that battles the bugs and from which our heroes derive is a quasi-fascist, militaristic one in which unquestioning nationalism and military service becomes an end unto itself.

In its initial release, the film was often wrongly accused of harbouring pro-fascist sentiments. The truth is, as Jamie Russell demonstrates, *Starship Troopers* uses a speculative future society in the context of war, to comment on militarised and ultra-nationalistic societies in the present. This is subversive because the film-going audience is preconditioned to identify with their protagonists, which we do here, until we ultimately discover that our heroes would have fitted in nicely with Hitler's National Socialist Party. We have met the enemy, and he is us.

This sort of metaphorical connection between speculation and real life is also explored by James Mottram in 'Jungle Fever: How Vietnam Changed the Hollywood War Movie', in which he recounts the cinematic steps leading up to the total annihilation of our world in films such as *Terminator 2: Judgment Day* (which I edited with Conrad Buff and Richard A. Harris), *Dr. Strangelove* and *On the Beach*, and by Sean Hogan who, in 'Ghosts of War' explores the spectral metaphor of soldiers returning from the dead, usually to prove a point about war to the living.

I first became of aware of Jay Slater quite a few years ago when a friend passed me a copy of his exhaustive analysis of the Italian post-apocalyptic movie (films that followed in the tradition of *Escape from New York* and *Mad Max 2*), a genre that previously hadn't been tackled in such depth. It knocked my socks off. We got in touch and have remained in contact ever since. Jay's love of genre and the war film in particular makes him the perfect curator of this cornucopia of cinema insights.

Endnotes

1. I would think that if he had, Sam Fuller would have been the man to direct it, having made such hard-hitting gems as *Fixed Bayonets* and *The Steel Helmet*. Now there's a filmic marriage that I would have loved to have seen.
2. I would add a complimentary sub-genre to this: the 'home-front' war film, which contains noir-ish elements, as spies try to infiltrate the US and create havoc (*All Through the Night*, many of the Mr. Moto titles, and even Hitchcock's *Saboteur*).
3. Aided by the immense contributions of director of photography John Schwartzman and production designer Nigel Phelps.

'C'EST LA GUERRE.'
'WAR IS WAR.'
'DIENST IST DIENST.'

How Hollywood Learned to Love the War Film

JAMES KIDD

SHOOTING WAR: THE BEGINNINGS OF A BEAUTIFUL FRIENDSHIP

If the 20th century was good for anything, it was good for making war and making movies. The same era that witnessed the rise and establishment of cinema as an art form and lucrative industry was also defined by unprecedented levels of mass conflict. As Niall Ferguson writes in *War of the Worlds*: 'The hundred years after 1900 were without question the bloodiest ... in modern history'. [1] Ferguson adds that there was 'not a single year before, between or after the world wars that did not see large-scale organised violence in one part of the world or another' (Ferguson, xxxiv – xxxv). It is hardly surprising, then, that cinemagoers would want to see their hopes and fears about violent conflict reflected on the big screen.

The alliance between shooting guns and shooting cameras was instant and enduring. The early history of the war film is really the early history of film as a whole. From the moment a camera could roll, it captured images and stories of martial life. Starting with R.W. Paul's primitive footage of marching soldiers and ending with Jean Renoir's anti-war masterpiece, *La Grande Illusion* (1937), the works of this period had to navigate the transition from short films to features, from silents to talkies, from motion pictures as circus side-show to the dominant field in the entertainment world. The first war films offer an eloquent 'plea for the art of the Motion Picture', as D.W. Griffith notes at the start of *Birth of a Nation* (1915). [2]

As a result, these two decades witnessed the slow birth of a genre, albeit a loose and baggy one. The early war films introduced the basic narrative structures, special effects and stock characters: the poetic hero, the grizzled veteran, the sympathetic clown. But the genre is really a cinematic Frankenstein's monster, constructed from the parts of many other genres. In addition to the bombs and the battles, there is romance, horror, gore, family drama, sex, adventure, comedy, and, of course, plenty of tragedy. In other words, precisely the sort of grandiose yet intimately human drama that has dominated both the box office and the Academy Awards for much of the past century.

So it was in the beginning. The American box office was dominated by military blockbusters during the early part of the 20th century: *Birth of a Nation* beat all-comers in the 1910s; *The Big Parade* (1925) and *The Four Horsemen of the Apocalypse* (1921) were the two most popular movies of the 1920s. [3] A third film from this decade, *Wings*, comes in at number nine, and also won the first Best Picture Oscar in 1927, and was the only silent movie to do so. Little wonder almost every major director, producer and star of Hollywood's first coming had a go – from King Vidor and Howard Hughes to Charlie Chaplin and Rudolph Valentino, from Buster Keaton and Greta Garbo to Jean Harlow and Gary Cooper, from Errol Flynn and David Niven to Laurel and Hardy.

While Hollywood has done much to shape our perception of war, so war has done much to shape Hollywood itself – and not just in terms of the kind of films it would produce. The pivotal moment was the outbreak of World War 1. Before 1914, US filmgoers were fed on what seems today to be an unlikely diet of foreign movies: Mark Cousins notes that in 1907, 40% of films shown in America were made by Pathé, while companies like Gaumont and Éclair also enjoyed significant market share. [4] The war decimated these hitherto dominant studios in both Germany and France, providing opportunistic American studios with a chance to cash in: 'importing few films between 1914 and 1918, [Hollywood] had a virtual monopoly on North American cinemagoers and visual entertainment' (Cousins, 58-9).

This protectionist stance meant that in 1918 Hollywood was ready and willing to deluge the world with its home-made work, leaving the other major film-producing territories in its wake. One notable exception was the Russian film industry, which also benefited from the Great War. [5] Yet it was Hollywood's golden age which would conquer the world, and the war film was central to its victory.

1898 – 1914: THE CONCEPTION OF A GENRE

The story of the war film begins some years before Hollywood's *coup d'état* – far from Los Angeles and rather closer to such glamorous locations as Muswell Hill golf course and the hills outside Blackburn. Dating back to the final years of Queen Victoria's reign, cinematic pioneers like R.W. Paul, Sagar Mitchell and James Kenyon recorded military marches, reconstructions of the Anglo-Boer war and vignettes of soldiers' lives. Only three years after agreeing to manufacture replicas of Edison's Kinetescope in 1894, Paul filmed the 'magnificent pageantry of royalties and troops from all parts of the world' that marked Victoria's Diamond Jubilee in 1897. [6]

These first works are not so much 'war films' as army photographs that happen to move a little. Paul interspersed these films with stories drawn from Edwardian life, from Dickens, and, given his own penchant for trick photography, with actual footage from the Anglo-Boer War – shot by an army doctor called Beevor, this includes film of General Piet Cronje crossing the veldt in a carriage only moments after surrendering to Lord Roberts in 1900. Paul's work tends to celebrate moments of patriotic and ceremonial grandeur: Lord Kitchener, then the 'Sirdar' of the Egyptian Army, receiving the freedom of the City of London; or his series of 33 films, *Army Life; or How Soldiers are Made*, which aimed to stimulate recruitment and also satisfy the public's growing interest about the army during the Boer War.

This widespread interest explains the vogue for reproductions of 'incidents' taken from the battlefield, one that would persist until the Great War with films like Walter Summers' *The Battle of Ypres* (1925) and *Mons* (1926). Having failed to capture much actual combat from Africa, Paul restaged scenes from the war on Muswell Hill golf course. *A Camp Smithy* begins something of a tradition of the blacksmith in war movies – they recur in both *Civilisation* (1916) and *J'Accuse!* (1919). *Attack on a Piquet* is rather more action-packed: a band of Boers ambush a dozing group of British soldiers, shooting them at close range.

Mitchell and Kenyon also shot their share of re-enactments, although they used the Yellow Hills outside Blackburn. *A Sneaky Boer* (1901) features the somewhat gymnastic death throes of another Tommy ambushed in the Transvaal. Mitchell and Kenyon often screened these re-enactments with live sound-effects of guns being fired: in one instance, the smoke billowed so successfully that it obscured the screen. The duo also filmed their share of documentary footage: of General Baden-Powell opening the Drill Hall in Accrington or the war hero Lieutenant Clive Wilson returning home to Hull in 1902.

These fragments suggest some rudimentary storylines that later directors would assemble and expand into feature-length movies. Paul's *Tommy Atkins in the Park* (1898), for instance, hints at the comic and romantic possibilities of army life. A remake of his first production, *A Soldier's Courtship* (1896), Paul's plot stars an off-duty 'Tommy' who kisses his girlfriend on a park bench. Interrupted by a forbidding matriarch, the less-than-chivalrous young warrior simply tips her onto the floor.

A couple of years later, the first filmmaker whose war movies would earn mass public and critical acclaim was beginning his career on the other side of the Atlantic. Best known today for the crude racial politics of *Birth of a Nation*, David Wark Griffith could nevertheless be christened the godfather of the war film. He did not invent the genre alone, but with works like *Birth of a Nation*, *Hearts of the World* (1918) and *America* (1924), he went a long way to establishing its basic conventions, themes and characters. As his biographer, Richard Schickel, states, when Griffith travelled to Europe in 1917 to film *Hearts of the World*, he was 'by common consent, the world's most pre-eminent director of military spectacle'. [7]

War was in Griffith's blood. The son of a Confederate colonel, he spent his child-hood 'listening to whittling oldsters by the horse-trough before the general store fight the Civil War over again – with ever-increasing victories' (Schickel, p.27). As a young actor, Griffith played Abraham Lincoln; as a young writer, he planned an epic about the American Revolution simply entitled *War*; this would eventually become his 1924 film, *America*.

Griffith's cinematic career would also be fuelled by conflict, both on and off-screen. His first years as a film director at Biograph (1900 to 1913) coincided with the 50th anniversary of the Civil War itself. With America in the mood to memorialise its dead, Griffith produced a number of short films that portrayed war as terrifying but exciting. An epic war film in miniature, 1911's *The Battle* anticipates many of Griffth's later preoccupations, not least his imaginative use of names: his lead couple are called 'Boy' and 'Girl'. For a short film, it required a cast of Homeric proportions and an array of explosive stunts and special effects. While Griffith later concentrated largely on depictions of macho heroism, here he offers a relatively sympathetic portrait of unadul-terated terror: before 'Boy' proves his manhood by guiding a wagon full of dynamite along a fire-strewn path, he can hardly bear to cross shaky swords with the enemy.

As audiences grew in size, so too did the scale of the films and the ambitions of their directors. As early as 1913, Giovanni Pastrone's *Cabiria* laid down a challenge that other directors would try to match. Made over six long months, the story included a series of set-piece adventures in Carthage and scenes of Hannibal crossing the Alps. As Mark Cousins notes in *The Story of Film*, '*Cabiria* is a gigantic work whose scale, even viewed from the era of computer-generated is still surprising' (Cousins, 47).

That same year, Thomas Ince, Griffith's main rival in the US market, tried his hand with a five-reel blockbuster entitled *The Battle of Gettysburg*. Griffith was already preparing his response: an adaptation of Thomas Dixon's White Supremacist novel, *The Clansman*. Griffith boasted that the resulting film "will be worth a hundred of the other movies." (Schickel, 207).

If Griffith's work for Biograph was where the popular war film gestated, the open-ing half of *Birth of a Nation* (as *The Clansman* was called) was where it was born. It is, Schickel notes, 'a miraculous production' in almost every respect: in terms of scale, cost, gross, popularity and controversy (Schickel, p.212). Although the movie does not share Dixon's ideology, its racial politics were crude enough to make even Griffith's heartfelt entreaty for freedom of speech sound infected by abhorrent innuendo: 'We [...] do demand, as a right, the liberty to show the *dark* side of wrong, that we may illuminate the *bright* side of virtue.'

The Birth of
a Nation
1915

© Epic/
The Kobal
Collection

Birth of a Nation is a film defined by similarly grand polarities: South against North, white against black, youth against age, the battlefront against home, male against female and the young against the old. Just about the most vulnerable person in Griffith's story is an elderly black woman enslaved in the Southern States. Not that she would have earned much sympathy from either Dixon or Griffith. As he states at the start of *Birth of a Nation*: 'The bringing of the African to America sowed the first seeds of disunity.' History may be written by the victors, but where *Birth of a Nation* is concerned, it can be rewritten by the self-righteous vanquished as well.

This prejudice suggests similar polarities within Griffith himself: a tension between fact and fiction, between authenticity and propaganda, between the personal and the epic and between didacticism and entertainment. How, for instance, do you make a film about that most un-American subject – defeat – and make it seem noble, heroic and entertaining?

Griffith's response seems paradoxical. He makes a film that conveys 'the ravages of war to the end that *war be held in abhorrence*', and also one that makes war seem thrilling and spectacular. By a similar token, Griffith promotes his personal interpretation of the Civil War and also stresses his objectivity. *Birth of a Nation* is punctuated by 'Historical Facsimiles' that attempt to lend veracity to the narrative: for instance, a portrait of Abraham Lincoln signing the proclamation requesting 75,000 volunteers.

These polarities also define *Birth of a Nation*'s plot: a simple tale of two families, the Southern Camerons and the northern Stonemans, who find themselves on opposing sides of the Civil War. The first casualty of conflict is not so much truth as a way of life: in this instance, one that 'runs in a quaintly way that is to be no more'. In the innocent opening scenes, the younger members of the two families make friends, horse about and fall in love. Yet even this pure vision is not untainted by the brutality to come: shots of a fighting cat and dog earn the screen card, 'Hostilities'.

This opening salvo sets a precedent that many subsequent war films (from *The Four Horsemen of the Apocalypse* to *Star Wars* (1977)) would follow: that of showing the world that would be torn to shreds by the looming conflict. Of course, just as many movies (*La Grande Illusion* (1937), *Apocalypse Now* (1979), *Platoon* (1986), *Saving Private Ryan* (1998)) follow Homer's injunction and begin *in medias res*. But for Griffith to make his central point – how the South was ruined by the North – he had to show the last days of bliss. Unsurprisingly, the portrait is both highly sentimentalised and idealised: the images of happy cotton-picking slaves dancing and smiling beggar belief.

Before hostilities proper get underway, Griffith provides another war film staple: the lengthy farewells. As the world prepares to divide itself into home-front and battle-front, he shows that the second casualty of war is the coherence of society in general and the family in particular. Men are separated from women, the young from the old, the soon to be glorious dead from those who will mourn them.

And there will be plenty of mourning. Griffith uses the family story to humanise the chaos of mass conflict he presents us. Having promised faithfully to meet again, the two youngest Cameron and Stoneman boys reunite on the battlefield. Recognition comes just in time to prevent Duke Cameron from bayoneting his 'chum'. Yet dramatic irony achieves what six inches of steel could not, and Tod Stoneman is killed before the smile has faded from Duke's face. Not an artist who favoured understatement, Griffith then kills Duke himself only a frame or two later. Collapsing beside his erstwhile friend, he initiates a noble tradition that mixes noble death with a splash of homoeroticism: draping his arm around Tod's neck, Duke Cameron moves in for a kiss, but ruins the moment by dying prematurely.

Griffith may have exaggerated the scale of his film (the estimate of 18,000 extras is about 17,500 over the top), but the sheer size of the Battle of Atlanta, for example, is mind-boggling. One minute, the camera offers a long shot of the two sides blowing each other to pieces; the next, it is on the ground in the middle of the action; the next there are superimposed images of the burning city and newly-created refugees running for their lives.

The combination of long shots and close-ups portrays the battle as vast, fast and thrilling, simultaneously beyond our comprehension and somehow within it too. The personal confrontation between Ben Cameron (the 'Little Colonel') and his friend Phil Stoneman engages our sympathies in the midst of the mortar fire, black clouds of smoke and waving flags. Half-crazed with the courage of the desperate, the 'Little Colonel' charges the Northern lines, Griffith's moving camera adding fervour to his attack. Suddenly, Griffith cuts again, not to the battle but all the way back to the Cameron family, sitting still and solemn around a table.

After a spot of chivalry (the Little Colonel helps an enemy soldier), he is wounded and taken to hospital, Griffith offers his most grandiloquent commentary to date: 'In the red lane of death others take their places and battle goes on into the night.' This is also the moment that *Birth of a Nation* ends as a war film: while the screen cards announce that 'The blight of war does not end when hostilities cease', the story begins its transformation into a kind of proto-fascist Western in which the Ku Klux Klan are a posse of courageous freedom fighters defending the racially pure homestead.

WORLD WAR 1 AND SILENT WAR FILMS

This final section of *Birth of a Nation* reminds you that it is a film of two wars – for example when Griffith shows images of dead soldiers strewn across the battlefield, described as 'War's peace' with a screen card. The moment may describe the American Civil War, but it also seems to belong to World War 1, which had just begun when *Birth of a Nation* was released in 1915. Griffith's tone of angry but plaintive irony would have chimed with poets like Siegfried Sassoon and Wilfred Owen, who over the next two years would write verse saturated by disillusion, weariness and loss.

World War 1 was a new kind of conflict, fought by amateurs as well as professionals, by everyday men from every part of society. Those who wrote about its despair experienced that despair first-hand; most classical martial verse is the invention of artists working far from the battlefield. But when *Birth of a Nation* was released, filmgoers were years from hearing such starkly candid accounts of the horror of war. The voices that tended to speak the loudest *during* the war – the stoic, jingoistic optimism of, say, Rupert Brooke – have all but been drowned out by those canonised by posterity.

As with poetry, so too with cinema. The declaration of war in August 1914 inspired a trickle of films – both fiction and documentary, features and shorts – that burst quickly into a torrent. Most were made to inform, boost morale or act as patriotic propaganda. [8] 1914 itself was relatively quiet, no surprise given that the war had just begun and that film has a relatively protracted composition period. Nevertheless, a few early Great War films did emerge: *The Bells of Rheims*, *It's a Long Way to Tipperary* and *Mike Joins the Force*, not to mention an adventure series starring Lieutenant Daring and the less rousingly named Lieutenant Pimple. Yet, these tended to be in the minority, crowded out by inspiring titles like *Algy Goes in for Physical Culture*, *Marjory's Goldfish* and the gloriously self-explanatory, *The Master Crook Outwitted by a Child*.

From 1915 until the armistice, however, a vast array of war films saw the light of day, slaking the public's thirst for news, comfort and, it should not be forgotten, entertainment. [9] The tone of these movies tended to be far closer to Rupert Brooke than Wilfred Owen. True, there was a film called *War is Hell* and another called *The Coward*, but most were made to educate (*Après 305 Jours de Guerre*, *The Battle of the Somme*) or to inspire: *France et Angleterre, Forever*, *I'm Glad my Boy Grew Up to be a Soldier* and *From Flower Girl to Red Cross Nurse*.

Some of the films sound self-explanatory: *Thrilling Feats of the Royal Flying Corps*, *Vive La France!* (both 1918). Some sound eccentric: *Rights of Man: A Story of War's Red Blotch* (1915), *When the German Entered Loos*. Rather a lot are crudely nationalist: *In the Clutches of the Hun*, *America's Answer to the Hun*, *Kaiser: The Beast of Berlin*, *The Hun Within*, *Kaiser's Finish*, *The Claws of the Hun*, *To Hell with the Kaiser*. One or two even succeed at being all three at once: 1918's *The Woman the Germans Shot*, for example.

Erich von Stroheim, who specialised in playing evil Germans – (*Sylvia of the Secret Service*, *For France* (both 1917) and *The Unbeliever* (1918) – probably never had so much work as an actor as he did during the war years. Until, that is, he crossed Douglas Fairbanks during the making of *His Picture in the Papers* (1916). Sent to collect some explosives for a special effects sequence, von Stroheim alarmed the munitions department by employing his most Teutonic accent and manner (Schickel, p.351). After the clerk called the authorities, von Stroheim was fired and seemed destined to disappear into obscurity until he was rescued by none other than D. W. Griffith, who was preparing a new war film, *Hearts of the World*. [10]

This new work was a commission. In either late 1916 or early 1917, the British War Office Cinematograph Committee asked Griffith to make an inspirational war film. Griffith preferred to boast that Lloyd George himself requested a picture that would 'make up America's mind to go to war for us' (Schickel, p.345). Whoever did the asking, it was a lucky break for Griffith, whose last film, the absurdly gigantic *Intolerance* (1916), had failed to cover its costs. The offer would also have appealed to his pursuit of authenticity: Griffith was given permission to visit the Western front, and film footage of trench warfare (Schickel, p.340). [11]

The resulting documentary images (some of which provide a prologue to screenings of the film proper) are probably the most compelling reason to see *Hearts of the World*. By the time it was eventually released in 1918, it had passed its propaganda sell-by date as America had long since entered the fray. Although it is accomplished enough, it is relatively hard to imagine anyone being inspired into battle by this lengthy melodrama of war-torn lovers.

On the plus side, Griffith is more generous to the Germans than he had been to the first African-Americans. On the minus, *Hearts of the World* is little more than a remake of *The Battle* and *Birth of a Nation*, one that obeys the law of diminishing returns. [12] Set initially in 1912, the plot again features two American families, this time (improbably enough) living side-by-side in a French village. Preparing us for the lack of subtlety to come, their address is Rue de la Paix. Griffith seems under the impression that the Great War was fought mainly by tourists: his evil German officer is also on holiday in the French village as the action begins. Once again, Griffith portrays an innocent way of life and a love story both ready to be shattered by looming war. As in *The Battle*, Griffith names his hero 'Boy' (Robert Harron) and his heroine 'Girl' (Lillian Gish). One suspects that this is meant to identify the couple as sympathetic archetypes, but it also hints at a certain laziness on Griffith's part.

Like the heroes of so many subsequent war films, 'Boy' is a brilliant artist who finds himself drawn into the global conflict. 'Girl' is basically a beautiful girl who likes to hoe her garden and offer prayers pure enough to make one gag a little: 'Please make me so nice and good that Boy will love me forever and ever.' Granted, Griffith inserts a feisty love rival in the shape of the 'Little Disturber' (played with charming abandon by Dorothy Gish). [13] Boy isn't having any of it, and besides, there is a sub-plot featuring a daft chap called Cuckoo that has the 'Little Disturber' written all over it.

This being a Griffith production, such innocence cannot survive intact and soon he is showing 'historical facsimiles' of Kaiser Wilhelm and barking gravely that war's ideal is 'the ruling of weaker nations and peoples by the Power of Might'. 'Boy' enlists in the French army, ruining his wedding plans with 'Girl'. Cuckoo also joins up and promises the Little Disturber that he will return with the Kaiser's moustache. Neither he nor 'Boy' goes far, as the German army lays siege to the village, singing 'War's old song of hate'. 'Girl' is driven insane and almost raped by a German officer. 'Boy' steps in but it is left to 'Girl' to kill the offending officer.

For Richard Schickel, this rather over-caffeinated plot not only suggests Griffith's unhealthy preoccupation with sexual violence (*Birth of a Nation* ends with a similar attack on female virtue), it reveals a narrative problem that Griffith saw as inherent in the war that he filmed. The critic Ronald Bergen may have written that 'Of all the wars, the First World War seems the most emblematic, and the one which probably lends itself best to cinematic treatment.' [14] Griffith, by contrast, seems to have found it something of a yawn: in a 1918 interview, he said 'viewed as a drama, the war is in some ways disappointing' (Schickel, 353). [15]

Although this comment sounds undeniably callous, it is perhaps best read as an act of self-criticism. Griffith failed to realise that World War 1 would require new kinds of language, new kinds of perspective and new kinds of dramatic form. Trained in the late 19th century theatre, his old tricks of emotional melodrama would not be enough to dramatise a conflict that on the surface was defined by boredom, stalemate and stasis, and whose wounds were not just physical, but internal, emotional and psychological.

Owen and Sassoon knew this from first-hand experience; over the subsequent decade, modernists like T. S. Eliot (with *The Wasteland*) and Virginia Woolf (with *Jacob's Room* and *Mrs Dalloway*) would realise it too. Theirs were narratives of fracture – of ruins and broken fragments, as Eliot would have it. In *Mrs Dalloway*, Woolf would use this elliptical and shattered form to evoke the inner life of the shell-shocked Septimus Warren Smith. In 1937, during the Spanish Civil War, Picasso would employ similar techniques to evoke the bombing of Guernica.

A few filmmakers were already experimenting with new forms. Whereas *Hearts of the World* is hamstrung by Griffith's dogged pursuit of authenticity, Thomas Ince's *Civilisation* (1916) has no problems departing from realism. A heavy-handed but enjoyably lunatic pacifist allegory, its unapologetically subversive approach to the war film expresses its unapologetically subversive message. In doing so, it suggested new directions for the genre. In one memorable sequence, Ince's gravely injured hero (a recent convert to pacifism called Count Ferdinand) experiences a dream vision in which he fuses with Christ in a heaven comprised of naked men.

As this implies, *Civilisation* possesses a storyline bizarre enough to make even the most far-fetched moments in Griffith seem probable. Set in the fictional city of Nurma, a dead ringer for Kaiser Wilhelm declares war on a neighbouring country. The Nurmans, who like nothing better than to argue abstractly about the relative merits of pacifism, are sent into a debating frenzy (no small thing for a silent film). Ironically, given the topic at hand, quite a lot of fights break out as a result.

Despite the fantastic surface, Ince grapples with contemporary events every bit as much as Griffith does. The King's chief inventor (the aforementioned Count Ferdinand) has built a sort of super-sub and is ordered to sink what amounts to a floating allegory, a cruise liner called the *Propatria* – another dead-ringer, this time for the *Lusitania*, whose sinking did rather more to push America into the war than *Hearts of the World*.

At this moment, Ferdinand experiences his first hallucination, visualising the deaths of the innocent passengers. When his pacifist arguments fail to sway his crew, Ferdinand opens fire – again, somewhat ironically given his anti-violence leanings. [16] Ferdinand, too, is not long for the naturalistic world. After his mind-meld with the Messiah, he is stoned, tried by the King – who is explicitly referred to as Pontius Pilate – and dies a second time. Although he loses the battle, Ferdinand wins the war: Christ emerges from his corpse to show the King the error of his ways. Peace breaks out.

Civilisation was ahead of its time (or at least slightly to one side) in a number of ways: for example, Ince's portrayal of women. If women in Griffith's films are passive victims of war – basically crying, mourning or on the verge of being raped – Ince's are active political animals and courageous rebels. Although our first sight of Count Ferdinand's wife has her running around after her dog, she later heads a mass peace march against the bellicose Nurman King. This fiercely pacifist stance would also find favour in years to come, when the rise of Adolf Hitler during the 1930s pushed the world towards a second world war. [17]

In its brave if bonkers narrative approach, *Civilisation* anticipated the coming of a far greater film – Abel Gance's *J'Accuse!*, a title that echoes Emile Zola's famous denunciation of France's political system during the Dreyfus Affair. Released in 1919, the film is at times naturalistic and surreal, tragic and comic, realistic and visionary, technically ambitious and narratively simple. In its most famous scene – where our latest poet-soldier, Jean Diaz, witnesses his dead comrades arise from their graves on the battlefield – it is almost all of these things at once. Little wonder D.W. Griffith was left 'emotionally devastated' and 'too moved to speak' when he saw it at its American premiere (Schickel, p.457).

In *J'Accuse!*, no one escapes the destructive shock of the war: not the soldiers, the women left behind or the older generation who fought in the 1870 Franco-Prussian War. Gance makes plain the devastation wreaked on individual lives and relationships as early as the opening credits, where the lead actors are introduced in character, only to change before our eyes into bleak shadows of themselves. Whereas a filmmaker like Griffith tended to juxtapose light and dark, Gance blends his narrative tones into one unsettling and ambivalent whole. Take the dancing skeletons that recur throughout, often superimposed over the action – both a mockery of human self-importance and a spectral reminder of our mortality.

What makes *J'Accuse!* revolutionary is how Gance tells the story, rather than the story itself. This is not unconventional: two rivals in love, Jean and François, become brothers in arms. What raises the moral stakes is the fact that the object of both men's affections, Edith, is François' wife. Pathologically jealous, François enlists and sends Edith away rather than allow her stay in the same village as the handsome and charismatic Jean. Unfortunately, he delivers her directly to a horde of vicious Huns, who rape and impregnate her.

Gance again mixes his feelings in a way Griffith's divided polarities never allowed him to: Edith is brutalised, but her child, Angele, is an angel indeed. Although she heals wounds (most notably in Jean), Angele is herself bullied by the local children when her true paternity is revealed. For Jean and François, the war too is a blessing and a curse: they are united in friendship and fellow-feeling for Edith at the very moment they are separated from her. Their mutual obsession can reach absurd proportions. In one scene, the pair are bombarded in a shell-hole, all the while swapping memories of Edith while their comrades die around them. The final shot shows François lost in reverie with a pair of dead man's feet beside him.

The remainder of *J'Accuse!* narrates the gradual disintegration of each side of our love triangle. Edith becomes a Christ-like metaphor of suffering: standing arms outstretched, she is a 'cross of sacrifice epitomising the Frenchwoman's agony'. For François, the degeneration is physical – the hunted look he wears throughout the film's final third speaks of exhaustion beyond endurance. For Jean, the collapse is mental – the visionary poet who wrote pacifist odes to the sun is, at the end, a broken man, beset by nightmare visions of death and the life he has lost. The war takes everything from him: his sanity, his mother and, in the end, Edith as well.

This final deprivation is rich with tragic irony. François dies, but not before asking Jean to take care of the woman he has loved from afar. Driven mad by what he has seen at the front, however, Jean can hardly recognise Edith much less look after her. Having shown the villagers his nightmare vision of their dead husbands, fathers, sons and brothers, all that remains is his new-found mantra, 'J'accuse'.

1920 : WAR AS BOX OFFICE

J'Accuse! represented a significant advance for the war film; if Griffith concentrated on personal stories, then Gance excavated the psychological horrors of the Great War. It is just possible that he, like Ince, was ahead of his time. As Bergen notes, after the armistice 'war films all but ceased'. As the troops returned home, or didn't, and the full extent of the destruction became apparent, the recent conflict became a tricky subject to tackle. Nowhere is this better illustrated than by Charlie Chaplin's *Shoulder Arms* (1918).

A short comedy about trench warfare, the plot put Chaplin's fundamental inadequacy for army life to comic effect: he messes up drills, lays waste to training camps, disrupts sleeping arrangements, and seems all but unaware that there is a war going on. Such an approach at such a time (filming began as late as May 1918) was risky indeed. Cecil B. DeMille noted that, 'It's dangerous at this time to make fun of the war.' [18] Having shot various sequences that he later withdrew, Chaplin was on the verge of withdrawing the entire film until 'Douglas Fairbanks' roars of laughter at a special screening' convinced him to release an edited version (Lynn, p.221).

Shoulder Arms, Bergen says, was released to howls of protest, with audiences not yet ready to be amused by the comic possibilities of incessant shelling and, in Chaplin's fantasy of heroic action, kicking Kaiser Wilhelm in the behind. Viewed with the benefit of 90 years' hindsight, however, there are moments when Chaplin approaches parts of the war that other artists (D.W. Griffith, for instance) had not reached: the minutiae, pettiness, claustrophobia and downright boredom of the trenches. Imagine *Carry on a Dulce et Decorum Est* and you are not far wide of the mark.

Although parts have dated, *Shoulder Arms* proved to be influential. Decades later, in *Love and Death* (1975), Woody Allen aped Chaplin's physical haplessness to mock the highly-disciplined and highly earnest requirements of army life: the wonderful scenes of both Allen and Chaplin in basic training suggest they were more dangerous to their own side than entire battalions of enemy soldiers. [19] In 1918, however, the spectre of the 'glorious dead' was simply too close for comfortable laughter; the comic war film wouldn't return properly until the 1930s when Laurel and Hardy used trench-life to propel the largely peace-time plots of *Pack Up Your Troubles* (1932) and *Block-Heads* (1938). Buster Keaton also weighed in with *Doughboys* (1930), which was largely based on his own experiences in the army.

Instead, the films from the 1920s that would succeed with the public, and succeed wildly, kept comedy in its proper Hollywood place. *The Four Horsemen of the Apocalypse*, *The Big Parade* and *Wings* (1927) all consign light relief to sub-plots or minor characters kept at one remove from the central story: for example, Herman Schwimpf, the hapless and Germanically named clown in *Wings*, who constantly proves his patriotic fervour for America by using his fists.

These three films prove that the war film might have fallen out of mass production, but could return in a refined and expanded form to win public and critical approval. Rex Ingram's *The Four Horsemen of the Apocalypse* is perhaps best remembered today as the film that launched the career of Rudolph Valentino. His portrayal of Julio Desnoyers, a tango-crazy libertine who gradually morphs into a sensitive but courageous soldier, injects some much needed sex appeal into the genre – this was the beginning of the Jazz Age, after all.

The film is not only memorable because Valentino looked so good on the dancefloor; it also unites various narrative strands first woven in the previous decade. On one level, *The Four Horsemen of the Apocalypse* is Hollywood's attempt to remake *J'Accuse!*: the plot revolves around an artistic young man who has an illicit dalliance with a married woman and learns how to experience ennobling feelings of courage, national pride and existential despair through his experiences on the Western front. [20] As with Gance's François, the husband cuckolded by Valentino is also redeemed through acts of martial bravery.

Ingram enlivens his largely realistic plot with vivid metaphorical touches: replacing Gance's dancing skeletons are recurring images of 'The Four Horsemen' themselves (Conquest, War, Pestilence and Famine, Death), skittering across ominous skies or through cross-laden cemeteries of Europe. In case audiences should miss this relatively transparent visual imagery, Ingram inserts a mysterious Russian mystic who provides a desolate running commentary about the cosmic implications of war. Citing Albrecht Dürer's *Revelation of St John* one moment, he meets Desnoyers Senior in the next. 'You knew my son?' Marcelo asks him after he learns of Julio's death. 'I knew them all!' the wild-eyed stranger replies.

Ingram's Great War is not simply allegorical, however. Taking his lead from Griffith, he personalises the national, political and cultural conflict through two families. In a plot that connects the 'Old World' to the 'New', the soon-to-be opposing French and German factions are first seen in Argentina. The Desnoyers and, in what must surely be an anti-German pun, the von Hartrotts, have both married into Don Madariaga's wealthy cattle-owning family. As with *Birth of a Nation*, future hostilities cast a long shadow over these pre-war days: the growing tension created by France and Germany's Empire-building finds an echo as the Desnoyers and von Hartrotts clash over who should inherit Madariaga's land.

Desnoyers Senior is a Socialist who lives to brood: about the dissipation of Julio, about his vast wealth, and his own conscientious objections to the Franco-Prussian conflict of 1870. The German father, Karl von Hartrott, instils Nietzchean values in his obedient, well-organised and eminently blond progeny: 'Man shall be trained for war and women for the procreation of the warrior: all else is folly', he opines early in the piece. In la belle et la decadent France, by contrast, the attitude to war is slightly less intense: 'Just imagine what war will mean!' cries the carefree Marguerite Laurier. 'No parties – no pretty clothes – women in mourning – nothing but misery'. Poor Marguerite.

Such nationalistic tensions are banished to the side-lines in King Vidor's *The Big Parade* (1925) by a story that concentrates upon America's role in the war. The culture clash, when eventually it raises its head, is not between competing European empires, but comprised of comic misunderstandings and romantic *frissons* between American soldiers and pretty French girls.

Vidor's is a story about men – about male bonding, about war as a great leveller of class and character, and about masculine lives accelerated first towards intimacy and then towards death. Our three heroes, glimpsed in Vidor's rapid-fire opening scenes, are a spoiled, wealthy socialite (Jim Apperson), a construction worker (Slim Jensen) and Bull, a barman in the Bowery. In the intensified context of war, friendships are built rapidly, with the prospect of a common enemy (not to mention mundane social lubricants like food and drink) healing potential differences of opinion: our three heroes are brought together initially by a cake sent to Jim. 'This ain't such a bad war', Slim says with what proves to be characteristic stoicism.

The gaps are not bridged completely. In this exaggeratedly masculine environment, no amount of male bonding makes the soldiers immune to sexual jealousy. Jim, who to start with is more a lover than a fighter, is roundly mocked as effeminate for his way with the girls – and, above all, for falling in love with the beautiful Melisande. Slim, by contrast, has no such luck. Instead, he is Hollywood's version of the brave, but mildly dim British Tommy, speaking in a sort of indomitable patriotic idiom: 'We're going to keep going until we can't go no farther,' he yells as a hail of bullets whiz past him; 'You don't want to live forever, do you?' he asks, rhetorically one hopes.

While Slim is too much the archetype to be bothered with inconveniences like character development, Jim begins what is already the familiar journey from innocence to disillusion. If *The Big Parade*'s first act was defined by the now familiar elevated ideals and light-hearted banter, the second shows the gradual erosion of those high spirits the closer our heroes get to the frontline. The first intimation that the romance of war is going sour occurs when romance of a different order is interrupted, and Jim is separated from Melisande. The shot in which she clings vainly to his leg will be echoed tragically before the end. The middle section of the story seems suspended between two tones. On the one hand, there is plenty of visceral excitement left over from the opening third. One of several impressive set-piece battles is narrated with as much breathless excitement as a boy's own adventure: 'MEN! Guns! MEN! More guns!' one screen card exclaims, as if it is surprised to see them there at all.

While the battle scenes are as thrilling as anything Griffith dreamed up, *The Big Parade* is not so in love with the drama of the battlefield as to ignore the futility of the battle. The tipping point is the climactic scene where Slim ventures out into no-man's-land and is shot while trying to defeat the German army singlehanded. This is the moment when Jim's taste for the fight vanishes completely. 'What the hell do we get out of the war anyway?' he cries before charging over the top to rescue a mortally wounded Slim. 'Who the hell cares… after this?' Vidor's Great War is utterly transformative. Unlike Gance or Ince, there is no hint of a transcendent visionary or spiritual dimension. Instead, the course of human lives, characters and bodies are changed forever. Both mentally and physically scarred by his experiences at the front, Jack limps home missing the leg to which Melisande clung so tightly.

Once there, he repeats the 'old lie' about the nobility of war to his family. Yet, family and home have lost all significance for him. The playboy has become a distinctly unplayful man, defined completely by the war. Jim finds that his heart and soul now belongs with Melisande, whom we last saw as a refugee trudging across the French horizon. Taking his mother's advice, he returns to France to search for her. The final heartbreaking scene shows Jim's stricken figure limping towards the love of his new life.

Unable to readjust to his former life on the homefront, he finds happiness in the love he found during the war. For Jim, the two have become indistinguishable.

Wings, the final film of the 20s triple bill, also ends with a romantic reunion between a war hero, Jack Powell (played by Charles Rogers) and his home-front sweetheart, Mary (Mary Pickford). Unlike Jim Apperson, Jack needs the war to realise that Mary really is his girl. Whilst this is affecting enough (Mary is a wonderfully tomboyish foil for Jack's boyish self-attention), *Wing's* true emotional core – indeed it's real love story – is between Jack and David, best friends, flying aces and sometime rivals in love whose bonds of friendship are far closer than any romantic relationship in the story.

Having butted heads over the sophisticated Sylvia (poor, tomboyish Mary), the pair end up fighting one another in the air. After one of many spectacular airborne battles, David crashes behind enemy lines, but escapes in a German plane; Jack, half-crazed with grief for his supposedly dead buddy, shoots every Iron Cross he possibly can, including the one borrowed by David. The climactic death scene makes Goose's crash-landing in *Top Gun* (1986) seem restrained by comparison. Fanciful as it is, this climax makes its point about the self-destructive futility of war. The final scenes, where Jack is confronted by David's parents, are truly affecting.

Wings is to the Jazz Age what its descendant, *Top Gun*, would be to Reaganite America. Like Tony Scott's tale of jets and jockstraps, it wants to be all things to all people: sexy and brutal, romantic and disillusioned, macho and vulnerable, youthful and mature. Hedonism and suffering are the order of the day. On leave in Paris, Jack tries to forget the conflict by holding a girl in one hand and a champagne bottle in the other; bewitched by animated bubbles that float into the air, he is quite oblivious that Mary is by his side.

The need for speed rises to the level of an existential statement about war's shortness of breath. *Wings* shows us *carpe diem* visions of boys grown old in a matter of months, of fleeting joys vanishing in the blink of an eye, and of youth extinguished in a flash. Nowhere is this more memorable than in Gary Cooper's blink-and-you-miss-it cameo. Having delivered some granite-jawed advice to the fledgling flyers, he climbs into his plane, swoops thrillingly and crashes all within a couple of minutes.

1930 : BOOM AND BUSTS

As *Wings* prophesied, the age was heading for a crash, both literally and figuratively. This trio of 20s films ushered in the end of an era – in fact, several eras all told. By the time Howard Hughes released *Hell's Angels* in 1930, the silent movie had just become a thing of the past. So too had the Jazz Age, and as economic depression spread across the globe, audiences started to yearn for the hard realities and high excitement of the war film all over again. Thanks to the revolution in sound technology, they also began to *listen* to it as well. The genre's renaissance also owed a debt to Adolf Hitler, whose rise to power in Germany was accompanied by the gradual realisation that a second world war was imminent. Anxiety about the present and the future inspired movies that kept one eye on the Great War, but glanced now and then at the possibility of a sequel.

Whether any of this was on Howard Hughes' mind when he conceived *Hell's Angels* seems debatable. Instead, his was a one-man mission to prove that size really is everything and to establish himself (and his Caddo production company) among

Hollywood's elite. Hughes had produced his first war film, *Two Arabian Nights*, a couple of years before. As the titular pun implies, this was a broadly comic tale about two hapless doughboys who find themselves escaping a POW camp on the Western Front only to get into trouble with the daughter of an Arabian king. It is mainly notable for being directed by Lewis Milestone, who in 1930 would make arguably the greatest war movie of them all with *All Quiet on the Western Front*. [21]

Two Arabian Nights proved two things to Hughes: firstly, the war film could be financially lucrative (it made a $300,000 profit); and secondly, it could be critically successful (it won an Academy Award for comedy). *Hell's Angels* was far more ambitious, especially in terms of its technical capabilities. This was due, in large part, to Hughes himself. Desperate to out-*Wing Wings*, and out-Hawk Howard Hawks, who was then shooting *Dawn Patrol* (1930), no expense was spared: the famous scene where a bomb-laden Zeppelin floats over Trafalgar Square was rumoured to have cost $100,000 alone.

Other pressures, however, were thrust upon Hughes. He had already spent in excess of $2.2 million when he realised that *The Jazz Singer* (1927) was no flash in the pan, and that words would literally have to be put in the mouths of the *Hells Angels'* cast (at a cost of another $1.9 million). The prime beneficiary was one Jean Harlow (credited as Jean Harlowe), drafted in at the last minute to replace Greta Nissen, whose thick Scandinavian accent meant she was better seen than heard.

If Valentino injected sex appeal into the war film, then Harlow gave it a treble shot of desirability. She was devastatingly sexy, never more so than in the scene when she seduces the rakish Monte Rutledge (Ben Lyon) using only a peculiar English accent, a backless dress and the line, "Would you be shocked if I put on something more comfortable?". "I'll try to survive," Monte says, looking less confident than he sounds. But more than this, Harlow was unapologetically sexual. Wartime not only allowed her character, Helen, to express her sexuality, it *demanded* that she did so. "I want to be free," she purrs, having just told Monte that she doesn't love his upright brother, Roy. "I want to be gay and have fun. Life's short and I want to live while I'm alive."

Harlow's *carpe diem* goddess seizes the day, then Monte, then a devilish English officer and finally the film as a whole. Her only competition in the scene-stealing stakes is Hughes' baroquely impressive aerobatic sequences; the plot, essentially a tale about mismatched brothers, is a thing of duty rather than beauty. Essentially posh updates of the trio in *The Big Parade*, the three male leads offer a contrast to Harlow's Helen. Whereas she was liberated by the war to find her true self, the men sacrifice their pre-war identities and destinies to the demands of battle. Their moral centre is the steadfast Roy (James Hall), whose optimistic faith in the world, and in Helen above all, is exposed as false. Seeking cold comfort with a sympathetic French girl, he is offered the traditional explanation of where it all went wrong: "Triste, c'est la guerre."

Then there is Karl Armstedt (John Darrow), Roy and Monte's German friend, whose rampant Anglophilia makes him initially unwilling to fight for the Fatherland. Later, suspended from the Zeppelin, he aims German bombs harmlessly at the Thames and not at Trafalgar Square. His goodness does not save him: as the Zeppelin starts to sink, Karl himself is unceremoniously dropped himself as the captain ejects unnecessary ballast.

Finally, there's Monte, whose mutation from playboy to existential soldier-philosopher guides the tone of the *Hell's Angels* as a whole. Although Monte echoes the journey of Jean Diaz and Jim Apperson, he adds something new to the canon of Hollywood heroes, being two parts pacifist to one part coward: his fear and guilt stem from his refusal to fly a night patrol, which leads to the death of his replacement.

As with many other films, the anti-war message sits somewhat uneasily beside the sheer excitement of the aerobatic spectacular that Hughes serves up: the set pieces, including several cloud-skimming tussles with von Richthofen's Flying Circus, are undeniably impressive. Yet, there is a stark, unflinching edge to Hughes' portrayal of violence. It is still shocking to watch German soldiers shouting 'For the Fatherland' before they jump to their death to lighten the load of the fast-sinking Zeppelin.

The sympathetic Karl would not look out of place in Lewis Milestone's *All Quiet on the Western Front* (1930). Adapted from Erich Maria Remarque's novel, its polished narrative, script and performances refine the classic war film structure to heartbreaking effect. There is the peace, optimism and enthusiasm for battle of the early scenes in a German village; there is the transition, frequently light-hearted, as the schoolboys harden into soldiers; and lastly the cruel revelation of what war really is, leading inexorably to the unhappy ending; the novel ends in more optimistic fashion.

Other filmmakers brought poetry to the war film – Griffith, Ingram and, above all, Gance – but no one had before captured the pathos of war like Milestone. His final close-up shows our hero, Paul Bauer, reaching out to touch a butterfly. Shots of his hand are intercut with an enemy sniper. Before he reaches his goal, Paul is killed and the film ends. The image is rich with possibility. It is a metaphor of youth cut down before its time: unlike the butterfly, Paul will never reach his adult state. It is a glimpse of gentleness, nature and the everyday amidst the unnatural destruction of violence. It is also a moving reminder of Paul's life before the war, and the artistic ambitions that will never reach fruition.

Whereas other mainstream films struggled to balance excitement with a serious message, *All Quiet on the Western Front* focuses on the human drama of the boys' attempts to survive the war. This structure certainly adds tension – one by one, the schoolboys are killed – but doesn't provide gratuitous thrills: 'death is not an adventure for those who stand face to face with it', reads the prologue taken verbatim from the novel. Tragically, this is the very message propagated by the stridently nationalistic school teacher in the opening scenes: "You are the life blood of the Fatherland", he exhorts. "You are the gay heroes who will repulse the enemy." As the boys rush to enlist, Milestone allows the shot of an empty classroom to linger, an eerie prophecy of what will be left of the class of 1914 in the months to come.

This opening section creates a hierarchy of age before youth that the remainder of the film turns on its head. [22] Whereas the experienced adults (almost exclusively male) talk knowingly about events at the front, the youngsters learn all too quickly what the conflict really means: boredom, bombs, loneliness, loss and fear. Once again, the constant proximity of instant death makes time move faster in the trenches than at home, propelling boys not long out of short lederhosen through manhood towards early graves. This is a generation where it was commonplace for parents to outlive their male children. Fear and its logical conclusion, cowardice, had been confronted before in war movies (Monte in *Hell's Angels*), but never like this: the scene in the dug-out where Paul's friend, Kemmerich, flinches and weeps every time that a whiz bang whizzes by is almost unbearable to watch. By the time Kemmerich careers into the trenches and is shot, one is almost relieved.

Milestone exploits the advent of sound in a way that Hughes was simply unable to. This was not only a case of using sheer volume to shock and awe – although the cannons and machine guns boom to ear-splitting effect – Milestone also employs silence to create passages of unearthly calm and increasing tension. In *All Quiet on the Western Front*, it is just as terrifying to wait for an attack as to experience it. Both Paul and his father-confessor, Stanislaus Katczinsky, are killed during lulls between the storm.

This relationship, between a tough older man and his quick-learning surrogate son, appears ironic beside the one between Paul and his father and between the deluded teacher and his pupils. Katczinsky shows the new recruits all the ropes they really need to know: how to find food, how to survive air raids, how to survive. Katczinsky becomes the father Paul actually requires; his own father still prefers to believe that it is sweet and proper to die for one's country. In this, Katczinsky even becomes the Fatherland that has long since abandoned the young soldiers. By adding depth and emotion to the role of the archetypal grizzled old hand, Katczinsky reminds us that the Great War was fought by civilians not soldiers, by privates not officers, by everymen not aristocrats.

Of course, not every film conveyed such realism. For every *All Quiet*, there was a *Mata Hari* (1931), a glossy star vehicle that allowed Greta Garbo to shake her money-maker and gaze with sultry intent at the dashing Ramon Navarro. If films like *Mata Hari* and *Dark Victory* (1937), starring Vivien Leigh and Conrad Veidt, helped install the spy movie as sexy and thrilling, then the 1932 version of *A Farewell to Arms* attempted to do the same for ambulance workers. Gary Cooper's granite chin earns rather more screen-time than it had in *Wings*, but the director seems far more keen on romance with Helen Hayes (playing Catherine Barkley). A precursor to *The English Patient* (both end with a desperate chase across barren terrain to reach a dying woman), the plot necessarily romanticises Hemingway's original.

A far better, if rather less cinematic film is James Whale's *Journey's End* (1930). Adapted from the play by RC Sherriff, it never quite escapes its theatrical origins. Indeed, Whale's camera basically sweeps back and forth across a stage set, albeit one that clearly influenced the dug-out used in *Blackadder Goes Forth*. In certain respects, however, its staginess is both the film's greatest strength and its greatest weakness. Although some scenes drag beyond their sell-by date, others brilliantly evoke the claustrophobia, boredom, angst, humour and humanity of trench life. As with the play, one feels that the real action – the war itself – is happening just off stage and always ready to engulf the characters passing the time before us.

This is the small scale and undramatic World War 1 that D.W. Griffith simply did not see, but which Owen and Sassoon laid bare in their work. R.C. Sherriff also saw it and remembered its banter, its longueurs and its pain. Sherriff understood that the English stiff upper lip was not only useful for keeping a moustache aloft – it spoke its own kind of stoic poetry, repressing violence, fear and death by chatter about gardens, rugger, topping girls and awful cooking. Mason saying to Stanhope, "Your sambridges, sir. 'Arf bully beef and 'arf sardine. Sardine on top, sir." Stanhope replying, "How delicious. No *pâté de foie gras?*"

It comes as no surprise to learn that the posh, sardonic and heavy-drinking Captain Stanhope (Colin Clive) was a model for Bruce Robinson's character of Withnail. Indeed, Stanhope is the role that 'I' wins at the end of the film, a part, it would seem, he has been unconsciously preparing for throughout *Withnail & I* (1987). Both drink to drown their sorrow that youth is ending. But while Withnail mourns the hideousness of middle-age, Stanhope knows he has no such luxury. His whiskey consumption buries the constant awareness of impending death and his own terror at the prospect: "…if I went up those steps into the front line – without being doped with whiskey – I'd go mad with fright," he confesses to his only friend, Captain Osborne (Ian Maclaren).

Whale's brilliant combination of ensemble acting, patrician hauteur and working class pluck would be perfected in what Bergen calls the finest World War 1 film of them all: Jean Renoir's *La Grande Illusion*. [23] Its spirit of defiant imagination and comic invention has made itself felt in films like *The Great Escape* (1963), *Catch-22* (1970), *MASH* (1970) and *Casablanca* (1942). Jim Jarmusch's *Down by Law* (1986) is not a war film but its plot, comprising prison breakers who find safety with a beautiful woman in a secluded farmhouse, is practically a remake of Renoir's.

La Grande Illusion provides arguably the most perfect articulation of war as futile, absurd and destructive. Its title alone suggests multiple strands. What is Renoir's grand illusion? The war? Patriotism? National rivalry? Class divisions? The skill of escaping prison? Cinema? Life itself? The plot centres on a ragged and somewhat eccentric band of French soldiers who escape from one German POW camp after another until they are locked in the prison to end all prisons, high in the German mountains.

Leading the group are the aristocratic Captain de Boëldieu (Pierre Fresnay), who puts the *froid* into *sang froid*, Lieutenant Maréchal, a working-class hero played by Jean Gabin, and Rosenthal, the son of a rich Jewish banker who escapes alongside him. The complex interactions of these characters who can be allies one moment and adversaries the next argues that human beings are simply more complicated than any ethnic, national and class distinctions. Boëldieu and Maréchal may both be French, but that does not mean they will be friends; Boëldieu and the German commander, von Rauffenstein (Erich von Stroheim) may be on opposing sides in the war, but that does not make them enemies. Then again, Boëldieu and von Rauffenstein may be simpatico aristocrats with mutual friends in common, but that will not prevent their eventual confrontation.

Time and again, Renoir builds specific expectations and relationships in one scene only to tear them down in the next. By the end, Germans are protecting French Jews; French soldiers are falling in love with Germans; German commandants are mourning the deaths of rivals they had far more in common with than their fellow countrymen. Little wonder Mussolini refused to watch the film. Joseph Goebbels, never the most discriminating film critic, condemned *La Grande Illusion* as 'Cinematic Public Enemy Number 1', before he banned it from German cinemas in 1940.

La Grande Illusion is a film that explicitly acknowledges the end of one era and the beginning of the next: Boëldieu and especially von Rauffenstein complain elegantly about the final days of their class superiority throughout. By the same token, the positive portrayal of Rosenthal offers a direct critique of anti-Semitism in general, but of Hitler's increasingly violent racial policies in particular. Renoir knew a second world war was coming and that it would require new kinds of film and even film stars. This would be a war fought not only on the battlefields of Europe, but in cinemas everywhere. Hollywood's elite would travel the world bringing cheer, laughter and hope to battered troops. And to think it all began on a golf course in Muswell Hill.

Endnotes

1. Niall Ferguson, *War of the Worlds* (Penguin: London, 2006).

2. With typical self-confidence, Griffith demands the same 'liberty to show the dark side of wrong [...] that is conceded to the art of the written word – that art to which we owe the Bible and the works of Shakespeare.'

3. The source is www.filmsite.org.

4. Mark Cousins, *The Story of Film* (Pavilion: London, 2004), p.45.

5. See Denise J. Youngblood, *Russian War Films: On the Cinema Front, 1914-2005* (University of Kansas Press: Kansas, 2006).

6. Paul himself quoted in the BFI pamphlet accompanying the DVD release of R.W. Paul: *The Collected Films, 1895-1908*, p.8.

7. Richard Schickel, *D.W. Griffith* (Pavilion: London, 1984), p.342.

8. See Nicholas Reeves, *Official British Film Propaganda During the First World War* (Croom Helm: London, 1986).

9. A guide to the numbers in question is provided by an admittedly unscientific search of imdb.com. An estimate of the numbers of 'war films' produced during the conflict is as follows: 70 in 1915; 46 in 1916; 54 in 1917; 89 in 1918; and 49 in 1919.

10. Von Stroheim is reputed to have said: 'For you, Mr Griffith, I would work for a ham sandwich a day' (Schickel, p.352).

11. Indeed, newsreel of Griffith working in the trenches as a shell passed overhead was shown as a preview to what became *Hearts of the World*.

12. Griffith half admits to his self-plagiarism at the very start when he writes that it is 'An old fashioned play with a new fashioned theme.'

13. Authenticity. Gish based the Little Disturber on a woman she and Griffith spotted in London and whom they followed for hours to copy her walk.

14. Ronald Bergen, 'Grand Illusions: Films of the First World War', the *Guardian*, 11 November 2008.

15. In the same 1918 interview, he flippantly compounded his insensitive misunderstanding of the actual war: 'The settings of the picture I took cost several billion dollars... I think I will be able to make good the claim that I will use the most expensive stage settings that ever have been or will be used in the making of the picture' (Schickel, p.353).

16. This plot may have some basis in fact. One apocryphal account of the sinking of the *Lusitania* suggested that the German quartermaster, Charles Voegele, also refused to open fire, a decision that resulted in his court-martial and a three year prison sentence. Des Hickey and Gus Smith, *Seven Days to Disaster: The Sinking of the Lusitania* (William Collins: London, 1981), p.221.

17. Re-released in 1931, *Civilisation* was introduced with a reminder that it was originally made at 'the height of the preparedness vs pacifism controversy in 1916', and that 'It is said to have helped Woodrow Wilson to his second election to the presidency.'

18. Quoted by Kenneth S. Lynn, *Charlie Chaplin and his Times* (Simon and Schuster: New York, 1997), p.221.

19. Allen would excavate another joke from *Shoulder Arms* in *Sleeper* (1973): Allen, like Chaplin, would use pungent cheese to incapacitate an enemy guard.

20. The connection between the two films is also suggested by the names of the two: Edith *Laurin* in *J'Accuse!* bears more than a passing resemblance to Marguerite *Laurier* in *The Four Horsemen*.

21. Milestone and Hughes had their moments, however. Keen to learn about film-making, in part to prepare himself for directing *Hell's Angels*, Hughes took Milestone's final cut and re-edited – purely for his own purposes. When the furious director burst in on the ingénue producer, he found Hughes covered in reels of film. 'Dunderhead,' he is supposed to have yelled. 'Artistic dunderhead [...] What in hell are you doing to *my* picture?' One hair-raising car ride later, Hughes explained that the final print had already been sent out for distribution. He, on the other hand, was merely trying to teach himself the finer points of editing. John Keats, *Howard Hughes* (Random House: New York, 1966), p.29.

22. In the novel, Paul muses: 'Youth! We are none of us more than twenty years old. But young? Youth. That is long ago. We are old folk.' p.26.

23. Bergen describes it as: 'a paradigm for all subsequent films on the subject'.

49TH PARALLEL

That's for Thomas Mann...
That's for Matisse...
That's for Picasso...
And... that's for me!

KIM NEWMAN

Strictly speaking, every film produced in Britain during World War 2 was a propaganda movie. When George Formby punched Hitler on the nose in *Let George Do It!* (1940) and Laurence Olivier trounced a foreign foe at Agincourt in *Henry V* (1944), they were selling the image of indomitable Britain to audiences in working class Essoldos and the carriage trade Odeons. But, to the British taste, propaganda movies were associated with what in the 1930s were called 'the dictator nations'. They meant Nuremberg rallies choreographed by Dr Goebbels and filmed with rapt fan girl awe by Leni Riefenstahl or odes to Soviet tractor production sanctioned by Stalin and filmed by whichever director had survived the latest purge. Your average filmgoer in Clapham or Chelsea wasn't having any of that, thank you very much. The British film industry's initial reaction to *Triumph of the Will/Triumph des Willens* (1935) was to doctor footage of a march-past of ranks of stern, dedicated Nazis so that it seemed Hitler's troops were goose-stepping to a popular dance tune, 'The Lambeth Walk'. Frankly, this was counter-propaganda – encouraging blitzed Brits to laugh at the Nazis was taken seriously by some of the biggest brains in the land, from Winston Churchill to Will Hay.

Though he never quite admitted it, it seems a prime attraction of working in propaganda for Michael Powell was that he could seek financing for a feature from the government rather than the established film industry. Having dealt with slippery studio bosses like Alexander Korda, and as big-scale movie production in Britain was liable to be curtailed, [1] Powell saw Minister of Information Duff Cooper as more biddable, and was prepared to bombard the Ministry of Information (i.e. the Ministry of Propaganda) with talk until they backed a project he had devised with his partner Emeric Pressburger. *49th Parallel* (1941) was initially funded by the MoI, who sprung for a Canadian research trip in the early days of the war – even Powell admitted this looked at the time like a dubious use of funds ('Imagine… France was falling, the Battle of Britain was looming, and here's some bastard who wants £50,000 or £80,000 to go and make a film in Canada'). As the script picked up buzz (Pressburger would win the Academy Award for Best Original Story) and prominent star names attached themselves, the Rank company came in on the production, which led to financial complications as a project some worked on at a reduced fee in aid of the war effort seemed to transform into a regular commercial venture. The commercial success of *49th Parallel* indicated its usefulness as propaganda, especially in the United States, but this early public-private finance initiative model of production would not become commonplace. Powell and Pressburger made *The Volunteer* (1943) for the MoI, a more conventional 46-minute recruiting film in which Ralph Richardson and his dresser join the Fleet Air Arm, but otherwise worked within the studio system – though, for the duration of hostilities, the Ministry had a say in films they hadn't actually put money into.

In *A Life in Movies*, the first of his two volumes of autobiography, Powell vividly – and with a little excusable dramatic flair – describes his pitch meeting with Duff Cooper and the sceptical holders of the Treasury's purse strings:

> I unfolded my map of Canada and spread it out on the Minister's desk. "This is a propaganda picture in which the only good Nazi is a dead Nazi," I began. "But as that kind of propaganda can be self-defeating, we have started out by making them human beings. There are all kinds of Nazis, as there are all kinds of human beings. Our group of seven are a composite of the Nazi character and creed. Emeric's story is about seven little Nazis, who are survivors of a

German U-boat's crew, which has been operating off the coast of Canada, sinking defenceless vessels. Their ship is tracked down and destroyed by the Canadian Navy and Air Force. The commandant is killed. He was a foolish great bullock of a man, unthinking, obedient, an executioner. The six survivors are left in a desperate position next to a Hudson's Bay post, where they meet their first two Canadians, a French-Canadian trapper and the factor of the post. This is the start of their trail of thefts and murders in an attempt to escape across Canada. One by one they are captured or killed. The first to go is the youngest of them, Jahner. He has been a Nazi since he was twelve. Murder and violence is his way of life. He is shot by an Eskimo.

"Then there are five in a stolen seaplane. They fly across Canada until the gas gives out. They crash land in a shallow lake near Winnipeg, and Kuhnecker, the engineer officer, is killed. He is the kind of Nazi who has been, since the beginning, a high-ranking officer in the Party. He had to be given a job, whether he was competent or not. He proves his competency by breaking his neck. Now there are four. They are in the heartland of Canada. A group of German-born immigrants, Christian communists of German descent (they call themselves the Hutterites) take them in without knowing who they are. Deceived by the kindness they have received, their leader, Lieutenant Hirth, second-in-command of the U-boat, makes a typical Nazi speech claiming them as brothers. A young girl whose father and mother have been killed by the Nazis threatens to denounce them. One of the Nazis, Vogel, is a decent fellow and wants to stay and become one of these friendly farmers. He is a baker by trade. Lieutenant Hirth orders the others to arrest him, and after a brief trial one of them executes him as a traitor to the Führer. Now there are three."

In spite of themselves, the Treasury men were listening intently. However much they disapproved of us, they wanted to know what happened next… Emeric was like a graven image. I went on:

"These three murder and rob their way across Canada to the West. They thumb a ride, kill the driver and steal his car and his money. They ditch the car and go on by railroad. They arrive at Banff in the Rockies on Indian Day. Now they are surrounded by people. The Mounties are looking for them, and are hot on their trail. Even the tourists at Banff are pressed into service. The nerve of one of the three remaining cold-blooded murderers breaks, and he is captured and nearly lynched by the mob. Now there are two. They escape into the high Rockies. They are not far from the border with America now – the 49th Parallel. This is, if I may remind you, Minister, the title of our film. They are given shelter in his camp, by a rich and easy-going writer. He seems to be a sitting duck for the ruthless Nazis. But when they become violent, it rebounds on them. Lohrman, the gunman of the group, tries to shoot his way out and is captured by the man he despises. Now there is only one, Lieutenant Hirth, the zealot, the fanatic, the devotee, the dyed-in-the-wool Nazi. He doubles back across Canada. The final scene between him and a Canadian soldier who has overstayed his leave takes place in a boxcar that will take them across the border into neutral America, by the suspension bridge below Niagara Falls. These two, the fanatical Nazi and the

Canadian soldier, end the film with a showdown of their very different beliefs and creeds."

The big room was very quiet. Duff Cooper hesitated. It was time to play my trumps.

"We are taking the actors who play the Nazis with us. They are cheap and we can get authentic scenes with them in Canada. The big parts are star parts which will be filmed here later in England. A Canadian trapper, Johnny, who is murdered by the Nazis at the Hudson's Bay post; the Hudson's Bay factor; the leader of the German-Canadian settlers; the charming, easy-going ethnologist in the Rockies; and finally the Canadian soldier. There is only one woman's part in the story, the Hutterite girl who threatens to denounce them and causes the death of the young Nazi who has fallen in love with her. This part will be played by Elisabeth Bergner. The leader of the Hutterites will be played by Anton Walbrook. Leslie Howard has agreed to play the charming gentleman in the Rockies. Raymond Massey has agreed to play the Canadian soldier, provided that his part can be filmed in Montreal, as he has rejoined the Canadian Army. Laurence Olivier hopes to be able to play the French-Canadian trapper, Johnny. We have contacted all these actors, and we have no reason to believe that they will go back on their promises. They have all agreed to work for the same flat fee."

Duff Cooper… turned to the Treasury officials and said rapidly and almost inaudibly: "Finance must not stand in the way of this project."

Between pitch and finished film, several things changed. In his outline, Powell gives Jahner (Basil Appleby) more character than he really shows in the movie, and describes a scene (the ditching of the stolen car) that was either not shot or trimmed from the picture by editor David Lean (whom Powell credits with tightening the film considerably). Powell also emphasised the murderousness of his Nazi villains in addressing the politicians, but downplayed that element in the film so that the comparatively few killings have more impact. Vogel, the most sympathetic German, is shot off-screen, but his death is still the film's big poignant moment. Death in the cinema is routine, especially in gangster movies and westerns – genres evoked when the Germans have shootouts with Native Canadians like beleaguered pioneers, and don sharp suits to barge in on Leslie Howard like Humphrey Bogart's gang in *The Petrified Forest* (1936). Often, as in *49th Parallel*, acts of non-lethal barbarism have more shock value. There are murders, though the apparently non-fatal rifle butt-bludgeoning of cheerful, embarrassingly loyal sidekick Nick the Eskimo (Ley On) and the burning of books and works of art prized by Philip Armstrong Scott (Howard) are somehow more upsetting. All the stars Powell promised the Treasury duly showed up, plus gravely Scot Finlay Currie – a busy character actor and veteran of Powell's previous 'runaway' production, *The Edge of the World* (1937), shot far from the London studios on the island of Foula – as the Hudson's Bay factor. However, 43-year-old Elisabeth Bergner, a leading lady in German and British films in the 1930s, left the movie in mid-production and was replaced by then-unknown Glynis Johns, certainly better cast as the 15-year-old Hutterite Anna; Bergner can be seen in some exterior shots, her face concealed by a big bonnet. Powell didn't flag it up in the pitch, but the movie has a score by Ralph Vaughan Williams, which gets equal billing with the famous stars.

Powell was always a contrarian. He brushed aside an official suggestion that he should make a film about minesweeping and let others turn out features designed to celebrate the heroic sacrifice of the British armed forces (*In Which We Serve*, 1942, *The Way Ahead*, 1944, *The Way to the Stars*, 1945), the merchant marine (*Convoy*, 1940), war-related boffins (Leslie Howard's *The First of the Few*, 1942), the fire brigade (*Fires Were Started*, 1943), women defence workers (*The Gentle Sex*, 1943) or indomitable civilian families (*This Happy Breed*, 1944, the Hollywood hit *Mrs Miniver*, 1942). The impetus for *49th Parallel* was that Canada had entered the war as part of the British

Commonwealth, despite grumblings from the traditionally anti-British French Canadian community; in the movie, Hirth (Eric Portman) tries to persuade trapper Johnnie (Olivier), who has been out of contact with civilisation for a year and only just found out there's a war on, that he should stay out of the fight because he's a member of an oppressed minority and Hitler will help him throw off the yoke of British rule. Johnnie [2] isn't convinced, and neither are we. However, the deeper point was neither to shore up Canadian confidence in the Allied cause or remind the world of Nazi barbarism. Powell told Kenneth Clark, Head of the MoI Films Division, 'Canada is in the war already… and is no more ready than we are to deal with Hitler. Sooner or later, their coast will be attacked and their ships sunk, and that will bring America into the war. I want to make a film in Canada to scare the pants off the Americans, and bring them into the war sooner.'

Powell, as it happens, was wrong about how America would go to war. He certainly remembered that the sinking of the unarmed liner *Lusitania*, torpedoed by a German U-boat, was a major factor in persuading the United States to enter World War 1. Nazi brutality had already featured in a run of American films, despite official protests from Germany, but there was still strong isolationist sentiment in America; German sympathisers in the US wrote off *Confessions of a Nazi Spy* (1939) or *The Mortal Storm* (1940) by characterising Hollywood as a Jewish propaganda machine. In the event, Hitler declared war on America to support his Japanese allies after Pearl Harbor – so it didn't really matter which way popular opinion in the US went about the Nazi regime. *49th Parallel*, released in America under the more blatant title *The Invaders*, [3] fudges several plot points in its attempt to get America 'on side'. At first, the marooned Nazis hope to make it across country to Vancouver where they can board a Japanese ship and be returned to Germany (to rejoin the Nazi war effort, presumably); only when Hirth is the sole survivor does he consider cutting his losses and crossing the 49th Parallel, the longest undefended border in the world, into the neutral America, which the film doesn't stress might be a safe haven for a Nazi naval hero. Thanks to a creative reading of the laws of international freight by two wink-wink American customs officials, the United States packs Hirth back to Canada – presumably to a prisoner-of-war camp, though it's possible AWOL Canuck soldier Andy Brock (Massey) beats Hirth to death in a box-car to get back his stolen uniform. 'Put 'em up, Nazi,' snarls the grinning Andy, prompting coward-at-the-last Hirth to raise his hands in surrender. 'Not that way,' says Andy, bringing up his dukes like a boxer. 'This way. Cause I'm not asking for those pants... I'm just takin' 'em!'

Co-writer Rodney Ackland objected to this finish on the grounds that Andy's brutality seems fairly fascist by itself. To be ridiculously fair-minded in this context, we're supposed to dislike Nazis for shoving the surrendering survivors of a just-sunk ship off their submarine (this early in the war, Powell doesn't machine gun them in the water) but approve of Allies beating up surrendering German sailors. In a neat, almost unnoticeable bit of humorous hypocrisy that prefigures the rigorous self-analysis of cinema ('all this filming... it's not healthy') in Powell's *Peeping Tom* (1959), gadget-minded Kuhnecker (Raymond Lovell) brings out a cine-camera and takes footage of bedraggled and bloodied allied seamen (for propaganda purposes, the swine!) only to have his camera knocked into the sea by a pissed-off second officer, who is then shoved off the submarine by the ill-tempered brute. Ackland might also have noted on a purely structural basis that Andy's crowd-pleasing punishment of Hirth at the fade-out was a bit too similar to an earlier scene in which diffident English author Scott treats the philistine book and painting-burning Lohrmann (John Chandos) to another off-screen thumping,

One of Our Aircraft is Missing
1942

© British National/ The Kobal Collection

hilariously hitting the whining kraut with 'that's for Thomas Mann… that's for Matisse… that's for Picasso… and… that's for me!'. In 1941, it seems, audiences couldn't get enough of Nazis being punched. They also enjoyed seeing the U-boat bombed to splinters, Jahner shot in the back, Kranz (Peter Moore) 'nearly lynched' by Indians and Kuhnecker shouted at by his superior officer for not remembering to check the plane's emergency petrol tank then getting his fool neck broken in the crash.

However, there's another peculiarity to *49th Parallel*, which didn't go unnoticed at the time. Despite the many instances of Nazi rottenness, cowardice and ineptitude displayed by the main characters, they are the main characters. Powell cited Agatha Christie's *Ten Little Niggers* as a precedent for the one-by-one whittling-down of his castaways, but in war movie sub-genres, *49th Parallel* is an entry in the cycle of 'lost patrol' movies named after John Ford's Iraq-set *The Lost Patrol* (1934) – soon to be remade by Zoltan Korda as Humphrey Bogart tank movie, *Sahara* (1943). The format of 'lost patrol' pictures, down to mutations like *Predator* (1987) and *The Bunker* (2001), is that a unit of military men are cut off from their support, behind enemy lines, and try to make it to safety, demonstrating their resourcefulness and ingenuity against the odds, harried by a usually-unseen enemy and harsh terrain. [4] The traditional 'lost patrol' ending has only one man left standing, and often he dies too. *One of Our Aircraft is Missing* (1942), which Powell and Pressburger made immediately after *49th Parallel*, is also a lost patrol movie: retelling the story of *49th Parallel* with a different slant, a British plane is shot down over occupied Holland and the crew, aided by heroic resistance fighters, have a difficult time getting back home. Of course, the good guy British airmen don't squabble or execute each other the way the baddie German sailors do, but their predicament is exactly the same. Both films have memorable, almost surreal plane crashes – the Germans' stolen seaplane goes down in a lake, with Kuhnecker ranting that the glare off the water means he can't judge height to make a landing, while the crew of the British bomber bail out and leave their unmanned aircraft to drone on into the Channel. Of course, the Brits buckle up and help each other with unflappable courage, while the krauts scream, panic and argue as they go down – but perversely the terrified Kuhnecker, who does nearly manage to avert disaster, is more credible than the RAF men of the later film.

Leutnant Hirth, played by Portman with a cold-eyed fanaticism, [5] is a ranting little Hitler – though Kuhnecker chides him for joining the Party late in the day – and a murdering coward. But Hirth is also determined, resourceful, wily and genuinely committed to his wrong-headed ideals and elements of him resurface in Portman's passionately strange performance as the 'glue-man' in Powell and Pressburger's late-in-the-war masterpiece *A Canterbury Tale* (1944). You can't sympathise with Hirth, but he is the film's hero, especially since guest stars Howard and Olivier give almost comic turns as the representatives of our side. Indeed, these Allies are more racially stereotyped than any of the film's Germans: Olivier's French-Canadian accent is worthy of Peter Sellers and his whiskery Catholic wild man act is so broad it must be taken as a lark, while Howard (whom Powell hated) sends up the unflappable pretend-twit aesthete image he established in *Pimpernel Smith* (1941) as a clot who smugly pokes fun at Hitler and Goebbels from the safety of the middle of nowhere and props up valued (and hideous) paintings next to the campfire in his tepee (which is asking for trouble even before the enemies of culture show up). When Hirth lectures Johnnie or Philip about their decadent democratic weaknesses, his points sound well made until these absurd people show by their actions that they draw the line. Even Andy, who has overstayed his leave because he has all sorts of gripes about the army, is a grotesque caveman figure rather than a righteous defender of democracy. This fair-minded tendency to give points to 'the other side' even as Germanic rigidity means they are doomed to be bested by romantic, free-thinking, improvisational amateurs would be revisited after the war in Powell and Pressburger's *The Battle of the River Plate* (1956) and *Ill Met By Moonlight* (1956), where Peter Finch and Marius Goring are surprisingly admirable Nazis.

In most British war films, there's a tendency to modest, clipped 'what we're fighting for' speeches delivered by Noel Coward or David Niven; here, the German gets to sound off about what he's fighting for, and we're supposed to be properly horrified. The most deeply-felt reaction comes after Hirth has made a speech to the Hutterites claiming them as his German brothers and stood up to give a 'heil Hitler' salute, and Peter (Anton Walbrook), the pacifist leader of the community, gives a humane response that combines tolerance with instinctive loathing. It's a dry-run for Walbrook's great anti-Nazi speech in Powell and Pressburger's *The Life and Death of Colonel Blimp* (1943), but also powerful enough on its own merits. Powell had just made two films with German émigré star Conrad Veidt; in *The Spy in Black* (1939), set in World War 1, Veidt is a jocular, less fascist version of Hirth, a swashbuckling German navy man thwarting the Allies while on the run in Scotland; in *Contraband* (1940), one of the first films to depict blacked-out London in the early days of World War 2, he's a Danish skipper running Nazi blockades and thwarting spies. Though stars in their homeland, Veidt, Walbrook (who changed his name from Adolf Wohlbruck for obvious reasons) and Bergner all had reasons not to stay in Nazi Germany (Walbrook was gay, Bergner Jewish). Veidt would become typecast as heel-clicking SS baddies in Hollywood (most memorably in *Casablanca*, 1943), but Walbrook – though a great screen villain in *Gaslight* (1939) – managed to sustain a screen career without ever playing a Nazi. It says something about the flexibility and relative lack of prejudice in Britain that a possible enemy alien could remain a popular romantic movie star during the height of the war. Reflecting Pressburger's own experience, *49th Parallel* alludes to the (debatably unjust) internment of innocent Germans in Canada (and Britain) in wartime. This sort of daring – raising uncomfortable issues at a time when a commitment to national unity and winning the war meant most critics let them slide – made Powell and Pressburger often unpopular with political censors. [6]

The reasons for Elisabeth Bergner's departure from the film remain vague: some suggest she only took the role as a way of escaping war-torn Europe and always intended to jump ship for Hollywood (where she made the little-known *Paris Calling*, 1941), others say she walked off the location shoot after a Hutterite extra found her painting her nails and/or smoking and slapped her for violating community standards. After the war, she was in a few German film and TV productions and was bizarrely cast as a witch in *Cry of the Banshee*, 1970. With Bergner on the cutting room floor, Walbrook is the nearest thing to a real German in the film (actually, like Bergner, he was Austrian). The U-boat Nazis were all at-the-time unfamiliar British actors – Portman seems to have picked up on Powell's offhand declaration to the treasury that they were 'cheap', which doubtless fed into his bad-tempered, paranoid performance – and most of them are limited to acting like goons or brutes. Roly-poly Raymond Lovell, channelling Hermann

Goering, would reprise his act bullying Will Hay in *The Goose Steps Out* (1942), while baby-faced John Chandos, a posh-accented thug, went on to be a theatre impresario and radio voice.

The most complicated character in the film is Vogel (Niall MacGinnis), a plodder with a conscience who has become a Nazi because it was the only way to stay in work in depressed 1930s Germany but isn't completely indoctrinated. MacGinnis is best-remembered as the chubby, perverse warlock villain of *Night of the Demon* (1958), but he'd been a virile, outdoorsy presence in *The Edge of the World* (1937); Powell makes him another earthy, peasant son of the soil in *49th Parallel*, but also encourages MacGinnis to show little weak touches that indict the tagalong Vogel in the crimes of his comrades. Vogel gives the dying Johnnie a rosary, but immediately balances this act of mercy by tearing down a picture of 'the King and Queen of Canada' and scratching a swastika into the wall of the Hudson's Bay post. Later, he warms to the Hutterite community, and reverts to his old trade of baking to help out – Powell is momentarily interested in the dough-mixing equipment and a mechanical bread-slicer he must have found on location, and treats bread-making with the rough, practical lyricism he would wood-turning in *A Canterbury Tale*. It's hinted that Vogel also takes a romantic interest in Anna – just as Chandos flashes a few leers that indicate Lohrmann would rape her if he got the chance; here, scenes scripted for the more mature Bergner take on a different meaning when played by Johns, who seems more like a substitute daughter than a possible wife. Vogel isn't as heroic as Walbrook's Theo von Kretschmar-Schuldorff in *The Life and Death of Colonel Blimp*, and – though likeable – the film essentially despises him for trudging along behind the goose-steppers, enabling their rottenness by keeping quiet, and only trying to opt out into an unworldly idyll rather than (as Theo does) turning against the whole notion of Nazism. Only when he is summarily tried in the open air and shot does the little man become a martyr.

It's in Vogel's story that we see the beginnings of the complicated world which Powell and Pressburger, who fused their credits and billed themselves as The Archers, would explore in their war-themed masterpieces, *The Life and Death of Colonel Blimp*, *A Canterbury Tale*, *A Matter of Life and Death* (1946) and *The Small Back Room* (1949) and meditations on art, sex and culture like *"I Know Where I'm Going"* (1945), *Black Narcissus* (1947), *The Red Shoes* (1948) and *The Tales of Hoffmann* (1951). Despite his pitch to the Ministry of Information, Powell was not by inclination a propagandist, and Pressburger had a lifetime of seeing things from the other fellow's point-of-view. An unstressed irony is that in the last act of the film, the stakes are upped because we see Nazi radio commentators commending Hirth as an intrepid hero of the Third Reich, [7] so we want him to fail so his exploits can't be used for propaganda purposes. He is smug enough to muse that his escape will become the subject of 'compulsory lectures' for the Hitler Youth, adding puffed-up vanity to his other failings. One of the points this propaganda film makes subtly is that the enemy are given to use propaganda blatantly. There are moments in *49th Parallel* when the strain of having to depict nasty Nazis and heroic allies tells and speeches become hectoring – which is never the case in the more sophisticated analysis of the British and German modes of behaviour in peace and war in *The Life and Death of Colonel Blimp*. Powell came to *49th Parallel* after serving as one of the directors of Korda's fantasy masterpiece *The Thief of Bagdad* (1940), with Conrad Veidt as a sub-liminally Hitlerian wicked sorcerer, and a great part of him yearned for fantasy (and

Technicolor); *49th Parallel* is black and white and down to earth. Canadian viewers have taken it to task for many distortions of the country's map and deployment of national stereotypes, perhaps missing a fine comic edge (arriving in Banff at the height of the tourist season, the Nazis clash with Indians in full battledress and Mounties in uniform). It's a big, simple film – but it does its job, and stakes a claim to the territory. However, to get where they were going, The Archers would have to transcend propaganda and aim for art.

Endnotes

1: In September 1939, when Great Britain entered the war, Korda shut down his in-progress super-production, *The Thief of Bagdad*, which Powell was directing, and shifted his base to Hollywood, where Tim Whelan took over. Korda reassigned Powell as one of three directors of *The Lion Has Wings* (1939), a morale-boosting salute to the Royal Air Force.

2: By the time he wrote *A Life in Movies*, Powell had forgotten how the name was spelled in the film.

3: *The Invaders* was also trimmed to 104 minutes from the *49th Parallel* running time of 123 minutes. Among the material edited for US audiences is the revelation that a pre-war German missionary to Canada was actually a map-making spy and some discussion of Nazi racial theory. It's possible that the latter talk was cut for fear that certain American audiences would agree with the villains' disparaging remarks about Eskimos, Indians, blacks and Jews.

4: The first film version of *Lost Patrol* (1929), based on a novel by Philip MacDonald, predates Ford's movie. The basic premise has been recycled by any number of war, western, crime, science fiction, disaster, jungle, horror or prison escape movies. Other 'lost patrol' pictures include *Bad Lands* (1939), *Bataan* (1943), *Seminole* (1943), *The Asphalt Jungle* (1951), *Too Late the Hero* (1970), *The Warriors* (1979), *Southern Comfort* (1983), *The Supernaturals* (1986). Even *Alien* (1979) and *The Blair Witch Project* (1999) are structurally lost patrol films.

5: Portman is also in the crew of downed bomber B-for-Bertie in *One of Our Aircraft is Missing*.

6: Winston Churchill tried hard to get the Colonel Blimp project squashed.

7: Dashing, daring Nazis like Field Marshal Rommel or SS man Otto Skorzeny were not in short supply during the war, but understandably the sort of brave, admirable kraut played by Conrad Veidt in *The Spy in Black* vanished from British and American movies. Whenever this type was revived in post-war films – Hardy Krüger as real-life POW escapee Franz von Werra in *The One That Got Away* (1957) or James Coburn as super-soldier Sergeant Steiner in *Cross of Iron* (1977) – it would be established that he was a rogue or a cynic rather than an idealist Nazi, and there would inevitably be a 'proper' Nazi villain, coward or thug in the film to be differentiated from the hero.

DON'T LET'S BE BEASTLY TO THE GERMANS

JULIAN PETLEY

Don't let's be beastly to the Germans
When our victory is ultimately won,
It was just those nasty Nazis who persuaded them to fight
And their Beethoven and Bach are really far worse than their bite.

Noel Coward

In most British and American World War 2 movies, when the German side is represented it tends to be largely in terms of undifferentiated, anonymous hostile forces. Sometimes, as in home front movies set during the London Blitz, it is virtually invisible, signified only by the devastating effects of its armaments. Although there are in fact a number of British and American films set during the war which feature German characters to a significant degree – for example *49th Parallel* (1941), *Went the Day Well?* (1942), *The Eagle Has Landed* (1976), and those revolving around the von Stauffenberg plot, from *The Night of the Generals* (1976) to *Valkyrie* (2008) – these do not involve battlefield action to any significant degree, and thus cannot easily be classified as war movies. We should also note, in this respect, *The Keep* (1983) and *The Bunker* (2002) which belong more to the horror than the war genre.

However, a number of war movies proper do feature segments of action shown from the German side – for example *The Desert Rats* (1953), *The Longest Day* (1962), *The Battle of the Bulge* (1965), *The Bridge at Remagen* (1968) and *A Bridge Too Far* (1977) – and in 1951 a whole film was devoted to a major German figure of World War 2. This was Field Marshal Rommel, played by James Mason, in the full-length biopic *Rommel: Desert Fox* (1951), which did in fact raise a few eyebrows at the time for its relatively sympathetic portrayal of the German warrior (and to which *The Desert Rats* can be seen as something of a riposte, although Mason once again plays Rommel, and does so in a similar manner). However, as *Rommel: Desert Fox* is what we would now call a dramatised documentary, and as a good deal of it is taken up with the Field Marshal's involvement in the von Stauffenberg plot, it doesn't really count as a fully-fledged war feature.

As was demonstrated by the negative reaction to *Rommel: Desert Fox* in some quarters, films set on the German side in wartime run the risk of being accused of painting the then enemy in too sympathetic a light. So it's perhaps unsurprising that there are only two Hollywood (and no British) war films set entirely in World War 2 on the German side: Douglas Sirk's *A Time to Love and a Time to Die* (1957) and Sam Peckinpah's *Cross of Iron* (1977). As we shall see, each film deals with the problems involved in a different fashion and, interestingly, does so in ways closely related to each director's major preoccupations, with Sirk producing one of his finest meditations on the terrible fragility of love and happiness, and Peckinpah delivering a savage blast against authority in all its forms and a paean to human solidarity in a brutally absurd world.

A Time to Love and a Time to Die is set partly on the Russian front in 1944 amidst the German retreat, and partly on the home front. It was based on the novel *Zeit zu leben und Zeit zu sterben* by Erich Maria Remarque, who wrote the famous *Im Westen nichts Neues/All Quiet on the Western Front*, and who appears in the film as a professor in hiding from the Nazis. The original title actually translates as 'a time to live and a time to die', but the English title of both the novel and the film substitutes 'love' for 'live'.

The film falls into three quite distinct parts. The first is set on the Russian front. Here we encounter the film's leading male character, Ernst Graeber (John Gavin), who,

out of the blue, is sent home on three weeks' leave. This leads on to the second, and longest, part of the film. Arriving home, Ernst discovers that his home, along with much of the rest of his town, has been destroyed by bombing raids. Desperately searching for his parents, he encounters Elizabeth Kruse (Lilo Pulver), the daughter of the family doctor; he, however, has been taken away by the Nazis and his house is now largely occupied on the authorities' orders by 'official tenants'. Managing to find a fragile happiness amongst the desolation and danger, Ernst and Elizabeth fall in love and get married. But Ernst has to return to the front where he receives the news that his parents are still alive and that Elizabeth is pregnant. Having witnessed the material destruction wrought by the war on his home town and the horrors brought upon it by the Nazis, Ernst is now no longer willing to obey orders with which he disagrees. Told by the Nazi officer and Gestapo informer Steinbrenner to shoot three Russian hostages, Ernst turns the gun on Steinbrenner instead and tells the uncomprehending Russians to run for their lives. Turning his back for a moment to re-read Elizabeth's letter, he fails to notice that one of the hostages has picked up Steinbrenner's gun and is shot dead.

A Time to Love and a Time to Die deals with the problem of how to represent the Germans in wartime by presenting us with a panorama of different kinds of people – in moral terms, the good, the bad and the merely indifferent. At the front, as well as the morally opposed Ernst and Steinbrenner we have Captain Rahe, the honourable but world-weary professional soldier, the hardened cynics Immerman and Sauer, and raw new recruit Hirschland who, having been forced to shoot Russian partisans as part of a firing squad, commits suicide. [1] The film thus does acknowledge (unlike *Cross of Iron*) that the Wehrmacht, and not simply the SS and the notorious *Einsatzgruppen*, took part in the murders of civilians on the Eastern front.

Back on the home front, the film's panorama broadens. Almost immediately Ernst is caught in an air raid, and is taken to a shelter by Elizabeth, whom he has just met. Just as in a film featuring the London Blitz, we are presented here with a spectrum of people all dealing with fear and loss in different ways – jocular bonhomie, clutching treasured possessions, petty quarrels over trifling matters ("Arnold, did you turn off the gas?" a woman irritably asks her husband), withdrawal into nervous collapse, and so on. A particularly fine touch here is the close-up of a chess game in which the hand moving a piece slightly but perceptibly shakes.

Searching for his parents Ernst encounters a brusque and unsympathetic bureaucrat who is more concerned with the fact that the bombing and its aftermath have left her records in a mess than with helping a long line of people desperate to find their loved ones. Again, such a figure might easily be encountered in a wartime Ealing comedy or Will Hay film, but the panorama of *A Time to Love and a Time to Die* also contains much darker, quite specifically Nazi elements. There is, for example, the harsh and authoritarian Frau Lieser, whom Ernst and Elizabeth call 'the crocodile': an 'official tenant' at Dr. Kruse's house and a member of the Nazi women's corps. More interesting, however, is Oscar Binding, an old school friend of Ernst who nearly runs him over in his posh official car. Once a nobody and expelled from school, he is now district leader and lives in a large house stuffed with hunting trophies and looted art works. As he himself puts it: "Just shows you anything can happen. Me, who couldn't even get a passing grade in history – political leader to keep the mayor straight." An archetypal petty bourgeois who has made good under Hitler, even he seems to find it barely believable that "I, a milkman's son, would be an art collector." However, there is something almost pathetic in the fact that the interiors of the house of which he is so proud are in fact incredibly vulgar and ostentatious in their excess, and that he seems to be so desperate to be liked by Ernst, telling him, apparently quite genuinely, that "you always have a home here with me". Indeed, there is something almost sexual, but more tender than predatory or threatening, about the way in which he sits by Ernst whilst the latter is in Binding's bath, plies him with brandy and douses him with his favourite lilac bath salts.

In a later scene at Binding's house, however, we encounter a far less ambivalent figure in the person of the SS officer Heini, who is the commandant of the local concentration camp. A full-blown Nazi, he plays classical music on Binding's piano whilst talking about how, when he was on the Eastern front, he poured vodka down Russians' throats and made human flame throwers out of them, and demonstrating with the aid of vodka and a pile of matches how he makes funeral pyres in the form of 'layer cakes' at the camp. Brutal and dissipated, yet at the same time a sensitive pianist and given to baby talk, he radiates an aura of sexual ambiguity, and the sexual overtones of this scene (which are quite absent from the way in which it plays in the novel) are further intensified by the presence of two scantily clad young women, the blonde one of whom is wearing an SS hat. The sinister Heini is quite unlike the petty bourgeois Binding who confides to Ernst after Heini has left: "I don't enjoy that sort of thing; you know me, much too soft hearted." But when Ernst replies: "But you think it's okay for him to do it", Binding retorts: "I don't think about it. I'm not responsible for what other people do," thus demonstrating the moral rottenness at the heart of his complicity with the Nazi system. It is partly this encounter which, as the narrative makes clear, causes Ernst to resolve to face his own moral responsibilities when he returns to the front, and partly a meeting with an absolutely reptilian Gestapo officer (chillingly incarnated by Klaus Kinski) who, in a shadowy basement, hands him Dr. Kruse's ashes in a cigar box. With these two characters we finally reach the Nazi heart of darkness. The only other indication of the true horrors of the Nazi regime is an effectively elliptical scene in which Ernst and Elizabeth look out of their window one night and see prisoners from the nearby concentration camp being forced to clear away the rubble left by the latest air raid.

Finally, in this panorama of Germans in wartime, there are those who actively resist the Nazi regime. The main figure here is Professor Pohlmann, whose fate is neatly summed up by Binding: "He was the reason why I had to quit school. He couldn't get it into his thick head that my work for the Hitler Youth was more important than his lousy examinations. Well, when I became party adviser to the school board I returned the favour. I had him put in a camp. Naturally that meant he was kicked out of his teaching post. He had me kicked out, so I had him kicked out. That's justice eh?" However, the 'soft hearted' former pupil had Pohlmann released after a few months, and he now lives, under surveillance and sufferance, in the ruins of the museum. In his view, "the war is lost, and, more terrifying, it must be lost before our country can regain its soul". This idea that Germany is lost but ultimately redeemable is also expressed by the Jewish fugitive, Josef, whom Pohlmann manages to shelter. When Ernst says "how you must hate us", Josef replies: "I remember the time before, the Germany I grew up in and loved" and asks, rhetorically, if he should hate Pohlmann and the pastor who hides him. Ernst then asks if there are many more like these people, to which Josef responds: "Yes, not enough, but many."

So this is how *A Time to Love and a Time to Die* deals with the admittedly difficult problem of representing people who, only twelve years before the film was made, were still the enemy – it establishes a continuum, with full-blown Nazis at one extreme and active opponents of the regime at the other. In between is a spectrum of more or less apolitical Germans, and the narrative is to some extent the story of Ernst's *prise de conscience*. But it is also a war film, which leads us to ask how it actually represents war.

From the above analysis, it might seem as if only the first and third parts of the triptych which constitutes the film's narrative concern war, and that it is absent from the second, and longest, part. But this is absolutely not the case. In the scenes on the Russian front, the Russians (apart from the civilian victims of the German firing squad) are never glimpsed – their presence is signified only by the deadly and almost constant rain of bombs and shells. War here is thus presented in an almost abstract fashion. But exactly the same applies to the home front scenes where bombs fall from unseen planes and buildings explode before our eyes as if of their own volition. All we see of 'action' in the conventional war film sense is a brief shot of two anti-aircraft guns firing. Here, particularly in the incredibly striking scene in which Ernst is caught in the open during a daylight raid and the landscape literally dissolves around him, we move from the abstract to the surreal. In this film there is absolutely no escape from war – it is, quite simply, everywhere and all-pervasive. So when Ernst first returns home and begins to explore the wrecked houses on the street where his parents lived, and an old man asks him: "In what hole have you been hibernating?" he responds: "The front. I just got back." To which he receives the scornful retort: "The front! And what do you think this is?" But this point is made even more strongly, and far more powerfully, by the absolutely heart-rending dissolve from the cross made by the window frame through which Elizabeth

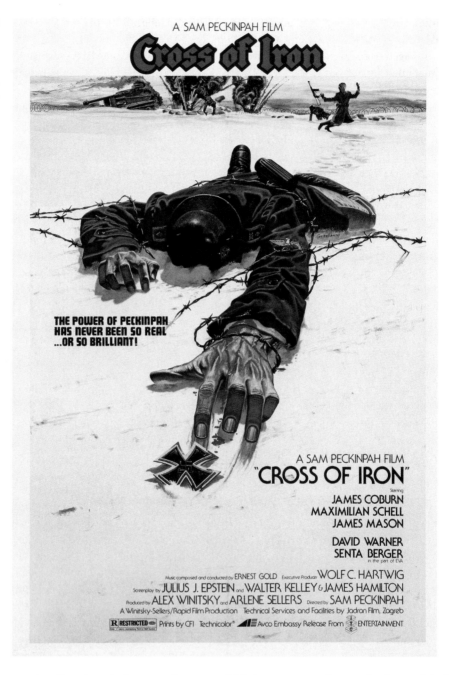

watches Ernst's train leave to the cross which he passes on the way back to rejoin his unit, whilst on the soundtrack the noise of the departing train dissolves into the whistle and explosion of falling shells. As Jean-Luc Godard wrote in 'Tears and Speed', his homage to *A Time to Love and a Time to Die* in *Cahiers du Cinéma*, Sirk's film 'is beautiful because one thinks of the war as one watches these images of love, and vice versa' (Milne 1972: 138). The central love story is not an interlude in or refuge from the war – it is a love story set in war. Or as Sirk himself so succinctly put it: 'What was interesting to me was a landscape of ruins and the two lovers' (Halliday 1997: p.144). Nothing could encapsulate the film more evocatively.

I have already suggested that Sirk made out of Remarque's novel one of his most poignant portraits of doomed love, but his film has an even more personal dimension to it than that.

As Ernst's train prepares to leave the station at the end of his leave, a very young soldier enters his carriage, and the camera quite noticeably lingers on him for a short while, prompting thoughts about what is all too likely to be a young life cut drastically short. But the moment has a much more specific resonance. In 1925, Detlef Sierck (the future Douglas Sirk, at this point a notable German theatre director and very much a man of the Left) had a son, Claus Detlef, by his actress wife Lydia Brinken. A few years later they divorced and she became a Nazi. When Hitler came to power, she obtained a court order banning her ex-husband from seeing his son, on the grounds that Sierck's second wife was Jewish. She also enrolled him in the Hitler Youth and launched him as a child actor, in which role he became the Third Reich's leading child star. The only way in which his father could see him was by watching him in movies – in which he sometimes played the role of a young Nazi. Sierck, who by this time had become a film director (and one of the very few interesting ones working in the Third Reich), finally left Germany in 1937. His son, just like Ernst Graeber, was killed on the Russian front in 1944. After the war, Sirk made an unsuccessful attempt to return to work in Europe, where he spent much of his time trying to find out exactly what had happened to his son in much the same way as Ernst tries to discover the fate of his parents, including scouring the same sort of makeshift notice-boards which play a key role in the home front section of *A Time to Live and a Time to Die*. [2]

Turning now to *Cross of Iron*, this is also set during the German retreat from Russia, but in 1943 on the Taman Peninsula. The action is based loosely on the Battle of Krymskaya, which took place near the Black Sea coast, and the film's original source is the novel *Das geduldige Fleisch/ The Willing Flesh* by Willi Heinrich, who himself fought on the Eastern front.

The story revolves around the conflict between Sergeant Rolf Steiner (James Coburn) and the newly arrived Captain Stransky (Maximilian Schell), who has been transferred to the Russian front at his own request – the reason being that he wants to be awarded the Iron Cross (which, to Stransky's chagrin, Steiner already possesses). Their superior officer is the resigned Colonel Brandt (James Mason), who is assisted by the even more world-weary Captain Kiesel (David Warner). When, in his efforts to be awarded the Iron Cross, Stransky submits a false report to Brandt about leading a successful counter-attack, which is endorsed by his adjutant Lieutenant Triebig (who is terrified that Stransky will reveal that he is gay), Steiner refuses to corroborate it. However, given his hatred of all forms of military authority, he also refuses to testify before a military tribunal that Stransky lied in his report. During a furious Soviet onslaught, Stransky engineers matters so that Steiner's platoon is unaware that their unit is retreating, and thus they find themselves cut off behind enemy lines. Making their way back to their unit, some of them disguised in Soviet uniforms, they manage to send a message announcing their imminent arrival and warning their comrades not to fire upon them. However, the transmission is intercepted by Stransky, who orders Triebig to open fire on anybody approaching the German position; consequently the platoon is cut to ribbons. However, Steiner survives, kills Triebig and forces Stransky, who has just heard that he is to be recalled away from the front, to join him in the desperate battle against the *Götterdämmerung* of the Soviet assault, in which he reveals himself to be a helpless incompetent, unable even to reload his gun.

The film's credits play over a montage which is accompanied on the soundtrack by a German military march intercut with a children's song; this tells the story of 'little Hans' who leaves his home one day and returns many years later so changed that his sister no longer recognises him. The montage intertwines four strands of images – young Germans climbing a mountain and planting swastika-bedecked flags on the peak, Nazi rallies, Hitler and his entourage at Berchtesgaden, and the horrors of warfare. The way in which the various images are combined clearly suggests that Nazi visual rhetoric concealed a grim reality, and the conspicuous presence of children in the images of the Nazi rallies emphasises the crucial importance which the regime attached to engaging German youth in its ideological programme. It also recalls a familiar Peckinpah theme – the implication of the young in the world's violence, an idea which might also be discerned in the song about 'little Hans'.

However, although the opening montage seems to suggest that the film will examine the gulf between the rhetoric and the reality of Nazism, *Cross of Iron* is not really concerned with Nazism at all. As Peckinpah himself wrote to the British film critic Colin McArthur: 'The film is very little concerned with politics – it is concerned with fighting soldiers, be they American, Japanese, Scottish, German.' (quoted in Prince 1998: p.154). In fact, the only character to be identified as a Nazi in the film is Zoll, who is seconded to Steiner's platoon from the SS by Stransky whilst Steiner is recovering in hospital from wounds which he receives in the film's first major battle scene. Significantly, Zoll is the only character in the film who actually commits an atrocity, forcing a female Russian soldier to engage in oral sex with him (as a consequence of which he gets his penis bitten off, and is abandoned by Steiner to his fate at the hands of his victim's comrades). Apart from the opening montage, the only sequence which prominently features a swastika is the one set in the hospital. Thus the film cannot be described as either anti- or pro-Nazi because, for the most part, it simply does not represent the Nazis or Nazism at all. The conflict, both between the Russians and the Germans, and between the Germans themselves, is not presented in political terms. The former is simply a brutal struggle for survival, in which it is frequently extremely difficult to tell the Russian and German soldiers apart; this is particularly apparent in the sequence in which members of Steiner's platoon don Russian uniforms to enable them to pass safely through the Russian lines as they make their way back to the unit from which they have been cut off by Stransky's perfidy. Meanwhile the conflict between Steiner and Stransky stems largely from the former's all-encompassing hatred of authority in general, of which his hatred of the upper classes is but an aspect.

Thus the conflicts which take place between the Germans in the film are not between Nazis and anti-Nazis. Stransky is keen to make it clear to Steiner from the start that he is not a Nazi, stating: "I am an officer of the Wehrmacht. I have never been a Party member. I'm a Prussian aristocrat and I don't want to be put into the same category." Stransky is thus clearly a member of the old, traditional ruling classes who, to an extent, were actually shouldered aside by the Nazis. This is very evident in his remark that: "In civilian, as well as in military life, a distinction is made between people… The difference is a matter of ethical and intellectual superiority which is caused, whether you like it or not, by blood and by class differences." The point is also emphasised by Lieutenant Meyer, who says of Stransky to Steiner: "This one is pure Prussian military aristocracy. And rich. You know the ruling classes… Stransky will survive this war one way or another, and he'll still have his land, his wealth and his status, but can be very dangerous in defeat. Be careful of him. He doesn't live in the same world we live in." This is most evident in their entirely different attitudes to the Iron Cross, Stransky confiding to Steiner that "if I go back without the Iron Cross I couldn't face my family", the latter dismissing it as "just a piece of worthless metal".

Steiner is perhaps the ultimate anti-authority figure in Peckinpah's oeuvre, at one point exploding to Brandt and Kiesel: "Do you think that because you and Colonel Brandt are more enlightened than many officers I hate you any less? I hate all officers – all the Stranskys, all the Triebigs, all the Iron Cross scavengers, and the whole German army… Do you know how much I hate this uniform and everything it stands for?" Significantly this passage is not in the original novel, and whether or not it was invented by Peckinpah it does very clearly relate to the hostility to authority figures which runs throughout so many of his films. In *Cross of Iron* this is evident not simply in Steiner's dialogue but infuses the whole film. Particularly striking in this respect is the hospital sequence, in which a visiting military bigwig extends his hand to a wounded man in a wheelchair; in return the soldier proffers one stump, then another, before finally proffering his leg in a grim parody of the Nazi salute or the goose step. The bigwig then orders the meat which has been laid on for his reception to be taken to a private dining room, leaving the wounded soldiers with just salad, and tells the staff that he wants the majority of the men returned to active service in three days.

Steiner has not the slightest truck with patriotism, or indeed 'isms' of any kind. He mockingly quotes von Clausewitz and von Bernhardi's famous aphorisms on war, and declares with bitter irony that "we are spreading the German culture throughout a desperate world". Bernard Dukore rightly describes him as an 'alienated existential man' inhabiting an absurd world (1999: p.54). As Steiner himself says to the Russian boy captured by his platoon, whose death Stransky orders but who is released by Steiner: "It's all an accident. An accident of hands – mine, others – all without mind. One extreme to another, and neither works, or will ever." And just to hammer home the point, the boy is almost immediately killed by his fellow Russians as they attack the German positions. In his excellent commentary on the Region 1 DVD edition of this film, Stephen Prince perceptively refers to its battlefield setting as "an existential no-man's land where the savagery of the fighting has extinguished all forms of political belief". Here the only imperative is survival, and the only responsibility which Steiner recognises is to the safety of his platoon. The film's profoundly nihilistic tone, which is highly characteristic of late Peckinpah, is perfectly expressed by Steiner's remark that "I believe God is a sadist but probably doesn't even know it", although it is constantly reinforced by the bloody chaos and turmoil of the battle scenes so brilliantly captured in all their murky horror by John Coquillon's cinematography.

In his attitude both to war and to Germany, Brandt is not at all dissimilar to Steiner, even though he is a traditional product of the officer class. Thus he states: "The German soldier no longer has any ideals. He's not fighting for the culture of the West, nor for one form of government he wants, not for the stinking party, he's fighting for his life." And, arranging for Kiesel's evacuation from the front, he says: "For many of us Germans, the exterminator is long overdue." However, he then adds: "But I have decided that you are worth saving... There's nothing wrong with you, except that you smoke too much. You're a brave man, braver than you think. One day there will be a need for brave civilians. In the new Germany, if such a thing is allowed to exist, there will be a need for builders, for thinkers, for poets. I begin to see now what your job will be... You will seek out and contact these – 'better people', you call them? – and together you will take on the responsibility that goes with survival." However, David Warner's portrayal of Kiesel as a weary cynic given to moaning about his health distinctly undercuts Brandt's optimistic view of a man whose cynicism serves simply to lend him an illusion of integrity and intellectual depth. Brandt asks Kiesel: "What will we do when we lose the war?" The latter replies wearily: "Prepare for the next one." This line is not in the novel, and the last we see of this 'better person' is, discouragingly, his exit slumped grotesquely in a motorcycle sidecar which is far too small for his large frame.

As Stephen Prince points out, in *Cross of Iron* Peckinpah "successfully stripped the combat of the patriotic heroism and glory that usually accrue to it in war films" (1998: p.154). But he also presents most of the film's characters at such a level of existential abstraction that it is difficult to feel much for them as their numbers remorselessly diminish; in spite of the overriding importance which the film's central character attaches to safeguarding the lives of the members of his platoon, and in spite of their being given clearly individuating features, they actually come across as somewhat cipher-like and rather unfortunately interchangeable. Furthermore, by refusing to engage with the political aspects of World War 2, and indeed of war in general, Peckinpah leaves himself with little to say other than 'war is hell' (which we know already, and which message is anyway somewhat undercut by the undeniably exciting and dramatic fashion in which the battle scenes are filmed and edited). This would matter less if both the opening and end credits did not indeed appear to be striving to suggest some kind of political or ideological perspective.

As we have seen, the opening credits use montage to comment upon the gulf between the rhetoric and the reality of Nazism. The end credits also employ montage. Here two strands of still images combine, one consisting of images of atrocities carried out against civilians by German troops, and the other of images from wars and conflicts more recent than World War 2, and in some cases contemporaneous with the film's production. Here there are two major problems. Firstly, with one exception, the foregoing film (like the novel) has entirely ignored the appalling atrocities which were systematically committed by the regular German army (and not, as is all too often claimed, simply by the SS and the various *Einsatzgruppen*) on the Eastern front. [3] Secondly, as Prince quite correctly points out, because of the depoliticised fashion in which Peckinpah has represented the war, 'he is left without a coherent social perspective that might connect this war with the other bloody conflicts' depicted in the still images. Thus all these become simply 'instances of the continuing human propensity to commit violence and examples of history as an ongoing parade of atrocities a portrait of timeless human barbarism.' (pp.154-5)

The final montage is actually one of a number of distancing devices which Peckinpah uses at the end of the film: these include apparently bringing back the dead character of the Russian boy (who shoots off Stransky's helmet with an amused shrug), reprising the 'little Hans' song from the opening credits, and counterpointing the awful still images with Steiner's ironic laughter, which recalls the end of *The Treasure of the Sierra Madre* (1948) and ends with a mumbled 'oh shit' which sounds as much Coburn's as Steiner's. But, most important of all, he also quotes from the end of Brecht's anti-Nazi parable *The Resistible Rise of Arturo Ui*. Written in 1941, this tells the story of a 1930s Chicago gangster who is determined to take over the cauliflower market, and is very clearly a satire on the rise of Hitler and Nazism. The film ends with a quote taken from the play's epilogue: 'Don't rejoice in his defeat, you men. For though the world stood up and stopped the bastard, the bitch that bore him is in heat again'.[4] But exactly who or what is being referred to here? Hitler (as in Brecht's play)? Clearly not. Germany in 1977? If so, why? Some kind of universal spirit of war? The general forces of reaction and repression? Quite possibly – but because Peckinpah has so resolutely both de-Nazified and de-politicised the war, Brecht's parting shot (which is extremely powerful in the play) no longer has any specific target and stands simply as a rather empty rhetorical device. Moreover, invoking Brecht at the end of a film whose battle scenes – Peckinpah's anti-war message notwithstanding – are undeniably both spectacular and involving, is not exactly a good idea, since Brecht disliked above all conventional theatrical (and, by extension, cinematic) spectacle and insisted on the importance of distancing the spectator from the action in order that they might learn something from it. *Cross of Iron*, for all its problems as a World War 2 film, is nonetheless a fine example of late Peckinpah at his darkest – but Brechtian it surely ain't. [5]

Endnotes

1. The scene in which the young female partisan curses those who are about to murder her is characteristically reprised in the superb *Les Carabiniers* (1963) by Jean Luc-Godard, a passionate admirer of this and other Sirk films.
2. This episode in Sirk's life forms part of the basis of the Hollywood novel *Out There in the Dark* – whose central character is a German émigré director called Dieter Seife – written by Wesley Strick, who also wrote the screenplays of *Cape Fear* (1991) and *Wolf* (1994) amongst others. Strick is interviewed about this on the French special edition DVD of the film.
3. This topic, still the subject of a great deal of controversy, is the subject of the Hamburg Institute for Social Research (1999).
4. A rather better (and complete) translation is that provided by Ralph Manheim:
    > Therefore learn to see and not to gape.
    > To act instead of talking all day long.
    > The world was almost won by such an ape!
    > The nations put him where his kind belong.
    > But don't rejoice too soon at your escape –
    > The womb he crawled from still is going strong. (Brecht 1981).
5. The above-mentioned *Les Carabiniers* is perhaps the best example of a genuinely Brechtian anti-war film.

Bibliography

Brecht, Bertolt (1981), *The Resistible Rise of Arturo Ui*. London: Eyre Methuen Ltd.

Dukore, Bernard F. (1999), *Sam Peckinpah's Feature Films*. Urbana and Chicago: University of Illinois Press.

Halliday, Jon (1997, second edition), *Sirk on Sirk: Conversations with Jon Halliday*. London: Faber and Faber.

Hamburg Institute for Social Research (1999), *The German Army and Genocide: Crimes Against War Prisoners, Jews, and Other Civilians*. New York: The New Press.

Heinrich, Willi (1999), *Cross of Iron*. London: Cassell. English translation originally published as *The Willing Flesh* (1956). London: Weidenfeld and Nicolson.

Prince, Stephen (1998), *Savage Cinema: Sam Peckinpah and the Rise of Ultraviolent Movies*. London: The Athlone Press.

Remarque, Erich Maria (1954), *A Time to Love and a Time to Die*, London: Hutchinson

Strick, Wesley (2006), *Out There in the Dark*, New York: Thomas Dunne Books.

BRITISH
PROPAGANDA FILMS
OF WORLD WAR 2

KAREN McCREEDY

War had been declared. The first air-raid sirens had wailed. Anxiety descended with the blackout, and everyone needed reassurance that Britain would prevail. In giving the people that reassurance, the Government had to produce 'propaganda' – posters, leaflets, radio announcements – to boost morale, counter enemy propaganda, and attempt to persuade neutral countries to side with the allies.

The Ministry of Information (MoI) took a while to catch on to the possibilities of film as a propaganda medium – indeed, at the outbreak of war, the Government temporarily closed all cinemas. The MoI's own Films Division did not even have a means of producing films in 1939, and gave no guidance to commercial producers. But, after a slow start, 'entertainment as propaganda' gradually became an essential part of the war effort. The first months of the war however produced only two propaganda films, both made on the initiative of their producers. *The First Days* (1939), a 23-minute documentary, was made by the GPO Film Unit to record the initial reaction to war. With a montage of different street scenes set to the echo of Chamberlain's sombre announcement, and a commentary stating that "filling sandbags is everybody's business", it gives the first hint of the "all in it together" slant that would help make later films such as *In Which We Serve* (1942) so successful.

London Films' *The Lion Has Wings* (1939) was filmed at Alexander Korda's behest, and released only two months after the war started. Its uneasy mix of documentary footage and studio-bound actors in stagey scenes does not make for timeless viewing, though it was regarded as a success at the time. Footage of shells, planes and tanks rolls by while Movietone News announcer E. V. H. Emmett announces that the country is well prepared for war – apparently, we had "the greatest navy the world has ever known", and the RAF were "undisputed masters of the sky". This may have helped the audience feel better, but it was a long way from reality. (In his book *The Big Lie*, John Baker White describes a Kent beach being defended 'by one under-strength rifle company with two Bren guns and a single aged Vickers machine-gun…') The film's portrayal of the RAF raid over the Kiel canal is about as accurate as the introduction, with bombs shown hurtling straight at a pack of German naval vessels, and barely a mention of the Blenheims that didn't return to base.

In early 1940, the Home Intelligence Unit was set up to monitor public morale and over thirty films were commissioned by the MoI. These had three aims: reassuring the public; making sure complacency didn't set in with the 'phoney war'; and warning against inadvertently passing information to the enemy. But it was again a commercial company that released the next big propaganda film: Gainsborough Pictures' *For Freedom* (1940). The battle of the River Plate and the sinking of the *Graf Spee* pocket battleship had dominated newsreels and reports in early December 1939, providing some much-needed cheer. Released in May 1940, just as the Nazis invaded France, Belgium and Holland, Gainsborough's fictionalised version of events provided a timely reminder that it was possible for the Empire to strike back.

On 10th May 1940, Churchill became Prime Minister and, among his early initiatives, he appointed Duff Cooper as Minister of Information. It was Cooper who grasped the lack of an official production agency and moved the GPO Film Unit to MoI's direct control. Under its patriotic new title, the Crown Film Unit (CFU) was handed the remit of producing instructional films and morale-boosters, and providing a filmic record of the war.

The Lion Has Wings 1939

© London Films/ The Kobal Collection

Following the fall of France and the evacuation of allied troops from Dunkirk, the threat of invasion increased daily with official propaganda and information struggling to keep pace with developments. For the Films Division, the 'Five-minute Film' was the answer – a weekly short, shown at every cinema in the country. Cheap and easy to make, they covered issues such as rationing, the dangers of rumours, and the importance of the blackout. *They Also Serve* (1940) reassured housewives that they were 'doing their bit' for the war, and was screened at WI meetings and similar female gatherings, presumably on the basis that, if they followed the example of the busy housewife in the film, women would never have a spare moment to get to the cinema.

Squadron 992 (1939), a 25-minute film that had been produced by the GPO Film Unit prior to its move to the MoI, was released in the summer of 1940. Unfortunately, its message that barrage balloons were a good defence against air attack had been over-taken by events. The Battle of Britain had begun and the balloons were clearly proving inadequate for the task. The solemn announcement: "These are the officers of Balloon Command" was never going to have the Luftwaffe begging for peace. In August 1940, one of the CFU's most noteworthy 'shorts' was released: *London Can Take It!* Made by Humphrey Jennings, the film – nominated for an Oscar for 'Best Short Subject' – endeavoured to capture the 'Blitz Spirit'. With laconic narration from American journalist Quentin Reynolds, and images of Londoners sweeping bomb debris from their steps, or walking past an upended double-decker bus to get to work, the message was clear: 'The British will not be beaten'. The public loved it – not only because the film reflected what they were going through and how they reacted to it, but because it didn't sermonise or give them orders. Wartime audiences disliked finger-wagging lectures just as much as people today detest nannying instructions to eat their fruit and veg.

However, it was not until 1941 that Brendan Bracken (the fourth wartime Minister of Information) told the War Cabinet that: "we must stop appealing to the public or lecturing at it. One makes it furious, the other resentful."

What the public did want was to be entertained, and in that respect Ealing's feature film *Convoy* (1940) delivered. Released at the end of September 1940, it told the fictional story of a British cruiser, HMS *Apollo*, to demonstrate the Navy's work in guarding the Atlantic merchant ships. Heavily outgunned by a German pocket battleship, the Apollo fights a delaying action that saves the convoy. *Monthly Film Bulletin* described it as 'the most exciting, lifelike and restrained account of the Navy's work in wartime yet seen on the screen', and audiences apparently agreed – the film became the biggest British box-office hit of 1940. It was the last feature-length propaganda film of that year. As the Germans bombed Coventry, and the air raids on London intensified, cinema audiences boarded *The Sea Hawk* (1940) with Errol Flynn, and did their best to escape the war for a few hours. Meanwhile, the CFU had been moved out of London to Pinewood studios, where they and the commercial filmmakers based there began to learn from each other.

1941 brought a new type of film: the resistance movie. Two Cities' *Freedom Radio* told the fictional story of a German underground radio station. However, an audience that was being bombed nightly by the Luftwaffe was not interested in making distinctions between 'good' and 'bad' Germans, even if the story had been more credible. Dr. Karl Roder (Clive Brook), the instigator of the radio station, cautiously tells a young electrician that he doesn't like living in a country "where you can't speak the truth for fear your best friend gives you away". But on the night he starts broadcasting, all his friends know when and how to tune in and duly phone him up to pass on a 'coded' message that they heard him! Small wonder he ended up getting shot.

The CFU short *Heart of Britain*, released in March 1941, captured the mood of the moment more successfully. Filmed as a northern companion-piece to *London Can Take It!*, the film sets the Yorkshire Dales and the Lake District to Elgar, before moving on to the towns and factories. In a stirring climax, the Huddersfield Choral Society sings the closing bars of the Hallelujah Chorus over images of Wellington bombers taking off to target Germany. *Words for Battle*, another CFU short, cleverly sets poetry and prose from the sixteenth to the twentieth centuries against a backdrop of contemporary images. Its release coincided with news of the German attack being repulsed at Tobruk, and the mass British bombing of Hamburg. Audiences would have listened to Laurence Olivier reciting lines such as Milton's 'mighty puissant nation rousing herself like a strong man after sleep,' and felt the words to be especially apt.

As the Germans turned on the Russians in the summer of 1941, the cinematic offerings were pretty lightweight fare, which used the war as a backdrop for lashings of heroic escapism. Anton Walbrook played a Polish airman in *Dangerous Moonlight*; and Leslie Howard starred as a professor smuggling refugees out of Germany in *Pimpernel Smith* (another film that suggested there was a German underground resistance). Once again the heavyweight propaganda came from the CFU. *Target for Tonight*, a fifty-minute narrative starring RAF personnel, was released in October. It told the story of a bomber ('B' for Bertie), its crew, and the supporting ground staff and personnel who planned and carried out a bombing raid. At this point in the war, errors in navigation and bomb aiming often meant that targets were missed by miles – but official policy was that precision bombing was destroying industrial targets. The film therefore delivered what the RAF could not – clusters of bombs falling directly on to the railway sidings they were aimed at, with the added bonus of every single plane returning safely home. Nevertheless, the *Monthly Film Bulletin* raved that it 'dramatises reality' and it won an 'honorary' Oscar for 'its vivid and dramatic presentation of the heroism of the RAF'.

The final propaganda film of 1941 was *49th Parallel* – the only feature film for which direct funding was provided by MoI. Filmed on location in Canada, and with an all-star cast headed by Laurence Olivier, it followed half-a-dozen survivors from a sunken German submarine as they crossed Canada in an attempt to reach the (then neutral) USA. Eric Portman's performance as the Nazi Leutnant Hirth made him a major star, while Emeric Pressburger won an Oscar for 'Best Original Story'. The critics praised it as being 'excellent propaganda' (MFB). Fortunately for the film's performance at the box-office, it also provided solid entertainment – for, only two weeks after its release, its anti-isolation message was rendered obsolete when the Japanese bombed Pearl Harbor. *Ships with Wings*, an Ealing story of heroics on the high seas, was released in January 1942 to a critical mauling. Its story of a rebellious young man redeeming himself by making the ultimate sacrifice to stave off disaster was too fantastic for the critics to swallow. Picturegoer's 1943 *Film Annual* commented that producers should 'determine the bounds of possibility before mixing studio stuff that strains the credibility of the most gullible'. However, a Mass Observation survey indicated that audiences liked it. Perhaps they enjoyed seeing footage of HMS *Ark Royal*, which had been used for some of the location work, but had been sunk prior to the film's release.

Wavell's 30,000, a documentary about the successes of the North African campaign, as filmed by the CFU and the Army Film and Photographic Unit, also sank without trace. Due for release in January 1942, and reviewed favourably by the critics, it had to be withdrawn from cinemas when Rommel counter-attacked. In March, *Listen to Britain* (1942) became another critical and popular success for the CFU. Running for almost twenty minutes, the film had no commentary telling its audience what to think. It simply took sounds and images of everyday life from train whistles to brass bands to remind people who they were and what they were fighting for. One sound the government did not want to hear was 'careless talk', and the public were given a reminder of the dangers of gossip via *Next of Kin* (1942), a film from Ealing studios which had originally been made for military training purposes. It showed how a British commando raid on a German-occupied port might be compromised by casual conversation, and suggested that the Germans had a network of unobtrusive spies taking advantage of overheard remarks. After the war, it became apparent that German efforts to establish a spy network in England had failed miserably, but in 1942, the threat seemed real enough for the film, and its message, to be given a general release. Ironically, its move into the public domain was held up because its fictional raid took place close to St. Nazaire, where a real commando operation was scheduled for the end of March. The St. Nazaire raid ensured that the German battleship Tirpitz did not have an Atlantic repair base, but by the time *Next of Kin* reached the cinemas, allied fortunes had taken a downturn. Sevastopol was besieged, Tobruk captured, and, in response to the assassination of SS leader Reinhart Heydrich in Prague, the Czech village of Lidice was wiped out. The last thing the public wanted to see in June 1942 was a film that ended in disaster for the British.

Fortunately, a more encouraging Ealing film, *The Foreman went to France* (1942) was released a week later. Based on the true story of factory foreman Melbourne Johns, it told how he travelled alone to France in 1940 in order to ensure that three special machines on loan to the French did not fall into enemy hands. The real Johns was indeed helped by two British soldiers (played in the film by Tommy Trinder and Gordon Jackson), though the film also wove in a fictional American girl, and added a daring escape with lots of shooting. The film's appeal however lay in its working class heroes, and the themes for which Ealing became famous: tenacity, teamwork and eccentricity, fighting against the odds and winning. The other two films released that month were resistance stories. *The Day will Dawn* (1942) starred Hugh Williams as a foreign correspondent in Norway. Fiction again coincidentally reflected fact, with its climactic commando raid on a U-boat base being compared by the critics to the real raid on Vaagso in December 1941.

In the case of *One of our Aircraft is Missing* (1942), the crossover between fact and fiction was intentional. Made by Powell and Pressburger, the film was based on the story of an RAF crew who had had to bail out of their Wellington bomber over occupied Holland, and made it safely back to England with the help of the Dutch resistance. The film had a documentary style that owed much to *Target for Tonight*, and won praise for its realistic approach, as well as two Oscar nominations (for 'Best Effects' and 'Best Screenplay'). A trio of propaganda films were released in September, all of them biopics of a sort. *The First of the Few* (1942) told the story of R. J. Mitchell, the inventor of the Supermarine Spitfire; and *The Young Mr Pitt* (1942) was a costume drama with contemporary overtones. But the biggest hit was Noel Coward's *In Which We Serve* (1942), the definitive Royal Navy film, which was based on the wartime exploits of Lord Mountbatten and his ship HMS *Kelly*. It is introduced as "the story of a ship" – though HMS *Torrin* is meant to represent all naval destroyers, just as her crew are meant to represent the men of the Royal Navy – with equal weight given to the lower ranks as well as the officers for the first time in a naval film. In the final scene, Coward's speech about "victory from defeat" and "strength through adversity" was aimed squarely at the audience, but the propaganda was wrapped in such terrific entertainment that the film topped a Mass Observation poll for the most popular film of the year. Nominated for two Academy Awards, it won Coward an 'honorary' Oscar and the New York Film Critics Circle Award for 'Best Film' of 1942.

The weekly five-minute films though had run their course, and it was decided to replace them with longer films, up to fifteen minutes, which would be released once a month. The first of these, *Lift Your Head, Comrade* (1943), told how German and Austrian anti-fascists, the Pioneer Corps, were fighting for the allies; though its message that there were 'friendly' Germans around may have been lost in cinemas where *Went the Day Well?* (1942) was playing. *Went the Day Well?* asked the question 'What if the Germans attempted to invade?' Though released too late for its message about remaining vigilant to be relevant, as the threat of invasion had passed, its violence and suspense had shock value in a film from Ealing studios. Reviews were mixed, and it did not do enough box-office business to trouble the *Kinematograph Weekly* annual surveys for either 1942 or 1943.

The beginning of 1943 brought good news on all fronts for the allies. The Eighth Army took Tripoli; the Americans made their first bombing raid over Germany; and the Germans surrendered to the Red Army at Stalingrad. It was not the best time to release a film whose key message of anti-isolationism was over a year out of date, but *Thunder Rock* (1942) – based on a 1939 stage play by Robert Ardrey – was released on 3 February. Scenes had been revised and reworked for the screen, and the critics were lukewarm about the changes. William Whitebait in *The New Statesman* wrote: "[If you have seen the play] the film is bound to be disappointing…" In April, a more pertinent film was released: *Desert Victory* (1943), an hour-long documentary about the Eighth Army's success in North Africa. Made by the Army Film and Photographic Unit and the RAF Production Unit, the actuality footage cost lives: four British army cameramen were killed, seven wounded, and six captured by the Germans. Their film though was as much a triumph as the victory it celebrated and it won the 1944 Oscar for 'Best Documentary'. *Monthly Film Bulletin* hailed it as 'the most notable film that has come from British filmmakers. [It is] as effective from the point of view of propaganda as it is successful from the points of view of cinematic art and factual narrative.'

From the triumphs of the services, the cinematic focus swung to uniformed civilians. *Fires Were Started* (1943), a feature-length film from the CFU, was a documentary-style tale of 'twenty-four hours with the Auxiliary Fire Service'. Real Fire Service personnel played the roles, with the result that some of the lines are unclear, and others are stilted. But the critical response was mainly directed at the effects: *Monthly Film Bulletin* wrote that 'the film fails to exploit the dramatic fury of acre upon acre of raging flames', while the *Daily Telegraph*'s Campbell Dixon felt that the action took 'an unconscionable amount of time to get started' and, when it did, 'the spectacle is disappointing'. The AFS also featured in Ealing's *The Bells Go Down* (1943), released only a few weeks later, with James Mason and Tommy Trinder in the lead roles. With a timeline ranging from the outbreak of war to the Blitz, the story had time to acknowledge the tensions between regular fire service personnel and the new recruits, and to cover some of the training involved. Made with the co-operation of the National Fire Service, the special effects, with flaming debris falling on and around the actors, and the use of real footage of blazing warehouses gave it a 'bigger scale' feel than the CFU film. *Monthly Film Bulletin*, which had been so unimpressed with *Fires Were Started*, wrote that this film was 'well above average, and thanks to a good story… and the tricks of cinematography, achieves its effect.'

The contribution of women to the war was explored in *The Gentle Sex* (1943), a Two Cities/Concanen film, which told the fictional story of seven new ATS recruits. Following them through basic training and in to service, the story was narrated by Leslie

Howard, who was killed shortly after the film's release when the Germans shot down his civilian airliner.

Meanwhile, Gainsborough pictures made sure that the Navy was not forgotten. *We Dive at Dawn* (1943) starred John Mills and Eric Portman in the fictional but gripping story of the submarine Sea Tiger and its mission to sink the German battleship Brandenburg. The absence of background music and the location shots in port enhance the film's documentary feel; while the scenes on shore are all set indoors, adding to the claustrophobic atmosphere established in the submarine. There are touches of black humour – "Talk about bundles for Britain," someone mutters, as they load anything that can float into the torpedo tubes – and a realistic feel when things go wrong. Nerves on edge, the captain loses his temper when the submarine cannot be kept level while he's trying to get the range on the Brandenburg, and both the captain and first officer have to repeat orders at crucial moments.

In June, the CFU asked the 'what if we'd been invaded?' question that had first been broached in *Went the Day Well?* (1942), but their 36-minute film took a very different approach. Inspired by a letter from Viktor Fischl, of the Czech Ministry of Information in London, *The Silent Village* (1943) showed how the massacre at Lidice might have happened in the Welsh mining village of Cwmgiedd, if the Nazis had managed to invade. The villagers play themselves, in naturalistic performances that seem unaware of the camera, their fate made more poignant by the music threaded through the film. 'Ar Hyd Y Nos' ('All through the Night') is heard as the resistance carry out their sabotage; later, the men sing the Welsh National Anthem as they are lined up to be shot. Wagner blasts triumphantly over images of blazing houses as the village is razed. In a coda to the main story, the people of Cwmgiedd vow that the name of Lidice has not been obliterated, but immortalised – and provide a reminder of why the war was worth fighting: "We have the power and the knowledge to liberate oppressed communities… to make sure there are no more Lidices."

Throughout the war, film characters had been allowed to criticise superior officers and the upper echelons of society. In *We Dive at Dawn*, John Mills' Lieutenant Taylor rants that "The trouble's at the top! Silly old buffers who couldn't run a regatta!"; and in *Went the Day Well?* it is the village squire who turns out to be a German sympathiser. But none of it had caused a fuss before *The Life and Death of Colonel Blimp* (1943) came along. Made in Technicolor with a running time of almost three hours (at a time when film stock was rationed), the film's title character was based on a newspaper cartoon that satirised military incompetence and establishment stalling. So the news that a film was to be made about the character caused enough alarm in Whitehall for Winston Churchill to become personally involved. Questions were asked about the possibility of prohibiting the film's release, but it was pointed out that a ban would make the British Government no better than the regime they were fighting. In fact, the film's 'Blimp' (named Clive Wynne-Candy for the screen) was a much more sympathetic character than the cartoon figure of fun he was based on, though the critics felt that the message was blurred. Cinemas promptly advertised it with hoardings saying: 'See the Banned film!' and the fuss doubtless led to people going to see the film who would not otherwise have bothered.

Cinematically, 1943 ended with two films that again emphasised the important work civilians were carrying out. Gainsborough's *Millions Like Us* (1943) starred Patricia

Roc as a young woman drafted in to do factory work, alongside Megs Jenkins and Anne Crawford. Though it did not shy away from showing some of the recruits complaining about their job (with the services regarded as being more glamorous), the message was that factory work was a vital and appreciated part of the war effort. The MoI assisted the production by arranging location work at the Castle Bromwich aircraft factory, adding a realistic feel to the fictional narrative.

A true story from the merchant navy provided the material for *San Demetrio London* (1943). The MV San Demetrio was an oil tanker that set off for Avonmouth at the end of October 1940. Torpedoed by a U-boat, she was at first abandoned, then re-boarded and salvaged by a half-dozen crewmen, including the second officer and chief engineer. An epic of teamwork and of triumph over the odds, the story was a gift for Ealing. Unfortunately for the real San Demetrio, she was repaired and returned to service, only to be sunk by another torpedo prior to the film's release.

By 1944, audiences were tiring of war films, and many commercial filmmakers turned their attention instead to more lightweight films about life on the home front, such as *This Happy Breed* and *A Canterbury Tale* (both 1944). But in April, another feature-length documentary from the armed forces was released. *Tunisian Victory* (1944) was directed by Frank Capra and filmed jointly by the Army Film and Photographic Unit and the US Service Film Units. With two narrators – one American, one British – the film followed up on *Desert Victory* (1943) with a reminder that the Eighth Army triumphs were just one part of a bigger plan. There is spectacular footage of the landings along the North African coast, and impressive battle scenes – though some footage had to be restaged and reshot by John Huston when the initial print was damaged. The saccharine quotient is much higher than in *Desert Victory*, notably in the Christmas scenes, and the cloying ending where a British and an American soldier swap ideas about post-war plans. "Bringing back the smiles to kids' faces" doesn't seem much of an ambition at the end of a campaign that cost 70,000 allied casualties! The North African campaign also provided the climax for *The Way Ahead* (1944), a Two Cities film that told the fictional account of a troop of reluctant draftees. It was well made and acted by all concerned – the cast included Stanley Holloway and David Niven. Unfortunately, as a tribute to 'the ordinary soldier', it was made redundant by a monumental piece of bad timing: it was released on 6 June 1944: D-Day.

Laurence Olivier's *The Chronicle History of King Henry the Fift with His Battell Fought at Agincourt in France* (1944) fared better. A stirring, patriotic riot of Technicolor, its story of victory against the odds matched the nation's mood perfectly. Even though it was the most expensive British production of the war, it still turned a handsome profit. Four Oscar nominations followed, along with two US Board of Review Awards, and the New York Film Critics Circle Award for Best Actor. Meanwhile, the RAF top brass felt that the important part their airmen had played in the D-Day landings had been overlooked, and were anxious to tell the public about it. Sir Arthur Harris, C-in-C Bomber Command, wrote to the Chief of Air Staff Sir Charles Portal in July 1944 about the 'lack of adequate or even reasonable credit to the RAF… for their efforts in the invasion'. *The Air Plan* (1944), made by the RAF Film Production Unit and narrated by Eric Portman, used gun-camera footage and scenes from airfields in France to show how the air force had been used to good effect in tactical support of the army. There is no mention though of Operation Taxable – the deception operation carried out on D-Day by

617 'Dambusters' Squadron. (Their planes dropped 'window' – metallic strips that confused the enemy's radar – over the Channel to fool the Germans into believing a large convoy was heading for the Pas-de-Calais.) It's possible that, at the time *The Air Plan* was made, the RAF wished to keep the method secret, in case it was needed again.

The RAF also featured in the last commercial film of the war to be set in the services – *The Way to the Stars*, which told the story of the personnel at a fictional airfield in South East England. The film's message was about sacrifice, and its sometime necessity, though it contained no combat sequences. Instead, the effect of the loss of the airmen was shown through the reactions of others – their ground crews, fellow flyers, and the people of the nearby village. Rosamund John loses two men (one her husband, the other a friend), yet she's able to tell John Mills, whose character has been dithering for four years over whether to marry the girl he loves, that it's all somehow worth it. The remaining propaganda films of the war years were filmed by the services. *The True Glory* (1945), filmed by the British Army Film Unit, and American and Allied Film Services, told the story of the allied landings from invasion preparations, through D-Day to Berlin. The film concentrates mainly on the British and American efforts, with the Commonwealth troops barely acknowledged in passing, though the commentary emphasises teamwork and co-operation. The setbacks as well as the breakthroughs of the campaign are covered and the film won an Oscar for 'Best Documentary Feature'. Teamwork and co-operation did not extend to the filming of the campaign in the Far East. After quibbling about who would film what, how and where the emphasis should be, the allies agreed to go their separate ways, film-wise, and the Army Film and Photographic Unit produced *Burma Victory* for release in late 1945.

The war ended with V-J Day on 2 September 1945. In Britain, Attlee had succeeded Churchill as Prime Minister, and people began to pick up the pieces of their lives and move on. The propaganda films had served their purpose and had developed from the patronising style of *The Lion Has Wings* to the 'all pull together' cross-class features of *In Which We Serve* and *San Demetrio London*. Even without much in the way of central direction, they fell into distinct phases: early 'gung-ho' flag-wavers; the 'resistance' genre; the uniformed services; 'everyone can help'; and the retrospective 'didn't we do well' summaries of the campaigns.

Of course they were 'blatant propaganda' (as they are sometimes dismissively described). That was the point. They were not disguised as something else – the audiences at the time were well aware that they were watching films designed to boost their morale and increase their efforts to win the war. But at their best, these films were not just propaganda. They were entertaining in their own right – and the best of them still are.

"DON'T COME TO ME WITH POLITICAL MATERIAL!"

Joseph Goebbels and Nazi Propaganda

ELLEN CHESHIRE

In 2007, ex-Roxy Music star Bryan Ferry had to make an open apology on his website stating that he finds 'the politics of fascism and Nazism to be abhorrent'.

A few days earlier the British press had reprinted sections of an interview he had given to the German newspaper *Welt am Sonntag* in which he said, 'My God, the Nazis knew how to put themselves in the limelight and present themselves. Leni Riefenstahl's movies and Albert Speer's buildings and the mass parades and the flags – just amazing. Really beautiful.' In his apology he put this comment into context: 'I apologise unreservedly for any offence caused by my comments on Nazi iconography, which were solely made from an art history perspective.'

The furore his comments on the Nazis' iconography and the subsequent media outrage highlights the dilemma of admiring an aesthetic whilst loathing the ideology. Therefore this chapter should not be seen in any way as an endorsement or glamorisation of the Nazi Party and its policies. Studying any period of history through its filmic output offers an insight into its past, which in this case may offer an understanding of how a well-orchestrated propaganda machine affected a whole generation of German citizens, and how these films and their use can be used as, to borrow the title of Laurence Rees' remarkable documentary series, 'a warning from history'. We will explore the filmic propaganda of the Nazis: cinema newsreels, key feature films (*Triumph of the Will/Triumph des Willens* (1935), *Olympia* (aka *Olympia 1. Teil – Fest der Völker* (*Festival of the People*) and *Olympia 2. Teil – Fest der Schönheit* (*Festival of Beauty*) (1938), *The Eternal Jew/Der Ewige Jude*, *Jud Süss/Jud Süß* (both 1940), *Münchhausen* (1943) and *Kolberg* (1945) and material transmitted on Germany's burgeoning television network.

Propaganda can take various forms, ranging from overt attempts to influence the public to covert means of persuasion through repetition. It is frequently thought of negatively and has become associated with ideas, facts or allegations deliberately spread to further a cause or to damage an opposing cause. Germany was not alone in producing propaganda throughout World War 2 – Karen McCreedy has written in this book of the British film industry's propaganda output during this same conflict.

In the introduction to *WWII Film and History*, Chambers and Culbert situate films' impact on World War 2: '…[it] was a cinematic war. From the outset, governments and national motion picture industries used moving images, newsreels, documentaries and feature films to help mobilize populations for war… Indeed the leaders of most of the major nations were all film enthusiasts. Roosevelt, Churchill, Stalin, Mussolini and Hitler had personal projectors and private screening rooms for nightly viewing of dramatic and documentary films.' [1]

But of all the people working through this period in the area of film production, it is Joseph Goebbels who has become synonymous with the term propaganda. The body of material that was produced under him has been much debated, studied, admired and contested. Each government has its own official slant on the way in which its 'history' is viewed through its artistic output. Artists (across all mediums) may offer opposing or endorsing views, but it is film's unique reproducibility and permanence that makes it one of the most significant art forms. A painting is limited to those who can visit the gallery in which it is housed (reproduced images in books or magazines never offering the same experience), a play to those who can visit the theatre during its usually short life. Books and poetry, although transportable, require more effort and commitment. Cinema however can transcend cultural, economical, social and education boundaries bringing people together for a collective common experience.

In January 1933, Hitler became chancellor, and that first year saw the introduction of two major factors that contributed to what was to follow in the area of film production under the Third Reich. Firstly, 1933 saw a mass exodus of creative personnel from Germany, fleeing an industry they had helped to build, but yet could not stay to see manipulated to promote the extremes of National Socialism. Many of Germany's innovative directors, musicians, composers, screenwriters, actors and technicians fled. Not everyone left. Some remained whether it was through choice, necessity or the belief that the more extreme policies would dissipate now that the Nazis were in power. Of course, there were those who admired Adolf Hitler and believed that National Socialism was the way to ensure Germany's economic, political and social growth. Those left behind were largely young and, lacking the influence or prestige to forge new careers elsewhere, were ambitious and eager to please.

The second factor would have a far greater impact: Hitler bestowed the position of Minister of Public Enlightenment and Propaganda for the State Chamber of Culture on Dr. Joseph Goebbels, and so brought art, music, theatre, authorship, the press, radio and film under the auspices of one man. Despite overseeing all these cultural forms, Goebbels' main focus and legacy was to be film. Fritz Hippler, director of *The Eternal Jew* said of Goebbels, 'He saw film as the medium best able to work powerfully on the subconscious. He placed film far above all other mediums like the visual arts and the press.' [2]

On 28 March 1933, Goebbels outlined the approach film would take towards the goal of public enlightenment and propaganda. In a speech to members of the film industry he said: "Ignore blatant ideological messages, concentrate on visual artistry, for this is vital to the communication of ideology. Production values, scale and cinematography suggest the power, solidity and vision of the state that produces it."

To formalise the work of the State Chamber of Culture in the area of film, the Reich Film Law of 1934 saw the establishment of a censorship committee, which allowed German films to be judged in six categories:

1. particularly valuable politically and artistically
2. valuable politically and artistically
3. valuable politically
4. valuable artistically
5. culturally valuable
6. educationally valuable

In addition the Film Law ensured that the Reich film supervisors:

- would examine all film scripts
- had full authority to reject any
- could advise on the selection and adaptation of film stories
- on completion all films had to receive a permit. These could be withheld if
  it deemed the film 'likely to endanger the vital interests of the state or public
  order or safety, or offend National Socialists, religions, moral or artistic feeling,
  to have a corrupting influence, or to prejudice Germany's prestige or German
  relationships with foreign countries'.

Despite the framework of judging films on their political, cultural, educational and artistic value Goebbels felt that entertainment was the best propaganda and as a consequence the vast majority of the feature films produced by the Third Reich had no overt propaganda messages. His aim was to entertain and get people off the streets and away from their homes. He wanted films to focus not on information and facts but on emotion and entertainment. In 1951, the Allied Control Commission examined the 1,097 feature films produced under the Third Reich and described only 141 of them as being politically debatable.

Wilfred Von Oven, attaché to Goebbels (1943-1945), recalls Goebbels' reaction to the 1933 film *Hitler Youth Quex*, in which a member of the Hitler Youth dies for his country: 'He kept telling his film people "Don't come to me with political material". All political films turned out dreadfully. He kept repeating "Hands off political films".' [3] As he soon saw, films featuring overt propaganda of an obvious nationalistic, political or patriotic nature were not well received critically or commercially. He solved the problem of adverse criticism in the press by banning all cultural criticism and the commercial problem by ensuring that there were always spoonfuls of sugar to help the message go down.

Historical films were a popular genre for entertaining and promoting the desired messages. From these epics audiences could draw parallels between previous periods of history and those of the current situation. These included biographies of famous men or women who could be seen as alternate Führers: *Joan the Girl/Das Mädchen Johanna* (1935) saw Joan of Arc as a leader who saved her people from despair; Frederick the Great in films such as *The Great King/Der Große König* (1942); and *Bismarck* (1940) in which the newly appointed prime minister defeats the Austrians, outwits the French and brings about the unification of a strong and powerful Germany. Another strand was the historic feature with a strong anti-British slant such as *Uncle Kruger/Ohm Krüger* (1941) set during the Boer War or *Titanic* (1943) which saw a German first officer spending most of the voyage observing that the arrogance of the captain and the shipping line will end in disaster.

Goebbels was the minister who travelled the most regularly meeting soldiers, the wounded and the homeless. But these meetings were not altruistic; their aim was to monitor the pulse of the ordinary German, thereby ensuring that all the media gave them the stories they wanted to hear and see. It is then perhaps ironic that for audiences studying this period of filmmaking today, the two most well-known feature films are Leni Riefenstahl's *Triumph of the Will* and *Olympia*, as they were not part of the canon of films overseen by Goebbels, but were commissioned by Hitler direct using general Nazi Party funds.

Riefenstahl's directorial debut *The Blue Light/Das Blaue Licht* (1932) was an artistic triumph, if not a commercial one. Hitler, who had long admired her as an actress, thought that she could capture the spectacle and romanticism of the Party. Her perceived lack of political interest meant that she could see the events through an inexpert eye, focusing on the overarching themes and power of the events and convert these real events into theatrical presentations that would move and inspire an audience regardless of their level of engagement with the politics.

Their first collaboration was a short film of the Nazi party's 1933 Nuremberg rally, *Victory of Faith* (1934). A year later, Hitler commissioned her to make a feature length film of the 1934 rally *Triumph of the Will* (1935). Another short followed, *Day of Freedom, Our Army* (1935) that focused on the German Army – a montage-driven piece which juxtaposes images of artillery preparation with the mythic images of earth and sky, fire and water. Her final film was *Olympia* (1938), a four-hour celebration of the 1936 Berlin Olympic Games. *Triumph of the Will* has been described as 'an impressive spectacle of Germany's adherence to Hitler', a 'Nazi masterpiece' and 'a masterpiece of romanticised propaganda' and is an oft cited example of propaganda at its most effective and manipulative.

Hitler's direct involvement meant Riefenstahl had huge resources at her disposal: an unlimited budget, a crew of 120 and between 30 and 40 cameras. It stands as a powerful artistic representation of the ideas in Hitler's book *Mein Kampf* (work, extreme nationalism, belief in corporative state socialism, a private army, a youth cult, the use of propaganda and the submission of all decisions to the supreme leader). Riefenstahl has consistently claimed that it was 'Not a documentary but a work of art, [there was] no commentary in the normal sense of the word. There's no commentator to explain everything. That's the way it differs from a documentary or a propaganda film. If it were propaganda, as many say, there'd be a commentator to explain the significance and value of the occasion. This wasn't the case.' [4] In contrast, Susan Sontag in her

Kolberg
1945

© NSDAP/
The Kobal
Collection

essay entitled 'Fascinating Fascism', claims that it is the 'most successful, most purely propagandistic film ever made, whose very conception negates the possibility of the film-makers having an aesthetic or visual concept independent of propaganda.' [5]

Riefenstahl has always denied that her films were designed as propaganda; they were merely film records of actual events. In an interview in 1964, Riefenstahl makes this clear: 'If you see this film again today you ascertain that it doesn't contain a single reconstructed scene. Everything in it is true. And it contains no tendentious commentary at all. It is history. A pure historical film... It is film-vérité. It reflects the truth that was then in 1934, history. It is therefore a documentary. Not a propaganda film. Oh! I know very well what propaganda is. That consists of recreating events in order to illustrate a thesis, or, in the face of certain events, to let one thing go in order to accentuate another. I found myself, me, at the heart of an event, which was the reality of a certain time and a certain place. My film is composed of what stemmed from that.' [6]

It cannot be denied that *Triumph of the Will* is a record of an event. It is a film of an actual event which occurred where and when the film says it did. In an account of the making of the film, Riefenstahl writes that she was involved in the rally's planning and conceived the event with filming in mind, as Susan Sontag reiterates in her article 'Fascinating Fascism': 'The rally was planned not only as a spectacular mass meeting, but as a spectacular propaganda film.' However, by 1993, Riefenstahl claimed that she was not involved in the design of the rally – 'I just observed and tried to film it well. The idea that I helped to plan it is downright absurd.' [7]

However, it has generally been accepted that the Nuremberg Rally was staged for the cameras, rather than the cameras having to accommodate the action: as was the case with the cinema newsreel crews. The film was cut to rhythm in time to anthems and music, creating choreographed images of endless numbers of men in uniform, marching in to and out of abstract shapes and patterns filmed from a variety of angles, reducing the men to geometrical designs. The passionate music, feeling and emotion builds up to a climatic frenzied finale when Hitler takes the stand. The dramatic intensity of the event was accentuated by the composition and editing. It is this deliberate manipulation of emotion that makes this film so effective. It is not only the messages in the film that were slanted towards Nazi beliefs and ideals, but the mise-en-scène, editing and music all combine to create a hypnotic and visually rich emotional experience, which would have undoubtedly influenced more people than, say, the crude propaganda films of Dr. Fritz Hippler or Veit Harlan.

The film commences with Hitler's arrival in Nuremberg by plane. Parallels can be made between Hitler's arrival through the skies and the descent of a god coming to meet his people – this is heightened by the endless views of clouds, the plane's shadow moving relentlessly over the sunlit streets of Nuremberg. Shots of the city's people in the streets staring up with a look of awed expectation on their faces. Our sense of perspective and reality is lost in the views, the music and the steady regal pace of the moving plane. The music played as Hitler's plane lands, the bands and singing, the beauty of Nuremberg, the hysteria of the crowds with their arms outstretched to greet him, combine to make up a display of Nazi passion and obsession. It is this emotional response of the people in the film and the emotional response the audience gains from these majestic shots that are at once inspirational, seductive and horrifying.

Throughout the remainder of the film one is stirred by the film's mix of power and certainty. The endless swastikas marching towards you, rows upon rows of Nazis in half profile staring mesmerically towards the 'great' leader, close-ups of Hitler, the constant movement of the camera, views from many angles, the resonance of banners, trumpets and torchlight processions seen through the waves of the giant flags, and the inter-cutting of shots of the isolated heroic father figure of Hitler, watching over his men.

Equally famous, and considered far less political, was Riefenstahl's coverage of the 1936 Olympic Games in Berlin. The four-hour epic *Olympia* (1938) offered a glorious view of Olympic athletes, which remains today powerful and popular. During the Olympics, the Government's anti-Semitic policies were toned down, the streets were cleared of Jews, disabled and beggars and the violence towards them ceased. The images in the newsreels and for the visiting dignitaries and sportsmen were ones of a prosperous Germany in the midst of an economic miracle. Riefenstahl's *Olympia* helped to perpetuate this façade. There are conflicting stories on how the commission for filming was given. Riefenstahl claimed she was approached by an International Committee coordinating the Games. However, it is now generally accepted it was Hitler, yet again, who made the suggestion for her to film the games. He once more provided the funding.

Her coverage of the Games was extensive. Editing took over a year. A key criticism of the film as a document of the Games is the film focuses more on the glorification of the human form than the sporting events. The athletes are kept at a distance, with the focus kept on their physiques and rippling muscles instead of their athletic achievements. For example, one can see an athlete preparing to put the shot in great detail, but not the shot in itself.

The message of the film is not political, in the way *The Triumph of the Will* is, but does focus on two of the seven main elements of Nazi ideology Hitler outlines in his book *Mein Kampf*. 1) His belief in the perfect Aryan-German race of athletic beautiful people, epitomised by the top athletes competing with each other for ultimate supremacy. 2) Hitler's ideology of a Youth Cult, emphasising sports and paramilitary outdoor activities. These, linked with shots of Nazi insignia on flags, bells and the athletes' shirts, the emphasis on the German activities and victories, the lingering shots of the triumphs of German sportsmen/women (lasting longer than those of other countries) combine to create an emotional patriotic film.

Riefenstahl's ambition when filming these two full-length feature films may well have been to create an artistic emotional view of two events in German history through the genre of 'documentary'. Susan Sontag's view in 'Fascinating Fascism' is that Riefenstahl was an artist whose personal preoccupations were primarily artistic and technical, not political, but that her films were used by Hitler and the Nazi party for their own political games. After the war she was arrested but never convicted of war crimes. Riefenstahl said her biggest regret was meeting Hitler: 'It was the biggest catastrophe of my life. Until the day I die people will keep saying, "Leni is a Nazi".' [8]

Far less contested are two films created as outright specific attacks on the Jewish community: *The Eternal Jew* (1940) and *Jud Süss*. These two overtly anti-Semitic propaganda films were created with the specific purpose of reinforcing prejudices and stereotypes, and to help make solutions to the 'Jewish problem' far more palatable to the German people. Indeed, so powerful is *The Eternal Jew*, that Richard Taylor feels that the film '…builds to a climax that can make even a Jew feel anti-Semitic'. [9] These two films clearly outline two different approaches to the use of film as a means of affecting an audience. The circulation of both these films is now strictly controlled.

In 1940, Goebbels, in close collaboration with Hitler, ordered the production of a direct propaganda film against the Jews. Fritz Hippler would direct one of the most infamous films of the period, a 'documentary film about world Jewry'. Following the war Hippler would be interrogated by the Allies, but ultimately not charged with war crimes for the contribution this film made to the acceptance of the Nazis' policies towards the Jews. He was an SS officer and was considered to be second only to Goebbels within the film industry. After the war it is purported [10] he worked on some West German documentaries with militant nationalist tendencies. It is not until an interview shown in the 2000 German documentary series *Holocaust* that the 90-year-old Hippler finally admitted that *The Eternal Jew* was "the most disgraceful example of anti-Semitism".

Triumph of the Will
1935

© NSDAP/
The Kobal
Collection

Speaking in 1992, he said "…with this film Hitler wanted to prove that the Jews were a parasitic race within mankind who had to be separated from the rest". [11] Using the conceit of documentary objectivity, Hippler combined archival material (both fiction and documentary) with newly-filmed sequences from the Polish ghettoes. These images were later combined with non-fiction and fiction film material, such as the Jewish actor Peter Lorre playing a child murderer in *M* (1931) and a sequence from the American film *The House of Rothschild* (1934) with misleading German subtitles.

Eventually it took 13 months to edit. Hippler oversaw the restructuring of the film in a dozen different ways, as it was decided what the film's tone should actually be. Various voiceovers were written and recorded which Hippler said "grew progressively more bloodthirsty and aggressive". [12] Finally a very aggressive tone was devised: "The civilised Jews that we know in Germany give us only an incomplete picture of their racial character. This film shows us genuine shots of the Polish ghettoes. It shows us the Jews as they really are, before they conceal themselves behind the mask of the civilised European."

It is now generally felt Hitler himself insisted on including the infamous inter-cutting of images between the men in the ghetto with rats in the sewers, over which the German actor Harry Giese narrates: "Wherever rats appear they bring destruction to the land – they destroy human property and food stuffs. They spread illnesses like leprosy, typhoid, cholera and dysentery. Rats are cunning, cowardly and inhuman among animals they represent deviousness and subversive destruction. Not much different from Jews among people." When the film opened in Berlin, the film was shown twice a day in two different versions. Contemporary advertisements exclaimed 'Since additional original material of Jewish animal slaughters will be shown at the 6.30 performance those of a sensitive disposition are recommended to see the 4 o'clock performances. Like-wise women will only be admitted to the 4 o' clock performance.' The film was a disaster at the box office. Goebbels was not at all surprised. On 5 July 1940, he commented in his diary: 'The Führer wants more polemic material in the script. I would rather have the pictures speak for themselves. And confine the script to explain what the audience would not otherwise understand. I consider this to be more effective, the viewer does not see the art in it.'

Commissioned after *The Eternal Jew* began filming, but released three months earlier was another anti-Jewish film, an historical drama *Jud Süss* directed by Veit Harlan and starring the 'Marilyn Monroe' of German Cinema and wife of the director, Kristina Söederbaum (Dorothea), Ferdinand Marian (Oppenheimer) and Werner Kraus (Rabbi Loew and Sekretar Levy). Inspired by the novel by Wilhelm Hauff, *Jud Süss*, set in the 18th century, sees a manipulative and conniving Jewish businessman (Oppenheimer) inveigling himself the position of treasurer within the court of the Duke of Württembürg. Oppenheimer cuts his hair and wears Christian clothes so he can move among the German people unnoticed – an echo of the opening narration of *The Eternal Jew* and the common fear at the time of Jews assimilating themselves among the civilised Europeans. Oppenheimer continues to win the favour of the Duke persuading him to repeal the law prohibiting Jews from living in Württemberg. At the film's climax he imprisons (and later tortures) the fiancé of the embodiment of German Aryan womanhood Dorothea, leaving him free to seduce and rape her. Following the Duke's death, Oppenheimer is condemned to death for having 'carnal knowledge of a Christian woman'. Söederbaum in an interview in 1992 said she lived in a "golden cage and was protected from seeing anything of the war". But "…looking at the films now, having seen the images from the concentration camps, I see a different film". [13]

Despite the film's 18th century setting, audience research of the time showed that they were able to make the link to 20th century Germany. They highlighted the stereotyped notions of Jews as being materialistic, immoral, cunning and untrustworthy, being portrayed in two caricatures: the unknown Jew moving among polite society unseen and unnoticed and the overt stereotyped Jews shown as dirty, physically unattractive complete with hooked nose and shuffling gait. On its release the audiences' enjoyment of the film made the removal of Jews from society more acceptable. Following film screenings there were reports of anti-Jewish violence. The film was a success within the Third Reich and became the number one film of the 1939-1940 season and seen by over twenty million people. It was shown to SS units about to be sent against Jews, to non-Jewish populations of areas where Jews were about to be deported and to concentration camp guards. After the war the film's director, Veit Harlan, was charged with participating in the anti-Semitic movement and aiding the Nazis, but was acquitted after successfully arguing that it was his superiors that interfered with his films. He continued making films until his death in the 1960s.

By 1942, it was becoming increasingly hard to convince German people they were winning the war. Goebbels' response was to go full colour with an extravagant fairytale featuring gallant officers, beautiful woman in harems, exotic fruit and far-away worlds. Made to celebrate the 25th anniversary of the UfA studios, *Münchhausen* was directed by Josef von Baky. Inspired by Alexander Korda's *Thief of Bagdad* (1940), David O Selznick's *Gone with the Wind* (1939) and Walt Disney's *Snow White* (1937), *Münchhausen* was the fourth German film shot in colour. [14] The film cost 5 million Reich marks. Hans Albers, playing Baron Munchausen, was the biggest star of the day and the film features many of the UfA's roster of stars in cameo or supporting roles. The film was designed to be a real celebration of the studios, colour, technology and movie magic.

The film opens in an opulent stately home in the midst of an 18th century ball. Sophie (Marina von Ditmar) is flirting with Baron Münchausen (Hans Albers). Lulled into the setting, language and location of 18th-century Lower Saxony, one then discovers that this is a party in 1940s Germany when the Baron switches on an electric light and Sophie runs from the party and jumps into a motor car. The following day Sophie and fiancé Freiherr von Hartenfeld (Hans Brausewetter), fascinated by the tales of the current Baron's famous ancestor, gather to hear the tales of the Baron and his servant Christian (Hermann Speelmanns) who travel from 18th century Lower Saxony to St Petersburg and the court of Empress Catherine the Great, to the harems of the Sultan in Turkey, to Venice and finally the moon. As the story draws to an end and we return to the 1940s, it soon becomes apparent that the Baron fails to relate his ancestor's adventures but his own. Ultimately, despite the magnificent adventures, it is a sad and lonely life where those he loves die as he carries on his eternal life.

Münchhausen is an episodic film in which the set pieces are lavishly mounted, but the film does not hang together, but the fantasy, frippery and fun epitomises Goebbels' notion that films should primarily entertain, with political messages buried beneath the shiny surface. At the beginning of the flashback the Baron returns triumphant from his overseas adventures and is welcomed by the whole town waving, laughing and celebrating –

reminiscent of the newsreel footage of Hitler and the invading armies arriving to a warm welcome. But it is hard to draw further allusions between the Baron and the Hitler portrayed by Goebbels. This leader openly drinks, gambles and womanises.

The Baron's servant Christian has the perfect Aryan family of five blonde-haired children and a jolly wife anxiously awaiting his safe return. Christian is surprised to see a child that he had not seen before and is told that he is "a souvenir of his last trip home". This could be seen as a nod towards the Nazis' eugenics policy, which itself was infiltrated into a number melodrama films and newsreels. Richard Grunberger [15] highlights a similar incident in *Leave on Parole* in which '…a lieutenant allows the men on troop training bound for the front six unscheduled hours home leave – in return for their promise not to desert. What startled the public was the officer's emphatic order to one of the men to "make sure you give your wife a child during those few hours!".'

The Russians are depicted as drunken, decadent brawlers and all other nationalities are shown as comic posing no threat to the sophisticated, cultured and beautiful Germans. Based on the novels of Raaspe and Burger, the screenplay was written by Erich Kastner, who had been banned from working in the industry. His books were amongst those burnt in 1933, so he wrote the screenplay under the pseudonym Berthold Bürger. After the war he continued writing, most notably in the area of children's literature. The womanising baron might be seen as a satirical dig at the private life of the Führer (who had a great following among women) and in *Great German Films* Ott asks: 'Did Kastner slip anti-National Socialist criticisms into the screenplay? When the devious Cagliostro suggests to Münchausen that they go into partnership, the Baron replies, "There is one thing we two will never agree upon. Principally, you want to rule, I want to live. Adventure, art, foreign lands and beautiful women, I want to use all of that but you want to abuse it." Or when the Sultan informs Münchausen that his religion is the better one, Münchausen answers: "Who can decide what is better when hardly anyone knows what is good?" And how should we interpret Casanova's declaration to Princess Isabella in the Venice sequence: "The state inquisition has 10,000 eyes and arms, and it has the power to act justly or unjustly." Does Cagliostro represent Hitler and should the comments of Münchausen and Casanova be construed as veiled criticisms of the National Socialist State? If so, Kastner risked a great deal given Goebbels' personal involvement in this prestigious production.' [16] The film opened on 5 March 1943 in Berlin, before going to general release in June. The fantasy and magic of the film ensured that it was a critical and popular film at a time when morale was low, a perfect antidote to the devastation that the German people were finding themselves surrounded by.

Berlin was in ruins and Goebbels was convinced audiences wanted to be diverted from the reality of life; therefore he commissioned the colourful and spectacular *Kolberg*. This film as well as being the most lavish production to date, was to feature a more overt political message supporting the popular party slogans of the day: 'One people! One Reich! One Führer!' and 'The community before the individual'. Veit Harlan, who had worked marvels across both feature films and newsreels, most notably *Jud Süss*, was hired to bring this true event to the big screen. Goebbels wished to draw out the parallels between the people of Kolberg (who put up great resistance against Napoleon's army) and those in present-day Germany. Kristina Söederbaum was cast as the innocent village maiden Maria, but unlike her naiveté when filming *Jud Süss* three years earlier, this time she '...found it ridiculous to be filming when the enemy was coming nearer and nearer – one knew about the war and everything that was happening...' [17]

With a budget of 8.5 million Reich marks this was an extraordinary production which featured 6,000 horses, 4,000 sailors and 187,000 soldiers diverted from the frontline to appear as extras – this was more men than had appeared in the original battle! Goebbels' attaché reported that Goebbels felt '...it was more important that the soldiers act in this film than fight at the front – which was no longer worth doing – since we were in the middle of total collapse'. [18]

Set in 1806-1807 when Napoleon had overrun much of the German states, the small city of Kolberg resisted and fought back. Loosely based on historical fact (some 'facts' were omitted, such as the British helping the beleaguered city of Kolberg), the film was to focus on the everyday heroism particularly of Nettlebeck (Heinrich George) and his niece Maria (Söederbaum). The film saw an untrained army stand up and vanquish its enemies, an act that Goebbels hoped would be repeated: "They can burn our houses but not our hearts", "Better to be burned in ruins than to capitulate" Nettlebeck cries out to the townsfolk. To his niece he says "You sacrificed all that you had here, Maria. But it was not in vain... The greatest things are always born out of pain. You stayed at your post, you did your duty. You too have won. You are a great woman."

Von Gneisenau (Horst Kaspar), a soldier who breaking ranks had helped to train the townsfolk, makes a dynamic and impassioned speech (again, epitomising Goebbels' intentions) before the French arrive at the city walls: "No love is more sacred than love for one's country. No joy is sweeter than that of freedom. You know our fate if we do not win this battle. Regardless of the sacrifice each individual must make, what matters is the sacred trust for which we will fight and win, unless we wish see cease being (Russians and) Germans... The best defence is attack." This is deliberate, consistent and controlled propaganda – a call to arms for everyone to pick up a rifle, pitchfork, spade or cooking pot to fight the enemy. Despite its big production and major German stars, very few people saw the film as it was released only months before the end of the war. Its reception with audiences is unknown but given the statement Goebbels made in a speech in March 1937 that "Propaganda becomes ineffective the moment we are aware of it", it is unlikely this film would have rallied citizens in the way he had hoped.

On 30 January 1945, the twelfth anniversary of the Nazi seizure of power, the film was premiered in Berlin. On 17 April, Goebbels showed the film to his colleagues at the ministry. At the end of the film his attaché said he turned to his staff saying that in 100 years a similar film would be made about their exploits, adding: "Gentlemen, don't you want to play a part in the film to be brought back to life in 100 years' time? I can assure you that it will be a fine and elevating picture, for the sake of this prospect it is worth standing firm. Hold out now so that 100 years hence the audience doesn't hoot and whistle when you appear on the screen." [19] Goebbels killed his wife, children and himself 14 days later.

The overt nature of the propaganda message seen in *Kolberg* was deemed unusual for the feature film genre. Goebbels saw effective propaganda as manipulating audiences on an emotional level. This indirect approach was the method he favoured for feature films, leaving the more direct approach for newsreels. Here he employed a systematic barrage of symbols, words, music, gestures, slogans, flags and uniforms to manipulate the attitudes, beliefs and actions of the people watching. Regardless of whatever the main feature film was, no audience could avoid seeing the newsreels. It was persistence rather than artistry that ensured that these newsreels were Goebbels' most powerful weapon. Here he freed himself of the constraints imposed by his desire for film to primarily entertain creating a constant stream of material with the aim of total manipulation, domination and indoctrination of the German people.

The repetitive thematic strands occur across all newsreel material produced: a weakness of Goebbels' propaganda was to adjust the style of stories produced to reflect the national mood or situation. Continually reinforcing key messages – working together we can achieve anything, German efficiency and superiority, British incompetence and criminality and Russian inferiority – were frequent news stories and phrases:

"Mr. Churchill – the most wanted war criminal of all time."

"The traitorous British pilots attacked Berlin during the night again and destroyed workers' homes with their senseless bombings."

"British pirates indiscriminately bomb German territories."

"[those] dreadful democratic warmongerers."

"German planes are the most advanced but British searchlights scour the skies in vain."

In 1940, newsreel production soared and the length of each one was quadrupled to 45 minutes. These newsreels were designed for domestic and overseas consumption. 1,000 copies were printed each week in fifteen languages. Within the year (by January 1941), 2,400 newsreel copies were produced each week reaching 30 million people. In *Great German Films*, Ott said: 'An official source in 1940 declared that the newsreels could not produce an objective truth but by using all decent means, it reveals that side of truth that is necessary to propagate in the interests of the German people.' [20]

The last newsreel to be shown was in April 1945 and lasted 11.5 minutes and only contained ten stories. It is the newsreel footage that is now most widely available commercially and features in documentaries about Hitler and the Nazis. This legacy offering a powerful visual record of Goebbels' love of Hitler and the lengths he went to make Hitler's dream of getting 'you all out of this poverty – if we all join in'. What is less well-known was Germany's use of television as a way of disseminating seemingly more innocent and low-key journalist led stories, light entertainment and consumer programming.

In March 1935, the Reich's Broadcasting Director, Eugen Hadamovsky, announced the launch of German television, Deutscher Fernseh-Rundfunk. Over the next nine years it broadcast programming on behalf of the Third Reich. Britain did not start broadcasting until almost a year later and stopped from the day war was declared on 3 September 1939. They did not resume until 7 June 1946. The Director's agenda was to promote the wonders of both German technology and National Socialism. In his March 1935 announcement he said "At this very hour the German broadcasting industry is called upon to fulfil its greatest and most sacred mission of imprinting an un-erasable image of the future on every German heart."

Unlike the more polished, professional and sophisticated cinematic newsreels and feature films, the output for television was much closer to the experience of German people. The television schedule was dominated by news and entertainment. Entertainment came in the form of leisure and variety music shows. A stream of cookery, health, beauty, gardening programmes aimed at the housewife highlighted ways of economising and making do in the war-deprived times, mixed in with music variety shows, journalistic reports and filming of live events. The number of people able to receive television was minute and therefore it is largely considered a small cog in the propaganda machine and little is mentioned in most studies of the subject. With its limited audience and technical infancy, the programme makers and journalists were largely left to their own devices. Heinz Riek, a TV journalist, said "No one gave any orders, but there was no critical journalism." He was unaware of any imposed censorship, but acknowledged that everyone involved was "Completely in tune with the party line… [Therefore] the political leaders did not have to bother monitoring or censorship." [21]

Initially broadcasting for a few hours a day, a few days a week, staff learned on the job. It was the 1936 Olympic Games that was to give television technicians the confidence and subject matter to develop the network further. TV parlours in large public spaces were set up with the express purpose of feeding material from the Games out to the masses. Over 160,000 people visited the parlours to watch the Games not quite live, but almost. The picture quality was poor (like looking through mist) and the cameramen, excluded from the best positions by newsreel or feature film crews, were often unable to provide the best coverage. Viewers often almost saw the winning shot. But the technology of near-live broadcast was a great achievement, especially impressive to the large number of overseas visitors in Berlin at the time.

The journalism was not sophisticated, and though they had the poorest angles and shots, when pushed into an obscure angle for a rally, meeting or grand event, the camera continued filming. The legacy is long unedited takes, views of these events not seen in the well-conceived and polished newsreels or in Riefenstahl's documentaries. Alison Graham writing in the *Radio Times* said that one of the sequences she found most memorable was '…of Mussolini on a visit to Germany casting around desperately for someone to rescue him from a hectoring Goebbels. He looks for all the world like a bored party guest.' By going out to capture what the commentary in *Secret History: TV in the Third Reich* described as "Wholesome, intimate and everyday – this was the carefully constructed image presented by German television, they also unwittingly captured what, in hindsight, was the chilling reality of National Socialism".

On 9 August 1936, one could settle down to watch a documentary about bridal schools set up to prepare young women to be perfect German wives. Elsewhere one saw documentaries about scientists conducting anthropological and race experiments. In 1938, production and transmission moved to larger studios with five sound stages, allowing them to branch out into new areas including TV dramas, especially written for the medium. In 1939, the post office and national radio planned further expansions of its TV broadcast service, but with the outbreak of war, these plans were put on hold.

However by 1940, Goebbels had lost interest in television, but supervisor Kurt Hanzmann wanted TV to be classified as essential to the war effort. Entertaining the troops was the plan: 'We want to make you happy and smile', their manifesto. Live theatre performances were held with soldiers in the audience and eleven military hospitals were linked up to receive television. Over the following four years, 100 live shows were transmitted. Over its nine years of transmission, thousands of hours of programming were broadcast featuring rallies, Nazi insignia, staff talking, driving, marching, meetings, pageantry of the Nazi regime, all sitting alongside domestic programming.

What is largely shown today in documentaries covering the period are those of orchestrated images of soldiers marching, waving crowds and large-scale events, but it is television's ability to broadcast the smaller-scale domestic visions of Germany beamed directly into sitting rooms which offer visions of a far more compelling and sinister nature: a jovial man with a fixed grin, immaculate dinner suit complete with bow-tie, looks to all the world the epitome of elegance. Held in a tight head and shoulder shot he talks directly to camera and therefore to you. He could be about to announce the next piece of music to be played but instead, without the grin shifting says the following: "It makes me very happy to see that everything is so harmonious today. Granted there are still a few sad notes and people playing out of tune. And maybe some who would prefer to march to a different drum. Take those so-called 'foreign-exchanged musicians'. We don't beat about the bush with them, do we? They're sent to 'concert camps' for their further education where they are taught to sing for their supper. And there they stay until they've changed their tune and can play along."

On 30 January 1945, Hitler broadcast his last radio address "…however grave the crisis may be at the moment, through our unalterable will, our readiness for sacrifice, and our own abilities we will overcome this crisis". But by this time even Goebbels' propaganda could not disguise the truth that Hitler had become a physical wreck. The last newsreel shots reveal Hitler's severe shaking paralysis in his right arm, a shuffling gait and blue glasses. Despite this he had lost none of his charisma.

The Nazis' use of the moving image has left a remarkable legacy not only of their own history, but on the history of cinema. The elusive question of how film can be used to affect and manipulate audiences has been one that is studied and leaves many with an open mistrust of the art form.

Recent outcries over a British production company deliberately editing documentary footage to make it appear as though the Queen was stomping off in a huff have brought into question the power of filmmakers to mislead an audience. Every filmmaker sets out to direct an audience's emotions whether towards fear, disgust or well-being. Even in advertising, the continual bombardment of images of how fabulous we could look if only we used this brand of shampoo is only propaganda in a seemingly more innocent form.

From the viewpoint of the 21st century, when one looks back at this body of material, we perceive a different set of materials to those viewed from 1933-1945. For contemporary audiences, being swept up in a continual barrage of visual images, audio messages only ever showing official national party line – with no voice of dissent or opposition to counteract this view – it is little wonder Lawrence Rees remarked "The majority of Germans had become racist through films about their superiority as a master race." [22]

Endnotes

1. *WWII Film and History*, edited by John Whiteclay Chambers II and David Culbert, Oxford University Press, 1996.
2. *We Have Ways of Making You Think*, written and produced by Laurence Rees, BBC TV, 1992.
3. *We Have Ways of Making You Think*, written and produced by Laurence Rees, BBC TV, 1992.
4. *The Wonderful, Horrible Life of Leni Riefenstahl*, written and directed by Ray Müller, Eureka Video, 1993.
5. Reprinted in *Movies and Methods Vol 1*, edited by Bill Nichols, University of California Press, 1976.
6. Reprinted in *A Biographical Dictionary of the Cinema*, by David Thomson, Andre Deutsch, 1994.
7. *The Wonderful, Horrible Life of Leni Riefenstahl*, written and directed by Ray Müller, Eureka Video, 1993.
8. Reprinted in Riefenstahl's Obituary by Val Williams in *The Independent*, 10 September 2003.
9. *Film Propaganda: Soviet Russia and Nazi Germany*, Richard Taylor, I. B. Tauris, 1997, first published in 1979.
10. *Politics and Film* by Leif Furhammar and Folke Isaksson, Studio Vista, 1971.
11. *We Have Ways of Making You Think*, written and produced by Laurence Rees, BBC TV, 1992.
12. Ibid.
13. *We Have Ways of Making You Think*, written and produced by Laurence Rees, BBC TV, 1992.
14. According to the German reference book *Deutscher Spielfilm Almanach – 1929-1950* by Dr. Alfred Bauer (editor of the new edition 1976: *Filmladen Christoph Winterberg*, Munchen), *Das Bad auf der Tenne* (1943) was the third, *Die Goldene Stadt* (1942) the second and *Frauen sind doch bessere Diplomaten* (1939-41) the first.
15. *A Social History of The Third Reich* by Richard Grunberger, Phoenix, 2005.
16. *Great German Films* by Frederick W. Ott, Citadel Press, 1986.
17. *We Have Ways of Making You Think*, written and produced by Laurence Rees, BBC TV, 1992.
18. Ibid.
19. Ibid.
20. *Great German Films* by Frederick W. Ott, Citadel Press, 1986.
21. *Secret History: Television in the Third Reich*, directed by Michael Kloft, Channel 4, 2001.
22. *The Nazis: A Warning from History*, written and directed by Laurence Rees, BBC TV, 1997.

WAR AND THE
FILM NOIR

EDDIE ROBSON

Film noir is inextricably linked to World War 2 in several ways. It benefited creatively from European film personnel who escaped the Nazis and brought an expressionist style to Hollywood genre movies. Its moody lighting was partly invented by Paramount art director Hans Drier as a means of disguising how cheap sets had become due to rationing of materials. After the war it was able to adopt a more street-level realistic style by using the lightweight equipment developed for wartime documentaries. And of course, as has been said many times, the movement reflected a darkening of the national mood. In fact, this has been somewhat overstated, as the movement began before America had entered the war and certainly before its true horror began to emerge, and it was rooted in the pulp fiction that had been created in the preceding decade. It's more interesting to look at how film noir engaged with the war directly, as the movement very quickly absorbed the end of the war as a means of generating characters and stories. Though these films were often lurid and stylised, they were arguably where the reality of the war was dealt with.

*This Gun
for Hire*
1942

© Paramount/
The Kobal
Collection

What film noir is 'about' has often been over-simplified into clichés about private eyes and femme-fatales. The only consistent subject matter is crime, and you could make a case for some films to be classed as noirs which don't even feature that. Attempts to lay down a set of criteria rarely get very far, yet as a phenomenon it undeniably exists. We can see a cycle of movies which use certain themes, narrative strategies and visual approaches running through the 1940s and 1950s, and within that we can also see mini-cycles of films that have particularly strong connections to each other. One such mini-cycle emerged as a direct reaction to the end of the war.

The use of the war as a plot device in noir dates back to Paramount's *This Gun for Hire* (1942), based on Graham Greene's novel *A Gun for Sale* (1936). The film falls into the noir category partly because Drier's influence created a murky, unstable visual style and partly because its central character, Raven, is very much an anti-hero. Greene's novel uses the pre-war tensions in Europe as a backdrop: in the film, the amoral hitman discovers that his revenge mission coincides with a plot to sell chemical weapons to the Japanese, and Raven eventually becomes a loyal American hero in a rather un-noirish way. (*Variety* thought the storyline 'improbable'.) Viewing the film in retrospect, it suggests why noir largely steered clear of the war whilst it was still going on, as to properly address it within the movement's emerging style would have run the risk of seeming unpatriotic. Indeed, the development of noir was generally limited during this time: as Paul Schrader notes, 'The need to produce Allied propaganda abroad and promote patriotism at home blunted the fledgling moves toward a dark cinema' [1] – films that were defined by grey morality and, often, unhappy endings. (It often goes unnoticed today that *Double Indemnity* (1944) is actually a period piece, using the 1935 setting of the novel: the selfish, greedy actions of its protagonists needed to be placed at a distance from the war effort.)

The war did not create film noir: on the contrary, it stifled the emerging dark cinema of the late 1930s. But 'As soon as the war was over… American films became markedly more sardonic – and there was a boom in the crime film,' as Schrader states. 'For fifteen years the pressures against America's amelioristic cinema had been building up, and, given the freedom, audiences and artists were eager to take a less optimistic view of things' [2]. As Reynold Humphries points out, the rise of Hollywood's liberal left in the post-war years contributed to 'a common political desire to criticise contemporary American society [3]', and film noir was a strong expression of that.

With its production-line approach, Hollywood was able to move fast in those days and the social fallout of the war was already emerging as potential subject matter before it was over. Samuel Goldwyn started developing the how-things-have-changed emotional epic *The Best Years of Our Lives* (1946) at RKO in 1944, and was rewarded when the result was widely praised and won seven Oscars. *Till The End of Time* (1946), which RKO released a few months earlier, covered very similar ground. At the same time, the noir movement was finally able to hit its stride and, whilst the subject of post-war readjustment was dealt with in other areas of filmmaking, as Andrew Spicer argues, 'the narrative patterns and visual style of film noir enabled it to explore this problem most extensively [4]'.

Noir often features characters that feel alienated from society and are haunted by their past, and hence such films were ideal vehicles for examining the plight of the returning veteran. Richard Maltby states that 'The central male protagonist in films

noirs of 1946-48 is almost invariably marked as a veteran by one means or another',
pointing out that the noir hero's situation often acted as a metaphor for that of the veteran: 'the narrative structure common to the majority of films noirs of this period is one
in which the protagonist has to account for a missing period of his life, when he was outside the world in which the film is set, and in which things happened which set him at
a distance from that world and its inhabitants'. Maltby cites the example of *Out of the
Past* (1947), in which the hero – a private detective played by Robert Mitchum who,
Maltby points out, 'was firmly identified with military roles' at that time – is prevented
from living a normal life 'by the guilt and obsessive neuroses he has acquired during his
period of absence from society'. [5] However, there are also many noirs in which the
leading character is literally a veteran, and it is these films we are concerned with here.
Schrader describes the typical plot as 'a serviceman returns from the war to find his
sweetheart unfaithful or dead, or his business partner cheating him, or the whole society
something less than worth fighting for. The war continues, but now the antagonism
turns with a new viciousness toward the American society itself. [6]

It is instructive to compare *This Gun for Hire*'s slightly awkward inclusion of
wartime issues with *Crossfire* (1947), made by the firmly left-wing director/producer
team of Edward Dmytryk and Adrian Scott, both members of the 'Hollywood Ten'
indicted by HUAC for communist sympathising. This is the post-war noir which
perhaps deals most explicitly with post-war issues. It clearly belongs in the noir
category: the plot revolves around a murder, the narrative is non-chronological and the
visual style is chiaroscuro. However, it is also an 'issue' picture – the murder is an
anti-Semitic hate crime and a scene towards the end effectively halts the plot for a few
minutes to discuss the murderer's motives in detail – and is often credited as the first
Hollywood production to deal directly with racism. At the same time 20th Century-Fox
was also developing a movie addressing anti-Semitism, *Gentleman's Agreement* (1947), but
with a speedy twenty-day shooting schedule *Crossfire* beat it into cinemas – demonstrating the quicker reaction times of cheaper genre pictures. (*Gentleman's Agreement* took the
Best Picture Oscar, but *Crossfire* got a nomination – very few noirs gained such recognition from the Academy.)

Although the main aim of the film is to address anti-Semitism, this issue is not
seen as specific to the war. This is partly because the novel on which the film is based,
The Brick Foxhole by Richard Brooks, was about homophobia, not anti-Semitism. The
Production Code which governed morality in Hollywood films prohibited any mention
of homosexuality, yet this aspect remains visible in the film: to an audience familiar with
gay narratives, the scene in which Jewish civilian Samuels (Sam Levene) speaks to
Corporal Mitchell (George Cooper) in the bar reads strongly like a pick-up. The
fortysomething man approaches the quiet, introverted, sensitive younger man who finds
him surprisingly easy to talk to, they discuss emotional strife and the older invites the
younger out for a meal. John Paxton's adaptation simply adds a girl for Samuels to elim-
inate this aspect (although she could be a 'beard' and Samuels could still be gay), but the
change demonstrates that the nature of the prejudice is not really important. The film
is about prejudice generally, and in a broader sense it is about hatred. This is a subject
which the tones and narratives of film noir accommodate far more easily than the
themes of duty and moral certitude which *This Gun for Hire* had to embrace.

Crossfire is also the noir closest in spirit to the *Best Years of Our Lives* type pictures, looking at different soldiers' reactions to a post-war world: as Spicer identifies, the film contains 'the widest range of maladjusted veterans' [7] of any noir. The characters, mostly demobilised soldiers in Washington, are still enlisted men and still in uniform, but find themselves back in the 'normal' world. Samuels is presumed by the anti-Semitic army officer Montgomery (Robert Ryan) to be a draft-dodger. Later the audience learns that Samuels was honourably discharged, which makes sense of the insight he demonstrates when telling Mitchell that, with the war over, 'We don't know what we're supposed to do, we don't know what's supposed to happen. We're too used to fighting, but we just don't know what to fight. You can feel the tension in the air. A whole lot of fight and hate that doesn't know where to go. Guy like you maybe starts hating himself.' A few hours later Samuels is killed by Montgomery (although suspicion first falls on the troubled Mitchell). Although the film notes that prejudice has always been with us, it's clear that Montgomery's hatred has been displaced and intensified by the war, and this makes it even more dangerous when he returns and no longer has a legitimate enemy.

Crossfire articulates two polarised responses to the end of the war: Montgomery, who lashes out, and Mitchell, who turns inwards. Montgomery's violent tendencies have been exacerbated by the military life, whilst Mitchell was clearly never comfortable with it: Sergeant Keeley (Robert Mitchum) claims 'He couldn't kill anybody,' although Keeley himself has – 'Where you get medals for it.' Keeley is placed between the two, a realist, aware of the difficulties that lie ahead: he's aware that his marriage may not have survived his absence, for example. Notably, Mitchell's only hope of an outlet – the understanding Samuels – is quickly destroyed, and he becomes lost and uncertain again, wandering from bars to strange apartments to all-night cinemas. Bearing in mind the homophobia-themed novel, this presumably has its roots in a bout of sexual confusion, with Mitchell's attempt to pick up Ginny (Gloria Grahame) aimed at reasserting his heterosexuality, but in the process of refashioning the film as a narrative about racism, this episode is slightly disconnected from the main plot and becomes a wider statement about the difficulty of readjustment. The fact that suspicion falls on Mitchell suggests that society doesn't want to accept his behaviour: the strange pattern of his evening makes it hard for him to provide an alibi. Spending time alone makes him a suspicious figure, particularly in a society which has been drilled in the importance of standing united. The ending, in which Montgomery runs from the police and is shot down in the street, affirms that we can prohibit the violence – and prejudice – that he embodied, but what future lies ahead for the likes of Mitchell is unclear.

The previous year's *The Blue Dahlia* (1946) was originally intended to follow a similar narrative path, as one ex-serviceman is suspected of murder only for another to be revealed as the true culprit. Johnny (Alan Ladd) returns from the war to discover that his old life has gone, his wife Helen (Doris Dowling) has a new boyfriend and Johnny's son has died as a consequence of Helen's alcoholic neglect. When Helen then turns up dead, suspicion naturally falls upon Johnny, then upon his army buddy Buzz (William Bendix), who is suffering blackouts as a result of a metal plate in his head. In fact, Chandler's intention had originally been that Buzz would be the murderer, before the navy protested at this depiction of their former troops as disturbed and unbalanced, thereby rather undermining the film's point that the war might indeed have left people disturbed and unbalanced. Ultimately a less likely, and less interesting, character was revealed to be responsible.

Broadly speaking, there are two categories of male noir protagonist: 'seeker-hero' and 'victim-hero'. The seeker is the detective figure, though in numerous cases he is not a professional detective or policeman, but someone who is simply motivated to find something out (even those who are professionals tend to go beyond their remit in the course of the story). The victim is the man who is overtaken by events and unwillingly pushed into an awkward situation. Characters can be a mixture of both, as Johnny is – he's the victim of suspicion and seeks to clear his name – and this demonstrates the mixed feelings of society towards the ex-GIs. The fact that Johnny can wrest control of the narrative shows his strength of character and brings audience sympathy on his side, but his victimisation happens because society is slightly afraid of him. Jon Tuska says that 'as a veteran, trained to live in a violent world, [Johnny] proves a match for the violence he encounters after his discharge' [8]: Johnny's dispatch of a goon who kidnaps him underlines the point, with Ladd's performance impassive and unflinching.

The fear is that, by sending these men away to kill, a door has been opened which can never be closed. In *Crossfire*, Montgomery bitterly suggests that civilians are indeed slightly afraid of soldiers: 'Not many civilians will take a soldier into their house like this for a quiet talk.' This is the price society is paying for victory, to put millions of people through this and then have to live with them afterwards. *In a Lonely Place* (1950) explores the notion that knowing someone could be capable of violence is just as disturbing as knowing they have actually committed violent acts: it's notable that we discover, in passing, that the film's protagonist Dixon Steele is a former military man. In *Gun Crazy* (1949) – based, like *The Best Years of Our Lives*, on a short story by MacKinlay Cantor – the story proper begins when Bart Tare, who has a longstanding fascination with guns but an aversion to killing, comes out of military service (although whether he would have fought in the war is unclear – the original story was published in 1940). Bart rejects the possibility of an ordinary life in favour of a transient, and ultimately criminal, existence.

However, as Michael Walker says (disagreeing slightly with Schrader), 'it is relatively rare for the fears to be made explicit, e.g. for a man to return from the services and find out that his wife has been unfaithful during his absence, as in *The Blue Dahlia*... or for the man's violence towards the woman to be linked in some way to the war, as in *In a Lonely Place*'. More commonly, the hero is given a more typical thriller dilemma to resolve, and the wider issues are implied. Walker goes on to state that 'A number of film noirs depict the plight of the returning veteran in terms of amnesia.' This is a common noir plot device as it creates uncertainty around the hero: in fact, amnesia is almost comically widespread in noir, but it has a more credible source where the ex-GIs are concerned. 'This is another example of the psychological threat that runs through [film noir]. Twenties and Thirties films about veterans of World War 1 tended to stress physical rather than psychological damage', Walker says, [9] The post-1945 films express the concern that the war has caused damage to people's personalities, their very sense of self: a nebulous malaise and one hard to dramatise. As a more extreme rendition of this, amnesia is easier to identify and offers obvious dramatic possibilities.

It doesn't necessarily have to be lengthy amnesia: short blackouts are central to *Deadline at Dawn* (1946), in which a sailor on leave has a gap in his memory due to alcohol, and *High Wall* (1947), in which a man suffers blackouts due to a brain injury sustained in the war. Like Buzz in *The Blue Dahlia*, they are both accused of murder and cannot remember whether or not they are guilty. Amnesia complicates the plot of *The Chase* (1946) when, in a bizarre development, a substantial chunk of the film turns out to be the dream of protagonist Chuck Scott (Robert Cummings): this vivid delusion is possibly caused by war trauma and is followed by a bout of amnesia, in which Chuck forgets he's supposed to be helping gangster's wife Lorna Roman to skip the country. The result is incoherent (and the audience would likely feel justly infuriated), but there does seem to be a genuine effort to communicate the disordered life of a traumatised veteran: 'It happened again,' says Chuck after the delusional episode. He no longer knows what is and isn't real.

In *The Clay Pigeon* (1949), directed by B-noir specialist Richard Fleischer and written by *High Noon* (1952) scriptwriter Carl Foreman, the gap in memory covers events from the war itself. Jim Fletcher (Bill Williams) – another seeker/victim protagonist – comes out of a coma suffering from amnesia covering part of his time in a POW camp, facing charges of treason. He escapes from the hospital to find Ted Niles, his best buddy from the camp, and establish whether or not he is guilty. Both of them suffered at the hands of the cruel guard Ken Tokoyama (Richard Loo) – or so Fletcher thinks. In reality, whilst Fletcher has been left with severe psychological problems due to his mal-treatment, his pal is working with Tokoyama to launder $10m of counterfeit American money forged by the Japanese in preparation for their invasion of American soil.

Though apparently based on a true story (we will have to take this claim at face value, as the plot is fairly absurd), *The Clay Pigeon* is more interesting as a metaphor for the psychological difficulties faced by veterans. Tokoyama acts as a physical manifesta-tion of the scars left on Fletcher by his wartime experiences: Fletcher would like to leave all this behind but it takes considerable strength to do so. Tokoyama has the effect of upsetting Fletcher's certainties, represented by the corrupted Niles, and the improbability of Tokoyama's appearance in California makes him seem all the more like a ghost who will not let Fletcher go. Amnesia always ups the ante in this kind of 'wrong man' thriller by preventing the accused from giving a true account of events, requiring him to search for the truth himself (and giving the accused cause to doubt himself). Here, however, the ambiguity this creates also reflects the uncertainty of those who fought in the war: Fletcher has emerged from a violent conflict unsure of whether he is a good man or not. He feels judged by people who weren't there and can't know what it was like.

The use of amnesia in *Somewhere in the Night* (1946) is more extreme. As soldiers in real life struggled to relocate their place in a changed world, so George Taylor (John Hodiak) returns from the war unable to remember anything about himself. This oper-ates as a thumpingly literal interpretation of the GI's dilemma, as he must rediscover who he is and his place in the world from scratch: even his face has been reconstructed after a major combat injury and so people won't necessarily be able to recognise him. Taylor returns to a disorientating, threatening Los Angeles, drifting from place to place with little sense of how one element relates to another, trying to piece together who he is and find the only man who knows him, a character by the name of Larry Cravat. As the narrative unfurls, Taylor realises that he joined the army in order to hide out, and must face up to the suspicion that he may have murdered someone and attempted to steal Nazi loot. (A later noir, *The Crooked Way* (1949), uses a similar premise, with an amnesiac veteran going to L.A. and being recognised by police as a gangster.)

Although *Somewhere in the Night* is given shape and immediate tension by its thriller elements, the broader question is explicit as Taylor openly wonders what sort of man he was. He is supported in his quest by nightclub singer Christy Smith (Nancy Guild), who at one point states that 'If it turns out that in your whole life you ever killed anything bigger than a horsefly, then I'm crazy and I want to be locked up'. Yet the fact is, Taylor may well have killed, and he certainly will have been trained to: he's just fought in a major war, after all. It's hard to tell whether or not this irony was intentional, as it is passed over fairly quickly, but generally the film suggests that the war has wiped the slate clean and we can make our own truth. Notably, although Taylor's detective work resolves the plot and offers some clues about his past life, this does not prompt the cloud of amnesia to lift. This may have come about due to simple good discipline on the part of the writers, resisting the temptation to have Taylor remember something critical at a point when the plot needs to be advanced, but it also means that the character we see building up on screen is the man who Taylor will continue to be. We are witnessing the start of the new George Taylor, and Taylor exits the film able to make a fresh start and leave his old life behind.

The notion of men using the war as a means of escape from problematic lives is also central to *Dead Reckoning* (1947), in which war hero Johnny Drake (William Prince) panics and flees when he realises that he is to be given the Medal of Honor – which will mean his picture will get in the papers. He turns up dead soon afterwards and it falls to his army buddy Rip Murdock (Humphrey Bogart) to figure out what happened (just as Bogart's Sam Spade in *The Maltese Falcon* (1941) felt obliged to do something about his partner's death, so Rip goes the distance for his comrade – their bond goes deeper than the war itself). In the process, Rip goes on his own journey of disillusionment, uncovering the betrayals his friend suffered. Roger Tailleur says of both this film and *The Blue Dahlia* that the protagonists 'discover a homefront reality not markedly different from that which they imagined they were fighting against overseas: a realm of arbitrariness and corruption [10]'.

It transpires that Johnny joined the army to escape a murder rap and evidently hoped to be able to make a new life upon his return to America – a plan foiled, ironically, by the attention drawn to him by his own heroics overseas. For some, the war gave them a higher purpose in their lives, leaving a substantial gap upon their return: for others, their inability to fit into society was given relief by the war, rather than being caused by it. Michael Walker identifies that 'domesticity almost invariably poses a threat to the noir hero [11]', a reaction that goes beyond the jarring contrast between military life and home life. This underlines that the tensions which emerge in post-war noir were, as Paul Schrader noted, not entirely attributable to the war itself. These issues dated back to before the war and had lain unresolved until the war either provided an excuse to air them or placed them in a fresh light.

The Clay Pigeon ultimately affirms American values when it contrives a small scene to avoid racism: whilst Fletcher is on the run, he briefly hides in the home of an Asian-American woman. Seeing a photograph of her husband in uniform, Fletcher is told that he died in combat as a member of the US Air Force and commiserates with her. This scene has no real plot relevance, serving to ensure that Tokoyama is not seen as representative of all Asians: however, it does create the impression that whilst Americans of all races are brothers fighting together under the flag and so on, those outside may well be psychopaths who deserve everything they get.

Xenophobia is not unusual in film noir. Mexico and South America in particular are frequently used as places which, although they seem to promise liberation from one's past/self, actually emerge as sites for dark and destructive passions to brew (as in *Gilda* (1946), *The Lady from Shanghai* (1948) and *Out of the Past*). Most post-war noir is concerned with the traumatic return home rather than going back out into the world, but there are notable exceptions such as *Cornered* (1945), made by the same writer/director/producer team as *Crossfire*. This revenge thriller is an interesting transitional film made immediately after the war's end with a story that belongs more in wartime but which is told in a very noirish way. Canadian airman Laurence Gerard (Dick Powell) is obsessed with tracking down the Vichy collaborator who caused the death of his French wife. The perpetrator, Marcel Jarnac (Luther Adler), is apparently dead, leaving Gerard with a lack of closure. Playing a small part in the war's vast narrative, his personal story is in danger of getting lost and the film addresses the unresolved tensions which the war may have left in its participants.

Gerard believes Jarnac to have survived and escaped to Argentina and, although he is repeatedly told to give up, he does track Jarnac down. The contrivance of the story that unfolds could be seen as an acknowledgement that, in reality, Gerard would be denied the closure of locating his nemesis and that his obsession would be ultimately self-destructive. Under this reading the film offers vicarious catharsis to anyone who feels similar unresolved tensions, whilst perhaps warning them to give up on finding it in the real world, for the sake of their own sanity. A lot of post-war noirs are ultimately kind to their heroes in this way: having established that these men have suffered in the war and then proceeded to put them through the wringer during the film's events, they are rarely then subjected to one of the famous unhappy endings of film noir (although the unhappy ending is another of the clichés about noir which is by no means the norm). In most of the films discussed here the hero ultimately survives, offering hope and/or catharsis to those for whom these issues were real. On the other hand, *Cornered* could be a message from an avowedly left-wing group of filmmakers – not only Dmytryk and Scott, but also actors Luther Adler and Morris Carnovsky, who both came from New York's Group Theatre – to remain vigilant against the return of fascism and never take its defeat for granted.

The grim tone of *Cornered* and the brutal approach of Gerard to his mission demonstrate how post-war film was able to take a new approach to the depiction of violence. The noirs of the late 1940s and the 1950s became markedly more violent and this was literally the expression of the real-life horrors experienced by a generation of Americans. The Production Code, which had been self-imposed by Hollywood in 1934 in response to intense pressure from religious groups, governed the portrayal of sex, violence and morality in Hollywood films. Film noir, which dealt heavily with all three of those, inevitably found itself pushing the Code's boundaries, and it was gradually unravelled by degrees: once the Code had permitted something, a precedent had been set and the boundaries shifted, ready for the next push. Billy Wilder skilfully slid *Double Indemnity* under the wire of what was acceptable as regards sex and morality, and began the erosion of the Code in those two areas. However, the Code accidentally undid itself where violence was concerned when it overlooked numerous transgressions during the war in the name of keeping national morale up: as Spicer notes, 'audiences had been shown Nazis or the Japanese as sexually twisted psychopathic killers in patriotic war films'. [12] Not only that, but a huge segment of the audience had experienced worse horrors for real. The sheer scale of the conflict, to the point where practically everybody had either fought or knew someone who had fought, was damaging to any notions of innocence. These were the tensions which were expressed in the post-war noir.

This caused obvious problems for the Code office when the war was over: having allowed violence in one context, it became harder to argue that it couldn't be done in others, *Cornered* being a prime example. It's not exactly a rousing flag waver, leaving the audience concerned for Gerard's state of mind – but his intent and his adversary are essentially the same as in a wartime film, the only difference being that there is no war. This raises the question, is war a justification for violent actions or an excuse? Similarly, *The Clay Pigeon* places an archetypal war movie villain into a crime narrative. Hollywood morality had shifted and the war had made things less black and white.

The finest example of this among the post-war noirs is the Anglo-American co-production *The Third Man* (1949). It's an atypical noir, as despite its American stars it fits more with the British noir tradition (it jars with the 'house style' established by the American studios, most notably in its soundtrack). This takes place in one of the most ambiguous spaces in noir, a Vienna occupied by the Allies and divided into British, French, American and Soviet quarters. The entire city is traumatised and its identity is in crisis. Against this, Holly Martins (Joseph Cotten) – an American author of pulp fiction – is the literal innocent abroad, a viewpoint character for anyone who didn't experience the war first hand. (Perhaps this is what makes the film so enduring – today, Martins makes a good representative for those generations born after the war.) He seeks his old friend Harry Lime (Orson Welles) who has invited him to Vienna to work with him, only to be told that Lime is dead. Martins eventually discovers this to be metaphorically true rather than actually true: Lime is no longer the man he knew.

The presence of Welles makes *The Third Man* a superior companion piece to his third film as director, *The Stranger* (1946) – credited as the first film to show footage of concentration camps. In both, Welles plays men who were involved in the war but did not fight in it, who both believe they can adapt to the post-war world, and who are both destroyed after the film's central character tracks them down. *The Stranger* portrays Nazi war criminal Franz Kindler as he seeks to build a new life in America as Charles Rankin, a university lecturer. His old opinions leak out in his teaching, but he believes he can leave his past behind and live quietly as an American citizen with his American wife. Yet, in a similar manner to *Cornered*, Kindler is located and exposed, and ultimately dies accidentally (conveniently saving the hero from having to dirty his hands). The message is quite simple and the film feels like a hangover from the wartime flag wavers, depicting a piece of unfinished business where the American authorities act effectively to vanquish a remaining menace. There's a little food for thought in the way that Kindler manages to ingratiate himself into American society up to a point, but ultimately there is no dilemma – Kindler was always an outsider and the simple solution is to cast him out.

Harry Lime in *The Third Man* is a more complex proposition. Where Kindler is a European trying to hide in America, Lime is an American hiding out in Europe. Assuming we trust Martins' opinion of his friend before the war, the conflict seems to have knocked all sense of morality out of Lime, leaving him content to profit from the black market with no apparent interest in the consequences of his actions. This could

The Third Man
1949

© London
Films/
The Kobal
Collection

be read as fitting in with those noirs which depict other countries as sites of corruption – Kurtz (Ernst Deutsch) admits that 'everyone in Vienna' is mixed up with some kind of racket, initially suggesting that Lime has simply adapted to his environment. However, Kurtz goes on to say that these things 'would have seemed unthinkable before the war' and expresses regret for the war's effect. By contrast, Lime seems without remorse and his activities have gone much further, as seen in his famous speech about shooting 'dots' from the Ferris wheel. He is a shiftless person without nationality: as Spicer notes, he is 'The true citizen of this distorted world [13]'.

Martins has made a career of fetishising outlaws in his western stories, and early on he draws a parallel between the British army's attitude towards Lime and one of his own books about a bullying sheriff. Martins assumes his friend to be a misunderstood figure, unfairly demonised by the authorities, with mitigating circumstances for any crimes, and the audience is also directed towards this expectation. In fact, the shock is that Lime, though charismatic, is amoral and unsympathetic. Martins' decision at the end of the film to kill Lime seems to represent an acceptance that the world has changed irrevocably, with no easy way back. The film rejects Lime's philosophy of amorality, as his death in the sewers is ignoble, unromantic, standing for nothing; he is not among those noir criminals who go out in a blaze of glory. However, the film also does not regard his defeat with triumph. Martins is technically the hero, and he has killed the film's notional villain, but in genre terms the emptiness of the victory is signalled by the fact that Martins does not win the girl, Anna (Alida Valli). In its final shot of Anna walking past Martins, failing to even acknowledge him, the film ends with a sense that much has been lost and nothing gained. We move out into an ambiguous and uncertain future.

The endpoints we put on periods in film are always slightly arbitrary and often

WAR AND THE FILM NOIR

contrived to fit a purpose, but *The Third Man* does serve well as an endpoint to noir's interest in the war. After a series of films which mostly deal with the war in terms of people returning home from it, *The Third Man* comes from outside Hollywood, takes an American to the heart of Europe and reveals the physical, as well as the mental, devastation. It acknowledges that we have all changed, and then looks to the painful process of rebuilding and moving on. Noir itself also moved on: by about 1950 the issue of post-war adjustment was no longer topical. Coincidentally, this is also roughly the point at which noir production peaked. Noir by this stage was entering its next mini-cycle, characterised by Schrader as one of 'psychotic action and suicidal impulse [14]', and although the unstable ex-servicemen of post-war noir had contributed to this, the subject matter now tended towards off-the-rails cops and gangsters. Yet these films had served a valuable purpose in bringing post-war tensions to the fore. 'Liberal critics took the movies as being symptomatic of a social condition they themselves were desperately in need of discovering,' says Maltby. 'The movies themselves are excessive representations of the normal as neurotic, providing confirmation, for anyone seeking it, that maladjustment was a normal response to post-war America.' [15]

Endnotes

1. Schrader, Paul, 'Notes on Film Noir', *The Film Noir Reader*.
2. Schrader, 'Notes on Film Noir'.
3. Humphries, Reynold, 'The Politics of Crime and the Crime of Politics: Postwar Noir, the Liberal Consensus and the Hollywood Left', *Film Noir Reader 4*, p.236.
4. Spicer, Andrew, *Film Noir*, pp.20-21.
5. Maltby, Richard, 'The Politics of the Maladjusted Text', *The Movie Book of Film Noir*.
6. Schrader, 'Notes on Film Noir'.
7. Spicer, *Film Noir*, p.86.
8. Tuska, Jon, *Dark Cinema: American Film Noir in Cultural Perspective*, p.178.
9. Walker, Michael, 'Introduction', *The Movie Book of Film Noir*.
10. Tailleur, Roger, 'The Pink Horse or the Pipe Dreams of the Human Condition', *Perspectives on Film Noir*, p.42.
11. Walker, 'Introduction'.
12. Spicer, *Film Noir*, p.38.
13. Spicer, *Film Noir*, p.188.
14. Schrader, 'Notes on Film Noir'.
15. Maltby, 'The Politics of the Maladjusted Text'.

Bibliography

Cameron, Ian (ed.), *The Movie Book of Film Noir*, Studio Vista, London, 1992.
Maltby, Richard, *Hollywood Cinema*, Blackwell, Oxford, 1995.
Palmer, Barton R., *Perspectives on Film Noir*, G. K. Hall & Co., New York, 1996.
Silver, Alain & Ursini, James (eds.), *The Film Noir Reader*, Limelight, New York, 1996.
Silver, Alain, Ursini, James & Porfirio, Robert (eds.), *Film Noir Reader 3*, Limelight Editions, New York, 2002.
Silver, Alain & Ursini, James (eds.), *Film Noir Reader 4*, Proscenium, New York, 2004.
Spicer, Andrew, *Film Noir*, Longman, Harlow, 2002.
Tuska, Jon, *Dark Cinema: American Film Noir in Cultural Perspective*, Greenwood Press, Westport, 1984.

1950S BRITISH WAR MOVIES AND THE MYTH OF WORLD WAR 2

TOM DAWSON

'What a comfort then, that in one field British studios should be supreme. No other country makes war films quite as well.'

Campbell Dixon, *The Daily Telegraph*, 22 February 1958.

Back in the 1950s, a decade when cinema was still the pre-eminent form of mass entertainment in Britain attracting audiences of some 23 million people a week, war movies were one of the dominant genres in British cinema. It's been estimated that some 100 World War 2 related films were made between 1946 and 1965, 10 times the number of Ealing comedies, and they provided some of the biggest box-office successes of the period: *The Dam Busters* was the top-grossing film in 1955, *Reach for the Sky* in 1956, *The Bridge on the River Kwai* in 1958 and *Sink the Bismarck* in 1960, whilst other major hits included *The Cruel Sea* (1953) and *The Battle of the River Plate* (1956). [1]

A number of theories have been advanced for the popularity of these war movies at this time. Partly producers, writers and directors were now able to draw on a steady flow of memoirs and biographies written by actual participants in the war and which recounted dramatic exploits. And as Britain faced up to the realities of the Cold War and its own imperial decline encapsulated in the Suez fiasco of 1956, it must have seemed comforting to return via the cinema and also through magazines, comics and books, to a time when the country was able to wield more influence in the world. Moreover writers such as Raymond Durgnat [2] and James Chapman [3] have persuasively argued that in terms of cinema the British war movie was the equivalent of the American Western: both genres were almost exclusively all-male, action-orientated affairs, which constructed mythical versions of national identity.

Unquestionably the British 1950s war movies, which have been endlessly repeated on television down the years, have played a crucial role in shaping the way different generations have come to think of 'the war'. Roland Barthes in his seminal *Mythologies* argued that myths turn the historical into the natural [4]: in other words in the process of myth-making the complexities and complications of actual events become stripped away, to be replaced with a simpler narrative of heroes and villains, of Good confronting Evil. On all sides of the British political spectrum World War 2 has come to represent 'our' island nation's 'finest hour', when 'we' stood alone but united against foreign tyranny. Dunkirk, thanks to the valiant efforts of the 'little ships', the Blitz and the Battle of Britain are in this analysis the twentieth-century equivalents of Agincourt, the repelling of the Armada and the Battle of Trafalgar. And many of the films discussed in this chapter have helped to buttress this mythical version of the past.

In watching these films from the perspective of 2009, one is struck by how the contributions to the Allied victory of both the Soviet Union and America are almost entirely ignored, whilst the Germans themselves are barely glimpsed. More troubling aspects of the British war effort – the firebombing of Dresden for example, the discovery of the concentration camps, the fact that crime rates soared in London during the Blitz, the inadequate provision of air raid shelters for British civilians – were also not considered worthy of cinematic investigation. The 1950s films present an almost exclusively middle-class perspective on the war, with working-class characters relegated to the periphery: these are officers' tales, and according to the critic Neil Rattigan, unlike the films made during the war itself, 'they show the British actually winning it', whether through bouncing bombs or the heroics of Spitfire pilots. [5] In terms of their casting, these films rely on a small number of dependable actors, in particular Jack Hawkins, John Mills, Kenneth More, Richard Todd and Anthony Steel, whose performances here often convey a sense of stoical duty during a crisis.

It would be hard to make a case for the directors of these films such as Guy Hamilton, Charles Frend and Lewis Gilbert to be considered as auteurs: certainly few take any formal risks in terms of how they tell their stories, in terms of narrative, mise-en-scène or montage. Yet these films continue to be ideologically revealing, not least in how they present Britishness, and in the way they explore masculinity. Two highly successful television advertising campaigns for Carling Black Label lager during the 1980s and 1990s playfully drawing on the visual imagery from *The Dam Busters* and *Ice Cold in Alex* (1958) suggest just how deeply these 1950s war films have become embedded in our collective consciousness.

WAR IN THE SKIES

Propelled by Eric Coates' thunderous theme music, *The Dam Busters* has come to be considered *the* definitive, patriotic 1950s British war film, and is currently the subject of a Hollywood remake. Based on real-life events – the raid by Lancaster bombers on the Möhne and Eder dams in the industrial heartland of Germany on 17 May 1943 – it calmly celebrates British scientific invention and military heroism, whilst presenting a world comprised almost entirely of middle-class characters. Directed by Michael Anderson from R. C. Sherriff's script, it's very much a film of two parts. The first concentrates on the eccentric figure of the scientist Barnes Wallis (Michael Redgrave) in his ingenious efforts to develop a 'bouncing bomb', with which to attack the Ruhr dams. He meets with considerable scepticism from Whitehall bureaucrats and high-ranking officers, but perseveres with his scheme, drawing the analogy with Nelson using his cannons at Trafalgar and "dismissing the French flagship with a yorker so to speak".

The second part of *The Dam Busters* switches its focus to Wing Commander Guy Gibson (Richard Todd) and the preparations and execution of the raid. Gibson himself cuts a remote presence. He has no wife or sweetheart (the 24-year-old real-life pilot was married) and he remains detached from his men, although he allows them to "let off steam" by debagging members of a fellow squadron, and he's entirely committed to his work – even on a theatre trip where he comes up with a solution to a navigational problem. His Labrador dog Nigger appears to be the most important figure emotionally in his life, and the creature is even buried outside its master's office after a hit-and-run incident.

Interestingly Gibson and Wallis are the only two significant characters in *The Dam Busters*: we learn very little about the identities of the other airmen who take part in the attacks. Yet despite its flag-waving status, there's a welcome reticence at key moments in the film. Gibson's words to the crews before take-off are simply, "Well chaps, my watch says it's time to go." Nor are we allowed to forget the terrible human cost of war. Admittedly we don't see any of the human victims in Germany, of which there were some 1500, the majority of whom were slave labourers. Wallis however is genuinely concerned about the numbers of British lives shed to reach the raid's objective. And in

the most moving scene, the camera simply pans around the living quarters of the airmen who won't be returning to base, picking out objects – a rowing oar, a clock, a clothes brush, neatly folded clothes – which are now the relics of their lives.

The Dam Busters, however, was something of an anomaly amongst 1950s war films in that it dealt with the activities of the Bomber Command section of the RAF. There have, of course, been the exploits of the 'Few', the Spitfire and Hurricane pilots over southern England during the Battle of Britain in 1940, which have tended to be mythologised in fictionalised versions of the war. Based on an original story by Wing Commander Pelham Groom and directed by George More O'Ferrall, the RAF drama *Angels One Five* (1952) begins with a burst of patriotic music and an excerpt from Churchill's 'Their Finest Hour' speech, yet it turns out to be a surprisingly melancholic affair. The setting is an unnamed fighter station in Kent during the summer of 1940 that serves as a metaphor for a whole nation at war. The group commander 'Tiger' Small, played by Jack Hawkins, is loyally supported by his squadron leaders. The German attackers may enjoy numerical superiority, but here everyone knows their role and works effectively as a team: the plummy-voiced women in the Operations Room, the cheery working-class mechanics and the fun-loving pilots, who indulge in a spot of *Dam Busters*-style horseplay in the officers' mess. [6]

Angels One Five follows how a new Scottish pilot T. B. 'Septic' Baird (John Gregson) learns to fit into this community and become a valued flier, despite initial setbacks such as crash-landing his plane on arrival and failing to switch off his wireless transmitter during a raid. He's given a tepid romance with a female ambulance driver, which is not allowed to be consummated. There are relatively few aerial sequences in the film, whose real centre is the Operations Room, and we learn of Baird's off-screen death through the messages relayed to its radio system. And there are some unusual details in the film's mise-en-scène. [7] The home and garden of Squadron Leader Clinton and his wife Dulcie (very much the base's mother-figure) adjoin the runaway. Despite the property having been badly damaged in a German attack, she continues to hang a lantern to guide the pilots home: in the final crane shot this light, even at a distance, continues to be visible, a symbol of British spirit that can't be extinguished. Another quote from Churchill, 'Never in the field of human conflict has so much been owed by so many to so few', closes proceedings, but it's the pragmatic observation of Hawkins' character that "We keep going, because we have to keep going", that resonates with the film's mood.

Lewis Gilbert's *Reach for the Sky* on the other hand is precisely the sort of work that has given British 1950s war films such a poor critical reputation. The opening inscription 'this is the story of Douglas Bader, a legend in his own time' announces its hagiographical intentions. Bader himself was the RAF pilot and brilliant sportsman, who despite losing both his legs in an accident, taught himself to fly again using his artificial limbs, and during the Battle of Britain was placed in charge of five squadrons. Shot down over France, he managed to escape from captivity despite his disability, before being placed by the Germans in Colditz. The voice-over to *Reach for the Sky* is provided by Bader's best friend Johnny Sanderson (Lynton Brook). The latter though barely registers on-screen, for this is very much a one-man show, celebrating an individual not a community. Not that Gilbert is interested in probing deeply into the character of his protagonist who regards aerial combat as another type of sport. The overblown score dictates our emotions, and whilst in real-life Bader's favoured tactic of 'big wings' – gathering as many aircraft as possible to attack the enemy en masse – was deeply controversial within Fighter Command, *Reach for the Sky* avoids complicating its reverence towards its subject matter.

THE DUTY TO ESCAPE: PRISONER OF WAR FILMS IN THE 1950S

Prisoner of war (POW) dramas formed a genre within a genre in terms of 1950s British war films. They were invariably based on the memoirs of real-life POWs and they laid further claim to authenticity by employing the authors as consultants for the actual filming, [8] even if the number of real-life escapes had been minimal. [9] As Cull points out, one of the reasons for the popularity of these films was that audiences got to experience the thrill of an escape story without the moral problems of identifying with a criminal, whilst the triumph of one escapee could represent in this war the success of a whole nation. [10]

The Wooden Horse for example, made in 1950, is based on a book by ex-POW Eric Williams and recounts the escape from Stalag Luft III in eastern Germany of a trio of British officers who are played by Leo Genn, David Tomlinson and Anthony Steel. Director Jack Lee, whose background lay in documentary filmmaking, pays careful attention to the physical details of constructing an escape. An ordinary piece of vaulting equipment becomes a Trojan horse: every day the vault is carried out into the yard for gym practice in full view of the German guards. The escapees take it in turns to hide in the chest and painstakingly dig a tunnel that extends beyond the perimeter. Morale seems high in the camp with the men cheerfully mocking their captors by singing 'Deutschland ist Kaput' in the showers. Even the colleague who criticises Peter (Genn) and John (Steel) for neglecting the communal chores is brought 'on-side' by the script: before they make their bid for freedom, he provides them with much needed foreign currency. The last half hour of *The Wooden Horse* follows Peter and John in their efforts to make their way through German-occupied territory to neutral Sweden. Lee generates some suspenseful sequences in night-time Lübeck where the British duo attempt to gain safe passage whilst fearing their accents will lead to their betrayal. The involvement of French and Danish resistance workers in spiriting the men to safety is a rare example of a 1950s British war film acknowledging an international dimension to one of 'our' stories.

Much more famous however than *The Wooden Horse* and *Albert R. N.* (Albert being a papier-mâché dummy used in an escape) is Guy Hamilton's *The Colditz Story* (1955), which paved the way for a long-running TV series. John Mills plays Major Pat Reid upon whose memoirs the film is based, and Eric Portman is the most senior British officer in the prison. When Reid arrives at Colditz, fellow POW Lionel Jeffries greets him with the line, "Forgive us for not coming to meet you at the station, but we were unavoidably detained." Alas this jokey, public school tone pervades the whole film, which resembles a Boy's Own yarn and fails to make use of its imposing setting. Of course, the other nationalities imprisoned in Colditz can't entirely be trusted: the traitor turns out to be Polish, and the French are prone to over-excitement. Reid and three colleagues end up escaping by dressing up in German uniforms, staging their exit at the same time as a theatrical show performed by the prisoners, which is the perfect excuse for some on-stage male cross-dressing. Imprisonment here appears to be treated as a game, and one has no sense of the psychological impact of confinement, nor of the nature of friendships between men in this enclosed environment. If you're looking for *The Colditz Story* in any way to match the humanity and social analysis of Renoir's *La Grande Illusion* (1937), you'll be disappointed.

Three years after *The Colditz Story* saw the release of David Lean's epic *The Bridge on the River Kwai*, which won seven Oscars and propelled the director into the ranks of international filmmakers. Set in a Burmese prisoner-of-war camp during World War 2, this big-budget Anglo-American production is very different from the likes of *The Wooden Horse* and *The Colditz Story* in that it offers both a much richer cinematic spectacle and a more meaningful character study of men at war. Colonel Nicholson (Alec Guinness) is the rule-bound British commander, locked in a battle of wills with his Japanese captor Colonel Saito (Sessue Hayakawa). Having withstood torture to prove a point of

The Bridge on the River Kwai
1957
© Columbia/
The Kobal
Collection

principle, Nicholson agrees that his men will build Saito's strategic bridge, partly to prove the superiority of British organisation and workmanship and partly to maintain discipline amongst his men. Meanwhile, a commando raiding party led by Jack Hawkins' Oxbridge academic Warden and including William Holden's Shears, an American escapee from the camp, are attempting to blow up the bridge.

Based on Pierre Boulle's novel, which was inspired by French officers whom the author knew in French Indochina, *The Bridge on the River Kwai* takes plenty of liberties with historical events. The Japanese themselves were highly skilled at designing and constructing bridges throughout Asia and didn't require Western expertise, [11] and the conditions endured by the slave-labourer prisoners were far, far worse than those depicted in the film. Equally no commando team was dispatched to destroy the Kwai bridge. Interestingly *The Bridge on the River Kwai* shows next-to-no interest in the experiences of the 'ordinary' troops under Nicholson's command who blindly follow his questionable leadership. Through its main characters however, the film explores notions of national identity. The virile American Shears turns out to be an individual who has been impersonating an officer in order to gain better treatment. The only figure allowed a female romantic interest, Shears' only concern appears to be self-preservation, until the heat of battle where he displays heroic bravery. The Japanese Saito is revealed to be trapped by the demands of his own nation's military code, which for example insists on the brutal treatment of enemy prisoners. And the Englishman is driven mad by his insistence on duty, which has blinded him to his own collaboration with the Japanese war machine. It's a lavishly photographed film of famous set-pieces – the soldiers marching into the camp whistling Colonel Bogey, their feet clad in tattered shoes, and the climactic destruction of the bridge – but there are also moments of quiet resonance, not least Nicholson, after 28 years of service, pondering "What the sum total of your life represents, and what difference does your career make." The final words belong to the doctor Clipton (James Donald), the only British officer to question Nicholson's wrong-headedness, who looks on to the carnage and cries, "Madness! Madness!" *The Bridge on the River Kwai* is one of the few British 1950s war films to dare utter such sentiments.

EALING GOES BACK TO WAR

During World War 2, Ealing studios made a number of war films including *Went the Day Well?*, *The Foreman Went to France* (both 1942), *Nine Men* and *San Demetrio London* (both 1943), and during the 1950s, it looked back on that momentous era. Based on Nicholas Montsarrat's best-selling autobiographical novel and drawing on documentary and newsreel footage, Charles Frend's *The Cruel Sea* (1953) offers a powerfully sombre account of the Battle of the Atlantic, by homing in on the story of one ship and its crew: of all the films discussed in this chapter, it's this one which has most stood the test of time and can be seen as a valuable precursor to the German submarine epic *Das Boot* (1981). The opening voice-over belongs to Captain Erickson (Jack Hawkins), a merchant seaman who has been placed in charge in 1940 of a Royal Navy corvette, the *Compass Rose*, whose task is to protect Allied shipping convoys from U-boat attacks. "This is the story of the Battle of the Atlantic", Erickson intones. "The men are the heroes, the ships are the heroines, and the villain is the sea, the cruel sea." Erickson's colleagues are drawn from a variety of peace-time professional occupations and geographical areas, allowing us to see *Compass Rose* as a metaphor for the nation at war: amongst the officers Lockhart (Donald Sinden) is a journalist, Ferraby a banker, Morrell (Denholm Elliot) a barrister, and Bennet a used-car salesman. It's telling that the aggressive and sexually boastful figure of the working-class Bennet is removed by screenwriter Eric Ambler at an early stage from the drama.

One of the most notable aspects of *The Cruel Sea* is that it dares to show the stiff-upper-lip mentality being challenged. In one sequence Erickson has to decide whether to fire depth-charges at a U-boat which he suspects is in the vicinity of *Compass Rose* or whether he should stop his ship to pick up stranded British sailors in the water. He goes after the U-boat, thereby running over those screaming for help, and is accused of being a "bloody murderer" by one of his own crew members. That evening Erickson is commiserated by three rescued merchant seamen captains, and Lockhart later apologises for his role in the incident – it was who he had told Erickson of a radar sounding, which turned out to be erroneous. The drunk Erickson is by now openly crying, an exceptionally rare sight in a British war film from the 1950s. "It's nobody's bloody fault. It's the war – the whole bloody war", he laments. "We have to do these things and say our prayers."

Comparisons with the flag-waving tone of *Reach for the Sky* are illuminating: in *The Cruel Sea*, war is primarily about survival. Over the course of five years, *Compass Rose* and its replacement vessel after it has been torpedoed only manage to sink two U-boats. When the British sailors do eventually come across their German counterparts, they don't, in Lockhart's words, "look very different from us". Erickson regrets how over time the demands of war had hardened his feelings towards fellow men. The academic Tony Williams, [12] sees in the increasingly obsessive Erickson 'a British version of Ethan Edwards in *The Searchers* (1956)'. And in modern-day terminology Erickson is shown to

The Cruel Sea
1953

© Ealing/
The Kobal
Collection

be suffering from Post Traumatic Stress Disorder, hearing in the funnels the screams of men who died when the *Compass Rose* sunk. Ferraby, we learn, experiences a nervous breakdown following the same sinking.

The officers in *The Cruel Sea* are given romantic interests. Erickson has a spouse, who remains off-screen, Morrell discovers that his actress wife has been unfaithful to him, whilst Lockhart who initially has "no ties to the shore", develops a relationship with a WREN Julie Hallam (Virginia McKenna). It's the understated, taciturn bond between Erickson and Lockhart however, which forms the emotional core of the film. Turning down the chance to command his own ship, Lockhart elects to remain Erickson's Number One officer. He even tells Hallam that his friendship with Erickson is the "only possible relationship war allows you", and she herself acknowledges the depth of feeling that exists between Lockhart and his captain, claiming that "women don't have that kind of relationship".

Towards the end of the 1950s, and significantly post-Suez, Ealing revisited one of World War 2's most mythologised events, namely the naval rescue operation from the Northern French port of Dunkirk of some 330,000 British and French troops in May and June 1940, which prompted Churchill's 'We shall fight them on the beaches' speech to the House of Commons. Directed by Leslie Norman, *Dunkirk* (1958) consists of two interconnected narratives. Firstly, a small group of men, reluctantly led by Corporal Binns (the ubiquitous John Mills), attempt to rejoin their unit, which is being evacuated. Secondly, a pair of English civilians – a forthright journalist (Bernard Lee) and a timid garage owner (Richard Attenborough) – pilot their private boats across the Channel to help in the crisis, and they encounter Binns and his men amidst the chaos of the evacuation.

Dunkirk doesn't shy away from depicting the utter lack of preparation on the part of the British authorities for waging war in 1940. Binns and his demoralised colleagues are forced to watch helplessly as fellow troops are wiped out by enemy artillery. On the beaches troops who are taking part in a Holy Communion service become sitting ducks for Stuka dive bombers. Casualties scream in agony. Medical officers draw lots to decide who will stay behind in France with the most wounded patients. As Lee points out, "Somebody has made a mess of things, and I don't think it's the army." The closing voice-over that accompanies images of Binns being drilled on a parade ground, testify that "there was no longer a distinction between fighting men and people" and that "the nation had been made whole", yet these claims sit uneasily with the rest of the film.

DERRING-DO IN FAR-FLUNG PLACES

As with POW dramas, stories of men-on-secret-missions form their own genre within British 1950s war films, the already discussed *The Dam Busters* being a prime example. Such stories tend to follow a familiar trajectory: the men, drawn from different parts of the country, are chosen for the task by senior officers, they are subject to a rigorous training programme and then carry out the behind-enemy-lines attacks, often with a heavy loss of life amongst their own team.

It makes sense to pair *They Who Dare* (1953) and *The Cockleshell Heroes* (1955), given they both interrogate notions of leadership. Directed by Lewis Milestone, who some two decades earlier had made the anti-war *All Quiet on the Western Front* (1930), *They Who Dare* recounts an SAS raid on the island of Rhodes, where the objective is to destroy two German airfields. An impressively quiffed Dirk Bogarde plays Lieutenant Graham, who leads a team of British and Greek men. Graham, however, makes a series of mistakes due to his seeming compulsion to take risks, and he's contrasted with the grammar school-educated and more intellectual Sergeant Corcoran (Denholm Elliot). [13] The Greek contingent prove unreliable, with one of them slipping off to his local village, which is full of Italian soldiers. On several occasions Graham refuses the sensible option of calling a halt to the mission and Corcoran eventually turns on him screaming, "I hate you because you never give up." Admittedly the action sequences in *They Who Dare* aren't especially convincing, notably the climactic submarine rescue of the last two survivors, yet the hysterical edge to Bogarde's performance suggests that beneath the surface of his character's suave façade lies a troubled personality.

Shot in Technicolor a couple of years later was the American-financed *The Cockleshell Heroes*, in which a small group of marines approach Bordeaux harbour by canoe and attempt to blow up with limpet mines the German ships garrisoned there. The two highest ranking officers in this film are soon at loggerheads. The nonchalant American Major Stringer (played by director José Ferrer) favours unorthodox training methods, which will teach the men to think for themselves. The laconic Captain Thomson (Trevor Howard) on the other hand, an army veteran of some 27 years, is horrified by the lack of discipline Stringer imposes and the lack of leadership he provides, leading him to declare that, "I am ashamed to be a member of this unit." Stringer defers to the Englishman's experience and the latter volunteers as a last-minute replacement for the actual mission. At times *The Cockleshell Heroes* heads into farcical *Carry On* territory – the long-running series actually began in 1958 with *Carry on Sergeant*

– as recruits, naked except for their swimming trunks, run across a firing range, whilst handling an explosive device like a hot potato. At the same time the film draws on very old-fashioned notions of British heroism. Under questioning, none of 'our' boys refuse to co-operate with their German captors, writing 'Rule Britannia' and 'Drop Dead' on their confession sheets, and they face the firing-squad without displaying fear. In this context it's interesting to note the media condemnation of certain Royal Naval personnel, who when captured by Iranian forces in 2007 were deemed to behave in a cowardly way. Particular opprobrium was reserved for 20-year-old Arthur Batchelor who allegedly cried because his iPod was taken away from him.

One of the few 1950s war films to focus on a female protagonist, *Carve Her Name with Pride* (1958) is based on the real-life story of Violette Szabo, a British Special Operations Executive (SOE) agent who ended up being executed by the Germans. *Reach for the Sky* director Lewis Gilbert delivers a workmanlike film, in which human emotions are kept firmly in check, even when our heroine faces death. Virginia McKenna plays the Brixton shop-girl, whose French husband is killed at El Alamein, leaving her with a young child. Wanting to "do her bit" for the war effort, Szabo is recruited by SOE enjoys some japes on the training course with her fellow female colleagues, and is then dropped into France to help organise Resistance networks. For some reason in *Carve Her Name with Pride* everyone, and that includes the Germans, seem to speak English, which makes Szabo's fluency in French redundant. Budgetary constraints meant that all the foreign locations, including the Gestapo torture rooms in Paris and the Ravensbruck concentration camp, had to be recreated in England. Presumably it was considered too downbeat to allow the film to end on Szabo's death, hence the sentimental coda in which her child, following a medal ceremony at Buckingham Palace, is shown playing in street with other children, symbolising her integration into society.

More interestingly *I Was Monty's Double* (1958) – whose American title was the memorable *Heaven, Hell, Hoboken* – cheerfully calls into question received notions of heroism. Inspired by M. E. Clifton James' book, it's a jaunty account of how in 1944, two MI5 officers (John Mills and Cecil Parker) persuaded an army clerk (Clifton James himself) to stand in for General Montgomery. In order to trick the Germans that the impending D-Day landings will take place in the Mediterranean, Monty's double is dispatched to complete a tour of inspections in North Africa. James turns out to be the most modest of men, the sort of self-effacing character you might find in *Dad's Army* alongside Sergeant Wilson. (John Le Mesurier has a cameo role in the film as James' army boss.) He bears a striking resemblance to 'Monty', yet he lacks confidence in his own acting abilities and doubts if he can trick high-ranking dignitaries. *I Was Monty's Double* observes how leadership can effectively be faked, that it is a question of perform-ance rather than about innate qualities. So persuasive is James in his public duties that the Germans alter the locations of their forces and they send a commando team to capture the doppelganger, whilst audiences cheer his speeches. The unlikely hero, who slips back into obscurity, is decorated because of his ability to preserve an illusion.

The final film under consideration in this chapter is *Ice Cold in Alex* (1958) that refutes the popular notion that British 1950s war films are all emotionally sterile, jingo-istic affairs. Scripted by writer Christopher London from his own novel and directed by J. Lee Thompson who went on to make *Cape Fear* (1962) in Hollywood, *Ice Cold in Alex* is set during the North African campaign of 1942. Eighth Army Officer Captain Anson

(John Mills) is entrusted with driving an ambulance from Tobruk all the way to Alexandria whilst avoiding enemy forces. He's accompanied by a sergeant (Harry Andrews) and two nurses (Sylvia Sims and Diana Clare), and along the way they pick up a stranded South African soldier Van der Poel (Anthony Quayle). The war-weary Anson couldn't be further removed from the traditional figures of Bader and Gibson depicted in *The Dam Busters* and *Reach for the Sky*. Guilt-ridden about leaving behind a fellow officer with whom he was competing for the same woman, he's a heavy drinker who seems to be crumbling under the pressures of leadership. As with *The Cruel Sea*, the struggle in *Ice Cold in Alex* is fundamentally against the hostile environment, in this case the Libyan desert rather than a human enemy. In their battered ambulance Anson and his team have to withstand the searing heat with limited water supplies, cross minefields and lethal quicksand, and drive their vehicle up steep desert slopes. The possibility of mechanical breakdown in the middle of this forbidding expanse is terrifying.

The suspenseful *Ice Cold in Alex* is much more dynamically directed and edited than other British war films from its period, and it feels closer in spirit to Henri-Georges

Ice Cold in Alex
1958

© Associated British/ The Kobal Collection

Clouzot's existential thriller *The Wages of Fear/Le Salaire de la peur* (1953). Moreover London's screenplay blurs the moral boundaries between hero and villain, when it's revealed that Van der Poel is actually a German spy, Otto Lutz. It's his physical strength – at one point he bears the weight of the ambulance on his back during a crucial repair – that saves their lives. The bonds forged by their collective experiences mean that when

they reach their final destination and that ice cold drink, Anson ensures that Lutz is treated as a POW. The final shot is of the latter being driven away, his last words being, "All against the desert, the greater enemy."

Another unusual dimension to *Ice Cold in Alex* is that it incorporates a heterosexual romance between the neurotic Anson and Syms' Diana, and it's the woman who is presented as the more emotionally mature figure, pointing out to her lover how little he understands women. One also notices the attention paid by Thompson to the physicality of his male characters. As Geraghty observes, [14] 'In general the British war hero, although courageous, does not engage in physical demonstrations of physical strength, and his body is covered by a formal uniform or a duffel coat, polo-necked sweater and scarf, which help him to endure the cold and damp.' In *Ice Cold in Alex* though, the men are stripped down to their shorts, and Quayle's tanned strapping frame dwarfs the pale, slender physique of Mills. We're left then with a British 1950s war film in which the British officer is the weak link in the chain and the supposed enemy is the saviour. The mythologising project of so many of the other films discussed in this chapter is absent: the war here isn't honourable or conventionally heroic; it's a bitter struggle against the physical elements where a stiff upper lip is no barrier against profound psychological distress.

POSTSCRIPT

'It is both tedious and disquieting, our addiction to war films… A dozen years after World War Two we find ourselves in the really quite desperate situation of being, not sick of war, but hideously in love with it.'

William Whitebait, *New Statesman*, 5 April 1958 [15]

The 'addiction' referred to by Whitebait began to wane however. By 1960, annual cinema attendances were half what they were in 1955. Fewer war films were being made, and those that were successful at the box-office such as *The Guns of Navarone* (1961) tended not to be based on real-life stories: instead they offered audiences more escapist virtues of spectacle, adventure and stylised violence. [16] Meanwhile from the late 1950s, a new wave of social realist films, which focused on working class experiences – the likes of *Look Back in Anger* (1958), *Room at the Top* (1959), *Saturday Night and Sunday Morning* (1960) – brought with them a new generation of stars such as Albert Finney, Richard Burton, Tom Courtenay and Laurence Harvey. The decent middle-class 'chaps', men like Jack Hawkins, John Mills and Kenneth More who had fought the war on screen during 1950s suddenly seemed out-of-date in this new era.

The 1950s war films discussed in this chapter remain interesting partly because they have contributed so much to a particular ideological version of the war, which has remained embedded in British society to this day. (See how for example after the suicide bombings in London in July 2005, newspapers were quick to remind readers of the city's enduring Blitz spirit.) Yet it would be wrong to ignore the diversity and popularity of war films made in this country during the 1950s. And the most interesting among them such as *The Cruel Sea* and *Ice Cold in Alex* eschew jingoistic heroism in favour of gripping stories about the struggle of men simply to survive in the most inhospitable of natural environments.

Endnotes

1. Ramsden, John, *The Dam Busters*, London, I.B. Tauris, 2003, pp30-32.
2. Durgnat, Raymond, *A Mirror for England: British Movies from Austerity to Affluence*, London, Faber and Faber, 1970, p.83.
3. Chapman, James, 'Our Finest Hour Revisited: The Second World War in British Feature Films since 1945', *Journal of Popular British Cinema*, Vol 1, no.1. pp72-73.
4. Barthes, Roland, *Mythologies*, Granada, 1973, pp142-143.
5. Rattigan, Neil, 'The Last Gasp of the Middle Class: British War Films of the 1950s', Wheeler Winston Dixon (ed), *Re-Viewing British Cinema*, New York, State University of New York Press, 1994, p.146.
6. Calder, Angus, *The Myth of the Blitz*, London, Pimlico, 1992. pp103-104. Calder points out the fascinating example of one Kent airfield, Manston, where hundreds of airmen refused to leave the safety of their shelters for a 12 day stretch during the Battle of Britain.
7. Medhurst, Andy, '1950s War Films', Geoff Hurd (ed.), *National Fictions in WW2 Films and Television*, London, BFI, 1984, p.36. I am indebted to Medhurst's insightful analsysis of this film [*Angels One Five*].
8. J. Cull, Nicholas, 'Great Escapes: "Englishness" and the Prisoner of War Genre', *Film History: An International Journal*, Volume 14, p.283.
9. Pronay, Nicholas, 'The British Post-Bellum Cinema: A Survey of the Films Relating to World War Two Made in Britain Between 1945 and 1960', *Historical Journal of Film, Radio and Television*, Vol.8, No.1, 1988.
10. Cull, ibid, p.288.
11. Crowdus, Gary, DVD review of *The Bridge on the River Kwai*, *Cineaste*, 22 March 2001, p50.
12. Williams, Tony, *Structures of Desire*, State University of New York Press, New York, 2000, p.189.
13. Murphy, Robert, *British Films and the Second World War*, Continuum International, London, 2001, p.210.
14. Geraghty, ibid, p.191.
15. Chapman, ibid, p.70.
16. Chapman, ibid, p.72.

MISSING IN ACTION

Where was John Wayne?

PAUL EDWARDS

As the penultimate warrior of American films, John Wayne portrayed America's national conflicts from the Whiskey Rebellion through World War 2. He even appeared, pot-bellied and over age, in his own version of the Vietnam War. But, in a revealing omission, none of Wayne's sixteen war films dealt with the Korean War (1950-1953). He did not believe the Korean War conveyed the true fortitude of the American military tradition. Instead Wayne made *The Alamo* (1960) because he believed that America had lost the courage and determination that had traditionally identified its fighting men, and he wanted to remind us all. [1]

These feelings were not limited to the Duke, however, for they reflect a widespread American ignorance and misunderstanding about the war. This attitude explains, in part, why there have been so few films produced about this dramatic conflict. Critics still argue if the movies are a cause of public opinion, or simply a reaction to it, but there is little doubt that the film response to the events in Korea has had a great deal to do with contemporary America's memory of the event. Unfortunately, the Korean War has become little more than a footnote in American history. It is also true that the tendency to pass it off as the 'the forgotten war' has added to the problem because it was much more than that. The Korean War has not simply been forgotten, it has become 'structurally absent' in American history. That is, the lack of national remembrance is not simply the waning of inertia, but has been a rather active scenario of denial and repression. Even during the heaviest fighting the war never captured America's attention.

A quick trip to your local bookstore will suggest just how insignificant it has become. Even if the history section has a unit on the Korean War, it will occupy little space, and most likely will be filled with accounts of Vietnam. The same is true of Korean War films for no matter how graciously you expand the definition it is difficult to identify more than 120 related films, in comparison to the several thousands about World War 2. Even films that are not necessarily well done, nor historically accurate, can be a valuable tool in the understanding of our history, reflecting how we see ourselves and the events of our lives. It must be assumed that the lack of Korean War films is a statement in itself. While the war was going on Hollywood was aware it might have box office appeal, but even from the beginning there were no major goals, no national images or significant messages to be delivered. And as the years have gone by, few of the films have provided a useful compass, even if several years behind, for the blowing winds of American opinion.

It terms of classic cinema, great dramatic portrayals, or even propaganda value, the majority of films produced about the Korean War are of minor stature. In the first place a good many are no more about the events in Korea than they are about the Boer War, and are all but indistinguishable from World War 2 movies. They are primarily formula films in which the war has a small part, providing the opportunity for interaction among small units, and saturated with often-inappropriate World War 2 footage. Among these would be early productions like *Air Cadet* (1951), *Korean Patrol* (1951), *Battle Zone* (1952), *Hell's Horizons* (1952), *Combat Squad* (1953), *Torpedo Alley* (1953) and *Sky Commandoes* (1952). These efforts even include an attempt to get Willie and Joe into the act in *Back to the Front* (1952), an early but futile attempt at comedy.

Quite a few, of course, simply use the war as a prop for telling a totally unrelated story. Claimed by the Korean War genre, they provide no reflection on the war or the climate in which it was fought. These would include films like *Mask of Korea* (1950),

Starlift (1951), *An Annapolis Story* (1955), *Cry for Happy* (1961), Bette Midler's *For the Boys* (1992), *The Great Imposer* (1960), Clint Eastwood's grasp for old glory in *Heartbreak Ridge* (1980), as well as the totally isolated stories in *Love is a Many-Splendored Thing* (1955) and James A. Michener's *Sayonara* (1957).

Unable to release themselves from the popular 'guilt' movies of World War 2, several films carried the 'haunting images' over into the Korean War. Examples would be *Battle Hymn* (1957), a highly stylised account of Dean Hess, a minister turned fighter pilot; *Submarine Command* (1951) that allows traumatised naval officer William Holden to prove his merit; and *Torpedo Alley* (1953) where Mark Stevens is able to find forgiveness for previous military failures. These sea stories also make use of a great deal of World War 2 footage, suggesting a naval involvement in Korea that is greatly exaggerated. In this same theme, the mental anguish of the Korean experience was seen as a potential excuse for later insane behaviour as in *A Step Out of Line* (1971) in which a battle-crazed veteran sets out to kill the children of a fallen companion and is then rescued by love.

There were, of course, some viable Korean War films at which we must look to see perhaps why there were so few and why they were generally unsuccessful. The answer is fairly simple: it is because they reflected the confusion, ambivalence and lack of understanding about the war that was held in common by the film companies as well as by the general public. Film historian Peter Biskind had it right when he suggested that not only did filmmakers not know why the Korean War was fought, they really did not care. While this may seem harsh it is primarily true and is a reflection of a rather extensive public inability to identify the goals of, or justification for, America's involvement. [2]

More important perhaps to the film industry was the fact the war in Korea was not a war about which most Americans felt any sense of pride. It was a considerable letdown from the rosy memories of World War 2, and Hollywood, which thrives on the extrapolation of real life, was faced with a tale of misdirection and an event that ended with the inability to find substitutes for victory. The fact that had to be dealt with was that America did not prevail. Following on the heels of World War 2, the nation's actions betrayed the tradition of total victory that had been the cry of the Jacksonian Democrats, to whom anything short of winning was incomprehensible and immoral.

It was not the intent of the war that was faulted, but its execution. The American purpose in fighting communism was not to be questioned. It was neither the idealism nor the goals of the American people that were in doubt. Rather the lack of victory and the indisputable fact that some Americans chose to remain with the communists, brought suspicions that reflected on the courage and determination of young Americans during a time of need. The intensity of American willingness to pay the price was in question, leaving many to wonder if we would prevail in the long haul.

The emergence of limited war was as foreign to the American public as it was to the servicemen who got the blame. Everyone involved – the Americans, United Nations, Chinese and Soviet sponsors – acknowledged that they did not want, nor could they profit from, an expanded war. Unable to win without further commitment and aware of the push for a decisive victory was far too risky, they opted for a negotiated settlement. Regardless of reasons, the fact that the war did not end in victory became a blight on the national morale. Since in Korea, Americans were fighting for geographical and political gain rather than survival and virtue as in World War 2, there was really very little about which they could negotiate. If war is billed as a contest between good and evil as this one was, then to arrive at a negotiated settlement is to compromise virtue. The negotiated peace suggested a loss of national nerve and gave birth to the myth of failure.

There was a second significant force involved that was quickly demonstrated in the films produced. This was the belief that the only way this change in American behaviour could be explained was as a betrayal. There was a similar sense of betrayal in the memory of Vietnam, but in that case it was focused on the betrayal of the home front, the media, the CIA as well as the politicians and the peaceniks. In this case it was the veteran that was betrayed. However, in Korea, the nation came to believe that the GI, especially the POW, had let the country down. This belief questioned the courage, maybe even the loyalty of the American fighting man. Many grew to suspect the resolve of the military. What was left was the undercurrent of belief that somehow the Korean veteran had betrayed the nation.

This attitude was primarily focused on the men who had been prisoners. There was a perceived weakness in the mere fact of capture and behaviour while in captivity led to concerns over the lack of masculinity and national spirit that allowed for collaboration and brainwashing to turn patriotic American citizens to communism. In the films, as with the American public, there was a wariness that identified a lack of confidence and vulnerability. The returning POWs were seen as men unable to prevail against unworthy opponents, causing many to worry that the nation, especially that of the military, did not have the guts to deal with another international crisis. Within the POW scene was an image of America's weakness and betrayal. This may well be the reason that there are so many prisoner of war movies, for certainly it is a significant sub-genre of the Korean War film. These films are unlike those produced for other wars, for captivity was no longer portrayed as an escape fable, but an inner trial. The prisoner of war, who had become so prominent in the ceasefire discussions, was quickly adopted by Hollywood, but not to tell the story of the ceasefire and their release. Rather film producers focused on the ideological struggle they represented.

A part of this was to do with the role of the collaborator. Despite the fact that nearly one third of Americans captured died in captivity, there were huge estimations about the numbers who collaborated with the enemy. A couple of early films tried to side step the situation and in *Prisoner of War* (1954) and *The Bamboo Prison* (1955), the film hero was a soldier who sneaked into the prison camp and pretended to be a collaborator to help others. *Prisoner of War* flopped with critics and the box office, the only praise being that the portrayal of torture was accurate. *The Bamboo Prison* was denied support from the Department of Defense as it was feared it would mislead Americans about the real threat of collaborating prisoners and introduce the notion of brainwashing. The collaborator is primarily ignored in films set during World War 2 and Vietnam; even the spy in *Stalag 17* (1953) was in reality a German soldier. In both World War 2 and Vietnam POW movies, the enemy was the nation holding their prisoner in captivity, but during the Korean War, the enemy was always portrayed as the individual soldier's own internal weakness. In the Korean War film some form of collaboration with the enemy is central in six feature films and a TV presentation about American POWs: *Prisoner of War*, *The Bamboo Prison*, *The Rack* (1956), *Time Limit* (1957), *The Manchurian Candidate* (1962), *Sergeant Ryker* (1968) and *Outer Limits* (episode 420: 'Nightmare' 2001) all fit this pattern.

The wide-scale misconception that there were hundreds of collaborators in Korean prisons led the American people to want to know whatever happened to 'name, rank and serial number,' a question the films answered by addressing the frailty, weakness and unfaithfulness of US servicemen. Perhaps the most successful of these films were those using the courtroom as the media. In reality there were very few trials, though the ones that were conducted drew high profiles. The courtroom drama, however, allowed the questions to be looked at without a great deal of portrayal of the events discussed.

It was clearly the intent of many of these films to question the integrity of the fighters in such a way as to avoid questioning the value of the fight. For in America's anti-communist surge the fight was paramount. In *The Rack*, collaboration was looked at as treason, but the film did so with some empathy for the anti-hero, acknowledging that brave, well-meaning men can falter. The same theme is repeated in the film *Sergeant Ryker* (the similarity of Stryker is too obvious) where it becomes evident that the United States serviceman was often out of control, and thus no longer capable of following his own conscience. The problem was brainwashing.

Lingering in most of these POW films is the call for the development of an unyielding Spartan code of behaviour. The obvious answer to the POW disgrace was to be found in a rededication of American's traditional moral values. These movies identified the failure to provide emotional and ideological preparation among men of the services. Almost in response, the Advisory Committee on Prisoners of War came to the same conclusion, and ended with the affirmation that 'the Korean story must never be permitted to happen again'. [3]

A second sub-genre looks at the other side of the war by identifying the military as the enemy. The Korean War army consisted of angry men who had been successful in World War 2 and then dragged back into combat. Filling the ranks were young inexperienced draftees with civilian mentalities who shared a common disregard for having been thrown into a war for which they had no passion and understanding. Not only does the theme of military inefficiency appear in most films that deal with the ground forces, but in a variety of others. The heartless bureaucracy appears in the made-for-television film *Afterburn* (1992), in which a Korean War widow fights the military to remove the stain of pilot error attached to her husband's crash. *Battle Flame* (1959) is a film in which the story takes a backseat to the men's bitches about the military establishment.

The vast majority of Korean War films were produced primarily as narratives of the conflict without much consideration for analysis or interpretation. They run the gauntlet from pretty good to downright awful. While there is a strong element of Korean War films that focus on the jet fighters and the men who flew them, the best of the stories are those told of the grunts, the soldiers and the Marines, who slogged it out on the ground. The common theme of ground action Korean War films focused on a small unit of men where inner conflict is as much in play as the battle they fought. Certainly among these would be *Fixed Bayonets* (1951), one of Samuel Fuller's two films that came out during the war and provided a surprisingly good look at the life of the soldier at the front. Intense and somewhat mystical it follows the interaction of a small unit who are trapped in a cave and try to fight their way out. The second of Fuller's films, and considered by many to be the best of the Korean War films, is *The Steel Helmet* (1951) made in California in twelve days for little more than $100,000. Unusual in its strong support of American involvement in Korea, it also does an excellent job of portraying the isolation of those in the war and the bitter observations of a situation for which there is no end. The writer/director realistically addressed many themes of the war – the old retread called back into service, the effect on the civilian population and the difficulties of integration. Unfortunately it was also a transition film, carrying over the 'typical unit' of geographically and ethnically mixed Americans from World War 2 to Korea.

One of the best ground-based movies would be *Pork Chop Hill* (1959) where Gregory Peck leads his men in the taking and holding of the infamous hill which was, more than once, a pawn in the battle of the negotiations table. This is a powerful film that addresses both the often-unimaginable pressures on those in combat, and the seeming meaninglessness of much of what was expected. *War Hunt* (1962) follows the actions of a soldier who cannot stop killing just because the armistice has been signed, but nevertheless provides a rather realistic look at what was going on. Lacking in sophistication and short on realism, *All the Young Men* (1960) also uses a small ground unit to provide a look at the difficulties in the forced integration of the armed forces. Here the face of racism is met and challenged in a purely pragmatic fashion, as the need for a blood-transfusion makes enemies 'blood-brothers'.

As with World War 2 movies, Hollywood produced a series of films through which they tried to reach the public by focusing on some specific military activities; units whose missions seemed more glorious than the average man at the front. *Battle Taxi* (1955) was a tribute to United States Air Rescue crews, *Battle Zone* focused on two Marine combat photographers, *Dragonfly Squadron* (1954) traced the efforts to create a South Korean Air Force; the maudlin tale involved in *Flight Nurse* (1953), a strained effort to depict women during the war.

Among the air films, attention must be drawn to *The Bridges of Toko-Ri*, (1954) with an all-star cast of Grace Kelly and William Holden, though it is really a thrilling story from World War 2 transferred to Korea. One of the better known of Korean War films, it appears on late television every once in a while. It steps out of the norm by including some serious dialogue that suggests an answer to the age-old question: 'why are we here?' Others, like *Jet Attack* (1958) and *Men of the Fighting Lady* (1954) are more designed to create character studies and deliver lines like 'a man's got to do what a man's got to do'. *Sabre Jet* (1953) is strong on scenes of flying jets but weak on comprehension of the difficult air war. The exploits of individual pilots are filmed in *The McConnell Story* (1955) a crude effort of depicting the life of Captain Joseph C. 'Mac' McConnell, and *Battle Hymn* (1957), a movie that film historian Lawrence J. Quirk dubs as 'diabetes with choral music'. [4] It stars Rock Hudson playing Colonel Dean Hess, who finds solace for past mistakes by taking care of orphans.

Before moving on it is necessary to mention *M*A*S*H* (1970) even though it is not a good film in its own right, nor does it provide a realistic portrayal of the mobile ambulance surgical units or address the confrontation in Korea. This military 'Animal House' was far more an anti-authority movie of the Vietnam era than in any way a reflection of the war in Korea, and more a tragedy than a comedy in the traditional use of those terms. In fact this cynical farce barely related to the actual events, and left more than a few veterans bitter that their sacrifice was portrayed in such a fashion. The screenplay by Ring Lardner Jr., who was blacklisted as a communist sympathiser

during the early 1950s, did not at first mention the Korean War and voiceovers had to be added to do so. Everything from the often-improvised dialogue to the cruelly obvious metaphoric football match expressed the black comedy counter-culture look of the era. Banned in all US military installations for several months, it was eventually accepted and has become something of a 'classic' making top-ten lists without much thought. This success, and that of the far better TV series, has had a great deal to do with America's incongruent view and massive misconceptions about the war.

Originally *M*A*S*H* was the name assigned to *Battle Circus* (1953), in which the highly sexed Humphrey Bogart finally stops chasing June Allyson long enough to demonstrate how the mobile units moved. As in most critiques, a good deal can be learned from Hollywood's attitude by looking at what they failed, or chose not to, record

on film. It is hard to account for the fact that the dismissal of General Douglas MacArthur, one of the great tacticians of the Korean War as well as a milestone in civilian/military control, is rarely seen in films of the period. The man is portrayed in *MacArthur* (1977) staring Gregory Peck as the general, but the film is limited in many respects and barely considers the causes for his dismissal. *Collision Course* (1975) pits Henry Fonda as MacArthur and E. G. Marshall as Truman in an effort to consider the conflict between these two great egos, but in this case the war plays a small part.

The same is true for the president of the Republic of South Korea, Syngman Rhee, who when rarely mentioned is treated as an insignificant character. Other than appearing briefly in *Inchon* (1982), this highly complex man who represented both the best and the worst of the Korean unification, remains a minor and insignificant character in Korean War films, very much like most Americans saw him at the time. President Dwight Eisenhower, who is perhaps unjustly given credit for getting America out of Korea, almost has no role in Korean War films or the prolonged and aggravating negotiations so essential to the outcome of the conflict or given much coverage other than to explain the hostilities. Even the behind-the-lines invasion at Inchon, an inspired UN operation, is barely mentioned, or given its due as a significant military operation. Other than *Inchon* that was produced by the Unification Church (Moonies) with their own personal agenda, it has not been seen as critical to movies about the war. [5] No real effort was made to deal with the complexity of the United Nations force or the many roles they played. *One Minute to Zero* (1952) allows Ann Blyth and Robert Mitchum to acknowledge the UN as a less-than-objective observer, and *The Glory Brigade* (1953) with Victor Mature uses an old story of combat bonding to overcome prejudice and to appreciate the Greek devotion to the cause.

The war at home received no better attention. They range in promise from the incredibly patriotic *I Want You* (1951), which is the Korean War version of the World War 2 propaganda film *The North Star* (1943), to the classic effort to warn America of the dangers of communism in *My Son John* (1952) where the communist sympathising son is turned in by his mother. Even less reflective was the weak look into the social and cultural attitudes portrayed in *Japanese War Bride* (1952). In these films there is very little offered to either instruct or represent the people at home. While the retreat from the Chosin Reservoir had its own film, *Retreat Hell* (1952), and played as a backdrop in several others such as *Hold Back the Night* (1956) and *Battle Flame* (1959), there was little produced that identified the equally dramatic retreat of the Eighth Army to the Pusan Perimeter in July and the advancing Chinese in December 1950. Nor is there any mention of the most heart-rending stories of all – the events in Operations Little and Big Switch and the release of prisoners of war.

The film industry completely misread the relationship between China and North Korea, treating it much as they had the German-Italian unification in World War 2, leaving a comprehension of North Korea that misses the point. This misconception was also a part of the movie studios' failure to understand the ceasefire process. Serving as a crutch to move along a less than credible story in *War Hunt* (1962) and the lacklustre *Sniper's Ridge* (1961), they narrate the final days of the conflict, but do so with little insight and no celebration. Owen Crump's *Cease Fire!* (1953) is probably the best overall film of the war's final days, but it ran into problems with the movie rating codes of the time, limiting screenings to low audience numbers. Perhaps the most realistic and most significant response to the ceasefire appears in *Pork Chop Hill*, which acknowledges the folly of the final days of negotiation, and leaves the audience with a real sense of the joyless frustration of a war whose only merit was that it was over.

John Frankenheimer's *The Manchurian Candidate* (1962) is perhaps the best-known Korean War movie. It was certainly one of the few films to do well at the box office, and has recently been reissued. Based on the almost universally held misunderstandings about brainwashing, it supported the belief – and provided an easy answer – that under the influence of such massive pressure, the POW was blameless because their free will had been taken away from them. The same thesis is to be found in *Outer Limits*, but the real topic of prisoner indoctrination has never been treated in the films.

More than twenty nations were represented in the United Nations force that fought the Korean War, and of these, comparatively few nations have produced any films dealing with the conflict. Those that were made, like many of the American movies, were often limited in scope and of poor quality. On the United Nations side of the conflict, Great Britain provided several films on the war. The best of the bunch was *A Hill in Korea* (1956) that starred Michael Caine who actually served in Korea on National Service. On the Communist side, Chinese films were more plentiful but generally so politically heavy that plot and narrative suffer as a consequence. Stressing unity rather than individualism, movies like *Battle of Shangganling Mountain / Shang gan ling* (1956) offer a story of national pride in the conflict with the Americans.

In term of quality and intensity, Korean War films produced by the North and South Koreans have been much more respectable. There was little opportunity during the war for either nation to produce films and after the end of hostilities the political restraints on the industry kept them primarily story-less propaganda. Heavy censorship of the South prevented any films that showed communists too kindly from being shown.

Brotherhood/
Taegukgi
Hwinalrimyeo
2004

© Kang Je-Kyu
Film Co. Ltd/
The Kobal
Collection

However, as of the 1980s, a staggering number of films from both nations began to emerge and many are available with English subtitles.

In both nations the weight of the war is heavy. While many of the young have forgotten or never knew the full extent of the war, the film industry does not appear to be interested in letting it drop. The more recent films have been strong on maintaining the historical events and addressing those issues particular to them. Other than the preservation of events for the sake of memory, they tend to focus on the desperate implications of the separation of families. Several recent films have portrayed the role of the patrician, men and women who found themselves in circumstances that forced them to fight against their own families.

The excellent *Brotherhood/Taegukgi Hwinalrimyeo* (2004) provides considerable grounds for sympathy for two brothers caught up in a war they do not understand, and interprets the conflict in a manner seemingly more designed to unify the nation than to intensify its separation. In the South, a consistent theme has been the presence of American troops that have been presented none too highly in the highly successful *Shiri/Swiri* (1999), a classic love story embedded in a tale of tension and intrigue between the North and South, and *Silver Stallion/Eunmaneun oji anhneunda* (1991) that attempts to understand the effect of American soldiers stationed in rural Korea. A significant number of films produced by South Korea are not so much designed for deep analysis or political idealisation, but for that of well-made entertainment for the masses. Among the best would be *8240 KLO* (1966) that tells the story of a partisan attack behind enemy lines; *A Brave Soldier Without a Serial Number/Kun-bon-eom-neun Yong-sa* (1966) where two brothers are haunted by their guilt of betraying their father's political doubts; and Jon Woo's *Last Words/Jgnu-ga nam-gin Han Madi*, a 1979 film in which a suicide unit is sent to destroy the final fortifications on Hill 598, a meaningless piece of land that was fought over 39 times during the course of the war. The film deals with the attempts to discover some value in what all involved considered a meaningless gesture.

The North Korean film industry produces around 60 movies a year. They have a tendency towards being ideological in character and orientated towards action. A significant number are still related to the events of the Fatherland Liberation War, and deal with the humanitarian aspect of combat and the life of the nation when under attack. As might be expected, they are generally identified by ideological considerations and the portrayals of individual martyrdom in behalf of the nation. Perhaps the most widely seen film produced in the North is *Unsung Heroes* (1971-1981), a twenty-part spy drama that takes place during the Korean War. Often translated as *Nameless Heroes*, it is of particular interest to Americans because Charles Robert Jenkins, one of the 21 'turncoats' who refused American repatriation, played the role of a villain and husband in the film. [6]

MISSING IN ACTION

The legacy of the Korean War film appears to be set with no new movies on the horizon. Somehow the prevailing themes that draw Hollywood such as fierce action, victory over incredible odds and stories of extended courage have not drawn them to new productions. Admittedly 'we fight because we are here' is hardly a moral crusade inclined to drive Hollywood as valid justifications for new productions. What has been left in the wake are some misconceptions about brainwashing, a humorous view of mobile hospitals and a vague sense of mystery about American's first all-Asian war.

When the American serviceman returned home he was not greeted with the joy of a victor, nor was he spat upon as a symbol of failed national policy – he was simply ignored. For the veteran it has been that way ever since; their war misunderstood, their contribution unrecognised, their victorious efforts unidentified. And the movies have done little to help. When there are such wonderful stories to be told, so many heroes to be identified, so much controversy and significance to be portrayed, it remains a question as to why Hollywood avoided, and continues to avoid, it as a subject. Indeed, Clint Eastwood has recently been seen in *Gran Torino* (2008). As far as movies go this is one of Eastwood's best, but he does no service to the Korean War veteran by carrying on into this otherwise fine film, the stereotype Korean veteran who still carries a grudge, brought home his M-1, and still carries a chip on his shoulder. Shame on you Clint Eastwood and Tom Hanks for yet another telling of Iwo Jima and D-Day and leaving the story of Gloster Hill, the evacuation at Hungnam or the defence of the Pusan Perimeter still untold.

Endnotes

1. Some have suggested that *Big Jim McCain* (1952), which had Wayne playing an agent for the House Un-American Activities Committee, could be counted as a Korean War film, but this is a long stretch.
2. Peter Biskind, *Seeing is Believing: How Hollywood Taught Us to Stop Worrying and Love the Fifties*. Pantheon Books: New York, 1983, p.100.
3. Called the Burgess Committee, it called for strict training and rededication to what was considered traditional behaviour.
4. Lawrence J. Quirk. *The Great War Film*. Carol Publishing Group: New York. 1994. p.148.
5. The movie received the Golden Raspberry Award as the worst film, worst screenplay, worst actor, worst director and worst supporting actor in 1982.
6. American audiences may not be as far from the North Korean film industry as they might think. Both *The Lion King* (1994) and *Pocahontas* (1995) were animated by North Korean filmmakers at the Science Education Korea Lab, by virtue of some overlapping subcontractors to avoid the law.

APOCALYPSE NOW

World War 3, WMDs and the
End of the World As We Know It

JAMES MOTTRAM

"I know not with what weapons World War III will be fought, but World War IV will be fought with sticks and stones."

Albert Einstein

Ever since the arrival of the atom bomb, the idea of World War 3 has fascinated film-makers. The key word being 'idea'. After all, World War 3 is a war of the imagination. A war of terror, rather than one on it, it's been built on our fears of annihilation, that the end of civilisation as we know it is just the press of a button away. While, as Einstein famously hints above, the fallout of such a global conflict would most likely send mankind spinning back into prehistoric times, very few filmmakers have dared to imagine such horror.

Too often, the preference has been for the post-apocalyptic, films that envisage the modern world in tatters. These range from the sublime to the ridiculous, from *Mad Max 2: The Road Warrior* (1981), where Australia is a wasteland short on gasoline and high on leather-clad biker gangs, to *The Postman* (1997), where Kevin Costner saves humanity by delivering first-class messages of hope. Other films set out to depict the world in ecological meltdown – such as the polar ice cap floods in *Waterworld* (1995), the deforestation of *Silent Running* (1972) or the overpopulation of *Soylent Green* (1973).

In this chapter, though, it's what leads us to the apocalypse that is of chief concern. Einstein may not have been able to envisage World War 3, but that has not stopped directors across the decades. And considering it's a war that has yet to happen – and hopefully never will – this is no mean feat. A conflict fought between politicians in war rooms rather than soldiers on the battlefield, it's not a war in the traditional sense. There are no heroes, no prisoners or allies here. The only certainty is the devastation left on our doorsteps.

In some ways, James Cameron came closest to capturing nuclear carnage in his groundbreaking SF sequel, *Terminator 2: Judgment Day* (1991). As any fan of the franchise knows, Judgement Day is August 29, 1997 – the day a revolutionary defence computer named Skynet became sentient. So the Terminator mythology goes, after operators attempt to pull the plug on the self-aware machine, it reacts by launching nuclear weapons at Russia, initiating a response that results in three billion deaths. While this is never seen, Cameron gives us a taste in a dream sequence when Sarah Connor (Linda Hamilton), mother of future resistance leader John Connor, imagines herself holding onto the chain-link fence of a children's playground that overlooks a city. Just at the moment she sees a younger version of herself in the enclosure, a white flash engulfs the sky and a firestorm terrifyingly tears buildings, buses and trees to shreds. Inside the playground, humans are incinerated with ease (even if the rocking horses remain a little tougher to burn).

If this image is not arresting enough, the sight of Sarah burning alive – before we see her skeleton left clinging to the fence – is simply staggering. Reputedly, the film's special effects team who were awarded an Oscar for their work, studied hours of nuclear test footage to make the scene as real as possible. Upon release of the film, members of several US federal nuclear testing labs unofficially declared it 'the most accurate depiction of a nuclear blast ever created for a fictional motion picture'. In many ways it felt like the culmination of years of work by filmmakers fixated by the nuclear nightmare – a fixation that can be traced back to the beginnings of the 'Manhattan Project'. The initiative that led the US to enter into a race to develop atomic weapons before Nazi Germany, the Manhattan Project resulted in the bombs dropped on Hiroshima and Nagasaki that brought Japan to its knees at the end of World War 2. Back in 1944, a year before Hiroshima, Alfred Hitchcock was already alert to the Manhattan Project as he plotted *Notorious* (1946) with screenwriter Ben Hecht. As he later told François Truffaut, 'A writer friend of mine had told me scientists were working on a secret project some place in New Mexico. It was so secret that once they went into the plant, they never emerged again.' [1]

It was 'these clues' as he put it that highly influenced the story of *Notorious*, an espionage caper peppered with romantic intrigue. Set in Rio, the film stars Cary Grant as the debonair US government agent T. R. Devlin, who's out to stop a ring of Nazi spies chasing after atomic secrets. With Ingrid Bergman as Alicia, the daughter of a convicted Nazi agent and the woman Devlin enjoys an affair with, the plot hinges on the discovery of a wine bottle containing uranium, stashed in the cellar of Claude Rains' Nazi-in-exile, Alex. Not everyone, though, was convinced. 'The producer was sceptical,' Hitchcock recalled, 'and he felt it was absurd to use the idea of an atom bomb as the basis for our story.' Evidently not – as Hitchcock later discovered that the FBI had kept him under surveillance for three months after he questioned a leading scientist about the development of the A-Bomb. While Hitchcock freely admitted he was never that interested in uranium as the plot device, his prescient selection perfectly tapped into the paranoia, fear and secrecy that symbolised the atomic age and, later, the Cold War.

If *Notorious* only obliquely touched on the topic, other films embraced it wholeheartedly. Officially, the first was *The Beginning or the End* (1947), an MGM drama starring Brian Donlevy as Manhattan Project Director Leslie Groves. Intended as a cautionary tale, it emerged as little more than propaganda as it traced the development of the A-Bomb from President Franklin D. Roosevelt's greenlight to the dropping of it on Hiroshima. Fudging events 'for dramatic licence' as the opening disclaimer put it, this was notable in a scene that shows Hiroshima, bombed without notice of course, showered with warning leaflets. As Harrison Brown, a veteran of the Manhattan Project later commented in a March 1947 edition of *Bulletin of the Atomic Scientists*, this was 'a most horrible falsification of history'.

Since then, however, the development of the nuclear war film could hardly be accused of being pro-war, with most filmmakers driven to supporting the need for disarmament. As we will see, the evolution of the genre went in tandem with world events. In the wake of the Cuban Missile Crisis, for example, which saw the US and

Soviet Union come perilously close to exchanging fatal blows, came films like Stanley Kubrick's black comedy *Dr. Strangelove or: How I Learned to Stop Worrying and Love the Bomb* (1964) and Sidney Lumet's more traditional thriller *Fail-Safe* (1964). With both films set in the upper echelons of US government, they showed just how the fate of the world was left in the hands of a few hapless politicians.

By the time the genre was revitalised in the 1980s when the Cold War heated up once more, filmmakers turned their attention to us, the innocent pawns in the deadliest game of chess there can be. Rather than make films about what might lead the president to push the button, we were given a series of movies that speculated on what would happen if he did. Depicting the brutal after-effects of a nuclear attack in differing degrees, films like *The Day After, Testament* (both 1983), *Threads* (1984) and *When The Wind Blows* (1986) all set out to show just how the so-called 'nuclear family' would be ripped apart.

A mix of two genres – horror and disaster – the World War 3 movie is unquestionably the bleakest of all war films. Rarely do we even know who or why we fight. With the exception of John Milius' *Red Dawn* (1984), an apocalyptic fantasy that depicts an invasion of the US by Soviet and Cuban troops, the enemy is invisible – not unlike the deadly radioactive fallout that invariably ravages survivors following a nuclear attack. It's only after the bomb drops that the battle truly begins, as former friends become foes in a quest for survival. With no winner in the stark horror of the nuclear winter, as Peter Watkins' sensational documentary *The War Game* (1965) notes, 'Would the survivors envy the dead?'

POST-HIROSHIMA AND THE ATOMIC AGE

By 1953, MGM's *Above and Beyond* was in cinemas. A biopic of Paul Tibbets, the pilot of Enola Gay – the plane responsible for dropping the Hiroshima bomb – it was as much a slice of spin as *The Beginning or The End*. As the credits stated, 'It is hoped that the story told here… can serve to illuminate the combined achievement of all.' Even at this stage, so early in the atomic age, its message felt out of date. Perhaps as a result of residual guilt over the Hiroshima bombing, nuclear trauma dominated the screens – most potently in science fiction B-movies like *Them!* (1954), *Tarantula* (1955) and *The Incredible Shrinking Man* (1957) – which plugged into fears about the effects of radiation with their depictions of mutant ants, spiders and even humans.

Meanwhile, a series of what has been dubbed by one critic as 'nuclear noir' films [2] followed on from *Notorious* – culminating with Robert Aldrich's *Kiss Me Deadly* (1955), which featured detective Mike Hammer (Ralph Meeker) in a quest for 'the Great Whatsit', a box containing radioactive, explosive material. Comparing the volatile contents to the morally unstable world of film noir, like *Notorious*, the film tapped into issues of secrecy, trust and freedom as well as casting suspicion over science, a recurring theme in films about World War 3. When the film's femme fatale, Gabrielle (Gaby Rodgers) finally opens the box, like a modern-day Pandora, a fiery holocaust envelops her and the house.

If this was no less a fantasy than the radioactive insects of the decade's B-movies, more serious attempts were also full of misinformation. Despite boasting the tagline 'Where Science Fiction Ends And Fact Begins!!', Ray Milland's *Panic in Year Zero!* (1962)

was speculative at best – not least that every character seemed entirely immune to radiation poisoning. Milland stars as Harry Baldwin, who leaves Los Angeles on a fishing trip with his family when a nuclear attack is launched against the city. With other blasts devastating the West Coast, as well as New York, Rome, Paris and London, Harry takes it upon himself to take his wife and two children and hide out in the Californian countryside. "When civilisation gets civilised again," he states, "I'll rejoin."

Primarily, the film is an attempt to portray what happens to society when it hits the brink of collapse. Faced with a survive-at-all-costs situation, Harry becomes a symbol for humanity sliding inexorably towards moral decay. His instincts become aggressive and animal-like as he steals guns and gasoline, much to the shock of his family and even himself. As he puts it, "I look for the worst in others and I found it in myself." Yet his belief that the destruction of world order is merely temporary (he estimates "the law will come back") indicates just how naïve filmmakers in the era were regarding the after-effects of a nuclear attack. While their innocence is understandable, given how atomic tests were still held in utmost secrecy, at this point the nuclear holocaust was nothing more than a dramatic device to conveniently explore the human condition.

Likewise, Ranald MacDougall's *The World, the Flesh and the Devil* (1959) uses the destruction of humanity through a nuclear war as a way to (rather clumsily) discuss racial issues. Harry Belafonte plays Ralph Burton, an African-American miner who gets inadvertently trapped in a shaft for five days. When he finds a way out and returns to the surface, he discovers mankind has been all but wiped out in a nuclear attack. Heading to New York – where he careers around the deserted streets in a new car – he eventually meets Sarah (Inger Stevens), "free, white and 21", who survived after finding her way into a decompression chamber. Bemoaning the fact that she'll "never get married now", Sarah soon makes a play for Ralph, who has taken it upon himself to contact survivors in other cities.

Rather than strike a blow for equality, he refuses her advances. "People might talk," he says, a comment on the racial divides in the US at the time, before claiming she wouldn't even know him in the world they left behind. The film then mutates into a muddled love triangle when a third survivor is discovered. An aggressive alpha-male, Ben (Mel Ferrer) comes to blows with Ralph – until the finale when the men, together with Sarah, walk down the deserted streets hand-in-hand, differences forgotten. Suggesting that friendship and tolerance will restore world peace, in a perfect fingers-down-the-throat moment, the traditional closing legend 'The End' is replaced with 'The Beginning' (echoing *Panic in Year Zero!* that finished, 'There Must Be No End – Only A New Beginning').

For all its flaws, Stanley Kramer's *On the Beach* (1959), the highest profile film about nuclear war made at the time, could not be accused of striking such false notes of hope. Adapted from Nevil Shute's 1957 novel, the story is set in 1964, in the aftermath of a nuclear war that has devastated the northern hemisphere and seen the majority of humanity destroyed. Only those in Australia are left alive – though inhabitants must face up to the fact that they have just a few months to live before winds spread the radioactive fallout to their shores. As nuclear scientist Julian Osborne (Fred Astaire) notes, he and his fellow survivors are "doomed by the air we're about to breathe". While Kramer was evidently enamoured with controversial material – he later made Nazi war crimes film *Judgement at Nuremberg* (1961) – *On the Beach* is something of a noble failure.

Arguably the most civilised account of a post-apocalyptic world you'll ever see, characters are left to contemplate their own demise at their leisure. Amongst these are US navy officer Dwight Towers (Gregory Peck), who only survived because his submarine, the Sawfish, was in the watery depths when war broke out. While it becomes clear he has lost his wife and child in the attacks, he subsequently gets close to Moira Davidson (Ava Gardner), a feisty singleton he meets at a party when he and his crew surface to safety in Melbourne.

Much like *Panic in Year Zero!*, the 'enemy' is anonymous here. We are given no indication of who started the war or where the bombs hit. In many ways, the film suggests it doesn't matter who fired first; the damage was done in holding a nuclear arsenal in the first place. As Julian puts it, "The war started when people accepted the idiotic principle that peace could be maintained by arranging to defend themselves with weapons they couldn't possibly use without committing suicide... The devices outgrew us. We couldn't control them." Indeed, the film is chiefly a cry for "a blind world", as one character puts it, to open its eyes. As a banner says in the film's final shot of an empty Melbourne, 'There is still time... brother.'

In the build-up to its release, anticipation was huge for the film, which had 17 simultaneous premieres in cities all over the world including Melbourne, Moscow and New York. Yet it failed to meet with much enthusiasm from the critics. 'This should have been the most controversial, vital and important film of the decade. Why isn't it?' said *Picturegoer*. 'Surely not everyone would prepare to meet the end quite so nobly.' It's a fair point. The final scene between Australian naval officer Peter (Anthony Perkins) and his wife Mary (Donna Anderson) is a prime example, as they spend their last hours reminiscing about when they first met – on a beach. "Now it's all over isn't it?" she says, quietly, entirely devoid of the hysteria one might expect.

If the film can be accused of being tame by today's standards, it was nevertheless viewed at the time in some quarters as incendiary (as well as inaccurate). Unsurprisingly, Kramer met with resistance in the US over the project during pre-production, presumably for fear of generating widespread panic. As he recalled, 'I needed an atomic submarine for the film, but the Pentagon told me, "No, your story says an atomic war would wipe out the world, and this isn't so. Only about five hundred million people would be killed." I told them that's the closest I'd like to get to a total wipeout. So since I wouldn't change the script, we didn't get the atomic sub.'

The overly earnest *On the Beach* wasn't an entire washout, however. In one of the film's most arresting sequences, Dwight returns to the US in his submarine, with one glorious shot showing the craft passing beneath a deserted Golden Gate Bridge (making Danny Boyle's efforts on London's Westminster Bridge in his zombie movie *28 Days Later* (2002) look puny by comparison). Likewise, the scene when one crewmember decides to jump ship and die in his hometown, rather than return to Australia and face the inevitable away from home, is very moving. Just as the obstinate attempts to carry on life as normal back in Australia with the hosting of the motor racing Grand Prix on Phillip Island are darkly touching.

Still, one letter published at the time in *Films in Review*, quoting from Earl Ubell, science editor of *The New York Herald Tribune*, summed up the film's lack of punch. 'An all-out saturation nuclear war involving the major powers would be far more grisly than the silent affair shown on the screen. Furthermore, the human race's gritty efforts to cling to civilisation after such a big nuclear war would be much higher drama than the quiet sentimentality of this film. Needless to say, a large "reasonable" nuclear war of 4,000 megatons would spell death for at least 100,000,000 persons. The ensuing social disorganisation may be far more disastrous than the radioactivity, leading to famine […] A city like Melbourne would turn into a human jungle, rather than remain the quiet, orderly place shown in Mr Kramer's picture.'

HOW WE LEARNED TO START WORRYING AND HATE THE BOMB

In October 1962, the Cuban missile crisis brought the world to within days, even hours, of a nuclear war, after US spy-planes spotted Soviet missile bases being built in Cuba. Yet if this emphasised the very real possibility of such a conflict, Stanley Kubrick was way ahead of the game. As far back as 1958, he was obsessed with making a film about thermonuclear war. Living in New York at the time, he was so convinced the city was a prime target for an attack, he told one friend he was considering moving to Australia (perhaps having seen *On the Beach*) where it was much safer.

While he immersed himself in some 46 books about nuclear war, including *The Effects of Nuclear Weapons* and *The Causes of World War III*, it was a novel that provided the template for what would become *Dr. Strangelove*. The book was *Red Alert*, the story of a US Air Force general who launches a nuclear attack on the Soviet Union, written in 1958 by Peter George. Kubrick initially decided to work on the adaptation with his then-regular producer James B. Harris who would go on to direct *The Bedford Incident* (1965), the Melville-esque tale about a captain of a US destroyer relentlessly pursuing a Soviet nuclear submarine.

Although Harris and Kubrick eventually parted company, it was during this phase that Kubrick began reimagining the story as a black comedy. 'The only way this thing really works for me is as a satire,' he told Harris. 'It's the same point but it's just a better way of making the point.' While such a bold decision was hardly socially acceptable at the time, Kubrick was convinced this was the way forward, so much so he brought in Terry Southern to work on the script. An author, essayist and hard-drinking hipster who later co-wrote the epoch-defining *Easy Rider* (1969), Southern's gifts were perfect for crafting a comedy about nuclear war.

The plot begins after US Air Force General Jack D. Ripper (Sterling Hayden) becomes mentally unhinged, ordering 34 B-52 bombers to launch an attack on the Soviet Union. This in turn, we learn, will trigger the Soviet Union's so-called Doomsday Machine, a device designed to retaliate against any nuclear attack that will lead to all-out annihilation. With the planes hovering at the 'fail-safe' point – beyond this, they cannot be recalled – it becomes a race against time to get the recall codes before, in his own words, US President Merkin Muffley (Peter Sellers) goes down in history as "the biggest mass murderer since Adolf Hitler".

While this is the nuclear-powered engine of the story, it barely hints at the genius behind Kubrick's vision. Like *Red Alert*, the film suggests that a balance of terror is required to keep world peace. As the wheelchair-bound Dr. Strangelove (also Sellers), a former Nazi now in charge of US weapons research explains to the President, "Deterrence is the art of producing in the mind of the enemy the fear of attack." While Ripper is seen as the lunatic – he believes Communist subversives will infiltrate the US and "de-purify all of our precious bodily fluids" – his behaviour is no more ludicrous than his compatriots. Who is madder is hard to say. First there is General 'Buck' Turgidson (George C. Scott) who suggests the President strike against the Soviets, wiping out ninety per cent of their nuclear capabilities while sustaining collateral damage of "no more than ten to twenty million people – tops". Meanwhile, Strangelove offers the idea of preserving human life by sending top scientists, politicians and so on to shelter in abandoned mines (with women outnumbering men ten to one for purposes of procreation, thus creating an Aryan-like master race). Then there is Major T. J. Kong (Slim Pickins) riding on the back of the missile when it finally launches (to the sound of Vera Lynn's World War 2 anthem 'We'll Meet Again').

While the only voice of reason comes from RAF Group Captain Lionel Mandrake (Sellers again), who attempts to extract the recall codes from Ripper, Kubrick ensures we're never left in doubt that the fate of the world rests in the hands of incompetent buffoons. Although the director famously cut out a cream pie fight in the US War Room that was set to conclude the film, presumably because it rather overegged an already farcical finale, his point was already perfectly made. Peace may be their profession, as a sign at the airbase says, but warmongering is their game.

It was during the production of *Dr. Strangelove* that Kubrick learned of another project about impending nuclear war in the works. Based on the best-selling 1962 book by Eugene Burdick and Harvey Wheeler, *Fail-Safe* was being directed by Sidney Lumet, then most famous for his courtroom classic *12 Angry Men* (1957). In response, Kubrick went nuclear, launching a plagiarism lawsuit against Burdick and Wheeler, among others, alleging that their work was 'copied largely from plaintiff Peter George's book'. Certainly, the two books bear considerable similarities – war rooms, doomsday devices and so on. The only difference was that *Red Alert* was more cynical about our need for fear to keep the peace.

While the *Fail-Safe* production went ahead regardless, Kubrick won this particular war of attrition, after Columbia – already distributing *Dr. Strangelove* – acquired *Fail-Safe* and promised to release it nine months after the opening of Kubrick's film. Not that it really helped him. Early screenings of *Dr. Strangelove* left executives nonplussed, many claiming it was a disgrace. Likewise, the reviews were initially negative. As influential *New York Times* critic Bosley Crowther noted, it was 'beyond any question the most shattering sick joke I've ever come across'. [3] Nevertheless, it was embraced by the industry winning four Academy Award nominations, including Best Picture and the first of Kubrick's four Best Director nods.

Even now, it's uncanny how similar the two resulting films are. Were it not for the fact both were in production simultaneously, *Dr. Strangelove* feels like a riposte to Lumet's effort, which details what happens when a series of events lead six supersonic bombers to mistakenly head towards Moscow to launch an attack. Walter Matthau's Professor Groeteschele, a civilian advisor to the Pentagon, is less Strangelove than he is Ripper, telling us that the Russians "are Marxist fanatics – not normal people" who do not feel normal emotions like rage or pity. Primarily played out, like Kubrick's film, in dimly-lit bunkers, conference rooms and a bomber cockpit, the story similarly shows the US President (Henry Fonda) contact the Soviet premier to urge him to shoot down the rogue US bombers.

Designed as a sweat-inducing thriller, Lumet's film took itself far more seriously than Kubrick's, preferring to emphasise that such an attack comes from mechanical failure rather than the idiocy of those with their fingers hovering over the red button. "We're to blame, both of us," says the President. "We let our machines get out of hand." Nevertheless, the film does not shirk its responsibilities at the end; unlike the Cuban missile crisis, disaster is not narrowly averted. As one bomber gets through to launch on Moscow, the US President orders an American plane to similarly bomb New York (where his wife is currently visiting) – the only way to convince the Soviets the attack on

their city was not premeditated and thus prevent further conflict. As he solemnly asks, "What do we say to the dead?"

Meanwhile as *Dr. Strangelove* and *Fail-Safe* were exploring issues about nuclear war in the rooms of power, Peter Watkins was planning something far more devastating. Originally produced for the BBC, *The War Game*, a no-holds-barred documentary depicting the nature of a nuclear attack, was intended for transmission in August of 1965, to mark the twentieth anniversary of Hiroshima. Such was its power the film was postponed before in November of that year, BBC Director-General Sir Hugh Greene announced that it would not be shown at all. As his statement read, 'The effect of the film has been judged by the BBC to be too horrifying for the medium of broadcasting.'

So began the half-life of what esteemed critic Kenneth Tynan dubbed what 'may well be the most important film ever made'. As is so often the case, such censorship served only to increase the film's notoriety and the public's awareness of it. By 1966, the BBC washed its hands of the film, announcing that it had sold worldwide distribution rights to *The War Game* to the British Film Institute. A move that seemed intent on keeping the film on a limited art-house circuit, it nevertheless meant Watkins' work was finally seen, ultimately leading to its Oscar for Best Documentary at the 1967 Academy Awards.

Ironically, despite media pressure for the BBC to screen the film, the reaction by critics was not entirely positive. 'It is about as dispassionate and balanced as a party political broadcast in aid of the Campaign for Nuclear Disarmament,' [4] wrote Peter Bostock in *The Daily Sketch*. He was not wrong. The film provided a perfect centrepiece for the CND's on-going efforts. As soon as the BFI acquired the rights, CND groups began hiring out the available prints for special screenings. Designed to help increase membership and stimulate discussion, the campaign even produced an accompanying 72-page booklet entitled *What We Do After We've Shown The War Game* (presumably provide viewers with a stiff drink).

By the time the television ban was eventually lifted by the BBC in 1985, forty years on from Hiroshima, *The War Game* had already been eclipsed by more harrowing efforts, notably *Threads* (1984). Yet even now, it's not difficult to imagine just what a profound effect it had on people who saw it back in the 1960s. Despite being shot in black and white and just 47 minutes long, its mixture of hard facts and vivid footage combine to create one of the most brutal documentary films ever made. And given the featured vox pops that showed just how ignorant members of the public were about the effects of radiation, it was evidently vital.

The film begins with news footage: the Chinese invade South Vietnam in support of the Vietcong, the US threatens to retaliate and the Russians ally with the Chinese. With this providing the international context, the film then turns its attention to Britain. The scenes are again typical: women and children evacuated, emergency rationing, hardware stores mobbed for sandbags. One man proudly shows off his gun "and I certainly intend to use it" he cries, as if he believes he'll be fighting them on the beaches. Then, as the air-raid siren sounds, sending one family into hysterics, the voiceover terrifyingly notes: "This could be the way the last two minutes of peace in Britain would look."

It's when the bomb explodes that *The War Game* truly comes into its own. At 9.16am, a single megaton nuclear missile overshoots its target – an airfield in Kent – and bursts in the sky (presumably this 'best case scenario' was used because had it landed there'd be little left to document). Furniture sets on fire. A boy 27 miles away from the blast receives retinal burns. His family cower in the kitchen as the blast waves rumble overhead – a phenomenon that's been "likened to a door slamming in the depths of Hell", we're told. Amid this panic, Watkins smartly recreates the resulting firestorm, not unlike the ones witnessed in Dresden, Tokyo and Hiroshima.

Using a hand-held camera and newsreel footage, we see firemen flattened by the winds in excess of 100mph. Faces are charred. Screams ring out. Cars explode. Finally we see figures collapse on the floor. "When the carbon monoxide content of inhaled air exceeds 1.28%, it will be followed by death in three minutes," informs the voiceover. "This is nuclear war." It's a frightening sequence, even by today's standards. Yet worse is to come, as doctors explain that patients with more than fifty per cent of their body covered in burns are left in a 'holding section' to die, primarily to preserve precious drugs for those with a better chance of surviving.

Those that do would no doubt wish they hadn't. Psychiatric problems are prevalent – "this too will be the legacy of a thermonuclear war" we're told. Corpses are disposed of by burning, the victims identified by their wedding rings. People become lethargic and apathetic, living in their own filth in a state of dejection. Firing squads roam the streets as looting begins and "behaviour becomes more primitive". At a refugee camp in Dover, four months after the attack, we see a pregnant woman – so often a symbol of the fragility of life in films about nuclear war – and are told she has no idea if her baby will be born alive. "Is there any real hope?" the voiceover asks. By Watkins' estimation, it seemed not.

TWO TRIBES GO TO WAR

In the 1970s, the arms race was far from over. It may have been the first UN Disarmament Decade but its 'meagre achievements' led the UN General Assembly to hold its first Special Session on Disarmament in 1978. As was stated in its final document issued on June 30, 'removing the threat of a world war – a nuclear war – is the most acute and urgent task of the present day'. Yet arguably due to America's involvement in the Vietnam War, diverting Hollywood's attention to Asia, films that were specifically about nuclear arms largely dropped from sight.

Admittedly, there was *The Omega Man* (1971), an adaptation of Richard Matheson's 1954 novel *I Am Legend*, first brought to screen as *The Last Man on Earth* (1964). But even this retelling, set in 1977, two years after a war between the People's Republic of China and the Soviet Union almost wipes out the entire human population, dealt with germ warfare. With humans turned into zombies, such apocalyptic devastation was very much in the realm of science fiction. When the nuclear issue was raised, it was in films like *The China Syndrome* (1979), in which Jane Fonda played a reporter who witnesses an accident at a nuclear power plant. Coincidentally released twelve days before there was a partial core meltdown at Pennsylvania plant Three Mile Island, it had little to do with impending Armageddon.

Yet by the 1980s, films about nuclear war returned with a bang. The Cold War intensified once again, not least after President Ronald Reagan called the Soviet Union an "evil empire" in March 1983, two weeks before he announced plans to proceed with the space-based missile defence system, which became known as 'Star Wars'. In Britain that November, the first of 96 US cruise missiles arrived at the RAF base at Greenham Common, each carrying a warhead with the explosive power of 16 Hiroshima bombs. A month later, 50,000 women – part of the Greenham Common Women's Peace Camp formed back in 1981 – encircled the base in protest.

The nuclear issue was now top of the agenda, something popular culture was swift to reflect. In the music charts, German singer Nena scored a hit with '99 Red Balloons', a Cold War protest song about the rising tensions between the superpowers. *OMD* referenced the Hiroshima bombing with 'Enola Gay' and, most potently, *Frankie Goes to Hollywood* delivered 'Two Tribes' in 1984. Featuring the unforgettable tones of Patrick Allen (who had voiced the *Protect and Survive* [5] ads two years earlier), the song came with a full-on video. Directed by Godley and Creme, it depicted look-alikes of Reagan and Soviet leader Konstantin Chernenko embroiled in a bloody fistfight as other world dignitaries look on.

Still, no song could ever match the power of the moving image and it was two television films that led the way: ABC's *The Day After* (1983) and the BBC's *Threads*. While feature films may lack the immediacy of news coverage, these two were different. Ripped from the headlines, they both tapped into our very primal fears about nuclear war. Watched by an estimated half the adult US population, as one critic put it, 'The biggest American media event of 1983 was the transmission of *The Day After*.' Akin to when Orson Welles broadcast his reading of *War of the Worlds* in 1938, its director, Nicholas Meyer, simply stated, 'I wanted to clobber sixty million people over the head.'

The film is credited as the brainchild of the then-president of ABC Motion Pictures, Brandon Stoddard. Inspired by the box-office success of *The China Syndrome*, he was determined to make a social conscience picture about nuclear war. In Meyer, best known for *Star Trek II: The Wrath of Khan* (1982), he found the perfect director – a man with vehement anti-nuclear beliefs. In principle, Meyer's concept for the movie was sound; as he wrote in a production diary, 'I tell ABC my overall idea: the more *The Day After* resembles a film, the less effective it is likely to be. No TV stars. What we don't want is another Hollywood disaster movie with viewers waiting to see Shelley Winters succumb to radiation poisoning.' [6]

The problem is that despite Meyer's good intentions, *The Day After* emerged as exactly what he didn't want. Yes, there are some remarkable scenes – none more so, perhaps, than the sight of Minutemen missiles being launched into the Kansas City sky, with the camera catching the horrified expressions of residents as the realisation dawns on them that equivalent bombs will soon be heading their way. Indeed, the film's size-able budget allowed Meyer to craft an unforgettable sequence when the bomb finally drops. Until Cameron's efforts in *Terminator 2*, the sight of people turned into skeletons, as buildings crumble and fire engulfs the landscape, was unquestionably the most pow-erful representation of a nuclear attack put on film. So much so, a disclaimer at the beginning advised 'parental discretion' when it came to showing it to younger viewers.

Set in the heart of America's Mid-West (it was shot in and around Lawrence, Kansas), the film relies not on showing the devastation of cities so much but of the surrounding countryside. With the ground left ashen-white, animal carcasses scatter the Great Outdoors – a sight just as symbolic to any American as the Statue of Liberty or the White House being torn to shreds. Still, *The Day After* often struggled to knit together a convincing narrative around its impressive set pieces and production design. Drawing from a mish-mash of genres – science fiction, documentary, melodrama – the hybrid nature of the film meant it was neither satisfying as conventional entertainment nor sufficiently informative when conveying the after-effects of nuclear war.

One of the biggest inaccuracies of the film was not properly hinting at the prospect of a nuclear winter, a major flaw given ABC reputedly brought on board a glut of technical advisors. Thus the scenes where members of the National Emergency Reconstruction Administration meet with farmers to discuss planting new crops and decontaminating the soil are laughable. That said, the filmmakers might point to the end caption: 'The catastrophic events you have witnessed are, in all likelihood, less severe than the destruction that would actually occur in the event of a full nuclear strike against the United States.'

While this hardly aids the film's credibility, neither does Meyer. He hits too many obvious notes, from the preacher reading from the Book of Revelation to the sight of a statue "in memory of our world war veterans" with two victims of the blast lying dead at the bottom of it. Everything from the Cuban missile crisis to Hiroshima is invoked, while the characters – primarily hick families living on farmsteads – feel like extras on *The Waltons*. Screenwriter Edward Hume has said the film is 'not about politics or politi-cians or military decision-makers. It is simply about you and me – doctors, farmers, teachers, students, brothers and kid sisters.' That may be true, but it didn't make it any more palatable.

Nine months later in September 1984, came the British response to *The Day After*. Written by Barry Hines (who had already penned three Ken Loach films including 1969's *Kes*), *Threads* was directed by Mick Jackson, who had previously helmed QED's *A Guide To Armageddon*, a documentary that speculated on what would happen if Britain was subjected to a nuclear attack. *Threads*, however, was a different prospect. Dubbed a 'mini-drama overtaken by a maxi-drama' by Jackson, as it primarily follows the fate of two families in Sheffield when the bomb falls on the city, it was meant as a riposte to the '*Dallas*-like' gloss of *The Day After*.

This it certainly is. Even now, as I write 25 years on from first seeing *Threads*, its power remains undiminished. If *The Day After*'s soap-opera sheen led it to be dubbed '*Peyton Place* with a nuclear explosion' by one US defence official, *Threads* was anything but, coming across more as a doom-laden docu-drama. Still, Hines nods his head to the soap opera in the build-up to the bomb, when we learn that nice middle-class girl Ruth (Karen Meagher) is pregnant. While boyfriend Jimmy (Reece Dinsdale) promises he'll stand by her, their subsequent decision to marry at such a young age shocks both families. Still, they let them get on with it, moving into a flat they will ultimately never use.

Just as this kitchen sink drama takes place, a series of international events unfold in the background. Primarily shown on televisions and heard on radios in homes, shops and pubs (which are often being turned off or over as more pressing everyday matters take precedence), the build-up to the war initially seems remote. US warships are deployed in the Gulf of Oman, two nuclear explosions occur in the Middle East and anti-Russian demonstrations take place in the US and so on. Slowly but surely, however, a nuclear conflict becomes a very real possibility to the residents of Sheffield, which lies just 17 miles from a NATO airbase used to house US Phantom jets in wartime.

Unlike *The Day After*, Jackson's film set out to document the disaster with factual evidence that puts it more in league with *The War Game*. Rather than include spurious characters – like John Lithgow's radiation expert seen in Meyer's film – the science fact came from a mix of impassive voiceover (provided by Paul Vaughan) and chilling onscreen captions estimating deaths, casualties and other consequences. What's more, rather than simply depict the immediate aftermath of the bomb, Hines' script dares to look into the future. Going as far as thirteen years on with Britain reduced to a wasteland and survivors little better than scavenging animals, it's the closest we have come to seeing Einstein's aforementioned prediction on screen.

If the film lacked the budget of *The Day After*, Jackson more than made up for it with his innovative approach to depicting the devastation. While both the make-up departments and the set designers excelled themselves, it was Jackson's clever reuse of material from his QED film that really left its mark. Punctuating the action are tableau-like black-and-white stills that seem to accentuate the horror of the holocaust, depicting burnt corpses, bombed-out buildings and the bleak skies of the nuclear winter. Combined with the stock scenes of panic buying, looting and martial law that were now *de rigueur* in such films, the effect is nothing less than harrowing.

Certainly there's an argument that the characters are reduced to little more than ciphers once the bomb drops – yet the film does a superlative job of depicting just how the threads of our society, culture and civilisation are left in tatters. The shot of a charred billboard showing a blonde-haired baby advertising Standard Life insurance with the slogan 'For all of your life'. The sight of Ruth's daughter carrying a Sainsbury's carrier bag or the sounds of Chuck Berry's 'Johnny B. Goode'. Most potently, the scene of a ragged group of survivors watching a videotape of the BBC's educational programme *Words and Pictures*, a great irony considering language has been reduced to little more than guttural sounds.

If *Threads* and *The Day After* were the most talked-about films to examine the nuclear holocaust, they weren't the only ones. Hollywood turned it into a game with surprising success, as Matthew Broderick's teenage techie hacks into a US Defense Department computer in John Badham's *WarGames* (1983). Designed to coordinate early warning systems and nuclear deterrents in the case of World War 2, when Broderick challenges it to a game of 'Global Thermo-Nuclear War', the machine begins what looks like a real-life countdown to Armageddon. Like an adolescent *Fail-Safe*, it may be primarily a thriller but the message was clear: there are no winners in nuclear war. As the programme concludes, 'The only winning move is not to play.'

More interesting, however, were two films that again preferred to examine the horror via the perspective of ordinary members of the public. Directed by Lynne Littman, *Testament* (1983) focuses on what happens to one family in a well-to-do middle-class suburb of Hamlin, California, after an unanticipated (and unseen) nuclear attack is launched. With the film refusing to provide any form of political context, the mother, Carol (Jane Alexander) and her children find out when a news flash interrupts an episode of *Sesame Street*. Just as we don't hear any news of her husband (William Devane), presumably dead after heading on a business trip to San Francisco, no indication of who launched the attack is given.

Narrated by Carol in a very detached manner, as she writes her diary cataloguing the days that follow the attack, the film follows the typical template of the before/after nuclear war film. Inevitable scenes of panic buying (in this case at the gas station) are followed by ones of looting. After a doctor at the community meeting at the church hall warns us that radiation will lead to vomiting, skin sores and loss of hair, Carol's children, one by one, begin to suffer the symptoms. Indeed, the theme of the film is prefigured by the primary school production of *The Pied Piper of Hamelin*. "Your children are not dead," the Pied Piper tells the townsfolk. "They will return. They are just waiting until the world deserves them."

Again, Britain managed to produce a far more moving examination of what happens when the bomb drops, courtesy of the animated version of Raymond Briggs' cartoon tale *When the Wind Blows* (1986). It's seen entirely from the viewpoint of Jim and Hilda Bloggs (voiced by Sir John Mills and Dame Peggy Ashcroft), a retired couple living in a remote Sussex cottage. Having survived World War 2, both believe that a bit more of the Dunkirk spirit will see them through again. "It'll take more than a few bombs to get me down," says Hilda, who shows such a lack of understanding about a nuclear attack, she frets her cake will burn in the oven when the three-minute warning sounds. While their naïve outlook provides the film's gentle humour (like the sweetest example ever of panic buying, as Hilda puts out a note for the milkman to deliver 28 pints of milk), it gives way to an inevitably tragic conclusion. Using live-action footage to show the devastation of the bomb, like *Threads* there is no redemption here. The teams of flying doctors that Jim envisages will soon be on their way never arrive. With no water ("such a shame we can't wash up," says Hilda) or telephone lines working, Briggs' story just gives us the merest hint of how civilisation collapses, when a rat scurries up the toilet.

Indeed, as the pair gradually succumbs to radiation sickness, it's like watching two *Daily Mail* readers die a slow, horrible death. But in many ways, the Bloggs are the perfect mirror for us all. Briggs' story utilises information from the *Protect and Survive* campaign (the title is evidently taken from a line in the pamphlet that notes, 'The radioactive dust, falling where the wind blows it, will bring the most widespread dangers of all'). While Jim follows the instructions, making a 'lean-to' from a door to shelter from the radiation, it shows just how naïve we all were if we thought such rudimentary protection would help us survive a nuclear blast.

JUDGEMENT DAY

In 1989, the Berlin Wall fell, leading to the dismantling of the Soviet Union and the Eastern Bloc. The Cold War was over. As a result, with the exception of *Terminator 2*, films about nuclear war were in decline. The writing was on the wall as far back as Steve De Jarnatt's *Miracle Mile* (1988), a ludicrously contrived (and unintentionally hilarious) day-glo story about a Los Angeles musician (Anthony Edwards) who accidentally becomes aware of an impending nuclear war between the US and Soviet Union. Having just met the girl of his dreams, Julie (Mare Winningham), his world implodes when he accidentally intercepts a payphone call. On the line is a voice, calling from a bunker in North Dakota, claiming the end of the world is nigh.

As Julie says of events, "We could probably make a TV movie out of it" – though evidently one nowhere near as good as *Threads* or *The Day After*. There's something horribly cut-price about *Miracle Mile*, inadvertently symbolised by the copy of the Cliff Notes guide to Thomas Pynchon's anti-war novel *Gravity's Rainbow* glimpsed in one character's briefcase. The same can be said of the HBO-produced *By Dawn's Early Light* (1990), another *Fail-Safe*-like drama about what happens when a terrorist attack on the Soviet Union, one that seems to originate from inside NATO ally Turkey, triggers a nuclear exchange between the superpowers.

While HBO subsequently became a byword for the production of sophisticated television drama, this was far from it. The film is primarily a power struggle, as the President (Martin Landau), who many believe dead after Washington is destroyed, attempts to wrest control from his gung-ho successor. Again recalling the soap bubbles of *The Day After*, the other subplot concentrates on the relationship between a veteran pilot (Powers Boothe) and his female co-pilot (Rebecca De Mornay) flying a B-52 bomber sent to attack the Soviet Union. With dreadful dialogue ("the fate of this planet is riding with you"), it further signalled that the half-life of nuclear films had almost expired.

The one exception in this period is Rod Lurie's *Deterrence* (1999), a smart attempt to replicate real-time terror. Entirely set in a Colorado diner where President-in-waiting Walter Emerson (Kevin Pollack) is forced to take shelter during a snowstorm, the film begins as Saddam Hussein's son sends Iraqi troops into Kuwait, with the intention of heading to Saudi Arabia. Emerson announces that he will drop a nuclear device on Baghdad unless Iraq withdraws from Kuwait inside the next one hour and twenty minutes. Interestingly, his advisors who surround him in the diner are not bucking for a conflict, but seem appalled at the President's nuclear brinkmanship. "Dropping an atom bomb isn't a war," he is told by Gayle Redford (Sheryl Lee Ralph), his national security advisor.

In many ways, the film grapples with the "moral certainty", as Redford puts, it takes to launch a nuclear attack. Emerson is aware that President Truman debated whether to forewarn the Japanese people before dropping the bomb on Hiroshima. "I'm determined to spare as many lives as I can," he claims. Yet, as it turns out, not unlike *WarGames*, *Deterrence* is a game, symbolised – in case you don't realise – by the rather obvious symbol of a chessboard in the diner. Well aware that the weapons owned by Iraq (cunningly sold to them, via the French government, by the US) were fakes, Emerson emerges as the winner. Given subsequent events in the Middle East, *Deterrence* now seems mightily prophetic.

After the events of 9/11 while Hollywood briefly turned its firepower towards thwarting Al-Qaeda, others imagined how further terrorist attacks could be inflicted on Uncle Sam. Take Chris Gorak's *Right At Your Door* (2006), a heart-racing thriller seen through the eyes of Los Angeles couple Lexi (Mary McCormack) and Brad (Rory Cochrane) as a so-called 'dirty bomb' is dropped on the city by unknown assailants. "It was a complete reaction to 9/11," says Gorak. "During 9/11, I was separated from my wife. I was in Vancouver and she was in Los Angeles. But she's originally from New York, and we have friends and family there and in Washington DC, and that feeling of isolation and separation played a lot into the concept of the film."

Rather than fall from fashion in the decade that has seen North Korea conducting a nuclear test and tensions concerning Pakistan's arsenal, the prospect of the apocalypse still hangs over us. Even Mr Hollywood himself, Steven Spielberg, recognised this fact, setting his long-awaited sequel *Indiana Jones and the Kingdom of the Crystal Skull* (2008) in the atomic age (with Harrison Ford's hero even sheltering from an accidentally triggered blast in a refrigerator). As Spielberg put it, "I thought that there was something quite iconic of a silhouette of Indiana Jones against a mushroom cloud."

While CBS series *Jericho* set about exploring what life was like for a series of characters after a nuclear war, Zack Snyder delivered *Watchmen* (2009), his much-anticipated adaptation of the graphic novel by Alan Moore and Dave Gibbons, which was first published in 1986. Set in an alternative 1985 where Richard Nixon has just been elected for a third term in the White House, it begins as the superpowers are edging ever closer to Armageddon. Primarily a tale of a jaded group of superheroes, the most prominent is the aptly named Dr. Manhattan, a character that embodies the very development of the atom bomb.

'Created' after a nuclear physicist, Jon Osterman, accidentally gets locked inside a test chamber and is torn apart, Dr. Manhattan re-emerges like a living WMD – a stark-naked, blue-skinned super-being so powerful, he's said to be able to "destroy large areas of Soviet territory instantly". With Dr. Manhattan an unwitting pawn in the Cold War after the US sends him in to finish the Vietnam conflict inside three months, it's little wonder Snyder estimates the film is "closer to *Dr. Strangelove* than it is [*The*] *Fantastic Four*". In the era that has ushered in the phrase Weapons of Mass Destruction, it's a sharp reminder that nuclear war is still a very real threat.

Endnotes

1. *Hitchcock-Truffaut* by François Truffaut, Simon and Schuster, 1967.
2. *The Big Secret: Film Noir and Nuclear Fear* by Mark Osteen, *Journal of Popular Film & Television*, Summer 1994.
3. *Kubrick Film Presents Sellers in 3 Roles* by Bosley Crowther, *The New York Times*, 30 January 1964.
4. *Brilliant But It Must Stay Banned* by Peter Bostock, *The Daily Sketch*, 9 February 1966.
5. Produced by the British government in the early 1980s, *Protect and Survive* was a series of pamphlets, radio broadcasts and public information films on civil defence designed to inform citizens about how to protect themselves during a nuclear attack.
6. *Bringing the Unwatchable to TV* by Nicholas Meyer, TV Guide, 19-25 November, 1983

THE EPIC VERSUS
THE B-MOVIE

ROBERT DAVENPORT

The epics (*The Bridge on the River Kwai* (1957), *The Longest Day*, *Lawrence of Arabia* (both 1962), *Apocalypse Now* (1979), *Battle of Britain* (1969)) versus the B-movies (*The Steel Helmet*, *Fixed Bayonets!* (both 1951), *Run Silent Run Deep* (1958), *Merrill's Marauders* (1962), *Where Eagles Dare* (1968), *Kelly's Heroes* (1970), *Aces High* (1976), *Cross of Iron* (1977) – which are better in their portrayal of wartime?

Hollywood came up with the idea of A-and-B pictures which became a standard for the way movies were shot and promoted from its inception during the early depression years until the concept was dropped in the early Seventies. An A-picture had all of the production values the public had come to expect: popular actors and actresses, lavish costumes, expensive and grandiose sets, outstanding musical accompaniment, high quality photography, often in colour, and a script with sharp dialogue, well developed characters, a clear concise storyline and a happy ending. These films were shown with a cartoon, a short subject one-reel film, a newsreel and the requisite previews of coming attractions. The only trouble with A-pictures was that they were expensive to make and tied up movie stars much longer than the B-pictures. Because of these constraints, most studios only made a certain number of A-pictures a year. Even so, because of all of these production values, the studios could usually rely on a good return on their investment as the public considered these to be 'must see' event films.

On the other side of the equation, B-pictures either featured once-popular actors whose careers were on the decline or actors studios were grooming for stardom and perceived to be on the way up. The films were shot in a hurry and on a tight budget. The scripts were penned by new writers and the dialogue, plot points and ultimate resolution could be mundane. Because these movies were usually shot on the studio lot, they used whatever costumes and sets were left over from other productions, thereby saving greatly on production costs, while at the same time contributing with their revenues to covering the substantial overhead which running a studio entailed. Because of their lower quality, however, it was difficult to convince the public to see a B-picture; therefore, the B-movies were often sold as a double feature consisting of two B-movies, cartoon, a short subject, newsreel and a travelogue or a one-reeler featuring a popular band and, of course, the mandatory previews of coming attractions. Because they were shown in double bills, a B-movie might run for seventy to eighty-five minutes, whereas an A-movie might run from ninety minutes to two hours. 'B' units became the place for new actors and actresses, directors, writers, composers and cameramen to learn their trade and to prove themselves.

The B-feature in the contemporary Saturday-morning line-up for children of a certain age would invariably be preceded by the latest instalment of a chapterplay, which in twelve or fifteen twenty-minute episodes would thrill the viewer with the exploits of intrepid G-men, superheroes and naval officers, and as the war commenced, became a handy vehicle for propaganda; noteworthy Republic serials of the wartime period include *Spy Smasher* (1942), in which the heroes combat a strikingly accurate rendition of a Horten flying wing, and *G-Men vs the Black Dragon* (1943), whereby Japanese subversives attempt to cripple America's war effort. Post-war, the Nazis and Japanese would metamorphose into Martians.

During the heyday of the studio system (1930-1975), most studios had A-and-B units which made the films for distribution – A-units spent the lion's share of the studio's money, but it was often the B-film units that made the most money. There were two reasons for this phenomenon. First, the B-units made more features than the A-units and since the cost of the movie tickets was the same they brought in proportionally more revenue to the studio. Also, it was known for a B-movie to turn out so well audiences would attend a B-picture as if it were an A-film.

Some found the A- and B-system confusing and thought it was a film ratings system, but nothing could be further from the truth. In those days, there were no age restrictions on movies because they had to have an MPCC seal to be distributed which meant that it conformed to a code that had been established in the mid-Thirties and was safe for family viewing. The idea of movie ratings did not come about until the end of the studio era, and film ratings had nothing to do with the A and B categories.

Lawrence of Arabia
1962

© Columbia/
The Kobal
Collection

The members of the Academy of Motion Picture Arts and Sciences who award the Oscars clearly differentiated be-tween the epics and the B-pictures, perhaps because they were in the studio system and felt that only A-pictures deserved such recognition. *Lawrence of Arabia* took best picture and best director, won a total of seven Oscars, and resulted in nominations for Peter O'Toole and Omar Sharif. *The Bridge on the River Kwai*, another David Lean-directed epic, swept the awards with seven wins, including best director, best picture, best screenplay, best actor for Alec Guinness and resulted in a nomination for best supporting actor for Sessue Hayakawa. *The Longest Day* received two Oscars from five nominations. *Apocalypse Now* had two Oscar wins out of eight nominations including best picture, best director, best screenplay and best actor in a supporting role for Robert Duvall.

While the war epics regularly sweep the Oscars, the B-movies are usually ignored, even when they are recognised by other awards. *The Steel Helmet*, while it received the Writer's Guild award for Best Written American Low-Budget Film, was completely ignored by the Oscars. The films with no awards include *Merrill's Marauders*, *Kelly's Heroes*, *The Tanks Are Coming* (1951) and *Fixed Bayonets!* And even if they were considered great movies in their own country such as *Aces High* and *Cross of Iron* and received foreign awards, these B-movies were still ignored by the Oscars.

But even though they were not officially recognised by the Oscars, such B-movies are often respected by those within the business. In one survey of the top 100 war movies, Steven Spielberg voted *Where Eagles Dare* as his favourite, despite its B-movie status – he even went so far as to quote the famous 'Broadsword calling Danny Boy' line. Casting is one hallmark that differentiated epics and the B-movies. Of course, fifty years later, it's hard to see that same distinction. While shooting the movie, one actor might be former A-list on their way down while a B-actor is on the up; those distinctions do not necessarily hold true half a century later. For example, *Run Silent Run Deep* is a good example of a B-movie in which the two leads, Clark Gable and Burt Lancaster, are on the opposite sides of the spectrum at the time, although they are now remembered as film legends.

Clark Gable was definitely a former A-list actor in the twilight of his career when *Run Silent Run Deep* was made. At the time of *Gone with the Wind* in 1939, Gable was one of the biggest movies stars in the world, but in 1958 had sunk to the point where he could only find work in B-pictures. After *Run Silent Run Deep*, Gable would only star in a further four pictures before dying of a heart attack while filming *The Misfits* (1961). Gable had been nominated as best actor three times and had won an Oscar for his performance in *It Happened One Night* (1934). But his heyday was prior to World War 2, and when he returned from fighting in Europe after three years of service, his career would never return to the mega-star level that he had previously held. Gable became increasingly unhappy with the mediocre roles offered to him by MGM as a mature actor and refused to renew his contract in 1953 and proceeded to work independently.

Burt Lancaster on the other hand, although already a well known actor, was considered by many at this point in his career to be 'Mr Muscles and Teeth,' a movie actor that was yet to be respected before winning an Oscar for Best Actor in *Elmer Gantry* (1960). Lancaster's movie image with the Academy might have prevented him from receiving the Oscar for his role in *From Here to Eternity* (1953), the award going to William Holden for *Stalag 17*. However, it was roles like that of the submariner in *Run Silent Run Deep* that helped to change this perception and Lancaster was ultimately nominated for the Oscar four times.

The ability of the B-movie to make use of rising and falling stars was of great value to studios since they could not hope to compete for the A-list actors. An A-list film such as *The Bridge on the River Kwai* would understandably attract the A-list actors. William Holden who had two Oscar nominations and one win got the role of Commander Shears and was supported by Alec Guiness and other A-list actors. However, the B-movie had to lure the past and future A-actors and this is perhaps why so many of these movies such as *Run Silent Run Deep*, which were considered to be B-movies at the time they were made, are now deemed to be war classics. With the passage of time and their original audience long gone, they are routinely screened on Midnight Movie and Netflix with a stature they never had in their first run.

A number of war films introduced the public to future stars for the first time. *Run Silent Run Deep* was the feature film debut for Don Rickles. *Fixed Bayonets!* was the first film role for screen legend James Dean. *Kelly's Heroes*, one of my personal favourites, is another good example of actors on the rise whose appearance in this well written B-list war comedy helped propel them up the showbiz career ladder. In retrospect, one would be mistaken that the movie featured an all-star cast; however, many of the lead actors were emerging from careers in television. Clint Eastwood had starred in the television series *Rawhide* from 1959 to 1965, was the man with no name in Sergio Leone's *The Good, the Bad and the Ugly / Il Buono, il brutto, il cattivo* (1966) and had yet to flex his directorial muscles. Of course, Eastwood was to shine for his seminal role as Harry Callahan in *Dirty Harry* (1971) and was to win Best Director and Best Picture Oscars for *Unforgiven* (1992) and *Million Dollar Baby* (2004). Telly Savalas was a television veteran but had yet to say his famous catchphrase "Who loves you, baby?" on *Kojak* (1973-1978). Carroll O'Connor who plays Major General Colt went straight from *Kelly's Heroes* to playing Archie Bunker in *All in the Family* (1968-1979). Gavin MacLeod was yet to star in *Mary Tyler Moore* (1970-1977) and *The Love Boat* (1977-1987) and Donald Sutherland was just about to do *M*A*S*H* (1970), a role that propelled him to national prominence.

A similar situation existed for writers – the B-movie often had great writers on the rise or fall. One of the greatest differences between the A-and B-movies is the production budget. The epics get the great battle scenes, the B-movies a lot less. Yet, it is the small scenes that are best remembered from both types of movie and for these we thank the writers. For example, in *Lawrence of Arabia*, it is the great and epic battle scenes that are remembered such as the taking of Aqaba and the massacre of Turkish troops. But it is the little scenes such as the following between Lawrence and General Allenby that really make the film outstanding, and for which they were honoured by an Oscar:

> *T. E. Lawrence:* I killed two people. One was... yesterday? He was just a boy and I led him into quicksand. The other was... well, before Aqaba. I had to execute him with my pistol and there was something about it that I didn't like.
>
> *General Allenby:* That's to be expected.
> *T. E. Lawrence:* No, something else.
> *General Allenby:* Well, then let it be a lesson.
> *T. E. Lawrence:* No... Something else.
> *General Allenby:* What then?
> *T. E. Lawrence:* I enjoyed it.

Another excellent scene that has nothing to do with big movie budgets but excellent scriptwriting is reproduced from *The Bridge on the River Kwai*. It's a simple scene between two people in a room and could have been in an epic or B-movie. Perhaps the argument could be made that a B-movie writer would not have delivered such a great scene. But in any event, it did not take a mega-budget to deliver this powerful exchange of dialogue and is wonderfully crafted. At its beginning, it would appear that Commander Shears (William Holden) holds all the cards, avoiding a mission to destroy the bridge to remain in hospital and chase the nurses. However, by the end of the scene, a completely different result ensues. After all, as Major Warden (Jack Hawkins) says throughout the movie (it's practically his tag line) "There is always the unexpected."

> *Commander Shears:* They can't do this to me. My navy's made a mistake. Look, I'm not a navy commander. I'm not even an officer. The whole thing's fake. I'm just an ordinary swab jockey, second class. When the Houston sunk, I made it ashore with an officer. Later, we ran into a Japanese patrol and he was killed. I figured I would be captured, so —
>
> *Major Warden:* So you changed uniforms with a dead man.

Commander Shears: I thought officers would get better treatment in prison camps.

Major Warden: Very sensible.

Commander Shears: Not that it did me any good. At Saito's camp, the officers worked along with the rest.

Major Warden: Yes, there's always the unexpected.

Commander Shears: I got used to being a commander... so when I arrived here at the hospital... I looked at the enlisted men's ward and the officers' ward... and I said to myself, 'Let's let it ride along for awhile.' There were certain definite advantages.

Major Warden: Yes, I saw one on the beach. [Referring to one of the nurses.]

Commander Shears: Anyway, that's the whole story. The point is that you can't use me. You want an American commander named Shears and he doesn't exist. When the navy brass learns the truth about me, they'll say 'Ship him home in irons for impersonating an officer!' Once that happens, I've got it made.

Major Warden: Got it what?

Commander Shears: Made. I'd like that drink now.

Major Warden: Of course.

Commander Shears: I'll apply for a medical discharge. I'll say I impersonated an officer because I went crazy in the jungle. I'm getting worse, you know? Sometimes I think I'm Admiral Halsey.

Major Warden: That's a clever plan.

Kelly's Heroes
1970

© MGM/The
Kobal
Collection

Commander Shears: It's not only clever, it's foolproof. When my navy finds out who I am... those temporary orders won't be worth the paper they're written on.

Major Warden: Is this your photograph?

Commander Shears: Where did you get this?

Major Warden: It took a bit of doing. Naturally, your people couldn't identify you at first. But finally your C in C Pacific sent us a copy of your service record: the photograph, fingerprints. It has everything. Would you care to have a look? We've known about your actual rank for nearly a week. Your navy's in an awkward position. In one sense, you're a hero for making an escape from the jungle. But they can't very well bring you home... and give you the Navy Cross for impersonating an officer. I suppose that's why they were happy to hand you over to us. You see?

Commander Shears: Hot potato.

Major Warden: As far as your present rank is concerned... we're fairly informal about those things in Force 316. So you'll have a simulated rank of major.

Commander Shears: A simulated major. That figures. As long as I'm hooked, I might as well volunteer.

Major Warden: Good show!

The scene ends with Colonel Green (André Morell), another British officer, being told that Shears is returning with the commando team to the bridge, at which point he also says 'Good show!' In this short scene, Shears has gone from being a gold brick impersonating an officer and chasing nurses to a classic and reluctant hero. Quite a feat for such a short scene!

Because such scenes are not dependent on expensive sets, B-movies can often manage the same great scenes on their threadbare budgets. For example, in a similar scene in *Kelly's Heroes*, Clint Eastwood talks two other diehard deadbeats, supply sergeant Crapgame (Don Rickles) and Oddball (Donald Sutherland), a tank commander, into volunteering for a dangerous mission behind enemy lines:

Kelly: I want the intelligence report for this whole sector in the next two hours.

Crapgame: That's nice. What's in it for me?

Kelly: A piece of the action.

Crapgame: What kind of action?

Kelly: This kind of action. [Kelly holds up a gold bar.]

Crapgame: [On telephone.] Hello, Izzy? Yeah, it's me. Listen, get me a quotation for gold on the Paris market. Yeah, now and hurry it up! [To Kelly.] How much more where this came from?

Kelly: Fourteen thousand bars.

Crapgame: Fourteen thousand bars?

Kelly: Fourteen thousand.

Crapgame: Hey sweetheart, have yourself a bottle of booze. You're beautiful! Fourteen thousand bars! That's beautiful! Where is it?

Kelly: In a bank.

Crapgame: In a bank? You're getting pretty ambitious, aren't you? To think you can blow a bank and get away with it?

Kelly: It's behind enemy lines.

Crapgame: Behind enemy lines. That could be the perfect crime. [On telephone.] Right. Right, I got you. [Crapgame works his calculator and then turns to Kelly.] $1.6 million. What else will you need?

Oddball: You could probably use some armor.

Crapgame: What are you doing up there?

Oddball: I crept in.

Kelly: Who the hell's that?

Crapgame: His name's Oddball.

Oddball: I got three Shermans outside.

Kelly: What outfit?

Oddball: Right now I don't have any outfit.

Kelly: Who's your commanding officer?

Oddball: He got decapitated by an eighty-eight about six weeks ago. But don't say you're sorry. He's been trying to get us killed ever since we landed at Omaha Beach.

Kelly: It's terrible.

Crapgame: He hasn't reported him dead yet. You see, I've been collecting his whiskey.

Oddball: We see our role as essentially defensive in nature. While our armies are advancing so fast and everyone's knocking themselves out to be heroes, we are holding ourselves in reserve in case the Krauts mount a counteroffensive which threatens Paris... or maybe even New York. Then we can move in and stop them. But for 1.6 million dollars, we could become heroes for three days.

Just like the A-list movie where William Holden is turned into a reluctant hero by a well-written scene, the same happens to Donald Sutherland and Don Rickles in *Kelly's Heroes* when they undertake their mission behind enemy lines. Rickles is so anxious to protect his investment that he fights alongside the combat troops. Of course, his character does not change and when he is assigned to haul the fifty calibre machine gun, he offers a soldier a hundred dollars to carry it for him.

Another area where great talent emerges in B-movies is the director. For example, Robert Wise directed *Run Silent Run Deep*, yet his credits prior to this film included *The Curse of the Cat People* (1944); however, after directing *Run Silent Run Deep*, Wise went on to make *West Side Story* (1961) that won a record number of ten Oscars including statues for Best Director and Best Picture. Was his talent any less when he directed 'B' pictures? I doubt it. And now decades later it does not matter that he directed *Run Silent Run Deep* before *West Side Story*. They are both great films and are a joy to watch.

An example of Wise's genius is in his dedication to the use of authentic military tactics. *Run Silent Run Deep* contains several accurate depictions of torpedo attacks being set up with periscope sightings, range and bearing calculations and the use of a Torpedo Data Computer to achieve a firing solution. When surfaced, the captain uses a Target

Bearing Transmitter mounted on the bridge to acquire the target visually and mark its bearing input for the firing party down below. Wise had real submariners work with the cast and crew until they could realistically depict the complexities of genuine torpedo attacks. Submarine veterans of World War 2 who viewed the film remarked on the accuracy of these scenes which now provide modern-day audiences with a fascinating look into what life was like aboard World War 2 submarines in action. One can only imagine how this dedication to drilling perfection paid off in *West Side Story* with its many choreographed routines in which the audience would have been able to detect almost any misstep in the dance numbers.

Not only can directors be excellent when they are on their way up, they can also be great when they are in the twilight of their career. When Sam Peckinpah made *Cross of Iron*, films like *Major Dundee* (1965) and *The Wild Bunch* (1969) were behind him and he only went on to direct a further three movies and a music video. But you are getting a Sam Peckinpah film in *Cross of Iron* and a friend of mine from my army days, Major Carlos Yguico, considers it as one of his favourite movies. While it did not garner an Oscar, it won the Golden Screen Award in Germany and ranked number 37 on the list of 100 greatest war films of all time compiled by Channel 4, a list voted by the public.

Another factor to consider with regards to epics and B-pictures is that location shooting is not the private preserve of epics, nor is the B-picture necessarily relegated to the back lot. In fact, many B-pictures were shot on location. *Kelly's Heroes* is an excellent example. It was shot in Yugoslavia while it was technically behind the Iron Curtain and *Kelly's Heroes* was the film where John Landis, director of *The Blues Brothers* (1980) and *An American Werewolf in London* (1981) got his start in the movie business as a production assistant. *Where Eagles Dare* was shot on location in Austria at the Schloss Hohenwerfen. *Cross of Iron* was also shot in Yugoslavia and ironically was Peckinpah's only war film, despite his reputation for depicting violence.

The public, in the final analysis, are those who determine as to what a great film is and what is not. And the rankings on this list of the Greatest 100 War Films, does not always directly correlate into epics and B-films. For example, A-list film *Lawrence of Arabia* at number 40 is beaten by both *Cross of Iron* (no.37) and *Kelly's Heroes* (no.36). At number 29, *Battle of Britain* is beaten by *Where Eagles Dare* (no.20). So ultimately, it is history and the movie-going public that are going to determine what qualifies as an A-list picture.

To conclude, we can see that in hindsight there is very little, other than large, expensive battle scenes, to distinguish the epic from the B-movie. Both can feature A-list stars but the A-list film would attract such acting talent in their prime whereas the B-movie would appeal to those on the wane or rise. Similarly, B-pictures can have great directors; filmmakers who at other points in their careers, either before or after, directed major A-list movies. And finally, the epic and B-picture can also benefit from great scripts as this is a part of pre-production that is not necessarily going to cost the studio a great deal of money. For example, *Kelly's Heroes* was written by Troy Kennedy-Martin who also wrote *The Italian Job* (1969), a script so great that it helped inspire a remake to be made in 2003.

JUNGLE FEVER

How Vietnam Changed the Hollywood War Movie

JAMES MOTTRAM

"Let's go and make the greatest war movie ever!"

Damien Cockburn, *Tropic Thunder*

August, 2008. Ben Stiller's *Tropic Thunder* has just knocked *The Dark Knight* off the number one slot in the US box office, taking close to $26 million on its opening weekend. 33 years since the last of the American troops were evacuated by helicopter from the roof of the US embassy in Saigon, the war is still raging – at least in Hollywood. In many ways, it was inevitable. Stiller's broad comedy, about the production of a Vietnam War movie, was first incubated two decades ago, after he unsuccessfully auditioned for Oliver Stone's Oscar-winning 'Nam effort *Platoon* (1986). At that point, the Vietnam War film became a rites-of-passage for any actor worth his salt and – for a time at least – a Hollywood staple.

Spearheaded by Stone, who went on to complete his Vietnam trilogy with *Born on the Fourth of July* (1989) and *Heaven and Earth* (1993), this second wave of 'Nam movies saw contributions from such venerable auteurs as Stanley Kubrick (*Full Metal Jacket*, 1987) and Brian De Palma (*Casualties of War*, 1989). Less celebrated directors got in on the act, with John Irvin delivering *Hamburger Hill* (1987), while Robin Williams was sent in to entertain the troops with *Good Morning, Vietnam* (1987). Even then, this trend was ripe for ribbing. In British sketch show *Alas Smith and Jones*, one skit featured a shaven-haired solider shot down in a hail of bullets, recalling Willem Dafoe's famous demise in *Platoon*, as a voiceover intoned: "Sassoon: the first casualty of war is your haircut."

Thus in its satirising of a filmmaking culture that made a veritable cottage industry out of the Vietnam War movie, *Tropic Thunder* felt twenty years too late. At least Stiller had paid attention in class: everything from military slang (like 'fragged') to the perennial late-Sixties rock soundtrack (including The Rolling Stones' 'Sympathy for the Devil') get a look in. Obligatory scenes such as the men discussing the girls they've left behind to the *Platoon*-inspired slow-motion shot of the lone soldier running through the jungle towards the airborne helicopter, also made the cut. Invariable nods to Vietnam classics also featured, in particular a direct reference to 'a saucier', taken from a line by Frederic Forrest's character Chef in Francis Ford Coppola's hallucinogenic 'Nam epic *Apocalypse Now* (1979).

Still, arriving some four decades after John Wayne delivered the first recognisable 'Nam film with *The Green Berets* (1968), Stiller's parody feels like a fitting conclusion to a sub-genre that started out as a lamentable, flag-waving exercise, before delivering some of the most stirring war films in living memory. It's no coincidence that the subject of the longest foreign war in America's history has attracted some of cinema's greatest maverick talents to its fertile ground. A conflict with no moral justification, this was not a so-called 'good war' like World War 2, but a combat zone where the murky jungle terrain reflected the mental state of many of the soldiers. Colonel Kurtz, the target Martin Sheen's Captain Willard is sent to assassinate in *Apocalypse Now*, may be "out there operating with any decent restraint" but he's hardly alone.

If anything, the Vietnam War was like a bloated Hollywood blockbuster in itself. As critic J. Hoberman wrote, it 'became the greatest episode in American show-business – the longest, costliest, most ambitious, best attended catastrophe ever staged…*Cleopatra* and *Heaven's Gate* had nothing on this debacle – a cost of billions, a cast of millions.' [1] With Vietnam the first modern war to receive blanket news coverage, it's little wonder there are numerous references to the media in the films it spawned. Coppola, for example, cameos in *Apocalypse Now* as a documentary director, yelling "don't look at the camera" to the soldiers running past, as if they are starring in what one character being similarly filmed in *Full Metal Jacket* calls "Vietnam the movie".

While this was a war being fought by young men brought up on Hollywood spectacle, from war films to westerns, it unfolded more like a disaster movie. Waged as a war to combat the spread of what Ronald Reagan referred to as the "Communist conspiracy", the US lent support to the government of South Vietnam as early as 1950, when military advisors began arriving in the country. By the time US combat units began arriving in the mid-Sixties, to fight against the North Vietnamese Army (NVA) and the insurgent guerrilla forces known as the Vietcong, it was intended by the American superpower as a show of force. It proved anything but, costing 60,000 American lives, countless more Vietnamese and creating scars on the US psyche that never truly healed.

Such is the potency of the Vietnam War, though; it has entered popular culture like few other conflicts before it. In film, just about every genre, from broad comedy (*Hot Shots! Part Deux*, 1993) to chilling horror (*Jacob's Ladder*, 1990) has used it as a source. Likewise, the Vietnam veteran has became a familiar figure on screen. Memorably played by John Goodman, Walter Sobchak is the foul-mouthed former grunt in Joel and Ethan Coen's stoner comedy *The Big Lebowski* (1998). The titular Tom Hanks character in *Forrest Gump* (1994) served in Vietnam, in one of his many moments where he and recent history collide. Equally famous was Robert De Niro's vengeful vet Travis Bickle in *Taxi Driver* (1976), a figure screenwriter Paul Schrader explored again with William Devane's returning war hero in *Rolling Thunder* (1977).

Primarily, the Vietnam War movie can be divided into four main categories. The first wave of films was dominated by what might be considered 'allegorical epics', *Apocalypse Now* and Michael Cimino's *The Deer Hunter* (1978). Moving on from merely presenting him as a psychotic, the 'veteran' movie sees the battle rage on back home, in films like Hal Ashby's *Coming Home* (1977), Coppola's *Gardens of Stone* (1987) and *Born on the Fourth of July*. The 'revisionist' movie, meanwhile, set out to rewrite history, in films such as *Rambo: First Blood Part II* (1985) and *Uncommon Valor* (1983). Last but by no means least there is the 'grunt ensemble' movie. Beginning with Sidney J. Furie's *The Boys of Company C* (1977), this took greater shape in the 1980s, with *Full Metal Jacket*, *Platoon*, *Hamburger Hill* and *Casualties of War* all showing the conflict from the bewildered soldiers' point-of-view.

Yet it took until the war was over before Hollywood even considered facing up to the war. During the ten years of America's involvement, the studios were united in the feeling that the subject was a landmine waiting to cripple them. Audiences plagued by nightly news reports of the carnage abroad, went the thinking, would have no wish to pay for a ticket to see this played out on the big screen. Even when it concluded in 1975, the war's built-in unhappy ending went against the Hollywood grain. *The Green Berets*, made when the US involvement was at its height, is the exception – yet this played out as a poorly articulated piece of propaganda co-directed (with Ray Kellogg) by The Duke himself. A ham-fisted attempt at justifying why American troops were fighting a war that wasn't their own, it was a job that fit the Commie-bashing Republican as neatly as his Stetson.

From the very first scene, it was clear the film – adapted by James Lee Barrett from a novel by Robin Moore – had no intention of questioning the war. "Foreign policy decisions are not made by the military," says Sgt. Muldoon (Aldo Ray), facing a gathering of sceptical reporters. "A soldier goes where he's told to go and fights whomever he's told to fight." The story effectively sees Wayne's Col. Mike Kirby lead a group of men on two separate missions: the first is to protect a compound – appropriately enough nicknamed 'Dodge City'. The second is to capture a North Vietnamese general. As Kirby warns, "We don't go back without the general. Not one of us." In Wayne's world, this is little more than a game of Cowboys and Indians.

Invariably, with the jungle laced with killer traps, the Vietnamese are portrayed as little more than savages – a trait that left its mark on the bulk of Hollywood films about 'Nam. At one point, Kirby tells a story about the Vietcong tying up a village chief and disembowelling him in front of his teenage daughter, while forty men "used his wife", before breaking every bone in her body with a steel rod. If that wasn't enough, the film concludes with the stomach-churning moment on the beach involving Kirby and the orphaned Vietnamese boy who his platoon adopted as a mascot of sorts. With the soundtrack blaring out 'The Ballad of the Green Berets', Kirby leads the boy towards the sunset, telling him, "You're what this is all about."

"The bullshit piled up so fast in Vietnam, you needed wings to stay above it."
Captain Willard, *Apocalypse Now*

When Francis Ford Coppola arrived at the Cannes Film Festival in 1979 with 'a work in progress' of *Apocalypse Now*, more than three years after it had gone into production, he famously stated at the press conference: "My film is not about Vietnam. It *is* Vietnam." As disrespectful as this seems to the thousands of Americans and Vietnamese that died, he had a point. Coppola's legendary production, battered by everything from typhoons to a heart attack endured by Martin Sheen, spiralled out of control. With the budget ballooning from $12 to $31 million, it almost sunk Coppola's American Zoetrope company as he ploughed his own money into the production to keep it afloat.

As Coppola told me, "I like to put myself in the situation of making the film that parallels what the story is about. *Apocalypse Now* is clearly a wild movie that almost got away from us in the same way that the Vietnamese War got away from the Americans." Like Kurtz (Marlon Brando), the AWOL US Colonel who refashions himself as a dictator ruling over a rogue army in Cambodia, Coppola conducted himself with a megalomania that reflected the American involvement in Vietnam. As he noted in the aforementioned press conference, "We were in the jungle. There were too many of us. We had access to too much money, too much equipment, and little by little, we went insane."

If the film's central theme is that of the madness of war – typified by Robert Duvall's napalm-loving, surf-obsessed Lt. Col Kilgore – it's fitting that it rubbed off on its filmmakers. In many ways, its protracted production took away from the fact it was written (at least according to screenwriter John Milius) back in 1969, just a year after the release of *The Green Berets*. Despite inspiring Walter in *The Big Lebowski*, avowed gun enthusiast Milius never saw any action in Vietnam, after he saw his application to join the Marine Corps rejected due to his chronic asthma. Rather *Apocalypse Now* spliced the river-journey structure of Joseph Conrad's novella *Heart of Darkness* with experiences he'd gleaned from veterans, fused together by LSD and the rock'n'roll of the era.

Given Milius took the title from hippie button badges that read 'Nirvana Now', it's little wonder the film's anti-war sentiments are somewhat obscured by its characters' gratuitous warmongering. "In this war, things get confused out there," the General tells Willard, when instructing him to "terminate" Kurtz "with extreme prejudice". Here, there's something decidedly seedy about the US operations – from the black marketeering to the Playboy bunny girls flown in to entertain the men. Unlike *The Green Berets*, there is no certainty in this war, reflected in the brutal monologue delivered by Kurtz to Willard near the end. He recalls a time when he was with Special Forces, when the Vietcong hacked off all the arms of village children inoculated by US soldiers for polio. "Then I realised they were stronger than we… They have the strength, the strength to do that."

As a sentiment, it prefigures James Earl Jones' speech in Coppola's *Gardens of Stone*, when he talks of how the Vietnamese soldier is willing to "march a hundred miles on no food through a jungle you would not believe, slaughter his own people, babies if he has to". Yet while Kurtz's words may hint at the impotency of the American intervention (a parallel to the European Colonialism in Congo as viewed by Conrad), the film has little interest in conveying the war, or its politics, in any accurate way. The closest it comes is in the French Plantation scene (cut from the original but restored for the extended 'Redux' version released in 2001) where Willard is told that America has ambitions of world domination – "yesterday it was Korea, today Vietnam, tomorrow Thailand, the Philippines, and then maybe Europe".

In the end, Coppola's film is an exploration of what Kurtz calls "moral terror", that this is necessary for civilisation to endure. In what is a deeply self-referential moment, Kurtz reads from T. S. Eliot's poem *The Hollow Men*, which itself quoted *Heart of Darkness* with the line "Mistah Kurtz – he dead". Indeed, just as Eliot was a scholar of Conrad, so Kurtz studies Eliot. On his shelf can be glimpsed both Sir James George Frazer's *The Golden Bough* and Jessie L. Weston's *From Ritual to Romance*, books cited by the poet in the notes to his seminal poem *The Waste Land* – which was originally set to open with "the horror, the horror", the infamous words uttered by Conrad (and Coppola's) Kurtz upon his demise.

If Coppola eschews discussing the particulars of the Vietnam War, his use of Eliot reflects on the very futility of such a conflict – given that *The Waste Land* was widely acknowledged as mirroring the disillusionment in Europe following World War 1. As Dennis Hopper's crazed photojournalist says, colourfully embellishing *The Hollow Men*, "This is the way the fucking world ends… Not with a bang but a whimper." Willard may already have passed through the "asshole of the world", when his boat sails through the last command post before Cambodia, but he's wound up dumped in the toilet. Whether its World War 1 or Vietnam, war – according to Coppola – can only leave one tainted by the stink of one's own actions.

It must certainly have been a bitter irony to Coppola that, deep into the mire that was the film's post-production, he was asked to present the Best Director Oscar to Michael Cimino for *The Deer Hunter* in 1979. Like Coppola, he strove to create a sprawling film about men whose lives were changed by the Vietnam War, but rather than bombard the viewer with grandiose images, his was an intimate epic, a slow-burner signalled by the soft-hearted main theme music by Stanley Myers. Three hours in length, it offers arguably the longest establishing sequence in history, as the first third is devoted to setting up foundry worker Michael (Robert De Niro) and his friends in expansive detail.

Set in the steel town of Clairton, Pennsylvania, in a tight Russian orthodox community, the first third centres on the wedding of Michael's buddy Steven (John Savage). As the banner that reads 'Serving God and Country' at the wedding reception hints, this celebration doubles as a goodbye to both men, along with Michael's flatmate Nick (Christopher Walken), before they head out to Vietnam. Yet Cimino swiftly ensures ominous warning signs punctuate this atmosphere of joy and revelry. A tanker thunders through the town at daybreak; a drop of wine spills on the wedding dress of Steven's bridge, Angela. More is to come when the boys meet a Green Beret at the bar, during the wedding reception. When they ask them what it's like in 'Nam, he simply replies, "Fuck it!"

It's a reply that washes over the men, who – despite their Russian Orthodox leanings – are red-blooded Middle Americans. Indeed, if *Apocalypse Now* set its protagonist up (at least initially) as a detached observer, Cimino's defiantly apolitical film presented him as a patriotic participant. Questioning the reasons behind America's involvement in the war doesn't even come into the minds of the blue-collar men at the heart of this narrative – even at the very end, with one of their number dead and another badly injured. Rather than bemoan the war, they raise their glasses to sing 'God Bless America', a contentious scene that caused outrage at the time with many believing it to be ironic. Even the televisions and radios that play in the background do so in silence, as if to mute any anti-war protests.

As one critic wrote, Cimino's film is a "spiritual descendant" [2] of *The Green Berets*. While Wayne coincidentally confirmed this when he presented the film with the Best Picture award at the Oscars, there is even a direct reference to the Duke in the script, regarding the stay-at-home womaniser Stan (John Cazale), who owns a gun that "he carries around like John Wayne". With such nods, it's little wonder that for all Cimino's attention to detail in the first third, the Vietnam sequence occupying the middle section feels like a myth-perpetuating portrait of combat. Cutting from the boys' solemn final drink, the first 'Nam sequence is Michael brandishing a flame-thrower, torching the Vietcong. After a dramatic ellipsis, the film cuts to the trio held captive by the NVA in a bamboo cage submerged in a river. Whilst there, they're pulled out indiscriminately to play Russian roulette in a nearby shack, where their callous jailers bet on their survival.

Arriving shortly after the scene where the friends stalk deer in the wilds before they leave for 'Nam, the hunters are now the hunted. And it's this scene that provides the film with its most potent image: that of an American soldier compelled to put a gun to his head and pull the trigger for the sake of his country. While it's been said there was no actual evidence of the Vietnamese torment-ing US soldiers in this way, Cimino believed Russian roulette was the perfect metaphor for the US government sending military personnel into Vietnam with no justification. Repeated to devastating effect later, when Michael returns to Saigon to find a heroin-ravaged Nick now playing the game for money, while *Apocalypse Now* showered the viewer with images of insanity, Cimino homes in on just one.

As Nick pulls the trigger in the Saigon bar, his luck runs out – causing a spurt of blood to leap from his head as he dies in Michael's arms. If anything, it recalls the infamous real-life footage of a young man in a check shirt who is shot in the head at point-blank range during the Tet Offensive of 1968. [3] But while Cimino's film may be a stirring essay on the white American men who went to war, not unlike *Apocalypse Now*, the politics are confused and misguided. As Pauline Kael put it in *The New Yorker*, "The Vietcong are treated in a standard inscrutable-evil Oriental style of the Japanese in the Second World War movies... The impression a viewer gets is that if we did some bad things there we did them ruthlessly but impersonally; the Vietcong were cruel and sadistic."

It hardly helps the film's credibility that the Vietnamese are all played by Thai actors while scriptwriter Deric Washburn (who had very limited military experience) did no research, due to time constraints. In the end, like *Apocalypse Now*, the film used the war as a backdrop to explore wider themes, such as the indelible bond of friendship, while paying little attention to historical accuracy. Indeed, even the production of *The Deer Hunter* seemed to mirror Coppola's. After spiralling over budget – notably in Thailand – Cimino's film similarly stalled in the editing room, as the director battled with the studio over everything from its running time to the violence. Just as Coppola became Kurtz, so Cimino became like Nick – though did not pull the trigger until his next film, the legendary disaster that was *Heaven's Gate* (1980).

"It ain't like it is in the movies."

Luke Martin, *Coming Home*

As it happens, *The Deer Hunter* was not the first significant film to deal with the Vietnam War. Released at the beginning of 1978, ten months before Cimino's film, was Hal Ashby's *Coming Home*. As Peter Biskind so faithfully reported [4] the two went to war at

The Deer Hunter 1978

© EMI/ Columbia/ Warners/ The Kobal Collection

the 1979 Oscars, with Ashby's film coming off worse – three statues, including Best Actor and Actress for leads Jon Voight and Jane Fonda, from eight nominations, compared to *The Deer Hunter*'s five from nine. At the time, *Coming Home* was regarded as the more worthy of the two; as Walken had said of *The Deer Hunter*, "In the making of it, I don't remember anyone ever mentioning Vietnam."

By comparison, *Coming Home* came six years after Fonda had determined to make a film about the Vietnam War. Curiously, she decided to focus on the plight of disabled vets after she met Ron Kovic at an anti-war rally in 1973. A Marine who was serving his second tour-of-duty in Vietnam when he was wounded and paralysed, Kovic's experiences ultimately fed into his book, *Born on the Fourth of July*, later filmed by Oliver Stone. In many ways, Kovic's story became the template for the 'veteran' movie: the soldier, crippled on duty, returns home to discover "people here don't give a shit about the war", as is said in Stone's film, and morphs from patriot to protester.

Still, *Coming Home* is not Kovic's story; rather it begins with its protagonist, Luke Martin (Voight), already back home and living in a Southern California veteran's hospital. Paralysed and embittered, he refuses to even use a wheelchair, scooting around – when he has to – on a trolley with a pair of walking sticks to guide him. Until, that is, he meets Sally (Fonda), the wife of a Marine Officer (Bruce Dern) who has just shipped out to Vietnam. Invariably, Sally and Luke begin an affair, leading to a confrontation in the clunky finale when her husband Bob returns to discover the truth after he is shot in the leg. "I'm not the enemy," yells Luke. "The enemy is the fucking war."

While *Coming Home* may be a more realistic assessment of the impact of the war than the kaleidoscopic snapshots that were *Apocalypse Now* and *The Deer Hunter*, it has aged poorly. Take the rather indiscriminate soundtrack – 'Hey Jude', 'White Rabbit', 'Born To Be Wild' to name but three – chosen by Ashby as if he'd just discovered a 'Best of the Sixties' album in his collection. With six tracks by The Rolling Stones, a band who probably fared better than any other when it came to receiving royalties for their work used in Vietnam War films, Ashby's choices are obvious at best. Simon and Garfunkel's 'Bookends', for example, with its line "a time of innocence, a time of confidences", playing over the sequence as Bob spends his last night with Sally before he goes to war.

To be fair, there are moments of power in Waldo Salt's script. The opening scene, as a group of veterans (played by non-actors) discuss the war, their justification for being there and coming home crippled, is an invigorating sequence. Were the rest of the film like this, *Coming Home* would have emerged as an angry, protest tale – rather than a sentimental story that concentrates on the power of love to regenerate and redeem. There are moments, such as when Luke chains himself to a marine embarkation depot or the scene at the end where he addresses a group of students and tells them "All you're seeing is a lot of death", but the effect is hardly hard-hitting.

While there's no doubt its heart is in the right place, *Coming Home* feels as removed from the war as Coppola or Cimino's film. The sun-kissed setting hardly helps, while casting such actors in their prime as Voight and Fonda, who buzz around in a Porsche Speedster no less, does not exactly lend the film credibility. Worse still, the script shies away from exploring the reasons behind America's intervention and has no interest whatsoever in the impact of the war on the Vietnamese, preferring to concentrate on how it affected US soldiers. Yet while it's easy to criticise the film as naïve, one has to see *Coming Home* as a product of its time. Daring to even reflect the growing mood of dissent amongst US veterans was a radical step forward for a Hollywood studio movie then.

Ironically, Stone wrote his script for *Born on the Fourth of July* at the time *Coming Home* was released. A screenwriter then – he won Best Adapted Screenplay for Alan Parker's *Midnight Express* the year *Coming Home* and *The Deer Hunter* were fighting it out at the Oscars – it would take him another eleven years before he got funding to tell Kovic's story. By this point, he had won a Best Director Oscar for *Platoon*, his semi-autobiographical account of his own time in Vietnam (between April 1967 and November 1968, he served in the 25th Infantry Division and the 1st Cavalry Division and was wounded twice) which also took Best Picture.

Despite this, Stone was furious it took so long to tell Kovic's story. "I wrote two scripts about the returning vets at that time and everyone said no one's going to make the goddamned things. Why? Well, it beats the shit out of me. A lot of post-modernist critics point the finger and say, 'You haven't told us anything new.' But before *Platoon*, nobody had ever told the truth before. The repression had gone on too long – there are stories out there that are primitive and true, and that are dying to be told. People were going around praising *Apocalypse Now*, which was a great piece of filmmaking but it wasn't 'Nam. As a vet, I was just dying for the truth about the vets to be told, and it's a shame it's taken me nineteen years to tell it." [5]

By comparison to *Coming Home*, Stone's film is a much angrier polemic and far more ambitious. It may have Tom Cruise as Kovic, echoing the glamour casting of Voight, but this is no glossy Hollywood biopic. As Stone told me, "I did my story, then I did Ron Kovic's story, because I thought it was a larger story about not only other people, which was outside my story, but it was also about America coming to terms with its war fever." Indeed, while Stone has consistently documented turbulent episodes in recent US history – *JFK* (1991), *Nixon* (1995) and *W* (2008) in particular – *Born on the Fourth of July* captured the growing disenchantment the American public felt after realising, as Ron's friend Steve tells him, "the government sold us a bill of goods".

For Stone, he couldn't have found a better embodiment of this than Kovic. Literally born on American Independence Day, this full-on flag-waver sees his belief systems become as shattered as his spine when he returns to his country to find that "people here don't give a shit about the war". Even the opening scene – set on Kovic's tenth birthday, in 1956 – warns us as such, as little Ron watches a veterans parade, and notices how the wheelchair-bound men all wince as explosions go off around them. Not that this puts him off signing up for four years in the marines after a recruitment drive comes to his school. "This is our chance to do something. To be part of history," he says. "You don't think you need to serve your country?"

Like many, Kovic fell for propaganda – from buying into John F. Kennedy's famous "ask not what your country can do for you" speech to believing that "Communism is moving in everywhere". Even when he returns to the US a paraplegic, after a horrific stint in a rat-infested veteran's hospital, to be told he will never have children or walk again, he remains a die-hard patriot, disgusted at protesters burning the American flag during the 1968 presidential election. When he heads home to Massapequa a year later, "everything looks so different," he notes. But it's not just his surroundings; Kovic's love for his country almost seems a thing of the past in the flower-power era.

If anything, Stone's film, which won him a second Best Director Oscar, reflects as much about American society at the time as it does the impact of the war. Vietnam is "a white man's war, a rich man's war", a black orderly in the hospital tells Kovic. If anything explains the indifference to the Vietnam War, it's that the Civil Rights Movement was spearheading a revolution much closer to home. And as the orderly puts it, "If you ain't part of the solution, you're part of the problem." Later, as he meets up with his childhood sweetheart (Kyra Sedgwick), who is now an anti-war protester, he watches an African-American veteran throw his Purple Heart and Bronze Star into the crowd moments before the police wade in with batons.

Impressively, Stone's telling of Kovic's story refuses to sanitise the author's darkest moments, from telling his religious mother "there's no god, there's no country" to the scene in Mexico when he meets Willem Dafoe's twisted veteran and the pair argue over who "killed gook babies". There is also a sense of bemusement about the war – notably expressed by the father of the marine Kovic accidentally shoots during combat, despite the fact his family fought in every war that America has ever been involved in. In a sequence set during Nixon's 1972 re-election campaign, Kovic tells a reporter that he and his comrades flew 13,000 miles to fight "poor, peasant people who have a proud history of resistance", having been fighting for their own independence for a thousand years.

If this attempted, albeit briefly, to do what few Hollywood films about Vietnam did, and give thought to why the US failed, Stone was not the first. Two years earlier, Coppola delivered one of his more overlooked films, *Gardens of Stone*, another 'home front' tale that faced up to the fact that the Americans were fighting a jungle war they were not equipped to win. With the title referring to the nickname given to Arlington military cemetery, the film is set in nearby Fort Myer, Virginia, where the Old Guard, a unit in the "burial business", is there to help put to rest the countless numbers being shipped back from Vietnam. With its fascination with such stately rituals, it's the very antithesis to *Apocalypse Now* – so much so you almost feel like Coppola feels guilty for the way he represented the war a decade earlier.

Certainly James Caan's ageing instructor, Sgt. Clell Hazard, is the polar opposite to Robert Duvall's Kilgore. A decorated Korea veteran, after also experiencing two tours of 'Nam, he is under no illusion of what it's like out there. "In this war, there is no front," he says. "It's not even a war. There's nothing to win and no way to win it." Labelled a "peacenik platoon sergeant" for his stance against the war, he even dates a *Washington Post* reporter (Angelica Huston) who believes the war is "genocide". Yet Hazard is desperate to head out to the frontline, if only to try and pass on his wisdom to a few wetbacks – notably the idealistic Willow (D. B. Sweeney), who is desperate to see some action and later pays the ultimate price.

With news footage of the war playing on almost every television set we see, suggesting the stark contrast between the horrors of battle and what is happening back home, Coppola manages to acutely express the feeling of sheer helplessness felt by Hazard and co. as they watch young men go off to war and come back in body bags. If there's a problem with the film, it's that this perspective – separating the warriors from the war – ensures it remains an emotionally detached experience. After the immediacy of the horrors of *Apocalypse Now*, *Gardens of Stone* feels like an examination of the war from a safe distance. Yet at least Coppola could never be accused of pandering to the disturbing trait of historical revisionism that had become prevalent in Hollywood in the early 1980s.

"Do we get to win this time?"
John Rambo, *Rambo: First Blood Part II*

Created by David Morrell from his 1972 novel *First Blood*, the figure of John Rambo supplied Hollywood with its most potent Vietnam veteran. Directed by Ted Kotcheff, the film version arrived a decade later, somewhat lagging behind the other 'psychotic veteran' movies that had begun as far back as the biker exploitation flick *The Born Losers* (1967). Like that film's protagonist, Billy Jack, Rambo (played by Sylvester Stallone) is a Green Beret with Indian heritage who returns to the US fuelled by anger. A former POW of the NVA, Rambo is a symbol of all veterans disowned by their country. As he puts it in the 1985 sequel, *Rambo: First Blood Part II*, "I want what… every other guy who came over here and spilt his guts wants. For our country to love us as much as we love it."

But we are getting ahead of ourselves. In *First Blood* (1982), Rambo drifts into a fictional Pacific Northwest town, looking for a former army buddy, who he later discovers has died of cancer following exposure to Agent Orange. Arrested for vagrancy by the local police force, it triggers a form of post-traumatic stress disorder as he begins to experience violent flashbacks to his time as a captive in Vietnam. Like the scene in *Taxi Driver*, where Travis Bickle suddenly moves into a martial arts stance when he is hassled in the New York Senator's campaign headquarters, the Rambo of *First Blood* is like a wound-up elastic band, waiting to snap. As he becomes the subject of a manhunt, Rambo takes cover in the nearby forest as the Washington State Patrol come gunning for him.

If the original film suggests men like Rambo are still fighting the war back home, be it on the inside or in a mountain-town, its sequel took far greater liberties. By the early 1980s, after the dust had settled on grandiose epics like *Apocalypse Now* and *The Deer Hunter*, Hollywood saw the opportunity to rewrite the history of the Vietnam War. A film so guilty of this it should be court-martialled, *Rambo: First Blood Part II* recast its embittered lead – jailed in a civilian maximum-security prison between the first two films – as a one-man wager of war. A "pure fighting machine", as his mentor and father-figure Col. Sam Trautman (Richard Crenna) dubs him, he's a nostalgic reflection of what Philip Caputo, in his 1977 book *A Rumor of War*, called 'that savage, heroic time… before America became a land of salesmen and shopping centres'.

Directed by George P. Cosmatos, *First Blood Part II* recast the Vietnam soldier from psychotic to victim, becoming the 1980s equivalent of the World War 1 veteran, the forgotten men of the Depression era. It perpetuates the rumour that American soldiers registered as Missing in Action are still being held in Southeast Asia. That MIAs are still a possibility is effectively confirmation that the US was morally justified to fight such a cruel and inhuman enemy as the Vietnamese in the first place. What's more, the fact the US government has refused to face up to this possibility suggests the spineless nature of an administration that previously withdrew troops from Vietnam in shameful defeat.

A rightwing revenge fantasy, *First Blood Part II* sets out to justify a private war of national retribution in an attempt to recognise the sacrifice made by veterans. Concentrating on the theme of abandonment, as he notes of his return to the States, "I found another war going on… The war against all the soldiers returning. The kind of war you never win." As a result, the film exonerates the culpability of Rambo and his fellow grunts, painting them out as innocent pawns in a game played out by politicians. Thus, the film boasts a significant distrust of authority – embodied by the figure of Marshall Murdock (Charles Napier), the pencil pusher in charge of a mission to find of evidence of MIAs.

Plucked from jail with the promise of a pardon, Rambo is instructed by Murdock to return to Vietnam and collect photographic proof that there are POWs still out there. This he does, freeing an American soldier in the process, but when Murdock learns of this, he aborts the mission. Already abandoned by his country and government, it happens again to Rambo in a symbolic scene when the helicopter about to pick up him and his charge is pulled back on Murdock's command. Highlighting how "expendable", as Rambo puts it, he and his fellow soldiers are, it emerges the mission was "a lie", as Trautman notes, "just like whole damn war".

As we learn, Rambo was supposed to fail, to return empty-handed and provide evidence that no such MIAs are in existence. When he proves otherwise, the mission is swiftly stopped. If not, Congress would be forced to appropriate billions in rescuing these men while damaging the international status quo by causing the war to begin all over again. Captured and tortured, Rambo invariably escapes, wiping out the old foe as he does, and rescues the groups of POWs held at the same camp – a series of cartoon-like scenes that both undermined the plot's credibility and saw the film hailed as a quest for manhood and a celebration of primeval patriotism.

Regarding the latter, a similar fate was ascribed to Bruce Springsteen's anthem 'Born in the U.S.A.' – when, like *First Blood Part II*, it was more a hymn to the forgotten veterans, with lines like, "Nowhere to run, ain't got nowhere to go." Yet Springsteen and Stallone were not the only ones to sing this song. Chuck Norris, the poor man's Stallone, went back to find captive POWs in Joseph Zito's *Missing in Action* (1984). A former POW himself, who like Rambo suffers from flashbacks to his traumatic capture, Norris' Colonel James Braddock heads back with a delegation to Ho Chi Minh City to investigate reports of Americans still held prisoner. A ludicrous slice of Reagan-era revisionism, the culmination of the film is another all-out war against a near-anonymous Vietcong.

A year after directing *First Blood*, Ted Kotcheff went on to contribute to this revisionist trend with 1983's *Uncommon Valor*. This time, the film does not put the onus on one man but a highly trained group of soldiers sent into Laos to rescue POWs. Gene Hackman plays Col. Cal Rhodes, who is still desperately searching for his missing soldier son, Frank, ten years after he disappeared. If it recalls Michael's return to Saigon to extract Nick in *The Deer Hunter*, the comparisons stop there. Despite the credibility lent to the film by the appearance of Hackman, the film is little more than another two-dimensional macho fantasy embodied by Sailor, the gung-ho, grenade-crazy soldier played by Randall 'Tex' Cobb.

Bankrolled by Texas businessman Paul MacGregor, who also is missing a son, Rhodes reunites his son's former unit to go back in and perform a rescue act like a latter-day *Dirty Dozen* (1967). The first half of the film is largely taken up with the men training for their mission at a Texan compound. There, Rhodes echoes Rambo's own assessment of the everyday Vietnam veteran. "You men seem to have a strong sense of loyalty because you're thought of as criminals, because of Vietnam," he says. This image of veterans as captives, even in the land of the free, is emphasised later when they use codenames, referring to famous prisons Sing-Sing and Alcatraz. "You know why?" he continues. "Because you lost. And in this country, that's like going bankrupt."

The suggestion here is that this demonising of veterans came about not just because the war was wrong but simply because they were failures. Losing the Vietnam War, it's suggested, was a slight against the American Dream. As for those who doubted the moral justification for America's involvement in the conflict, as Rhodes said, "This time nobody can dispute the rightness of what we're doing." Again echoing the plot of *First Blood Part II*, the story sees CIA agents attempt to derail the mission and the theme of abandonment rears its head when one of the unit utters "We can't leave anybody behind this time." In the end, four MIAs are reclaimed, including MacGregor's son. While we learn that Frank died of illness some weeks earlier, it's enough to help his father to allow his memory – and the Vietnam War – rest for good.

Platoon
1986

© Orion/
The Kobal
Collection

"We're the unwanted. Yet we're fighting for our society."
Pvt. Chris Taylor, *Platoon*

While Rambo set out to rewrite history, in many ways his speech about how "expendable" he and others like him were set the tone for what was to come. Led by *Platoon*, there followed a spate of what became called 'grunt ensemble' movies that set out to demonstrate Rambo's ruminations. What is more, these movies were determined to examine the deplorable conduct of American soldiers during the war. As *Casualties of War*'s PFC Eriksson (Michael J. Fox) puts it, "Everybody's acting like we can do anything." As if Hollywood filmmakers were finally facing up to the US's own shameful part in the Vietnam conflict, the films felt almost confessional and cathartic in tone by comparison to the earlier waves of 'Nam movies. "We did not fight the enemy," as *Platoon*'s Pvt. Chris Taylor (Charlie Sheen) notes. "We fought ourselves and the enemy within us."

If one considers *Platoon*, along with the other three main examples of this – *Full Metal Jacket, Hamburger Hill* and *Casualties of War* – they all share certain preoccupations.

Seen from the subjective perspective of either one or more of the rank-and-file soldiers, the protagonists were often naïve innocents who had just signed up for military service, such as Taylor or Eriksson. These are the moral pillars of the story. Taylor, for example, stops one platoon member raping a Vietnamese girl by yelling, "She's a fucking human being, man." Likewise, Eriksson, balking when one fellow soldier compares their activities to Genghis Khan, says: "It's the Twentieth Century… Jesus, we're supposed to be helping these guys."

Not that the films shirk on showing the horrors perpetrated by American soldiers. *Platoon* features a scene where the pent-up soldiers unleash a 'scorched earth' policy on one unsuspecting village, much in the way Kilgore's men do in *Apocalypse Now*. Meanwhile, *Casualties of War* – based on a true story first reported in *The New Yorker* by Daniel Lang in 1969 – dealt with a platoon of five American soldiers who kidnap a Vietnamese woman from her village for "portable R&R". Forcing her to march with them, at the urging of their sergeant (Sean Penn), they then brutally gang rape her. While Eriksson refuses to participate, it's ultimately his testimony that brings the perpetrators to justice after they kill her. A neat expression of what constitutes individual moral responsibility in a combat zone, it asks the question: how far do you go before enough is enough?

In *Platoon*, Stone strains, perhaps too much, for religious significance. Taylor refers to Sgt. Bob Barnes (Tom Berenger) and Sgt. Elias Grodin (Willem Dafoe) fighting for "possession of his soul". Likewise, when Elias dies in the jungle, falling to the ground with his arms in the air – reputedly a recreation of a photograph taken in 1968 by Art Greenspon – the image is too Christ-like to be a coincidence. If suggesting that the soldiers' sacrifice was akin to Christ's crucifixion was somewhat stretching it, Stone's reverent tone – dedicating the film to "the men who fought and died in the Vietnam War" – coincided with attitudes in the US softening towards veterans. Back in 1982, the Vietnam Veterans Memorial in Washington D.C. had been completed and *Platoon* arrived just as US citizens were beginning to face up to the country's recent history.

Yet in many ways, *Platoon* and its peers were no less guilty than their earlier counterparts of certain traits. Notably, the enemy is still a near-invisible force, hidden in the jungle undergrowth or in bombed out buildings. Those Vietnamese that are seen in more detail are often female – either victims, as in *Platoon* and *Casualties of War*, or antagonists, such as the sniper in *Full Metal Jacket*. The ever-present figure of John Wayne is also yet again invoked; in Kubrick's film, Pvt. Joker (Matthew Modine) frequently invokes The Duke with his impersonation, while one of his fellow soldiers says, "We'll let the gooks play the Indians." And to further this mythologising of the war, nostalgic Sixties rock'n'roll blares from every radio wherever possible.

With virtually all of these films set during the peak of America's involvement, before President Nixon began withdrawing troops and sapping morale, all concentrated on the theme of abandonment that seems to haunt these grunts (again picking up on something seen in *Rambo: First Blood Part II* and *Uncommon Valor*). In *Platoon*, this is shown in the above-mentioned sequence, when the dying Elias misses the departing helicopter after Barnes has shot him in cold blood. In *Full Metal Jacket*, it's the scene in Vietnam where Eightball (Dorian Harewood) is gunned down by the female sniper in no-man's-land, plugged with bullets one at a time, leaving him isolated and very expendable.

In the case of *Hamburger Hill*, a true story that chronicles the ten-day assault on Hill 937 in the Ashau Valley, the film is a grass-roots account of the absurdity of war. Arguably more 'real' than even *Platoon*, which on a superficial level features some very visceral combat scenes, it's a harrowing watch. Called 'Hamburger Hill' because the bullets were turning men into shredded meat, this is a strength-sapping, mud-caked, rain-soaked mission that seems to have no intrinsic meaning, strategic or otherwise. We never really find out why this hill is such an important piece of land to conquer – and when they do, in the finale, they sit about dazed by burning tree stumps as if they still don't know.

The least celebrated of this quartet of 'grunt ensemble' films (doubtless due to its journeyman director and relatively obscure cast, bar Don Cheadle in an early role), *Hamburger Hill* has much going for it. While the others all focused on white protagonists, the platoon in *Hamburger Hill* featured a considerable number of African-American soldiers and the film sets out to investigate the racial tensions that exist within the US army. Showing how many of the black grunts are in the war because they lack education, as one is told, "They don't take niggers back in headquarters." Yet, unfortunately like its peers, the film doesn't investigate the very racism of the American intervention that underpins the whole war.

Wearing its heart on its sleeve far more than the other films, *Hamburger Hill* actually shows its protagonists showing emotion as their comrades are blown up around them. This is not the romanticising of Oliver Stone, setting Elias' death scene to Samuel Barber's heart-wrenching *Adagio for Strings*. These deaths are violent, bloody and shocking – flesh severed and smoked, pierced and ripped. It seems a world away from Kubrick's clinical view of the war, fought out in bombed-out urban environments as a war of attrition. These men cry when their girlfriends write to them, scream when their buddies die. As the poem by Major Michael Davis O'Donnell quoted at the end says, "Take one moment to embrace those gentle heroes you left behind."

The problem with focusing on the war from the grunt's eye view is that it left the perspective as myopic at best. Certainly *Platoon*'s detail of Taylor's deadly day-to-day routine is commendable yet it hardly allows for a wider analysis of America's involvement in the war. With its sensational first half set on Parris Island in South Carolina, *Full Metal Jacket* may be the best film ever made about basic training. But the battle between the gunnery sergeant (R. Lee Ermey) and the overweight misfit recruit Pvt. Gomer Pyle (Vincent D'Onofrio) is so compelling, the film's concluding half in Vietnam feels almost like an afterthought. Indeed, Kubrick's film, coming after *Platoon* and *Hamburger Hill*, felt like too little too late.

By the early 1990s, after America had dubiously restored its pride with the first Gulf War and Operation Desert Storm, the Vietnam War movie was on the wane. There was a new enemy now. Nevertheless, Stone attempted to examine the conflict from a more global perspective, with 1993's *Heaven & Earth*, which told the true story of Le Ly Hayslip, a Vietnamese girl who grows up during the war and ultimately marries a US marine. "The third story, *Heaven & Earth*, was an attempt to even go further, to make it global, to reach across the waters and reach out to the Vietnamese people who suffered so greatly and bring her back home," he says. "She came to America, so she covered both cultures. I love that movie. I still do. It still brings tears to me."

Yet while Stone's attempts to show the Vietnamese perspective in this third film was commendable, the execution was far from it. Hamstrung by its attempt to splice two of Hayslip's books, *When Heaven and Earth Changed Place* and *Child of War, Woman of Peace*, the clunky script is far too episodic to remain cohesive. Tortured by non-communist Vietnamese for suspected political treachery, raped by the Vietcong, banished from her Central Vietnamese village, Le Ly (Hiep Thi Le) winds up in Saigon, where she refuses to prostitute herself. Instead, hooking up with the genial marine Steve Butler (Tommy Lee Jones), the plot takes her with her new husband to San Diego, California, where she lands slap bang in the middle of the American Dream.

Stone makes some concession to considering the impact of the war on the Vietnamese, when Le Ly returns to her homeland thirteen years later to find her brother telling her the Americans caused much suffering in the country. Yet it is somewhat ironic that this comes fifteen minutes from the end of the film. With *Heaven & Earth* arriving when it did, it felt as if Hollywood was finally giving an almost cursory glance towards the Vietnamese, right at the tail end of the cycle of Vietnam War movies. Covering this war was never meant as an examination of global politics, just as it wasn't about die-hard heroism. The Vietnam War movie, in the end, was about guilt-ridden reflection, looking in the mirror to see the collateral damage sustained by the American psyche.

Bibliography/Endnotes

1. *America Dearest* by J. Hoberman, *American Film*, May 1988.
2. *Vietnam on Film* by Keith Connolly, *Cinema Papers*, May-June 1978.
3. The Tet Offensive was a military campaign conducted by the Vietcong and NVA in 1968 to strike at military and civilian command and control centres throughout South Vietnam.
4. *The Vietnam Oscars* by Peter Biskind, *Vanity Fair*, March 2008.
5. *A Story That's Dying to Be Told* by Graham Fuller, *The Listener*, 14 December, 1989.

ILSA, KITTY, UNDERWATER ZOMBIES, TESTICLE TRANSPLANTS AND TRAMPOLINES

The Nazi Exploitation Film

MIKE MAYO

Ever since the days of silent film, movies have promised incomparable depictions of sex, violence and other exotic naughtiness. The advertising campaign for 1924's *Alimony* breathlessly claimed 'brilliant men, beautiful jazz babies, champagne baths, midnight revels, petting parties in the purple dawn, all ending in one terrific smashing climax that makes you gasp.' Alas, no one was able to deliver on those promises until the late 1960s and early '70s when societal pressures and governmental restrictions were relaxed and the movies finally were able to give viewers the tastelessness that they'd wanted to see for decades.

Mainstream exploitation was born.

For our purposes, exploitation is defined as a film that is made quickly to exploit either a subject that's in the news or another profitable film. Exploitation also exaggerates the most sensational aspects of its story. In the United States, the Motion Picture Association of America (MPAA) 'Production Code' specifically forbade the very acts and attitudes that exploitation is built upon (and that moviegoers want to see) with a detailed list of 'thou shalt nots'. Created in the 1930s and amended and expanded over the years, it was enforced with varying degrees of severity until 1968 when Jack Valenti became President of the MPAA. He did away with the code and in its place installed a ratings system, loosely based on the classification system that had been in use in England for decades. His system describes the content of a film without judging its artistic merit or propriety. At the same time in other countries, government censorship and religious restrictions were giving way to a more relaxed and accepting attitude toward art in general, movies in particular. Gone was the idea that the state and the church should tell people what to watch, or that it was the job of the movies to elevate and ennoble their audience. Let the marketplace decide.

By the early 1960s, World War 2 films set in the European theatre had already evolved through three stages. The first, made during the war, were propaganda – *In Which We Serve* (1942), *Action in the North Atlantic* (1943) and *The Way Ahead* (1944). The second wave, made in late 1940s and 1950s, took a more serious psychological approach as seen in *Battleground* and *Twelve O'Clock High* (both 1949). Around a decade later, the war became violent escapist entertainment (Hollywood's bread and butter) with *The Great Escape* (1963), *Where Eagles Dare* (1968) and many others. At roughly the same time on American television, *Hogan's Heroes* (1965-1971) turned the European war into situation comedy. Once those lines had been crossed, it was a short step for the war film to morph into exploitation.

The exploitation films based on Nazi atrocities fall into three overlapping categories: action, horror and sex. The films focused on sex are by far the most salacious and astonishing. As a group, they're notable for atrocious acting, impoverished production values, fevered plotting and gamy excesses of every stripe. There is a consistency of tone, titles, imagery, cast and plotlines across the subgenre, and three of the films, maybe four, are bizarre masterpieces. As a group they have displayed enduring popularity on tape and DVD. They were also at the centre of the 'video nasties' censorship controversy in the United Kingdom during the 1980s. Over the years, many of the films have been re-edited and/or re-named numerous times to cash in on a star's popularity or to appeal to a different segment of the exploitation audience.

As Joe Bob Briggs wrote in his excellent book *Profoundly Disturbing: Shocking Movies That Changed History*, referring to exploitation in general, 'These movies were released during the golden age of exploitation from about 1972 to 1983, when flicks destined for downtown grindhouses and drive-ins were routinely passed by the MPAA classification board and given "R" ratings, apparently under the assumption that no one except the already depraved would see them.' He's correct in calling those years the 'golden age' of exploitation, and the Nazi movies were the strongest and most disreputable of the bunch. They utilise the iconography of German National Socialism, particularly in political symbols and costuming, and they're based tacitly or explicitly on the all-too-real horror of the Holocaust.

ACTION!

Both *The Guns of Navarone* (1961) and *The Dirty Dozen* (1967) topped the American box office in the years they were released, and that success made imitations of the small-group-working-behind-enemy-lines story inevitable. The nature of the protagonists, however, changed significantly. In *The Guns of Navarone*, the heroes are conventional soldiers and partisans. In *The Dirty Dozen*, they are convicted criminals, murders and rapists who face a death sentence or long stretches in prison. Of course, there are enough rationalisations – racism, arrogant officers, etc. – to make the characters fairly sympathetic, but they're still a questionable lot. As the trend continued in such films as *Commandos* (1968), where Lee Van Cleef leads a group of saboteurs against Italians in North Africa, and *Kelly's Heroes* (1970), where Clint Eastwood and company's motivation is sheer greed, the characters become considerably more anti-authoritarian, reflecting the tenor of the times. Still, those films have solid production values and tell relatively complicated stories.

The first real action exploitation picture is the rarely seen and curious *The Cut-Throats* (1969) from writer director John Hayes, who'd been nominated for an Academy Award in 1958 for his short film *The Kiss*. *The Cut-Throats* begins with the credits rolling over a painting of a guy wearing a cowboy hat and throwing a lasso with an M-1 Garand rifle at his feet. Another character carries a Colt single-action revolver, further confusing the Western and war iconography. Those details aside, Hayes was one of the first to understand how inexpensively Nazi ideology could be represented on screen. (In discussing exploitation, economic considerations cannot be overestimated.) The first German soldier to appear wears a black SS uniform. (He, by the way, is a rapist.) Later, one of the softcore sex scenes is played out with a Hitler speech on the radio to set the mood and a long Nazi banner – bright red with a white circle and a black swastika – for decoration. The image of the black uniform and the simple banner, and the hectoring voice first became familiar to moviegoers in Leni Riefenstahl's *Triumph of the Will/Triumph des Willens* (1935). The Nazi exploitation filmmakers of the 1970s would make even more extensive use of them. Why not? The speeches are free and English-speaking audiences understand the tone even if they know nothing of the exact meaning. The banners make an immediate, unmistakable visual statement. More about the uniforms later.

Hayes' plot also provides a partial template for the war exploitation films that would follow. It involves a villainous captain who cons his superiors into letting him lead a mission behind German lines to a 'golf course and country club' used by Wehrmacht officers for R&R with willing young women. The war is almost over and he tells them that the plans for the counter offensive are hidden there. Actually, he's after a Nazi horde of gold and jewels and is ready to kill anyone, American or German, to get it. The important idea, which is found in almost all of these films, is that the end of the war is within sight. For the Germans, all is lost and normal rules of behaviour no longer apply. The characters are then allowed to indulge in any sensual excess, the more sadistic, sick and imaginative the better. To that end, Uschi Digard, one of the more prominent actresses in softcore low-budget films of the period, makes a welcome appearance. The sets are also worth noting. The allegedly luxurious country club looks like a long-abandoned housing project. Attempts to make the interiors appear luxurious are equally futile. The entire film has a dingy, anaemic look that would become the standard for the subgenre.

Released the same year, *Five for Hell/5 per l'inferno* tells essentially the same story about a group of American GIs heading behind the lines to Villa Verde to steal the details of 'Plan K,' the Fuhrer's personal counter offensive. Directed by low-budget veteran Gianfranco Parolini, it's notable mostly for an intense performance by Klaus Kinski as the evil SS officer, near comedic action sequences (some involving a trampoline) and an incongruously bouncy theme that might have come from a TV gameshow of the time. The script was co-written by Sergio Garrone who would make his own mark in the field with much stronger material.

Prolific writer-director Lee Frost's *Black Gestapo* (1975) is really more a part of the 'blaxploitation' wave of the 1970s, but it deserves mention in this context, too. It concerns the conflict between a black power movement called the People's Army and Italian-American gangsters over the drug and numbers rackets. In the first half, the black protagonists wear khaki uniforms and red armbands with a black clenched fist inside a white circle. In the second half, when they've been corrupted by their success, they adopt conventional black SS regalia and shout 'Sieg Heil' over a general's inspirational speech. Frost, who plays the effeminate capo Vince, crams a commendable amount of crazed violence and kinky sex (including another appearance by la divine Uschi) into the proceedings. If the comparison between the actual Nazi rise to power and Frost's creations is tenuous, he understood how to use the symbols and images, as he had demonstrated several years earlier in 1968 with *Love Camp 7*, forerunner of the sexual exploitation films that would become so popular in the 1970s.

Certainly the most popular of the action exploitation films, if not the best, is Enzo G. Castellari's *The Inglorious Bastards/Quel maledetto treno blindato* (1978). Effervescently plotted, it begins in France, 1944, where five American soldiers are being shipped off to prison for various infractions. When their convoy is strafed by a German plane, the commanding officer orders the MPs to shoot any prisoners who try to escape from the truck that is the airplane's primary target. Pvt. Canfield (Fred Williamson) quite reasonably strangles him. Having established a moral equivalency between the Germans and the American officers, the film then becomes an episodic road movie, as Lt. Yeager (Bo Svenson) leads the escapees toward Switzerland. They meet good Germans who see the war for the waste that it is, bad Germans who want to execute all prisoners, and ten naked women. Whenever the action slows, more shelling commences and they're off to another adventure until they're united with resistance fighters who mistake them for commandos and enlist them in an elaborate train heist.

Throughout, the pace is quick and the tone is light. Some of the violence is

heightened with slow motion but most of it is less than intense. That febrile plotting, cheerful cynicism and fierce energy account for the film's enduring popularity and the big-budget Quentin Tarantino remake with Brad Pitt, *Inglourious Basterds* (2009).

A rare shot of director Enzo G. Castellari on the set of *The Inglorious Bastards* 1978

© Enzo G. Castellari

HORROR!

The Nazi exploitation horror film are variations on Armando de Ossorio's *Blind Dead* films, featuring the resurrected Knights Templar, and George Romero's zombie movies. In all of them, slow-moving ghastly figures rise up from the grave to prey on the living. The first and arguably the best of this spotty lot is Ken Wiederhorn's *Shock Waves* (1977). It's the ploddingly paced story of a group of tourists in the Caribbean who are marooned on an island. Its sole inhabitant, living in an abandoned hotel, is a German scientist (Peter Cushing) who was helping to create invincible SS troops – 'not dead, not alive but somewhere in between' – at the end of the war. He escaped in a ship with his semi-deceased bunch and scuttled them on a reef. For unexplained reasons that appear to be celestial in origin and involve a bilious orange lighting effect, the submerged soldiers are reanimated with the arrival of the tourists. The tropical setting is seedy and mosquito-infested, and Brooke Adams is fetching in a yellow bikini, but the only power that the film generates is in the images of those lurching men with jackboots, grey uniforms, goggles and wafting blond hair.

Ishiro Honda's *Frankenstein Conquers the World/Furankenshutain tai chitei kaijû Baragon* (1965) also involves Nazi scientists who hope to create invincible soldiers by shipping the still-beating heart of Frankenstein's monster in a U-Boat to Hiroshima on 6 August 1945. The atomic bomb explosion causes the irradiated organ to be transformed into a dog-eating hydrocephalatic Caucasian boy who grows into a towering, city-stomping monster and fights an equally giant floppy-eared armadillo with a light-emitting horn on its head, and a huge octopus while scientists led by Dr. Bowen (Nick Adams) look on in bewildered amazement. However, it does not really engage any significant Nazi elements.

More underwater reanimated Germans populate Jean Rollin's *Zombie Lake/Le Lac des morts vivants* (1980). They are soldiers who were tossed in a lake by resistance fighters at the end of the war. It's revealed later that during the Inquisition, a black mass was held at the same lake and children were sacrificed, so apparently it's the supernatural connection that has kept these guys in some sort of suspended animation. They are jump-started when a nubile young woman chooses to ignore the 'No Swimming' skull and crossbones sign and takes a skinny dip. Moments later the first Nazi rises up from the muck. Presently, the members of a women's basketball team doff their duds and more of the undead are released. A laborious flashback explains that it all has to do with a 'good' soldier who wants to visit his daughter in the nearby village.

The cheesy organ lounge music score is entirely appropriate for an effort that's pretty poor, even for the prolific Rollin. It's extremely silly and a bit sexy and it manages to be marginally better than Jesus Franco's *Oasis of the Zombies/L'Abîme des morts vivants* (1981). These undead Nazis live under the North African sand and guard $6 million in gold. The plot follows the same sins-of-the-father line that Rollin used. The effects are equally cheap and long stretches of the action are so dark that you can tell nothing about what's happening. As a group, these horror films use German uniforms and rotting-flesh make-up effects to create inexpensive and ineffective monsters. The exploitation films of the era that deal directly with sex are far more frightening.

SEX!

Lee Frost's *Love Camp 7/Nazi Love Camp 7* (1969) establishes several of the basic premises that films of the 1970s would copy and embroider upon. Because it was made in a time when exploitation had to wear a fig leaf of artistic or historical respectability, it begins with a talky 'the story you are about to see is true' prologue in present-day London. Two WACs (Maria Lease and Kathy Williams) who have near-psychic memorisation skills volunteer to infiltrate a concentration camp where women are forced to be sex toys for German officers. Why? Our heroines are to pick the brain of Jewish scientist Martha Grossman who is imprisoned there and has important knowledge about jet engines. But, as the spymaster tells them, it will "be necessary for you to cooperate with Jerry in any manner that they order."

Director Frost realised that it doesn't take much to create the setting. The camp barracks where most of the action takes place is threadbare, bleak and believably grim.

In other scenes, red Nazi wall hangings are the primary set dressing. A few uniforms and period weapons do the rest. Much of the violence occurs off screen but judging by the actresses' facial expressions, at least some of the humiliation and embarrassment was real. Brief mention is made of scientific experiments, but the real point is sexual subjugation and, despite the talky filler scenes, the film is about as explicit as late '60s softcore could be. Writer and producer Bob Cresse is convincingly piggish as the commandant. If reports of his contemporaries are to be believed, he brought real commitment to the character's lip-smacking excesses. Cresse is also responsible for the two basic storylines that these films follow: (1) the concentration camp where the guards, male and female, abuse the women prisoners and (2) the brothel where officers relax. *Love Camp 7* also leads directly to the first masterpiece of the subgenre. The cigar smoking Col. Kemp is played by Dave Friedman. Friedman was also a rival producer of Cresse in the softcore business. When *Love Camp 7* proved to be a box office hit, Canadian investors approached Friedman to create a more graphic and expensive version, *Ilsa, She Wolf of the SS*.

Erwin Dietrich's *Frauleins in Uniform/Eine Armee Gretchen* (1973) is little more than an elaborately plotted softcore skin flick that almost turns into a real war film in the third act when Soviet tanks appear. It follows a German doctor and his two daughters who are pressed into service near the end of the war. He's sent to the front while they go into a 'special division' to support the troops. The combat sequences at the end have virtually nothing to do with what has gone before. Footage from those scenes is recycled in Bruno Mattei's *SS Girls/Casa privata per le SS* (1977), one of the crazier entries in the genre with bondage, orgies, debauchery, suicide, bestiality and a main character who's insane.

In 1975, *Ilsa, She Wolf of the SS* appeared. It is the most famous and infamous of these films in America, if not in Europe. (In the early 1980s, I lived in a college town where *Ilsa* replaced *The Rocky Horror Picture Show* (1975) as the weekend midnight feature at one cinema for months.) A pious foreword explains that the film is based on 'documented fact', and, astonishingly, that is the case. (The foreword is signed 'Herman Traeger, Producer' because Friedman was embarrassed to associate his name with the finished product. Such is the power of film.) A woman named Ilse Koch was married to the commandant of the Buchenwald concentration camp and she participated in all manner of sexual exploits. Though photographs taken of her in later years are unflattering, in her prime, she was quite the looker. But historical truth was the last thing that director Don Edmonds and producer Friedman were interested in. Their Ilsa (Dyanne Thorne, an absolutely perfect name for the actress playing the part) is a flint-hard buxom blonde commandant who revels in her power. She's first seen naked astride a man, one of the inmates. When she's finished with him, she proclaims, "Once a prisoner has slept with me, he will never sleep with another woman again. If he lives, he'll remember only the pain of the knife. Castrate him."

That's precisely what Ilsa and her two equally imposing blonde aides proceed to do, with the focus on sharp, glittering surgical instruments and the screaming terror-stricken subject. The setting is Medical Camp Nine and much of the action involves horrific experiments. Naked women are tortured with various combinations of electric shocks, boiling water, impalement with grotesque instruments, surgery, disease-infected maggots and the like, all presented with sickening verisimilitude.

Similarly, rape is depicted with more realistic violence than titillation. Compared to most other works in the genre, *Ilsa* has a highly polished look. It was filmed on the long-unused sets of *Hogan's Heroes* (1965-1971), and care was taken with Nazi regalia, particularly the black SS uniforms with their death's head decoration and silver piping. Like the red banners and wall hangings, those uniforms are immediately recognisable and ominous. While the simple grey Wehrmacht uniform tends to fade into the background, the SS uniform commands attention. That's what Heinrich Himmler intended when he personally designed the outfit to separate his racially pure Nordic men, who supervised the Holocaust, from other police services. Himmler also obsessed over the insignia. The SS lightning bolts suggest runes, and the silver death's head was adapted from a 19th century military unit. The black numbers worn by Ilsa and her cohorts are tightly tailored and décolleté, adding blatant sexuality to the mix.

But the strongest element in the film is the stomach-churning medical torture. Having produced the original gore movie, *Blood Feast* (1963), Friedman was an old hand at this sort of material. He, Edmonds and make-up artist Joe Blasco are all too effective with the depravities. Despite the advances in visual effects, that part of the film is still unsettling. The sexual side also becomes increasingly extreme, to the point where even Ilsa herself is a bit put off by the outré demands made upon her by a visiting general, and the big finish brings it all to a fittingly destructive conclusion. Few of the films that followed are able to match *Ilsa* for sheer inventiveness and bravado.

Pier Pasolini's *Salò, or the 120 Days of Sodom / Salò o le 120 giornate di Sodoma* (1975) should not be considered with these films. It's a deadly serious work, not exploitation, but it's so extreme and so moving that it is a major influence on the others and must be mentioned. Pasolini's father was an officer in the Italian fascist army. His son was passionately anti-fascist. Pasolini wrote in a foreword: '[The] entire film with its unheard-of atrocities which are almost unmentionable is presented as an immense sadistic metaphor of what was the Nazi-Fascist dissociation from its crimes against humanity… The film is a mad dream which does not explain what happened in the world during the Forties. A dream which has an awful logic in its entirety, but chaos in the details.'

A respected poet, essayist, novelist and filmmaker, Pasolini was murdered before the film was released. His death may have been the result of a sexual encounter gone wrong or a politically motivated assassination. He had angered the Italian rightwing with essays attacking the government, and the communists had expelled him for his homosexuality. Whatever the case, the film is a work of profound personal and political despair with an autobiographical element. Pasolini's brother Guido had joined the Italian resistance toward the end of the war, but was brutally murdered in an unexplained internal conflict.

Based on a novel by the Marquis de Sade and presented with the formal simplicity of a fable, *Salò, or the 120 Days of Sodom* revolves around four prosperous middle-aged men who are religious, judicial, political and aristocratic leaders. Near the end of the war, they round up a large group of attractive young women and men, some the children of resistance fighters. With the help of young guards, the older men hold them prisoner at a rural villa. There they subject the kids to escalating tortures and indulge their sadistic sexual and coprophilic proclivities. Throughout, the young people are bizarrely passive.

One of the men introduces their atrocities with this bit of verse:

> Within a budding grove
> The young girls bloom
> All unaware of their impending doom.
> They listen to the radio; they drink their tea
> Not knowing they must soon forgo their liberty.
> The bourgeoisie does not recoil from slaughter
> Though the victims be their loving sons and daughters."

(This version comes from the English language version of the Criterion DVD. The subtitled Italian is slightly different.) The acts become increasingly extreme and nihilistic as the film progresses, but the tone remains muted, the pace stately. As Pasolini said, it is an allegory on the nature of evil, of deliberate well-organised cruelty, depravity and murder. Without question, it is a singular masterpiece of horror, one of the most disquieting films ever made.

Liliana Cavani's *The Night Porter/Il Portiere di notte* (1974) has more serious aspirations than exploitation, and it, too, is a strong influence on the low-budget efforts that followed. Dirk Bogarde is the title character, Max, an SS filmmaker who made propaganda in concentration camps. In 1957, he works in a Vienna hotel. He still has his old uniforms in the closet and hangs around with his Nazi pals. They're trying to erase the last traces of their past when Lucia Atherton (Charlotte Rampling) shows up. She was a prisoner with whom Max had a masochistic sexual relationship during the war. In a sort of doomed *Repulsion* (1965)/*Last Tango in Paris* (1972) way, they are drawn back into their old roles. Even considering the time when it was made and the surreal flourishes, it's still bizarrely overwrought and quite possibly the least sexy movie ever made about sexual obsession. For all the artistic pretensions, it still works with the same images that power the exploitation – swastika banners, black uniforms and overall kinkiness.

Tinto Brass' *Salon Kitty* (1976) combines the seriousness of *Night Porter* and *Salò* with the horrific subject matter of *Ilsa*. But where the American/Canadian production is a fairly straightforward, low-budget film staged on one set, the Italo/German/French co-production is a raunchy surreal, operatic extravaganza with elaborate production values, dance numbers, careful lighting, lush colour photography and fart jokes. Aldo Valletti, who plays one of the main characters in *Salò, or the 120 Days of Sodom*, appears in an important cameo. The loose plot concerns the establishment of a brothel that has been surreptitiously wired for sound so Nazi officials can ferret out dissent within the officer corps. A patriotic young German woman (Teresa Ann Savoy) volunteers to work there. But the story is merely a framework for Brass to indulge his sumptuous excesses, mixing images of warm sensuality with horror. He pumps up traditional Nazi imagery to rococo extremes with a huge swastika banner repeatedly reflected on a highly polished floor. The main character (Helmut Berger) sports red and white silk scarves with decorated swastikas, swastika wristbands, and a skintight silvery SS outfit. In perhaps the most bizarre of several bizarre moments, a naked German officer and a whore wearing a swastika garter go foaming-at-the-mouth insane, literally, while propaganda footage of Hitler is being projected on their bodies. The scene comes after the 20-couple synchronized orgy, the pig slaughter and dwarf sex. That shifting tone makes the film difficult to synopsise or describe, but it is undeniably successful as bizarre entertainment, and so it spawned immediate imitations. As a group, these pictures are much more narrowly focused on sexual sadism, rape and mutilation under the guise of scientific experimentation.

Deported Women of the SS Special Section/Le Deportate della sezione speciale SS (1976) was made as the cycle was winding down and so it amps up the key elements that had made the earlier films successful. In this case, that means mutilation, rape, torture, degradation, death and a really bizarre ending. John Steiner returns as the effete commandant, a role that's based on his work in *Salon Kitty*, and suffers a variation on the 'fate worse than death'. The plot concerns women who are brought to the 'Joy Division' camp where they're used as sex slaves. As one inmate sums it up, "The war is lost for the Germans, but in this hellhole nothing ever changes. They've become more beastly. They don't feed us; they screw us and kill us." That really describes the basic plot of most of these movies.

Sergio Garrone's *SS Experiment Camp/Lager SSadis Kastrat Kommandantur* (1976) and *SS Camp 5: Women's Hell/SS Lager 5: L'Inferno delle donne* (1977) were produced together in seven days on the same cheapjack concentration camp and laboratory sets with many of the same cast members and the same Grand Guignol sensibility. The first film concerns a testicle transplant from an unwitting guard to the camp commandant (Giorgio Cerioni); the second, a Jewish doctor and his daughter who are trapped in a brothel/research camp. Both are heavy on nudity, torture and graphic surgery. (Actually, the most remarkable thing about both films is Cerioni's hair. It's a long carefully coiffed platinum blond pompadour that has an eerie phosphorescent glow.) In interview, Garrone defends himself by comparing his work to reality TV. "It's true I made semi-porno Nazi films, but I'd never make disgusting crap like that! Nazi-fascist movies aren't exactly exorcisms, they're a product. But they are cathartic – people get it out of their system! They are exposed to such strong material that they feel a repulsion." No one who's seen his movies could argue with that.

Perhaps the best of the dubious bunch is *The Beast in Heat/La Bestia in Calore* (1977). Again we have the blonde Nazi, Dr. Kratsch (Macha Magall), who uses an apelike guy (Salvatore Baccaro, who played a similar character in *Salon Kitty*) to rape women as part of her research. She introduces him by saying, "I'm certain that my creature will give you a demonstration of its virility that no human being would be capable of imagining. We must see, dear doctor, and appreciate the immolation of the chosen virgin who, without realising it, will be sacrificing herself for science!" Most of the sexual content, like the violence and the overripe dialogue, is so exaggerated and athletic that it's almost humorous. Director Luigi Batzella makes particular use of Nazi symbols, notably a large outdoor swastika sculpture. In one shot, the shadows of the camera and crew on the thing are so obvious, so blatant that Batzella might have meant to show them. That's probably giving the low-budget production more credit than it's due. Everything else about the film looks like it was done in a rush.

Mario Caiano's *Nazi Love Camp 27/La Svastica nel ventre* (1977) begins as a relatively placid softcore romance in pre-war Germany where Jewish Hannah Meyer (Sirpa Lane) falls for a typical Aryan guy. Soon, though, her family is killed and she's shipped off to a concentration camp where she's subjected to repeated rapes, shown in some versions with hardcore inserts. The camp commandant makes her his mistress and partner when he is tasked with setting up a brothel for officers. At times, the overall level of weirdness comes close to *Salon Kitty*, and the ending cranks up the mixture of violence and madness

SS EXPERIMENT CAMP

EXPERIMENT CAMP

to a manic level. Alain Payet's *Nathalie, Fugitive from Hell / Nathalie rescapée de l'enfer* (1978) is a slow silly little trifle where the titular heroine, a doctor, wears high heels while she's riding her bicycle or being tossed into a prison camp. Even judged by the impossibly lax standards of the subgenre, it's cheap looking and slow.

Cesare Canevari's *Gestapo's Last Orgy / L'Ultima orgia del III Reich* (1977) almost manages to live up to its unsavoury reputation. If it's not the equal of *Salon Kitty* or *Salò, or the 120 Days of Sodom*, it's close to them in its excesses. It begins with voiceover testimony of atrocities at the post-war trial of concentration camp Commandant Starker (Adriano Micantoni). Flashbacks reveal his relationship with inmate Lise (Daniela Poggi). The rest of the film mixes serious drama that emphasises anti-Semitism with hysterical sadism and bawdy sex.

As a group, the European films tend to be more pessimistic and, perhaps, more personal. Garrone mentions the 'exorcism' aspect of his work and there is certainly a degree of truth to that. All of these films are excessively violent, and most of them end with bodies littering the screen and many of the main characters dead. Resistance or escape from the horror is impossible. By contrast, the American films have more conventional plotting and heroic protagonists who occasionally prevail. The European films implicitly admit that everyone who had anything to do with the Nazi or fascist atrocities bears a degree of responsibility. No one could say that any of these films, except *Salò, or the 120 Days of Sodom* and *Salon Kitty*, attempt serious comment on their subject. Neither do they explain any sort of national guilt, even if they recognise the 'mad dream' that Pasolini saw in the heart of Nazi-fascism. Their purpose is to show naked women and explosive violence, combined with immediately recognisable symbols of the great horror of the 20th century. At their best, they provide the atavistic jolt of unembarrassed sleaze. Even now when graphic violence and all forms of sexual activity have become commonplace on screen and digital effects have made them more realistic, Nazi exploitation still has the power to shock, amaze and disgust.

In North America, these films are available for rent from Netflix and Blockbuster, and for sale from Amazon, Movies Unlimited (moviesunlimited.com), Something Weird Video (somethingweird.com), Blue Underground (blue-underground.com) and Luminous Film and Video Wurks (lfvw.com). In the UK, many are heavily cut or banned outright.

UNDER PRESSURE

Depth-charging, Confined Drama
and Life on and Under the Water
in the Submarine War Movie

DANIEL ETHERINGTON

Das Boot, the 1981 epic that's now considered among the best ever submarine-based war movies, opens to the sight of the bow of the titular U-boat, U-96, pushing through the green-tinged, murky depths. Although the ensuing film proceeds to go into the lives of men serving about the boat in great detail this opening sequence, as well as the very name of the film – The Boat – makes it very clear who the main character is here. It's not Jürgen Prochnow's Captain or Herbert Grönemeyer's Lieutenant Werner, the war correspondent who narrates the film and is the fictionalised equivalent of Lothar-Günther Buchheim, who wrote the source novel about his old experiences aboard a U-boat in 1941. No, it's U-96 itself.

   Throughout the submarine sub-genre of war movies, the submarines themselves have felt like characters in their own rights, from the USS *Copperfin* of *Destination Tokyo* (1943), to Cary Grant's second vessel, the put-upon USS *Sea Tiger* of *Operation Petticoat* (1957), to the boats featured in the 1990s resurgence of the genre like the Red October

Das Boot
1981

© Bavaria/
Radiant/
The Kobal
Collection

and USS *Dallas* of *The Hunt for Red October* (1990), or even the titular vessel of the controversial *U-571* (2000). More so than any other sub-genre of the war movie, the submarine war movie is defined by its vehicles, by its hardware. The Lancaster bomber may play a starring role in *The Dam Busters* (1954), the Spitfire in *Battle of Britain* (1969), or the Sherman tank in *Kelly's Heroes* (1970), but while this hardware may move the protagonists around and be used in combat, none of it serves as a long-term home, none of it confines them so dangerously and so persistently, none of it provides a setting for so much of the drama.

Arguably, the submarine war movie is an offshoot of the naval war movie more generally, but in many ways it's distinct. The submarine itself contains the drama as it contains the protagonists, the officers and men of the submarines and *Unterseeboots*. Although the submarines of World War 2 operated predominantly on the surface, and by and large only dived and remained underwater during combat situations or for strategic considerations, they still confined and contained their crews in a way that's very unlike that experienced by the crews of surface vessels. This confinement is at the heart of what makes the submarine war movie distinct from other war movies.

World War 1 warfare was evocatively captured in such fictions as R. C. Sherriff's 1928 play *Journey's End*, adapted for the screen by James Whale in 1930, and Erich Maria Remarque's landmark novel of the same year, *All Quiet on the Western Front*, adapted into the quintessential anti-war film of the same name in 1930. The drama in such cases is intensified by its setting in the dugouts, trenches and shell craters. In narratives of wartime aviation, the flyboys can leave their planes at the end of their missions – which generally last only hours. Aerial dogfighting seen on film might have an incomparable intensity, but it's generally comparatively brief. Likewise, even the scenes of the Normandy landings we see in such films as *The Longest Day* (1962), *The Big Red One* (1980) and *Saving Private Ryan* (1998) are passing events. No matter how potent and horrifying the incidents we're witnessing as Tom Hanks and co-battle on Omaha Beach, eventually they are able to move on, the air clears and the intensity abates. In the case of submarine movies, particularly the best of the genre – *Das Boot*, *The Enemy Below* (1957), *Run Silent Run Deep* (1958) – the submariners have no let up, the intensity of the experience portrayed on screen is maintained by the very fact of being confined in these metal tubes, or 'iron coffins' as the U-boats were sometimes called. Of course, the entire running time of these films is not taken up by the grim horrors of being depth charged, but even when they're not engaged in combat, the submariners are living a life most of us cannot contemplate. In terms of cinema's evocations of wartime experiences, the submarine movie surpasses all others in terms of how prolonged the intense drama is, and how sustained the elements of tension, claustrophobia, discomfort and fear are.

As a sub-genre, the submarine war movie evolved slowly, coming to fruition in World War 2, at a time when the output of war movies was greatly increased to serve propaganda purposes. The sub-genre continued to be popular for more than a decade after the end of the war, but, as with the war movie genre more broadly, changed subtly, reflecting how the world was changing. The sub-genre would resurface at the start of the 1980s for one major classic, and then be revitalised once more, briefly, during the 1990s and around the turn of the millennium. This chapter will track those changes, but also look at the factors consistent to the submarine war movie: their confined drama, their familiar visual motifs.

DIVE! DIVE! DIVE!

For non-submariners, the very idea of being in a submarine is deeply perturbing. The psychological implications of being aboard a submarine and in a combat situation are profound. As Murrell, the destroyer captain in *The Enemy Below* says, "being inside a submarine under attack is the worst experience you can imagine". Since the rise of the submarine war movie, filmmakers have exploited the dramatic potential of the submarine, of the unique implications of what it means to be sealed inside a metal tube, hatches and watertight doors sealed, and, effectively, alone at sea.

In her work defining and categorising combat movies, renowned US academic Jeanine Basinger suggests that while the infantry movie represents the combat movie at its purest, the submarine movie comes a close second. The submarine may be providing 'a self-contained and home-like unit' but 'it is also in the midst of danger from both nature and the enemy'. [1] This is particularly evident in *Das Boot*, where the two-month patrol involves three dangerous encounters with the enemy, but also a terrible north Atlantic storm that rages for more than three weeks. Of course, the crews of surfaces vessels may have faced similar dangers from both the enemy and nature, but at least they had endless supplies of air to breathe and, relative to the cramped World War 2 era submarines, a modicum of space to move around.

Even when Hollywood takes liberties with the dimensions of subs in its World War 2 movies, one consistent factor in all these films is that of the 'home-like unit'. Again, *Das Boot* is arguably the most evocative film when it comes to presenting the lives and routines of the crewmen, with its imagery of the military, the machine and the domestic all mixed up together – the food hanging between the equipment, the crew of 50 forced to use just one toilet as the other is filled with supplies, men scraping the mould off salamis and cured meats hanging in the control room. Even the less epic feature films, those built around more conventional plots and standard 100 minute running times, give us plenty of views of the men bunked alongside torpedoes, eating their dinner adjacent to crewmates at work. Sure, other genres of war movie show elements of domesticity – airmen in their mess, infantrymen cooking up meals in their fox-holes – but again, submarine movies have a unique variation on the theme, as domestic rubs shoulders so closely with war-like, in such confined spaces.

The war movie is a broad, perennial genre and one that serves numerous functions; it's highly mutable. It can be patriotic propaganda or pure entertainment. It can offer visceral action and thrills or gritty realism. It can illuminate through historical, factual veracity. Or it can be pure myth-making. And some of the best war movies are actually *anti*-war movies. The submarine war movie over the years has fulfilled all these roles. Whatever the agenda of the filmmakers, and however different the tones and messages, submarine war movies are almost always unified by the same, very specific elements and motifs, many of them dictated by that torpedo-spitting, tube-shaped central character, the submarine itself.

The submarine sub-genre is deeply codified in terms of its structural elements. So watching any submarine war movie, you're more than likely to see most if not all of the following: the crew getting bounced around inside their sub during a depth-charge attack; the sub skipper surveying enemy shipping or warships through the periscope, quite possibly turning his cap backwards before he does so; torpedoes being fired at enemy shipping (often accompanied by such utterances as "Torpedo number one running hot straight and normal"); the sub being shelled by a destroyer or Q-ship (armed merchant) while on the surface; the sub being strafed and bombed by enemy planes; the sub crash-diving after one or other of these attacks; the sub being damaged and sinking to dangerous depths; the sub miraculously surviving said depths, though with leaks and popping rivets; the sub captain ordering "rig for silent running"; the captain trying to fool a destroyer by shooting debris and even the bodies of their dead out of a torpedo tube; the sonar and/or hydrophone operator clutching his headphones while listening to enemy movements accompanied by the ping of sonar; red lighting; orders being relayed and repeated; shots of the helmsman pushing the wheel to initiate an order to dive deeper; and many subtle variations and combinations thereon.

In terms of the actual drama played out between the characters in the narrative, there are similarly recurring elements. So for example, the captain and the executive officer might have differing attitudes or ideologies that bring them close to coming to blows. They may even form two points in a love triangle with the same woman. Furthermore, differences between the officers may lead near mutiny, but ultimately result in a handing over of the baton, from the older, more experienced captain to the younger XO. The main lesson passed with that baton is that leadership involves terrible, difficult decisions that have to be made fast. Such motifs can be found in even the very earliest submarine war movies.

AHEAD ONE THIRD

The submarine rose to military viability late in the 19th century. Although submersibles had existed previously, submarines designed around a familiar tube-shape really began to appear in the middle of the 19th century. By 1864, the technology had advanced sufficiently for the Confederate States of America to successfully sink the Union's USS *Housatonic* with the CSS *H.L. Hunley*. By 1870, the submarine had made such an impact on the public imagination that Jules Verne had a hit with his novel *20,000 Leagues Under the Sea*. By the turn of the century, the use of diesel motors, which recharged previously limiting batteries, became standardised. The first decade of the 20th century also saw the rise of another, very different, but also very significant technology: cinema. Since its incremental 'invention' in the late 19th century, film moved fast from side-show oddity to highly commercial mainstream entertainment. Before World War 1 had given submarine technology a new imperative, the film industry had started dallying with the vessels. One early appearance of the submarine on film was in 1915 when Mack Sennett's Keystone Studios made *A Submarine Pirate* (1915), a comedy starring and co-directed by Syd Chaplin (Charlie's half-brother). This silent film was a landmark for the involvement of the US Navy, which allowed the filmmakers to use a submarine for exterior shots. It was the start of a long relationship between navies and filmmakers.

Thirteen years later, up-and-coming Hollywood professional Frank Capra had one of his first hits as a director with *Submarine* (1928). The film was in part inspired by the tragedy of US submarine S-51, which sank after being hit by a steamship in 1925, though *Submarine* was more preoccupied with a love-wrangle between two navy buddies and the single object of their affections. Another film that drew more on the very real tragedies of submarines sinking was John Ford's *Men Without Women* (1930), which saw the submarine movie enter the sound era. Although much of the early part of the film involves shenanigans by crewmen in Shanghai, submarine drama does ensue, building towards the film's sub, S-13, sinking and having to hold on until rescuers can reach it. The film's story involves a British officer, shamed after his vessel was sunk by the Germans with a field marshal aboard and now living incognito as a US Navy torpedo-man. This narrative element was likely inspired by the 1916 sinking of the British HMS *Oak*, which struck a mine planted by a U-boat. Among the casualties of the sinking of the *Oak* was Field Marshal Kitchener (he of the famed recruitment poster). This incident was to be again fictionalised for the seminal submarine war movie *Morgenrot*, 1933).

Along with the US *Hell Below* of the same year, *Morgenrot* helped introduce the submarine war movie as we'd recognise it. Its status as such was for a long time overshadowed by the fact that the film was the first to be released in Germany after Hitler became chancellor; it was appropriated by the Nazi party and used as a propaganda tool. *Morgenrot* is not, however, a Nazi film and is in fact not just a great precursor of the submarine war movie generally, but also a clear predecessor to *Das Boot* in the realism of its marine and submarine scenes.

Like *Das Boot* half a century later, *Morgenrot*'s first image is that of a submarine. The ensuing story then involves the requisite love triangle, as fellow officers Kapeu (short for Kapitänleutnant) Liers (Rudolf Forster) and Oberleutnant 'Phipps' Fredericks (Fritz Genschow) are both involved with the same woman. Despite the film spending a fair portion of its running time on dry land, it does incorporate many elements that would become familiar in later films. The familial, domestic atmosphere among the crew; crash diving; being depth-charged; torpedoing the enemy; a sequence in which they're tricked by a British sloop that's actually a Q-ship; the crewmen bravely going on with their duties when the sub is terribly damaged and sunk. One dive sequence involves shots from a camera mounted on the exterior of a real U-boat; 35 years later, John Sturges received acclaim for ostensibly innovating similar shots in *Ice Station Zebra* (1968). Alongside the gripping drama, which climaxes with a moral dilemma among the shipmates who survive the sinking but are faced with fewer pieces of escape equipment than there are men, the film is technically astonishing in places: in another memorable shot rushes, the camera through the interior, passing through bulkhead doors, giving the viewer a concise tour of the boat. It's a remarkable film, and deserves to shake off the Nazi associations that led to it remaining little-seen for decades. Interestingly, the film was co-directed by Briton Vernon Sewell, making his debut. Ten years later he co-wrote and co-directed *The Silver Fleet* (1943), a film produced by masters Emeric Pressburger and Michael Powell that was very much a British propaganda piece, with its story of a Dutch resistance operative secretly fighting the Germans from his position of influence running a shipyard making submarines.

Hell Below was another World War 1-set film that presaged the World War 2 submarine movie. As well as using genuine World War 1 footage, the film features the tensions and drama of life – and combat – aboard a submarine, as well as the personal dramas between the main protagonists. Here that means by-the-book sub captain Lieutenant Commander Toler (Walter Houston) and Lieutenant Tommy Knowlton (Robert Montgomery), who just happens to meet and fall in love with the captain's married daughter. Classic scenes in the film include one where Toler is forced to make a decision to dive when enemy planes attack, despite Tommy's best friend being topside, the sub being sent to the bottom by a depth-charge attack, and the ultimate message of the younger officer learning about duty and sacrifice from the older, stricter man. Like *Morgenrot*, much of the film is played out on land, but there are still enough of the submarine war movie elements here to make the film an essential step in the evolution of the genre. Both films are seminal but of *Morgenrot*, British academic Jonathan Rayner says it 'exhibits the continuities of style, narrative and characterisations which come to define the submarine film in later decades. A claustrophobic mise-en-scène, the representation of submarine attacks and depth-charge reprisals, and the stoical endurance of submariners are present in its impartial rendering of the patrol.' [2] While US military historian and film biographer Lawrence H. Suid calls *Hell Below* 'a convincing submarine production, at least to eyes inexpert in the mysteries of torpedo tubes, control-room gadgets and oxygen tanks.' [3]

RIG FOR SILENT RUNNING

Submarines made occasional further appearances on film through the 1930s, such as in the John Ford-directed tale of a submarine-chaser, *Submarine Patrol* (1938), but as Basinger says, 'It took World War 2 to make the submarine into a real genre setting for viewers.' [4] Among the first American wartime movies to feature subs was the Lew Landers-directed *Submarine Raider* (1942), a B-movie melodrama that, against the backdrop of the attack on Pearl Harbor on 7 December 1941, is more concerned with a love story between a sub captain and a woman who survived a Japanese attack on her yacht. The film that really consolidated the submarine war movie, where most of the action takes place aboard a sub, was *Destination Tokyo* (1943), which Basinger describes as 'the submarine warfare section of *Hell Below* dilated to become an entire movie'. [5]

In 1940, Cary Grant had reportedly tried to enlist for the Royal Navy. The application may have been rejected on the grounds of his age (36), though other rumours continue to circulate that he was involved with British Intelligence, keeping an eye on Nazi activity in Hollywood. Whatever the reality, Grant's contribution to the war was more complex than is suggested by the contemporary movie magazine criticism that he should 'come home like David Niven'[6] (who served in the British army and remained absent from the screen during the war). Not only did he contribute much of his earnings to war charities, he contributed his inimitable charms to several propaganda and morale movies. Even before the war, Grant had made his first fictional foray aboard a sub when he played a lieutenant in a supporting role in the submarine melodrama *Devil and the Deep* (1932). By 1943, when he was a major star, he had become a submarine commander in *Destination Tokyo*, with his Captain Cassidy in charge of the USS *Copperfin*, which is dispatched from its pens in San Francisco on a top secret mission. This involves picking up a meteorologist from the Aleutian Islands then proceeding to Tokyo Bay, where he is sent ashore to gather information vital for the Doolittle Raid. This was America's first bombing strike on Tokyo which in reality took place in April 1942 and would famously feature in such other movies as *Thirty Seconds over Tokyo* (1944).

The *Copperfin*'s 'eight thousand miles of historic adventure' (in the words of the promotional tagline) involves the chummy, familial crew, working its way across the Pacific nudging their way through the mine fields and submarine nets defending Tokyo under the benign, fatherly eye of Cassidy and fed and tended to by the motherly cook (Alan Hale). The underwater work is realised with model work that has not stood the test of time, notably because the tank includes anemones and weeds that look monstrously large alongside the model submarine. The interior scenes work better, however, with plenty of technical talk of 'zero bubble' and 'all vents open'. We even get some tense depth-charging scenes and added pathos when the mascot kid of the crew has to have an emergency appendectomy. Although the film seems hoary and clichéd today, much of its story had basis in fact. Submarines did go on fact-gathering missions to Japan, though they did not send parties ashore in Tokyo Bay, and amateur appendectomies were reported. The drama may not have been exactly naturalistic, but the film gives a sense of realism through the 'filmmakers' adherence to detail and concern for accuracy of procedure.' [7]

The 'first big-budget submarine movie of World War 2 combat' [8] introduced audiences more widely to conditions of life aboard wartime submarines, with their arcane controls and parlance, cramped conditions and status of being at the mercy of depth-charges. Basinger suggests the 'challenge of limited space to be explored by the camera, coupled with the various possibilities for dramatic action – both above and below the sea – make it [the submarine] a natural for the film medium' [9] though arguably the submarine interior and ocean exterior are actually somewhat counter-intuitive in visual, cinematic terms. Cinema is all about the drama in the image, and the film image can achieve so much that cannot, say, be achieved on stage. The confines of a submarine are almost like a stage in that they're a limited space, while the imagery of curved walls, equipment, bunks squeezed beside torpedoes, as well as that of men with binoculars surveying endless sea and sky from the bridge, are not 'natural' for cinematic imagery, they're essentially very limited and limiting. Hence, like on stage, the emphasis in submarine films always returns to the human drama. In these early submarine war movies, even the imagery of the action sequences, of the model subs being depth-charged, or firing their 'fish' at shipping, was limited and served more of a role in punctuating the narrative drama. The submarine movie works best when characters are well drawn and the audience becomes acquainted with them – and then can relate to their suffering inside a submarine being depth-charged. The actors and their characters are more important than special effects shots of submarines. Ironically, however, the submarine war film was more generally lauded for its special effects work than for its storytelling or acting: although *Destination Tokyo* earned a Best Writing, Original Story Oscar nomination in 1944, it was the next big American propaganda submarine movie, *Crash Dive* (1943), that took a golden statuette that year in the Best Effects, Special Effects category. *The Enemy Below* (1957) won the same category in 1958, while *Torpedo Run* (1958) was nominated for it in 1959. *Ice Station Zebra* won Best Cinematography and Best Special Effects Academy Awards in 1969.

Unlike *Destination Tokyo*, *Crash Dive* had no basis in actual incident, though tonally it is similar, designed to have contemporary audiences cheering on their brave boys. The first colour feature in the submarine war movie genre, the film opens to striking shots of PT boats at work on the deep blue sea. Commanding one of them is Lt. Ward Stewart (Tyrone Power), who, due to "a shortage of trained officers" is transferred to submarine duties, aboard the USS *Corsair*, under Lt. Cmdr. Dewey Connors (Dana Andrews). The first half hour of the film is romantic, even screwball, comedy, as Ward falls for Jean Hewlett (Anne Baxter), who just happens to be the same woman Dewey plans to propose to when he gets an extra stripe on his sleeve. This inevitably results in complications when the truth emerges, but the two officers still manage to work together to complete a commando raid on a German island base, which they discover after a run-in with a Q-ship. The film is packed with stirring, heroic stuff, and even ends with an incredible homily to the US Navy delivered by Ward, who has overcome his boyish adoration of PT boats. "It isn't one branch of the service, it's all branches, and it isn't all ships, it's men," he says, as the film closes to a close-up of the Stars and Stripes.

Britain's major submarine movie of the same year, *We Dive at Dawn*, closes on a very different note – with a breezy joke, an adjunct to the stiff upper lip drama that defines the rest of the film. Directed by Anthony Asquith and starring John Mills as the captain of HMS *Sea Tiger*, this one involves another top secret mission, to take out the formidable German battleship the *Brandenberg*. Whereas the American war film will often feature an ethnic and regional smorgasbord of characters, the British version involves Cockneys, Scots and Yorkshiremen, like Eric Portman's hydrophone operator, Hobson, whose marital difficulties are making him a surly chap. Yes, melodrama elements are present and correct here too, but so are the familiar combat elements of crash diving, torpedoing and being depth-charged. When the submarine runs low on fuel, a party goes ashore in Denmark, and the climax of the film is not unlike that of *Crash Dive*, with Allied heroes giving Jerry a good bashing, but with the pure wish-fulfilment and intimacy of small arms ashore, not the cold anonymity of torpedo warfare – something that in reality was largely concerned with sinking shipping. Just as the German U-boat effort in World War 2 was concerned with trying to cripple the Allies by sinking Atlantic merchant shipping, so the US efforts in the Pacific were generally focused on attacking Japanese supply lines. However, such warfare was not entirely suitable for movie drama: for audiences back home, it was more important to show a clear-cut war with our subs by and large sinking warships, not merchantmen. Post-war, however, the genre shifted somewhat, as the necessity for such tidy propaganda passed.

The British *Morning Departure* (aka *Operation Disaster*, 1950), featuring John Mills again, returned to the stricken, sunken submarine theme. The Douglas Sirk-directed *Mystery Submarine* (1950) was more a thriller than a combat film and featured an intelligence agent on a mission to save a scientist in South America. You could rely on John Wayne to wave the flag, however, which is just what he did in *Operation Pacific* (1951). The US was entering its next war, in Korea, but this feature returned to the World War 2 setting for its tale of bashing an Asian foe. The film, which crudely combines model work with period footage and is full of clichés, such as a love triangle, a captain who sacrifices himself while on the bridge so that his sub can dive and escape, and a depth-charging sequence ("There's a bad leak down here, Captain."). The film has a few notable elements too though, particularly how it addresses the US Navy's notorious problems with dud torpedoes during World War 2. There's also a cameo appearance by none other than *Destination Tokyo*, which the crew of Wayne's sub watches in some down-time. "The things those Hollywood guys can do with a submarine," muses one officer, dismissively.

BRACE FOR DEPTH CHARGES!

The 1950s were an interesting period for the submarine war movie. Global politics had shifted from the open combat and comparative clarity of World War 2 to the murk of the Cold War. The atomic age had come, transforming how the submarine operated. The new generation of nuclear submarines, which appeared in the middle of the decade, could remain submerged for long periods, and their combat role now involved ICBMs and cruise missiles. The submarine genre went in several directions at once. There was the science fiction and fantasy of films like *The Atomic Submarine* (1959) and Disney's version of *20,000 Leagues Under the Sea* (1961). There were appraisals of the implications of nuclear weapons, like Sam Fuller's *Hell and High Water* (1954), which concerned the efforts of mercenary Richard Widmark and international consortium to foil a fiendish Commie plan is an old Japanese 'sewer pipe' submarine; Nevil Shute's *On the Beach* (1959), with its bizarrely calm take on the apocalypse; and *The Bedford Incident* (1965), with Richard Widmark's white destroyer captain coming into conflict with Sidney Poitier's black journalist. Then there were the films that took us back to the relative comfort of World War 2. The latter produced plenty of generic films, like *Hellcats of the Navy* (1957), a film most notable for being the only time Ronald Reagan and Nancy Davis (Reagan) appeared together; the comparable *Submarine Command* (1951) and *Torpedo Alley* (1953), which both dealt with the ensuing guilt felt by commanders who have had to make terrible, difficult decisions; this issue was also dealt with in *Torpedo Run* (1958), which also featured another perennial submarine movie theme, that of Ahab-like obsession. This was the main theme of one of the decade's best submarine films set during World War 2: *Run Silent Run Deep* (1958).

The Enemy Below 1957

© 20th Century Fox/ The Kobal Collection

John Gay, the screenwriter of *Run Silent Run Deep*, effectively shaped his story around this theme of obsession. The source book, by US Naval captain Edward L. Beach, only very loosely featured the film's main themes of obsession, and a classic rivalry set-up between an older, wiser captain and a younger, feistier XO, but Hollywood apparently needed this type of drama. It actually works well in the film, despite such material already feeling tired by this stage in the genre's lifespan. The film, directed by Robert Wise, was made by Burt Lancaster's production company and the actor, then at the height of his fame, cast himself in the role of the XO, Jim Bledsoe. To go toe to toe with the formidable Lancaster, the role of the captain, commander 'Rich' Richardson, went to Hollywood legend Clark Gable, who was twelve years his senior. The film was criticised for casting these men, aged 45 and 56, as submarine officers, as the boats were in reality commanded by younger officers, but such concerns, and other glaring flaws like how Rich survives his sub being destroyed in the prologue, can be overlooked due to the power of the film's drama.

Bledsoe is on the verge of his own command of the USS *Nerka*, but Rich persuades the brass to let him have one last crack at 'Bungo Pete', a Japanese vessel that has been racking up the US subs, among them Rich's previous command, in Japan's Bungo Straits. Bledsoe is angered, but has to follow orders, even when he starts to get dismayed about Rich's relentless drilling and his refusal to engage certain enemies. Despite Rich's rule-bending and Ahab-like obsession, the film ultimately follows the traditional course of the older man passing on lessons to the younger man. The film also features numerous of the established genre elements – the man left up top, the crash dives, the depth-charging, the silent running, the strafing runs of enemy planes – but unlike the earlier films, with their more upbeat morale-boosting approach, here Wise keeps things tight and harsh, the drama taking on intense psychological levels as the conflict between the officers escalates along with the danger of their circumstances.

Alongside the Moby Dick motif, sub movies also often featured duels between sub and ship, as each determines to sink the other and the drama ratchets up with each successive cat and mouse encounter. The paradigm of this narrative structure is *The Enemy Below* (1957). Initially, *The Enemy Below*, directed by Dick Powell and based on the novel by British naval officer Denys Rayner, would appear to be a more traditional maritime war movie, set aboard a destroyer escort, the USS *Haynes*, commanded by Captain Murrell (Robert Mitchum). However, the film soon introduces the *Haynes'* foe, a U-boat, captained by Von Stolberg (Curd Jürgens). Unlike in US films set during the war, the German captain is no vicious antagonist, and the film establishes early on he has no time for Nazism. In dramatic terms, Murrell and Von Stolberg are both portrayed simply as old warriors. Screenwriter Wendell Mayes even feeds Murrell lines that speak of a deeper problem with humanity and our proclivity for warfare: "That there's no end to misery and destruction. You cut the head off a snake and it grows another one. You cut that one off and you find another. You can't kill it because it's something within ourselves. You can call it the enemy if you want to, but it's part of us; we're all men." The film reworks the ending of Rayner's novel to, famously, have both Murrell's and Von Stolberg's vessels destroyed, then the two men uniting to save the latter's injured first officer. In the words of Lawrence Suid, '*The Enemy Below* contains perhaps the final comment on how the world has changed.' [10]

Despite the fact that the late-1950s produced these two classics of submarine war movies, for the most part the public was tiring of the sub sub-genre. Filmmakers took the submarine war movie into other areas, with such films as *Above Us the Waves* (1955), another one starring John Mills, but here retelling some of the story of the efforts by the Royal Navy to sink the German warship Tirpitz using 'Mark I Human Torpedoes', then later 'X-Type midget submarines'. And the American *Up Periscope* (1959), which shifted the focus to a navy diver (James Garner) getting involved with life aboard a sub while on his way to perform a dangerous solo mission. The last word in submarine war movies for the decade was, however, a comedy. Directed by Blake Edwards, *Operation Petticoat* (1959) gently spoofed the sub-genre, right down to having Cary Grant in some ways reprise his *Destination Tokyo* role as the captain. It also played with many of the elements covered with decidedly more machismo in *Operation Pacific*, such as taking civilians – and a distracting group of army nurses – on board the knackered USS *Sea Tiger*. This brave old submarine, sunk and refloated at the start of the film, farting its way across the Pacific, even suffers the indignity of being painted pink (a result of the lack of red lead paint, which has to be mixed with white lead paint). The heart of the film is a humorous rivalry between Grant's by-the-book captain Matt Sherman and Tony Curtis' Lt. J.G. Nicholas Holden, a playboy who finds his niche as a dubious 'requisitions officer'. Despite the film's streak of silliness, double entendre ("A woman just shouldn't mess with a man's machinery") and irreverence, it still manages to adhere to many of the plot devices you'd expect from a submarine war movie – though in this case when they try to stop a (US) destroyer from depth-charging them, rather than using the trick of sending up rubbish and oil, they send up women's underwear.

The submarine war movie had passed its prime by the 1960s, but a few films were still made in the sub-genre, among them a British film that recycled the title *Mystery Submarine* (1963). *Brassey's Guide to War Films* uses the term 'nonsense picture' [11] for both films. Grander, more robust entertainment value came in the form of *Ice Station Zebra* (1968). Despite a somewhat incomprehensible plot, this film directed by John Sturges from the novel by Alistair MacLean and starring Rock Hudson, captured in colour and somewhat cramped CinemaScope, something of life aboard nuclear submarines. Despite being bigger and better supplied with air than their World War 2 diesel forebears, nuclear subs apparently experienced many of the same travails, with the crew of the film's USS *Tigerfish* gritting their teeth through more confined, intensified drama despite the Cold War setting. There's even the requisite sinking incident, though here it's caused by a spy aboard sabotaging the torpedo tube doors. Like so many other movie sub crews, the men aboard go about their business professionally and efficiently, despite the threat of death in the depths. "It's impossible. 1230 feet. Must be 40 tons of pressure per square foot," notes one dryly while working to resolve the crisis.

The submarine war movie genre effectively left the big screen for several years during this period. Though during the 1970s heyday of the disaster movie, Hollywood returned to sunken sub territory, and after the appearance of the likes of Lancaster and Hudson, gave another granite-jawed heroic leading man, Charlton Heston, his turn in submarines. The film was *Gray Lady Down* (1977) and it concerns Heston's captain, Blanchard, on his final tour on a US nuclear sub, the *Neptune*, facing tragedy when it collides with a freighter. Their only hope is with a small rescue submersible. The film recycled footage from *Ice Station Zebra* and is hardly a classic. It was at this time, however, that the submarine war movie was about to undergo a remarkable revival and take a very different look at life on (and under) the ocean wave during World War 2.

Das Boot
1981

© Bavaria/
Radiant/
The Kobal
Collection

UP PERISCOPE

The most remarkable thing about *Das Boot* is how Wolfgang Petersen, who directed and adapted the film from the book by Lothar G. Buchheim, managed to build an entire film around familiar elements of the submarine war movie sub-genre, yet utterly revitalise them. Although the two-and-a-half-hour feature film version released in 1981/82 was powerful, the subsequent four-and-three-quarter-hour version ('the original uncut version'), based on the 1985 and 1988 TV mini-series cuts, enabled Petersen to more comprehensively realise his vision of the travails of the U-96 and its crew. In great detail, we see – become intimately acquainted with – the life of the men: their domestic arrangements (from the officers having to stand up from their meal whenever a crewman has to pass them in the narrow gangway, to an outbreak of crabs), the depths of their boredom while far from home and not involved with any combat, and their fears when that combat finally comes.

Das Boot is a true wartime epic, and alongside its submarine facts of life, it also incorporates thematic explorations of notions of duty, patriotism and the place of ideology when faced by the grim realities of war, and the futility of war ("We are ordered to sink ships where we find them. You can ask the men who started the war about the rest."). For much of *Das Boot* the men aren't fighting the enemy, they're fighting their own anxieties and boredom, their own physical discomfort as they go for weeks without sun or fresh food. The film took two years to make (with around *190 miles* of film shot) and over the course of the photography principal cast members were instructed to not go outside, so they became suitably pallid; the film was shot in sequence, to retain continuity as their beards and hair grew. In the majority of previous submarine war movies, the interiors of the boats are clean, tidy, relatively light places, but Petersen and his collaborators created a more realistic U-boat, and it's a place that fully exploits our anxious preconceptions about submarine life. The film's U-96, its sets

UNDER PRESSURE

based on genuine U-boat plans from a Chicago museum, is crammed and cramped; it's gloomy, even when they're not on red lights; it's dank and dripping with condensation, the inevitable side effect of 50 men sharing a confined, frequently sealed space. It's an oppressive place, yet it's also homely. Like those men played years before by Cary Grant and others, Prochnow's Captain – or Kaleu, or 'Der Alte', 'the old man' as, in his thirties, he was older than the rest of the crew – is a benign father figure, who by and large retains a calm and decency that helps keep the crew confident and functional. Other than the stiff, token Nazi 1st Lieutenant (Hubertus Bengsch) and the mentally unstable chief mechanic Johann (Erwin Leder), the crew is mostly defined by its cama- raderie and bond, and when times get tough, when they're depth-charged and even sunk in the Strait of Gibraltar, by their professionalism. Here, when they're struggling to raise the boat from a shelf 280m below the surface of the Mediterranean, the abject, absolute horror of their circumstances, the tangibility of death at the bottom of the ocean, is evoked with unprecedented power. However, the ultimate achievement of *Das Boot* may not be in these moments of powerful drama and action, it may be in Petersen's evocation of the time between the intense incidents, the crew's downtime. As Werner says in voiceover, "The routine never changes, day in, day out, always the same. Every day the same routine, whether on watch or off watch. Everywhere you smell the acrid stench of oil, sweat, bilge and damp clothing." The boredom of being tossed around on the Atlantic is only broken up by "the chirping of Morse code from the hydrophone". The boredom and lethargy are compounded by malnutrition and ill-health, as well as storms. Werner calls it, "An experiment to sound out the limits of our ability to suffer."

Although *Das Boot* provided the ultimate portrait of submarine life (and death), it wasn't the last entry in the genre. The 1990s saw a slight resurgence in interest in the submarine war movie, though in a highly diversified form. The climax of the Cold War, and the changing world after the collapse of Russia, produced two Hollywood features set aboard submarines. *The Hunt for Red October* (1990) involved author Tom Clancy's

CIA analyst Jack Ryan (Alec Baldwin) trying to avert nuclear war when a veteran Soviet submarine captain (Sean Connery) defects with a state-of-the-art vessel. It's very much a thriller, though being set aboard submarines it inevitably strays into the territory established by its World War 2-set forebears. Even more indebted to the history of the submarine war movie is *Crimson Tide* (1995), a drama entirely constructed around the conventional device of conflict between a veteran captain (Gene Hackman) and a younger XO (Denzel Washington) who respond very differently to the threat, again, of nuclear war. The film's racial dynamic, meanwhile, very much recalled *The Bedford Incident*. The following year the sub-genre also received another comic entry with *Down Periscope* (1996). It's the tale of captain who is passed over for command of a nuclear sub and instead assigned to a dilapidated World War 2 diesel sub.

The turn of the century saw the first of two late period Hollywood submarine war movies that took on board the grittier approach of *Das Boot*. *U-571* (2000) was a reasonably effective submarine action movie, but, for British audiences at least, went down as the film that rewrote history to have the US Navy seize the all-important Enigma code machine from a U-boat in the north Atlantic. In reality, the first Enigma machine was captured by the crew of the British HMS *Bulldog* in May 1941 – before the US had even entered the war. The issue was even mentioned in the House of Commons where one MP called it an 'affront to the memories of the British sailors who lost their lives in this action'. [12] Despite this posturing among politicians and ire in some quarters, however, David Balme, a sub-lieutenant on the *Bulldog* who led the boarding party to capture the Enigma machine, thought the controversy missed the point. He suggested that only Hollywood could afford to tell this story and bring 'home the whole Battle of the Atlantic to a generation who otherwise would have known nothing about it'. [13] He said he enjoyed the film, telling the BBC 'It's a great film. It's all blood and thunder and the young people will love it.' [14]

A more interesting variation on the gritty World War 2 submarine movie was *Below* (2002). Directed by David Twohy and co-written by him, Darren Aronofsky and Lucas Sussman, the film essentially uses the setting of a submarine to present an 'old dark house'-type horror thriller. Although the film was not an enormous success in cinemas, in retrospect, this blending of genres makes absolute sense. The old dark house story has its origins with the 19th century creators of the horror and mystery thriller genre, Edgar Allan Poe and Sheridan LeFanu, who crafted spooky tales of the supernatural and pseudo-supernatural, set in gloomy, isolated, literally dreadful buildings. Considering the cinematic submarine, the realistic submarine as shown in *Das Boot*, had similar traits of gloom, isolation and strained mental states, the combination is a natural fit. In Twohy's film, after three survivors of a hospital ship sunk by a torpedo are picked up by the USS *Tiger Shark*, strange things start happening on board. The crew superstitiously believe it's because one of the survivors is a woman, considered back luck, but as the film progresses, dark secrets emerge. Submarine dramas have always dealt with the psychology of being aboard a vessel that takes men into the hostile realm of the under the water, but Twohy pushed this further, so that the film plays out like a ghost story where cracks begin to appear in the mental health of protagonists.

Given that the submarine war movie sub-genre became deeply codified during its heyday in the 1940s and 1950s, and that subsequent decades saw it simultaneously rely on the old motifs and elements while narratively diversifying into other genres like the espionage thriller and the mystery thriller, is there anywhere else for it left to go? After Kathryn Bigelow's commercially disappointing *K-19: The Widowmaker* (2002), which dramatised the true story of a Soviet submarine that suffered a potentially disastrous malfunction with its nuclear reactor, the genre seems to have pretty much petered out. A last gasp seems to have been *In Enemy Hands* (*U-Boat*, 2004), a US film featuring American star William H. Macy and German Thomas Kretschmann. The film was never released in the UK and went straight to DVD in the US. Like audiences in the late 1950s, are we finally bored of the submarine war movie? Considering how many classic war movies the submarine sub-genre has produced, it's not likely – *The Enemy Below* and *Das Boot* will continue to stand the test of time. No other sub-genre can offer the unique qualities of the submarine war movie, with its focus on war machines that can take men under the water and attack enemies unseen; with its portrayal of how the crews of these machines live, cheek by jowl, bunk by torpedo, frequently overseen by paternal captains and aspiring, argumentative first officers; how these men face warfare, under pressure.

Endnotes

1. Jeanine Basinger, *The WWII Combat Film: Anatomy of a Genre*, Wesleyan University Press, 2003. p.21.
2. Jonathan Rayner, *The Naval War Film*, Manchester University Press, 2007. p.27.
3. Lawrence H. Suid, *Sailing on the Silver Screen*, US Naval Institute Press, 1996. p.24.
4. Basinger, p.106.
5. Ibid, p.67.
6. Sheridan Morley, *Tales from the Hollywood Raj: The British Film Colony On Screen and Off*, Weidenfeld and Nicolson, 1983, p.176, quoted in Graham McCann, *Cary Grant A Class Apart*, Fourth Estate, 1996. p.159.
7. Suid, p.66.
8. Basinger, p.63.
9. Ibid, p.63.
10. Suid, p.128.
11. Alun Evans, *Brassey's Guide to War Films*, Brassey's Inc, 2007.
12. BBC news online, 'Storm over U-boat film', 2 June 2002. http://news.bbc.co.uk/1/hi/entertainment/773913.stm
13. BBC news online, 'Capturing the real U-571', 2 June 2002. http://news.bbc.co.uk/1/hi/uk/774427.stm
14. Ibid.

YOUNG HEARTS AND MINDS IN A TIME OF SOUND AND FURY

The War Movie and Childhood

JAMES CLARKE

'As soon as it is formed, the skin of history peels off as film.'

André Bazin [1]

Rampaging through the Warsaw ghetto, Nazi soldiers fail to notice a little girl in a red coat moving delicately through the crushing chaos and violence. She is watched from a hilltop overlooking the ghetto by Oskar Schindler. This transformative moment for Schindler, the film's title character, is one of the most well remembered scenes from Steven Spielberg's *Schindler's List* (1993) and it goes some way to encapsulating the fascination and storytelling tradition of putting a child in the midst of the action of a war film. In this extremity the collision of innocence and experience could be no stronger. Vulnerability and physical force, and the omnipresence of death engulf the child, symbol of life and better days. If life is a battle of some kind then this is the great conflict of heart and mind that is endured. For sure, sentiment tends to play its significant part in how childhood is placed amidst war. The movie evidence of this storytelling approach is wide ranging and includes titles as recent and awards-lavished as Roberto Benigni's *Life Is Beautiful/La Vita è bella* and *Saving Private Ryan* (both 1998). In this latter title, director Steven Spielberg unsurprisingly renders one of the film's best scenes around the plight of a child. Indeed, Vicky Lebeau in her book *Childhood and Cinema* talks about 'the genre of the child' (p.13) and goes on to explain and explore how 'cinema… (is) closer to perception, it can come closer to the child…' (p.16).

French filmmaker François Truffaut wisely observed that the great bind in which war films forever find themselves is that whilst they may sincerely strive to condemn war, or at least represent its traumas, they simultaneously make it entertaining because of the very allure that cinema possesses as spectacle. Even the humblest, most bare bones, plain and simple close-up of a face is inviting, appealing to the voyeurism and narcissism that the movies satisfy in all of us. This may be something of a dead end idea to pursue but arguably the war film, no matter how hard it strives to, can't help but someway, somehow enjoy putting images of the combat and horror of war on screen. War films are about many actions, feelings and ideas. One of the undeniable subjects of so many war films is courage and when it comes to a child-focused war story this concern runs like gold through the Klondike. For a child in a war story the act of courage carries a particular charge.

Childhood is an experience everyone has in common if only at its most fundamental level of the world looking so huge and 'up there' and often utterly confusing and terrifying. Getting through a day can be its own mini war when young, battling to secure attention and safety. The three films dealt with in this chapter all put kids into the heart of the warzone, where severe crises are the crucible in which growing up poignantly plays out in all its Sturm und Drang. Other war films with children at their centre include Louis Malle's *Au revoir les enfants* (1987), Bahram Beizai's *Bashu/Bashu, gharibeye koochak* (1989), Agnieszka Holland's *Europa Europa* (1990), Bahman Ghobadi's *A Time for Drunken Horses/Zamani barayé masti asbha* (2000) and *Turtles Can Fly/Lakposhtha parvaz mikonand* (2004) and Mohsen Makhmalbaf's documentary *The Afghan Alphabet/Alefbay-e afghan* (2002). Think too of Mark Herman's *The Boy in the Striped Pyjamas* (2008).

Mesmerisingly, the late Stanley Kubrick had planned to make a feature film focused on an adult and a child during the Holocaust. It was to have been titled *The*

Aryan Papers. When *Schindler's List* was released to such success, Kubrick brought his project's development to a close. In early 2009, at the British Film Institute, a video installation at the Southbank in London was opened called 'Unfolding the Aryan Papers', based around the material on the film based in the Stanley Kubrick Archive at the University of London.

In her book *Childhood and Cinema*, Lebeau observes that childhood is often used in cinema as the mechanism by which the wider culture can test out the subjects that most concern it at a given moment in time. As such, childhood and mortality are intertwined, and the convention of childhood being represented as a special time of innocence and wide-eyed wonder is only thrown into starker relief by the presence of children under threat and peril in a time of war. This dynamic is what fuels the powerhouses of cinema that are Roberto Rossellini's *Rome, Open City / Roma, città aperta* (1945), Spielberg's *Empire of the Sun* (1987) and a more recent movie that stands in stark stylistic contrast to these other titles, Guillermo del Toro's *Pan's Labyrinth / El Laberinto del fauno* (2006). Other films that we can at least name check on this occasion are John Boorman's *Hope and Glory* (1987) and *Welcome to Sarajevo* (1997), Michael Winterbottom's compelling dramatisation of aspects of the Balkan war of the early 1990s. In Winterbottom's film a key dramatic catalyst is provided by a war journalist's fast track commitment to adopt a child from an orphanage. Then too, and on a very different scale, the undying appeal of the image of a plucky kid against the canvas of a bombed out, war torn world is central to the 2008 UK television commercial for Hovis bread that showed a boy running through a number of key moments in modern British history. This short film commercial forged a link between a household name for bread with wider national identity and the language of images of war.

As I mention elsewhere in this book in my chapter about war's treatment in the animated film, childhood is ripe for interpretation against the backdrop of the culture clash of war. Just consider the Japanese film *Grave of the Fireflies / Hotaru no haka* (1988) and the way it takes its audience through a perspective on war as seen by a boy and his toddler sister.

The mission of this chapter is to consider three distinct feature films. The list comprises one old time Italian classic, one Hollywood classic and, finally, one Latin American modern classic. Each of these movies justifiably works across a range of genres and certainly evidences the great storytelling skill and sensitivity of their makers. The films that drift into the crosshairs here are *Rome, Open City* (the old school title), *Empire of the Sun* (the Hollywood title) and *Pan's Labyrinth* (the Latin American title, that's already too well known to be considered a cult piece I'd suggest). Each of them is the work of a major filmmaker and so is a satisfying war movie experience in its own right as well as being ample evidence of the elegance and thoughtfulness of their makers. The war film, then, is often most effective when removed from the battlefield itself. Certainly, this seems largely true of the three films that we'll talk about here.

Rome, Open City concerns itself with the Italian capital in the moment of rebuilding itself after World War 2. *Empire of the Sun* is set primarily in a POW camp for British nationals in China during World War 2 and *Pan's Labyrinth* is set in the forests of Spain where the resistance movement seeks to fight Fascism during the Spanish Civil War in the late 1930s. In *Empire of the Sun*, and *Pan's Labyrinth* particularly, there is a keen edge to the story fascinated by the role of fantasy and imagination in allowing a young heart and soul to endure the horror of war and ultimately rise above it. In *Rome, Open City* a far more 'realist' sensibility pervades. All in all, though, these films make a dazzling, inventive and moving trilogy of war movies.

EMPIRE OF THE SUN

In *Empire of the Sun*, Steven Spielberg adapted J. G. Ballard's semi-autobiographical novel of the same name. The film is a Spielberg classic and at the time was seen as quite a leap in subject and tone for the filmmaker who, when he made the movie, was still very much synonymous with fantasy and adventure. To put it starkly, the film was not popular commercially. No matter. That said, why is it that so many films that don't make it commercially first time around prove to be such long distance runners when it comes to repeat viewing appeal? A classic is a story that has not finished with what it wants to say as the great writer Italo Calvino usefully observed.

Undoubtedly now, in my mind, and my memory of growing up (which isn't the same as what actually happened growing up necessarily), what so connected with me about Spielberg's movie heroes, and particularly those who were children, was their essential loneliness and imaginative capacities. In times of enforced solitude it was the imaginations of these heroes that became their constant companion and salvation. To borrow the phrase Captain Miller whispers at the close of *Saving Private Ryan*, Spielberg's heroes have creativity as the "angel on their shoulders". Poems about loneliness are what Spielberg's greatest movies are, whether they be fantasy, history or war movie.

Empire of the Sun is a war movie poem and as Nigel Morris observes in his book about Spielberg's cinema, *Empire of Light* (Wallflower Press), the character of Jamie embodies ideas around '…wish fulfilment, (and) the relationship between "escapism" and the "rest of life" (p.136). Are these issues not the very problem that engulfs us when we watch war movies? Frame by frame they trade on the thrills of visual spectacle and movie-style narrative structure that we never seem to tire of. Is it dangerous to suggest that perhaps it's immoral and tasteless to sit and watch a war movie of any kind? With that in mind, let's throw out a bunch of Shakespeare plays and Greek tragedy whilst we're at it. Alright, maybe I am being a little too much of a spoilsport. Of *Empire of the Sun*, so replete with historical detail in the recreation of Shanghai and the physical terrain of a prisoner of war camp, we could say that it was Spielberg's movie in which he most confidently channelled the David Lean vibe. One has to imagine that Spielberg revisited Lean's marvellous *The Bridge on the River Kwai* (1957) in preparation for the film.

Lean was originally to have directed the film with Spielberg producing. He had tried to persuade Lean to direct an episode of *Amazing Stories* (1985) on a schedule of a week for a twenty-two minute episode, but he joked that he required seventy days. In the *Amazing Stories* series, Spielberg directed a war movie fantasy entitled *The Mission* which is a highly obscure Spielberg gem having been produced for television and is a legitimate companion piece to his feature-length war stories. Indeed, *The Mission*'s central drama around saving a young soldier who is trapped in the line of fire slightly pre-empts Spielberg's award winning *Saving Private Ryan* though unlike *The Mission*, *Saving Private Ryan* does not invest its action with the lustre of all-out fantasy. If anything, *The Mission* in Spielberg's hands becomes more about the power of art to save and the bonds between men under fire.

Moving from the more overt fantasy of *Close Encounters of the Third Kind* (1977), *Raiders of the Lost Ark* (1981), and *E.T.: The Extra-Terrestrial* (1982), Spielberg sought to enrich his work in terms of subject matter and its treatment, though for me *The Sugarland Express* (1974), *Jaws* (1975) and *Close Encounters of the Third Kind* are just as dazzling. *Empire of the Sun* is perhaps the most lyrical film he has yet made and for screenwriter Tom Stoppard, the film was something of a chance to draw on the narrative elements of classic Hollywood. Stoppard has commented that 'Steven was really fascinated with the relationship between Jim and Basie. In Steven's mind, it was connected with other stories of boys coming under the formative influence of experienced men: Captains Courageous, for instance, which he often mentioned.' (p.323 of Baxter)

To its great credit, *Empire of the Sun* is *so* visually driven, that particular images and sequences retain their place in the retina of the audience long after the film has finished. Take the sequence in which Jim discovers a bombed-out plane and proceeds to imagine being engaged in a fast and furious dogfight. It is one of the scenes that wordlessly and perfectly express the confusion Jim has in distinguishing between fantasy and reality. This confusion will be undone and clarity attained but only through a number of experiences in which almost all certainties slide and distort right in front of his eyes. How perfectly expressed this is by the comment he makes upon seeing the white light thrown by the Hiroshima bomb. He describes it as being like God having taken a photograph. Twenty-one years later, Spielberg revisited the atomic blast image at the beginning of the knockabout *Indiana Jones and the Kingdom of the Crystal Skull* (2008). As an aside, are Spielberg's Indy movies war films or not? Indeed, Spielberg's war movie comedy *1941* (1979), widely perceived as a misfire, might also be worth a second look. It was *Empire*

Empire of the Sun
1987

© Warner Bros/
The Kobal Collection

of the Sun, though, that really marked a watershed moment in Spielberg's cinema and embraced the shadows of human experience and the eeriness of destruction and displacement as evidenced by the unreal, off-kilter reality of the Olympic stadium sequence in which the entire arena has become a storehouse of furniture and cars culled from English ex-pat homes in suburban Shanghai.

American film critic Henry Sheehan wrote of *Empire of the Sun* as a landmark Spielberg film and indeed the moment at which he transitioned into something closer to artful filmmaking than any of his previous efforts had. He wrote in a landmark essay published in *Film Comment* in 1992 entitled 'The Panning of Steven Spielberg' (and now available on Sheehan's website) that 'though there was an intersection of interest among Spielberg and the British ironists Ballard and Stoppard, the director made his own particular adjustments. Instead of using the character of a boy as a vicarious vessel of feelings, he actually invited the viewer to step back and examine rather than identify. The adventure was not just mounted for affect, but scrutinised for effect.'

One of the key relationships in *Empire of the Sun* is the one between Jim and the Japanese boy on the other side of the camp wire. They are united by their shared love of flight and in this relationship Spielberg uses the wire as a symbol for all the disagreement, debate, discussion and confusion that results in war. It might be naïve but the act of imagination is what allows the wire to become 'meaningless' as Jim and the boy develop a friendship. Late in the film the Japanese boy becomes the victim of a trigger-happy American who is compelled to protect Jim in the face of any apparent danger that the Japanese boy presents. Spielberg's film presents an intelligent, motivated, curious boy who finds a way to survive the typically larger than life forces that utterly destroy his comfortable suburban life. In this, the film is a more elaborately designed, epic variation on the drama of John Boorman's *Hope and Glory* (1987) which sets it story in suburban London during the Blitz.

Like Elliott in *E.T.: The Extra-Terrestrial*, Jim must become his own hero. For Jim, there are two obsessions: fighter planes and American comic books. The film uses the motif of flying recurrently such as in the scene where Jim climbs into a fallen plane and imagines himself engaged in an air battle, the film's music soaring wistfully as the camera mimics the moves around the stationary plane that would typically be used in combat footage. A little later Jim goes into ecstasy, an almost primal state, as he watches American planes fly in and bomb Japanese air hangars near the prisoner of war camp. Jim has become a savage. In the early twentieth century, playwright J. M. Barrie created a savage child character that fought a pirate. At the time of promoting the release of *Empire of the Sun*, Spielberg commented that Jim '…was the opposite of Peter Pan. This was a boy who had grown up too quickly.' (*The New York Times* interview, 1987).

When Jim arrives at the POW camp Spielberg's penchant for colour and the foregrounding of music with image reach something of a career apogee as Jim sights a plane and moves reverently towards it, placing his hand on its hull then turning to salute the three Japanese flying aces that stand in silhouette. The sequence acknowledges our readiness to valorise the winged heroes of war. In an interview I conducted in autumn 2007 with film producer Rick McCallum about the forthcoming war film *Red Tails* (2009), McCallum noted of American audiences particularly that "they've always something about fighter pilots in our imagination, they've always had the right stuff. There's a lot of pilots out there when there probably wouldn't (be) if Bush wasn't president. It's always been such an integral part of the American psyche and so we have that audience."

In *Empire of the Sun* Jim is a cosmically attuned kid, rather like countless other Spielberg heroes, notably Cinque in *Amistad* (1997), Elliott in *E.T: The Extra-Terrestrial* and David in *Artificial Intelligence: AI* (2001). *Empire of the Sun* is a Hollywood film not afraid to chart loss rather than accomplishment in the acknowledging what we lose as we gain in other ways. Security falls away, we gain anxiety, but we also gain courage and going home will never again be what we thought it could be.

ROME. OPEN CITY

Amidst the rubble and the austerity of Rome rebuilding its heart and soul what endures in Rossellini's film is the image of boys watching their beloved priest in his final, most courageous moment.

It is 1944/1945 and Rome is beginning to emerge from the shadow of Nazi occupation; Hitler's troops are still very present, though. The film follows a number of different lives intercutting between them, rather like a soap opera. We are introduced to Pina and her son Marcello. His father is dead and Pina is preparing to wed Francesco, another resistance fighter. Giorgio comes to Pina's looking for Francesco. In another part of the city, Don Pietro the priest undertakes a mission to collect money being printed in secret to take to the resistance militia. Marcello and his young friends play amidst the rubble of the city and call themselves comrade. The Nazi Major is relentless in hunting Manfredi down and sure enough Don Pietro gets hunted. Giorgio and Don Pietro are eventually captured by the Nazis. Pina is killed by a Nazi soldier when she runs after Francesco as the Nazis flush out an apartment block. Giorgio is tortured and Don Pietro put in front of the firing squad with his young charges watching.

Rome, Open City is a war film that does what it can to strip away the spectacle of conflict and instead document the lives of the downtrodden. The film is one of the key titles of the Italian neo-realist film movement which emphasised a commitment to 'telling the truth' rather than using the fantast that cinema can so easily become to engage its audiences. Italian screenwriter, Cesar Zavattini, commented that 'For the directors who used the neo-realist form the aim was the recreation of moments of truth focused around issues of unemployment, social injustice, impoverished circumstance.' Actually, it's worth considering that rather like Japanese cinema there was an idea in Italy that neo-realist cinema had power to bring a kind of salvation to its audiences. Films could be entertainment, reflection and illumination. Generally speaking the Italian neo-realist films reacted against the tradition of the bourgeois 'white telephone' films of Italian cinema that pre-dated World War 2 and which had no engagement with 'real life'. For neo-realist director Vittorio De Sica, the underlying impulse of the neo-realist movement was that it showed 'reality transposed into the realm of poetry'. (p.32 of *Bonadella*). Italian neo-realism, like any other film movement, has a context and a tradition that it relates and responds to; and which it potentially rejects and seeks to radically revise.

In the long shadow of World War 2, Italian cinema saw and seized an opportunity to revise, refresh and renew itself in the years after 1945. It may seem a little unsurprising now but this journalistic quality would have been somewhat arresting to audiences. Defining neo-realism, then, is, in part, about citing its realistic approach to a

Roma,
città aperta
1945

© Excelsa/
Mayer-
Burstyn/
The Kobal
Collection

subject, a sense of social content, 'historical actuality and political commitment'. ('The Masters of Neorealism: Rossellini, De Sica and Visconti' from P. Bonadella, *Italian Cinema: From Neorealism to the Present*, New York, Continuum, 1998, p.31).

Much of the film's power comes from its immediate root in the actual events it recreates and depicts and indeed some of the film's narrative threads based on events previously reported, such as two priests who had been arrested and executed in 1944. *Rome, Open City* was shot in early 1945 when the war was at its earliest aftermath and so a number of images and settings that we see are as real as can be. At the time German soldiers still occupied northern Italy. The screenplay for the film had been written between September and December 1944 and famously the assistant screenwriter on the project was Federico Fellini who went on to become a major director of the post neo-realist Italian cinema with films such as *La Dolce Vita* (1960), *8½* (1963) and *Fellini – Satyricon* (1969).

Like many independently produced films the funding for *Rome, Open City* was fragile and somewhat convoluted in its history. Nonetheless, the film endured its financial woes during production and went on to become a major commercial success in Italy. The film put familiar still images of war into moving pictures for the Italian audience. In his BFI monograph about the film David Forgacs notes that certain images in the film reference drawings and paintings by artists such as Ennio Morlotti, Aligi Sassu, and Ernesto Treccani that would have been familiar in 1943-1944 showing anti-fascists being shot. Like so many of the most affecting war films, combat is not really the focus of *Rome, Open City*'s story. Instead, the concern is with the emotional toll of war on ordinary people. Rightly so, *Rome, Open City* has a melancholy about it, but it is not without a sense of hope. The film often uses very sentimental music that leads us out of a given scene to amplify the feeling.

Things are never simple. Anti-fascist though *Rome, Open City* is, the historical record shows that in his earliest years as a filmmaker, Rossellini directed three fascist propaganda feature films. Amidst *Rome, Open City*'s stark presentation and recreation of the trauma of war on individuals and families, there is a sense of the film functioning as a something of a rallying cry for the Italian people as they emerge from the war. Indeed, perhaps the film's 'heartbeat' scene is the one on the stairway where the exhausted Pina and her fiancé Francesco, who is so still and placid, Christ-like you might say, talk about how to endure. Francesco quietly says that "We mustn't be afraid because we're on the just path."

Whilst the film valorises the anti-fascist movement, and rightly so, the film also late on suggests that not all of the Nazi soldiers were as monstrous as the major, who is the film's personification of the brutality and inhumanity of fascism. In the lounge, a drunken Nazi speaks openly about the immorality of their project and the major tries to silence the captain as he talks about the futility of the situation. In a line that is echoed many years later in Brian De Palma's war film *Casualties of War* (1989), Don Pietro says before dying, "It's not difficult to die well. The difficult thing is to live right."

Rome, Open City was first shown on 24 September 1945. Rossellini felt the film could have been more positively received by the press, but it was the most popular Italian movie of that year and its two stars, Aldo Fabrizi and Anna Magnini, would have helped the box office. In keeping with its overall tone of restraint, the film does not explicitly show its two most violent incidents, both centred on the priest towards the end of the film. Inevitably, our imaginations can do a more powerful job of rendering horror.

The film is surely one of the greatest war films ever, yet, inevitably, already seems lost to a younger audience. *Rome, Open City*, like the fantastic, and again little known, *Kanal* (1957), must surely have informed the visual style of the almost globally recognised *Schindler's List*. Rossellini's film is powerful because of its restraint and because of how it measures the immensity of war against the smallness of domestic life and childhood friendships. Rossellini once said: "I am not a pessimist; to perceive evil where it exists is, in my opinion, a form of optimism." In this, Rossellini's sensibility with *Rome, Open City* sets something of a benchmark for all other war films to follow and work from.

PAN'S LABYRINTH

A fairy tale. Can there be any more exciting way of relating the perils and possibilities of human experience? To combine the war movie with the fairy tale makes for a heady, thrilling fusion. At the centre of this dazzling feature is a young girl and her curiosity and courage.

It is 1944. A forest in Spain serves as a hideout for anti-fascist Spanish rebels. They are being hunted down by a sinister soldier, Captain Vidal who has taken an old mill as headquarters from which to run down the rebels. Vidal is there with his wife and step-daughter, Ofelia. During their arrival, Ofelia begins to explore the forest and discovers the route into an underground labyrinth where she is met by the faun of the film's title. The faun charges Ofelia with three quests that relate to a larger, fantastical narrative. Ofelia undertakes each challenge and these adventures intercut their way through the story of the captain seeking to root out the anti-fascist rebels in the forest. Ofelia's friend, the housekeeper, is an ally of the guerrillas.

In Guillermo del Toro's lavish horror fantasy war film a young girl enters the labyrinth on a rites of passage adventure that serves as a spiritual response to the trauma of the Spanish Civil War that unfolds in the forest above the underworld. The film explores the experience of terror, the adult world and the world of twisted loyalties.

Pan's Labyrinth /
El Laberinto
Del Fauno
2006

© Tequila
Gang/WB/
The Kobal
Collection

As such the film presents us with the power of fantasy to speak allegorically about the pain of growing up that leads to the age old discovery that there's a lot out there that isn't what it seems. The war movie is an ideal opportunity to dramatise these hostilities that take the heart hostage.

A key strand of the film follows the captain's housekeeper and her covert support of the rebels hiding out in the forest that surrounds the mill. She supplies them with food and even attempts to run a knife out to them. In these sequences the war movie aesthetic is strong and is built around the tension the audience is made to feel as to whether or not the housekeeper will be discovered by the captain. Blasé in his treatment of life, the captain's overwhelming evil is registered early on when he kills two animal poachers.

Pan's Labyrinth is ultimately a war film with a fantasy strand that counterpoints its specific historical moment. What the fantasy does is allow for an allegorical engagement with the subjects of violence, choice, selfishness and compassion. The film is elaborately designed, rooted in fairy tale, mythological language, Catholic sensibilities and the traditions of the war film. Of the film del Toro clearly stated his basic method: 'A maze is a place where you get lost but a labyrinth is essentially a place of transit: an ethical, moral transit to one inevitable centre.' (*Sight and Sound*, December 2006). It's also useful to acknowledge how the film serves as a complement to del Toro's earlier war story/ghost story *The Devil's Backbone/El Espinazo del Diablo* (2001).

Like *Rome, Open City* and *Empire of the Sun*, *Pan's Labyrinth* charts the death of innocence and ignorant bliss of childhood in the moment that adult violence, prejudice and fear morph into the realities of war and combat. Unlike the other titles discussed here del Toro's film explicitly recreates several moments of viciousness. By his own admission, del Toro used the film as a parable and as a chance to explore his fascination with violence and the choice to be, or not be, violent. Del Toro is aware of the violence inherent in fairy tales and the concept for *Pan's Labyrinth* bears this out. In a piece he wrote to promote the release of the film in the UK in late 2006, del Toro commented that 'To have a fairy tale logic but not in a sanitised way, not in a clean, nice sort of child's story, but a much more rough – edged type of illustration or painting I thought of Arthur Hughes, who had a very perverse sense of design in the Victorian illustration of fables that he did.' (*Empire*, p.109, December 2006).

Pan's Labyrinth, like many war films, charts the clash of civilisation at its worst and best. The film is built around connections between youth and nature, innocence and imagination and the emotional and intellectual fortitude of its young hero. There's the feeling that Ofelia would have got on just fine with Jim in the POW camp of *Empire of the Sun*. In *Pan's Labyrinth* (somewhat misleading in its translation to English), Ofelia, like Jim in *Empire of the Sun*, is protected in her odyssey far from home. The faun is her guide and he is not a figment of her imagination, but a real, living, ancient creature. In a poster (rendered by the great movie poster artist Drew Struzan) not eventually used for the film it is clear just how important this protective relationship is that the faun has towards Ofelia. Of Mexican cinema del Toro's contemporary Alejandro Iñárritu commented that what makes Mexican cinema distinct (and it's a cinema with a history going back to the late 19th century) is that 'Our films are more concerned with the visceral side of life and not the money side, and we shoot from the pelvis and not from the intellect.' ('Mexican Cinema: The New Aztec Camera', *The Independent*, 8 Sept 2006, by Chris Sullivan).

Pan's Labyrinth fascinates for its fusion of generic impulses. Whilst the film's advertising campaign emphasised the fantasy trappings of the story, my immediate reaction to seeing the film was that it was a war film with a fantastical subplot rooted in the power of nature and the unconscious. *Pan's Labyrinth*, then, explores choices made to give life and choices made to sustain a reign of death. When the evil captain holds Ofelia's hand early in the film he grips it hard, nearly crushing it. The captain is all about destruction and Ofelia is all about life. As an aside, the film makes interesting viewing when placed next to Ken Loach's take on the Spanish Civil War, *Land and Freedom* (1995). The film is elegantly made and reminds us of the need for the imaginative process and a sense that the indefinable and the unseen can weave its magic and in doing so empower in our lives.

Maybe it's enough to say here that it will be fascinating viewing to see how contemporary conflict is duly represented and imagined within the format of popular cinema especially. Putting the appropriate voice to the pain and trauma of conflict is a delicate mission.

Bibliography

1. Originally published in *Esprit* (1946) and quoted on p.23 of BFI classics, *Rome, Open City*.

NOT SO SILENT NIGHT

The World War 2 Hollywood Christmas Film

JAMES EVANS

Superficially, at least, linking the topics of Christmas and war might seem an unlikely if not eccentric undertaking which should perhaps be restricted to addressing the seasonal coming together of members of dysfunctional families – a convention incidentally, much explored in Christmas films in the last quarter century. Certainly in terms of critical cinematic discourse there is a dearth of examples of writing about the wartime – or indeed, peacetime – Christmas film. One need only consult the indices of almost all cinema/film studies texts to see that an entry for 'Christmas' will yield negative results. There are plenty of references to 'war' but little or none to 'Christmas'. Whether 'Christmas' is so special a category in the culture as to be deemed almost untouchable – why problematise Christmas? – or considered too ephemeral an object of study will be left for the reader to speculate upon, but the sheer quantity of Christmas films and the attendance and box office relevance of these productions cannot be so easily dismissed.

Rooted in both received and original literary texts, the Christmas theme has been invoked in a myriad of cinematic treatments and it has for decades now, been adapted to almost all genres, some examples being: Christmas film noir (*Christmas Holiday* (1944)), screwball comedy (*Christmas in Connecticut* (1945)), musicals (*Meet Me In St. Louis* (1944), *Holiday Inn* (1942), *White Christmas* (1954)), science fiction (*Santa Claus Conquers the Martians* (1964)) and from 1974 onwards the Christmas slasher cycle (*Black Christmas* (1974) followed by the so-called psycho Santa films (*Christmas Evil* (1980)). [1] Of course, the 'special Christmas episode' pervades television history from *I Love Lucy* to *Father Ted* and from *The Good Life* to *Dr. Who*. It is the aim of this chapter then, to peer through some of the mist of critical amnesia that seems to descend whenever a Christmas film appears in the larger cultural arena – especially with regard to the wartime Christmas film in general and the World War 2 Hollywood Christmas film in particular.

THE WARTIME CHRISTMAS FILM

Audiences on both sides of the Atlantic who were drawn to wartime Christmas films came to them already weighted down with a considerable amount of seasonal cultural baggage. Their received notions of Christmas with all of its associations of virtue of charity, home, family, kindness and as a time of transformation (sometimes given a help-ing hand by supernatural intervention) rather than transgression, and redemption rather than revenge was an historical inheritance bequeathed to them from the Victorians. Those Victorian ideas are due largely to two men: Charles Dickens [2] and Albert, the Prince Consort. The mediation of their ideas had been aided and abetted by the rise of the middle classes, increased literacy and by new modes of mass produc-tion, distribution and consumption. Their ideas eventually percolated down to inform the modern American Christmas with its own highly charged and potent narratives of nation, home and hearth, family gatherings, notions of generosity, love, peace on earth and 'counting your blessings' which are all a part of an ideological (and largely imagi-nary) Norman Rockwell-esque [3] vision of Christmas. In stark contrast to that is the materialistic American Christmas which is all about sending and receiving greetings cards, buying and exchanging gifts, eating, drinking and consuming large dollops of Santa Claus, kitsch, crassness, hucksterism and insincerity. Within these conflicting dual-ities are to be found the dramatic and cinematic elements of the larger whole that is the

American Christmas, now more recognised and consumed than any of the many and varied Christian and European traditions that were appropriated and absorbed by it. The Western world and many areas of the East, North and South as well, now celebrate or at least occupy some of this hegemonic seasonal space. So alluring and potent is this siren call of American (Hollywood) Christmas that as Penne Restad points out:

'When Christmas is not the central theme nor even a minor one in a film's story line, directors, screenwriters, and others have codified the fragmented reminders of the holiday into highly telegraphic renditions. A quarter, and perhaps even a majority of top-grossing motion pictures released in recent years at least mention Christmas or have a scene with a Christmas icon – a fleeting cameo of a Christmas tree, or the trailing melody of a soft-hummed carol – regardless of the movie's actual theme. These further circumscribe Christmas in order to convey a... highly condensed expression of American faith and values ... In the Christmas celebration reside all goodness, kindness, hope and tranquillity. It stands as the all-purpose point against which the greed, violence, selfishness and dishonesty of the late twentieth century are gauged.' (Restad, 1995: pp.170-171)

The roots of the American (Hollywood) Christmas then are a unique blend of many other societies' customs and traditions. It is a culturally layered and constructed idea that is a rich and varied stew of historical ingredients made up of pagan rituals, European and Siberian tribal ceremonies, Saturnalian and medieval festivals featuring 'Lords of Misrule' and carnivalesque days of role-swapping where 'the world turned upside down' briefly becomes the norm. Fools, clowns, miscreants, gift-bearers and all manner of things natural and supernatural were all conflated with an evolving Christianity which finally decreed 25 December as its focal point. With the American additions of an anti-abolitionist's poem, *The Night Before Christmas*, a pinch of Thomas Nast and the Coca-Cola-sponsored illustrative work of Haddon Sundblom, the 'down home' illustrations of Norman Rockwell all stirred in with hundreds of carols and songs reaffirming the elementals of Christmas and then finally mediated through a jumble of patriotism, family values, capitalist consumption, biblical homilies and Madison Avenue promotions and there you have it – the American Christmas. A seasonal pudding to be endlessly used – and abused – by Hollywood.

The fascinating story of the American Santa Claus is regrettably beyond the scope of this chapter because his cinematic presence is much more notable in post-war American Christmas films than in the more realistic and 'practical' wartime Christmas films. The war years – perhaps paradoxically – were not times conducive to looking for supernatural or magical influences to alter events or effect change. 'Making do', hoping for the best and getting on with it were the more pragmatic concerns of wartime audiences. [4]

What requires emphasis in this account however, is the notion of Christmas that is most commonly represented in the cinema – that of the 'domesticated Christian' Christmas which, as mentioned, has its roots in Victorian England. As Mark Connelly writes: 'The Victorians took up Christmas and all its trappings and used them to celebrate home, family and charity ... This was the inheritance handed to the cinema, an inheritance that was also felt, and continues to be felt, in European and US society today.' (Connelly 2000:3) He goes on to note that Hollywood grasped that yuletide feeling and reproduced it in many early films including *The Old Folks' Christmas* (1913), *Christmas Day in the Workhouse* (1914) and *One Winter's Night* (1920). There were in addition of course, many versions of *A Christmas Carol* made [5] and although, as Connelly observes, the Christmas movie seemed to lapse during the 1920s and 1930s, there were many radio versions of the Scrooge story produced to fill the void. Wartime governments and military advisors were not slow to realise the tremendous power of cinema and to see potential for seasonal films as witness an early British World War 1 example, *Christmas Without Daddy*, a 1914 British and Colonial Production – but cinemas were soon to be closed during that war. Twenty-seven years later in the dark days of 1941 another similarly toned film – though this time a documentary – was commissioned, *Christmas Under Fire* (pc. Crown Film Unit) directed by Charles Hasse and Harry Watt. But in World War 2, unlike the First, the British Ministry of Information (MoI) kept cinemas open during the war realising the tremendous potential of the cinema for information and propaganda dissemination. But these small and modest British films were as nothing in comparison to the real masters of the wartime Christmas film, those producers and directors ensconced in the ubiquitous and resilient dream factory that is Hollywood.

HOLLYWOOD AND WORLD WAR 2

With the declaration of war by Britain and the Commonwealth in September 1939, Hollywood was about to enter a period of profound change. Though America remained neutral at the outset of the war, events in Europe were having a profound effect on Hollywood distribution and receipts:

'By the summer of 1940 Hitler's conquests in Eastern and Western Europe had closed 11 countries to American films. At the end of 1940, with the exception of Sweden, Switzerland and Portugal, the whole of continental Europe was closed to American films … With the disappearance of the European market, Latin America was now Hollywood's only strong foreign outlet. (Thus) the ebullient Carmen Miranda found herself in the vanguard of a concerted export drive.' (Cross in Karney, ed: p.306)

The mood of the country and thus of its audiences however, was determinedly isolationist and the studios made few films which would run counter to this mood and possibly damage revenues, no matter the sensitivities of many of the European – especially Jewish – emigré community in Hollywood. But as the old adage goes, 'War is good for business!' And amidst the increasing problems that Hollywood was facing at the time with anti-trust investigations, labour and union problems, personnel politics of both right and left, theatre owners lamenting unfair booking practices and the down-turn in business that had been affecting profits (which had never been able to match the 1929-1930 high watershed of receipts), Hollywood quickly gleaned that a different era with unique opportunities was dawning.

Upon declaration of war in December 1941, the American domestic war machine moved into high gear. Almost immediately a network of government agencies sprang up, of which the main ones were: the War Production Board (WPB), the War Manpower Board (WMB), the War Labour Board (WLB), the Office of Price Administration (OPA) and the Office of War Information (OWI). They respectively:

'…coordinated the wartime economy and the production of war goods …
coordinated and allocated the overall human resources required for military, industrial, agricultural, and other civilian needs … handled all labour-

management disputes in defence-related industries … controlled prices and regulated the production and availability of civilian goods, including all the necessities of day-to-day life … (and the OWI) which handled all government news released to the press, served to liaise between press and government, and supervised the dissemination of information and propaganda through the media, notably motion pictures and radio'. (Schatz, 1997: p.134)

Hollywood found that it could make truces and compromises with these government agencies in exchange for putting its cinematic shoulder to the war wheel and converting its resources to wartime ends. In fact, all of America was called upon to do the same:

'This effort required additional workers and increased productivity … In 1939-1940 8 million people – nearly 15% of the workforce were unemployed … and the average factory was in operation for forty hours per week … By early 1942 … unemployment had fallen to 3.6 million. By 1944 the US workforce had increased by 18.7 million and the unemployment bottomed out at 800,000. A total of 64 million Americans were at work, including some 10 million in the armed services. By then, the average factory was in operation for ninety hours weekly, and the United States was producing 40% of the world's armaments.' (Schatz, 1997: pp.134-135)

Of overwhelming social and cultural significance however, was the fact that millions of these factory workers were women – and film goers – and as Schatz points out:

'The war had a greater impact upon the employment and economic status of American women than any other event this century. More than 6 million women took jobs during the war, increasing the female workforce by more than 50%. Much of the work was in traditionally male roles, particularly factory work.' (Schatz, 1997: p.135)

Much of this work was in the aircraft and shipbuilding industries, previously male-only occupational enclaves, and apart from the more obvious social implications of this for women – and for Hollywood – came a degree of financial independence:

'Conversion to a war economy boosted salaries… with total wages and salaries increasing from $52 billion in 1939 to $113 billion in 1944. Under government-imposed salary limits on raises, average weekly earnings in manufacturing rose 65% during the war from $32.18 in 1942 to $47.12 in 1945.' (Schatz, 1997: p.135)

This was an unprecedented rise in individual prosperity. But here was the rub:

'… the production of civilian goods fell by about one third as US workers found themselves with greater purchasing power but increasingly less available for purchase. Shortages and restrictions became a way of life, and as the war pro gressed virtually everything that Americans wore, ate, drank, drove or otherwise was rationed by the OPA.' (Schatz, 1997: p.135)

Added to the fact, already mentioned of the movement of Americans to urban areas was a change in demographics due to:

'… the millions of men going into the service … the early 1940s saw something of a 'marriage boom' and a mild 'baby boom' ... From 1940 to 1943, one million more families were formed than would have occurred under normal conditions, while the birth rate rose about 15%. The number of family households increased by about two million during the war, despite a sizeable countertrend toward 'merging households' due to shortages of housing and consumer goods. The number of households with married women at the head and husbands absent increased from 770,000 in 1940 to 2,770,000 in 1945.' (Schatz, 1997: p.136)

The repercussions of some of these facts will be evidenced in the filmic texts that will be presently explored, but it is worth noting here that in the Vincente Minnelli film, *Meet Me in St. Louis*, there are not only six women in the household but a largely ineffectual grandfather (Harry Davenport) and a superficially patriarchal father-figure (Leon Ames). Revealingly, in one sequence during which a domestic crisis is unfolding, one of the children opines that their father should be immediately summoned and the matriarch, Mrs. Smith (Mary Astor) who is very much in control of the situation – disparagingly replies, "Oh, what good would he do?"

The equation of prosperity plus rationed goods (or few goods) to purchase could only add up, in an era without television, to increased demand for audio, theatre, records and films. Especially films. For among many other factors cinemas were places where women could safely (and respectably) go to at night. [6] And children could be dropped off or taken at weekends – a lucrative double market that Walt Disney, the Fleishers and other animators were quick to exploit. Another cultural phenomenon was also being observed:

'In July, the *Motion Picture Herald* reported that "customers are leaving the neighbourhood second-and subsequent-run theatres for first-run houses downtown" and it suggested two principal reasons. First, patrons had more spending money and were willing to pay the increased admission price ... and second, first-run pictures were taking longer to move out of the downtown houses and into the 'nabes' (neighbourhood theatres). The latter point was crucial, as films were enjoying increasingly longer runs and thus generating more money for all concerned – even the subsequent-run exhibitors, who also ran top features longer than ever when they finally were able to get them.' (Schatz, 1997: p.152)

With this came a problem for the out-of-town exhibitors: how to get enough product. And this was solved by an increased offering of reissues, a relatively new phenomenon for Hollywood studios who found that healthy profits could be made by judicious selection of the back catalogue. As Schatz states:

'The governing wisdom was that star vehicles released from two to ten years previously were the best candidates for reissue; the *Motion Picture Herald* reported that these pictures routinely returned $400,000-$600,000 at the box office – a tremendous unexpected windfall for the studios and exhibitors alike.' (Schatz, 1997: p.152)

Even more pleasing – with regard to studio coffers – in the days before residual fees were in existence. But the big studios B-pictures suffered, 'because of the overheated first-run market, the success of reissues, and decree-related selling policies, the majors of all but eliminated low-budget production during the war'. (Schatz, 1997: p.152)

Demand for the B-movies remained however and they continued to be shot by smaller as well as independent studios – a phenomenon that was to later prove fruitful to post-war producers and filmmakers especially in the light of the increasing numbers of car owners and the inevitable rise of drive-in theatres. The construction of drive-ins had stalled during the war – rationing of rubber tyres and petrol put paid to that – but they mushroomed in the post-war period.

In spite of restricted overseas markets, the economy of Hollywood had, through a series of deals and cooperation, managed to pull off quite a coup – maintaining high-end salaries, left free to 'get on with it' so long as wartime propaganda was being produced, and maintaining the status quo. New markets were encouraged in Latin America. Most Commonwealth countries and the Middle East were still able to rent films and the American distribution system remained incredibly efficient. England became a bigger market [7] than before the war and with the limited filmmaking taking place in England itself, demand surged. The British government relaxed the quotas it had previously placed on foreign films – due to the lack of British films being made because of shortages of manpower and materials – by 1942:

'After turning out two hundred or more features per year before the war, British production fell drastically in the 1940s. The board of Trade registered only forty-eight features in 1942 and, between sixty and seventy in each of the next three years, when British product occupied only 15-20% of screen time in British theatres ... attendance climbed (however) surpassing 30 million in 1944 and 1945 – 25% above pre-war figures.' (Schatz, 1997: p.155)

Demand everywhere, as in America itself, 'for diversion, relaxation, and the collective ritual of mass-mediated entertainment' (Schatz, 1997: p.153) was running at record levels. And importantly, the Government, the unions, the theatre-owners and the anti-trust lawyers were, for the duration, off of Hollywood's back. But if war is good for business, then it is also good for Christmas.

WAR IS GOOD FOR CHRISTMAS

'Unless you have experienced a totally blacked-out town, limited food and shops that were almost empty, you cannot comprehend the part films played in our lives.'

(Gwyneth Wathern quoted in *Turner*, 2002: p.437)

With unprecedented revenues pouring into Hollywood coffers and entirely new audience profiles and geographies to contend with, Hollywood was required to sail with the prevailing winds. Studios were recruited to produce films addressed to the military and to the home front, films running the gambit from documentary to propaganda, from instructional to educational. There were discernible trends in Hollywood films of the time: a creeping realism into war and other films influenced by documentary modes (no lesser a figure than Frank Capra was responsible for seven films in the series, *Why We Fight*), the beginnings of a genre of film that was to later be identified by French critics as *film noir*, the screwball comedy cycle, the 'woman's film' addressing issues of infidelity and finally the 'home front' films dealing with the domestic realm and the problems of absent or ineffectual male presences and the new situation of women heading households and having to balance this with factory or other work – all of these individually, beyond the scope of this particular chapter, but many of the issues and trends will be evidenced in the wartime Christmas films that will be discussed. As will one of Hollywood's greatest emotional ploys: the secular Christmas song.

Christmas – with its profound psychological, symbolic, cultural, social and historical roots deeply embedded in American audiences – was bound to become an even more poignant and emotional idea during wartime. Yet Hollywood seemed slow to understand or respond to this, perhaps due to the distractions of having to shift into wartime consensus production or perhaps the idea of reconciling the time of 'Peace on Earth and Goodwill to Men' with a world war seemed a concept too far. Whatever reasons may be conjectured – apart from the already noted lack of Christmas films previous to the war – the first attempts to utilise the Christmas theme were the 1940 film *Remember the Night* (Mitchell Leisen from a story by Preston Sturges) and *The Man Who Came To Dinner* 1941 (from a play by George Kaufman and Moss Hart). But work was already under way on a third studio Christmas-themed effort and in this case, it was third time lucky.

HOLIDAY INN

Holiday Inn (Paramount Pictures, d. Mark Sandrich 1942) as a cultural production within the remit of this essay is unique: it was developed before the war, in production during the war, near wrapping up when Japan attacked Pearl Harbor and was released by Paramount when America was actually at war. As such it displays characteristics which illustrate some of the points made in   section one – a primary one being how quickly the Hollywood industry could turn its production around and respond to the new mood of the country. Particularly telling is the war montage that appears behind the character Jim Hardy (Bing Crosby) as he is performing the 'Song of Freedom' in the Independence Day segment. Not written into the original version of the script, the producers were able to insert a specially made montage into the narrative in which is seen a triumphal march of images of America's war mobilisation. It is the only allusion to the war in the entire film and does appear to be, if not gratuitous, certainly pasted in. Mark Glancy comments:

> 'While many holidays are treated lightly, Independence Day and Christmas Day are taken very seriously. Independence Day is celebrated with two songs. First "Song of Freedom" is sung by Jim to celebrate both well-established freedoms (the Bill of Rights) and newly prized freedoms (two of President Roosevelt's Four Freedoms are acknowledged in the lines 'freedom from want/freedom from fear') … Ted (Fred Astaire) then appears on stage for show stopping tap-dance routine in which he throws firecrackers down around his feet. "Let's Say It with Firecrackers" is a violent response to the threats referred to, however indirectly,

in "Song of Freedom". It provides a cathartic release from the momentary glimpse of war and as a blasting and triumphant finale to this sequence, it signifies victory and effectively banishes all thoughts of war from the film.' (Connelly, ed. 2000: p.66)

While Glancy is correct in mentioning the accent placed upon Independence Day and Christmas Day in the film, it is no less significant that all the holidays that are stressed are just regular 'working days' for Jim and company, entertainers continually toiling to keep these cultural memories in the public mind. Quintessential dates in the American calendar: Lincoln's birthday, Washington's birthday [8], Easter Sunday, Independence Day, Thanksgiving Day [9], Christmas Eve and New Year's Day. The entire cycle runs through the film as if to assert that, no matter what, life goes on. But it is Christmas (and to a lesser degree) New Year's that get dealt with – in substance – twice. In both cases the problems and tensions which have arisen at Christmas have been put aside by New Year, signalling a fresh and positive future – and the film's end.

Most famously this is the film that introduced the Irving Berlin song, 'White Christmas', which was destined to be not only the biggest-selling record of Bing Crosby's singing career but would eventually enter the *Guinness Book of World Records* as the best-selling and most recorded song of all time. Stories and tales about this song abound but in the context of the Hollywood wartime Christmas film, its importance is not only in its fantastic reception, but that it defied the expectations of the producers of the film – 'Be Careful With My Heart' was expected to be the standout hit – by appealing to the sentiments, longings and homesickness of contemporary viewers. It also struck a chord with radio audiences but was given velocity when it became an especial favourite of fighting troops who adopted it for themselves after repeated requests for

airplay on Armed Forces radio. It must surely have been the first American secular 'carol' and is still a Christmas essential today as is the film itself. The song caught perfectly the nostalgia, romance, wistfulness and displacement being experienced at the time and the longing for 'home' and security that was imagined and hoped for by contemporary   listeners. Sung twice in the film, it also became the template for the musical Christmas hit which was to feature in future film productions as will be seen.

With its universal lyrics – and with an eternal debt of gratitude for a tough editor who fought with Berlin over the original opening lyrics [10] 'The sun is shining, the grass is green/The orange and palm trees sway/I've never seen such a day/In Beverly Hills L.A.' – 'White Christmas' became a seasonal anthem for wartime listeners and has since sold some 120 million copies. Such was the power of Berlin's genius and Hollywood's wartime Christmas cultural dominance. So iconic and ubiquitous is this song, and so much associated with the American military and Armed Forces Radio that the recording was broadcast as a pre-arranged signal during the Vietnam War for the start of the U.S. evacuation of Saigon in April 1975 and one can be certain it has played a part in almost every military adventure – American or otherwise – since.

In the safe hands of Hollywood's top male box-office stars, [11] with a score by Irving Berlin alongside an entertaining story of roots and reunification which moves from the bright lights of the city to the earthy and comfy security of a New England inn where couples get reunited, it is not hard to see how Hollywood's first proper foray into a specific wartime seasonal Christmas theme was a great triumph. Not just for supplying the needs of the audience but also for reassuring the Government that Hollywood was more than up to the job of wartime production and morale building without too much heavy-handed interference from Washington. With the release of *Holiday Inn*, Americans felt temporarily soothed, reassured and comforted about the future. [12] They must have been. *Holiday Inn* was the fifth highest earner of 1942 (Schatz 1997: p.466) and Paramount recycled it as *White Christmas* in 1954. Not surprisingly, *Holiday Inn* won an Academy Award for its musical score – an Oscar made not of metal due to rationing that year, but plaster (Barnes: 2002). MGM was the next big studio to tackle a Christmas segment in the popular musical genre.

MEET ME IN ST. LOUIS

It could be fairly claimed that Vincente Minnelli's *Meet Me in St. Louis* (MGM, 1944) almost doesn't qualify as a fully-fledged wartime Christmas film, centring as it does one full cycle of the seasons. But the Christmas section is lengthy and the most poignant and psychologically revealing of all of the seasonal texts within the film. Also, many of the successful themes and subtexts that the other studios realised made a success of *Holiday Inn* found their way into the narrative of Minnelli's film: there are changing seasons, changing relationships and songs for various occasions including another future Christmas classic, 'Have Yourself a Merry Little Christmas' written by Ralph Blane and Hugh Martin. There is also the attempt to make a 'feel good' escapist movie which reinforces the message of basic American goodness and the ability to triumph over adversity if 'we stick together' – and unlike its predecessor devoid of even the merest mention of the war. This was intentional. As Mark Glancy has remarked, by 1943 even the journal *Variety* was warning producers that audiences – largely female – were weary of seeing combat movies and war references at the cinema. In 1944, audiences were deeply in the grip of war, hardship and separation. Charles Higham describes *Meet Me in St. Louis* as:

> '…about a family which learns, in the St. Louis of 1903, and on the brink of the
> World's Fair, that father is to be transferred to New York and their whole world
> of peaceful provincial happiness is going to be shattered. The parallel with the
> disappearance of an innocent America is carefully stressed, and the film –
> photographed in chocolate box colours, pretty, cluttered and a trifle airless –
> is as formally nostalgic as a cameo brooch … the Halloween sequence … has a
> deliberately artificial charm, a studio-made period flow, that is very appealing.'
> (Higham and Greenberg, 1968: p.173)

Meet Me in St. Louis follows the domestic travails of the Smith family – an 'everyman' name and identity, throughout four calendar seasons in the year of 1903 – thereby distancing the audience from contemporary times. Each seasonal episode is signalled by:

> 'A tintype drawing that dissolves into live action Technicolor. In these picture-
> postcard views, nature becomes a fashion plate; and in the four dramatic
> episodes, clothing and furniture are carefully selected to suggest what Roland
> Barthes might call "seasoness".' (Naremore 1993: p.173)

Here again, the Norman Rockwell-esque view of consensual American society can be clearly seen. The film is centred on a household where women actualise almost all of the action and control most of the domestic and emotional lives of the protagonists. It is a household where men are noticeably absent. The only son is whisked off to college early in the film and only reappears at the end. The father is mostly away at the office working and when he is home is rather ineffectual in advising or understanding events on the domestic front and the granddad who does live at home is more of a cutesy, old duffer figure. While the father ostensibly 'rules the roost' when he enters the home, his authority is usually subverted or given lip-service and his main importance in the plot is the declaration of the family move to New York in order for him to advance in his company. It is also a move that will occur just before the eagerly awaited opening of the Louisiana Exposition throwing the stability of home and hearth in St. Louis into chaos because all of the family have their hearts set on being a part of the festivities and of seeing their lives unfold in the secure environment of provincial St. Louis.

In further contrast to the men, the domestic feminine household are enthusiastic about the emerging culture of consumption – a frequent trope of the time within which is embedded several pejorative meanings – and the females, unlike the males, are seen to be flexible in their attitudes and ideas. Although as Naremore cautions:

> 'The glorious vision of domestic economy ... hardly looks like an economy at all. Catsup making is a communal activity, and the various parties, meals, or celebrations that mark different stages of the narrative seem to emerge effortlessly ... Clearly MGM was imagining a peaceful time before the two world wars, when women were not yet fully socialised into politics and the workforce.
> Just when these women were entering public life in greater numbers than ever before, the film suggested that old-fashioned domestic labour was more natural and far less boring than shop keeping or business. In the same breath, it depicted the Smith women as ideal consumers of fashion and spectacle and as harbingers of the post-war move to suburbia.' (Naremore 1993: p.74)

These notions would have been well suited for a female wartime audience. The threat of disrupted families, the control by men of events beyond women's influence – i.e., warfare – and the necessity for women to keep the home fires burning while men are absent was bound to strike a chord.

But it is the Christmas sequence that concerns the present text and it is in this sequence that several dramatic things occur: there is a case of mix-up and mistiming surrounding the Christmas Eve dance but everyone eventually 'finds' everyone else and order (especially romantic order) is restored, and on a parallel plane young Tootie (Margaret O'Brien) has dug up all her 'dead dolls' from the garden in readiness for the move to New York. The looming crisis has already been established with a mise-en-scène of the children building snowmen which represent family members and which will come to play a symbolic and dramatic role later. It is when Esther (Judy Garland) returns to the house after the romantic dance sequence that she sees Tootie curled up, playing her music box and looking out from the warmth of her window (inside the home) into the cold night hoping to catch a glimpse of Santa Claus (what really is out there beyond the house?). She poignantly asks Esther how Santa (good fortune/bounty/continuity) will find her next year – a question sure to have been on many of the audience's minds. As they both look out the window the camera moves the eye to a shot of the boy next door, John (reality), when we might have almost expected a glimpse of Santa (fantasy). In order to comfort Tootie, who has accepted that she can't take her snow people to New York, Esther begins to sing, 'Have Yourself a Merry Little Christmas'. This song written by Ralph Blane with lyrics by Hugh Martin which made its debut in this movie, could not have failed to move its largely female audience to near or actual tears. It is an unusually melancholy song about separation that managed to express all the 'confused feelings of Christmas into a few short stanzas – the love, sadness, and longing for perfection'. (Svehla, 1998: p.12). It intones:

'Some day soon we all will be together if the fates allow/Until then we'll have to muddle through somehow' – no comment needed. [13] The song causes the impressionable Tootie to dash outside where she begins to destroy the symbolic family snowmen. Meanwhile Mr. Smith, who has been observing this family trauma endures a 'dark night of the soul' and in a transformative Scrooge-like moment realises that what is most important in life is family and home, not money and worldly advancement. He decides to reject the New York offer and to stay in St. Louis where in spite of encroaching modernity (worldly and domestically), transience and incursions into life he realises that all manner of disruption can be overcome by a strong sense of community, roots and familial connection. A message that wartime audiences then and audiences today still fervently wish to believe. Once again, as in *Holiday Inn*, an innocent, more wholesome past, in which life is centred on the family, the home and the small town, is affirmed and reified. And like *Holiday Inn*, one sure-fire way to get this particular propaganda to seep into and remain in the audience's unconscious was a fantastic Christmas setting and song – and within these frameworks both films came up trumps.

Two other important Christmas films would appear in 1944, *Since You Went Away* (pc. Vanguard Films, d. John Cromwell) and *I'll Be Seeing You* (pc. Dore Schary Productions, d. William Dieterle), the former about the trials and tribulations of an

Christmas in Connecticut 1945

© Universal/ The Kobal Collection

all-female household coping without father, and the latter about a decorated but shell-shocked returning soldier who meets and falls in love with a woman on Christmas release from prison. But it is to the differently nuanced Warner Brothers entry into the Hollywood Christmas film that attention will now be drawn – appearing as it does at the end of the war.

CHRISTMAS IN CONNECTICUT

You can forget Nigella Lawson. In 1945, there was only one domestic goddess and that was Elizabeth Lane (Barbara Stanwyck) in *Christmas in Connecticut*. (pc. Warner Brothers, d. Peter Godfrey 1945). Apart from Stanwyck, the film stars Reginald Gardner as John Sloan, her rather dull and pompous architect suitor, Dennis Morgan as war hero Jefferson Jones and Sydney Greenstreet as publishing magnate Alexander Yardley. Though released when the end of the war appeared to be nearing, the lobby card tagline reminded audiences: So Far…Sooooo Good! It's that Double-Trouble Dame. It's that 'God is my Co-pilot' Guy! They're   having the time of their love-life in the teasin' and squeezin' hit of the season! Buy War Bonds at this theatre! [14]

An undeservedly little-seen production today, the narrative and plotlines in this film signal quite a shift from other wartime movies – Christmas or otherwise. Even by 1945 standards, when Hollywood and America were beginning to look forward to mass

Christmas in Connecticut
1945

© Universal/ The Kobal Collection

demobilisation and the winning of the war, some texts within the film were daring, perhaps even racy. Certainly some thought so, as Mark Connelly writes:

> '...it was feared that the film treats Christmas and marriage too lightly. Warner Brothers decided to release (the film) in July rather than during the holiday season. A review in *The New York Times* warned its viewers that... the film is not a "folksy fable that will put the kiddies in the proper spirit for Santa's next visit". Similarly, the *Motion Picture Herald* complained the film "is by no means the gently sentimental items of Americana that the title indicates". The Catholic Legion of Decency gave the film a 'B' rating, indicating that it considered it to be 'objectionable in part'. And in Britain, the title was changed to the more judgemental *Indiscretion*. (Connelly, 2000: p.74)

Clearly this example of the wartime Christmas film is looking forward to a post-war world, specifically a post-war America. According to this Hollywood text, post-war life will be different, full of new changes and challenges, but it will be upbeat and positive. The film is sprightly and has elements of both farce and 'screwball' comedy: the humour is based on clever dialogue, rapid-fire delivery, mistaken identity and above all, the introduction of a new female type who is career minded, independent, not ostensibly concerned with marriage and who clearly has her own very clever, sometimes devious, mind.

As the final script of 1944 describes her character, Elizabeth Lane is:

> '... in her late twenties, attractive, intelligent, with a bright, wry sense of humour. Although she has attained quite a success as a magazine writer, she is still at heart a white-collar girl, a typical American business girl who might step out of any advertising office or department store. She is feminine, definitely not sophisticated. She's impulsive, she's impressionable. But there is, as with all the thousands of swell American girls like her, a veneer of outward wisdom that covers an inner core of gentle femininity and ideals.' [15]

Against all previous feminine types so far encountered, this independent-minded journalist (who writes a famous domestic column in the fictional magazine, *American Housekeeping*) is thought by her publisher – and her adoring reading public – to be a fine American wife and mother. She is a celebrity housewife who is famous for her recipes and her tales of an idyllic life in a Connecticut country house replete with husband and baby. The only problem is that Elizabeth Lane lives all alone in a small apartment in New York. As she cannot cook, she gets her recipes and food from her friend, a Hungarian restaurateur Felix (S. Z. Sakall) and her tales of Connecticut living from her suitor John Sloan. Her most prized possession is a mink coat which, unable to afford she has bought on credit (rash female consumer trope) and in order to pay for it, accepts a raise from editor Yardley if she will entertain returned war hero Jefferson Jones – whose Christian name resonates with American ideas of 'liberty' and whose surname with 'everyman' – to show him why marriage and domestic bliss are so necessary to pursue in the soon to be demobilised world. She attempts to present a traditional Christmas at Sloan's country house, which he has offered up for this ruse contingent upon her actually marrying him there, making it 'legit'. To complete the dream scenario Sloan even procures a baby (or two) from women working in the nearby munitions factory – a real scenario that female audiences could certainly relate to, along with the reality of doing shifts in the factories even during Christmastime and everyone mucking in with baby care. But the real dream in this film is the Hollywood version of the returned soldier – he is a war hero, handsome, fit in body and mind, and as it soon becomes evident one who can cook, wash dishes, bathe babies, change nappies, play piano, sing, and most importantly can resist the temptation of succumbing to what he thinks is a married woman. He is also not mentally or morally damaged by the war, he seems to have left it all behind. In short he is a near-perfect male and presumably the one female audiences hoped would be returning to them from the war. Lane on the other hand, finds it difficult to adapt to a strictly domestic role and her self-made career and city-smarts are not about to be sacrificed by a return to a restrictive home life – a reversal in social progress that her World War 1 female counterparts would have to forbear. Lessons had been learned!

The idea of transformation and new expectations of gender roles are strongly hinted at here and seem to be tipping off audiences about what to expect in post-war times. That it is finally Yardley, another sort of Scrooge-like figure, who changes in the end, is one of the several turnarounds in the film suggesting that inflexible and outmoded patriarchal attitudes and moralities will have to adjust to the forthcoming era. Of course, the Christmas setting accomplishes what it is intended to do; the love that develops between Jones and Lane unfolds within customary Christmas 'poetics' such as snow, tree-trimming, singing songs, taking a sleigh-ride and within the social context of reassuring small-town American values. The architect John Sloan finds that he is given support to implement his visionary plans for post-war housing and modernist develop-ments, but tellingly, within a framework of traditional vernacular architecture. The future is about innovation but not changes of traditional values. This tension (anxiety?) is plotted within the film in relation to the forthcoming post-war culture and changing gender roles not to mention a new multi-cultural social consensus. In *Christmas in Connecticut*, American, English, Hungarian, Irish and Black American all co-exist seam-lessly, happily and unproblematically in that supposed big melting pot – the United States of America.

But it is in the presenting of future possibilities open to post-war women to make their own choices: about partners, about the possibility of marrying later in age becom-ing a bachelorette in the meantime and about not having to rely wholly upon men to support them. Alongside this, it is the lightness made of love and marriage that makes this wartime Hollywood Christmas film unique and prescient – Elizabeth Lane does not have to compromise and become transformed (the usual Christmas text) and Jefferson Jones does not have to become the dominant partner because of his gender. In fact, Jefferson Jones *is* a liberator; he is a model of the post-war 'new man' – which is more than can be said of the director of the 1992 remake, Arnold Schwarzenegger.

CONCLUSION

> 'For a few hours it made you forget about the war in the 1940s and after the war the drabness of everything in post-war Britain ... We went more often during the war because you could forget the war for a few hours and the air raids that were often going on at the same time, also it was a place to be warm in the winter months, as coal was in short supply'
>
> (Joan Draper, cinema goer quoted in Stacey in *Turner*, ed 2002: p.431)

The provision by Hollywood – under limited control from US government agencies during the war years – of films that could satisfy the sort of visual and narrative pleasures that the cinema goer quoted above craved in those years is a testament to the studios' uncanny ability to survive. And thrive. Statistics mentioned in the text attest to this.

Hollywood's ability to adapt to the changed circumstances combined with its keen awareness of wartime audiences' needs proved instrumental in helping to sustain domestic and military morale. It also was instrumental in disseminating straightforward instructional and propagandist materials. Perhaps at no time had Hollywood fulfilled so many of the conditions outlined in Richard Dyer's model of the appeal of entertainment forms where the cinema spectator is seen as:

> 'the missing line between the social tension/inadequacy/absence outside the cinema and the utopian solution offered on the screen which is accomplished by "pleasuring" scarcity with abundance; exhaustion with energy; dreariness with intensity; manipulation with transparency; and fragmentation with community.'
>
> (Dyer in *Turner*, ed 2002: p.430)

The Christmas season provided a unique and particular cultural and social space (and challenge) within which Hollywood could focus upon social tensions and provide utopian solutions with very specific reference to the latter of Dyer's dialectical 'pleasuring' accentuations: fragmentation and community. All of the films discussed display an element of people pulling together to triumph over adversity (one of the wartime home front's most cherished, promoted and key goals), all of them focus upon received notions of small town (American) values and make reference to a simpler and more idealised Christmas past; very little reference is made, as Connelly observed, to a 'Santa Claus', 'Father Christmas' or any other supernatural figure who would become so prominent in post-war films, the notion of the 'here and now' and individual effort and sacrifice being the prevailing wartime ideology. The utopian mood is sustained by use of comedic, nostalgic, romantic and idyllic settings where plentiful food, drink and comfort are much in evidence. Longed for security and tranquillity are also on offer in large quantities as a reminder of the desired and presumed outcome at the end of the conflict:

> 'The heartaches and anxieties of wartime ... were largely unsolvable and insurmountable, but Christmas was seen to have a transformative power. This .... was an established concept that many in the audience would have brought with them to the cinema, but it derived a particular power in wartime. Audiences enduring long separations from their families, a loss of community and uncertainty for the future were eager to see these threats banished, and found the resolutions all the more convincing and fulfilling for arriving at Christmastime. A key component of the Christmas film is the climactic and

joyous scene that occurs ... on Christmas Eve or Christmas Day. Christmas was used as the *deus ex machina* that could deliver all that they had hoped for: not only a white Christmas, but a Christmas of intact families and established homes, of reunion and renewal, the return to the past, and most remarkably, an almost complete disavowal of the war and the world beyond small town America.
(Glancy in Connelly, ed 2004: p.75)

Christmas is a special time in the Western calendar when hopes of redemption, transformation and transcendence are rife, when reflecting on seasonal cycles and new beginnings are foremost in the cultural consciousness. When seeking solace in ritual, family and loved ones and taking comfort in thoughts of some imagined past – a 'better', innocent and more harmonious time – becomes, briefly, the norm. Hollywood provided comfort, escape and pleasure for a war-weary, uprooted and displaced American population in their wartime Christmas offerings. When most of the audience could only dream of walking out of the theatre and into the scenarios that were on display, Hollywood rose to the challenge of providing them for a couple of out-of-life hours. And wartime audiences loved Hollywood for it.

Endnotes

1. For more on this, see Evans 2008.
2. Notably the reception and influence of Charles Dickens' Christmas books and the story *A Christmas Carol*.
3. Norman Rockwell is the famous and beloved American illustrator of Americana and images of small-town life painted in a highly sentimental and charming style. He illustrated dozens of covers of the *Saturday Evening Post*.
4. There was of course, one lingering, poignant and near-mythological cultural Christmas war memory from World War 1 when Christmas truces spontaneously occurred on the Western Front between British/Allied forces and German troops resulting in the exchanging of toasts, small gifts, food and the singing of carols. By Boxing Day – in some cases not until New Year's – the slaughter resumed. This has been referenced in various songs and accounts and is the subject of the 2005 film, *Joyeux Noel*. The theme was also taken up in Keith Gordon's *A Midnight Clear* (1992).
5. The rarely seen but most well-known early version that actually made it to video is the 1938 version directed by Edward L. Marin and starring Reginald Owen and Gene Lockhart.
6. Or day… or the wee hours. As Schatz recounts: '…many downtown theatres were soon forced to expand their schedules. In Detroit… a UAW request induced the 5,000 seat Fox Theatre to offer pictures from 1:00 am to 5.30 am for swing shift workers – a contingent of at least 100,000 workers … By late 1942 midnight shows were becoming commonplace in theatres in defence plant areas, where exhibitors tried, as *Variety* put it, "to catch the trade piling into downtown zones at the late hour".'
7. Frozen assets being held in countries such as Britain did prove problematic to the studios though they were able to negotiate part payments to some extent in exchange for co-production deals or easing quota restrictions. Source: Schatz, 1997.
8. Here it is interesting to note the use of the now controversial – if not culturally repressed memory – of blackface, a tradition well known by Crosby who had used the device in previous films and was also known to be a huge fan of Al Jolson. Here blackface is used to reference the stage tradition, signify Lincoln's importance in freeing the black community and also to hide the identity of the Linda character (Marjorie Reynolds) from Ted rendering her 'invisible'; a trope that would later be taken up in Ralph Ellison's great American 1952 novel, *Invisible Man*. This scene is routinely cut out of most television presentations today.
9. Film historian Ken Barnes note that the 'in-joke' of the turkey hopping from one date to the other refers to the fact that in 1939 Franklin Roosevelt had proposed a policy by which the third Thursday in November would henceforth be declared Thanksgiving Day rather than the traditional fourth Thursday in order that a longer consumer run-in to Christmas Day could be effected, hence profiting the economy. In 1941 when the film was being shot this was a controversial issue in US politics and was not resolved until after the film's wrap-up. Congress overruled and the fourth Thursday stayed. The affair was referred to as 'Franksgiving'.
10. Interesting to think that according to Ken Barnes, Berlin fought hard to keep his original lyrics in the song, which had been rejected by head of Decca, Jack Kappa, as too localised and made the song less universal. You may judge for yourself, the original lyrics were: 'The sun is shining, the grass is green/The orange and palm trees sway/There's never been such a day/In Beverly Hills, L.A./But it's December the 24th/And I'm longing to be up North/I'm dreaming of a white Christmas…' (Quoted by Barnes: 2002)
11. Due to the high salaries of the two male stars, the preferred female stars being considered for the roles of the women, Ginger Rogers and Rita Hayworth, were deemed too expensive and the two lesser knowns, Virginia Dale and Marjory Reynolds, were cast. Reynolds' singing was dubbed by Martha Mears. (Svehla & Svehla 1998: p.63)
12. If this is not more than enough afterlife for any film, it was while watching a television broadcast of the film in 1951 that one Kemmons Wilson conceived of a chain of motels to be called 'Holiday Inn'. (Connelly, ed 2000: p.68)
13. Well, perhaps one comment. As melancholic as the recorded version of the song sounds, the original lyrics which Garland thought too sad to sing went: 'Have yourself a merry little Christmas/Make the Yuletide gay/Next year we may all be many miles away/No good times like the olden days/Happy golden days of yore/Faithful friends who were dear to us will be near to us no more' and 'But at least we will all be together if the fates allow/And we'll have to muddle through somehow/So have yourself a merry little Christmas now'. And another version went, 'Have yourself a merry little Christmas/ It may be your last/Next year we may all be living in the past' and 'Faithful friends who were dear to

us/Will be near to us no more'. The lyrics were dropped and the song was rewritten by a reluctant Martin. (John Fricke audio commentary *Meet Me in St. Louis*, 2001)

14. This reference is from the *Christmas in Connecticut* production files held at the Warner Bros. Archive at the University of Southern California and I am indebted to Barbara Stanwyck researcher, Linda Berkvens, for pointing it out to me.

15. Ibid.

16. Hollywood never missed a step in the post-war cinematic Christmas sweepstakes as film followed film, classic examples being: *The Cheaters* (1945), *It's a Wonderful Life* (1946), *Miracle On 34th Street* (1947), *The Bishop's Wife* (1947) and *Christmas Eve* (1947). And as we know, this relentless festive march carries on...

Bibliography

Butler, Ivan. *The War Film* (London: Tantivy Press, 1974).

Clark, James. *War Films* (London: Virgin, 2006).

Connelly, Mark. *Christmas: A Social History* (London: IB Taurus, 1999).

Connelly, Mark. *Christmas at the Movies* (London: IB Taurus, 2000).

Evans, James. 'Psycho Santa, Qu'est-ce que c'est?: The Christmas Slasher Film' (*Electric Sheep Magazine*, winter 2008).

Glancy, Mark H. W*hen Hollywood Loved Britain* (Manchester: M.U.P, 1999).

Higham, Charles and Greenberg, Joel. *Hollywood in the Forties* (London: Tantivy Press, 1968).

Izod, John. *Hollywood and the Box Office 1895-1986* (London: Macmillan, 1988).

Karney, Robyn, Ed. *Cinema Year by Year* (London: DK, 2004).

Marsh, Dave and Steve Propes. *Merry Christmas, Baby: Holiday Music from Bing to Sting* (New York: Little, Brown and Co., 1993).

Miller, Daniel, Ed. *Unwrapping Christmas* (Oxford: Clarendon Press, 1993).

Naremore, James. *The Films of Vincente Minnelli* (Cambridge: C.U.P, 1993).

Pimlott, J A R. *The Englishman's Christmas* (Hassocks: Harvester Press, 1978).

Restad, Penne. *Christmas in America* (Oxford: O.U.P, 1995).

Rosen, Jody. *White Christmas: The Story of a Song* (London: First Estate, 2002).

Ryall, Tom. *Britain and the American Cinema* (London: Sage, 2001).

Schatz, Thomas. *Boom and Bust: The American Cinema in the 1940s* (New York: Charles Scribners, 1997).

Svehla, Gary and Susan Svehla. *It's Christmas Time at the Movies* (Baltimore: Midnight Marquee Press, 1998).

Turner, Graeme, Ed. *The Film Cultures Reader* (London: Routledge, 2002).

Audio Visual Sources

Barnes, Ken. *Holiday Inn* (Film Commentary) (London: Universal Pictures, UK, 2002).

Fricke, John. *Meet Me in St. Louis* (Film Commentary) (London: Warner-Brothers, 2004).

GOOSE-STEPPING IN SPACE

Fascism, World War 2
and Giant Bugs in
Starship Troopers

JAMIE RUSSELL

'What Riefenstahl did you can't compare to a movie about young adults fighting giant bugs. It is really very different.'

Paul Verhoeven [1]

Picture this: Aryan men with angular features stand to attention in regimental formation. "We are the Reich's young manhood!" proclaims one, staring into the middle distance with fervour in his eyes. Militaristic music plays on the soundtrack as Adolf Hitler addresses the crowd from a podium. "Just as you serve this Germany proudly," he shouts to the assembled young men, "all of Germany today will see its sons marching in you with proud joy." On-screen a flag emblazoned with a swastika flaps in the breeze.

Now picture this: handsome young soldiers – men and women – stand to attention in regimental formation. "I'm doing my part," proclaims a black girl straight to camera. "I'm doing my part," says a white college jock. Militaristic music plays on the soundtrack as a perky voiceover tells us "Join the Mobile Infantry and save the world." On-screen a flag emblazoned with what looks like a robotic eagle flaps in the breeze.

A lot of things separate these two sequences: sixty-odd years of history, the skin-colour of the soldiers and a hefty dose of postmodern irony. The first clip comes straight out of Leni Riefenstahl's documentary cum propaganda movie *Triumph of the Will* (1935) shot at the Nazi Party Congress in Nuremberg in 1934. The second is from Paul Verhoeven's $100 million SF war movie *Starship Troopers* (1997). Verhoeven's echo is deliberate and subversive. No one Sieg Heils, no one waves swastika emblazoned flags, but the unease remains – the shot of these good-looking, space-faring All-American teens you're watching could have been masterminded by a futuristic, colour-blind Goebbels. *Would you like to know more?*

THEY SUCKED HIS BRAINS OUT!

Paul Verhoeven is no stranger to controversy. Since swapping Holland for Hollywood in the mid-1980s, the Dutch director has developed the art of turning each new movie release into the perfect storm. *Basic Instinct* (1992) stirred outrage after Sharon Stone flashed her muff; *Robocop*'s (1987) violence was labelled gratuitous; *Showgirls*' (1995) exposé of the Las Vegas lap-dancing biz simply exposed its nubile actresses. American Puritanism was offended, headlines were generated and tickets were sold. Yet, in 1997, not even Verhoeven was prepared for the furore surrounding *Starship Troopers*.

The project went into pre-production as *Bug Hunt*, a SF adventure described by producer Jon Davidson as 'kind of *Lost Patrol* with arachnids'. [2] After the producer and screenwriter Ed Neumeier realised that the rights to Robert A. Heinlein's novel *Starship Troopers* were available, though, they shifted focus and decided to update the novel for the screen. Heinlein's story came with a certain notoriety. In 1959, the author's long-standing publisher Scribner's refused to release the novel, appalled by its militarism. The book – 'a bugle-blowing, drum-beating glorification of the hero's life in military service' [3] – was eventually published by Putnam's and went on to win the Hugo award

Starship Troopers
1997

© Columbia
Tristar/
The Kobal
Collection

for Best SF Novel the following year. Awards success did little to placate left-leaning critics who were concerned that Heinlein's vision of a future 'utopia', in which military service gave citizens the right to vote, was neo-fascist. Debate about the novel's politics has continued ever since. [4]

Verhoeven and his production team came to the material intent on turning this big screen adaptation into an ironic reading of Heinlein's tub-thumping patriotism. When the movie was released in 1997, though, the Dutchman was shocked by the response. Audiences apparently didn't appreciate the joke. It wasn't just irony-deficient Americans either. European audiences seemed particularly resistant to the satire. Instead of reading the film as a critique of contemporary America (as the director claimed he'd intended), Verhoeven says many European critics accused him of stamping the jackboot of fascism on the audience's face:

'When I came with *Starship Troopers* to Europe, to promote the movie, in general, in all the countries – with the exception of England, in fact – in all the European countries that had been fascist or Nazi, notably Germany, Italy and France – there was an enormous resistance and anger about this movie – they told me that I had made a fascist movie. I thought I had made a movie about the United States, revealing fascist tendencies that were perceptible, in my opinion, in that society. [5]

Not since Jonathan Swift's *A Modest Proposal* was misread by audiences convinced it was prompting baby-eating among the Irish, has an artist's satirical intent and its reception been so far out of joint. But what is it about *Starship Troopers* use of Riefenstahl and other World War 2-era movies that causes such a knee-jerk response in viewers?

THE ONLY GOOD BUG'S A DEAD BUG!

Starship Troopers opens with a 'newsvert' from the Federal Network, the mouthpiece of the global Terran Federation that runs the Earth at this unspecified point in the future. 'Join Up Now!' advises chunky on-screen text as a narrator tells us that 'Young people from all over the globe are joining up to fight for the future.' It's a stirring sequence that anyone with even a passing familiarity with *Triumph of the Will*'s rhetorical visuals is likely to recognise immediately. Verhoeven makes no bones about his cinematic plagiarism. 'When the soldiers look at the camera and say, "I'm doing my part!" that's from Riefenstahl,' he told *Entertainment Weekly* just before *Starship Troopers*' release. 'We copied it. It's wink-wink Riefenstahl.' [6] Such deliberate echoing of World War 2 era iconography is one of *Starship Troopers*' recurring tricks. It's not just Nazi propaganda – and that, perhaps is where the confusion begins. Verhoeven's ironic recycling of the past also encompasses World War 2 combat movies and 1940s newsreels.

Some might argue that the film's World War 2-references could be explained away as an attempt to put some window-dressing on a SF movie. Compare it with, for instance, the Heinlein-indebted *Aliens* (1986) that reworked the Vietnam War movie with its story of US Marines on a 'bug hunt' in space ('This time it's war' promised the tagline; a rare example of a studio publicity department being doggedly literal). James Cameron's film redeployed a series of familiar Vietnam War movie tropes: the cowardly lieutenant who loses it under fire; a general air of cynicism about the military authorities

Starship Troopers 1997

© Columbia Tristar/ The Kobal Collection

that leads one character to ask, in a blatant reference to the events of 'Nam 'Do we get to win this time?' Strip *Aliens* of these allusions, though, and you'd lose very little of what makes *Aliens* so successful; the allusions weren't necessarily a key part of the film's subtext (which was arguably more psychosexual than political).

In contrast, *Starship Troopers* isn't content with simply redeploying genre staples to buff up its SF war story. No, it's far more subversive than that. Although it looks at first sight like a popcorn movie about giant bugs being splattered by futuristic weaponry, *Starship Troopers* is actually a cartoonish attempt to coax the viewer into asking some awkward questions about our identifications with our heroes and the ideology of the Hollywood action genre itself. The film's magpie-like pillaging of past cinematic references – from pro-Hitler to pro-Allies – is all part of this strategy. Such familiar iconography seduces us into the film's world and encourages us to identify with its All-American heroes. Then we're left reeling as Verhoeven unmasks these heroes as futuristic fascists who are just one rendition of the Horst Wessel song away from being card-carrying Nazis. The aim is to make you choke on your popcorn.

Glance at the film's parade of perma-tanned, perma-grinning cast of human heroes and it's hard not to be fooled into thinking you're watching *Beverly Hills 90210* in space (the suspicion is aided, of course, by the fact that a couple of the actors including Casper Van Dien had passed through that series on their way to Verhoeven's casting couch). [7] *Starship Troopers* begins like a teen movie with high school jock Johnny Rico (Van Dien) smitten with prom queen Carmen (Denise Richards). Muscular and broad-shouldered, he's the star of track and field but a little light up top when it comes to mathematics. Carmen's bright and beautiful, though, and in the film's future society she can have her pick of assignments with the space navy. Gender equality means girls with brains can be space pilots. Jocks with low averages however get shunted straight to the Mobile Infantry – the grunt outfit that does the Terran Federation's heavy lifting.

It almost looks utopian; after all, in this world gender and race are no longer the tools of discrimination they once were in the twentieth century. Yet there is a new discrimination – one between those who have served in the military and those who haven't. Slavish patriotism – to and beyond the point of paying the ultimate price on the battlefield – is the only thing that gives citizens the freedom to go into politics or be guaranteed a licence to have children. Already the cracks in *Starship Troopers'* multiracial, post-feminist future are beginning to show. As the Earth goes to war against a race of giant bugs – the arachnids – who're jostling our colonial interests in the depths of space, those cracks are ripped open.

Suddenly we realise that this world isn't as utopian as it looks – at least not for any left-leaning liberals in the audience. The film's future is an Anglo-American global state where even Buenos Aires has become an extension of L.A. suburbia and the franchise is only available to military veterans. If you want to vote in this fascist 'democracy' you'll have to serve first – two years of hard graft to get the right to put an 'X' on a ballot paper. As History and Moral Philosophy teacher Jean Rasczak (Michael Ironside) tells his charges, while prodding them with the stumpy remains of the arm he lost during his own tour of duty, "When you vote, you're exercising political authority. You're using force. And force, my friends, is violence, the supreme authority from which all other authority derives."

So Earth's global 'democracy' isn't a bastion of freedom at all. Instead, it's a military dictatorship where criminals are executed on live TV, leaders talk about 'cleansing' planets of the alien threat and military officers are decked out in black and grey dress uniforms that owe more to the Waffen-SS than the United States Marine Corps. Propaganda is rife, condensed into sixty-second newsverts that explain 'Why We Fight' in a creepy echo of the title of Frank Capra's World War 2 series of information films that shared the same name. Is Verhoeven simply ticking off World War 2 references from Riefenstahl's Nazi iconography to Capra's pro-American patriotism? Or should we read something more into the appropriation of American World War 2 propaganda and its use in this future fascist dictatorship?

SERVICE GUARANTEES CITIZENSHIP

Capra's *Why We Fight* series was a collection of seven information films produced during World War 2 by the Office of War Information. The Hollywood director – who'd previously shown his commitment to wholesome, small-town Americana in films like *Mr Deeds Goes To Town* (1936) – had volunteered his services to the War Department in December 1941. With titles like *Prelude to War*, *The Nazis Strike* and *The Battle of Russia*, the seven films were designed to bring the American military and public up to speed with a war that had been raging for two years before the Pearl Harbor attacks. As Richard Griffiths, the *Why We Fight* unit's researcher, later explained: 'The problem in 1942 was how to turn the youth of a nation, so recently and so predominantly isolationist into a fighting force not only effectively trained and equipped but armed too, with the conviction that his country's entry into a war was not only just but the inevitable answer to serious wrongs.' [8]

In other words, the *Why We Fight* series was pure propaganda. Capra, who'd seen Riefenstahl's films, knew he had a tough act to follow. According to historian Ian S. Scott, Capra's verdict on *Triumph of the Will* was that 'Satan couldn't have devised a more blood-chilling super-spectacle.' [9] The director was apparently 'so dumbstruck by the force of Riefenstahl's imagery that [he] felt compelled to resist by using it'. [10] The *Why We Fight* series unashamedly steals Riefenstahl's filmmaking toolkit and recalibrates the ideological rhetoric it espoused in favour of a pro-democratic, pro-American thrust. The result was a new type of American propaganda as slickly put together as a Madison Avenue ad campaign with animated segments courtesy of Disney.

In *Prelude to War*, the first film in the *Why We Fight* series, the groundwork for Capra's rhetoric is quickly laid down. "Why are we Americans on the march?" asks the narrator. "Is it because of Pearl Harbor?" [Cue newsreel footage of bombs dropping and ships burning] "Is that why we're fighting?" "Or because of England?" [Here come shots of the Blitz]. Later, a quote from Vice President Henry A. Wallace – 'This is a fight between a free world and a slave world' – leads into a creaky special effects shot. Two planets, Earth and its black Nazi twin, stand side by side. It's as if the Universal Studios logo has been cloned by Ming the Merciless. A crash course in democracy, from Moses to Lincoln and beyond, follows. The upshot? 'Give me liberty or give me death.'

Is it weird that a fascist documentary could inspire a pro-American information film? Verhoeven certainly seems to think so. In *Starship Troopers*, the *Why We Fight* series is gleefully subverted. Here Capra's graphics of European territory are turned into intergalactic star maps showing the bug threat (complete with 'You Are Here' legends);

shots of Japanese bombing raids are replaced by footage from the destroyed city of Buenos Aires, the Pearl Harbor of the Arachnid War, where a man mourns his dead dog before turning straight to camera to intone: "The only good bug is a dead bug." Elsewhere the human war effort is goaded on by military chiefs in Geneva (!) where Americans like Sky Marshal Dienes (Bruce Gray) display the oratory skills of a Nazi rally leader (and a uniform to match): "We must meet the threat with our valour, our blood, indeed with our very lives, to ensure that human civilisation, not insect, dominates this galaxy now and always!" It's the bastard love child of Capra and Goebbels jettisoned into space.

Why We Fight and Triumph of the Will aren't the only '40s artefacts that Verhoeven turns his attention on. Even the humble World War 2 platoon movie – that creaky beacon of democratic values – is subverted in Starship Troopers' dystopian future. Recalling his work on the script, screenwriter Ed Neumeier told Cinefantastique: 'I was fed a steady diet of World War 2 propaganda pictures [by producer Jon Davidson and Verhoeven]. I'm not talking about the Why We Fight series – although I looked at the stuff too – I'm talking about movies the big studios made in the middle of the war, like Airforce and Action in the North Atlantic. I just said, "That's what I want to do; I want to embrace that! I want to make a big rootin', tootin' propaganda film, but use it as a form of social satire."' [11]

COME ON YOU APES, DO YOU WANT TO LIVE FOREVER?

The Jew with smelly feet, the comedy Irishman, the noble African-American, the cranky, terrier-like Polack: these were the kind of stereotypes that the World War 2 platoon movie focused on. Films like Bataan (1943) and A Walk in the Sun (1945) epitomise the cycle of movies in which the multiracial platoon group came to symbolise the democratic impetus that Americans were fighting the Axis to defend: in America, men were equals, brothers who fought side-by-side against a common, racist enemy who had no time for liberty. Of course, America in the 1940s was no beacon of liberty if you happened to be black and live in the South and for much of the war infantry regiments were carefully segregated. Yet the platoon movie's 'melting pot' of racial stereotypes suggested what America could be – a less imperfect democracy where race was no longer an issue. Like Capra's Why We Fight series, these platoon movies were another kind of propaganda, a way of mobilising a nation's mindset for war.

Written in 1959, Heinlein's novel is clearly influenced by the platoon movies of World War 2 and also the Korean War like Sam Fuller's Fixed Bayonets (1951). The movie adaptation of Starship Troopers makes the influence even more apparent, focusing in on Rico's platoon as they go through basic training and head to the frontline. The soldiers are the usual collection of stereotypes popularised by World War 2 movies. There's the hardened drill sergeant Zim (Clancy Brown); the punk joker Ace (Jake Busey); a token African-American (Seth Gilliam). There are even, since this future society is post-feminist, female soldiers like Dizzy Flores (Dina Meyer) who's had a crush on Johnny since high school.

'The "melting pot" roll call has become a basic trope of the war movie, a cinematic cliché,' suggests historian Richard Slotkin. 'But it also exposes a myth of American nationality that remains vital in our political and cultural life: the idealised self-image of a multiethnic, multiracial democracy, hospitable to difference but united by a sense of national belonging.' [12] Other film historians agree. Looking over several decades worth of World War 2 set films Jeanine Basinger claims that in these films 'the war brings a need for us to work together as a group, to set aside individual needs, and to bring our melting pot tradition together to function as a true democracy since, after all, that is what we are fighting for: the Democratic way of life.' [13] The platoon movie then, with its melting pot of stereotypes, became a repudiation of master race fascism, a kind of American myth of inclusivity and democratic meritocracy. It didn't matter that it didn't exist in reality – myths don't have to. They only have to speak to their audience.

By nodding to the platoon movie in its focus on Rasczak's – and later Rico's – Roughnecks, *Starship Troopers* pulls off quite a coup. Rather than reinforcing the platoon movie's ideology of democracy and freedom, Verhoeven's film actively undermines all this by linking it with explicit Nazi iconography. The effect is unsettling; slowly we begin to realise that these men and women we've been cheering may not be so heroic after all. With their might-is-right philosophy and commitment to a policy of extermination, a term that brings to mind both Rentokil and Auschwitz in a deliriously disturbing coincidence of cartoon SF and historical atrocity – they're less defenders of freedom than militaristic aggressors.

By the time Neil Patrick Harris' psychic officer turns up dressed in full Nazi regalia (well, almost) we begin to wonder if we've been cheering the wrong side. All along the bugs have been presented as mindless, sub-human insects by the Federation's propaganda. [14] But suddenly, there's a captured 'Brain Bug' and when Harris' psychic communicates with it he tells the cheering troops 'It's afraid!' Hold on a minute. That means the arachnids are sentient life, then... no?

In interview, Verhoeven has explained that his aim was to leave the audience questioning their allegiances. 'I wanted to do something more than just a movie about giant bugs. What I tried to do is use subversive imagery to make a point about society. I tried to seduce the audience to join [this] society, but then ask, "What are you really joining up for?" [15] 'What I was saying was that your heroes in this movie have a fascist ideology and you should be aware of that. What we did was seduce the audience to follow us and then present them with the bill, which is basically "You're a fascist", because you went for this route and you enjoyed it. The Neil Patrick Harris character in a SS uniform clearly should indicate to the audience that there was something wrong with these people.' [16]

In referencing *Triumph of the Will*, *Why We Fight* and the World War 2 combat movie, Verhoeven not only throws the dormant right-wing ideology of the action movie into stark relief. He also makes an audacious claim: is America itself fascistic? Was World War 2 really the 'good' war that we're always told it was? How much of a line separates fascism and democracy? *Starship Troopers* isn't interested in giving answers. Instead it wants to shock us with its questions. In effect, it's a kind of anti-propaganda – an action movie that subverts its own militaristic thunder by highlighting the role between filmmaking and propaganda.

Such a technique is so audacious arguably only a European could have achieved it; after all, World War 2 holds a very special place in American mythology as movie historian Jeanine Basinger explains: 'World War 2 seems to be the combat that speaks to the American soul. Perhaps it's our total victory, or the sense of our righteousness, or the conviction that it wasn't our fault, or the influence of technology on art – in which the ability to take cameras into the field created images of power that would and could not be forgotten.' [17] Verhoeven's film is not *Saving Private Ryan* (released the following year). It's the anti-*Ryan*, a movie that discovers not decency and democracy in the violence but instead the seeds of totalitarianism and asks: *Would you like to know more?*

Endnotes

1. Verhoeven quoted in Benjamin Svetkey, 'The Reich Stuff', *Entertainment Weekly*, 21 November 1997, p.9.
2. Jon Davidson quoted in Dan Persons, 'Starship Troopers', *Cinefantastique* (December, 1997), p.18.
3. H. Bruce Franklin, *Robert A. Heinlein: America as Science Fiction*, New York and Oxford: Oxford University Press, 1980, p.111.
4. For an overview of Heinlein's novel and its reception see Franklin's *Robert A. Heinlein: America as Science Fiction* and Everett Carl Dolman, 'Military, Democracy and the State in Robert A. Heinlein's *Starship Troopers*' in Donald M. Hassler and Clyde Wilcox (eds.), *Political Science Fiction*, Columbia: University of South Carolina Press, 1997, pp.196-213.
5. Verhoeven quoted in Christine Cornea, *Science Fiction Cinema: Between Fantasy and Reality*, Edinburgh: Edinburgh University Press, 2007, p.141.
6. Verhoeven quoted by Svetkey, p.8.
7. The director himself has described his too perfect cast as having a certain 'lobotomised' manner. 'If you look at the faces, you get the feel of those German movies of the 1930s or Leni Riefenstahl's *Triumph of the Will*. See Cornea, p.172.
8. Richard Griffiths quoted by Roger Manvell, *Films and the Second World War*, South Brunswick, New York, London: A. S. Barnes, J. M. Dent, 1974, p.168.
9. Ian S. Scott, 'Why We Fight and Projections of America', in Peter C. Rollins and John E. O'Connor (eds.), *Why We Fought: America's Wars in Film and History*, Kentucky: University of Kentucky Press, 2008, p.249.
10. Ibid., p.249.
11. Ed Neumeier quoted by Persons, p.19.
12. Richard Slotkin, 'Unit Pride: Ethnic Platoons and the Myth of American Nationality', *American Literary History* Volume 13, Number 3, (Fall 2001), pp.469-498.
13. Jeanine Basinger, *The WWII Combat Film: Anatomy of a Genre*, New York, 1988, p.37.
14. Verhoeven has said that the film's treatment of the bugs is similar to the way the Axis were characterised in World War 2 movies. 'I think what I saw in the script was the possibility to create an enemy that was politically correct, that you could kill, in a certain way, [as you could one] do in a movie about the German enemy. It's the attitude that we – the Europeans and the Americans, at the same time – had about the Second World War: the enemy was Japanese or German, and they were definitely devilish; they were not seen in any human way. If you listened to documentaries at that time, the enemy is completely dehumanised.' See Persons, p.21.
15. Verhoeven quoted in Svetkey, p.9.
16. Verhoeven quoted in Jeff Bond, 'Another Bug Hunt', *Cinefantastique*, (August/September, 2003), p.6.
17. Basinger, p.81.

Bibliography

Basinger, Jeanine, *The WWII Combat Film: Anatomy of a Genre*, New York, 1988.

Bond, Jeff, 'Another Bug Hunt', *Cinefantastique* (August/September, 2003), pp.5-6.

Cornea, Christine, *Science Fiction Cinema: Between Fantasy and Reality*, Edinburgh: Edinburgh University Press, 2007.

Dolman, Everett Carl, 'Military, Democracy and the State in Robert A. Heinlein's Starship Troopers', in Donald M. Hassler and Clyde Wilcox (eds.), pp.196-213.

Franklin, H. Bruce, *Robert A. Heinlein: America as Science Fiction*, New York and Oxford: Oxford University Press, 1980.

Hassler, Donald M. and Clyde Wilcox (eds.), *Political Science Fiction*, Columbia: University of South Carolina Press, 1997.

Manvell, Roger M, *Films and the Second World War*, South Brunswick, New York, London: A. S. Barnes, J. M. Dent, 1974.

Persons, Dan, 'Starship Troopers', *Cinefantastique* (December, 1997), pp.17-31.

Rollins Peter C. and John E. O'Connor (eds.), *Why We Fought: America's Wars in Film and History*, Kentucky: University of Kentucky Press, 2008.

Scott, Ian S., 'Why We Fight and Projections of America', in Peter C. Rollins and John E. O'Connor, (eds.), pp.242-258.

Slotkin, Richard, 'Unit Pride: Ethnic Platoons and the Myth of American Nationality', *American Literary History*, Volume 13, Number 3, (Fall 2001), pp.469-498.

Svetkey, Benjamin, 'The Reich Stuff', *Entertainment Weekly* (21 November 1997), pp.8-9.

DRAWING FIRE

Animation and the War Film

JAMES CLARKE

'I truly believe that the lack of adequate imagery is a danger. It is as serious a defect as being without memory. What have we done to our images? What have we done to our embarrassed landscapes? I have said this before and I will repeat it again as long as I am able to talk: if we do not develop adequate images we will die out like dinosaurs.'

Werner Herzog

War stories and the animated film have a long, rich history together. The war movie as adventure, as rallying cry for peace and as propaganda document and public service announcement all have their place in the context of the animated film. Even the kinetic, broad comedy of *Who Framed Roger Rabbit?* (1988) which proved so popular that a sequel was considered entitled *Toon Patrol* in which Roger and his animated buddies went up against Fascism. It would have been a fascinating film and would fit so much with how the Nazi party considered Mickey Mouse. I quote: animated war films can be narrative based, character based or alternatively based as far from these two foundation stones as possible.

An animated film is such a deliberately fashioned film format that it is arguably the most worthy of consideration. Nothing in an animated film is left to chance. Much less than in a live action film at least. Everything has been selected and emphasised for a particular reason: colour, absence of colour, camera placement, camera movement, camera stillness, the place of sound, the place of silence and so forth. A film's meaning and value is *never* only embedded in the spoken word. Meanings, and a sense of how a given film's drama assesses the world, are found in what characters do say, what they imply, what their gestures and actions suggest. As in life, every moment of a movie matters in every way, each take on the subject informed by point of view, experience and frames of reference, and the control that the filmmaker can exert in very subtle and intended ways. Animated films are amongst the richest texts we can take time to understand. Animated movies are an immensely common frame of reference for people. Animation transforms and heightens reality, often making clearer to us our fears and wishes. Animated films have an apparently innate capacity to express and imagine the concept of transformation and in doing so transform our own perceptions of things we might typically take for granted. Animation scholar Paul Wells states that animation has the capacity to subvert expectations and that it is not necessarily bound by the imperatives of photorealism. Subsequently, animation carries a conceptual freedom and might just open the eyes and mind of the viewer in a range of startling and thoughtful ways. Like any cultural product, animation can be considered historically, economically, aesthetically, technologically and in terms of a given production context.

Animated films, then, reveal the world to us with great thought, invention and a sense of vivid metaphor. It seems to me that animated film tends to be unfairly ghettoised as separate to the rest of cinema and yet before any other considerations it is still filmmaking and is arguably the most pure of film forms. Animated films have visualised and dramatised questions such as: What it is to be human? What it is to live with technology? After all, war is fought with technology.

Animation and the idea of innocence of being 'just for kids' (as though young viewers were less worthy of being treated intelligently by film producers) needs to be

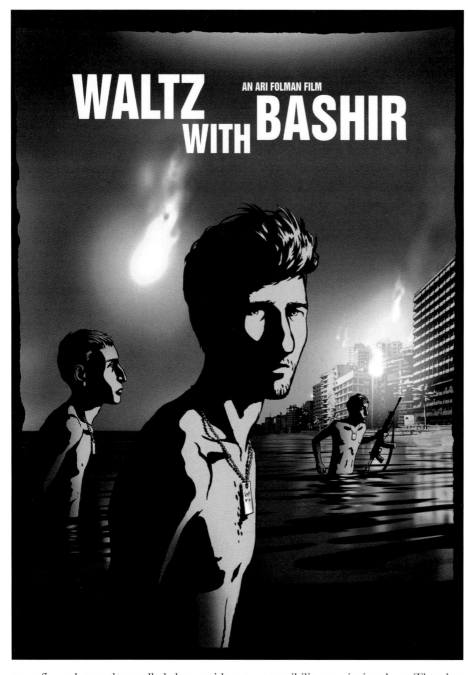

Waltz with Bashir
2008

© Bridgit
Folman Film
Gang /
The Kobal
Collection

reconfigured or rather pulled down with a new sensibility put in its place. There's a more compelling reality. Paul Wells has written that the animated film 'essentially offers an alternative vocabulary to the filmmaker by which alternative and perspectives and levels of address are possible'. Style creates substance and creative choices are packed out with implicit or explicit ideological statements. Nothing is without a view of the world fixed beneath the image. Certainly, in the animated war film, or in certain cased film made during wartime, national identity gets an especially vivid visual workout. The

animated film, then, is perfectly poised to express and explore subjects and themes that might be considered mature for younger students. Animation has developed in a wide range of ways globally and this has been the case since the earliest days of cinema.

In 2008, the film *Waltz with Bashir/Vals Im Bashir*, written and directed by Ari Folman, and realised as a rotoscoped film (that is to say, as a film which uses live action footage as the basis over which 'animated' characters and action are traced) was received with great enthusiasm for being both visually and politically engaged. A film exploring the Israeli-Palestinian conflict was distributed by Sony who also distributed the recently released *Persepolis* (2007). *Waltz with Bashir*, then, is another high profile animated project that explicitly engages with culturally specific and contested issues that carry a range of powerful and controversial resonances. Like *Persepolis*, the film explores the place of memory, or in the case of *Waltz with Bashir*, the lack of memory. *Waltz with Bashir* centres on a protagonist who has been traumatised by his experience as a teenager in the Israeli army in the early 1980s and the first Lebanon war.

How, then, do we define animation? What is it about its form and content that fit with a thoughtful study of film and of our perception of reality in all its diversity?

ANIMATION, REALISM AND ENTERTAINMENT

Perhaps the first, best place to start is with a quick sketch of the relationship that is generally understood to exist between realism and film. To do this we need to step back to the 1930s and the writing of French philosopher and cineaste André Bazin, most famously in *What Is Cinema?* (1958–1962). For him realism and cinema was bound up in terms of a certain claim to truth and rested on a form of integrity borne from photographing the world that exists all around us. Clearly, animation does not typically show us objects that 'live and breathe' in the world and yet it arguably somehow finds a 'truth' that live action sometime fails to attain.

Adding further interest is the typical equation of cinema with entertainment which, to some degree, is a view that has a root in the medium's origins as a 'cinema of attractions', as a novelty into which narrative devices were subsequently integrated. In the development of narrative moviemaking, cinema drew reference from literature, theatre and other arts and like those arranged its productions in terms of genre. There is no room here to explore it so extensively but genre is regarded as ideologically loaded, each generic narrative (western, horror, romance, thriller, science fiction to name a few) goes some way in expressing the sensibilities and attitudes of a given culture; typically of the dominant ideology in that culture. Richard Dyer wrote a landmark essay, 'Entertainment and Utopia', which elaborates on the relationship between cinema and ideology. Dyer writes that 'Entertainment does not present models of utopian worlds… Rather, the utopianism is contained in the feelings it embodies. It presents, head on as it were, what utopia would feel like rather than how it would be organised…' Given how readily we use the term 'entertainment' as a descriptive and evaluative term, it is productive to properly engage with what the term might actually mean and refer to. It also bears repeating that animation is not a genre but rather a form, or series of forms, into which any genre can be placed and worked through with varying degrees of fidelity to its particular generic tradition and to the world outside our windows.

In her study of animation history and the various forms of animation that have developed, Maureen Furniss in her book *Art in Motion: Animation Aesthetics* suggests that animated films exist on a spectrum that has, at one extreme, the capacity for mimesis, the copying of reality. At the other end of the spectrum lies abstraction. Any given animated film can be placed at the relevant place on this scale depending on the degree to which it can be regarded as transforming the reality it represents. Transforming reality can occur at two levels: i) the surface level of the visual, sound and narrative elements and ii) the deeper level of a film's capacity to assess or, judge its subject, this process being the expression of a network of cultural and ideological relationships.

WHEN THE WIND BLOWS

In the mid-1980s, the threat of nuclear war was palpable, as ever-present in the news as terrorist issues are today. A sense of developing tragedy characterises the story of *When the Wind Blows* (1986). The film documents a passage of time as the elderly couple succumb to the effects of nuclear pollution. Atypically, the film begins with live action news footage of protests at Greenham Common, the site of a US nuclear airbase on British soil, thus locating the film specifically in time and place. Like *The Plague Dogs* (1982), this film is a critique of a very specific situation which nonetheless remains pertinent two decades on.

Like the Japanese animated feature *Grave of the Fireflies / Hotaru no haka* (1988), *When the Wind Blows* is a war film, or rather an anti-war film. Although the film emphasises its realist tendencies, it vividly deploys a small number of contrasting animation styles that move towards the abstract in order to express animation's transformative powers. This more expressionistic, hyper-animation style is used carefully in order to give the viewer a more powerful sense of the two characters' outlooks and imaginings and is, for example, adopted to show us Hilda's memories of youth and pastoral bliss and also the couple's fear of a Russian soldier storming into their quiet countryside home.

When the Wind Blows, in its original graphic novel form, by Raymond Briggs who created *The Snowman*, uses rusty colours and the film faithfully translates this palette. Autumnal hues are used for the moment of nuclear fallout, in which we see houses blowing in the wind. These images contrast powerfully with the healthy, lush greens seen at the opening of the film and the soft, pastel colours that characterise Hilda's dream memories. This colour coded contrast is a recurrent and recognisable device of cinema, and is as much a part of *Grave of the Fireflies* and *The Mighty River* (1993), both equally conscious in their representation of social breakdown and chaos.

When the Wind Blows adopts an interesting device: its backgrounds are photographed model sets of the house interior and over these have been placed painted animated figures. This unusual but very effective contrast of approaches allows for certain camera positions and movements and placements that adhere to the realist mode of British cinema which we can usefully understand in the way that film historian and critic Richard Armstrong suggests here: 'Better than any other genre, social realism has shown us to ourselves, pushing the boundaries in the effort to put the experiences of real Britons on the screen, and shaping an idea of what British cinema can be.' This is a welcome and useful contrast to the dialogue elements and the use of animation in this way can serve as a useful trigger for considerations of how animation is best deployed in service of a kind of emotional integrity. As such, *When the Wind Blows* is fascinating in its outright refusal to use animation for more 'frivolous' ends and in this it shares much with *The Plague Dogs*. The fidelity to realism of *When the Wind Blows* is key to understanding it. As with *The Plague Dogs* this contrasts with a sense of only suggesting the real rather than seeking to more mimetically recording it. As such, one might argue that the aesthetic choice is a matter of philosophy and reflects how one chooses to view the world.

The war film has a strong thread through British cinema and is an important component of our national identity (which we might consider a construction in itself). In this genre, *When the Wind Blows* is a relatively overlooked title. Based on the book by writer and illustrator Raymond Briggs the film charts the attempts of elderly couple Jim and Hilda to survive a nuclear explosion. The film was produced in the mid-1980s when there was a palpable fear and concern around nuclear war as tensions between the US (under the administration of Ronald Reagan) and Russia and Libya worsened. The film is very consciously a cautionary tale. By contrast, the major animated American film release of 1986 was *An American Tail*, a very traditional family orientated animated feature in 'the Disney tradition' of anthropomorphised animals.

In *When the Wind Blows*, Jim and Hilda are innocents who have put their faith in the government completely and who are ignorant of the real threat of nuclear fallout, imagining the bombing to be like that of World War 2. The character of Jim play-acts war at several moments in the film, in so doing indicating the difficulty in reconciling the sense of 'old' war with the new war he is about to become the victim of. Furthermore, the tragedy of Jim and Hilda is as much about their misguided, naïve trust in the government and its guidelines in the event of war as it is about their physical struggle to survive. Jim's misunderstandings annoyingly and yet touchingly lead him to observe that 'the bomb won't cost us a penny. We'll be well covered.' Perhaps ignorance *is* bliss.

GRAVE OF THE FIREFLIES

Grave of the Fireflies is a massively popular and well known anime film outside of its country of production and original release. Whilst not commercially popular upon original release in 1988 – it has a starkness akin to *When the Wind Blows* and *The Plague Dogs* – *Grave of the Fireflies* has assumed a cult following of sorts and you may find that a significant number of students have already seen it as part of a fairly widespread fascination with Manga, anime and East Asian culture that has developed over the past ten years.

One of the most appealing aspects of Japanese animation (and let's not forget its relationship to Manga) is its expressive use of background, rather than background being deployed in a more prosaic way. The poetic and lyrical sensibility underpins much anime, and Japanese cinema more generally. What we are venturing into here is the issue of the mise-en-scène of animation which is fundamentally based on the form's ability to be very elastic in its presentation of space.

There is a determined realist aesthetic that dominates *Grave of the Fireflies*. The film does not shy away from illustrating the physical trauma and horror of war. Consider the image of the protagonist's mother bandaged and bloodied after an air strike. We are then shown her body and many others being committed to a mass burial site. *Grave of the Fireflies* possesses a quality that echoes similar moments in *When the Wind Blows*. *Grave of the Fireflies* presents images of nature enduring the ravaging force of war and the film's drama turns very much on ideas of duty and the struggle to survive and find something of beauty amidst war, suffering and trauma.

Few animated feature films would be expected to start with the following spoken words 'September 21st 1945. That was the day I died.' The film uses animation to be absolutely realistic but also to transform the 'real' into something more metaphorical and to communicate the states of mind of its protagonists. As in *When the Wind Blows*, this film plays up the contrast between the light greens and blues of nature with the reds, browns and rust palette associated with war and a burning world. There is a scene that arguably runs longer than it would in a British or American film where the brother and sister look out at the ravaged city. The brother begins swinging on a frame and his sister crouches sadly and the moment is lingered on as a crystallising experience for them.

UNDER FIRE: A CENTURY OF WAR MOVIES

The background, the setting, is as important to the scene as the actions of the children. In the Japanese idiom, realism is often secondary to emotion and subsequently backgrounds can be used in more expressive ways in order to indicate inner emotional and psychological states.

Over the past ten years, Studio Ghibli has powerfully embedded itself in non-Japanese territories, proving very popular with young people. The studio's output and exhibition and distribution in Europe and North America has opened up the wider field of anime and built on the impact of *Akira* (1988), the first anime feature film to receive widespread attention in Britain and America. The name most often invoked in material about Studio Ghibli is Hayao Miyazaki. Miyazaki co-founded the studio and his directorial efforts include the first Ghibli film *Nausicaa: Valley of the Wind/Kaze no tani no Naushika* (1984), and *Princess Mononoke/Mononoke-hime* (1997), *Spirited Away/Sen to Chihiro no kamikakushi* (2001) and *Ponyo on the Cliff/Gake no ue no Ponyo* (2008).

The Studio Ghibli films, aside from being produced with the intention of generating profit and the largest audience possible, also continue the grand tradition of Japanese cinema in its largest, most generous sense which was set down for the ages almost way back in 1924 when Kido Shiro who was head of Japan's Shochiku Studios observed that 'There are two ways to view humanity… cheerful and gloomy. But the latter will not do… To inspire despair in our viewers would be unforgivable. The bottom line is that the basis of film must be salvation.'

Interestingly, Miyazaki has spoken of his relative lack of interest in securing overseas audiences for his productions. Indeed, to get a useful handle on the message and value systems on offer in the animated films from Japan being discussed here one can usefully refer to the book *The Chrysanthemum and the Sword* which neatly unpacks many of the fundamental and longstanding sensibilities and cultural traditions that underpin Japanese life and which find expression in a wide variety of ways across Japanese cinema and certainly in its anime form. We have an understandable tendency to think of Japanese anime being rooted very much in their own culture. However, this may not quite be the case as Andrew Osmond notes in his essay *Castles in the Sky*: 'World children's literature is an integral part of anime… It's an irony of cross cultural exchange that Japanese people are probably more likely to recognise an anime version of Heidi than… *Akira*.'

Arguably, Japanese cinema has quite self-consciously engaged with matters of social import to its island culture and, critically, the tension between (often ancient) tradition and modernity. Anime is also notable for being about and for young people. This fusion of national trauma and focus on the young finds powerful expression in Japanese cinema evoked in a very powerful realist style. In the wake of World War 2 and the atomic bombing of Hiroshima and Nagasaki, Japanese culture and identity centred on a way to negotiate the power and potential threats of science and technology. The live action movie *Godzilla/Gojira* (1954) embodies this concern and in turn anticipates many of the subjects that anime would take on board.

Grave of the Fireflies was based on a partly autobiographical novel of the same name. The film charts the experiences ('adventures' would give the wrong idea) of a brother and sister, teenager Seito and his young sister, Setsuko. When their town is bombed they are sent to live with their aunt in the country. They struggle to survive. One could say that like the most effective war films, *Grave of the Fireflies* seeks to dramatise ways in which one can sustain humanity amidst the trauma of war. Their survival is as much emotional and spiritual as it is physical, and the Japanese construction of beauty and death underpins the movie.

Just as *When the Wind Blows* and *The Plague Dogs* deal with dangers of mechanised, military worlds, so *Grave of the Fireflies* fits consistently alongside them. Film scholar Donald Richie commented in 1961 that: '...the Japanese failure to cope with Hiroshima is one which is shared by everybody in the world today. No one has come to terms with the bomb – least of all, perhaps, the people upon whom it was originally inflicted. When the thing itself has become the very epitome of chaos unleashed, it would be expecting too much that an ordered and directed reply could be instantly appreciated.'

THE ANIMATED FILMS OF NORMAN MCLAREN: A SELECTION – NEIGHBOURS AND OTHERS

Neighbours (1952) is perhaps one of Norman McLaren's most famous pieces of animation wonderwork. We see a very neat and tidy garden into which arrive two 'cutout' suburban houses and also two men dressed very similarly and rather innocuously. They sit down in deck chairs to enjoy the sunshine and read their newspapers, emblazoned with headlines about war and peace. A little flower suddenly sprouts and the men find themselves first of all delighting in its beauty (even leaving the ground at one point) before finally fighting over whose property it is on. The film becomes genuinely horrific in its climax and nature is shown to endure over human folly.

If you thought vibrant screensavers were a relatively new thing you need to immerse yourself in the work and world of Norman McLaren for surely he will renew your delight in what films can be, what they can do, how they can transport you totally and re-imagine the world. A Cold War allegory and a significant step in the development of pixilation, the film – in my experience of screening it for students of film – has been that it never fails to amuse, startle, intrigue and finally unsettle. That's a lot of movie magic to pack into not even a ten-minute running time. To borrow an idea from the great André Bazin, McLaren's filmmaking very much puts its faith in film. Yet, like so many animators, he successfully gets to the 'heart and soul' of reality. As such, *Neighbours* is a powerfully clear example of how animation (and maybe all films are animated but let's not dwell on that) as a means of exploring explosive and difficult concerns and themes.

McLaren made fifty-nine variations on the idea of the animated film and his work reminds us that movies are about the spirit of movement and energy and he reminds us of how, in many ways, the role of dialogue in movies has been a loss to what moving pictures can express. McLaren has been dubbed 'the poet of animation'. More or less true as there are other such filmmakers equally deserving of the term. Certain McLaren movies were made without cameras. Instead, McLaren scratched shapes, forms and figures directly onto the film strip and projected that. Film was not necessarily about representing the world that we observe and have some kind of consensus about regarding its 'appearance' and workings.

McLaren's filmmaking, then, is arguably amongst the purest filmmaking available in that he shows us images, actions and sequences that can *only* exist because of the use of the filmmaking process. McLaren once said that 'Handmade cinema is like watching thought, if thought could be seen.' Beginning as an art college student at the Glasgow School of Fine Arts in 1932, McLaren soon recognised that his interests and abilities would be maximised in moving pictures. He began painting directly onto film not realising that elsewhere animator Len Lye was engaged in the same dynamic frontier busting.

In 1936, McLaren served as a camera operator in Spain during the civil war, an experience that inevitably left some kind of impression on him. In 1939, McLaren moved to Canada where John Grierson (who had offered McLaren a post at the GPO Film Unit in London in the mid-1930s) had become Canada's first Government Film Commissioner. McLaren became a member of the National Film Board and it was under the NFB's aegis that he produced his initial films, all of them designed to promote the war effort as titles such as *V for Victory* (1941) and *Keep Your Mouth Shut* (1944) indicate. McLaren's output was considerable. McLaren's work, I think, reminds you why you started falling in love with cinema in the first place.

Beyond the view of McLaren's left field sensibilities we can also bring to our attention to Frédéric Back's *The Man Who Planted Trees/L'Homme qui plantait des arbres* (1987) which so eloquently suggests the contrast between a man solitarily tending to his garden whilst the destruction of war thunders beyond his valley. The film is a call not only for attentiveness to nature but also attentiveness to peaceful work and living.

DISNEY AND THE WAR EFFORT

Throughout World War 2, the Walt Disney Studio played a major part in keeping morale high amongst moviegoers by providing a range of propaganda pieces. The first image I ever saw of the Disney characters making one of their many war effort contributions was a drawing showing Donald Duck wielding a fountain pen like a great mace, leading his studio buddies towards justice and an unseen enemy, under a stars and stripes streaked sky. Mickey manned (moused?) a tank and Dumbo circled in the air. This image was originally published in *Coronet* magazine in September 1942 and had been drawn by Hank Porter. Certainly, the Disney studio effort reinforces our sense of animation's capacity to get under the skin of a subject and connect.

Amidst its wartime comic books, insignia artwork for various military divisions (check out Hank Porter's various designs such as the one for the 127th Airborne Engineer Battalion) the Disney studio produced a number of inventively told short films, notably *Victory Through Airpower* and *Reason and Emotion* (both 1943). In *Victory Through Airpower* the studio adapted the book of the same name indicating how the American people could support the war effort through war bonds. "Keep your money fighting." In the film and trailer we hear the boldly spoken words "Only the medium of Walt Disney... only in a democracy could this film be made." Very clearly the film satisfies Truffaut's reservations about even the best war film title. In the film *All Together* (1942), the importance of war bonds to the American military effort is reinforced. Even Pinocchio and Gepetto get in on the act carrying a banner together.

Reason and Emotion is often seen as the real propaganda classic from the Disney studio. Tellingly it is not overtly focused on battlefields but instead on the conflict between, as the title says, reason and emotion. We are taken inside a toddler's head and see reason depicted as a meek little old lady and emotion as a childish 'cave man'. The contrast is immediate and the general idea of the film well presented. Reason is duly presented as the driving force of adulthood with emotion taking a backseat. The key moment, though, occurs when the average man is described as being taunted by fears and hearsay about the effects of war. Emotion and fear are presented as weak and the point is bluntly made that Hitler will prey on the weakness engendered by emotion and fear.

"I know that when Walt Disney decided to make the screen version of Major Alexander de Seversky's best selling and controversial book *Victory Through Air Power* he was motivated not by the promise of financial reward but by a sincere desire to place before our people a theory which he believed as firmly as the author. He knew that we are the most air-minded people in the world, because after all the aeroplane is an American creation...Nevertheless, he understood that too few were cognizant of the role that the air power must and will play in the wiping out of our enemies." [1]

With *Victory Through Airpower*, then, the Disney Studio had adapted the book with what Wanger calls 'simplicity, yet with such comprehensiveness that a nine year old can understand the whole outlook of the worldwide conflict'. (p.45 of Smoodin). Indeed ninety per cent of the studio's capacity was directed towards films for the armed services and American government.

In 1988, the Disney studio released *Who Framed Roger Rabbit?* The film was hugely popular and a sequel was considered that would have pitted Roger and his animated films against the forces of Nazism. The validity of this idea is borne out by the historical record: the Nazi party hated Mickey Mouse and the way he represented the mix of ethnicities and cultures that formed the modern United States of America. With this in mind, we are reminded again of how powerful the animated film, the silly cartoon, is in provoking. Let's hope that the holy fool that animation is often seen as continues to fight against the tyrannical and oppressive. There has never been anything more seriously minded than a thoughtfully considered and animated film.

Bibliography

1. *Disney Discourse – Producing the Magic Kingdom*, edited by Eric Smoodin, Routledge, NY, London, 1994. The quote is from an included essay in the anthology entitled 'Mickey Icarus, 1943: Fusing Ideas with the Art of the Animated Cartoon' by Walter Wanger, first published in *Saturday Review of Literature*, 4 September 1943, pp.18-19 and in Smoodin on pp.44-47.

GHOSTS OF WAR

SEAN HOGAN

"You have scooped the many diseased psyches out of the German gutter. You have infected millions with your twisted fantasies. What are you meeting in the granite corridors of this keep? Yourself?"

The Keep

"We must find a way to safeguard our town from the mad murdering zombies!"

Zombie Lake/Le Lac des morts vivants

Stories of war and the supernatural have always gone hand in hand, both in fact and fiction. Famous battlefields from Gettysburg to the Normandy beaches have provided fertile soil for the classic ghost story; sites supposedly haunted by the spirits of men cut down before their time, and consequently unable to find peace. Humanity's fear of death is never more apparent than when confronted with slaughter on such a massive scale. If we struggle to comprehend the senseless demise of a single person, then what of hundreds and thousands? And in the 20th century, where we saw war waged on a greater scale than ever before, it stood to reason that cinema, the primary story-telling medium of the age (and arguably the best equipped to visualise the full horror of warfare), would attempt to dramatise and rationalise these conflicts. Of course, the dominant approach of war cinema has been naturalism, or at least the illusion of it. Driven by a desire for historical fidelity and humanist empathy, films ranging from *All Quiet on the Western Front* (1930) through *Paths of Glory* (1950) to *Saving Private Ryan* (1998) have all prided themselves on their supposed realism (and in some instances been castigated for it). And whilst Stanley Kubrick's inherent distrust of authority and misanthropic leanings result in a very different film from Steven Spielberg's tidy and conventional jingoism, the mode of representation is similar. War is hell and we're going to splash it all over the screen in as much realistic detail as budgets can muster.

All well and good. But dating back to the very origins of the medium, there has been another approach to depicting warfare and its costs and consequences – a more symbolic, metaphorical approach. In *J'Accuse!* (1919), Abel Gance moves from a literal depiction of battle in the film's early stages to a full-on climactic shift into the supernatural, depicting legions of the dead returning to accuse the 'unfaithful wives, war profiteers, politicians and president'. Indeed, Gance's leap into poetic propaganda proved so resonant that he remade it in 1938 as a protest against the looming spectre of World War 2. Alas, as is so often the case with anti-war films, no one appeared to be listening.

Nevertheless, it's not difficult to trace a line from Gance's two films up through such later works as Bob Clark's *Dead of Night/Deathdream* (1974) to Joe Dante's *Homecoming* (2005). All employ the notion of the restless dead returning to protest their deaths in unjust wars, and despite the differences in approach (Gance's grand spectacle-with-a-conscience, Clark's cheap and cheerful grindhousing, Dante's slick TV satire), we are left in no doubt as to the seriousness of their intent. The image of tormented, monstrous Andy returning to his own grave at the climax of *Dead of Night* still says more than

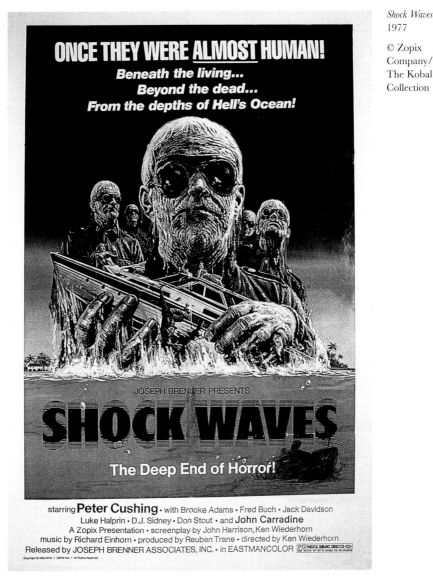

Tom Hanks carving the ham thickly sliced and imploring Matt Damon to 'earn it'. In the following essay, I shall attempt to look at how these films and others use the supernatural as a different means of engaging with the modern war film, whether it is for serious, metaphorical ends or simply as another twist on the exploitation formula. The marriage of cinema and World War 2 quickly proved to be a happy one. Both a visually spectacular widescreen spectacle and a 'just war' with clearly defined good and guys, World War 2 arrived as a ready-made Hollywood pitch. And judging by the amount of modern-day Oscar nominations garnered by such films as *Saving Private Ryan*, *The Thin Red Line* (1998) and *Letters from Iwo Jima* (2006), it hasn't lost any of its lustre. The story at the other end of the prestige spectrum has been a similar one. Supernaturally themed World War 2 works far outweigh the number of horror/exploitation movies made about any of the other major conflicts this century. But one doubts that the lure of critical

acclaim is the factor here. Rather, the popular glut of crypto-historic studies on Nazi occultism would seem to have provided the impetus for many of these films. Despite the questionable historical veracity of the majority of these accounts, their continued popularity was noted by B-movie producers everywhere, less interested in portraying an accurate account of Third Reich ideology than in selling the admittedly evocative pairing of the supernatural and Nazi iconography.

Given the predominantly low budget nature of these works, they often eschew any direct representation of the war itself in favour of adopting Abel Gance's notion of fallen soldiers rising from their battlefield graves to confront the living (usually after sufficient time has elapsed to preclude the need for any expensive period production design). The difference being that these unquiet spirits are not symbolic of a pacifist filmmaker's anguished conscience, but are merely the same old money-making B-movie monsters dressed up in crisp German uniforms. Ken Weiderhorn's *Shock Waves* (1979), in which a boatload of tourists stumble across a deserted Caribbean island inhabited by Nazi refugee Peter Cushing, provided something of an early template for the subgenre. It transpires that Cushing was the leader of a cadre of superhuman Nazi troops, genetically adapted to fight in any habitat or terrain. But because the test subjects had been recruited only from the most violent and sociopathic men available, they had proved impossible to control, and Cushing had finally ordered their vessel sunk off the coast of the island.

Needless to say, the waterlogged ghouls still lurk in the depths below, and after somehow raising their rusted ship to the surface, proceed to menace the assembled holidaymakers. Weiderhorn unaccountably missed a trick here. Instead of copying the then newly minted template for flesh-eating zombies, he is content to simply have his Nazi undead drown their victims, which, after you've watched a screaming victim get dunked for the second or third time, becomes slightly tiresome after a while. As does the film, which having exhausted its plot innovations in the first 20 minutes, has no other ideas other than to have its cast run around the jungle looking slightly worried for the rest of the running time. The occasional shots of the black-clad undead goose-stepping across the ocean floor are undeniably striking however, and one wonders whether it was these alone that led to a brief vogue for underwater Nazi zombie films. In which case Ken Weiderhorn has a lot to answer for.

Über-hack Jesus Franco apparently wrote the original screenplay for *Zombies Lake/Le Lac des morts vivants* (1980), but then bailed from the director's chair shortly before production was to begin, leaving his replacement Jean Rollin little or no time to prepare. Not that anything but a ritual burning could have saved Franco's laughable script from its own retarded incoherency. Towards the end of the war the local resistance ambushes a number of German troops and their bodies are dumped in a nearby lake. But as legend has it, the waters are cursed and only a blood sacrifice can protect the villagers from their malign influence. As a result, green-faced goons are soon bobbing to the surface and stumbling around the picturesque French countryside in search of nubile victims. Rollin's grasp of narrative pacing is undead to say the least and his guiding tenet seems to be to throw in as many naked ladies as possible in the hope that this will keep the audience awake.

And if his pacing is slipshod, Rollin's understanding of the space-time continuum is seemingly akin to that of a backward child. In a long, flabbily expository flashback sequence, we learn that one of the soldiers fathered a baby daughter with a local girl. In the main timeframe of the film, the daughter has now grown to 10 years old. But somehow, the rest of the world has shifted from 1945 to 1980. Perhaps it's something in the water; certainly none of the villagers seem to have aged a day since the war. As his undead comrades proceed to lay waste to the village, the until-now absent father returns from his watery grave to befriend the daughter he never knew, who somehow manages not to collapse in hysterical laughter every time her ineptly-greasepainted pop enters the room. Apparently the production could afford a set of German uniforms but not the zombie make-up to go with them.

There were possibly the seeds of an interesting film about the ghosts of Nazi occupation and collaboration, but Franco has never given much indication of being interested in narrative subtext, or indeed text. Nevertheless, he was obviously taken with the vast cinematic potential of Nazi zombies and returned to them in his next film, *Oasis of the Zombies / L'Abîme des morts vivants* (1981). The story involves a shipment of Nazi gold that is lost in the African desert when Allied forces ambush its German guards. (The resulting battle is so inept as to put the lie to the notion that Franco had any particularly constructive input into the battle scene of Orson Welles' *Chimes at Midnight* (1966), despite being credited with second unit work on the production.) Somehow, both sides are wiped out with the only survivor being a British officer who is then rescued by the local tribespeople. Years later, his son returns to the oasis in search of the gold, only to discover that it is jealously watched over by its Nazi guards, now a bunch of papier-mâché zombies (a favourite being a grinning decomposed head puppet on a stick; this being a Franco movie, said stick is often visible in shot). A lot of people are unconvincingly eaten whilst in pursuit of the buried gold, and ultimately, the officer's son has to settle for a few life lessons in lieu of a pile of loot. After escaping empty handed, he is asked what he found in the oasis. "I found myself," he replies portentously, thus demonstrating that Franco straining for significance is even more painful for the viewer than Franco going through his usual slack-jawed cinematic motions.

This trashy Eurohorror double-bill seemed to have done what its protagonists couldn't and laid the Nazi undead to rest. But in recent years, there have again been stirrings amongst Hitler's stirring dead. Steve Barker's *Outpost* (2008) revives the notion of undead SS supertroops and throws in a spot of quantum physics for good measure. A group of mercenaries are enlisted by a typically sinister and untrustworthy corporation to locate and secure a hidden bunker in an unnamed war-torn Eastern European country. What they find is a laboratory used by the Nazis for groundbreaking research into unified field theory, instrumental in the creation of a team of invincible zombie stormtroopers who can appear and disappear at will, oblivious to whatever physical barriers or booby-traps might stand in their way. Whilst the film never convinces you that the filmmakers have anything but the vaguest understanding of its supposed scientific underpinnings (one might question why a team of undead soldiers that can materialise at will can be forced into laying siege to the bunker from the *outside*), the muted, atmospheric production design and slow build of tension do at least make for diverting viewing, even if the narrative does finally fall apart in a mass of inconsistencies and general paucity of ideas. *Outpost* is to be followed by the Norwegian production *Dead Snow / Død snø* (2009), which looks to be an attempt to go one better than Jesus Franco and add some for once intentional comedy into the Nazi living dead remix.

Certain films attempted to do away with the decaying trappings of the Nazi undead subgenre and instead focused on a more spiritual form of evil. In Alvin Rakoff's *Death Ship* (1980), the titular vessel is a haunted Nazi freighter used during the war as a floating torture chamber. Now manned by the unseen ghosts of its crew, the rusted hulk continues to prowl the seas in search for new victims. Early on in the film it rams and sinks a pleasure cruiser, forcing the survivors to take refuge aboard the menacing black ship. Gradually, they all begin to lose their minds and perish in a series of unlikely supernatural accidents (a wiseass Jewish comedian is the first to go), the boiled sweets that cause a woman's flesh to putrefy being a highlight. Ultimately, the film becomes a replay of *The Shining* (1980) on the seven seas with reliable old ham George Kennedy standing in for Jack Nicholson and gradually becoming possessed by the ghosts of the Nazi crew. The script is nonsense and the direction crude, but *Death Ship* does achieve the occasional frisson, not least in the scene where one unfortunate is dragged down and drowned by the bloated corpses of the ship's previous victims. And the vessel herself is more of a character than any of the human beings aboard, with the desolate corridors, rusted decks and the shrieks and moans of the decaying engines doing a better job of building atmosphere than anything in the filmmaking itself.

Lucio Fulci found a different inspiration for his *The Ghosts of Sodom / Il Fantasma di Sodoma* (1988), the title seemingly being a reference to Pier Paolo Pasolini's fascist atrocity movie *Salò, or the 120 Days of Sodom / Salò o le 120 giornate di Sodoma* (1975). Similarly to the Pasolini film, *The Ghosts of Sodom* opens in an Italian villa where Nazis are enjoying a perverse orgy; however, their fun is soon cut short when they are bombed in a scene cobbled from old stock footage. Cut to the present day as a lost group of annoyingly garrulous tourist kids stumble across the abandoned villa and take refuge overnight. And not a lot proceeds to happen, at least for about two thirds of the film. Fulci, with his usual sure grasp of narrative timing, has the group stay there for three nights before anything remotely scary takes place. And even then most of the horrors revolve around a slightly camp Nazi leering from behind a mirror. One of the boys dies by falling down a couple of steps and banging his head; his corpse then decays at an advanced rate for no good reason. Ultimately, the kids manage to break the spell and wake up amongst the rubble of the now-ruined villa, and given that the aforementioned fall victim has been magically restored to the ranks of the living, one can only deduce that the preceding film was ALL A DREAM. When Mario Bava attempted a similar twist in *Lisa and the Devil / Lisa e il diavolo* (1973), his sure handling of the film means the effect is authentically dreamlike; when Fulci does it, it's merely dunce-like. By this point in his career Fulci was a washed-up journeyman, with even the dubious salad days of *Zombie Flesh Eaters / Zombi 2* (1979) and *The Beyond / E tu vivrai nel terrore – L'aldilà* (1981) far behind him. Often overrated by genre fans because of the sheer vulgar gore and gusto of some of his earlier works, *The Ghosts of Sodom* lacks even those incidental pleasures and is simply indefensible rubbish.

Of course, the subject of Nazi occultism has provided the fuel for more than just a glut of marginal B-movies. Before he decided that war was a Serious Business and not to be trivialised, Steven Spielberg was quite happy to use comic book Nazis and their occult dabblings as the antagonists of *Raiders of the Lost Ark* (1981) and *Indiana Jones and the Last Crusade* (1989). In truth, these films have little more substance than *Oasis of the Zombies*, but the snappy scripts, winning performances and directorial verve (more so in the case of *Raiders of the Lost Ark* than the slapdash later sequel) mean that they'll no doubt be remembered after the likes of Jesus Franco have deservedly been forgotten. Guillermo del Toro's *Hellboy* (2004) follows a similar tack in its Lovecraftian mash up of Nazis and demons, but as entertaining as the film is, del Toro used the fantasy/horror genre to comment on warfare with much greater effect in his Spanish language productions *The Devil's Backbone/El Espinazo del diablo* (2001) and *Pan's Labyrinth/El Laberinto del fauno* (2006), and it is to those works that I shall return later in this essay.

The flawed masterpiece of the Nazi occult genre is doubtlessly Michael Mann's *The Keep* (1983). Typically, the supernatural threat here is not Nazi in origin; instead Mann uses an ancient, metaphysical evil to undermine and destroy the Hitlerian myth of German supremacy. A garrison of German soldiers occupy an ancient keep in the Romanian mountains, only to unsuspectingly unleash a malignant force far more powerful than themselves. Allegedly cut down from a three-hour running time, the release version of *The Keep* makes little sense (much like David Lynch's *Dune* (1984), it helps to have read the source novel) and suffers from dated, unfinished special effects and poor casting, but nevertheless exerts an atmospheric power. The wordless opening depicting the Nazis' arrival at the keep is still one of Mann's finest directorial set pieces. And the visual design of the film is masterful, the monochrome greys and blacks of the Nazi uniforms and granite walls serving to create a stark unrelenting gloom that says more about Nazi ideology than many more conventional war movies ever do. Mann, unhappy with the studio release version, has supposedly blocked its release on DVD, but imperfect as it is, *The Keep* deserves to be seen.

The Keep
1983

© Paramount/
The Kobal
Collection

Only nominally supernatural, Rob Green's briskly efficient *The Bunker* (2001) is nevertheless the best of the recent mini-spate of British war/horror films. Although hauntings in the film may ultimately be purely psychological, it differs from other works covered here in that it uses Nazi spectres to torment other German soldiers. A small group of troops are in retreat from invading Allied forces in 1944. Low on morale and ammunition, they take refuge in a small bunker manned by an old man and a teenager. Convinced they are surrounded by American soldiers and torn apart by infighting, the German unit implodes. Desperate to find a way out, they attempt to explore the tunnels beneath the bunker only to find something may already be lurking in the depths. The film does not really attempt to answer whether the soldiers are actually being haunted or merely tormented by the memory of past atrocities (and does perhaps err on the side of fudging the issue somewhat), but it's an impressive, albeit low-key work with some creditable directorial flourishes.

David Twohy's *Below* (2002) covers similar territory to *The Bunker*, but from an Allied perspective. A US submarine picks up the last three survivors from a sunken hospital ship, only to find its mission endangered by a pursuing German vessel and a spate of bizarre onboard events. And once again, the consequences of past crimes begin to threaten the sanity and safety of the crewmembers. Much like *The Bunker*, Twohy's film attempts to play it both ways in terms of its supernatural events, which can again be read as merely being the product of guilty consciences; however *Below* is ultimately rather better at evoking the claustrophobic terror of life at war on a submarine than it is at outright genre horror. But Twohy's fluid direction and the immersive technical detail do at least suggest that the film deserves more attention than it received on its brief initial release.

"It's war!" "What's war?" "I don't know."

J'Accuse!

Gance's original *J'Accuse!* remains one of the few supernaturally-themed World War 2 movies. Whether for reasons of budget or because Nazi iconography has proven more attractive to genre filmmakers, the conflict has generally been overlooked within the field. Edgar G. Ulmer's *The Black Cat* (1934) used the war as the crux of the enmity between the two antagonists, but despite the film's morbid air of satanic gloom, it never truly veers into the supernatural. However, in 2002, Michael J. Bassett took his cameras into the World War 1 trenches for the messily allegorical *Deathwatch*. Unfortunately, whilst the film's evocation of the muck and filth endured by the combatants is impressive, the script proves far less so. Seemingly a riff on *Jacob's Ladder* (1990), the narrative concerns a group of soldiers whom, after going 'over the top', are lost in a foggy wasteland and take refuge in a near-deserted German trench.

The few enemy survivors they find appear terrified of some nameless evil, but the language barrier precludes any further understanding of what the threat might be, and one by one the men die. Whilst the film gleefully lingers on scenes of men being torn apart by computer-generated barbed wire, it perhaps says a lot that the most horrific moment comes when a crippled soldier discovers that his legs have been devoured by rats whilst he slept. The ill-thought-out narrative construction hobbles the proceedings from the get-go. It's obvious as soon as the soldiers find themselves lost in the fog that they are clearly meant to have perished in battle, so the film quickly becomes a wearying slog through the afterlife as we attempt to discern why the men are being tormented. Perhaps aware that he has revealed his hand too early, Bassett tries to obscure the issue as much as possible; the group never really seem to realise their situation, and wind up in purgatorial underground limbo whilst sole escapee Jamie Bell makes his way out of the trench into the usual brightly-lit heaven lying somewhere beyond the frame line.

Quite why some of the men deserve to stay behind and suffer is unclear; certainly Bell's character is set up as a coward at the beginning of the film, and his final redemption ultimately seems largely unearned. Add to this a woefully ham-fisted final punch line, and what you have is a film far more memorable for its marvellously detailed production design than for any of its second hand ideas.

"I'd only been in jail thirteen hours.
I thought 'Nam couldn't be any worse."
"Shows how little you knew."

Jacob's Ladder

"Nobody wants to read about the goddamn Vietnam
War anymore. They wanna read a good horror story!"

House

In stark contrast to the cut and dried heroics of World War 2, the Vietnam conflict understandably made Hollywood very nervous. An unpopular war, it was not originally considered the stuff hits were made of. John Wayne's early attempt to transplant the jingoistic World War 2 movie template to the Far East, *The Green Berets* (1968), made money on the back of the Duke's star power, but was widely considered an embarrassment even then. In time, *The Deer Hunter* (1978), *Coming Home* (1978) and *Apocalypse Now* (1979) would point the way towards Oscars and sizeable box-office, but originally it was left to a small independent horror movie to attempt an intelligent treatment of the Vietnam War and its consequences. Bob Clark's aforementioned *Dead of Night* takes the same unhappy couple (John Marley, Lynn Carlin) that John Cassavetes previously located at the heart of dysfunctional American domesticity in *Faces* (1968), and uses them in an expanded reworking of W. W. Jacobs' *The Monkey's Paw*.

Patrolling a Vietnam jungle that would appear to be located somewhere in rural America, US soldier Andy is gunned down in a pre-credit sequence that makes up in intensity for what it lacks in geographical verisimilitude. The gloomy visuals and incessant dying screams on the soundtrack make it clear from the outset that this is to be no flag-waving exercise. When his parents are subsequently informed of their son's death, the stricken Carlin tearfully wishes him home. And as in the Jacobs story, the parents are soon surprised by a late night visitor – their seemingly resurrected son. However, the difference here is that they open the door and welcome him with open arms, assuming the reports of his death were greatly exaggerated. After all, Andy certainly looks normal, if a little withdrawn. But his return soon opens fault lines in the family unit. Carlin becomes overprotective of the son she thought she had lost, whilst Marley begins to resent and fear Andy's strange behaviour and lash out at what he believes to be his wife's attempts to turn their offspring into a mama's boy. He begins to drink heavily, causing further domestic divisions; Andy has brought the ravages of the war back home. Needless to say, the young vet is soon revealed as an undead monster, one who must feed on human blood to survive. However, the film eschews any gothic vampire trappings and rather than a set of fangs, Andy relies on a syringe and tubing to shoot up his regular fix of plasma. The parallel here with the real life drug problems suffered by many actual veterans is too obvious to ignore.

*Dead of Night/
Deathdream*
1974

© Impact
Films/
The Kobal
Collection

IT WRINGS THE VICTIMS OUT..
AND HANGS THEM UP TO DIE!!!

DEATHDREAM

STARRING:
JOHN MARLEY • LYNN CARLIN WITH: RICHARD BACKUS • HENDERSON FORSYTH
Screenplay Written by: ALAN ORMSBY Music by: CARL ZITTRER Executive Producers: JOHN TRENT & PETER JAMES
Produced and Directed by: BOB CLARK

A QUADRANT IMPACT FILM   **PG** PARENTAL GUIDANCE SUGGESTED Some material may not be suitable for pre-teenagers   Color by: TECHNICOLOR
An ENTERTAINMENT INTERNATIONAL PICTURES RELEASE   DEATHDREAM-76/19S

Interestingly, Clark avoids any actual mention of Vietnam (the location of the war is only ever referred to as 'over there'). Whether this was due to skittishness on the part of the producers or simply an attempt at universality is unclear. Regardless, the film wears its intentions on its sleeve, a point driven home by the contrast drawn between the sullen Andy and a family friend, a cheerful World War 2 vet who expounds at length on his experiences in what he clearly regards as a just war. Finally forced to accept their part in what Andy has become, Marley shoots himself and Carlin escapes with her rapidly decaying son to the local cemetery, where she tearfully helps Andy return to his grave. There is to be no climactic catharsis here; despite its rough edges, *Dead of Night* is an admirable, albeit grim and depressing work, entirely in tune with the mood of its time. Clark's film was probably too bitter a pill for most drive-in audiences to swallow, and whilst many independent horror films of the 1970s deal with the psychic fallout from Vietnam in one way or another, it wasn't until the Reagan Eighties that the genre attempted to deal directly with the conflict, however superficial. The rubbery ghouls inhabiting Steve Miner's *House* (1986) turn out to be part of a plot marshalled by William Katt's undead army buddy, looking for payback after Katt abandoned him to the Vietcong years before. But the Vietnam back story is the MacGuffin driving this blandly nonsensical potpourri of comedy horror, and the wartime flashbacks to a brightly-lit plastic jungle are possibly the most unconvincing aspect on display, which is saying something. The freeze-frame happy ending is entirely symptomatic of the film, which, true to its time, fits snugly into the pandering niche occupied by other mid-Eighties triumphant Vietnam fantasias such as *Missing in Action* (1984) and *Rambo: First Blood Part II* (1985). No guts, no glory.

It was not until *Jacob's Ladder* (1990) that a genre film dealt with the Vietnam War on such a level of seriousness as *Dead of Night*. Long regarded as one of Hollywood's best unproduced scripts, the success of *Ghost* (1990) finally gave screenwriter Bruce Joel Rubin the clout to get his pet project made. And whilst he was perceived to be less than ideal, director Adrian Lyne put aside his usual preference for peddling softly-perverse pap and delivered a gritty, frightening study of the twin horrors of war and mind. An opening sequence finds Tim Robbins' Vietnam platoon attacked from both within and without. Shelled by attacking VC, the men are felled by uncontrollable seizures. Robbins flees into the jungle only to be knifed by an unseen assailant. He then awakes on a New York subway train, apparently some years removed from the conflict. Shaken by his nightmare, he soon witnesses the first of a series of demonic visions or hallucinations; people with tails and horns, screaming faces gazing at him through windows. Tormented by flashbacks to the jungle in his dreams and continued glimpses of various creatures and apparitions in his waking life, Robbins questions his sanity. Determined to get to the root of his visions, he discovers a plot by the US military to dose soldiers with an experimental drug called 'The Ladder', designed to increase aggression. Apparently Robbins' unit had been given a small dose whilst in country, but instead of stoking their desire to fight the enemy, he and his comrades had turned on each other. (This plot element is supposedly based on real-life events; a caption at the end of the film states that the US military allegedly experimented on troops with a hallucinogen codenamed BZ, although this was denied by the Pentagon.) The narrative continues to slip between different levels of reality, until we finally learn that Robbins never made it out of Vietnam, that his devilish tormentors are merely embodiments of his vain struggle to resist death, and that his entire subsequent life in New York was nothing but a dying dream experienced on the operating table à la Ambrose Bierce's story *An Occurrence at Owl Creek Bridge*. (Where this leaves the plot assertions about military drug testing is ambiguous.)

However vague the film's ultimate intentions, it nevertheless manages to both raise questions about US military policy in Vietnam and build a sympathetic portrait of the veterans' lot. Although flawed slightly by a somewhat clumsy and conventional visual rendering of the final narrative revelation (not helped by a cameo from insufferable Hollywood moppet Macaulay Culkin) *Jacob's Ladder* remains an engrossing, visceral work, anchored by Robbins' strong performance and some striking direction and design. The various demonic assailants deserve special mention; apparently inspired by the work of Francis Bacon, they are disturbingly fleshy and organic, and light years away from the usual latex monsters found in much genre fare.

Another look at Vietnam came in the South Korean *R-Point* (2004). Su-Chang Kong's film follows a group of troops sent into the field in search of a missing platoon. Upon arrival in the eponymous region, they are confronted with the usual legends of cursed burial grounds and whatnot, and the lines between reality and madness soon begin to blur. Aided immeasurably by the high degree of visual ability commonly found in Korean cinema and actual location shooting in Cambodia and Vietnam, *R-Point* holds few surprises, but is for most of its running time an atmospheric and effective yarn with a handful of standout shocks. It does degenerate into the usual Asian horror clichés by the end, unfortunately; the spirits of *R-Point* being personified by none other than the typical longhaired ghost girl in a white dress. And the director's assertion that he intended it as an anti-war parable is all hot air – the film's only real subtext being a warning not to mess with countries and cultures you do not understand, not by any means an atypical message for a horror movie.

"You're getting older, and you'll see that life isn't like your fairy tales. The world is a cruel place. And you'll learn that, even if it hurts."
Pan's Labyrinth

Guillermo del Toro's diptych of Spanish Civil War narratives, the aforementioned *The Devil's Backbone* and *Pan's Labyrinth*, arguably represent the pinnacle of what has been achieved by the small number of films that have attempted to fuse the fantasy/horror genres with that of the war movie. The two works, closely linked in their structural and thematic approaches, both look at the effect of warfare on children and the families around them (adoptive or otherwise). By doing so, go full circle to *J'accuse!* by demonstrating the haunting poetry that can be achieved by using the supernatural as a means to examine that all too natural state of human affairs, warfare.

The Devil's Backbone tells the story of a young orphan boy, abandoned in a rural orphanage during the Spanish Civil War. Despite being short of money and supplies, the heads of the facility welcome him into what seems to be a relatively happy community. However, we soon learn of the various tensions and secrets concealed within the building's walls. The leftist heads of the orphanage are concealing gold for the local Republican forces, yet are clearly expecting the Fascists to triumph and fearing the consequences (one subtly elegant sequence shows them removing all Republican symbols from the walls and replacing them with Catholic ornamentation in unspoken anticipation of a Franco victory). The proto-fascist handyman, a former pupil of the orphanage, has discovered the secret of the gold and is busily plotting to make off with it, all the while continuing to sleep with the middle-aged headmistress. The unquiet spirit of a small boy roams the corridors at night, eager for someone to solve the mystery of his disappearance. And a clearly symbolic unexploded bomb sits half-buried in the building's courtyard, taunting us as to whether it or one of the above sub-plots will detonate first.

Both a political parable and a look at the fall of innocence, del Toro's film seamlessly melds a naturalistic look at life under the spectre of Franco with a poetic evocation of a world where death is everywhere and unhappy ghosts are a fact of life. Whilst clearly not of the right, del Toro manages to hint at the schisms and weaknesses of the left during that era; the elderly teacher, too frail to fight, and unable to declare his love for the headmistress due to his impotence; the headmistress herself, crippled by the loss of a leg, strongly supportive of the Republican resistance but yet still driven to share her bed with the brutish Franco-sympathising handyman. Meanwhile the supernatural sequences are some of the finest in the cinema; the skilful cinematography, sound design and deft yet sparing use of CGI combining to summon up a time and place where childhood terrors prove to be all too real. And whilst the film's mysteries are eventually solved, the director offers no easy answers. Fleeing back to independent foreign-language cinema after the fights and compromises of his previous Hollywood film *Mimic* (1997), del Toro had the freedom to show how war not only brutalises, corrupts and destroys those who fight in it, but also those who should offer hope for the future: the children. Certainly the sequence in which a large explosion kills or maims several of the orphans would be practically unthinkable in a mainstream US movie. The tragic climax leaves the orphanage in ruins and all of the adults dead, the children left alone to make their way in an uncaring world. Their subsequent journey into adulthood then involves them turning on their tormentor, the handyman, and violently attacking him with sharpened sticks, the primitive weapons marking their induction into the ways of killing. The lessons of war have been passed on and learned.

In a pointed in-joke, del Toro was then to show the two main boys from *The Devil's Backbone* dying in battle with the triumphant fascist forces in its 2006 companion film, *Pan's Labyrinth*. Whilst *The Devil's Backbone* had certainly enjoyed its fair share of acclaim and represented a much-needed liberation for del Toro after his trials in Hollywood, perhaps somewhat ghettoised by its supernatural themes it never really crossed over in terms of box-office success. *Pan's Labyrinth* was to prove a very different story; critically adored and financially successful, the film even won over mainstream US audiences, a notoriously hard market for subtitled films to crack. It went on to be nominated for six Oscars, winning three. And yet the two films are intentionally similar, two variations on the same theme.

Set just after the end of the civil war, *Pan's Labyrinth* also tells the story of a young child's entry into an adoptive home. But whilst *The Devil's Backbone*'s hero eventually found acceptance in his, Ofelia, *Pan's Labyrinth*'s heroine, finds only fear, torment and death. Fearful of her ability to bring up a child alone in Franco's Spain, Ofelia's widowed mother marries a Fascist army captain and soon falls pregnant. Ofelia and her mother then move to the captain's estate in the country, but the girl soon finds that her bullying stepfather is only interested in his unborn child, which he declares will be a son and ergo his rightful heir. Her mother, enduring a difficult pregnancy, becomes increasingly ill and takes to her bed. Too sick to defend her daughter from her new husband's callousness and largely unwilling to rock the boat, she begins to abandon Ofelia to her own devices. The lonely child begins to seek refuge in an ancient labyrinth located on the grounds of the estate, and quickly falls into a fantasy world as a refuge from the coldness and cruelty around her.

Whilst *The Devil's Backbone* employs the language of the horror film, *Pan's Labyrinth* is nominally a fantasy, structured as a fairy tale. The characters are more archetypal, the narrative built around a series of quests that Ofelia must complete to gain entry into the fantasy realm and regain her rightful heritage. Del Toro's scheme here is to leave it open as to whether Ofelia's other world is real or simply an imaginative construct, but regardless of one how chooses to read it (the director has stated that he had a specific interpretation in mind, but is happy for the film to be understood either way), what is clear is that the two realms increasingly begin to parallel and comment on each other. (For instance, close inspection shows that the different colour schemes used in the initial design of the separate worlds eventually start to merge together, before then swapping places entirely.) In essence, the film uses its supernatural metaphors to shed some light on the brutal word of post-civil war Spain. Ofelia's fascist stepfather is as much a monster as the terrifying Pale Man she meets on the second of her quests (who, as a symbol of repressive authority, is tellingly shown to feast on children), and it is by overcoming the creatures in the faerie realm that she ultimately gains the strength to face down the monstrous captain. Whilst nominally more of an overt tragedy than *The Devil's Backbone*, *Pan's Labyrinth* does move beyond that film's despairing look at the impotence of the Left and how violence is passed from generation to generation; the Republican rebels here at least gain a small victory at the end, and when they tell the doomed captain that his son will never know anything of him, the implication is of a hopeful future at least. Of course, Ofelia dies in the course of her final quest, but the fantastical climax of the film still allows that sacrifice to be read as a triumph, whether only as a vision of her dying imagination or otherwise.

Pan's Labyrinth is ultimately a lament for the death of fantasy and the imagination. Del Toro demonstrates in the film how much we lose when we put aside so-called childish fantasies in favour of cold, hard *realpolitik*. The narrative message seems to be that we have much to learn from children, not the other way around, and indeed, the few characters that survive to the end of the film are the ones least dismissive of Ofelia's visions. Possibly there is a message for the war movie here too: that there is another means of looking at and portraying these events, beyond simple po-faced flag-waving or anti-war sloganeering; a more poetic, metaphorical approach. In these two small masterpieces, del Toro has shown the way. And another way of looking at warfare and its consequences may be just what is needed right now, especially given the recent failure of so many Iraq-themed war movies. Certainly one of the most successful looks at the current middle-eastern conflict has been Joe Dante's aforementioned TV production *Homecoming*, which portrays the Iraq war dead rising from their graves to vote against the corrupt political administration that sent them into battle. *Homecoming* often paints in too broad strokes and is somewhat shrill, but its vision of dead US troops clambering out of their flag-covered coffins is certainly one of the more startling war-related images I've seen onscreen recently (especially given the Bush administration's well-publicised refusal to let TV news broadcast any real-life images of said coffins being shipped back to the US). So perhaps the tradition of Abel Gance is indeed alive and well in the hands of auteurs like del Toro and Dante. It will be interesting to see who else follows in their footsteps.

LIGHTS, CAMERA, INCOMING!

How YouTube Rewrote the War Movie

JAMIE RUSSELL

"This ain't the fucking movies over here."

Michael Herr, Dispatches

CLICK PLAY. The street is dusty, heat-baked and full of crumbling buildings. Bricks are sandwiched together with an excess of mortar. Everything looks brittle, ready to crack. Outside an unfinished house – no windows, just empty holes – a group of US Marines huddle together. There's an explosion, then gunfire. In the fog of war, chaos reigns: "Over there on the left!"; "The house is surrounded"; "Where'd it hit me? It got me in my face"; "Is there still someone up there?"; "The fucking room is booby trapped!"

CUT TO: the building's roof. Three Marines in dusty body armour poke their M16s into the gaping mouth of a collapsed stairwell. They're all tense. "I don't know what the fuck he's doing. I can't see. I don't like this," complains one. "He's gone," says another. "He was fucking laying right there and he's not there no more. I shot him like five times." They edge down the stairwell in single file then retreat in a blind panic as someone in the darkness fires at them with a handgun. "Motherfucker's got a fortified bunker in there!" From deep inside the building comes the chilling sound of voices chanting 'Allahu Akbar'.

With their position on the roof compromised, the Marines decide to clear out the building. They edge down the stairs again. This time there's no resistance. Has the enemy gone? Or are they hiding somewhere deeper inside? The Marines creep forwards, weapons sweeping in a nervous arc, left to right. It's a nail-biting scene worthy of any war movie, perhaps even a horror film. Except this is a real, life or death moment. Spooked, the grunts open fire into empty rooms. The enemy has vanished, holed up somewhere inside.

Back outside with their squad, the Marines unleash their full arsenal on the building from a safe distance. As the bullets turn masonry into dust, a lone dog wanders through the hail of lead. The building vanishes in a plume of smoke. When the dust settles, the Marines head back inside and discover two corpses half-buried in the rubble. The screen fades to black. SHARE. REPLAY.

THE YOUTUBE WAR

The clip you have been watching is *Close Combat in Iraq*, a five-minute short uploaded to YouTube and shot by one of the Marines in the squad. In a year on the site this 'grunt video' has been watched more than 621,000 times and has attracted 2,618 user comments. The responses range from the banal ('Fuckin Intense'), to the offensive ('Haha! Wasted those mujji assholes!') and the ironic ('I played this map on BF2 [military videogame *Battlefront 2*]. It's really cool. These guys are good though.'). *Close Combat in Iraq* has also stirred pro- and anti-war sentiment as well as spirited discussions among viewers about the Marines' alleged lack of professionalism. It has also, somewhat predictably, caused lengthy arguments about the fate of the dog. [1]

Every war intersects with the media in different ways. American civilians in World War 2 experienced the frontline vicariously through newsreel footage and propaganda films. Vietnam was the first 'living room war' with television reports broadcasting pictures of soldiers getting shot to bits in South East Asian rice paddies back into American homes. Meanwhile, the Gulf War was – according to French philosopher Jean

Baudrillard's provocative claim – 'the war that did not take place' since it was pre-packaged for an audience of passive viewers as a mass media spectacle. [2] In contrast, many commentators have described the Iraq War as the first 'YouTube War'. [3]

Unlike previous wars with their embedded reporters and censored letters home, the Iraq War is the first to be recorded independently by the soldiers fighting it. The amateur filmmakers are the grunts on the ground in places like Falluja and Tikrit who are manning the checkpoints, doing the house-to-house searches and dodging the IEDs. A US Marine's best friend may still be his rifle but it now has competition from his helmet cam, laptop and broadband Internet connection. Being able to shoot a camera as well as a gun is now a valued skill – being able to do both at once doubly so.

It's not only soldiers. This is a war in which everyone, no matter what side they're on or whether they're combatants or civilians, seems determined to document their involvement: US prison guards take snapshots of abuse at Abu Ghraib; insurgent videos show trophy footage of attacks on US forces. Even Iraqi civilians have picked up cameras, mocking the occupying forces by teaching soldiers on patrol bad Arabic and then uploading the resulting hilarity online. Meanwhile, in the US, anti-war protesters have taken to posting impassioned video diatribes on YouTube. We're all filmmakers now.

Such a seismic shift in the way war is both fought and reported raises thorny issues for the military and conventional news media. Yet it also begs serious questions of professional filmmakers too. In a conflict where everyone is making movies, what role is left for the traditional war movie? It seems no small irony that the popularity of grunt videos on YouTube is in direct contrast with the apparent antipathy towards mainstream movies about the Iraq War. In an era when combatants themselves are becoming soldier/filmmakers are we seeing a new kind of battlefield authenticity on our screens, or just a different kind of propaganda?

SHOOT TO KILL

Search YouTube for dispatches from the frontline and you quickly realise that grunt videos shot by US troops don't conform to any one genre. There are comedy goof-offs in which participants engage in *Jackass*-style stunts like overturning a 'port-a-potty' containing an unsuspecting comrade or throwing flashbang grenades into a flock of sheep. There are also sombre tribute videos for fallen comrades and aggressive 'we're gonna fuck you up' showreels cut to speed metal tracks in which troops display their firepower and play tough for the camera. [5] The visual influences for these clips are various: gonzo skater/surfer movies; MTV music videos; *Jackass* and *America's Funniest Home Videos*; and Vietnam War movies.

Such clips offer an uncensored view of the Iraq War that obviously appeals to both the filmmakers themselves and their audience (both military and civilian). 'I was there' is the function of all war stories and these videos are often seized on as a kind of authentic, unquestionable truth of the fighting man's experience in Iraq and Afghanistan. For instance, *Iraq Uploaded*, one of the first offline responses to the phenomenon, premiered on MTV in 2006; the programme was billed as 'The War Network TV Won't Show You, Shot By Soldiers and Posted Online'. The implication is that these videos present us with a window onto reality that the mainstream media – whether network news or Hollywood movies – can't match.

For the Pentagon, the issue of grunt videos is a serious one. Vietnam proved that images from the frontline can sway public opinion about a war. Today's Internet culture makes that danger even more extreme and the widespread use of recording equipment by troops is obviously ripe for producing compromising situations in which photographic and or video evidence of brutality, atrocities and war crimes come to public attention. In fact it's the lure of seeing such acts that draws many viewers to YouTube and similar websites in the first place, in an attempt to gain access to material denied by the circumspection of a mainstream media that has already been coy about showing images such as the coffins of dead soldiers.

Some of the titles of the grunt videos themselves seem to explicitly encourage this voyeuristic desire. One clip, for example, is called *OMG [Oh My God] US Troops Killing Kids!!!!* It actually turns out to be harmless footage of soldiers dancing in the street of an Iraqi village and entertaining a group of clapping children (the title is a bad pun: they're killing the kids with laughter). [6] Other videos, though, live up to their names. In *British Troops Beating Young Iraqis on Camera* we see graphic footage of British troops assaulting Iraqi kids captured during a riot. In long shot we see the teenagers begging for mercy as they're hit with riot sticks. [7] Meanwhile the off-screen camera operator mocks their cries and shouts encouragement to his comrades. Some videos are more explicit, showing the apparent killing of alleged insurgents. They could be described as a kind of online snuff; the Internet era's answer to ageing video nasty *Faces of Death* (1978). [8] Conversely, insurgent videos show IED attacks on coalition forces and jihadists killing hostages like the now infamous clip of British contractor Ken Bigley's beheading. [9]

The politics of war and the politics of representation go hand in glove. Perhaps in recognition of this the Department of Defense blocked serving troops from accessing YouTube and social networking sites on DoD networks in May 2007. It claimed there were bandwidth and security issues. [10] Two months earlier it had launched its own YouTube channel, Multi-National Force-Iraq, giving 'viewers around the world a "boots on the ground" perspective of Operation Iraqi Freedom from those who are fighting it'. [11] One of the obvious aims of the channel was to give the US military a video presence online and so counter Al-Qaeda's use of the Internet to distribute martyrdom and jihad videos. A new front in the war had opened into cyberspace.

While jihad videos are frequently touted in the West as Al-Qaeda propaganda, grunt videos are rarely approached with such scepticism. Instead they have become part of a larger, pro-troop narrative that argues that the only people who have access to the truth about the war are those soldiers on the ground. With the spectre of Vietnam hanging over Iraq – a war in which returning veterans felt their experience had been woefully misunderstood by civilians – these grunt videos have taken on a hallowed sanctity for a nation obsessed with supporting the troops. However, what these videos don't show is often more intriguing than what they do. Where are the images of US soldiers being killed in action? Where is the footage of friendly fire incidents? Where are images of the thousands of Iraqi civilians killed since the invasion?

YouTube's community guidelines explicitly warn users that 'Graphic or gratuitous violence is not allowed. If your video shows someone getting hurt, attacked, or humiliated, don't post it. YouTube is not a shock site. Don't post gross-out videos of accidents, dead bodies and similar things.' [12] However, it's obvious that a double standard exists. One can easily find videos showing dead insurgents (like those at the end of *Close Combat*), blooper reels of suicide bombers blowing themselves up accidentally or graphic camera phone footage of Saddam Hussein's execution. Likewise there are numerous clips shot in sickly green night-vision that show enemy combatants being cut down by US gunships. The implication is that YouTube snuff is permissible as long as it's patriotic snuff.

Simultaneously, instead of widening debate about the politics behind the war, the uncritical, narrow focus on the soldiers on the ground in videos like *Close Combat in Iraq* refuses to acknowledge that there is a bigger picture beyond the frame. Shorn of context – What regiment are we watching? Where are they? Who's filming? – these videos encourage the viewer's disengagement from the larger debate surrounding the war itself. Simple sentiment or patriotic/militaristic bombast frequently wins out over insightful critique. [13]

THE MOVIES GO TO WAR

Since 9/11 and the subsequent occupation of Iraq in 2003, there has been no shortage of attempts to harness the War on Terror for the purposes of multiplex entertainment. 2007 was a bumper year with movies like *Lions For Lambs*, *In The Valley of Elah*, *Rendition* and even *The Kingdom* (a popcorn-friendly post-9/11 action movie about FBI agents investigating a terrorist attack in Saudi Arabia) tackling the subject. These films shared one common denominator: they all bombed like Bin Laden at the US box office. Received wisdom now suggests that American audiences are not interested in watching movies about a war that's been so divisive.

Stop-Loss
2008

© MTV Films/
The Kobal
Collection

What's interesting about the current cycle of Iraq War films, though, is how redundant so many of them seem in the wake of YouTube's archive of grunt videos. The sight of Tom Cruise, Meryl Streep and Robert Redford arguing for and against the War on Terror in *Lions For Lambs* seems a million miles removed from the gritty, shaky-cam vérité found online. Indeed, there's something fitting about the fact that Hollywood's only major A-list outing about the war keeps its major stars safely ensconced in Washington D.C. arguing over US foreign policy while the bullets fly elsewhere.

That doesn't mean that American filmmakers haven't tried to rise to the challenge that the current conflict represents. Significantly, several directors of both fiction and documentary films have attempted to appropriate the visual immediacy of these grunt videos, clearly recognising that the YouTube War requires a new aesthetic response from traditional cinema. Deborah Scranton's documentary *The War Tapes* (2006) was one of the first films to demonstrate this new awareness as it turned the conventions of 'embedded' war reporting on their head. Given the opportunity to accompany members of the New Hampshire National Guard to Iraq, Scranton decided to stay at home and instead issue the soldiers themselves with Sony MiniDV cameras. The agreement was that the troops would record their experiences in country while Scranton interviewed their families back home and edited the resulting material into a documentary.

The end result not only suggests the impact that the rise of the soldier/filmmaker is likely to have on the war documentary genre (something beyond the scope of this essay), it also highlights the way in which the culture of reality television is intruding onto the modern battlefield. The soldiers who fight and film aren't simply interested in videotaping what happens on the ground. Rather, the war becomes a personal journey of self-discovery for each of these grunt filmmakers and their responses to events become more important than their recording of them. When an Iraqi civilian is accidentally run over by a US Humvee, the focus is less on what happened or the fallout that follows and more on how the soldier who witnessed it feels. Even the wives at home are co-opted into becoming props for their husbands' self-absorption. "Mike needed to do this," says one. "If I'd held him back he would have been bitter towards me." The war is presented less as an invasion and occupation of a foreign country than as an arena for a very contemporary kind of self-expression framed through video diary confessionals.

In *The War Tapes*, the soldiers' videos become an important way of getting those back home to identify with the troops who are fighting. Families unite to watch the videos in an attempt to understand what their fathers, brothers and sons have been through. One soldier complains about how his friends ask to see his photos from Iraq then switch off halfway through, bored by a war that is so distant to them. As one of the soldiers argues, the videos offer civilians a way of appreciating 'what he must have seen, what he must have done to earn [the combat veteran] badge'. Along the way, solipsism eradicates any pretence of political, historical or military analysis.

Looking over what he calls the 'grunt documentaries' about the Iraq War – films like *The War Tapes*, *Gunner Palace* (2004) and *Occupation: Dreamland* (2005) that focus on the perspective of soldiers on the ground – critic Tony Grajeda claims that these films always foreground the subjective responses of their subjects. 'By privileging personal experience over historical awareness, these accounts construct a version of the war in which it becomes impossible to apprehend such atrocities as Haditha, Ramadi, Abu Ghraib,' he argues. He goes on to suggest that part of the reason for this tunnel vision is that the dominant discourse of contemporary American patriotism post-9/11 is one in which 'to confront such issues as military policy, government decision-making and the like would be to "politicize" the war, and thus in the logic of these documentaries somehow betray the troops'. [14]

Narrowing the focus down to the level of the individual soldier these feature length documentaries seduce us into thinking we're seeing the war as it really is, when all we're really seeing is a limited viewpoint shorn of wider perspective. Online grunt videos are arguably an acute illustration of Grajeda's point – in particular his suggestion that the films he discusses 'seek to make an epistemological argument by which the truth of the Iraq war, and perhaps every war, can only be had from the soldiers themselves, that their experience alone grounds the reality of war.' [15]

Shot in 2004 and released two years later, Scranton's documentary was certainly ahead of the curve in terms of reacting to the widespread popularity of letting soldiers tell their own stories. Other directors have since scrambled to keep pace. Director Kimberly Peirce's *Stop-Loss* (2008) – about traumatised soldiers returning home and being shipped back to Iraq through the controversial government policy of 'stop-lossing'

– was inspired by her eighteen-year-old brother's service in Iraq. On his first leave home, Peirce discovered him watching grunt videos and was intrigued by their raw energy:

'I found my brother in our living room sitting a few inches from an oversized TV, mesmerized by what was playing: soldier-shot and edited images of life and war in Iraq cut to rock music. There was something completely unique and immediate about these images – images of soldiers doing raids, seeing combat, cruising in Humvees – mostly shot with lightweight, one-chip cameras that the soldiers had mounted on guns, Humvees, sandbags, or whatever they could attach them to; images of weapons, fighter jets, bombs going off (downloaded from other soldiers and from the Internet from Defense Weapons companies such as Lockheed Martin and Boeing) then edited on iMovie or Final Cut and put to music – rock, sentimental, patriotic. It was a personal, unadulterated look at combat as these young men were experiencing and signifying it. I studied the videos he brought home and located more videos through other soldiers. These small home movies were like anthropological finds – told entirely from the soldiers' point-of-view. They opened many windows into the lives of these guys and my brother.' [16]

Convinced that she had access to an authentic window onto the reality on the ground, Peirce tried to replicate the style of these clips in *Stop-Loss* by shooting her own grunt video – a tribute to one of the fictional soldiers killed in the opening in country sequence set in Iraq. It's possibly the film's most memorable sequence although it is largely at odds with the visual conservatism of the rest of her thoughtful, low-key drama.

In interview, Peirce has suggested the ways in which contemporary filmmakers are aware of the change in visual grammar that the current conflict has created and its use for propaganda purposes:

Battle for Haditha
2007

© CH4 Films/
The Kobal
Collection

263

'This is the first war in which every soldier is a filmmaker. It's the combination of the video camera, cheap editing software and the Internet as a distribution system. On a bunch of these videos they have credits – shot by, edited by, directed by – it's almost like a Hollywood movie. We watched these films on an endless loop in the office. These soldiers are totally making themselves into movie stars. It's all about airplanes, big guns, tanks. It's all 'We are tough, we will fuck you up, don't mess with us!' It's an assertion of US power and its glorification of violence and the strength that America has to do damage to anybody who messes with us.' [17]

Of course, this propaganda value cuts both ways. British documentary director Nick Broomfield recognised as much in his docudrama *Battle for Haditha* (2007) based on the November 2005 massacre of civilians in the Iraqi town of the same name. His film cast non-professional actors – real-life ex-grunts – to play the members of a US platoon that goes off the rails after an IED kills one of their comrades. In an obvious nod to the way that filmmaking itself has become an integral part of the Iraq War, Broomfield focuses on the way in which the atrocity itself makes good footage for the insurgents who laid the IED. They spend most of the running time shooting US troops with their video camera, making a movie-within-the-movie that has obvious propaganda purposes. "Now the world will see how the Americans behave," comments an insurgent. It's a line that speaks volumes about the various ways in which today's global, increasingly media-savvy audience are using images from the frontline to support their own agendas.

HOLLYWOOD COMES TO YOUTUBE

Another filmmaker who came to a similar conclusion about the role of filmmaking in this war after watching YouTube clips is Brian De Palma. Instead of merely aping the style of grunt videos, however, De Palma's *Redacted* (2007) addresses the very issue of the manner in which the Iraq War has created a new visual lexicon.

When *Redacted* was released in America in November 2007, it stirred up a storm of controversy. The screenplay's semi-fictionalised drama was based on the real-life rape and murder of a teenage Iraqi and the massacre of her family by US forces in 2006. It was a My Lai style war crime that few Americans wanted to be reminded about. By diverging from the usual 'boots on the ground' viewpoint of the grunt videos and offering a wider critique of American foreign policy, De Palma and his film were vilified by US conservatives for being anti-war, anti-troop and anti-American. One of the many commentators who attacked De Palma was radio host and film critic Michael Medved who gave a vitriolic on-air review: "I honestly was close to vomiting when I saw the film. I have seen a lot of unspeakable garbage in years and years of reviewing movies. Nothing quite like this. It is a slander on the United States of America. It is a slander on the Marine Corps. It is a slander on our troops." [18]

With so much negative publicity surrounding the film's release, it was easy to overlook what made *Redacted* such a groundbreaking addition to the on-going cycle of films to have come out of the Iraq War. De Palma approaches the material in a unique manner that's obviously inspired by the collision of the battlefield and YouTube. Everything here is treated as 'found' footage, shot as if it was recorded within the film's world. The action is presented as a mosaic of viewpoints edited together from camcorder footage, CCTV surveillance tapes, jihad websites showing IED attacks and anti-war monologues

Redacted
2007

© Hdnet
Films/
The Kobal
Collection

posted on YouTube. Admittedly the film is more impressive as a filmmaking exercise than as a piece of cinema. Poor performances, a schematic screenplay and some risible moments don't help the film's impact and its structural approach frequently puts tech above effect. However, it is arguably the first war movie released during the conflict to explicitly grapple with the shift in cinematic grammar that YouTube and the Internet have brought about.

Redacted centres on a squad of US soldiers manning a checkpoint in Samarra in Iraq. Among them is Private Angel 'Sally' Salazar (Izzy Diaz), a Hispanic recruit who hopes to get into film school by making a video diary of his time in country. De Palma cuts between Sally's footage and various other fictionalised perspectives including a French documentary about the soldiers' work on the checkpoint. The shooting styles are naturally very different: Sally's video camera segments are rough and ready; the French doc uses arty zooms, Peckinpah homages and the same classical score as Stanley Kubrick's *Barry Lyndon* (1975). Later, grainy footage from websites, news footage from Arabic and American TV channels and night vision sequences are mixed into the main action to present us with a range of supposedly authentic material. The artifice involved won't fool anyone into thinking that this is a documentary; yet the intention is to ask broader questions about the representation of war in the media. The film's title makes this apparent: 'redaction' is military jargon for the act of editing or censoring.

In several interviews around the time of the film's competition in the 2007 Cannes Film Festival, De Palma drew explicit comparisons between the wars in Vietnam and Iraq and the role of images in each. According to the filmmaker, Vietnam was fought (and ultimately lost) because of pictures sent back from the battlefield. 'We saw fallen soldiers, we saw suffering Vietnamese. We don't see any of that now,' he told one journalist. 'We see bombs go off, but where do they come down? Who do they hit?' [19] In a separate interview he suggested there was a conspiracy of silence surrounding images from Iraq. 'As an American taxpayer I am financing a war that I totally don't believe in;

and if we're going to finance the bombing and destruction of a country, I'd like to see the pictures from it. Where are the pictures?' [20] The implication, clearly, is that mainstream war reporting is itself being redacted – a reaction, no doubt, to the legacy of Vietnam where frontline pictures were splashed across the cover of magazines like *Life*.

Trawling the Internet as part of his research for *Redacted*, De Palma concluded that the World Wide Web theoretically offered the public access to these missing images redacted from the nightly news ('Nobody's seen any images from the war. I mean, if you go on the Net you can find them. But if you don't look for them, you don't know they exist'). [21] However, he clearly remains sceptical about the myth of grunt videos as authentic, uncensored documents.

"So don't be expecting any Hollywood action flick," Salazar warns us at the beginning of *Redacted* as he shoots the introduction to the film-within-the-film video diary that he somewhat naïvely calls *Tell Me No Lies*. "There's not going to be smash cuts, no adrenalin pumping soundtrack, no logical narrative to help make sense of it. Basically, here, shit happens." Later, Salazar tells his comrades that his video diary will be "the truth 24/7" because "this camera never lies". One of the squad, the bookish Blix (Kel O'Neill), counters with a statement that could have come straight from the director's mouth: "Dude, that is bullshit."

Much as in De Palma's Vietnam drama *Casualties of War* (1989) – with which *Redacted* shares its tagline 'Truth is the first casualty of war' – the director's point is that veracity is lost between the film's multiple viewpoints. It's not just the military authorities who erode truth: every filmmaker within the film has their own agenda, their own slant on events. The very notion of authenticity and veracity itself are thrown into question. Indeed, the more competing pieces of footage we're shown the more we're inclined to believe that film *lies* at twenty-four frames a second.

In the crossfire between propaganda and objectivity, events on the ground – the rape, murder and massacre of civilians by US troops – are lost from sight. Even *Redacted* itself isn't absolved from this muddying of the waters: the film explicitly conflates fact and fiction with its based-on-a-true-story screenplay. De Palma even found his own work being redacted when the film's distributor, Magnolia Pictures, decided that the final sequence – which showed real pictures of dead civilians – was unacceptable. Although the images had already been shown in the press and online, the director was told their faces would have to be blanked out for legal reasons. [22] The final montage in the finished film – with the faces of victims crossed out with thick black lines – ironically makes De Palma's point about truth and censorship more pertinently than their un-doctored use would have done.

Redacted is arguably the first Iraq War movie to address such issues of representation, truth and censorship. Unlike the grunt videos it refers back to, De Palma's film displays an awareness of the wider context of the Iraq War, subtly historicising it in relation to America's misadventure in Vietnam and positioning it in relation to contemporary media theory. Ironically, though, it was a film that few people went to see (estimates of the opening weekend box office in the US were a shockingly paltry $25,628) put off by mixed reviews and the controversy that suggested it was an unpatriotic piece of filmmaking. [23]

Audiences weren't prepared to engage with *Redacted* and it's something that the film itself acknowledges when Salazar complains: "People watch, and they do nothing.

Or they make a video for people to watch, and they do nothing." At a time when America and Britain remain caught up in the quagmire of Iraq, it seems that most audiences would prefer their war movie fixes to come with less insight, politics or bite. Many of those viewers eager to vicariously experience *Close Combat in Iraq* want to be taken to the frontline without having to consider the implications of what it actually means to be there are either an audience or a nation. The popularity of the YouTube grunt video is that it can offer exactly that.

Endnotes

1. The dog's fate remains unconfirmed but the discussion is surely prompted in part by the case of 22-year-old US Marine Lance Corporal David Motari who was shown throwing a puppy off a cliff in Haditha, Iraq. Posted on YouTube in March 2008, the clip became a viral hit with 150,000 views in the two days it was available before it was taken down. The incident sparked outrage, endless news reports and the eventual discharge of Motari from the USMC.
2. Jean Baudrillard, *The Gulf War Did Not Take Place*, Bloomington: Indiana University Press, 1995.
3. See for instance Ana Marie Cox, 'The YouTube War', *Time*, 19 July 2006: www.time.com/time/nation/ article /0,8599,1216501,00.html
4. See AFP, 'Iraqis Mock US Soldiers and Themselves on YouTube', AFP (28 January 2008): http://afp.google.com/article/ALeqM5jdb_pS3Wf216-aXFTVmNFnY8c57w
5. See for instance the following video clips: *American Soldiers Attack on Terrorist Sheep* (sic), http://uk.youtube.com/watch?v=3TQdgyEapvw; *Stupid Americans in Iraq*, http://uk.youtube.com/watch?v=QvyUUQdf4Ts; *Iraq Marines Kicking Butt*, http://uk.youtube.com/watch?v=OLeoWskPUpw; *Patriot Guard Escorts Fallen Soldier from Caddo Mills, Texas*, http://uk.youtube.com/watch?v=pnp9idOEj4g
6. See *OMG US Troops Killing Kids!!!!*: http://www.youtube.com/watch?v=3bq3bsGyZUQ
7. See *British Troops Beating Young Iraqis on Camera*: http://uk.youtube.com/watch?v=fxi5kxzx3V0
8. See *Tribute to Marines* (WARNING: graphic content at 3:10): http://uk.youtube.com/watch?v=M4CgYSIdkJQ
9. Jihadists regularly distribute martyrdom attacks on coalition forces on jihad websites and video sharing services like AqsaTube. Sometimes they even appear on YouTube - although they are usually removed once discovered by the site administrators. The Bigley execution video has long been expunged from the site but remains available in various forms on several so-called shock sites (such as Justsickshit.com) at the time of writing in November 2008.
10. See 'US blocks soldiers from websites', BBC News, 14 May 2007, http://news.bbc.co.uk/1/hi/world/americas/6655153.stm
11. See Multi-National Force – Iraq's channel on YouTube at: http://www.youtube.com/profile?user=MNFIRAQ
12. See YouTube's guidelines: http://uk.youtube.com/t/community_guidelines
13. That's not to say YouTube doesn't host more than its fair share of anti-war dissent. Many veterans and fallen soldiers' families have used the site to speak out against the conflict from various positions. See, for example, *KILL EVERYBODY: American soldier exposes US policy in Iraq*: http://uk.youtube.com/watch?v=VwwMF6biCJU
14. Tony Grajeda, 'The Winning and Losing of Hearts and Minds: Vietnam, Iraq, and the Claims of the War Documentary', *Jump Cut* 49 (2007), p.16.
15. Ibid., p.16.
16. Kimberly Peirce quotes in Anonymous, '*Stop-Loss* Production Notes', (Paramount) 2008, p.5.
17. Peirce, unpublished interview transcript with the author. This interview was the basis for Russell, Jamie. 'Between Iraq and a Hard Place', *Total Film* 139 (April, 2008), pp.122-124.
18. Michael Medved's review can be found on YouTube at: http://uk.youtube.com/watch?v=SP6_Dm9gLzU
19. De Palma, quoted in 'Director De Palma Disturbed Over Iraq Film Edit', *Reuters.com*, 19 October 2007: http://www.reuters.com/article/entertainmentNews/idUSN1846489220071019
20. De Palma, quoted in Simon Hattenstone, 'No One Wants To Know', the *Guardian*, 8 March 2008. Reprinted online at: http://www.guardian.co.uk/film/2008/mar/08/features.iraqandthemedia

21. De Palma, quoted in Charles Taylor, 'A Need To Know More', *Los Angeles Times*, 4 November 2007. Reprinted online at: http://articles.latimes.com/2007/nov/04/entertainment/ca-depalma4
22. See 'Director De Palma Disturbed Over Iraq Film Edit', *Reuters.com*, 19 October 2007: http://www.reuters.com/article/entertainmentNews/idUSN1846489220071019
23. Box office figures from Box Office Mojo.com in November 2008: http://www.boxofficemojo.com/movies/? id=Redacted.htm

Bibliography

AFP, 'Iraqis Mock US Soldiers and Themselves on YouTube', *AFP* (28 January, 2008):http://afp.google.com/article/ALeqM5jdb_pS3Wf216-aXFTVmNFnY8c57w

Anonymous, '*Stop-Loss* Production Notes', (Paramount Pictures, 2007).

Baudrillard, Jean, *The Gulf War Did Not Take Place*, Bloomington: Indiana University Press, 1995.

BBC News, 'US blocks soldiers from websites', BBC News (14 May 2007): http://news.bbc.co.uk/1/hi/world/americas/6655153.stm

Chown, Jeffrey, 'Documentary and the Iraq War: A New Genre For New Realities', in Peter C. Rollins and John E. O'Connor (eds.), *Why We Fought: America's Wars in Film and History*, Lexington, Ky: University Press of Kentucky, 2008, pp.458-487.

Cox, Ana Marie, 'The YouTube War', *Time*, 19 July 2006: http://www.time.com/time/nation/article/0,8599,1216501,00.html

Grajeda, Tony, 'The Winning and Losing of Hearts and Minds: Vietnam, Iraq, and the Claims of the War Documentary', *Jump Cut* 49 (2007), pp.1-17.

Gritten, David, 'Brian de Palma: Veteran Comes Out All Guns Blazing', *The Telegraph* (7 March 2008).

Hattenstone, Simon, 'No One Wants To Know', the *Guardian* (8 March 2008), http://www.guardian.co.uk/film/2008/mar/08/features.iraqandthemedia

Reuters, 'Director De Palma Disturbed Over Iraq Film Edit,' *Reuters.com* (19 October 2007): http://www.reuters.com/article/entertainmentNews/idUSN1846489220071019

Rollins, Peter C. and John E. O'Connor (eds.), *Why We Fought: America's Wars in Film and History*, Lexington, Ky: University Press of Kentucky, 2008.

Russell, Jamie, 'Between Iraq and a Hard Place', *Total Film* 139 (April, 2008), pp.122-124.

Taylor, Charles, 'A Need To Know More', *Los Angeles Times* (4 November, 2007): http://articles.latimes.com/2007/nov/04/entertainment/ca-depalma4

Winter, Jessica, 'I Love the Smell of Celluloid in the Morning', *Slate.com* (16 November, 2007): http://www.slate.com/id/2178071/

BATTLEGROUND

Storming the Beaches –
Recent Popular Culture and the
Representation of Warfare

ESTHER MACCALLUM-STEWART

Only a tiny fraction of the Western population is directly involved in military matters, yet a widespread fascination with warfare has ensured the popularity of the war film throughout the history of cinema. However, in recent years the ways that war can be presented, current events that have changed attitudes towards conflict, and finally the ability of the viewer to become both player and active agent in their own wargames, have dramatically altered perceptions of warfare. This chapter looks at some of these changes, suggesting reasons why this may have happened, as well as demonstrating how the representation of war has been displaced, moving away from film and into other popular genres.

War as a direct topic is currently avoided by Hollywood producers; even directors such as Oliver Stone have been critiqued for recent films in which they produce 'by the numbers' accounts of current events which do not challenge cinema audiences, most notably in his production of *World Trade Center* (2006). At present war is often displaced into other genres; science fiction and fantasy in particular have seem huge increases in popularity, catering to audiences who wish to emerge themselves in what are often mistakenly assumed to be more optimistic or linear worlds. In particular, worlds that bear a strong resemblance to our own have become very popular indeed, presenting 'Elseworlds' where the mystic, superhuman or spiritual is emphasised. *Bones* (2005-present), *Medium* (2005-present) and *Twilight* (2008) remake the world with a twist, whereas more exaggerated fantasies such as *The Lord of the Rings* (2001-2003), *Eragon* (2006) and *The Chronicles of Narnia* (2005-2008) provide the viewer with more traditional fantasy vistas.

However, despite their sunny presentations of other worlds, or the representation of the world we know as more supernatural, more easily explained through recourse to the occult, none of these series entirely escape the ghost of 9/11, or the conflict that followed. In many of these series, an escape to the spiritual provides answers to moral questions about wrong and right, good and evil – questions that became uppermost in the American psyche post-9/11. In the latter, blockbuster films present warfare on a grander, more retrograde scale. These films often specifically identify warfare as functioning almost solely through codes or chivalry, and yet always tinged with the tropes of loss, waste and destruction. The political and social commentary usually witnessed in pure war films is far from absent in these productions, and even those that do not address war directly often express anxieties about the current state of world affairs. One might perhaps look to the extreme popularity of a series like *Heroes* (2006-present) in its attempt to refigure a strong American identity, for example, with key figures playing wholesome roles such as cheerleaders, policemen, politicians and academics. Even the time-hopping Hiro cries an ecstatic 'Ya-Ta' ('I did it!') when he accidentally ports himself to Times Square and thus out of his native Japan (*Heroes* 1.1). Similarly, whilst the *Twilight* series is criticised for lacking in feminist spirit, it also presents not simply wholesome American life as the ideal state, but also seems to suggest that in the land of the vampire, it is the ones who embrace a suburban existence just outside Seattle where they can eat the local wildlife and pretend to be a family unit, rather than those who live rough and travel around the world to avoid being caught for murder, who are esteemed because of their desire to fit in, settle down and live like a family.

All of these series and films show an anxiety however, a difficulty in understanding what is correct when clear opposition from around the world has surfaced against a country that prided itself on being the land of the free. Cynthia Weber's book, *Imagining America at War*, specifically argues that post-9/11 war films were often contextualised through America's self-questioning and frequent bafflement over its moral character. War films often present an internal struggle to save a family or families, and as Stephanie Coontz points out in *The Way We Never Were: American Families and the Nostalgia Trip*, this idealised unit rarely exists. The reconstruction of atypical family units in subsequent popular culture, for example, the pilots from *Battlestar Galactica* (2003-2009), the castaways from *Lost* (2004-present), the gifted individuals in *Heroes* and the 'good' vampires in the *Twilight* series, all demonstrate an unease with the American family – a recognition that more diversity is needed, even if these figures are eventually subsumed into 'normative' practices. Significantly, the series also avoids warfare directly, veering away from traditionalist depictions of conflict and resetting it elsewhere, presenting racial tensions between groups as an individualist act, enemies as misinterpreted or sympathetic, and the American citizen as a more unilateral, diverse figure.

However, the War(s) on Terror also coincided with other changes in the ways and means with which audiences accessed entertainment technology. The growth of mediums such as long haul television series, online gaming and Web 2.0 have given audiences new ways with which to access and gain control of media representations. The growing interactivity of these texts, and their tendency to rely on more than one medium to produce a cohesive whole (Jenkins: 2006), has given audiences a more hands-on approach to popular media. Given the simultaneous development of CGI, game engines and special effects, the realism and tangibility of these convergence texts directly affects the audience, meaning that the impression that they are getting their hands dirty is much stronger than before. Connecting this relative immersion and agency of the player/viewer with the 'business as usual' response to warfare, as well as the deeply personal response that 9/11 prompted in America, it is easy to see that the desire to be actively criticised about one's military motivations (as most war films do in some part), is not currently present in mainstream culture.

THE REALITY OF WAR

9/11 gave audiences around the world a film to watch – a film of towering infernos, of unexpected collisions, and of hopeless bodies falling through the air. In the aftermath of that, in the cinematic yet real life search for truth and redemption, came a confusing pseudo-war against an enemy that could never be found, and against people that turned out to be horribly, realistically human. The main bad guys, the 'boss' fights, slipped through people's fingers. The war didn't seem to be about anything, and yet it was exerting a horrible, vicious toll on everyone. The leader of the war was clearly not a hero, he was instead a man who was unable to form a coherent sentence and was prone, when he did, to making vainglorious but ultimately counterproductive statements such as the claim that America is 'the world's oldest democracy' (30 November 2008). America was forced to realise that it was not on the 'good' side, because the sides didn't make sense. All of these confusing and contradictory factors helped to reshape the ways that warfare was perceived, but also brought it into the world of the American citizen in a far more direct, personalised manner. As Cynthia Weber argues in the opening chapter of her book on the subject:

'September 11, 2001 arguably rendered another rethinking of US morality possible ... about who "Americans" are, about what "America" represents to the rest of the world, and about what Americans and America might be in this new world order. ... what many of them repeatedly posed as the simple question "why do they hate us?"' (Weber, 2006:2)

Whereas the film industry has had a long and productive relationship with the military (Westhall: 2006), 9/11 and the War on Terror provided American society with a more problematic interchange. Firstly, the enemy was nebulous, intangible. Shortly after the bombings, the head of The Motion Picture Association of America, Jack Valenti, announced that Hollywood would not be producing films which depicted Islamic Terrorists in order to prevent a racist backlash against Islamic Americans. James Castonguay contests this decision, arguing that by restricting these depictions, Americans were largely kept ignorant of Islamic customs and behaviour (2004). Certainly at points during the War on Terror, the conflation of terms such as 'Arab', 'Islamic', 'Muslim' and 'fundamentalist' have indeed been problematic. The touchstones of the conflict – and the obvious political representations of truth and fabrication – appeared interchangeable. Weblogs, forums and mobile phones supported this split, presenting personalised views of warfare – exactly the type of depiction that war films and authors have specialised in, and which viewers are accustomed to accessing when they need cultural depictions of warfare. These accounts brought the age-old adage 'we are not so different, you and I' into constant focus, as well as exposing more official sources as mendacious at worst, and to have very real, often clearly argued opposition from 'normal' people around the world at best.

Although there were a handful of war films released post 9/11, the two that stand out during this era as specifically 'anti-war' are *Fahrenheit 9/11* (2004) and *Jarhead* (2007). These are often commended as new attempts to recover the war film. As is done within this chapter, the events of 9/11 and the subsequent conflicts are often regarded in an interchangeable manner – with 9/11 as the catalyst (or the excuse, since American foreign policy had been reaching a particularly militant critical mass before the event) for the subsequent wars. Attention is given to these films, however, because they stand out in a medium that is quite deliberately avoiding the subject. Michael Moore's documentary notoriously won the Palme d'Or at Cannes, but it is also a low budget polemic about the state of American politics post 9/11 with no attempt at neutrality. *Jarhead* was also unsuccessful at the box office, leaving many viewers confused about the messages they were supposed to be receiving. [1] As one reviewer for *Rolling Stone* online comments, 'I went to see *Jarhead* with a friend, not because I really wanted to see it but just for the trip to the theater. War movies are usually not my favorites.' The apathetic response towards hard-hitting depictions of warfare is clear here.

It is fashionable nowadays to mock the attitudes of the general public during World War 1. Their patriotic response to the war effort and their obsession with 'business as usual' is often derided, or reinterpreted as a deliberate blindness to the 'true' conditions of war. Books such as Sebastian Faulks' *Birdsong* (1996) represent civilians as wilfully ignoring the obvious even when presented, head on, with the horrors of war by returning soldiers. A 'them and us' dichotomy within this type of fiction presents the soldier as a hero, and the general public as an amorphous, passive-aggressive villain. However, the general public has now found themselves in this position. Given the option, they have chosen not to wallow in self pity, horror and futility, but instead to largely ignore, or indeed support the efforts of the 'war on terror'. This trend has been frequently noted by critics who bewail the lack of war films, but at the same time often answer their own question 'where have all the war films gone', with answers similar to the ones above. Whilst war films have temporarily all but disappeared from the filmic spectrum, there is a clear understanding why this has happened.

THE RUN-UP TO 9/11 –
SAVING PRIVATE RYAN AND THE DEATH OF THE WAR FILM

Why are war films seen as so constricting at present? One of the main reasons is that which has gone before. The defining moments of war cinema often take the experience of warfare to extremes, but in the latter part of the 20th century, they have also presented defining moments in the American cinematic psyche (Boggs and Pollard: 2007). This is epitomised in the film *Saving Private Ryan* (1998). Commended at the time for its realism, most notably in the opening scenes in the film which recreate the Omaha beach landings on 6 June 1944, the film can also be re-examined post 9/11 as presenting some of the more vainglorious, pro-American attitudes that made the USA a target. In the light of modern analysis, *Saving Private Ryan*'s core fault line is not the extremism of the special effects used, but that it conflates the ideal of the individual at war with the representation of the American soldier as a moral paragon.

Saving Private Ryan contains many standard war motifs, such as representing the military establishment as inherently victimising (again playing on the 'generals in chateaux' myth of World War 1), but it also touts traditionalist values of patriotism, family identity and the self in war. In the final scene of the film, the elderly Ryan is vindicated as he weeps on the gravestone of Tom Hanks, asking his family if he has 'earned' him life after war (as Hanks has ordered him to upon his own death). The

Saving Private Ryan
1998

© Dreamworks LLC/
The Kobal Collection

wholesome representation of the graveside watchers as a nuclear, middle-class family of intelligence and success with many progeny provides silent approbation. The message here, and in other parts of the film is very clear: 'Live well, especially if you have known suffering, and thou shalt be rewarded.' The reward Ryan has been given as a result of his well-lived life is clearly an idealised American life. This lifestyle as implicitly moral, upright and desirable is additionally supported throughout the film by Tom Hanks' (as Captain Miller) adherence to the value system of the army, and his recognition that whilst its micro objectives may present his men with dangerous, even foolish objectives, on a grand scale, the moral rightness of their mission (and therefore of war in general) still holds true because it is at heart, a mission to rescue an American family and reunite it.

As propaganda, *Saving Private Ryan* supports an idea of the American at war with

Ewan McGregor in *Black Hawk Down* 2001

© Columbia/ Revolution Studios/ The Kobal Collection

vigour despite the horrific conditions; a brief perusal of the film would suggest that the only sides fighting in World War 2 at all are (good) Americans vs. (probably similar but nevertheless oppositional) Germans. Most importantly in this respect, the German soldier that Miller decides to free during the film is the one who kills him at the end. On a small scale, it is the decisions of Miller (as a good American) that help to save Ryan; in this respect Hanks (as both actor and character) represents stereotypical American forthrightness and credibility. This is complemented by Spielberg's presentation of the 'alternative' to American life as holocaust in *Schindler's List* (1993), and the 'other' as German Nazi. The two films clearly counterpoise each other in this respect with their presentations of good and evil forces at war. Blatant appropriations of warfare as a duty by America to keep the world safe can also be seen in earlier films such as *Independence Day* (1996) during which the American president bequeaths the 4th of July celebration to the rest of the world as 'our Independence Day', in the shameless accreditation of the recovery of the Enigma machine to Americans (not the historically correct British) in *U-571* (2000), and even ironically, through the unveiling of the alien flag, speared through the president's dead body in *Mars Attacks!* (1996).

Saving Private Ryan is over ten years old, passing into cinematic history. This time span is important – Spielberg's epic has had few successors, the most notable being *Black Hawk Down* (2001). It is glaringly obvious that since 9/11, very few films indeed have been made by mainstream cinema about warfare. Thus it can be seen as a cut off point for the modern war film, after which historical events also intervened to change the ways that warfare is currently regarded. *Black Hawk Down* specifically targets the war in Somalia, which few people knew of in a political sense. The film made traditional usage of army equipment, most notably the helicopters used during filming and the pre-training of the actors by army personnel. The traditional link between army and war film, where support is often provided by the military, and a pro-war slant which presents warfare as a necessary but dirty event, remains intact here. The film had however already been made pre-9/11 and was released only 2½ months after the event, in many ways making it a film produced before the event and thus adopting more secure tropes of Americans at war and at large internationally.

MENTIONED IT ONCE. THINK I GOT AWAY WITH IT...

The tendency to comment on the war from a distance has directly affected other media. Partly, this is due to the constrictive representation of direct acts of warfare through official channels. Castonguay argues that the normative, patriotic representations of the war on terror, including such elements as the broadcasting of the 'Battle for Baghdad' were overwritten by simultaneous broadcasting through the web by individuals. In an era conditioned to reality television, audiences were more open to the multiplicity of mundane accounts available and able to digest them in counterpoise to those images being broadcast on the major networks. This included, for example, eyewitness accounts documenting the fact that behind the camera lens filming the 'crowds' around the statue of Saddam Hussein being torn down by Americans and civilians alike, there were very few people. The growing ability of the general public to make its own news and to consume one media product across multiple different channels has also been one that has made the public more aware of the nuance of representations.

A very strong example of this is the re-imagining of the 1970s science fiction series *Battlestar Galactica* (2003-2009). The new series has repeatedly won awards and praise for its complex, often challenging representation of people in conflict. Subjects have included the daily grind, the identity and religious politics of warfare, the humanitarian treatment of prisoners and the morality of leadership. However, the series has also taken advantage of the growing use of YouTube. Between each series, more edgy ideas have been expressed in short 'webisode' series. In the first webisode series, the human resistance endorse and carry out a suicide bombing and in the second, flashbacks show the Battlestar fleet admiral, William Adama, deliberately violating the peace treaty between Cylons and humans under order of the military. The episodes were initially shown commercially and then broadcast online through the Sci-Fi Channel and spread across the Internet via sites such as YouTube. By presenting this deliberately contentious content, the producers deliberately wanted to show audiences a more dubious political angle to war, filmed and presented through the same media that had given alternatives to the war on terror.

Battlestar Galactica is an extreme response to the war on terror, able to comment explicitly because it is science fiction (and therefore hypothetical), and also based on a previous series (and therefore working at a remove that seeks to remake a previous product which may or may not have expressed the same values). However, it is absolutely not alone in being both popular, and in using a long-haul television series to integrate ideas about the state of America at war. *24* (2001-present), *The West Wing* (1999-2006) and *Spooks* (2002-present) all provide political, thriller-type responses to the escalation, and in 2005, the Sky network aired *Over There*, a fictional account of soldiers and their families on active service in Iraq. All of these series contain threats to both American society and the American government (or both USA and UK, in the case of *Spooks*, with Americans typically presented as neurotic and hypersensitive to home and international security). Other series such as *Lost*, deal with multiculturalism and social politics, again reaching for a re-imagination of the American citizen on more compatible internationalist terms. The juxtaposition of the character Sayid Hassan Jarrah, a former communications officer in the Iraqi Republican Guard and James 'Sawyer' Ford presents interesting issues about tolerance. The fact that despite Sawyer's initial racist claims, Sayid does in fact turn out to be involved with terrorist acts, presents the audience with conflicting responses, both through their 'unseen' knowledge about Sayid (gleamed through the use of flashbacks in the series) and his behaviour on the island itself. The storyline is resolved in a muddleheaded manner however, symptomatic of the unsure nature which these debates now provoke.

Most of the series involved deal with an Elseworld, even if the deviation from real and fictional universes is very slight – in both *24* and *The West Wing*, for example, a black president is elected pre-Obama. In all of these series, however, what stands out the most is that war is mentioned cautiously. If it is a central theme, the war is not 'real' but almost deliberately removed into a genre of the imaginary. If characters are involved, their relationship with war is approached tentatively. Sayid in *Lost* is not religious, for example, the members of Blue Watch simply disappear; there is little reference in the series as to what has happened to them; *The West Wing* episode 'Isaac and Ishmael' (3.1) is prefaced by an out of character announcement by cast members stating that the episode does not exist within the series' continuity frame, and is intended to show a hypothetical reaction by the characters of the series (fictional characters responding to a fictional scenario) to a terrorist threat.

CGI AND WARGAMES

Saving Private Ryan was produced at a time where presenting the hyper-real in films was taking on an almost obsession quality. Spielberg uses this to great effect – the violence seems not only appropriate, but was lauded for its truthful representation of the wounding, danger and actions of war. These depictions of realistic violence, which are echoed in films such as *Black Hawk Down*, spread to the representation of violence in general within cinema. This can be seen in films such as those by Quentin Tarantino and Oliver Stone, in which violence is shown brutally and without finesse, but also extends even to fist-fests such as martial arts films. In *Romeo Must Die* (2000), special effects are used to portray the effect of every major break, snap and punch upon the human body. The glamour of wounding was lost, replaced by more true-to-life depictions of injury and death. Again a direct parallel can be drawn between largely unrealistic or glamorous depictions of warfare as seen in adventure films, and the ways that war films, like the war writers of the 1920s, developed more hard hitting, realistic portrayals of war which present the reality as harsh, horrific and dehumanising. In the same way that authors such as Blunden, Sassoon, Graves and Owen wanted to present the 'truth' of war, developed CGI allowed directors with similar passions to make war films explicit. As a result, this very realism killed the war film off in a time when realism equalled remembering. Fewer films about war and more fantasy and science fiction films entered the market. Superhero movies became extremely popular, heralded by Peter Jackson's *The Lord of the Rings* films, but also through productions of Batman, Spiderman, The Fantastic Four, even the Bourne saga and the new James Bond films veered towards superhuman figures, rather than real soldiers. Spies replaced soldiers, and elves took over from the army.

Post 9/11, a change in the way that special effects are employed to depict the actions of warfare and even combat are apparent. In superhero films this is more obvious, with an emphasis on the extreme. Bodies can fly, toss cars out of their way, morph into mechanical or animalistic representations of themselves, stretch or simply disappear in a blur of speed. All of these actions can be used to make fighting in films less about combat, and more about a demonstration of special effects, inhuman actions or simply a performative act by the participants. Much of this fighting is about avoidance – we hardly ever see bodies collide; Spiderman traps people in webs, Sue Storm repels them with her magic shield. Post 9/11, the nature of fighting has changed – James Bond, Neo and Jason Bourne twist balletically (and falsely) around each other, and this is taken to extremes in films such as *Sin City* (2005) and *300* (2007) where even the colour of violence is emphasised. Blood may spurt red but it is quickly rendered into smooth animated lines. If we witness a fight in a film, the camera work deliberately makes it hyper-real; so fast that actions are blurred. The people fighting are technically brilliant. We see individual 'moves' highlighted, paused or even freeze framed. Combat is graceful, artistic, proficient. It is not gristly, slow, haphazard or random. All of this encourages the reader to see any fighting as artistic but also beyond their ken – rendered safe by the beauty of the special effect and removed from reality by the conversion of the human to carefully rendered pixels.

GAME ON!

The blurring between human and CGI animation on the screen is one which naturally overlaps into games. In this instance, the unreal splendour of the fighting that we saw on the screen becomes infinitely possible in the hands of the player. In the new millennium, the technology and capacity available to digital games has undergone huge increases. Whereas in 1988, the Sega Megadrive boasted a 16 Meg processor, current computers can hold several gigs of information. As a result, their complexity has increased radically. Graphics and the size of games, as well as the ability to include lengthy spoken sections, sound effects, music, additional background detail and other ephemera have greatly aided the development of video games as a medium in their own right with distinctive narrative and ludic trends. In particular, the representation of the human body in games has become increasingly more detailed.

From the moment that digital games developed enough to be able to render recognisably humanoid figures in their graphics, they have had an uneasy relationship with critics. The claim that video games are violent, and therefore induce violent behaviour in their players, has been a prescient concern throughout their history. This is also linked to the fact that many (although by no means all) digital games represent some sort of violent activity and have done since their inception – from destroying blocks to shooting space invaders. In the new millennium, this concern became even greater when some games appeared to also use immoral behaviour (such as the *Grand Theft Auto* games), and others, most notably first person shooting games (FPS), began to produce extremely realistic graphics. The history of first person shooting games reflects this –

early attempts such as *Doom* focus mainly on amorphous monsters or aliens – since these creations are fictional, there is no benchmark with which to compare them. As graphics developed in complexity, so the objects displayed to the player become both more complex, and proceed towards more realistic depictions of recognisable objects, creatures or people. In this way, the images of first person shooter games in particular become both more recognisable as people, and are able to behave in more complex ways. Accompanying this was also the capacity to provide more extraneous detail, including special effects such as death animations, the appearance of wounds or blood, or sound effects including screams and moans from the wounded, as well as gunshots and sounds of movement or pain. Sound files with more extended periods of conversation or movement also become much more plausible within games, allowing for the development of more extended narratives.

The concern with moral representations of war can be seen in both extremist and conformist examples within digital games. The best selling franchises *Medal of Honor* (1999-present) and *Call of Duty* (2003-present) both use heavily directional narratives, as well as providing players with sections of the game which contain 'Easter Egg' bonuses to uncover. Frequently, these rewards come in the form of historical information about the era (*Medal of Honor* uses sound files, photographs and first person witness accounts), as well as tangible ludic rewards such as different weapons or scenarios. To give the *Medal of Honor* plot arc more gravitas, the overall narrative was directed by Steven Spielberg. Throughout the games, the emphasis on correct military detail is a constant factor. These games are representations of conflict; this is unavoidable – it is simply part of what they are. However, designers are conscious of the fact that players engage directly with these scenarios, and whilst they are representative and necessarily counterfactual (through the thousands of possible actions the player may take), they are also relatively responsible in presenting morally loaded situations. Frequently, therefore, more points are awarded for avoiding killing enemy NPCs unnecessarily, and as the capacity for more actions in games increased, so too do the options to escape or simply avoid these targets. The *Metal Gear Solid* (1998-present) and *Max Payne* (2001-3) series, whilst not directly related to warfare, both emphasise stealth over combat; neutralising enemies rather than killing them outright. On the other hand, there are many games that embrace their enfant terrible status; *Battlefield: Bad Company* (2008) satirically represents the soldier as the bad guy. *S.T.A.L.K.E.R Shadow of Chernobyl* reinvents the disaster at Chernobyl under a conspiracy story context, with multiple 'good' and 'bad' endings which reflect upon the player's behaviour. Digital games where the player realises halfway through their game that they have been fighting for the 'wrong' side are also popular (*Max Payne, Bioshock, Fallout 3*). It is no accident that the twin genres of science fiction and digital games, genres which have always carried a strong connection with diffracted or subversive representations of society, are now able to turn their considerable scrutiny towards the ways that war is played out, understood and simply lived through.

The development of games has enabled a more rounded narrative and ludic experience. These images of combat proved difficult however, when audiences wanted to shy away from violence. Regardless of the self-justification used, the identification of player with main avatar has caused a similar drop in the production of war gaming. The same change, from war to fantasy, can be seen in digital games as elsewhere. Perhaps because of their position as a medium with little cultural recognition, this also means that often, subversive or simply alternative views have been presented. Although wargames are still popular, the huge growth of online gaming has interestingly moved away from simply linking together so that they can 'frag' each other, and has instead enabled them to inhabit complex worlds in which they enact characters, develop extensive social relationships, and are able to think at greater length about the conflicts they encounter within it.

"You have your orders. Now obey them!"
Counterfactual beach landings in World of Warcraft.

Arthas: This city has got to be purged.
Uther the Lightbringer: How can you even consider that?
There must be some other way!
Dialogue from 'The Culling of Stratholme' Instance.

Since its release in 2004, the online MMORPG (Massively Multiplayer Online Roleplaying Game) *World of Warcraft* has persistently challenged what it means to be at war, and in this respect it is a clear product of its time. The game shows confusion however, with the paradoxical representation of a world at war, in which designers can make pertinent commentary through pertinent narrative story arcs and a place where the main function of the player is to subdue this world through violent means.

From the battlegrounds that allow players to break the nominal truce between the two playable sides (Alliance and Horde), to ongoing narratives within the plot that records a history of conflict, the game also has strong ties to the real world events and politics that surround it (see also MacCallum-Stewart: 2008). In a game where thousands of players interact together at once and simultaneously engage with the content of the game, *World of Warcraft* is a strong indicator of how digital games can challenge what it means to be at war. As the game has developed, so too has the complexity of its responses towards warfare. This is particularly true in the 2008 expansion to the game, *Wrath of the Lich King* (WOTLK), which develops both the internal narrative of the game and uses counterfactualism to display new, challenging representations of ethnic cleansing and the Omaha beach landings.

"Why do you aid the Magus? Just think of how many lives could be saved if the portal is never opened, if the resulting wars could be erased …"
Chrono Lord Deja in 'The Opening of the Dark Portal' Instance,
World of Warcraft: The Burning Crusade.

The *World of Warcraft* has a substantial narrative background, previously established throughout the earlier *Warcraft* games (2000-2004), and supported through a plethora of convergence texts including novelisations, huge forums maintained by Blizzard itself and the second largest wiki in existence (Dybwad: 2008). In the first expansion to the game, *World of Warcraft: The Burning Crusade*, players are introduced to the idea of counterfactualist events through a series of dungeons (also known as 'Instances') where they are asked to support leading characters within the world to accomplish certain tasks. Groups of players are transported back in time to perform tasks vital to the history of Azeroth. These include escorting the leader of one side to safety after the original person to do it is captured, aiding sometime villain Medivh in opening a portal that allows the Horde into Azeroth (and thus paves the way for years of slaughter and bloodshed between the two sides), and fighting a climactic battle on Mount Hyjal, where historically, Horde and Alliance groups were forced to come together to finally drive back their collective enemy, the Burning Crusade itself. All three Instances are deliberately problematised as 'what if' situations, but in order to complete the Instance (and thus, 'win'), players must follow a predetermined course where they cannot deviate from 'what really happened'. Thus, counterfactualist arguments are expressed (as with Chrono Lord Deja's battle cry, above), but in order to succeed, the player must allow history to take its course.

Wrath of the Lich King takes this counterfactualism to a far greater extent in the Instance *The Culling of Stratholme*. In *Wrath of the Lich King*, the narrative focus has changed and much of the plot involves a protracted struggle against one villain, the Lich King Arthas. Arthas' back story is in turn taken from an earlier *Warcraft* game, *Warcraft III* (2002) and is a rather simplistic retelling of Arthurian legend (Arthas' mentor is called Uther and there are other obvious parallels such as the magic sword he wields) with the twist that Arthur is in fact more of a Darth Vader character whose passion and commitment have swayed him to the 'dark side'. Throughout most of the game, Arthas is posited as 'other'; his 'lich king' moniker prompts metonymic parallels with otherness and vampirism (Williamson: 2005), and players are also awarded for completing major story arcs which permanently alter the gamescape to demonstrate his cruelty (indirectly causing a gas attack upon an army composed of both sides in the Dragonblight area being the most obvious example). *The Culling of Stratholme* however, goes back to a time previously enacted in *Warcraft III* and discussed briefly in the loading screen credits of *Wrath of the Lich King*. Wowwiki explains the plot of the Instance:

'Prince Arthas arrives outside of Stratholme, realising that the people have been infected by the Plague of Undeath by the Dreadlord Mal'Ganis. Arthas orders Uther the Lightbringer to purge the town. Uther utterly refuses, so Arthas disbands the Knights of the Silver Hand. He then takes it upon himself to burn down the city and kill everyone in it, to prevent the citizens from becoming part of the Scourge. The purging of Stratholme is one of the first acts in Arthas' descent into madness and evil, setting him down the path of becoming the Lich King's greatest death knight and later the Lich King himself.'

The players must help Arthas do this. This includes exposing plague-poisoned grain for him to find as well as rampaging through the city after him, keeping him alive during combat, slaughtering the inhabitants (Arthas gets to the human ones first, the players must tackle the more obvious and less ethically offensive undead) and fighting off the Infinite Dragonflight, a faction of time travellers who are attempting to alter the course of history by killing Arthas and thus preventing these events from happening. On some levels, *The Culling of Stratholme* is fast paced and enjoyable where players encounter ghouls, zombies and other nightmare creatures, and destroy them before it is too late. On the other, they are engaging in what is clearly posited by all-round narrative good guys Jainia Proudmoore and Uther the Lightbringer as a despicable act of genocide [2]. The fact that Arthas refuses to consider any other option than what can only be described as a Kristallnacht, and that the players have no other option than to follow is disturbing in the extreme. Throughout the Instance, his tonal inflection and actions are still clearly posited as evil – he may look like a goodly paladin, but his actions clearly state otherwise.

What is the *World of Warcraft* doing by creating this scenario? The player is forced to notice that their actions are clearly not ethically right and that the dubious morality of the events in Stratholme should be severely questioned. The Instance is deliberately unsettling; bunting hangs from houses and cheerful music plays, and although the plagued citizens are transformed into ravening undead, the niggling questions of Proudmoore and Uther remain; perhaps there was another way. Historically within the *Warcraft* chronology, this act is seen as the one that definitively corrupts Arthas and starts him down the path to lichdom, and within the Instance he is not sympathetic, barking orders and attacking monsters at a breakneck pace that precludes clear thought. The question of whether this path is rightful, despite its historical 'necessity' is a harsh one. Blizzard have deliberately designed the encounter to have an unsettling effect, and to leave the player with the sensation that the means (culling Stratholme), should not be justified by the ends ('Arthas told me to' and 'it's what happened in the past').

In contrast, the dark tones of Stratholme are totally reversed in battleground The Strand of the Ancients, which takes us back to a more playful environment with a satirical look at the Normandy landings. One might think that such as serious event, rather like the pogrom of Stratholme, cannot be taken lightly, and yet from the moment that the player appears on the steam powered boat chugging towards the shoreline, it is clear that the game is clearly trying to insert some levity into the representation of war, and indeed, the seriousness with which players often regard this in-game. Perhaps it is the 20 minute time frame of the game that draws us immediately back to Tom Hanks' slightly longer 23 minutes on Spielberg's beach, or the gigantic 'seaforium charges' that the player totteringly carries up the beach, surrounded by steampunk tanks puffing smoke, that alert us to a very different way of making pointed statements about the representation of warfare in popular culture without the sting of ethnic cleansing. This is not a satire of war, it is a satire of cinematic, even digital war. The beach landings are so stagey in their exposition that despite their clearly historical roots, one also sees deliberate camera angles, sounds and graphics meant to present a tongue-in-cheek representation of the time honoured 'war is hell' scenario, and, most often, players charging around in this chaos with real delight.

CONCLUSION

The War on Terror was not a war of decisive battles, grand moments or heroes. The most dramatic moment (the bombing of the twin towers) was a loss, not a victory. Subsequent events did not really seem to link closely to it; there was no or little connection to the American events and those abroad. The last thing that mainstream audiences wanted, therefore, was to visit a cinema and see this confused, devastating event acted out in any form, and when people are really dying, have really died, watching the umpteenth limbless body being dragged towards the shore is not comforting, redemptive or patriotic. It is simply cruel. As America struggled to redefine itself, the emergence of narratives that tried to separate the war film from reality meant an increasing reliance on alternative texts; ones which looked at war from the corners of their eyes. Most frequently, these texts have not been cinematic; instead games, long haul series and other 'trash' culture have stepped into the breach. The results are often surprising, thoughtful and often subversive.

The success of *Battlestar Galactica*, which has won numerous awards as well as being awarded best TV series by *Time Magazine*, demonstrates that whilst the public do not want direct representations of the war they are quite happy to digest commentary about it when it comes from other media. Hardly any of these new representations indulge in 'blood and entrails' representations of conflict. Computer games, which do the same thing are also showing a marked popularity. The magic and mayhem of *World of Warcraft* is cartoonish rather than graphic. *The Call of Duty* series is rapidly becoming more of a franchise, drifting into the area of fantasy as the demand for battle-bred killers fades, and series such as *24*, *The West Wing* and *Spooks* work towards the prevention of violence, not the making of it. The critical, confused eye of America has turned upon itself, and whilst attempts to restore a sense of humanitarian self are not always wholly successful (especially to those who are not American themselves), they are more than present. What is most apparent is that trash culture is prepared to ask hard ethical questions about the morality of being at war, and it is also prepared, often because it no longer knows the 'right' answer itself, to leave these questions open; to trust the reader/player/writer to think, if not to decide what possibilities may be presenting themselves.

Endnotes

1. See for example the mixed reviews at *Rolling Stone* online at www.rollingstone.com/reviews/movie/6824323/review/8749082/jarhead and Amazon Books www.amazon.co.uk/review/product/B000F2DCRG. These reviews often find the central issues of the film puzzling or unclear, argue that the film has all the elements of a good war film but never puts them together, or simply comment that the book by Anthony Swofford which the film was based on has a far stronger impact overall.

2. A video of the whole conversation can be seen here: www.wowwiki.com/Culling_of_Stratholme

Bibliography

Boggs, Carl and Pollard, Tom, *The Hollywood War Machine, US Militarism and Popular Culture*, New York, Paradigm Press, 2007.

Castonguay James 'Conglomeration, New Media, and the Cultural Production of the "War on Terror"' *Cinema Journal*, Vol. 43, No. 4 (summer 2004), pp.102-108.

Coontz, Stephanie. *The Way We Never Were: American Families and the Nostalgia Trap*, New York, Basic Books, 2000.

Dybwad, Barb. (2008). 'SXS08: how gamers are adopting the wiki way' at Massively www.massively.com/2008/03/08/sxsw08-how-gamers-are-adopting-the-wiki-way

Faulks, Sebastian, *Birdsong*, London, Vintage Books, 1994.

Feministing.com (2008) 'Stephenie Meyer's Twilight and its "independent" heroine'. http://community.feministing.com/2008/11/stephenie-meyers-twilight-and.html

Jenkins, Henry, *Convergence Culture: Where Old and New Media Collide*. New York: New York University Press, 2006.

Ruby Rich, B, 'After the Fall: Cinema Studies Post-9/11'. *Cinema Journal*, Vol. 43, No. 2 (winter 2004), pp.109-115.

Weber, Cynthia, *Imagining America at War, Morality, Politics and Film*, London: Routledge, 2006.

Westwell, Guy, *War Cinema, Hollywood on the Front Line*, London, Wallflower Press, 2006.

Williamson, Milly, *The Lure of the Vampire, Gender Fiction and Fandom from Bram Stoker to Buffy*. London: Wallflower Press, 2005.

Index of films
Figures in italics refer to illustrations